THE PRACTICAL WOODWORKER

A COMPLETE GUIDE TO THE ART
AND PRACTICE OF WOODWORKING

Written and Illustrated by Experts

and Edited by

BERNARD E. JONES

Editor of "Work," "The Amateur Mechanic," etc.

VOLUME IV

Copyright © 2013 Read Books Ltd.
This book is copyright and may not be
reproduced or copied in any way without
the express permission of the publisher in writing

British Library Cataloguing-in-Publication Data
A catalogue record for this book is available from the
British Library

Woodworking

Woodworking is the process of making items from wood. Along with stone, mud and animal parts, wood was one of the first materials worked by early humans. There are incredibly early examples of woodwork, evidenced in Mousterian stone tools used by Neanderthal man, which demonstrate our affinity with the wooden medium. In fact, the very development of civilisation is linked to the advancement of increasingly greater degrees of skill in working with these materials.

Examples of Bronze Age wood-carving include tree trunks worked into coffins from northern Germany and Denmark and wooden folding-chairs. The site of Fellbach-Schmieden in Germany has provided fine examples of wooden animal statues from the Iron Age. Woodworking is depicted in many ancient Egyptian drawings, and a considerable amount of ancient Egyptian furniture (such as stools, chairs, tables, beds, chests) has been preserved in tombs. The inner coffins found in the tombs were also made of wood. The metal used by the Egyptians for woodworking tools was originally copper and eventually, after 2000 BC, bronze - as ironworking was unknown until much later. Historically, woodworkers relied upon the woods native to their region, until transportation and trade innovations made more exotic woods available to the craftsman.

Today, often as a contemporary artistic and 'craft' medium, wood is used both in traditional and modern styles; an excellent material for delicate as well as forceful artworks. Wood is used in forms of sculpture, trade, and decoration including chip carving, wood burning, and marquetry, offering a fascination, beauty, and complexity in the grain that often shows even when the medium is painted. It is in some ways easier to shape than harder substances, but an artist or craftsman must develop specific skills to carve it properly. 'Wood carving' is really an entire genre itself, and involves cutting wood generally with a knife in one hand, or a chisel by two hands - or, with one hand on a chisel and one hand on a mallet. The phrase may also refer to the finished product, from individual sculptures to hand-worked mouldings composing part of a tracery.

The making of sculpture in wood has been extremely widely practiced but survives much less well than the other main materials such as stone and bronze, as it is vulnerable to decay, insect damage, and fire. It therefore forms an important hidden element in the arts and crafts history of many cultures. Outdoor wood sculptures do not last long in most parts of the world, so we have little idea how the totem pole tradition developed. Many of the most important sculptures of China and Japan in particular are in wood, and the great majority of African sculptures and that of Oceania also use this medium. There are various forms of carving which can be utilised; 'chip carving' (a style of carving in which knives or chisels are used to remove small chips of the material), 'relief carving' (where figures are carved in a flat panel of wood), 'Scandinavian flat-plane' (where figures are carved in large flat planes, created primarily using a carving knife - and rarely rounded or sanded afterwards) and 'whittling' (simply carving shapes using just a knife). Each of these techniques will need slightly varying tools, but broadly speaking, a specialised 'carving knife' is essential, alongside a 'gouge' (a tool with a curved cutting edge used in a variety of forms and sizes for carving hollows, rounds and sweeping curves), a 'chisel' and a 'coping saw' (a small saw, used to cut off chunks of wood at once).

Wood turning is another common form of woodworking, used to create wooden objects on a lathe. Woodturning differs from most other forms of woodworking in that the wood is moving while a stationary tool is used to cut and shape it. There are two distinct methods of turning wood: 'spindle turning' and 'bowl' or 'faceplate turning'. Their key difference is in the orientation of the wood grain, relative to the axis of the lathe. This variation in orientation changes the tools and techniques used. In spindle turning, the grain runs lengthways along the lathe bed, as if a log was mounted in the lathe. Grain is thus always perpendicular to the direction of rotation under the tool. In bowl turning, the grain runs at right angles to the axis, as if a plank were mounted across the chuck. When a bowl blank rotates, the angle that the grain makes with the cutting tool continually changes between the easy cuts of lengthways and downwards across the grain to two places per rotation where the tool is cutting across the grain and even upwards across it. This varying grain angle limits some of the tools that may be used and requires additional skill in order to cope with it.

The origin of woodturning dates to around 1300 BC when the Egyptians first developed a two-person lathe. One person would turn the wood with a rope while the other used a sharp tool to cut shapes in the wood. The Romans improved the Egyptian design with the addition of a turning bow. Early bow lathes were also developed and used in Germany, France and Britain. In the Middle Ages a pedal replaced hand-operated turning, freeing both the craftsman's hands to hold the woodturning tools. The pedal was usually connected to a pole, often a straight-grained sapling. The system today is called the 'spring pole' lathe. Alternatively, a two-person lathe, called a 'great lathe', allowed a piece to turn continuously (like today's power lathes). A master would cut the wood while an apprentice turned the crank.

As an interesting aside, the term 'bodger' stems from pole lathe turners who used to make chair legs and spindles. A bodger would typically purchase all the trees on a plot of land, set up camp on the plot, and then fell the trees and turn the wood. The spindles and legs that were produced were sold in bulk, for pence per dozen. The bodger's job was considered unfinished because he only made component parts. The term now describes a person who leaves a job unfinished, or does it badly. This could not be more different from perceptions of modern carpentry; a highly skilled trade in which work involves the construction of buildings, ships, timber bridges and concrete framework. The word 'carpenter' is the English rendering of the Old French word *carpentier* (later, *charpentier*) which is derived from the Latin *carpentrius;* '(maker) of a carriage.' Carpenters traditionally worked with natural wood and did the rougher work such as framing, but today many other materials are also used and sometimes the finer trades of cabinet-making and furniture building are considered carpentry.

As is evident from this brief historical and practical overview of woodwork, it is an incredibly varied and exciting genre of arts and crafts; an ancient tradition still relevant in the modern day. Woodworkers range from hobbyists, individuals operating from the home environment, to artisan professionals with specialist workshops, and eventually large-scale factory operations. We hope the reader is inspired by this book to create some woodwork of their own.

CONTENTS

	PAGE
LIST OF THE CHIEF CONTRIBUTORS	vii
ROLL-TOP DESK (38 *Illustrations*)	1225
OTHER OFFICE FURNITURE (87 *Illustrations*)	1238
MANTEL FITMENTS (18 *Illustrations*)	1261
SLEIGHS AND TOBOGGANS (20 *Illustrations*)	1268
AEROPLANE WOODWORK (37 *Illustrations*)	1275
PICTURE FRAMING (9 *Illustrations*)	1290
WOOD TURNING (47 *Illustrations*)	1295
VENEERING (32 *Illustrations*)	1315
INLAY AND MARQUETRY WORK (36 *Illustrations*)	1330
WOODCARVING (76 *Illustrations*)	1345
FRETCUTTING AND PYROGRAPHY (9 *Illustrations*)	1381
THE FIXING OF METAL FITTINGS (56 *Illustrations*)	1387
WOOD FINISHING, PAINTING AND ENAMELLING (3 *Illustrations*) .	1401
UPHOLSTERY (15 *Illustrations*)	1416
TOYS (42 *Illustrations*)	1429
EASY PATTERNMAKING (55 *Illustrations*)	1438
WOODWORKING BY MACHINERY (100 *Illustrations*)	1461
DRAWING FOR WOODWORKERS (134 *Illustrations*)	1497
TIMBER : VARIETIES AND USES	1543
INDEX	1591

List of the Chief Contributors

H. ALEXANDER	Machine Woodworking
I. ATKINSON	Toys, etc.
A.M.	Upholstery
W. A. C. BALL	Examples
J. D. BATES	Metal Fittings
R. V. BOUGHTON	Drawing
G. S. BOULGER	Woods and Timber
JOHN BOVINGDON	Veneering and Examples
R. S. BOWERS	Examples
C. W. D. BOXALL	Equipment, Examples, etc.
SYDNEY CAMM	Aeroplane Woodworking
A. CLAYDON	Examples, etc.
T. W. CORKHILL	Joint Making, Construction, etc.
J. L. DEVONSHIRE	Examples
G. ELDRIDGE	Examples
H. E. V. GILLHAM	Examples
P. R. GREEN	Examples
R. GREENHALGH	Tools, Processes, etc.
T. HOLT	Joint Making
W. J. HORNER	Turning, Pattern Making, etc.
H. JARVIS	Joint Making, etc.
F. W. LOASBY	Billiard-table Making
R. H. LOMAS	Barrow Making
W. J. MOSELEY	Wood Finishing
G. F. RHEAD	Inlaying, etc.
W. S. ROGERS	Picture Framing, etc.
C. F. SHACKLETON	Examples
G. STRETHILL-SMITH	Examples
C. S. TAYLOR	Upholstery, etc.
H. TURNER	Wood Carving
C. E. A. WYATT	Examples

Roll-top Desk

The principal views of a 5-ft. roll-top desk are shown by Figs. 1 to 8.

Fig. 1 shows the desk in perspective, and elevations and half plans are given by Figs. 2, 3 and 4.

Roll-top desks as commonly known are more often made of oak than any other wood, probably on account of so many being made abroad, where the particular kind of oak is plentiful and cheap, besides being of a very suitable texture; but, of course, there is no reason why any other hardwood should not be used, the only question being one of expense. Some of the superior specimens sometimes seen are constructed of mahogany, and have a very beautiful appearance.

With these introductory remarks the worker will be left to use his own judgment and taste in selecting the material. The following methods and principles of construction are suitable for any wood.

For a job of this character working drawings of a full-size horizontal section (a half section is shown in Fig. 4) and vertical section (Fig. 5) should at least be made, and will be found of great advantage for setting out the parts.

The following is a list of the sizes of material required for the various parts:

Lower Framing of Carcase of Desk. —Four front corner stiles F S (Fig. 3), 2 ft. 6 in. by $2\frac{5}{8}$ in. by 2 in.; four angle stiles A S (Fig. 3), 2 ft. 6 in. by $1\frac{1}{4}$ in. by $2\frac{5}{8}$ in.; two inner stiles I S (Fig. 3), 2 ft. 6 in. by $1\frac{1}{8}$ in. by $2\frac{5}{8}$ in.; one bottom rail for back B R (Fig. 4), 4 ft. 11 in. by $3\frac{1}{2}$ in. by $1\frac{1}{8}$ in.; two bottom rails for kneehole framing, 2 ft. 5 in. by $3\frac{1}{2}$ in. by $1\frac{1}{8}$ in.; one middle rail for back M R (Fig. 2), 4 ft. 11 in. by $3\frac{1}{2}$ in. by $1\frac{1}{8}$ in.; two middle rails for kneehole framing, 2 ft. 5 in. by $3\frac{1}{8}$ in. by $1\frac{1}{8}$ in.; one top rail for back T R (Fig. 2), 4 ft. 11 in. by $2\frac{5}{8}$ in. by $1\frac{1}{8}$ in.; two top rails for kneehole framing, 2 ft. 5 in. by $2\frac{5}{8}$ in. by $1\frac{1}{8}$ in.; two top rails for ends T R (Fig. 4), 2 ft. 5 in. by $2\frac{5}{8}$ in. by $1\frac{1}{8}$ in.; fourteen lower muntins for back, ends, sides, and kneehole framing, 1 ft. $3\frac{1}{2}$ in. by $3\frac{1}{8}$ in. by $1\frac{1}{8}$ in.; fourteen upper muntins for back, ends, sides, and kneehole framing, 8 in. by $3\frac{1}{8}$ in. by $1\frac{1}{8}$ in.; four lower panels for back, 1 ft. $1\frac{1}{2}$ in. by $6\frac{1}{2}$ in. by $\frac{3}{4}$ in.; three lower panels for back, 1 ft. $1\frac{1}{2}$ in. by $6\frac{1}{2}$ in. by $\frac{3}{4}$ in.; moulded on each side; seven middle panels for back, $6\frac{1}{2}$ in. by $5\frac{1}{4}$ in. by $\frac{3}{4}$ in.; six lower panels for ends, 1 ft. $1\frac{1}{2}$ in. by $7\frac{1}{2}$ in. by $\frac{3}{4}$ in.; six upper panels for ends, $7\frac{1}{2}$ in. by $5\frac{1}{2}$ in. by $\frac{3}{4}$ in.; six lower panels for kneehole framing, 1 ft. $1\frac{1}{2}$ in. by 7 in. by $\frac{3}{4}$ in.; six upper panels for kneehole framing, $5\frac{1}{4}$ in. by $7\frac{1}{2}$ in. by $\frac{3}{4}$ in.; one plinth for back, 5 ft. 2 in. by $4\frac{1}{4}$ in. by $\frac{3}{4}$ in.; two plinths for ends, 2 ft. 8 in. by $4\frac{1}{4}$ in. by $\frac{3}{4}$ in.; two plinths for kneehole, 2 ft. $6\frac{1}{2}$ in. by $4\frac{1}{4}$ in. by $\frac{3}{4}$ in.; one plinth for back of kneehole, 2 ft. 1 in. by $4\frac{1}{4}$ in. by $\frac{3}{4}$ in.; two plinths for front, 1 ft. 8 in. by $4\frac{1}{4}$ in. by $\frac{3}{4}$ in.; eight division rails between drawers D R (Fig. 5), 1 ft. 4 in. by 2 in. by 1 in.

Framing for Outer Edge of Desk.—

For the top T F (Fig. 5) two pieces 5 ft. 4 in. by 3¾ in. by 1 in., and two pieces 2 ft. 10 in. by 3¾ in. by 1 in. will be required.

Panel for Top Framing.—As this is usually covered with leather or similar material it may be made of the best pine; but whatever wood is used it must be obtained thoroughly well seasoned. It will following runners and panels may be of deal or pine; Fourteen runners, 2 ft. 4½ in. by 1½ in. by 1 in.; and six panels, 1 ft. 1½ in. by 2 ft. by ⅜ in. It should be noted that the straight grain runs the short way of these panels, therefore they will require to be made of probably three boards jointed up. One panel under

Fig. 1.—Roll-top Desk

probably have to be made of two or three boards jointed up. The size of this panel will require to be 4 ft. 10 in. by 2 ft. 3 in. by ¾ in. There will be required : Two pull flaps, 1 ft. 6 in. by 1 ft. 3 in. by ¾ in.; two clamps for same, 1 ft. 3 in. by 2¼ in. by 1 in.; and one rail over kneehole drawer, 2 ft. 3½ in. by 1⅝ in. by ¾ in. The central drawer, 1 ft. 11 in. by 2 ft. 2½ in. by ½ in., is also required.

Upper Carcase Framing of Desk.—Four angle stiles A S (Fig. 4), 1 ft. 10 in. by 2⅝ in. by 1⅛ in.; one bottom rail to back B R (Fig. 2), 4 ft. 11 in. by 2⅝ in. by 1⅛ in.; one middle rail to back M R (Fig. 2), 4 ft. 11 in. by 3⅛ in. by 1¼ in.; one top rail to back T R (Fig. 2), 4 ft. 11 in. by 2⅝ in. by 1⅛ in.; two bottom rails for ends B R (Fig. 4), 2 ft. 4½ in. by 2⅝ in. by 1⅛ in.; and two middle rails for ends M R (Fig. 2), 1 ft. 7 in. by 3⅛ in. by 1⅛ in. The curved rail and piece of top rail will receive special attention later. There are also required: Six lower muntins for back, 11 in. by 3⅛ in. by 1⅛ in.; six upper muntins for back, 9 in. by 3⅛ in. by 1⅛ in.; four lower muntins for ends, 11 in. by 3⅛ in. by 1⅛ in.; two upper muntins for ends, 9 in. by 3⅛ in. by 1⅛ in.; seven lower panels for back, 9 in. by 6½ in. by ¾ in.; seven upper panels for back, 7 in. by 6½ in. by ¾ in.; four lower panels for ends, 9 in. by 7½ in. by 1 in.; and two upper panels for ends, 7 in. by 7½ in. by 1 in. The four special panels at the ends can be got out of about 2-ft. run of 8 in. by 1 in.

It will be seen that the top is formed of two thicknesses as shown by T and M (Fig. 5), the portion M being framed together. For this the following will be required: Two pieces, 5 ft. 3 in. by 2½ in. by 1⅛ in.; two pieces, 1 ft. 3 in. by 2½ in. by ⅛ in.; and one 5 ft. 3 in. by 1 ft. 2 in. by ⅝ in.

Drawers.—By reference to the illustrations it will be seen that there are two deep bottom drawers, which have the appearance of four drawers. The following pieces will be required for the drawer fronts, 1 ft. 2½ in. by 1 ft. by 1⅛ in.; two drawer fronts, 1 ft. 2½ in. by 1 ft. by 1⅛ in.; made in two pieces, one drawer front over kneehole, 2 ft. 1½ in. by 3½ in. by 1 in.; eight drawer sides, 2 ft. 2 in. by 5¾ in. by ½ in.; four drawer sides, 2 ft. 2 in. by 1 ft. by ½ in.; two drawer sides for kneehole drawer, 2 ft. 2 in. by 3½ in. by ½ in.; four drawer backs, 1 ft. 2½ in. by 5¼ in. by ½ in.; two drawer backs, 1 ft. 2½ in. by 11½ in. by ½ in.; one drawer back for kneehole drawer, 2 ft. 1½ in. by 3 in. by ½ in.; six drawer bottoms, 2 ft. 1½ in. by 1 ft. 2 in. by ⅜ in., which will be jointed up in about three pieces, the straight grain running the short way of the wood; and one drawer bottom, 2 ft. 2 in. by 2 ft. 1 in. by ½ in.

Roll.—For this will be required three boards about 5 ft. long, 11 in. wide, and 1¼ in. thick, and one slamming rail for roll 5 ft. by 3 in. by 1 in.

Drawer Pulls.—For these eight will be required, 7 in. by 2 in. by 1 in., and two 5 in. by 1¼ in. by 1 in.

Locking Arrangement.—This will require four pieces 2 ft. by 1¼ in. by 2 in., two pieces 1 ft. 3 in. by 2 in. by 1¼ in., and two blocks 5 in. by 2½ in. by ½ in.

The sizes given are from the saw, and allow only a fair margin for planing. The next procedure will be to face up and plane square the edge of each piece, and then gauge and plane to thickness and breadth to the finished sizes. After this the setting out can be proceeded with.

The four angle stiles joining the back and side framings should be placed in pairs face to face, and set out on the edges for mortising, haunching, and mitreing as shown by Fig. 6. By reference to the illustrations it will be seen that the moulding, which is made on the solid of the framing, is as wide on the face as the depth of the plough groove to receive the panels. Therefore the distance A A (Fig. 6) shows the full breadth of the rails, the distances A B the depth of the plough groove and width of moulding, and at the upper end of the stiles the distance C A shows the width for the haunching. A mortise gauge should now be set to $\frac{5}{16}$ in., and so that the fixed tooth is the same distance from the face of the work as the front arris of the plough groove. Fig. 7 shows the stile mortised, and Fig. 8 the stile ploughed, moulded, mitred, and shouldered.

Taking the piece for the bottom rail for back, say, the edge, face, and back should be set out for shoulders of tenons, mortises for tenons of muntins, mitreing, etc., as shown in Fig. 9. By reference to the illustrations it will be seen that the front mouldings project beyond the back shoulders the exact distance of the breadth of the moulding. Special attention must be given to this matter throughout the setting out of the framing, otherwise a mistake is very liable to occur, by not allowing for this prolonging of the front shoulders, and thus making the rails too short. The mortises for the tenons of the muntins

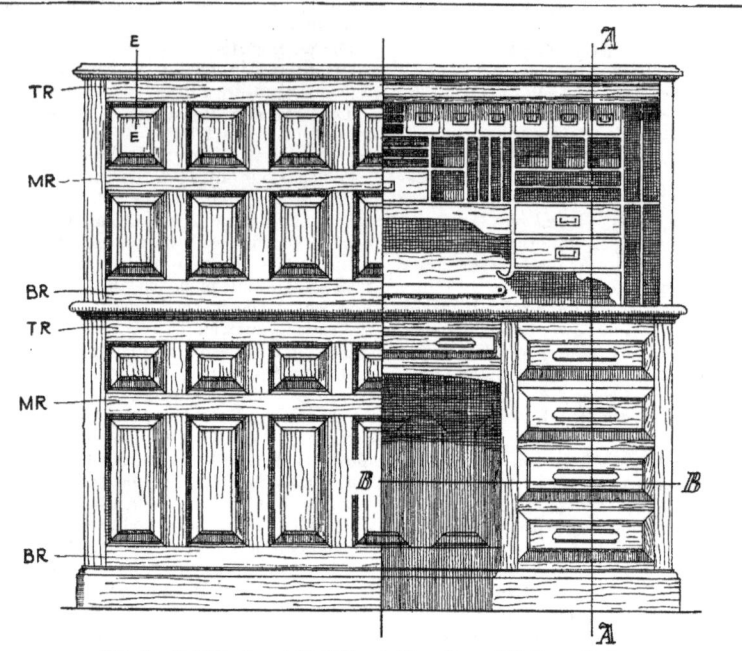

Fig. 2.—Half Back and Half Front Elevations of Roll-top Desk

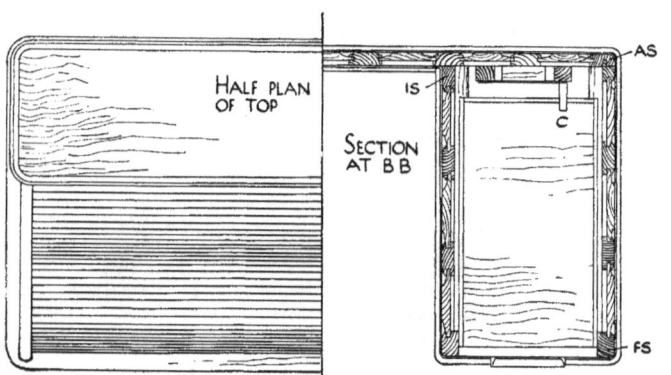

Fig. 3.—Half Plan at Top and Half Sectional Plan

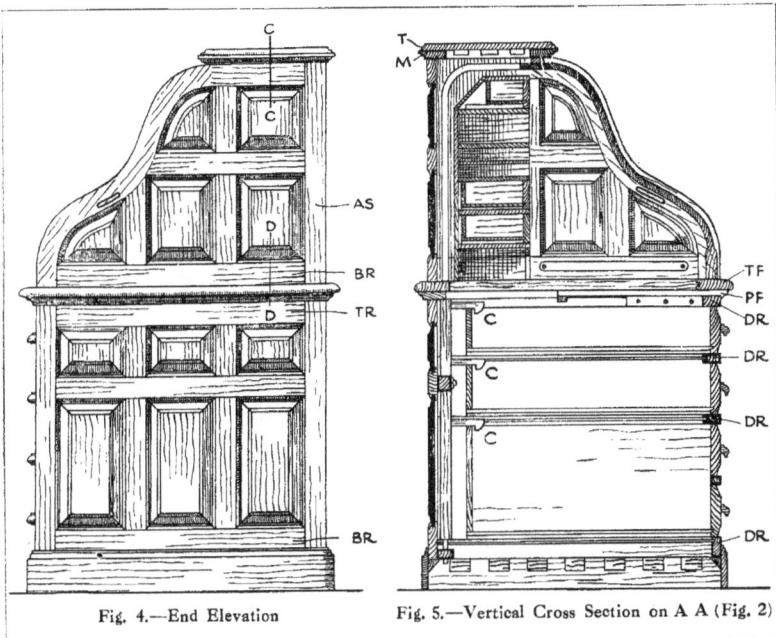

Fig. 4.—End Elevation

Fig. 5.—Vertical Cross Section on A A (Fig. 2)

should next be set out as shown in Fig. 9, the distance A A being the full breadth of the mouldings, and thus shows the beginning of the mitres, whereas B B shows the breadth of the mortises in each case. Fig. 10 shows the end of the bottom rail mortised and the tenon cut, and Fig. 11 shows the end of the bottom rail completed.

The bottom rail, middle rail, and top rail should be placed together with their face edges outwards, and the top and middle rails thus set out from the bottom rail. Having set out one edge of the middle rail, the line should be squared across the face and continued on the opposite edge. Now take one of the upper muntins, and mark off from a stile the exact distances for the front and back shoulders, and from these set out the shoulder lines on the face side and back side, as shown in Fig. 12. The remaining upper muntins should be placed face to face and with the one set out on the top. Then the face edge of each should be scribed down from the one already set out, and then the shoulder lines scribed on each in turn. Fig. 13 shows a muntin tenoned and moulded, and Fig. 14 shows a completed muntin. The procedure for setting out the lower muntins will be precisely similar to that just described for the upper muntins. The gauging for the mortising and tenoning can now be done.

The setting out for the stiles, rails, and muntins for the ends can next be proceeded with if desired, and in method will not differ from what has been described for the back framing. It will be clear that the two front corner stiles, and also the two stiles of the kneehole, form part of the framing of the ends and the kneehole respectively. The setting out for mortising, etc., for the edges of the stiles which

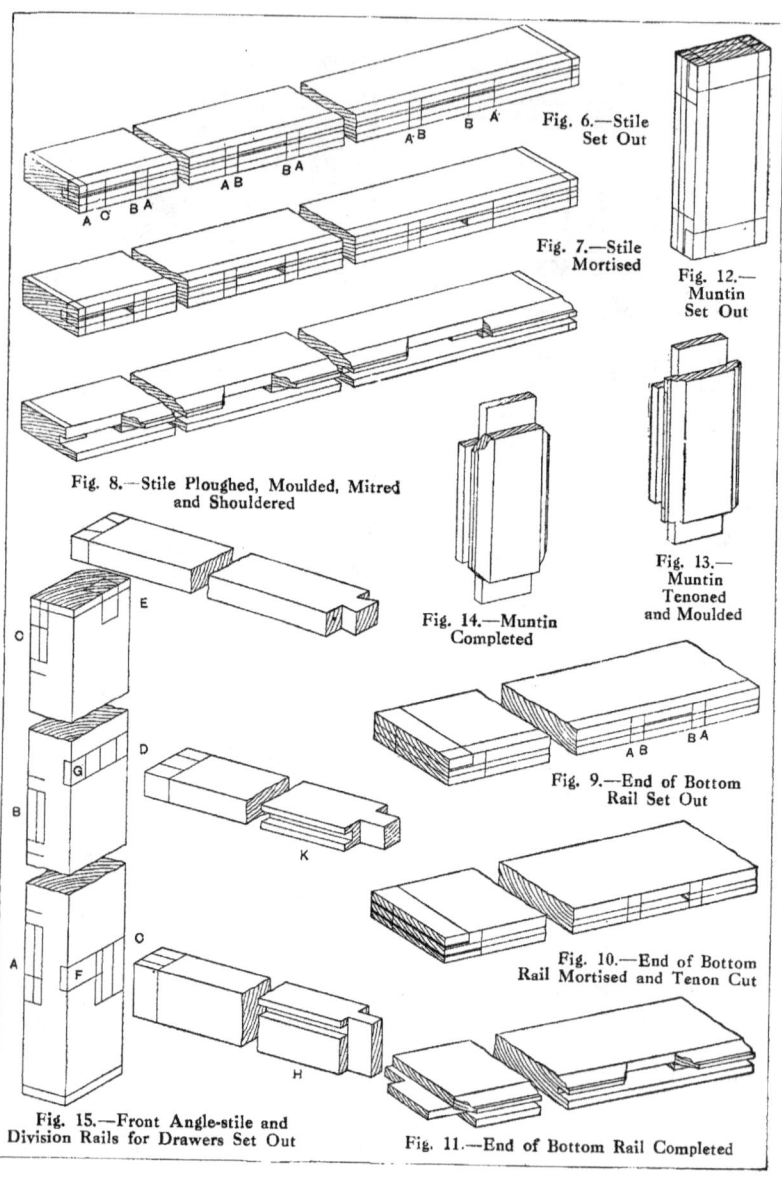

ROLL-TOP DESK

are to be part of the panel framing is shown at A, B and C (Fig. 15). The form of the completed stile is shown in Fig. 16. The setting out for rails, muntins, and kneehole framing can next be proceeded with, and should present no difficulty.

Taking one of the front stiles, it should be set out on its proper edge for mortises to receive the tenons of the bottom and top, and two horizontal divisional rails for the drawers. The proper relation for this setting out to the adjacent edge of framing is shown at C, D, and E (Fig. 15). A shallow housing is shown set out at F and G for the reception of the ends of the runners. It will be seen in Fig. 15 that the top rail is connected with the stile by a dovetail joint; this is a better method than having simply a mortise and tenon. The setting out of these front rails is comparatively a simple matter, as the front and back shoulders are of equal length.

The front stiles for the kneehole will require setting out for the two rails which are to receive the drawer. It should be observed that the faces of these rails are set back from the face of the stiles about ¾ in., as shown in Fig. 17, so that the circular corner of the stile may be continued to the underside of the top. All the necessary gauging for mortising and tenoning may now be completed.

All the mortises should next be made, and, as a rule, the depth of these should be about two-thirds the breadth of the material, except, of course, the middle rails, where the mortises should be made right through, working half from each side. Of course, great care should be taken to make the mortises parallel to the face of the wood, otherwise there will be a difficulty in keeping the surfaces of the material truly in plane when fitting them together.

The tenons should next be sawn, carefully observing to stop sawing at the proper shoulder line at the front and back. The shoulders should not be sawn at this stage.

A mortise gauge should be set to the exact width of the plough iron, and all the pieces gauged. This will be found to obviate the chances of ragged edges, which are liable otherwise to be left from the plough iron where the stuff is crossgrained. All the pieces should now be ploughed to the proper depth.

Of course, it is important that the plane required for moulding the edges of the framing should have been at hand before any setting out was done. If the worker has not one already in stock, it may be necessary to make one; but there should be no difficulty in purchasing a new one, or even a second-hand one, and care should be taken to adjust or make it so as to be in proper working order. Then a short length of moulding should be worked on a spare piece of wood, and from this two gauges should be set, one for the exact distance it works on the face, and the other for the exact distance it works down. All the stiles, rails, and muntins should now be gauged with these two gauges A stile, rail, and muntin are shown gauged in Figs. 6, 9, and 12 respectively.

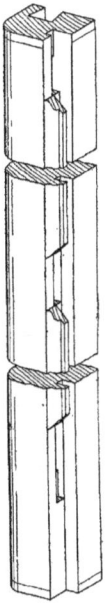

Fig. 16.—Front Angle-stile Completed

The shoulders of the tenons should be cut with a fine tenon saw. The best method for the front shoulders will be to saw just a shade from the scribe line, and then slightly inclining the saw inwards. Then the remaining slight amount of waste should be removed by means of a metal shoulder plane. This will leave the greater part of the shoulder as a square surface for fitting against the shoulders of the stile or rail, as the case may be.

The moulding in front of the mortises should be cut away by paring a little from what will be the finished mitres, and a square shoulder made so that its outer arris and that of the moulding are in one and the same line as shown. Then with a mitre template and a freshly ground chisel (*see* Fig. 18) all the mitres can be pared exactly to the setting-out marks made on each of the stiles, rails, and muntins. These parts when completed will have the appearance shown in Figs. 8, 11, 14 and 19. The two parts forming each joint of the framing should now be fitted together used on the face ; then the panels may be set out as shown in Fig. 20. If desired, the sunk surfaces may be moulded as shown, for which a plane will have to be made or obtained. But if simply a flat splayed surface is required, a skew-mouth rebate plane will be found most suitable

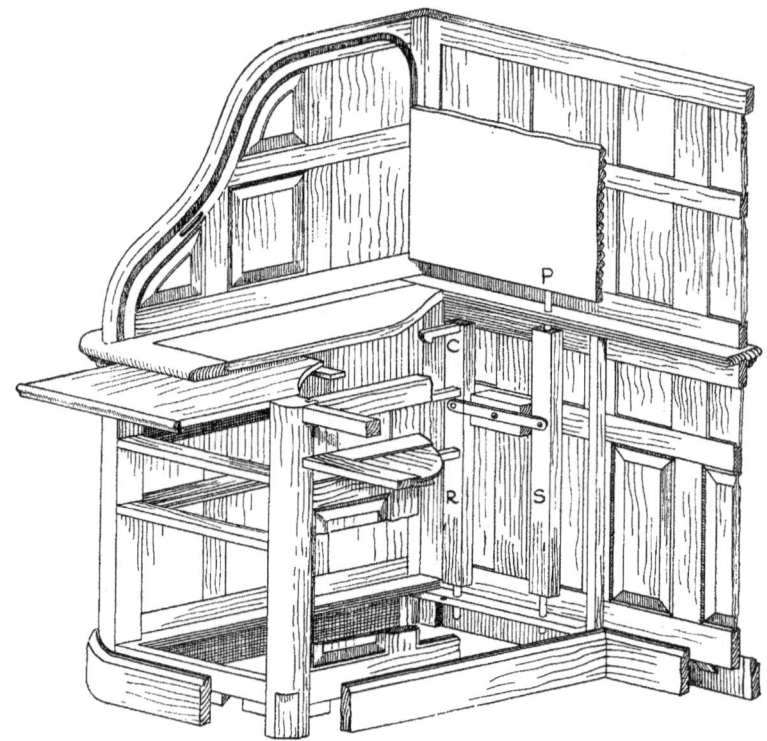

Fig. 17.—Details of Construction of Carcase

and numbered. The tenons of the top rails will require to be reduced in breadth, so as to form the haunchings.

The panels should first be trued up exactly to length and breadth. Then a gauge should be set to the distance of the sinking, the edges gauged, and another gauge set to the breadth of the sinking and for the purpose, especially when being used against the grain. In working the sinkings it will be found to be the best to work the two across the grain first, as shown in Fig. 21, and the two with the grain afterwards. If the small hollow is to be worked on the edge of the field of the panel, it will be found an advantage to

ROLL-TOP DESK

also work the two arrises at the ends before the sinking is done for the sides of the panel, as shown in Fig. 21. Fig. 22 shows the moulding with the grain completed. It will be observed that the three lower panels at the back are moulded on each side. A conventional view of a portion of the back framing is given in Fig. 23.

The next thing will be to fit in all the panels, and when the different parts are found to fit satisfactorily the joints should be glued and cramped up in the usual manner. The next process will be to true and smooth off the front of each piece of framing.

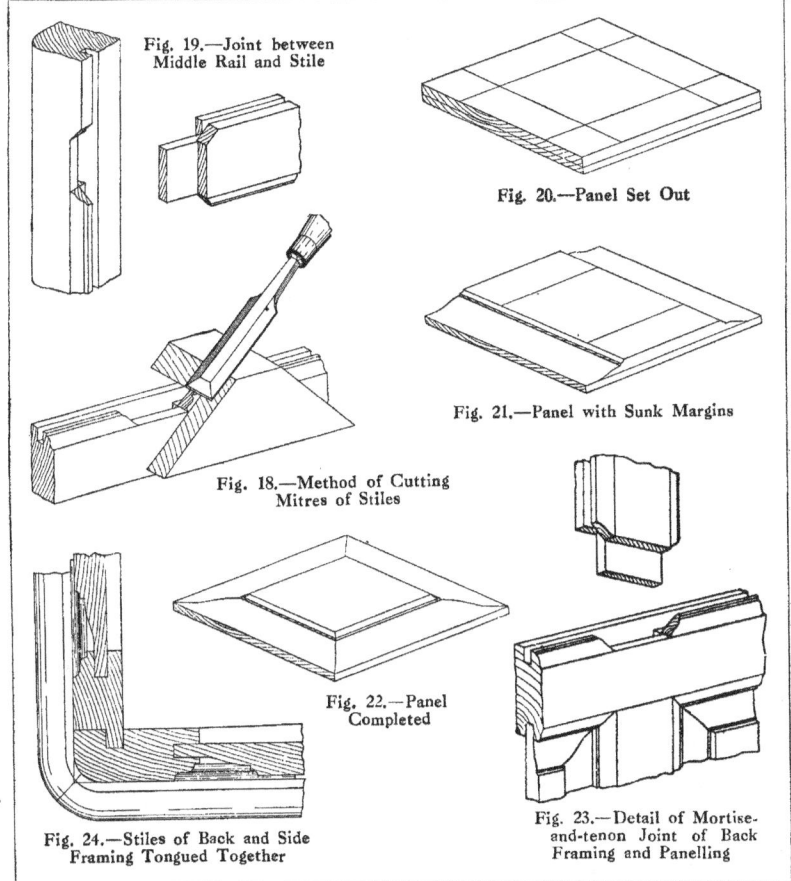

Fig. 19.—Joint between Middle Rail and Stile
Fig. 20.—Panel Set Out
Fig. 21.—Panel with Sunk Margins
Fig. 18.—Method of Cutting Mitres of Stiles
Fig. 22.—Panel Completed
Fig. 23.—Detail of Mortise-and-tenon Joint of Back Framing and Panelling
Fig. 24.—Stiles of Back and Side Framing Tongued Together

The angle-stiles of the ends and back which meet should be ploughed and tongued, so as to fit together, as shown in section by Fig. 24. The stiles of the kneehole framing adjacent to the back should be fitted, and these parts prepared to fit together with two or three hardwood dowels. The divisional rails for drawers should be tenoned and ploughed for receiving the panels as indicated at H and K (Fig. 15). Having proceeded thus far, the several pieces can be glued together, forming the main portion of the carcase. A few small blocks should be glued in the angles between the back and end framings as to form a bed for these triangular pieces glued on the back of the plinth, as shown by the section (Fig. 26). The top edge of each piece of plinth should now be moulded. The circular ends should now be worked to within a little of the finished size, and the top edges moulded. The carved portions of the mouldings will, of course, have to be worked by means of a chisel and gouge. The plinth should next

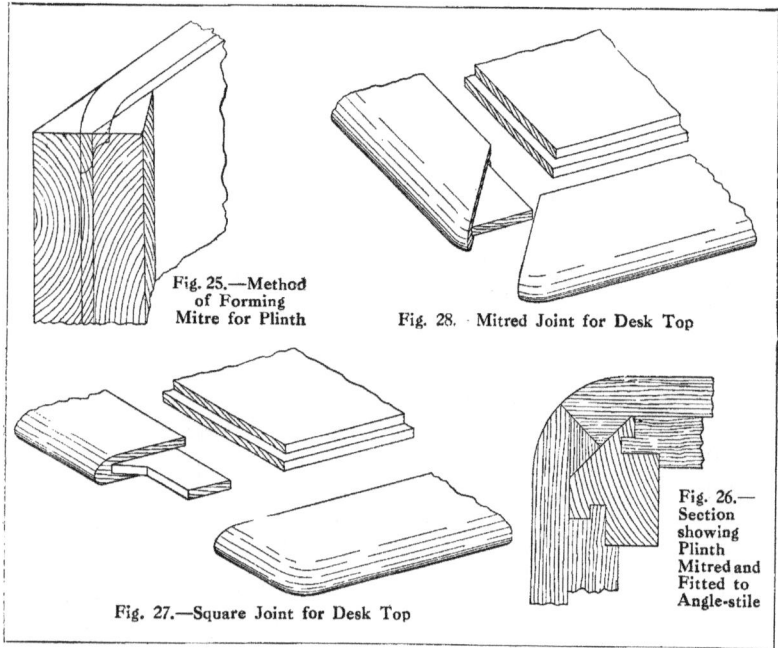

Fig. 25.—Method of Forming Mitre for Plinth

Fig. 28. Mitred Joint for Desk Top

Fig. 27.—Square Joint for Desk Top

Fig. 26.—Section showing Plinth Mitred and Fitted to Angle-stile

and the back and kneehole framings, as shown in Fig. 5.

The pieces for the plinth should be fitted round and mitred. Then at the angles a triangular piece should be prepared so that its grain is running in the same direction as the piece of the plinth, and then glued on the back of same, as shown in Fig. 25. Next the bottom portion of the angle-stiles should be pared away carefully to a surface angle of 45°, so be fixed. This may be done by gluing, holding in position by hand screws, and the insertion of a few screws from the back of the stiles.

The desk top is formed by two rails and stiles with a panel which is nearly flush with the top of the rails. The reason of this sinking is to allow for the thickness of the leather or cloth with which the top is to be finished. In Fig. 27 is shown the ordinary method of forming the joint between the stile and rail where a square shoulder is used for the rail. Fig. 28 shows the method by which the stiles and rails would be mitred and tenoned together. Of course, in each case the stile and rails should be ploughed to receive the tongue of the panel as shown. Four strips should next be prepared, mitred, moulded and fitted, and fixed on the top of the carcase immediately under the desk top. This is shown in section at A (Fig. 29). It should here be observed that a portion of this moulding forms the front edge of the pull flap. An enlarged detail of the construction of the flap A (Fig. 17) is given by Fig. 30.

After having made the framing for the lower part of the desk, the preparing of the framing for the roll top should present little difficulty. The only part where such might occur will be in the curved rail, and for this the worker is strongly advised to make a full-size elevation of the end, from which a mould should be made for the curved rail. Having prepared and fitted together the three pieces of the framing, the groove for the roll should be made. This, of course, will have to be principally done by gauging, and then cutting and paring out with a chisel, working the groove to an even depth by using a router. The groove is shown in section in Fig. 29.

Probably the simplest method of preparing the moulded laths for the roll will be to obtain a good, straight-grained, and mellow board, whose thickness is a little more than the breadth the laths will be

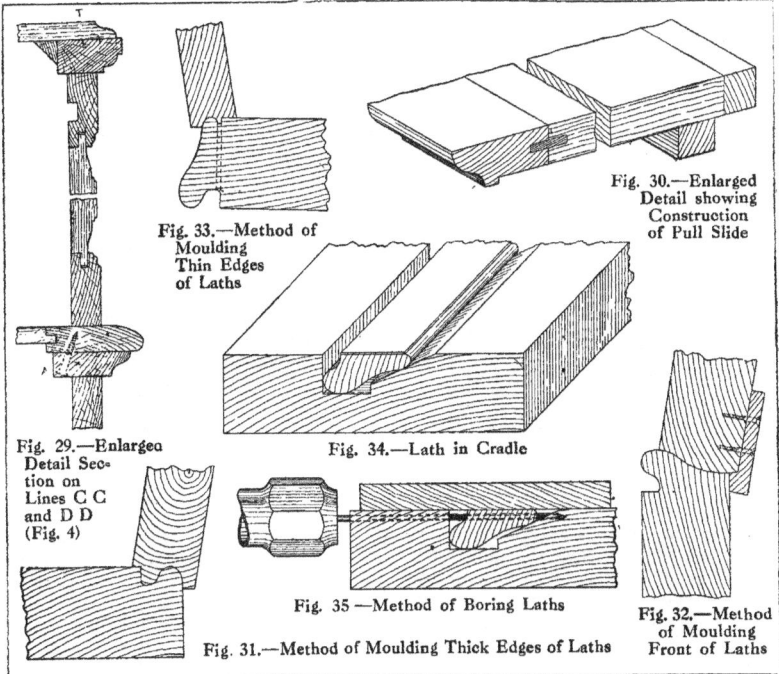

Fig. 29.—Enlarged Detail Section on Lines C C and D D (Fig. 4)

Fig. 30.—Enlarged Detail showing Construction of Pull Slide

Fig. 33.—Method of Moulding Thin Edges of Laths

Fig. 34.—Lath in Cradle

Fig. 31.—Method of Moulding Thick Edges of Laths

Fig. 35 —Method of Boring Laths

Fig. 32.—Method of Moulding Front of Laths

when finished. Then by altering an old bead plane, or making one, the thicker edge of the laths can be worked, as shown in Fig. 31. An old round or a rebate plane can be adapted with a fence screwed on it, as shown in Fig. 32, for working on the edge. Of course, a gauge must be used, so as to work down to exactly the right distance. Then an ordinary small bead plane can be used for working the small rounded edge, as shown in Fig. 33. Now, taking the quirk as a guide, the strip can be sawn off. The edge of the board can be re-shot, and the process above described repeated for each lath in turn.

For backing off and getting the laths exactly to a thickness a cradle can be made by ploughing and splaying a piece of board, so that the laths can rest in, just to the proper depth. Then the upper surface of the cradle will be an exact guide for planing down to the proper thickness, as shown in Fig. 34.

The length of the desk being 5 ft., it will not be well to depend solely on the canvas backing for keeping the laths properly together, therefore the two following methods are offered : All the laths may be bored with four holes and cords passed through. Each of the holes will have to be at the same distances in all the laths. The cradle which was used for planing to thickness can be bored at the proper intervals and distance from the top with a fine bit. Then each lath in turn can be held firmly in the cradle, and the four holes bored through, as shown in Fig. 35. The second method, which perhaps may prove the best, will be to obtain three or four strips of $\tfrac{5}{8}$-in. by $\tfrac{1}{16}$-in. untempered steel, which should be drilled and countersunk for $\tfrac{3}{4}$-in. No. 3 screws. The distance apart, of course, should be equal to the breadth of the strips of the roll, so that the steel is then fastened by the screws to each strip (see Fig. 36).

The back of the roll may be covered by gluing on canvas. Of course, great care must be taken not to allow the glue to get between the joint of the strips. A good method of obviating this will be to coat with moderate thin glue one side of a few sheets of thin drawing paper, then when dry cut them into strips about $\tfrac{1}{4}$ in. wide.

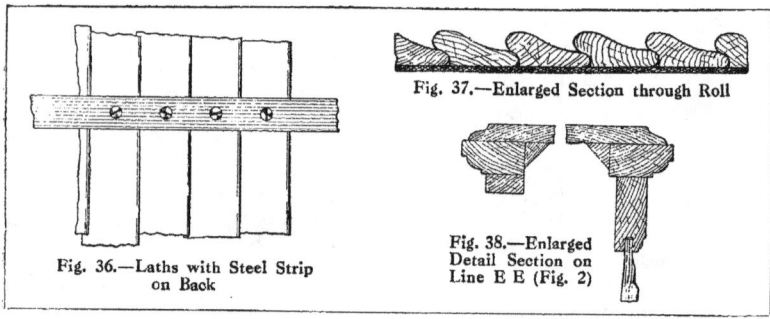

Fig. 36.—Laths with Steel Strip on Back

Fig. 37.—Enlarged Section through Roll

Fig. 38.—Enlarged Detail Section on Line E E (Fig. 2)

The glued side should then be damped, and stuck over all the joints at the back whilst the roll is laid on a flat surface. The strips of paper should be allowed to stand an hour or two to dry, after which the canvas should be glued and applied to the back of the strips and pressed to them, taking care not to disturb the paper strip. Thin american cloth, although more expensive, has its advantages over canvas, because the fabric side can be glued without the glue running through to the other side. The ends of the roll should be sawn off true to size, and they should afterwards be fitted into their respective grooves in the sides, and, of course, any necessary easing done. An enlarged section of the roll is shown by Fig. 37. When this is

ROLL-TOP DESK

satisfactory, the side and back framings should be fitted together, the shutter being inserted, and the desk top screwed from its underside into the bottom edges of the framing.

The top can next be prepared and fixed on; an enlarged section of this is given in detail by Fig. 29. A section through the front and back of the top is given in Fig. 38. For connecting the upper part of the desk to the lower, a few screws should be inserted upwards through the moulded fillet, which was fixed to the top of the carcase, as shown at A (Fig. 29), into the underside of the stiles and rails of the desk top. Thus it will be seen that for the purpose of removal, etc., the roll top portion of the desk can be separated from the pedestal portion.

It will be seen that by an ingenious contrivance when the roll top is open the drawers are unfastened; but immediately the roll is drawn the drawers are fastened at the back. This arrangement is clearly shown in Figs. 5 and 17, where it will be observed that the edge of the roll strikes a projection pin P, forcing it down, and at the same time the sliding piece S, which is connected by a metal lever working on a pivot at its centre as shown. This causes a second sliding piece R to rise, and at the same time raises hardwood or metal clip fasteners C, which are fixed to it, as shown in Figs. 3, 5 and 17. These clips when down engage in the back of the drawers as shown; but on the slide being raised they disengage themselves from the back of the drawers, thus allowing them to be opened. To bring about this action properly the sliding piece R must be considerably heavier than S.

The fronts of the drawers should be carefully fitted in by the usual method, and the sides connected to these and the back by dovetailing.

Other Office Furniture

PEDESTAL WRITING-TABLE

THE writing-table illustrated by Fig. 1 is a typical example of this class of work, the same construction applying however much the design, details, or dimensions may be varied. For convenience in making and moving, the table is made in three distinct portions, namely, the top with the three drawers immediately below it, the left-hand pedestal subdivided into four drawers, and the right-hand pedestal, which can be devoted to drawers or used as a cupboard, as in the case illustrated.

While it is desirable to use hardwood practically throughout for furniture of this type, there is a good deal of concealed work which can, if necessary, be carried out in pine, and this is indicated on the details where it occurs by the lighter cross-hatching. Front and end elevations are shown by Figs. 2 and 3. Fig. 4 is a half back elevation.

Fig. 1.—Pedestal Writing-table

Each pedestal consists of 1-in. (nominal) panelled framing for the back and sides, tongued and **V**-jointed at the angles A (Fig. 5). Where drawers occur the side panels should finish flush internally (see B, Fig. 5). As a skirting will ultimately be mitred round each pedestal, the bottom rails of the framing can be made out with pine behind this, as at C in Fig. 6. This figure gives a detailed section of the main parts of a pedestal, showing at D a $\frac{3}{4}$-in. solid top rebated into the sides and back, and at E two of the drawer divisions, which can be panelled with three-ply as shown, or more probably where extra work is a consideration made solid like the top D. In no case should the divisions be left open in the middle. The bottom F will resemble the divisions, and like them should be housed into the sides, the joint stopping $\frac{1}{4}$ in. back from the front face of the work. The drawers are of the usual type, but with the backs set forward

OTHER OFFICE FURNITURE

several inches as at G, to prevent them from being pulled too far out. They should have ¾-in. front (which may with advantage finish $\frac{1}{16}$ in. behind the front face of the framing when shut), ½-in. sides and back, and moulded wooden pulls as

The top consists of 4½-in. by 1-in. sides and back H (Fig. 7) tongued and **V**-jointed as before, connected along the front by two 2½-in. by 1-in. rails J (Fig. 8) dovetailed at the ends K (Fig. 7), and having two short uprights stub-tenoned between

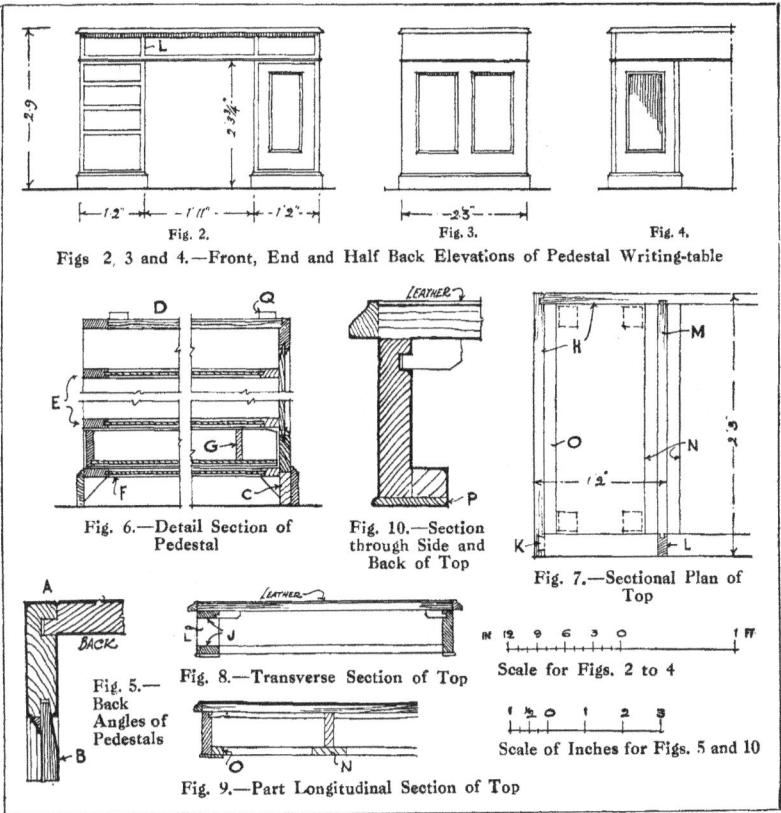

Figs 2, 3 and 4.—Front, End and Half Back Elevations of Pedestal Writing-table

Fig. 6.—Detail Section of Pedestal

Fig. 10.—Section through Side and Back of Top

Fig. 7.—Sectional Plan of Top

Fig. 5.—Back Angles of Pedestals

Fig. 8.—Transverse Section of Top

Scale for Figs. 2 to 4

Scale of Inches for Figs. 5 and 10

Fig. 9.—Part Longitudinal Section of Top

in Fig. 1. If the sides of the horizontal divisions are not of oak, the drawers should have wide fillets fixed underneath, so that in use they may not wear grooves in the parts on which they run. The cupboard pedestal hardly calls for special description.

them, as at L in Figs. 2, 7 and 8. Drawer divisions are tongued into these and dovetailed to the back, as at M in Fig. 7, and fitted with bottom rails 3½ in. wide to act as drawer-runners N (Figs. 7 and 9), corresponding fillets being fixed at the ends as at O in the same figures.

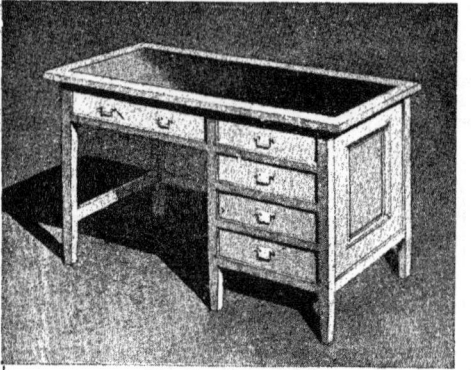

Fig. 11.—Office Table

This will complete the framing of the top portion, which should have a small fillet P (Fig. 10) on the undersides to cover the joint with the pedestals on which it rests being kept in position by means of small square blocks fixed on the tops of the latter, as at Q in Fig. 6 and where dotted in Fig. 7.

The actual table-top can be framed up as a large panel with a moulded edge, or made more simply as shown from several well-seasoned widths 1 in. thick, cross-tongued together, surrounded with a mitred moulding (*see* Fig. 10). In each case it should be secured with small oak

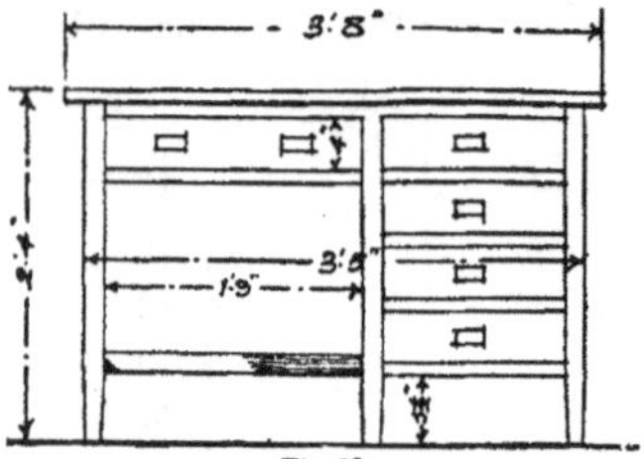

Fig. 12.

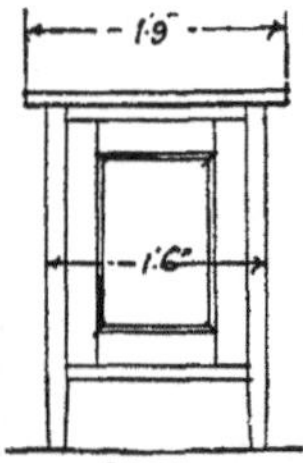

Fig. 13.

Figs. 12 and 13.—Front and Drawer-end Elevations

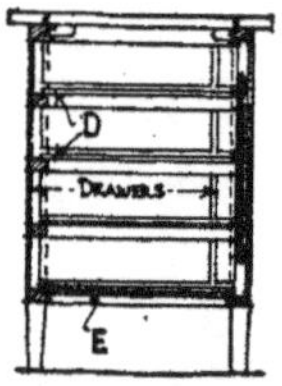

Fig. 17.—Section through Drawers

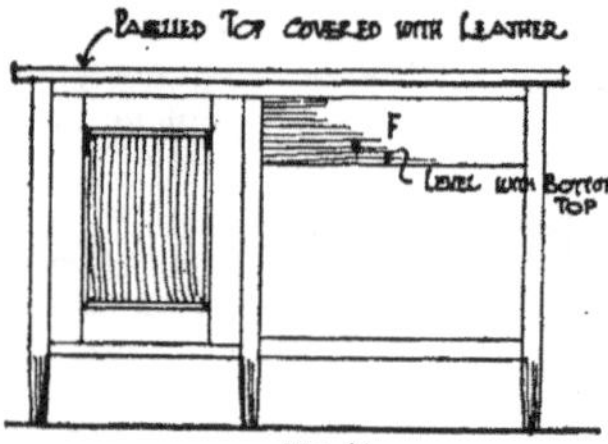

Fig. 14.

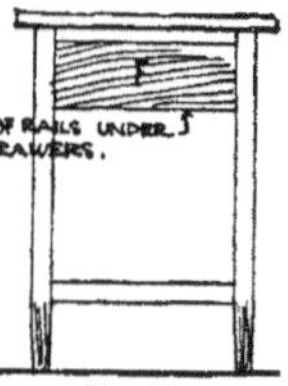

Fig. 15.

Figs. 14 and 15.—Back and Open-end Elevations

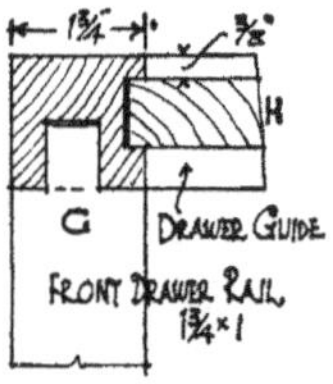

Fig 20. — Detail of Drawer Rail and Leg

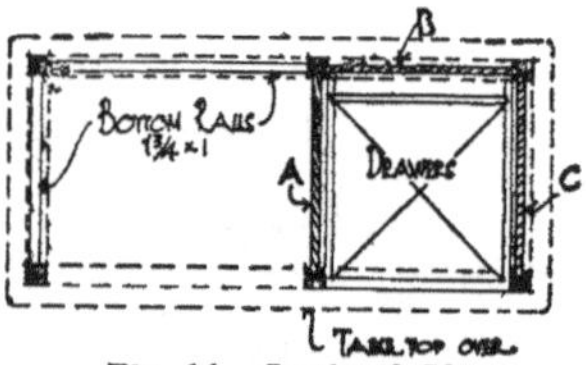

Fig. 16.—Sectional Plan

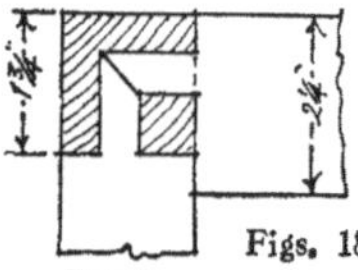

Fig. 18.

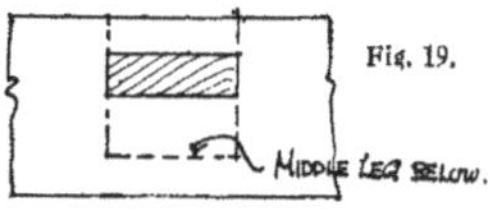

Fig. 19.

Figs. 18 and 19.—Details of Corner and Middle Legs

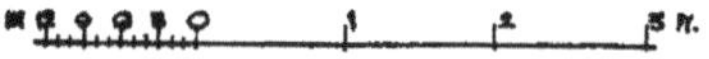

buttons fitting rebates in the framing as indicated.

OFFICE TABLE

The writing-table shown by the half-tone reproduction (Fig. 11) would look well with or without inlaid lines, and can be executed in any class of wood. Four elevational drawings of the table are shown by Figs. 12, 13, 14 and 15, and a plan by Fig. 16. Its six legs are 2 ft. 3 in. long, finished 1¾ in. square, and slightly tapered at the bottoms.

The various rails are tenoned into the legs in the usual manner, and four of these, as well as the corresponding rails, will require grooving, in order to take the enclosure to the sides and back of the tier of drawers. This enclosure, on the side marked A in Fig. 16, would be plain-tongued boarding, which would also serve for the exposed sides B and C. A better effect, however, is produced by the introduction of 1-in. framing and panels in these positions, as illustrated.

Fig. 17 is a transverse section of the table, taken through the four drawers. The three intermediate rails between the drawer fronts can be 1¾ in. by 1 in., but the two top and two bottom ones should be ½ in. wider. The wearing surface at the front of each drawer should be increased by means of a small fillet, as at D, and oak runners should be screwed to the sides of the compartments level with the front rails, to support the drawers. The bottom can be filled in as at E, or not, as desired. The 1-in. rails at F in Figs. 14 and 15 should line with those under the top drawers, and as the legs are connected at top and bottom need only be housed ¾ in. into them.

Fig. 18 shows how the various rails are tenoned into the corner legs, the wider rail being used on the long sides at the top and all round the bottom of the tier of drawers. The middle legs can be tenoned through the top rails, as in Fig. 19. One of the intermediate drawer-rails is shown tenoned into the middle leg at G in. Fig. 20, which also shows at H the side filling (as at A in Fig. 16), housed into a groove in the leg. Owing to the break between the inner faces of the filling and the leg, drawn guides will be required, fixed to the sides flush with the leg, in addition to the runners previously mentioned.

For the table-top, a 1-in. board, enclosed by 3-in. by 1-in. framing with haunched tenons at the corners, will be required, the board or panel being finished about ⅛ in. below the surface of the framing, to suit the leather covering. A moulding could be worked round the top if desired, and it

Fig. 21.—Inexpensive Double Desk

can either be screwed through the top rails from below, or preferably "buttoned" in place, as shown in Fig. 17.

The drawers are of the usual type, and will look best if made to close with their faces ⅛ in. behind those of the front legs and rails.

INEXPENSIVE DOUBLE DESK

The double desk, shown by the photographic reproduction (Fig. 21), could be executed in cheap wood, either with or without a mahogany top.

Front and end elevations and a cross section are given by Figs. 22, 23 and 24 respectively.

For a very cheap job the drawers could

be eliminated, and the sloping tops arranged to hinge upwards with one large box or several small compartments in the space shown filled with drawers. If preferred, the legs of the under-framing could be turned, although this is seldom really worth while. This framing is made independently of the upper part, and, as shown, consists of 2-in. by 2½-in. square stuff, all tenoned together with the exception of the long top rails, which are dovetailed to the tops of the legs, the dovetail coming above the tenon at the end of the short rail in each case, as in Fig. 25.

The central tie near the floor serves as a foot-rest, and should be in oak. It is tenoned to the end bottom rails, as in Fig. 26, where one of the latter is shown in section at A and the foot-rest at B.

All exposed angles should be well rounded, and the feet of the legs chamfered all round as shown. The two portions of the desk can be screwed or

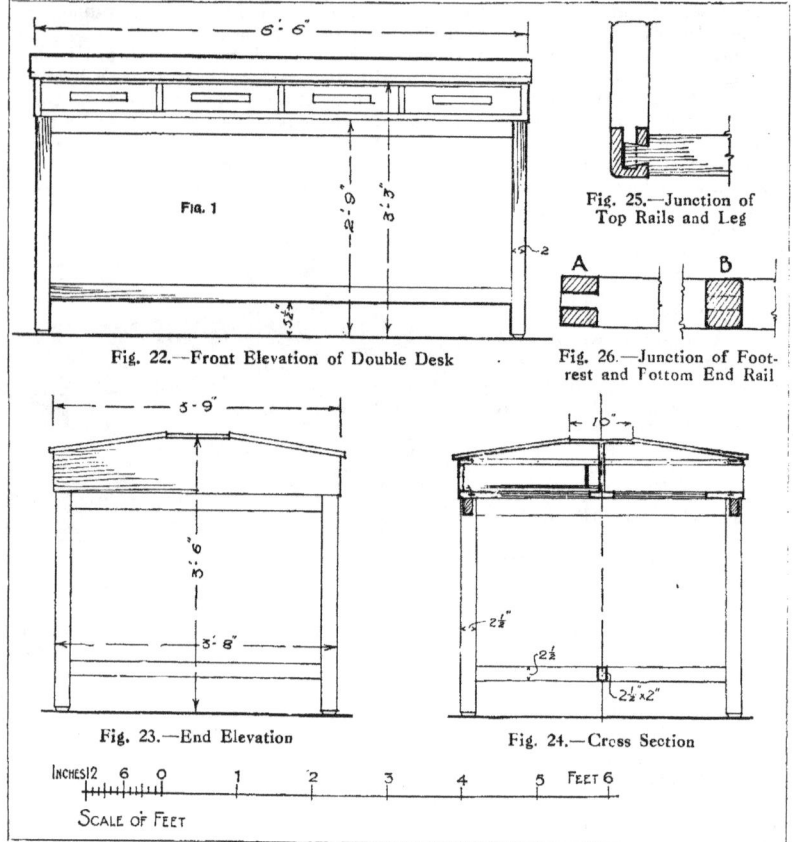

Fig. 22.—Front Elevation of Double Desk

Fig. 23.—End Elevation

Fig. 24.—Cross Section

Fig. 25.—Junction of Top Rails and Leg

Fig. 26.—Junction of Foot-rest and Bottom End Rail

OTHER OFFICE FURNITURE

buttoned together. Wooden pulls are suggested for the drawers.

OFFICE DESK FOR FOUR

With a desk of the class shown in the half-tone reproduction (Fig. 27) the top is framed up separately from the pedestals, upon which it is fitted by means of hardwood dowels. Three alternative arrangements of the pedestals are given in the front elevation (Fig. 28): one in which the mounted have solid sides, except at each end of the desk where they are framed, moulded, and returned. It will be seen by reference to the plan (Fig. 31)—the right-hand half of which represents a section through the upper portion of the desk, and the left-hand half a section through the pedestals—that each pedestal goes right through from one face to the other in one unit. If preferred, however, the half-pedestals can be framed separately, and placed back to back with about

Fig. 27.—Office Desk for Four

extra height is occupied with small drawers, one with a drawer and a cupboard, and the third with two drawers and some vertical divisions to take ledgers or other large books. If these are heavy, friction-rollers should be fitted at the bottom of each space.

The upper part of the desk consists of a double slope and flat (see Fig. 29), with solid returned ends and framed fronts and bottom; it is fitted with brass standard rails for books. Fig. 30 is a half sectional plan through the writing space. The three fitted pedestals on which it is

¾ in. between them, the face side of one pedestal being arranged to run over the back and fit close to the other. This is sometimes a more convenient and economical method of construction than to make each pair of pedestals in one fitting, as, when made as above described, they are lighter to handle, there is less danger of the sides splitting through shrinkage, and the drawers are easier to fit, as the backs can be seen.

It is usual in narrow fittings like these to make the drawer divisions solid, as the value of the stuff is less than that of the

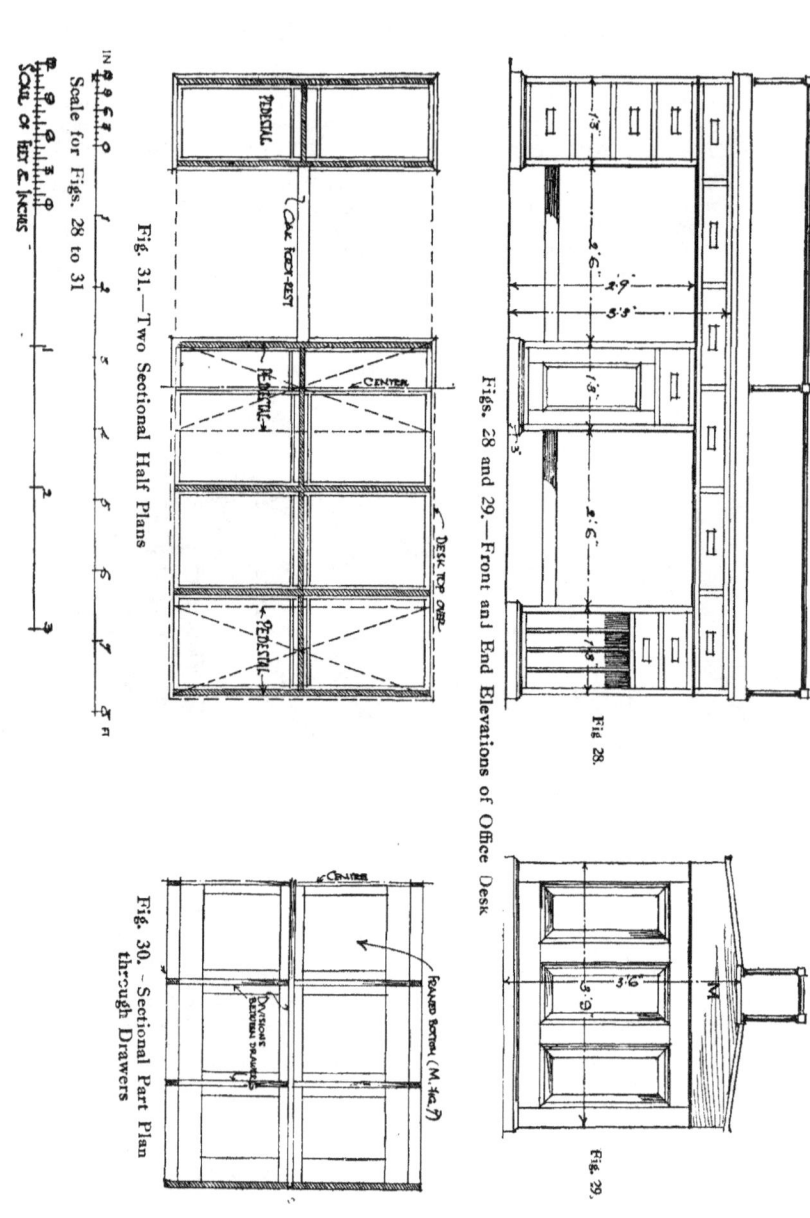

OTHER OFFICE FURNITURE

labour in preparing framed divisions; the divisions can be of white deal, edged with mahogany from 1½ in. to 2 in. wide, as at A in Fig. 32, the joints being ploughed and tongued. There is no necessity to dovetail-groove for framed divisions, as they will be quite strong enough if fitted tightly and glued. The ends are secured by angle-screwing them to the side at the back edge, thus obviating any danger of the drawers starting them.

The tops are fitted into the sides with lap dovetails. They must be kept flush with the rebates at the back. The divisions between the drawers are housed ¼ in. into the sides, and the grooves stopped ⅜ in. from the front edge. The plinth consists of a deal base, as at B in Fig. 32, with all necessary angle-blocks, and is concealed by means of a 3-in. by 1-in. moulded skirting.

When setting out the divisions, mark a small mortise on the underside of each for the bolt of the locks, as the mortises are awkward to make after the framework is fitted together. The position for the mortise can easily be found by laying the lock with its keyhole in the centre of the opening; keep the mortise in a trifle, so that there will be no play if a front happens to be thin. It will look well if all drawer fronts and cupboard doors close with their faces $\frac{1}{16}$ in. back from that of the framing.

Before setting out the framed slope it will be well to run over the plan (Fig. 31) and the section (Fig. 32), and to note how the various parts are put together. The top is formed of two wide pieces of 1-in. mahogany running lengthwise, and overhanging the frame ¾ in. all round; they are secured to the flat, centre portion with a glued-and-tongued joint. Note the break between the two surfaces, as at C in Fig. 32, which will serve to prevent pens, etc., from rolling down the slope. A fillet as at D will also be useful at the bottom of the sloping portions B.

The fronts are framed, by means of rails and cross-divisions, into a number of openings for the reception of drawers; the cross-divisions are formed with upright pieces of 1-in. mahogany E clamped on each end of shaped deal pieces F (Figs. 33 and 34) that are notched half-way through in the middle to receive a longitudinal centre division G (Fig. 33). Top rails (Figs. 32 and 34) are double mortised for the divisions and dovetailed into the ends, as shown at J in Fig. 34.

The bottom rails K K (Fig. 33) are tongued and glued to the framed bottom L, which is also shown by Fig. 35. It is 1 in. thick and has a beaded lower edge to break the joint of the desk. The ends of the top are shaped to suit the slopes, as at M in Fig. 29, and rebated to receive the ends of the bottom (L, Fig. 33), as at N in Fig. 36, which shows the bottom rail dovetailed in position.

In setting out the case, great accuracy must be observed, as errors in double-faced work are very difficult to correct. Take one of the top rails, and lay it on the plan rod, face up. Mark the divisions a trifle small, and draw the dovetails. Two mortise gauges will be required for the division mortises (E, Fig. 33); use a ¼-in. chisel ⅜ in. from each edge; no wedging need be allowed, as the paring of the tenons for entry will be sufficient. Gauge the front edge ⅝ in. thick from the underside; the rail will be bevelled to this after mortising, etc. Pair the corresponding rail to this one, also pair the bottom rails; handscrew them all together, and square the lines over; transfer these to the faces, and gauge. The longitudinal division G may be set out from one of these rails, the mortises giving the lines for the notches to receive the cross-divisions (see Fig. 33); do not cut the length till the case is together.

The divisions next claim attention. The clamps will be set out from the section (Fig. 32), the length between the shoulders being equal to the width of the drawers, the tenons at each end being gauged with the rail gauges. A stump mortise must be set out on the back edge 1½ in. by ¼ in., and this should be in the middle of the thickness; if mortise gauges are scarce, one of the others may be used, but care must be taken to gauge both deal and mahogany from the same side. The deal portion of the divisions should be set out from the same section, with shoulder

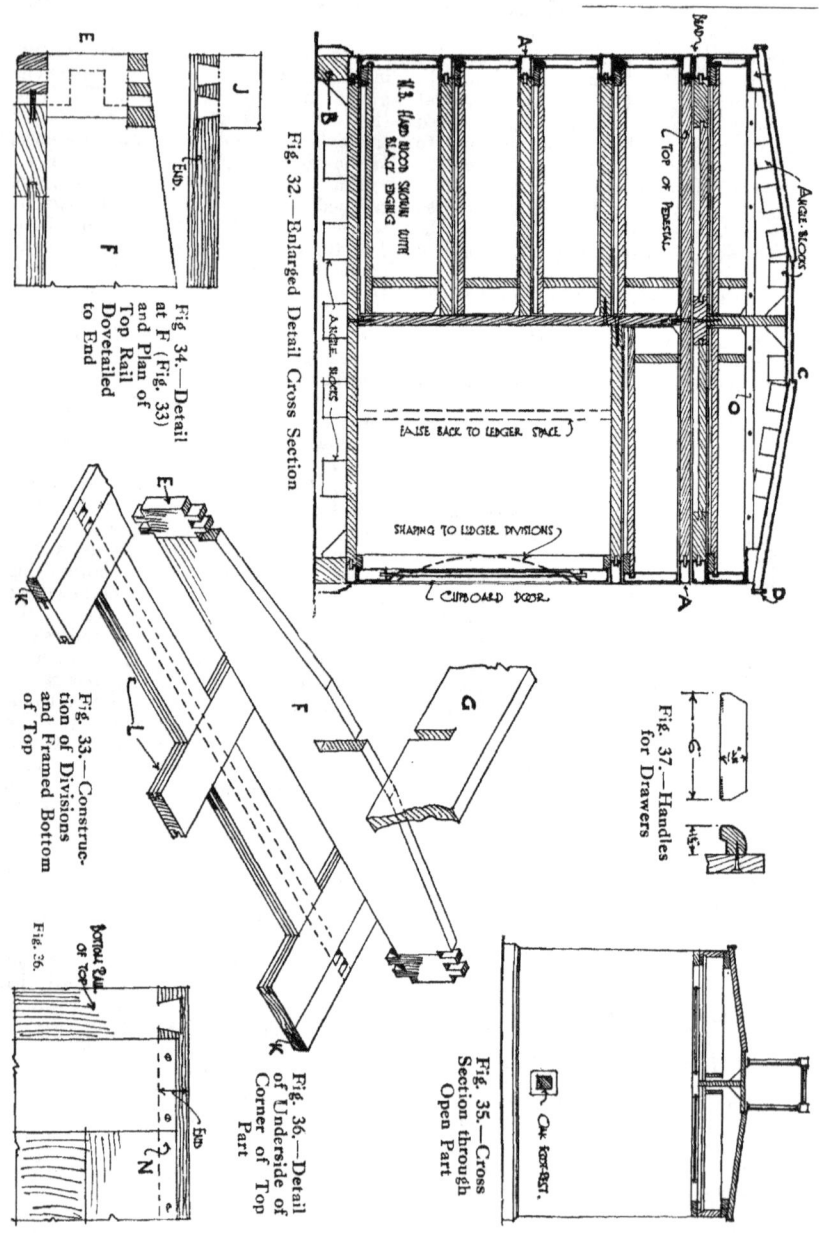

OTHER OFFICE FURNITURE

lines, the notches for the centre division in the middle, and tenons at the ends; one of the divisions should be cut to shape at the top, and used as a template for marking the others. The two ends must be paired, the total width of the case outside squared up, and a bevel set to 45 degrees applied at the top edge, the inside bottom edge gauged for rebating $\frac{3}{4}$ in. by $\frac{5}{8}$ in., and the top edge marked with the template.

The bottom will be set out from the plan; the two side rails should run through, and be mortised to receive the end-rails and muntins, by which arrangement end grain will not come in the joints. The mortises can come through and the tenons be wedged, but their ends must be cut back $\frac{1}{8}$ in. The framing is to be ploughed from the face side with a $\frac{1}{4}$-in. groove $\frac{3}{8}$ in. deep for the panels. Gauge from the face side a full $\frac{1}{4}$-in. tongue.

The top can be marked from the plan, cut to size, full in width, the joints shot to the bevel obtained from the section, and ploughed square with the edge from the underside, and the groove stopped 1 in. from the ends. If it has to be ploughed by hand, a piece of stuff should be tacked on the back and planed square with the joint; this will form a fence for the plough to work against.

When all mortising, tenoning and ploughing is done, fit and glue the clamps on the divisions; clean off flush when dry. Fit the divisions into the front rails, marking each as done; cut and fit the dovetails in the ends. Glue up the bottom, and put a screw in the tenons not wedged. When the work is dry, level off, and shoot to the exact width and glue on the bottom rails; when these are dry, the remaining mortises will have to be made for the divisions. Nail or screw the drawer guides O (Fig. 32) upon the cross-divisions parallel with the bottom edge, and make the lock mortises in the top rails.

Lay the bottom on the bench, face side up, glue the lower tenons of the divisions, insert in the bottom, drive the ends on, and screw; put the top rails on, glue, cramp, and wedge up carefully, trying for square in both directions. Next apply the centre division in place, mark to length, and cut dovetails in the ends, as at P in Fig. 30 (these need only go halfway down), glue, and drive home; clean the case off, turn it over, and clean out the rebate.

At this stage it will be convenient to fit the drawers, as it will be easier to see where they bind before the top goes on. To fit on the top, lay it flat on the bench, face down, and turn the case up on it; put a handscrew on the end, to keep it steady, and turn in the screws; glue in plenty of angle-blocks. Then turn the case right side up, and fit the slopes, correcting the nosing or joints where required.

A cramp should be provided for each 2 ft. of length, and a stiff piece of quartering to run along the top for the cramps to pull against; hollow out several pieces of stuff for the nosing end of the cramps, and put some shavings inside under the joints to catch the glue that may fall. Rub a little chalk on the joints, glue in the tongues and joints, and cramp up both sides equally; leave the cramps on for at least six hours, then block the underside, and clean off. If plenty of help is not available, it will be advisable to glue only one side at a time, letting the first side dry before the second side is done.

All that is now required is to fit on the locks and handles; the brass fitting on the top is screwed in position after the desk is fixed. As the pedestals are of precisely similar character to the top they call for no special description. They can be brought to the exact width of the desk, and the plinth fixed, the sockets for the foot-rails screwed on, and the oak rails cut in.

In place of metal handles it is suggested that wooden pull-handles be made on the lines shown in Fig. 37. These consist of a piece of moulding of the required section cut up into 6-in. lengths and splayed and rounded at the ends. They should be secured by means of countersunk screws from the inner face of the drawers.

TYPEWRITER TABLE

It is generally wise to have a special table or desk for a typewriter, because ordinary tables and desks are too high if the operator is seated on a chair of the ordinary height. Very often, also, a small table is not sufficiently steady under the constant use of a heavy typewriter.

A suitable table or desk is shown by Fig. 38. The suggested dimensions are given on the two elevations and plan (Figs. 39, 40, and 41). A back elevation and section are shown by Figs. 42 and 43. Its height is 2 ft. 4 in., which is about sufficient to allow the fore-arm of the operator, when seated on an ordinary chair, to be level with the keyboard. The other dimensions are, to a great extent, a matter of convenience, but the top may measure 3 ft. long by 1 ft. 8 in. wide. A pedestal of drawers, hinged extension to the top, and a pull-out slide, all of which are incorporated in the present design, make for the utility of the table, and add to its convenience from the point of view of the operator.

The main support of the table-top takes the form of a panelled enclosure to the back and ends. This can be about 1 in. thick, jointed together at the angles, as in Fig. 44, a small quadrant-bead being planted on the external corners, as at A. An inner side to the pedestal is also required, as at B in Fig. 41; this can be plain or panelled as preferred. It is secured at the back by means of a rough back C (Figs. 41 and 43), and its bottom edge, as well as the undersides of the framing of the main enclosure, is finished with a grooved and twice chamfered 2¼-in. by 1¼-in. base, as in Fig. 45, screwed on from below. The parts B and D are kept in proper relationship by means of a foot-rail at the bottom, and a top rail 4 in. by 1 in., as at E in Figs. 39 and 41, dovetailed at the ends, as in Fig. 46. The top is screwed or buttoned on from below, and angle-blocks as dotted behind the rail E (Fig. 39) can be added if necessary. On three sides the top is moulded, as at F in Fig. 47, the remaining edge being worked to a "rule-joint" to suit the hinged flap, which is moulded all round. This joint, together with the method of hinging, is clearly shown, and is much superior to the mere straight or butt joint. A shaped

Fig. 38.—Typewriter Table

OTHER OFFICE FURNITURE

bracket, as at G in Figs. 39 and 41, is required to support the flap, which should fold down over it when closed, as in Fig. 42.

The pedestal has drawers closing with their fronts $\frac{1}{16}$ in. behind the framing, wooden pulls, and solid divisions between

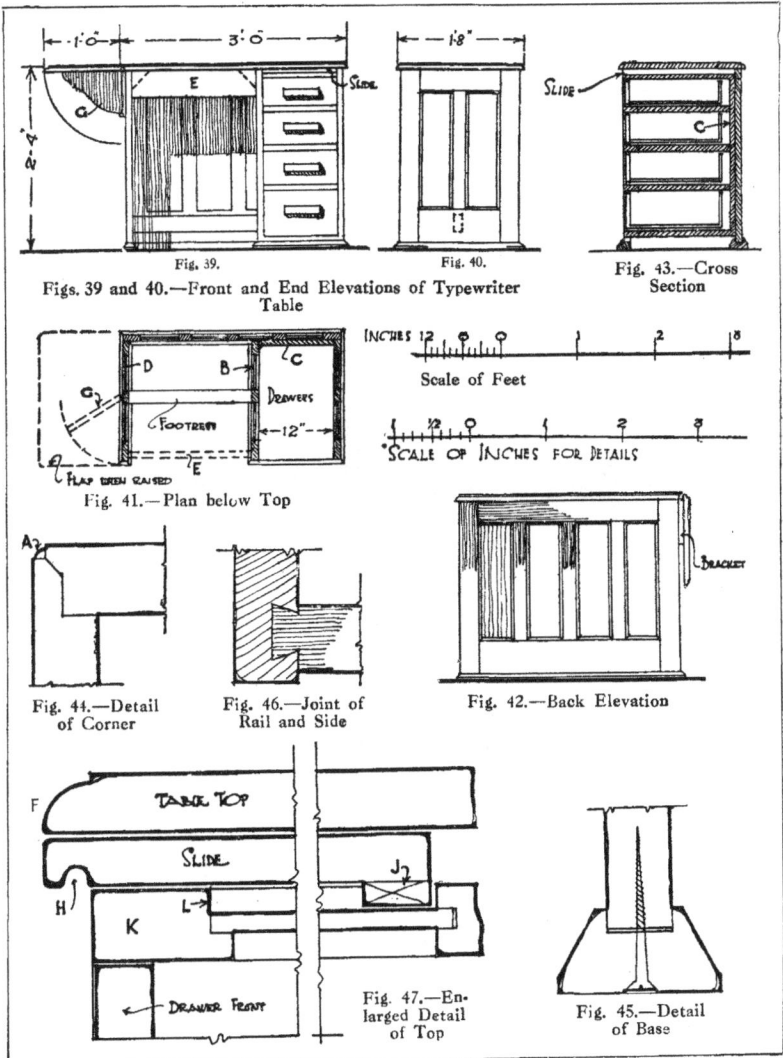

Fig. 39.
Fig. 40.
Figs. 39 and 40.—Front and End Elevations of Typewriter Table

Fig. 43.—Cross Section

Fig. 41.—Plan below Top

Fig. 44.—Detail of Corner

Fig. 46.—Joint of Rail and Side

Fig. 42.—Back Elevation

Fig. 47.—Enlarged Detail of Top

Fig. 45.—Detail of Base

the drawers. These divisions are simpler in construction than the panelled forms, and the difference in material required is negligible. At the top is a narrow compartment for a slide $\frac{1}{2}$ in. thick, as in Figs. 39 and 47. This has a sinking, as at H, to facilitate pulling out, and in order to prevent its sliding too far a small stop, as at J, should be fixed to the back edge. To provide a ledge for this to strike against, the top cover to the pedestal K might be panelled as shown. Otherwise, a groove stopping at L can be worked for the stop to run in. This part of the work must obviously be completed prior to the final fixing of the table-top.

The material may be $\frac{3}{8}$-in. pine, clean and free from knots, though the case may be $\frac{1}{2}$ in. thick with advantage, while the upright divisions could be reduced to $\frac{1}{4}$ in. The depth from back to front is not important; it may be just the width of the board from which the job is to be made, probably 9 in. at most.

First prepare two pieces 2 ft. 3 in. long, and two 1 ft. long. These form the top, bottom, and ends of the case, and are nailed or dovetailed together. The shelves should now be cut to fit tightly within the ends. They are the same width as the top and bottom, and should be cut perfectly square. Do not fasten

Fig. 48.—Nest of Pigeon-holes

NESTS OF PIGEON-HOLES

A nest of pigeon-holes for ordinary office use can suitably contain twenty-six holes, one for each letter of the alphabet; though as that number is an inconvenient one to arrange in equal tiers, it is more usual to have twenty-seven, or only twenty-four.

Fig. 48 shows a nest of pigeon-holes ornamented with the bracket pieces and with the top and bottom moulded. Tall compartments are suggested at the ends, to suit books, etc. (see also Fig. 49). In the first instance the more simple set as shown by Fig. 50 will be described and reversion made to the more elaborate set later.

them in until the upright partitions are ready and until the grooves have been cut for their reception.

The joint of the shelves and the partitions are shown by Fig. 51; the edge of each partition is sunk in a $\frac{1}{8}$-in. groove cut for it in the shelf. The width of the grooves is just enough to allow of the partitions fitting tightly into them. To mark and cut these grooves, at equal distances from each other, mark out, either with compasses or by other convenient means, the positions of the divisions, remembering that at the ends of the shelves the spaces must be shorter by half the thickness of the partitions than the others. Square lines across, representing the width of the grooves, and cut these lines down

OTHER OFFICE FURNITURE

to a uniform depth with a wide chisel, or, guided by a straightedge, draw the chisel along so that it cuts into the wood. Remove the waste wood with a ⅜-in. chisel.

by the grooves and partly by a few nails through the top and bottom. Or the top and bottom could also be slightly grooved to receive them. If very thin the partitions might be merely **V**-jointed into the

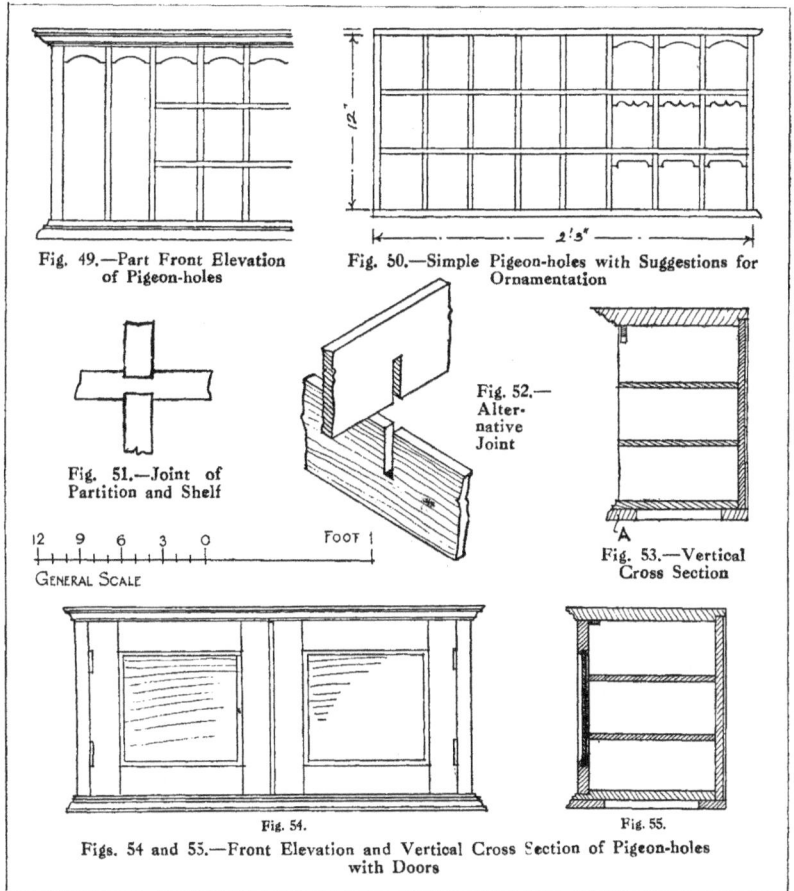

Fig. 49.—Part Front Elevation of Pigeon-holes

Fig. 50.—Simple Pigeon-holes with Suggestions for Ornamentation

Fig. 51.—Joint of Partition and Shelf

Fig. 52.—Alternative Joint

Fig. 53.—Vertical Cross Section

Fig. 54.

Fig. 55.

Figs. 54 and 55.—Front Elevation and Vertical Cross Section of Pigeon-holes with Doors

The shelves now may be fitted in their places, and the upright partitions forced in. The grooves will hold those between the shelves, while those above the top and below the bottom shelf will be held partly shelves, or another method as shown by Fig. 52 might be adopted.

It only remains to fasten thin wood on the back, and the nest of pigeon-holes is complete, as far as actual construction is concerned, as shown on the left-hand half of Fig. 50. It is a good plan to mark each hole with a letter of the alphabet, or according to the documents it is intended to hold.

An excellent finish, relieving the stiff, straight lines, may be easily formed by putting thin shaped pieces of wood at the top of each hole. They are cut with a fretsaw, and fastened by means of small blocks of wood glued in behind them. The right-hand half of Fig. 50 will give some suggestions for these. This figure also shows the top and bottom pieces projected ⅜ in. and simply moulded, thus improving the appearance and enabling the ends to be housed into them instead of dovetailed.

Reverting to the pattern shown by Fig. 48, the construction of this set is virtually the same as those already described. The top is of 1¼-in. pine, and the ends are thicker. The bottom is moulded and thickened up by a piece of stuff, 1 in. thick and, say, 2 in. wide, as at A (Fig. 53), fastened on to the bottom boards by means of screws driven through from below. The front piece should be the whole length of the job and the end pieces shouldered up behind it, so that they need not be mitred at the corners. If these end pieces are cut off across the grain of the wood, instead of with it, they will look better. The edges can easily be rounded off, as shown, with the plane, and finished with glasspaper.

Doors may be added to the nest of holes made as described, and would constitute a great improvement. The doors should be hinged within the ends, their fronts then being flush with, or a trifle back from, the edges of the ends, top, and bottom. It is in consequence necessary to have the partitions and shelves less by the thickness of the door—say, ¾ in.—than the depth of the casing. On the left-hand door a bolt should be fitted to shoot into either the top or bottom of the case, or, if preferred, two bolts, one at top and one at bottom. On the right-hand door a cupboard lock with bolt shooting to the left should be fixed. The nest of pigeon-holes so made will be as shown by Figs. 54 and 55. Ornamentation in the way of mouldings, etc., can be added as desired.

For a small nest, possibly one door may be preferable to two. In a long, low nest, if one door is preferred, it should be hinged at the top or bottom rather than at the end. If hinged at the top, a stay of some kind will be advisable to keep it open when the contents are being got at; but this arrangement will be more awkward generally than if the door is hinged at the bottom. In the latter case the door remains open by its own weight, and, if not allowed to hang down, forms a convenient table on which to sort or look over any of the contents of the holes.

The door hinged at the bottom may be used easily as a writing flap, in which case, of course, the panel and framing must be flush on the inside, and will be pleasanter if lined with leather. To prevent the flap falling farther than required, a rule-joint or similar stay may be used, or instead a simple chain or cord fastened to the insides of the flap ends. If the flap is to be used for writing purposes, part of the space occupied by the pigeon-holes may be devoted to stationery—such as notepaper, envelopes, ink, pens, etc.

DRAWING-OFFICE CHEST OF DRAWERS

A good modern type of cabinet for drawings, etc., is shown in front elevation by Fig. 56. It has eight drawers of double-elephant size, and being rather bulky is made in two sections, the upper one being kept in position on the lower by means of dowels and a few screws put in from below.

The ends take most of the weight (which is considerable when all the drawers are filled), and are flush-panelled on the inner faces. They should finish 1 in. thick, and be rebated for a back which will be best if panelled; it is screwed to the sides. The front of the carcase consists merely of four 3½-in. by 1-in. flat rails, as at A in Fig. 56. The top can be moulded and polished, a small bead should be worked where the two sections meet, while the base is strengthened with rough blocks in the

OTHER OFFICE FURNITURE

usual way, and it can either be finished square or with a small mitred plinth next the floor as dotted. A side elevation of the cabinet is shown by Fig. 57.

The drawers call for good, conscientious workmanship if they are to give satisfactory service. Sometimes they are lightly made, and have three-ply bottoms, and the result is that they rack badly and become jammed, while the weight of the contents bulges the bottoms, forcing them away from the sides.

A sketch of the form of drawer advocated is shown in Fig. 58; it has a front finished 1 in. thick, rebated for the bottom (below which it should project $\frac{1}{16}$ in., as at B in Fig. 59), and is dovetailed to $\frac{7}{8}$-in. oak sides, which, in turn, are rebated for a $\frac{3}{4}$-in. back. A light strip, as at C (Figs. 58 and 59), stiffens the whole, prevents the drawers from being pulled out too far, and

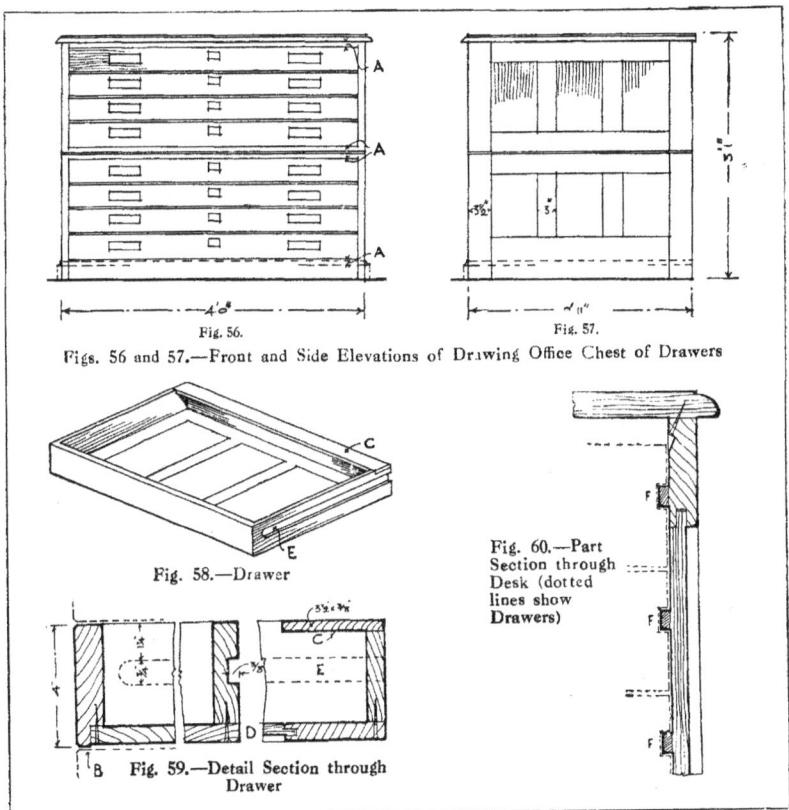

Figs. 56 and 57.—Front and Side Elevations of Drawing Office Chest of Drawers

Fig. 58.—Drawer

Fig. 59.—Detail Section through Drawer

Fig. 60.—Part Section through Desk (dotted lines show Drawers)

also stops the drawings from curling up and getting damaged. A flush-panelled bottom (D, Fig. 59), $\frac{5}{8}$ in. thick, is screwed (*not* grooved) to the sides, back and front. It will be observed that the drawers do not work on runners in the more usual way. Instead of this a groove (as at E in Figs.

58 and 59) is worked on each side, so that the drawers may be carried on oak strips, as at F in Fig. 60, strongly screwed to the to hold cards or labels will be found very convenient. A hinged upright bar at one or both ends can be arranged to fold over

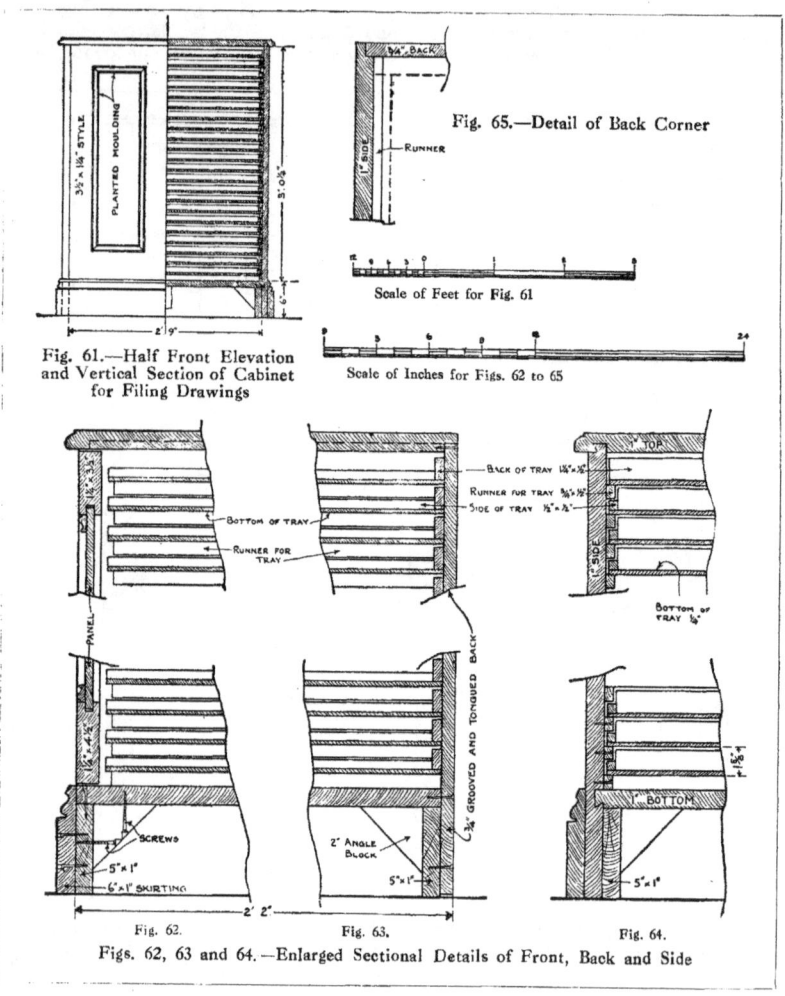

Fig. 65.—Detail of Back Corner

Fig. 61.—Half Front Elevation and Vertical Section of Cabinet for Filing Drawings

Figs. 62, 63 and 64.—Enlarged Sectional Details of Front, Back and Side

sides, and very accurately adjusted. The drawers can have shell handles or moulded hardwood pulls, and small metal frames and secure all the drawers with one lock if desired. In a case where the chest is not required for use as a table, additional

OTHER OFFICE FURNITURE

drawers can very suitably be obtained by the introduction of a third section, similar in height and design to the top and bottom ones, between which it is placed, thus producing an imposing piece about 4 ft. 6 in. high.

An imperial size chest can be made if desired, but although it entails almost as much work and material, will not be found nearly so convenient and capacious as that described. Sometimes the bottom drawer of all is made deeper in order to accommodate rolls of drawings, but it is infinitely preferable to keep all sheets flat as they are much easier for reference.

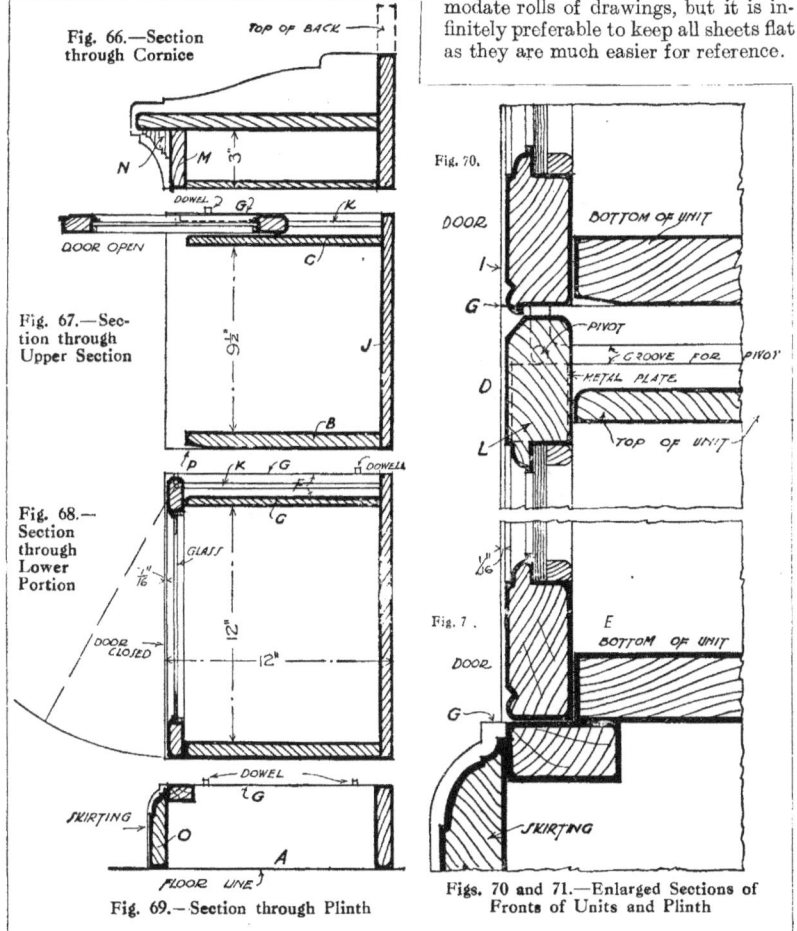

Fig. 66.—Section through Cornice

Fig. 67.—Section through Upper Section

Fig. 68.—Section through Lower Portion

Fig. 69.—Section through Plinth

Figs. 70 and 71.—Enlarged Sections of Fronts of Units and Plinth

ANOTHER CABINET FOR FILING DRAWINGS

Another small cabinet fitted with trays for filing drawings is shown by Figs. 61 to 65.

THE PRACTICAL WOODWORKER

Fig. 61 is a half-front elevation and half-longitudinal section of the cabinet; Fig. 62 is a detail of section through front; Fig. 63 is a detail of section through back; The construction of the cabinet is apparent from the drawings, and as it is on very similar lines to the one just described need not be detailed.

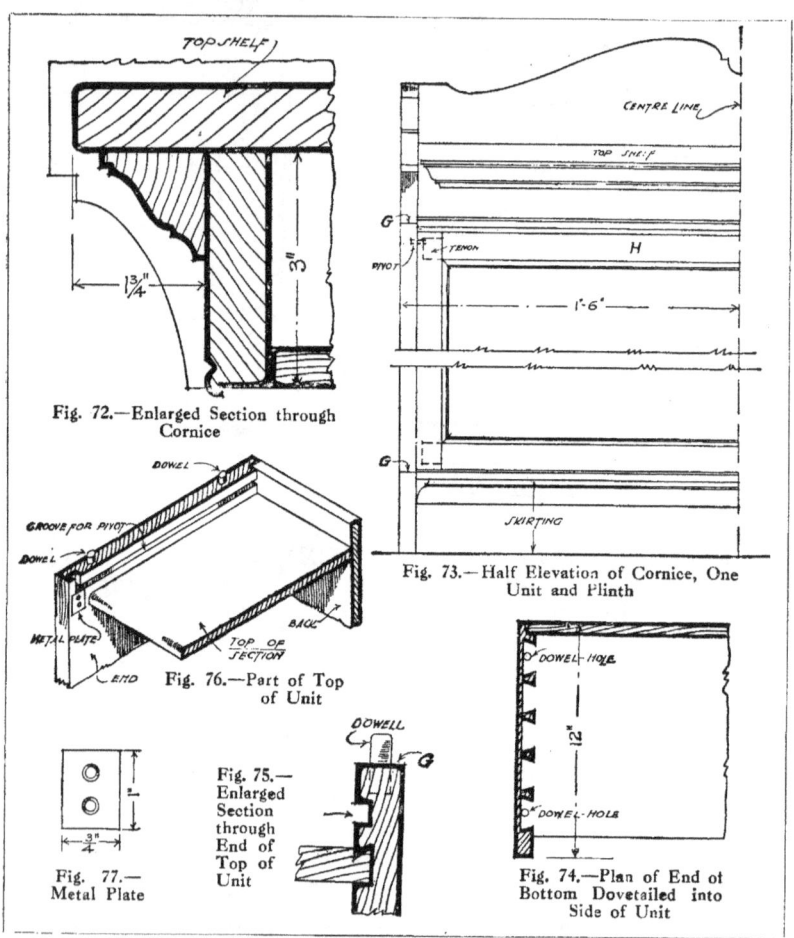

Fig. 72.—Enlarged Section through Cornice

Fig. 76.—Part of Top of Unit

Fig. 73.—Half Elevation of Cornice, One Unit and Plinth

Fig. 75.—Enlarged Section through End of Top of Unit

Fig. 77.—Metal Plate

Fig. 74.—Plan of End of Bottom Dovetailed into Side of Unit

Fig. 64 is a detail of section through side; Fig. 65 is a detail of plan through one of the back corners. The size of the cabinet from back to front over all is 2 ft. 2 in. All other dimensions are shown.

SECTIONAL BOOKCASES

The sectional type of bookcase consists of a number of separate units which are built up as necessity demands. A book-

OTHER OFFICE FURNITURE

case of this type may be said to be never complete, for it grows with the requirements of book accommodation, and its only limitation is space. The convenience of this system is apparent and need not be dwelt upon. The general appearance of such a bookcase is perhaps rather severe, which renders it more suitable for office furnishing than for home use, but its adaptiveness should not be lost sight of when considering it in the latter capacity. Figs. 66 to 69 explain the construction. The cases about to be described are easily made and require no elaborate fittings. As will be gathered from the illustrations, the glass fronts are pivoted at the top to open outwards (see Fig. 67 and 68), and when raised to a horizontal position, slide into compartments contrived for their reception.

The first figure is termed the cornice, and is detachable from the sections below, as is also the base or plinth (Fig. 69). The width across the front is 3 ft., and the depth of the end at the narrow part is 12 in. (see Fig. 68), or a little less if desired.

Mahogany or American walnut will look well with a finish of french-polish, as will also oak with a wax polish. The interior parts may be made of pine, stained to match the outside. Stuff 1 in. or $\frac{7}{8}$ in. thick is employed in the main, while the backs, etc., can be quite thin.

Commence operations by first making a full-size drawing of the sections as follows: Get a piece of drawing paper or wallpaper (using the reverse side of the latter) and pin it to a table-top or drawing-board. Start with the base line A in Fig. 69, and

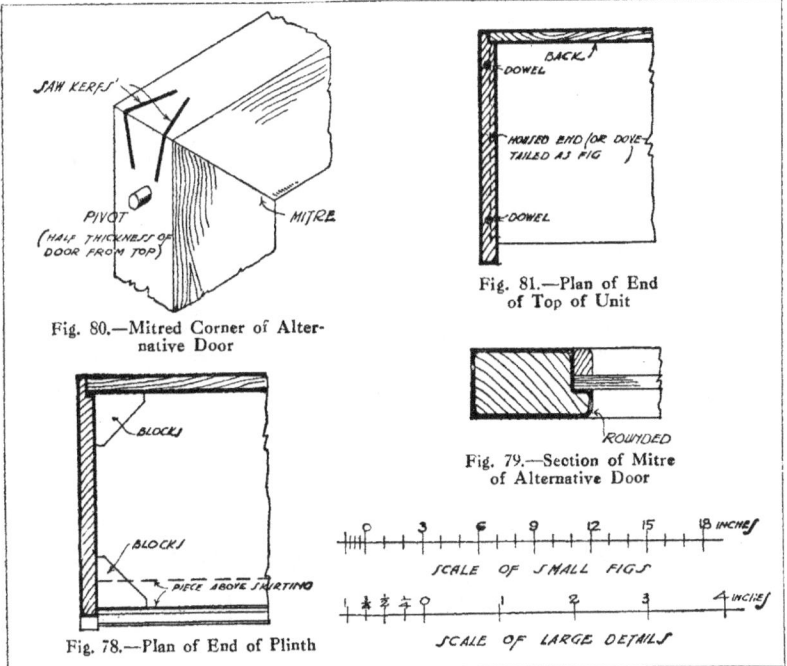

Fig. 80.—Mitred Corner of Alternative Door

Fig. 81.—Plan of End of Top of Unit

Fig. 79.—Section of Mitre of Alternative Door

Fig. 78.—Plan of End of Plinth

SCALE OF SMALL FIGS

SCALE OF LARGE DETAILS

set out two vertical lines 12 in. apart. Then, with a pair of dividers or compasses, ascertain the various sizes, etc., in Figs. 70, 71, 72, etc. (some of these will be found figured on the illustrations), by reference to the scales given. Transfer the measurements full size to the working drawing, and so deal with all the different parts. Draw bottom B of the lower section, taking the thickness, etc., from Fig. 71. From this decide on the height of space required for the books. The lower section (Fig. 68) allows for 12 in., and the section above

drawn, allowing the front H (Fig. 73) to drop $\frac{1}{8}$ in. lower than G; likewise the lower rail I (top of Fig. 70). The details of the plinth may now be put in. Let the doors stand back a full $\frac{1}{16}$ in. from the front edges of the ends. Half the front view (Fig. 73) may now be drawn, the horizontal lines of the cornice, doors, and plinth being obtained from the sections first drawn.

Regarding the construction, first make the sections, dovetailing the bottoms B to the ends, as shown in Fig. 74. The tops C

Fig. 82.—Office Wardrobe or Cupboard

9$\frac{1}{2}$ in. Next mark the position of the section top C. Insert a full-size copy of the rails D and E, as in Figs. 70 and 71. Between the top C allow for the space F equal to $\frac{3}{16}$ in. larger than the thickness of the doors, for clearance when they are lifted and pushed into this space while taking out books. Above the space F begin with the bottom of the upper section, and proceed as for the lower section. Note the line G in all figures represents the top point of each section.

The cornice (Fig. 66) should next be

(Figs. 67 and 68), of $\frac{1}{2}$-in. stuff, are dovetail-grooved as in Fig. 75. Of course, this groove must not come through to the front.

A back J (Figs. 67 and 68) of $\frac{1}{2}$-in. stuff is fitted in rebated ends, and fixed with screws, or $\frac{1}{4}$-in. three-ply might be substituted. Two $\frac{3}{8}$-in. diameter dowels protruding about $\frac{3}{8}$ in. are fixed in the top of the section ends, as in Figs. 67, 68, 74, etc., and corresponding holes bored into the bottom of the ends. Before the top and bottom of the sections are glued to the ends, a groove

OTHER OFFICE FURNITURE

K (Figs. 67 and 68) must be made. This groove is for an iron or brass pin, shown by the dotted circle in Fig. 70 (*see also* Fig. 73, etc.). These pins should be put in half the thickness of the door down from the top edge, and may suitably consist of screws with the heads filed off, leaving a projection of about $\frac{8}{16}$ in. This groove, instead of coming out at the front, is turned upwards, as in Fig. 76, in order to drop the pins of the doors into position, the upper section of the cornice being tilted to do this.

As by constant usage the pin would wear the bottom of the groove, and thus let the door down and interfere with its true hanging, a metal plate L (Fig. 70), and shown in Figs. 76 and 77, is fixed with a couple of countersunk screws. The lower side of the pin in the door will then ride on the top edge of the plate, which may be made out of a piece of sheet-brass or hoop-iron. The groove at the entrance should be the same size as the iron pin in the door, but farther inwards it should be wider, to avoid friction. In fact, for ease of running, the door should rest on the top C (Figs. 67 and 68) when pushed in, as shown in Fig. 67. The space F (Fig. 68) should have a good application of powdered

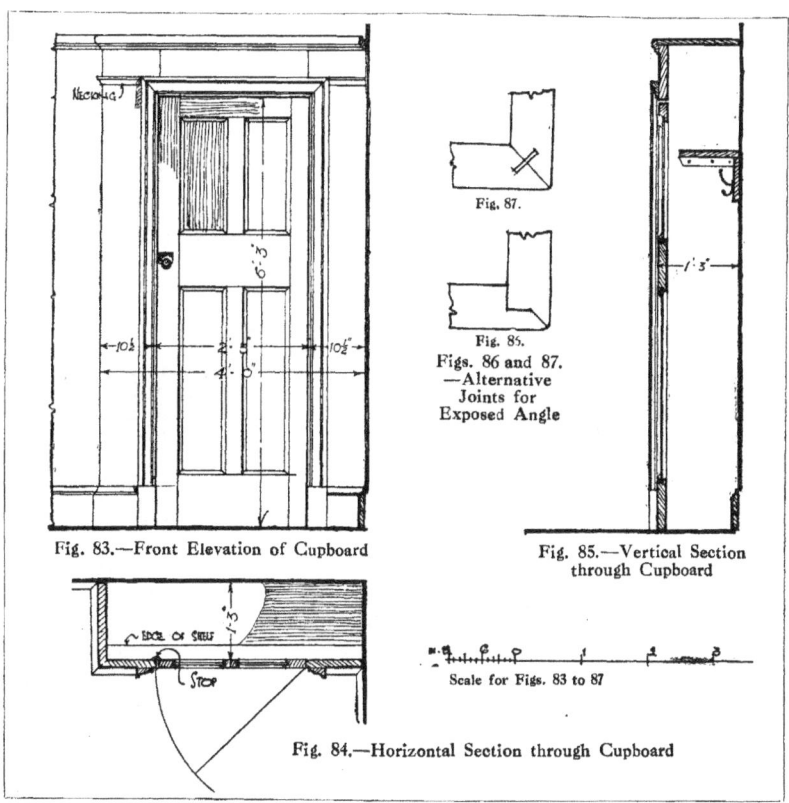

Fig. 83.—Front Elevation of Cupboard

Figs. 86 and 87.—Alternative Joints for Exposed Angle

Fig. 85.—Vertical Section through Cupboard

Scale for Figs. 83 to 87

Fig. 84.—Horizontal Section through Cupboard

french chalk or blacklead, to help the easy sliding of the door.

The cornice (Fig. 66) top may be housed into the ends as described for the top O (Figs. 68 and 75), the bottom dovetailed as in Fig. 74, and the front M have short tenons fitting into mortises going three-quarters through the ends. The back is continued above the top, and shaped as shown in Fig. 73. The moulding N is simply fitted between the ends. The plinth (Fig. 69) need not have a top ; the front portion O is tenoned into the ends the same as M (Fig. 66). Angle pieces, as in Fig. 78, are fixed in the corners, and secured with glue and screws. The back is fitted as for the sections, and further secured with blocks. The skirting is fitted between the ends as described for the cornice.

The doors are tenoned and mortised together and have moulded edges as in Figs. 70 and 71, which also show the fixing of transparent glass with beads. Leaded glass of a lighter type would look very well, and can be obtained made to order. The doors could be formed in a simpler manner by using 1½-in. by 1-in. stuff rebated and rounded, as in Fig. 79, then mitred together and glued up. A piece of strong cord should then be tied round, and eight small blocks inserted between the cord and the frame, gradually working towards the mitres until sufficient pressure is obtained to thoroughly close them. When the glue is hard, a couple of saw kerfs are run in, the mitre dovetailing, and a slip of veneer glued in, as shown in Fig. 80. Glass slips may be prepared and mitred in the door ; or, if preferred, the glass can be fixed in with coloured putty to match the wood. Figs. 74 and 81 show the positions of the dowels. The weight of the books will help to keep one section to the other ; but for further security slanting screws may be driven from the upper face of the bottom into the ends beneath. Care must be taken that they do not interfere with the sliding in of the doors. To prevent the doors from jamming when being pushed inwards, the bottoms of sections must be bevelled as at P (Fig. 67) ; also the front edges of the tops O should be rounded as shown.

Great care must be taken in framing the section together to have them true— that is, the tops and bottoms must be at right angles to the ends ; and to ensure the nice running of the doors in the space F (Fig. 68), the tops and bottoms B and C must be $\frac{1}{16}$ in. wider at the back than at the front.

OFFICE WARDROBE OR CUPBOARD

The average fitted cupboard has few claims to rank as a thing of beauty. It is usually rather mean in appearance and out of harmony with the other parts of the room, and yet only a very little initial care is required in order to make it quite refined and pleasing in appearance. One inexpensive design, shown by Fig. 82, is explained by Figs. 83 to 87. It is obvious that such a fitment is not necessarily only suited to office use. Finished in a suitable style it could quite well be adapted as a wardrobe for the bedroom, or to occupy some available space on a landing.

A 1½-in. door, 6 ft. 3 in. by 2 ft. 3 in., is hung to a perfectly plain cupboard front and returned end, kept quite free from the beaded angles and V-joints so often found. The angle between front and end should be slightly rounded, and can be formed in accordance with one of the two methods shown by Figs. 86 and 87.

Having fixed the cupboard in position an architrave moulding with plinth blocks is mitred round the door opening, and the general skirting is carried round the bottom up to the plinth-blocks. Next the top is filled in with tongued boarding, and a capping moulding added as shown. If this moulding can match and line with the general frieze-rail, so much the better for the harmonious appearance of cupboard and room. A small necking should be added, level with the shoulders of the architrave, as in Fig. 83, and a stop planted on inside, as in Fig. 84, to form a rebate for the door, which is hung in the usual manner, thus completing the cupboard with the exception of the shelf.

Mantel Fitments

THE wooden mantelpiece is tending almost entirely to supersede the metal one in even small houses. This is almost entirely due to improved taste and the consequent demand for mantelpieces which are decorative in themselves, and harmonise with the surrounding woodwork.

Now that panelling in oak, mahogany and walnut is coming so much into vogue, cast-iron mantels are practically ruled out because of their limitations with regard to the finish. Painting and graining is not satisfactory in connection with fireplace work, hence the demand for wooden mantels in character with the surrounding interior trim.

The treatment of the stove or actual fireplace part allows of many variations and, generally speaking, one can devise many successful treatments. Well-coloured tiles in many sizes and shades are easily procurable at a price which enables them to be used in even small houses, and a great variety of well-designed grates enables one to make a selection which will actually enhance the design of the woodwork.

In addition to the open grate illustrated by Fig. 1, two alternative treatments can be adopted for the fireplace proper. Anthracite slow-combustion stoves can be used quite well in conjunction with a mantel such as that shown, in which case it is customary to fill in the opening with tiles, a small space being cut through to the flue to take off the fumes and smoke.

Another treatment is in connection with gas fires, which can be obtained in many varieties. Dog grates fitted with imitation logs set back in a tiled or brick opening are very effective, or they can be obtained to almost exactly match an ordinary open fire. It will thus be seen that grates or stoves can be obtained specially designed for either coal, wood, gas, or anthracite, and consequently the fireplace can be made most attractive and a distinct decorative feature of any room.

There are a few general constructive points in fireplace work which should be borne in mind. In the first place it almost goes without saying that the wood must be thoroughly well seasoned and dry, otherwise shakes are bound to appear in the work after a few months. Secondly, in addition to tongueing the joints, screws should be inserted from the back for additional security ; and, as a last precaution, it is customary to glue blocks in the angles wherever possible at the back. In cases where wooden mantels are fixed against very fresh walls, it will be found a good plan to well coat the wall with paint and varnish bottoms mixed together, this being applied also to the back of the mantel as a guard against dampness working out of the wall.

First example.—The mantel illustrated by Fig. 1 is intended to be executed in oak, with an ammonia-fumed and wax finish ; or, if American or Canadian oak is employed, an almost similar effect can be

Fig 1.

Fig. 3.

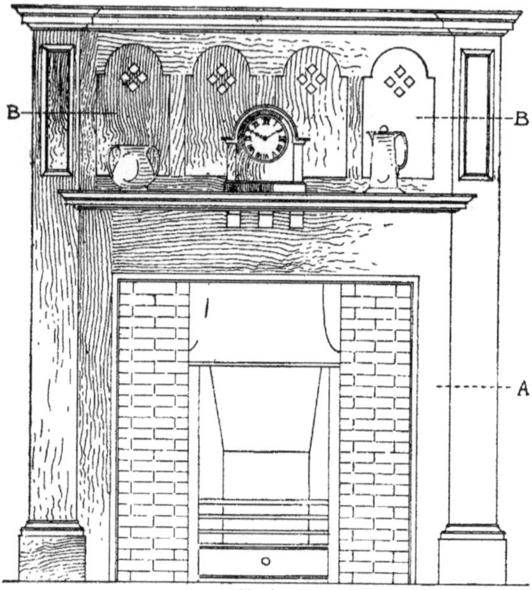

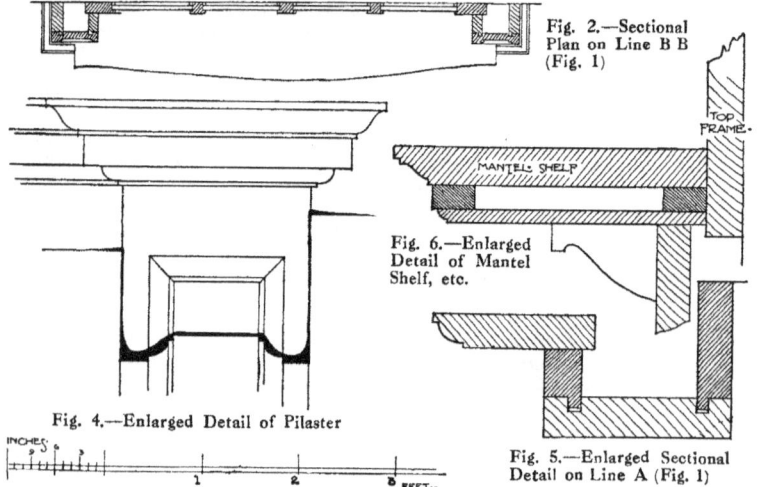

Figs. 1 and 3.—Front Elevation and Vertical Section of Mantel Fitment

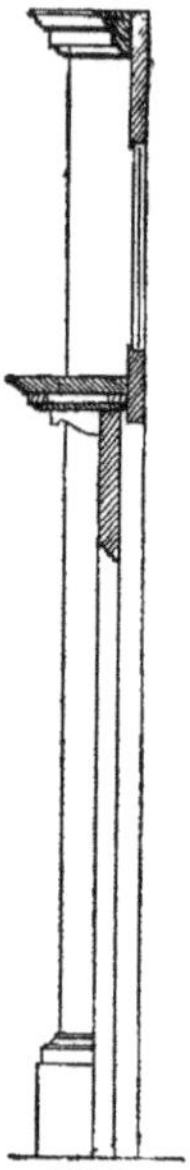

Fig. 2.—Sectional Plan on Line B B (Fig. 1)

Fig. 6.—Enlarged Detail of Mantel Shelf, etc.

Fig. 4.—Enlarged Detail of Pilaster

Fig. 5.—Enlarged Sectional Detail on Line A (Fig. 1)

MANTEL FITMENTS

produced with caustic soda or American potash for the colouring medium. The design shown would harmonise quite well with a modern Jacobean or Elizabethan treatment, or in conjunction with slatted and papered walls, or even plain distempered walls. The tiles in the example shown would be slabbed as indicated on wooden frames, and a better effect is produced if these are splayed inwards to it will be seen, are simply made with three pieces tongued together, panels being recessed as shown near the tops (see Fig. 4). Blocks should, of course, be glued in the inside angles to increase the strength of the joints. An enlarged sectional detail (Fig. 5) shows the necessary moulding detail for the recessed panels.

Between the pilasters two frames are necessary, the fronts of which lie in separate

Fig. 7.—Second Example of Mantel Fitment

the front of the grate, thus giving a recessed effect to the latter.

The elevation (Fig. 1) is drawn to scale and indicates normal sizes; it is, however, always a good plan to ascertain the exact size of the stove it is proposed to use, so that the opening can be made accordingly. The sectional plan (Fig. 2) under the elevation represents a sectional view through the upper part of the mantel. A vertical section is given by Fig. 3. The pilasters, planes. This will be more clearly seen by referring to the enlarged section (Fig. 6) showing the construction of the mantelshelf, etc. The bottom frame is brought forward in order that sufficient space may be left between the frame and the wall to receive the tiled front. One and a half inches is a customary space for this part.

The enlarged section of the mantelshelf (Fig. 6) shows the construction necessary for the shelf. If made in the solid it would not stand well, and would almost certainly split after a short time. It is therefore built up as indicated, two narrow pieces are same direction all through, so that if shrinkage occurs the whole built-up shelf will shrink together. An additional precau-

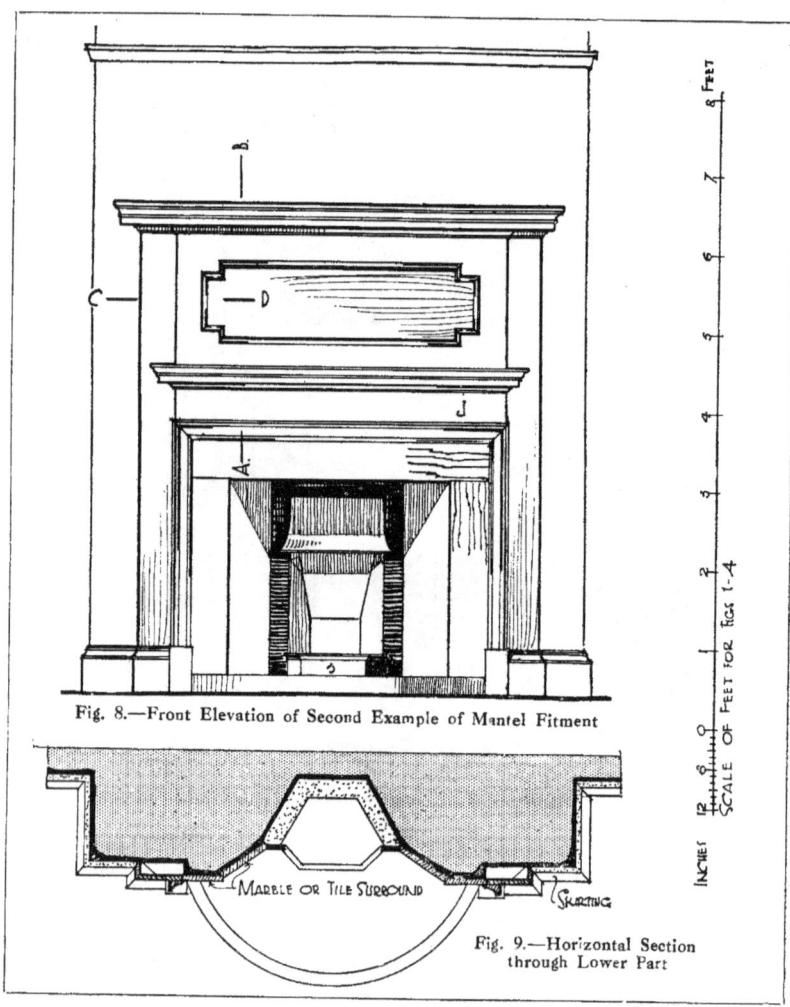

Fig. 8.—Front Elevation of Second Example of Mantel Fitment

Fig. 9.—Horizontal Section through Lower Part

glued in between, and it is also necessary to fill in the resulting spaces at the ends. The grain of the wood must run in the tion to ensure solidity is effected by gluing two cross-grained pieces of wood equally spaced between the end-filling pieces and

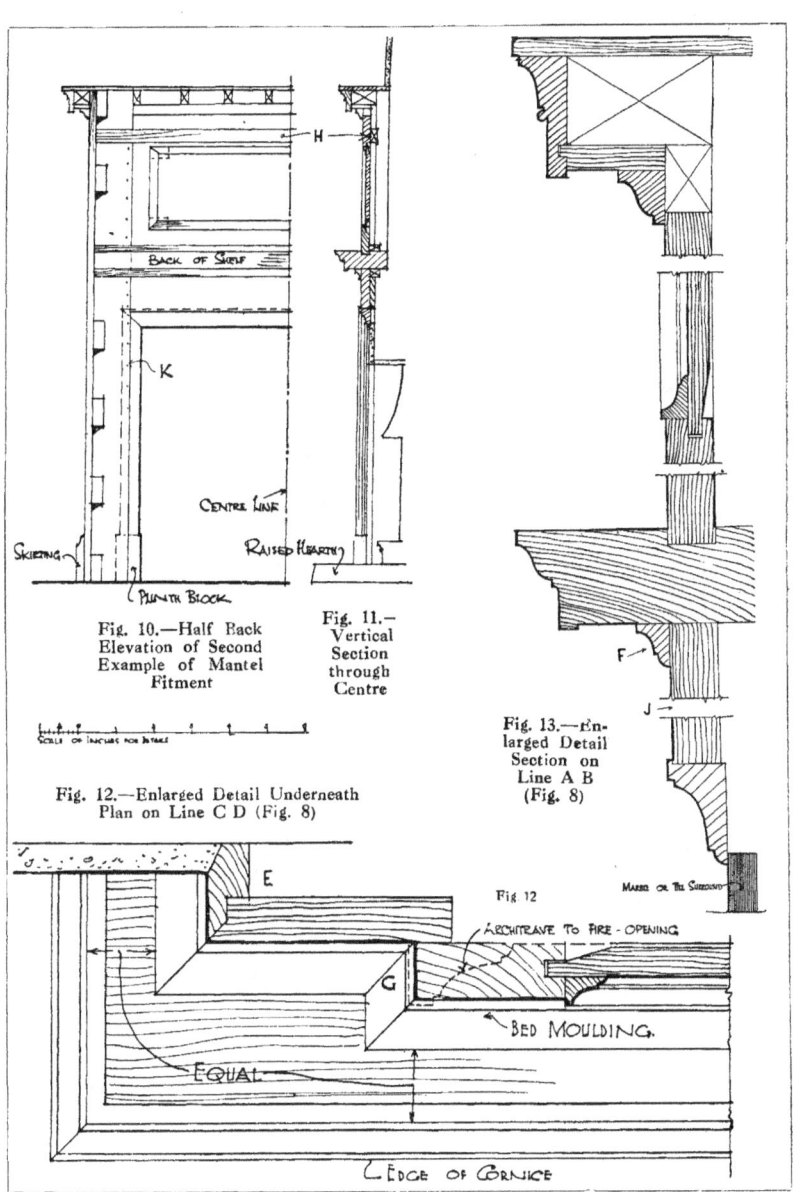

Fig. 10.—Half Back Elevation of Second Example of Mantel Fitment

Fig. 11.—Vertical Section through Centre

Fig. 13.—Enlarged Detail Section on Line A B (Fig. 8)

Fig. 12.—Enlarged Detail Underneath Plan on Line C D (Fig. 8)

the boards in order to keep them the proper distance apart.

It will be seen from Fig. 3 that the insides of the pilasters must be cut away so that the frames can be screwed on from the back. When fixed to the pilasters the shelf and brackets should be added, and then the skirting and brackets mouldings are mitred round to complete the job.

Second example.—An alternative design is shown by the half-tone reproduc-

panel and its frame projects in front of the jambs as G (Fig. 12), and is secured to them by means of horizontal rails across the back, as at H in Fig. 10. The top is completed by a boxed cornice, slightly larger than the lower solid one, as in Fig. 13, having the bed-mould only broken round the projecting panelled front, thus obtaining a slightly pronounced overhang at the corners (see Fig. 12), the top being filled in with a cover-board.

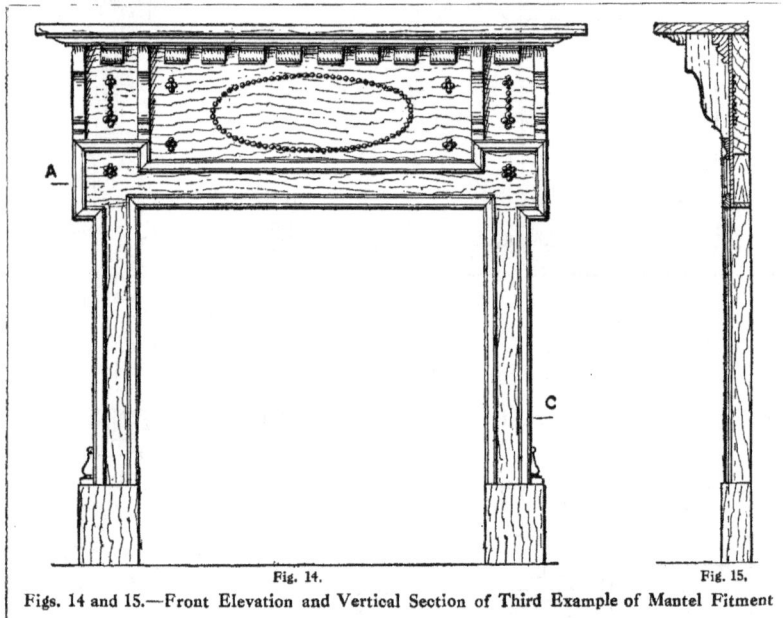

Figs. 14 and 15.—Front Elevation and Vertical Section of Third Example of Mantel Fitment

tion Fig. 7. An elevation and horizontal section are given by Figs. 8 and 9.

Figs. 10 and 11 show the suggested construction, the jambs being boxed out as at E in Fig. 12, and connected in the middle by the solid lower shelf, which is moulded and made into a complete cornice by the addition of a bed mould, as at F in Fig. 13. Above this shelf is a panelled front, having a moulding on the face broken round small rectangular blocks at the corners. This

Below the lower shelf is a frieze J (Figs. 8 and 13) exactly in the same place as the framing above, and below this again is the moulded architrave, mitred round the fireplace opening and finished next the floor with plinth blocks to stop the moulded skirting, which should match, or at least line with, that of the room concerned. Architrave, plinth, blocks, etc., can be held in position by screwing from behind through the jambs as at K

MANTEL FITMENTS

in Fig. 10, which also shows angle-blocks strengthening the main corners.

Third example.—The making of this example is of a more simple nature than the two already given, and it is intended as a covering to an existing mantel rather than a separate construction. Dimensions will, of course, vary according to existing conditions, but the proportions shown by the elevation and vertical section (Figs. 14 and 15) should be retained as nearly as possible.

The panel should be of one piece of poplar ½ in. thick, and the two jambs about 5 in. wide and ½ in. thick. The four brackets are prepared and fixed to support the shelf, as shown in Fig. 16, which is a vertical section taken near the centre line. At regular intervals, ten dentils cut from suitable architrave moulding are secured to the shelf and the top of the panel to form a decorative feature. Another length of suitable moulding is planted on the underside of the shelf and is mitred at the angle of return to the wall, and this tends to relieve the plain appearance of the square-edge shelf.

At the bottom of the jambs a square-edge plinth of the same height as the existing skirting boards, and having sufficient thickness to come flush with the moulding used for the border of the jambs, can be fixed. This is shown enlarged in Fig. 17. At this stage of the work the moulding at the edges of jambs and panel can be bradded on.

For the decorative feature in the panel brass-headed nails, as used in furniture upholstery may be chosen in place of the composition ornament of the manufacturer, and the effect is most pleasing when the mantelpiece is finished in white enamel paint.

Some little care and patience are necessary to ensure the nails entering and bedding to the wood symmetrically. Therefore a centre line should be drawn with the spaces divided off and then small holes made with a fine bradawl as a guide for the nails. Then a hardwood block tapered down and hollowed to fit the brass heads will prevent damage to their surface when driving them in. Any nails out of centre with their heads should be discarded.

The outline for the oval or ellipse can be made by the following method (*see* Fig. 18). Draw the long centre line E D to the predetermined length, then also draw the shorter diameter F G. These lines will intersect at H, and using H as centre and G H as radius, strike a circle, and where the circle cuts the long diameter at I and J, insert a brad. Now fasten a piece of fine twine to the brad at I, insert another brad at G, draw the string lightly round this brad, and finally secure it to the brad at J. Remove the brad at G, place the point of a lead-pencil firmly against the twine, and move it steadily forward, when it will trace the ellipse as shown by the dotted line G to D, and may be continued until the complete outline is drawn.

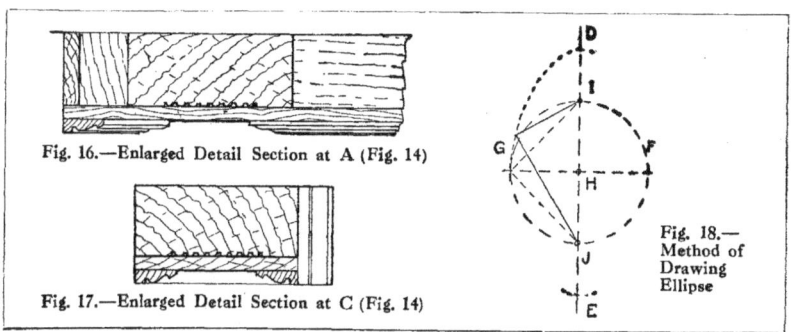

Fig. 16.—Enlarged Detail Section at A (Fig. 14)

Fig. 17.—Enlarged Detail Section at C (Fig. 14)

Fig. 18.—Method of Drawing Ellipse

Sleighs and Toboggans

EASILY-MADE SLEDGE

A TOBOGGAN may be so simple that it may be nailed together of rough boards, but desirable improvements are to shape and plane the runners, cross-seat, and foot-rail, to provide hand-holes, and to screw strips of half-round or D-shaped iron to the under edges of the runners (see Fig. 1). Such a coaster for a single passenger need not be more than 3 ft. long and 1 ft. 3 in. wide, the runners, of 1-in. or 1½-in. wood, being about 6 in. deep. The seat and foot-rail should be let into notches (preferably dovetailed),

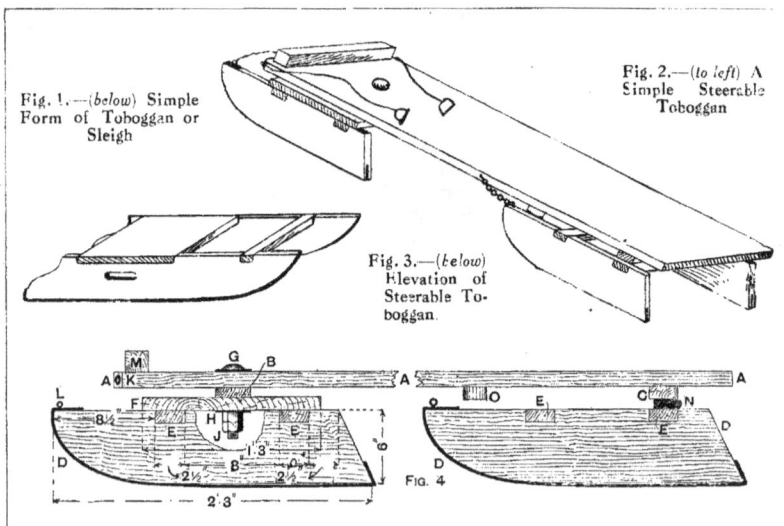

Fig. 1.—(below) Simple Form of Toboggan or Sleigh

Fig. 2.—(to left) A Simple Steerable Toboggan

Fig. 3.—(below) Elevation of Steerable Toboggan.

as illustrated, and held by stout screws. For two or more persons the coaster should be lengthened, the hindermost passenger steering with a pole held across his knees, a touch on the ground with

SLEIGHS AND TOBOGGANS

either end deflecting the course of the coaster to one side or other of the track. A rope is attached to the foot-rail for dragging up-hill.

A steerable toboggan (Figs. 2 and 3) may be made from the following material: a top board A, 6 ft. long, 1 ft. 6 in. wide, and 1 in. or $1\frac{1}{4}$ in. thick, and two cross-pieces, one B, 3 in. by $\frac{3}{4}$ in. by 1 ft. 6 in., and the other C, $2\frac{1}{2}$ in. by 1 in. by 1 ft. 6 in. Screw on the former (B) 9 in. or 10 in. from the front end, and the other (C) 5 in. or 6 in. from the opposite end of the top board. For the runners, prepare four pieces D of 1-in. board, 6 in. wide and 2 ft. 3 in. long, making notches 1 in. by $2\frac{1}{2}$ in., as shown, to carry cross-pieces E 1 ft. 6 in. long, fitted (dovetailed, if preferred), and screwed so as to hold together each pair of runners. Over the front pair, screw firmly to the crosspieces E a piece F of 1-in. board 1 ft. 3 in. by 1 ft. 6 in. long. To the underside of the cross-piece C right at the rear of the toboggan screw two or three strong hinges N, and fix the three flaps as shown.

Now place the whole in position on the floor, and, having the sides of the front pair of runners flush with those of the top board, and the crosspiece B in the centre of the board F, bore a $\frac{3}{4}$-in. or 1-in. hole right through A, B and F, exactly in the centre. Through this, pass a round-headed bolt fitted with two washers, a nut H, and lock nut J, and bolt up H tight enough to allow the front bogie to move freely without too much play; then tighten up the lock nut J. A front foot-rail M and screw-eyes on each side at K and L, with strings crossed from L and leading to the handles, will complete the toboggan. An indiarubber door-stop might, however, be screwed on at O to take any undue stress off the hinges in case of a very rough track. A short chain-stay at each side, as illustrated, is also desirable. The steering can easily be done by means of the crossed cords, and feet outstretched in front will act as brakes when necessary.

CANADIAN BOX SLEIGH

Fig. 5 is a side elevation of a Canadian box sleigh with two deep lazy-backed seats for four passengers, and suitable for either one or a pair of horses. Fig. 6 is a half-front view, showing the side bend of the runner meeting the dash iron in one continuous sweep, also the position of the forked shaft eye. Fig. 7 is a half-back view, from which the various side bevels and half-widths are obtained; it shows one of the side raves or running boards, which serve as a step. Fig. 8 is a half plan, bottom upwards. The hind seat may be taken out and the front one slid back for use by two people only.

The principal dimensions are as follow: Size of body on top line, 5 ft. 8 in, by 2 ft. $11\frac{1}{4}$ in.; depth of body panels, $9\frac{1}{2}$ in.; sides and ends of body splayed $\frac{3}{4}$ in.; height from bottom boards to top of seat, 1 ft. 2 in.; seat boards, 3 ft. 6 in. by 1 ft. 4 in.; depth of seat panels, measured on a vertical line, 9 in. at front and $9\frac{1}{2}$ in. at back; sides and back of seats splayed 4 in.; depth of lazy-back, 9 in.; distance between lazy-back and top of seat panel, 2 in.; distance of front seat from front of body, 1 ft. 9 in.; length of runners over the bend, 6 ft. 9 in.; width of track over runners, 3 ft. 6 in.; height from ground line to top of rave, 1 ft. 2 in.; height of dash from top of body, 1 ft. 8 in.; and width of dash, 2 ft. 8 in. The runners A (Fig. 5), the beams B, and the knees C (Figs. 5 to 8) should be of fine white oak, the runners $1\frac{3}{8}$ in. deep by $1\frac{1}{2}$ in. thick, beams 3 ft. 6 in. long by $2\frac{1}{4}$ in. deep by $1\frac{1}{8}$ in. thick, and the knees $1\frac{3}{4}$ in. wide at the beam, tapering to $1\frac{1}{8}$ in. at the runner by $1\frac{1}{8}$ in. thick. The front ends of the runners terminate at the upper edge of the body, where they taper to the dash-board thickness; they are bent with the end-grain or annual rings vertical.

In framing up the underwork, set the foot of the front knee 3 in. in advance of the beginning of the bend of the runner, and the beam 6 in. from the front of the body. Set the back beam 6 in. from the back of the body to the same angle as the front knee. Tenon the knees into the beams and runners to the required bevel, as shown by Fig. 9, the ends of the beam

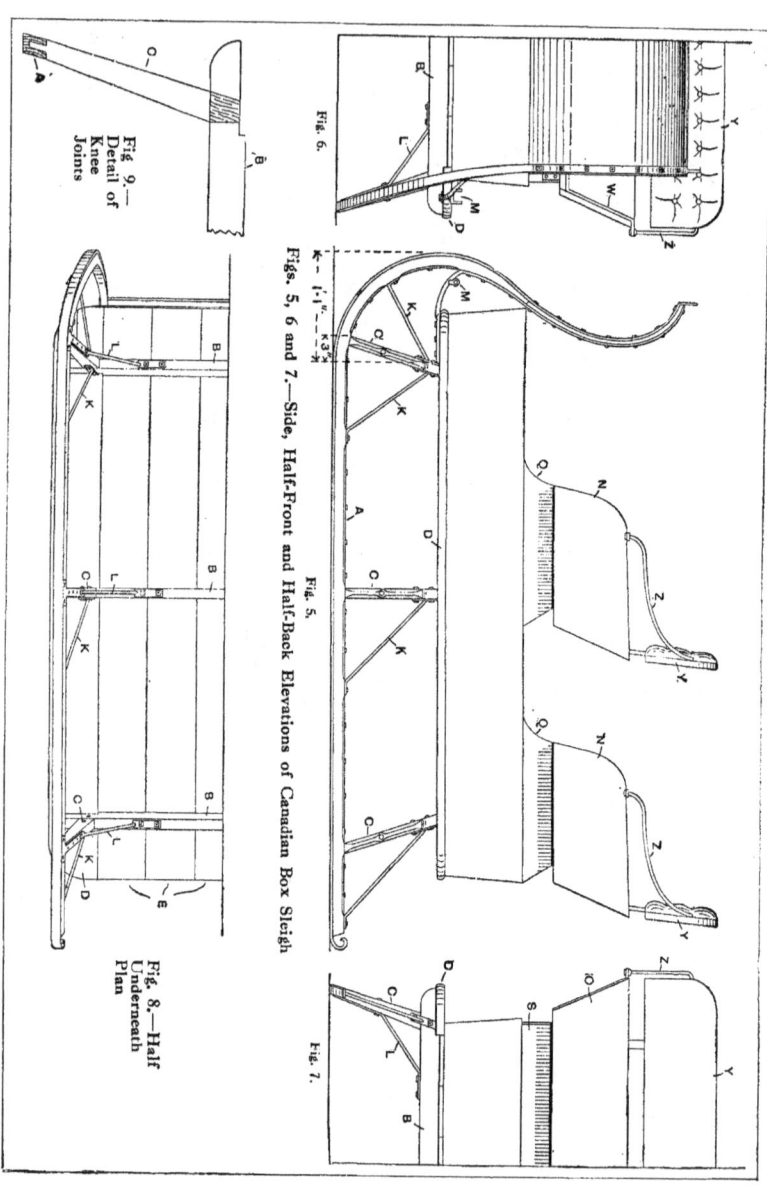

Figs. 5, 6 and 7.—Side, Half-Front and Half-Back Elevations of Canadian Box Sleigh

Fig. 8.—Half Underneath Plan

Fig. 9.—Detail of Knee Joints

SLEIGHS AND TOBOGGANS

projecting 3 in. Do not weaken the runners by mortising right through, but leave ⅜ in. of wood underneath and make the mortises a little wider at the bottom than at the top to allow for wedging. Having cut all the tenons, set up the knees and beams, and lay them together to see that the tenons are all in line. Next put on the runners, and test for accuracy, correcting all joints. Then, after marking all the bearings, take the frame apart and shave up the edges, leaving the back of the knees flat. Glue up the knees and beams, and when the glue is set, give the jecting ½ in. over the ends of the beams, and fix them with screws. Fill in the space between the raves with ⅝-in. boards lengthwise of the frame for the floor, nailing them to the beams.

If the sleigh is to be painted, American whitewood will be suitable for the panels and dash-board. A longitudinal sectional elevation of the body is given by Fig. 10, the frame of which is of ash 9 in. high, the panels extending ½ in. above to form a guard for the seat risers. As the panels are ½ in. thick, the frame should be made 1 in. less in length and width than the

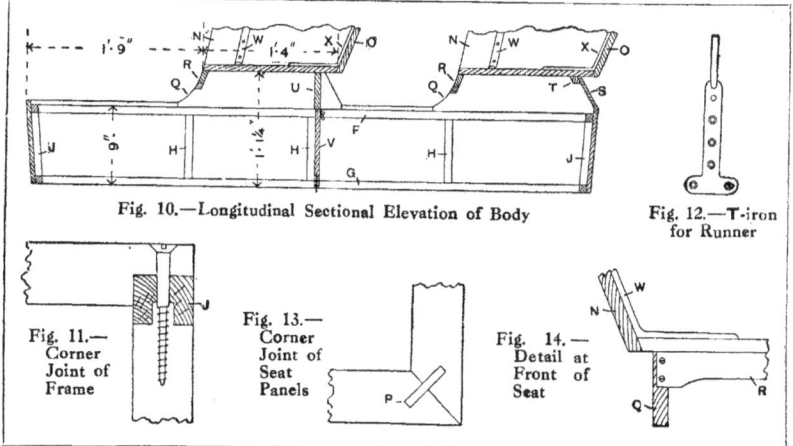

Fig. 10.—Longitudinal Sectional Elevation of Body

Fig. 11.—Corner Joint of Frame

Fig. 12.—T-iron for Runner

Fig. 13.—Corner Joint of Seat Panels

Fig. 14.—Detail at Front of Seat

tenons at the lower end of the knees a coat of white-lead mixed with raw linseed oil, insert a small wedge in the end of each, and drive them into the mortises in the runners. Place the runners between timbers fixed to the floor of the workshop, forming parallel grooves the required distance apart for the width of track, and secure them temporarily with top buttons. See that the beams are in the exact position in which they are to remain, and fix them with cleats. The raves D (Figs. 5 to 8) and the bottom boards E may be of deal. The raves are 5 ft. 7½ in. long by 6 in. wide by 1 in. thick. Let them into the beams ⅜ in., with the outer edge projecting ½ in., with the outer edge pro- dimensions previously given. The rails F, sills G, and standards H are all ⅞ in. by ⅞ in., while the corner pillars J are 1⅛ in. by ⅞ in. A standard is also framed in at the centre of the front and back of the frame. Fig. 11 is an enlarged plan of the corner joints. The standards are half-lapped into the rails and sills from the outside, the joints being glued and screwed together. Mitre the panels together at the ends, then fix them to the frame with glue and brads, and punch the latter well below the surface. Then dress the face of the panels slightly convex (otherwise they will appear hollow when painted and varnished), and fix on the corner plates. The lower corners of the frame should be strengthened with knee plates. If it is intended to have the body removable, it can be fixed to the raves with light bolts and wing-nuts; but if not, through the knees and beams, making the joints secure. The runners are further secured to the knees with **T**-irons (Fig. 12), which may either be welded or lapped into the lower flap of the under-braces L (Figs.

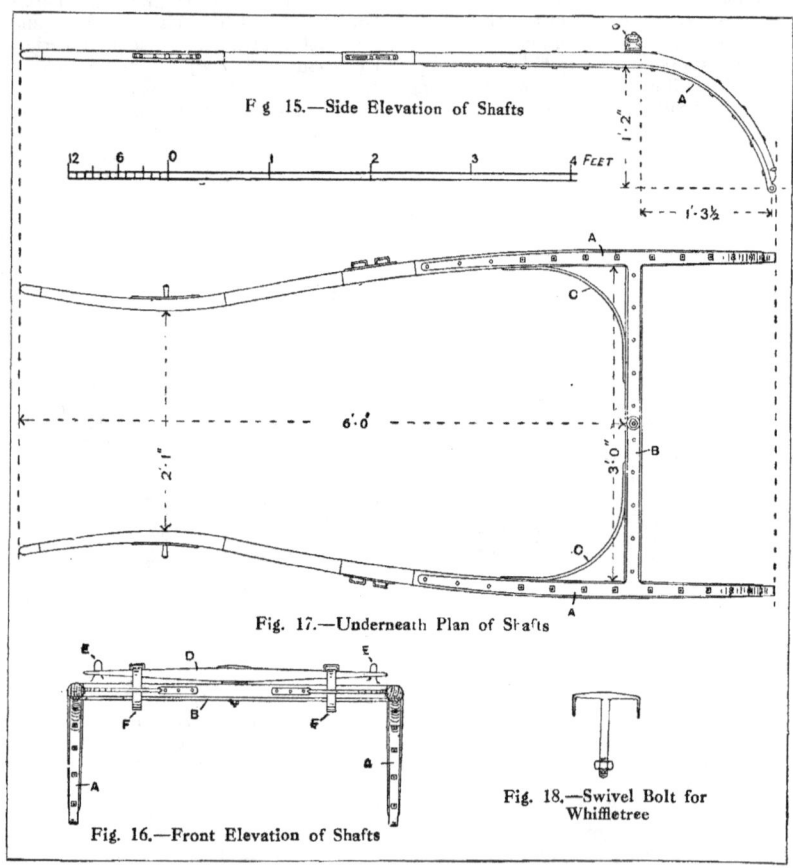

Fig. 15.—Side Elevation of Shafts

Fig. 17.—Underneath Plan of Shafts

Fig. 16.—Front Elevation of Shafts

Fig. 18.—Swivel Bolt for Whiffletree

it can be fixed with screws put in from underneath.

The runners can now be removed from their fixings, and the ironing-up of the underwork proceeded with. The flaps at the top of the side braces K (Fig. 5) are each fixed with a couple of light bolts put 6, 7, and 8). The forked shaft eyes M (Figs. 5 and 6) have a flap at both ends, one fixed underneath the front end of the raves, and the other to the back of the runners with bolts. The runners are shod with soft cast-steel shoes, $1\frac{1}{4}$ in. wide on the top and 1 in. on the tread by $\frac{3}{8}$ in. thick

SLEIGHS AND TOBOGGANS

fixed with ¼-in. bolts with countersunk heads. The shoes are lapped into the front plates, of 1-in. by ⅜-in. half-round iron, which continue to the top of the dash, terminating in a spill at the end. There is a similar plate at the back of the dash, the lower end of which is lapped into the upper end of the shaft-eye flap, the dashboard, of ½-in. wood, being fixed between the two plates with ¼-in. bolts. The dashboard can be bent to shape by wetting or steaming the back, and subjecting the face to heat.

The seats may now be taken in hand. Dress off the three bevelled edges of the seat boards the required amount, as indicated in Figs. 5, 6 and 7, but narrow the back of the board ₁³⁄₈ in. on each end. This is done to ensure the width at the top of the end panels measuring across front and back alike, which they will not do otherwise if the front corner is lower than the back. The seat panels N and O, of ¾-in. whitewood, are mitred at the back corners and screwed to the edges of the seat board. With a coarse saw, run a slot in the corner joint as shown at P in Fig. 13. Glue and screw the panels in position, secure the top of the joints with corner cramps, and drive into the slot a glued strip of ash. When the glue is set, dress off level, and secure the joints with corner plates on the top. The seat risers Q (Figs. 5 and 10) should be of ⅞-in. close-grained hardwood, such as cherry. They are fixed underneath the seats with screws, the front rails R, of 2-in. by ¾-in. ash, being checked and screwed into the front ends of the risers, as shown by the enlarged view (Fig. 14). The space between the back seat and the body is closed in with a ⅜-in. panel S boxed into the back ends of the seat risers, and a fillet T is fixed on inside underneath the seat. The space below the front seat is closed in by a ¾-in. board U, stump-tenoned and glued into the risers, and a ⅜-in. removable board V, secured in position with a couple of studs at the bottom, and two small brass bolts at the top, on each side of the body. Hoop-iron should be fixed along the top of the side rails F for the seat risers to slide on, the risers having studs fixed underneath registering with holes in the plates and rails to hold the seats in position. The lower part of the seat irons is shown at W and X (Fig. 10). They are 1-in. by ⅜-in. half-round iron. The lazybacks Y (Figs. 5, 6, and 7) are fixed with screws to the back irons X and the side stays Z, the threaded pin at the front end of the stay passing through a hole in the top end of the front irons W, a nut being screwed on underneath.

The shafts or thills are of the American buggy type, bent downwards at the heel, the size chosen being suitable for a 15-hands horse. Fig. 15 is a side view of the shafts, Fig. 16 a front view, and Fig. 17 a plan of the underside. The best kind of wood for the shafts and bars is hickory ; but if this is too expensive, or difficult to obtain, a good substitute will be either South American locust or best fine-grained English ash. The dimensions of the shafts are as follow : Length from cross-bar to point, 6 ft. ; distance from cross-bar to tug-stop, 4 ft. 6½ in. ; distance from cross-bar to back screw hole of breeching staple, 2 ft. 3½ in. ; width between the shafts, 3 ft. at the bar and 2 ft. 1 in. at the tugs. At the cross-bar the shafts are 1⅞ in. wide by 1½ in. thick, and the cross-bar, 2 in. by 1½ in., is framed into them with tenons 1 in. long. The back parts of the shafts are strengthened with 1½-in. by ⅜-in. half-round plates A, fixed underneath with bolts and screws, the end bolt next to the eye having a T-head clipped round the sides of the shaft to prevent its splitting. The bar plate B, of 1½-in. by ⅜-in. half-round iron, has a boss in the centre to take the whiffletree bolt, the ends of the plate being welded into the shaft plates. Light braces C are fixed to the inner edge of the shafts and cross-bar for additional security. The whiffletree D is 2 in. by 1½ in. at the centre, tapering to 1¼ in. by ⅞ in. at the ends, which pass through the slotted holes in the end of the traces, the latter being kept in position by pieces of leather lace put through two small holes bored through the whiffletree, as shown at E (Fig. 16). The swivel bolt (Fig. 18) is ½-in. in diameter, and has a T-head with fangs at the ends to drive into the whiffletree. Washer-plates are interposed between the cross-bar and whiffletree, to which they are fixed with screws. The bolt passes through the centre of the bars, and is secured with a hexagon nut and a split-pin underneath. A couple of leather check straps F hang loosely round the two bars near the ends.

the cross-bar D, and regulating the pressure on either end as required. An eye-bolt is fixed in the centre of the front cross-rail E for the attachment of a line to haul up the sleigh to the top of the track.

The hind bob F is hinged to the body-board at G, so as to accommodate itself to inequalities in the ground, the two

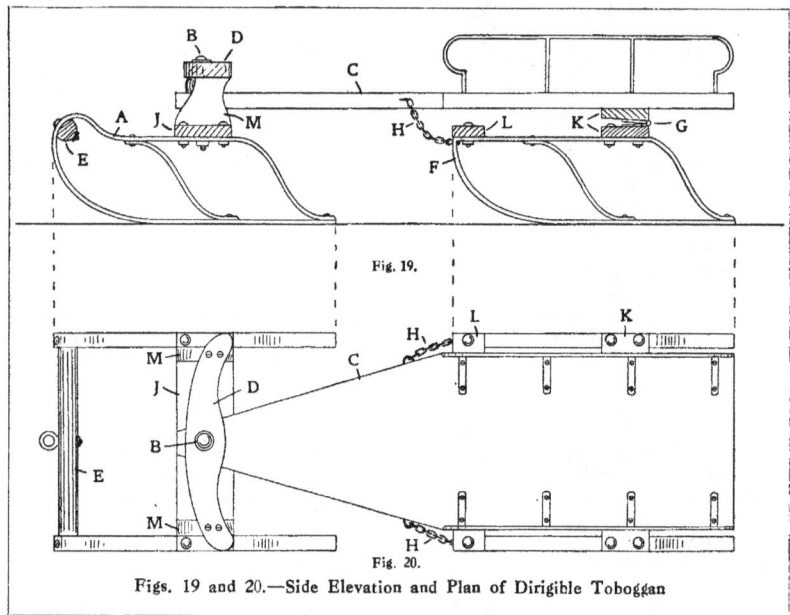

Figs. 19 and 20.—Side Elevation and Plan of Dirigible Toboggan

DIRIGIBLE TOBOGGAN

An improved dirigible toboggan or bob-sleigh mounted on a pair of bobs with light, flexible runners made of spring-steel is shown in side elevation by Fig. 19 and in plan by Fig. 20.

The front bob A turns on a king-bolt B passing through the front end of the body-board C, which is made taper, as shown in Fig. 20, to allow sufficient locking movement, the steering being effected by the front occupant placing his or her feet on

chains H checking any undue movement. A suitable size for four adults will be: Body-board C, 8 ft. long by 1 ft. 6 in. wide by $1\frac{3}{8}$ in. thick; bobs, 2 ft. 6 in. long by 1 ft. 10 in. wide by 9 in. high; front bolster J, 1 ft. 10 in. by 6 in. by $1\frac{1}{2}$ in.; front cross-rail E, 1 ft. 10 in. by $1\frac{3}{4}$ in. in diameter; hind bolsters K, 1 ft. 10 in. by 5 in. by $\frac{7}{8}$ in.; light rail L, 3 in. by $\frac{7}{8}$ in. The steering bar is got out of a piece of stuff 1 ft. 10 in. by 5 in. by $1\frac{1}{4}$ in., and is screwed to the two pedestals M, which are fixed to the bolster.

Aeroplane Woodwork

THE employment of wood as a material for the construction of aeroplanes has resulted in an extension of the woodworker's sphere and the formation of an important branch of the industry, and although there is a tendency towards the substitution of steel in the construction of various components hitherto made of wood, the fact that the use of the latter material tends towards a lower initial cost is certain to enforce its retention for some considerable time. Apart from this there are certain items in aircraft construction which cannot as yet be successfully made of steel, outstanding examples being the airscrew and the floats of the seaplane.

Principal Woods in Use.—The chief woods in use are silver or sitka spruce, Douglas fir, ash, hickory, mahogany, walnut, birch and poplar. Of these varieties silver spruce is most extensively employed, being very strong for its weight, of uniform quality, and, what is possibly its most useful characteristic, is straight of grain and relatively free from knots. It is obtained from North America, the best varieties from British Columbia. The trees average from 150 to 200 ft. in height and are about 4 ft. in diameter. The balks obtainable vary from 10 ft. to 30 ft. in length and from 9 to 20 inches in width. It is a fairly soft wood to work, but is inclined to woolliness.

Douglas fir, or as it is sometimes called, Oregon pine, is chiefly used as a substitute for silver spruce. It possesses a more pronounced grain than spruce, is heavier, and has a tendency to develop shakes and checks during and subsequent to manufacture. For this reason great care is necessary in the selection of the planks before conversion into finished parts, and the latter in turn must be carefully examined before assembly in the structure.

Of the various species of ash, the English variety is preferred in this country. It is used for all bent work and for such parts as skids, longerons, engine bearers and for any part in which hardness is desired.

Hickory, obtained from North America, possesses similar qualities and is used for the same purposes as ash. It is not so reliable as the latter, and is more liable to decay on exposure.

Mahogany is mainly used for floats, seaplane hulls and airscrews, the Honduras variety being preferred.

Walnut, either French or American, is used almost exclusively for airscrews. It is an extremely valuable wood for this purpose as it does not warp, and, when properly seasoned, shrinks very little. A comparative scarcity of this timber has necessitated the employment of other woods for airscrew construction, its substitute in this country, as already noted, being Honduras mahogany, while in America birch and white oak have been used.

The poplar species, which includes

American whitewood, basswood and cottonwood, are used for various minor details, and also as a core for plywood.

Plywoods enter very extensively into aeroplane construction, the most important varieties being three-ply birch and ash, varying in thickness from $\frac{1}{16}$ in. to 1 in., although above $\frac{1}{4}$ in. the layers are usually increased to five and sometimes seven.

The careful selection and examination of the wood to be used is an important preliminary to the actual woodworking operations. The chief requirements of an average specification for aircraft timber are cleanness and straightness of grain, and freedom from knots, resin pockets, dote and deleterious shakes. Cross breaks or "thunder shakes" are also defects to which particular attention must be paid, the detection of these faults being rendered more difficult by reason of the fact that they are often only existent towards the centre of the tree, and therefore only become visible when the timber is sawn into pieces of small scantling. Although these cross breaks are more often found in mahogany, they are occasionally met with in the various grades of spruce. Pronounced spiral and diagonal grain are also detrimental defects for aircraft timber, the limit for the inclination of the grain to the length of the plank being 1 in 20 for spruce and other approved substitutes. A further requirement for spruce is that it must possess not less than six annual rings per inch.

It is of fundamental importance for the timber to be thoroughly seasoned, preferably by a natural process, although certain methods of kiln-drying are allowed. It is also necessary for aircraft timber to fulfil certain tests as to strength, but these do not concern the woodworker. To limit as far as possible the amount of shrinkage which almost inevitably occurs after timber is freshly sawn, it should be quarter sawn, that is, the width of the plank should run from the centre to the outside of the tree and not, as in the case of flat-sawn boards, tangential to the circumference. For reasons of economy it is not always possible to adhere to this procedure, but it is a point that should receive attention in the mill. It becomes of importance when the timber is required for items of laminated construction, in which a number of layers are glued together. It then becomes necessary, if the best results are to be obtained, to use in one item, such as a spar, only boards which have approximately the same direction of end grain. The reason for this is that quarter-sawn boards have a different rate of shrinkage from that of flat-sawn boards, and it is therefore apparent that in a member composed of flat and quarter-sawn boards, the natural drying subsequent to gluing up will impose a considerable strain, either on the glued joints or the lamination, this resulting in a considerably weakened spar. The importance of this varies with the class of work, but is at a maximum in airscrew construction.

Gluing.—While glue and the operation of gluing is of great importance to the woodworker on any class of woodwork, it is of the utmost importance in aircraft work, this, of course, being due to the fact that the various glued members of the aeroplane are subject to considerable variations in temperature and the weather. For this reason most aircraft glues are to a certain extent waterproof, and require some care in use. When preparing glue for use the directions accompanying the make of glue used must be adhered to. The stipulated amount of water should not be exceeded, as this will result in a reduction of strength, apart from the detrimental effects on its waterproof qualities. The room for gluing should be as warm as possible and free from draughts. The glued surfaces should be clamped together as quickly as possible; but it is important to note that excessive clamping pressure may result in the glue being pressed out to a greater extent than is consistent with a good joint. The tendency to use stale glue, or glue which has been excessively heated, is detrimental to the efficiency of the joint, mainly because, although the glue may thicken, it loses its strength and cannot be improved by the addition of water. The employ-

AEROPLANE WOODWORK

ment of fresh water and clean utensils is absolutely necessary. Care should also be taken when washing off the surplus glue from a joint, as the water is liable to penetrate the joint, with a consequent weakening effect.

Division of Woodwork Operations.—It is usual to divide the various woodworking operations into sections, a typical arrangement being:

(1) Sawmill and machine shop.
(2) Parts preparation shop.
(3) Plane assembly shop.
(4) Fuselage assembly shop.
(5) Complete erection.

The sawmill and machine shop is concerned with the conversion of the timber from the balk into the necessary sizes, and to spindling or channelling of the various sections, which are passed on to the parts shop. The parts shop deals with such work as the preparation for assembly of wing spars, struts, fuselage, seating details, etc.

Fuselage Assembling.—The assembly or erection of the fuselage, or body of the aeroplane, is one of the chief sections of aeroplane woodworking. From Figs. 1 and 2, which show a typical fuselage in plan and side elevation, it will be seen that it is a braced framework, composed of longitudinal rails, or longerons, and vertical and cross-struts, braced in the front portion by plywood and in the rear by wire or tie-rods. The longerons and struts may be either solid, channelled, or hollow in section, as shown by Fig. 3. In some cases the longerons are tapered. The first operation is the preparation of the longerons and struts, which are usually machined up to the approximate sizes and then finished accurately by hand and cut to length. To ensure the greatest accuracy in the sizes of the longeron at the various points to which fittings are to be attached, small templates may be cut from $\frac{1}{8}$-in. mild steel for the different sizes necessary, allowance being made for a shrinkage of about $\frac{1}{64}$ inch. These can then be tried on as the member is planed down. To ensure that the member is accurately cut to size, a companion template

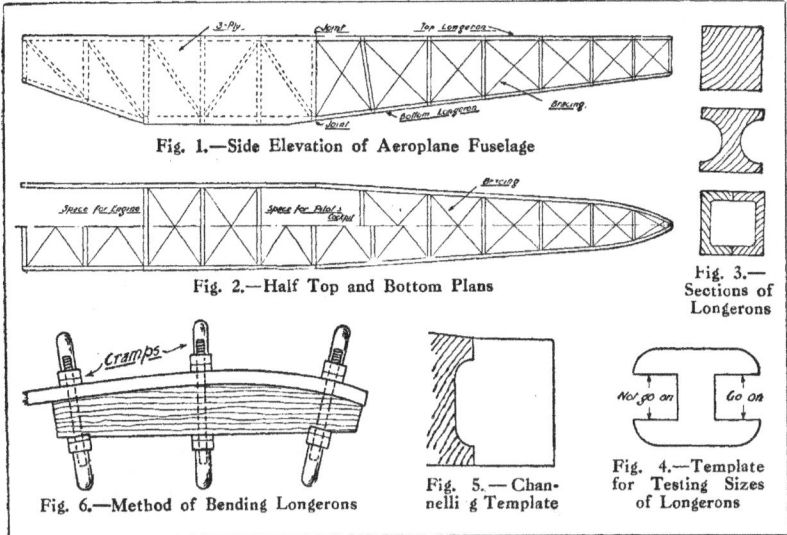

Fig. 1.—Side Elevation of Aeroplane Fuselage

Fig. 2.—Half Top and Bottom Plans

Fig. 3.—Sections of Longerons

Fig. 6.—Method of Bending Longerons

Fig. 5.—Channelling Template

Fig. 4.—Template for Testing Sizes of Longerons

should be made for each different section, and this should be cut to ·01 under the size the longeron is required to finish. The first template should just go on, the second not. For convenience in handling the two can be cut from one piece of metal, as shown by Fig. 4.

When finished to size, the longerons are drilled for the attachment of the fittings, to take the struts, wiring, etc. For accurate drilling it is preferable to use a jig, into which the rail may be clamped, and to drill through suitable guides placed in the jig. This ensures uniformity, and permits of greater rapidity in drilling. It is not always possible, on account of length, to arrange the jig to run the whole length of rail, and in such cases a short jig can be used with suitable locating points. As it is necessary that all holes should permit of the bolt being pushed through, i.e. neither a tight nor a slack fit, the absolute coincidence of the holes with the bolt sizes is essential, which necessitates the use of Morse drills. When the longerons are of the hollow box variety, blocks are inserted during gluing up at those points at which fittings are to be attached.

For testing the spindling or channelling, templates may be cut out as shown by Fig. 5. In some cases the fuselage has a curved outline, and the longerons have therefore to be steamed to the desired curve. The usual practice is to cut bending blocks, as shown by Fig. 6, these being of sufficient thickness to allow about four members being clamped at a time. In marking out, the bending block should be made sharper than the finished curve, to allow for the straightening out of the members after drying. It may be noted that ash, when used for bent work, must not be kiln-dried, and should be preferably in an unseasoned state, and in order that the fibres should not be damaged the maximum temperature of the steam should not exceed 220° F. (2 lb. per square inch). As soon as the wood has reached the necessary pliability it must be withdrawn from the steaming chamber. If the period of steaming is unduly prolonged serious weakening of its strength will result. In the preparation of the struts care must be taken to ensure that they are perfectly straight, this necessitating the rejection of those containing diagonal grain, as the latter is certain to result in a bowed strut. Struts exhibiting the slightest tendency to bow or warp must on no account be used, as the strength value of a strut initially bent, that is before the load is applied, is considerably reduced. Generally speaking, wood possessing a pronounced hard grain has a tendency to warp after standing in the shops for any length of time.

In cutting the struts to length a jig, as shown by Fig. 7, may be used. This is composed of a board of dry material, such as American white wood, planed perfectly true, to which is glued and screwed hardwood fillets, spliced at distances which will depend on the various sizes of the struts. In fixing the length blocks it is convenient to cut templates of plywood for each strut, these being dead to length with correct end-bevels. These can then be laid in the grooves formed by the fillets, and the length blocks fixed to suit. To ensure even bedding down in the sockets during erection, the strut ends must be trimmed to length, and not left from the saw. A strut left with ends from the saw is difficult to properly check for length and end cuts.

Assembling Operations. — Generally the fuselage is built in two portions, the rear portion being assembled first, and the wires roughly tensioned. In the case of the fuselage, shown by Figs. 1 and 2, it would be necessary to make a bench assembling jig, shown in plan form by Fig. 8. The various members should be accurately set out on this and hardwood blocks or fillets screwed and glued to it, so that the struts and longerons can be dropped in place.

The three-ply covering, having previously been cut to shape, with a small allowance for cleaning off, can then be applied. In order that the plywood may make a proper joint with the various members, the guide blocks should be slightly under the thickness of the latter.

AEROPLANE WOODWORK

To facilitate the application of the plywood covering it is usual to drill and countersink beforehand the holes necessary for the nails or screws. This is best accomplished by clamping six or more plywood sides together and drilling them from a plywood pattern.

The next operation is the attachment of the various fittings which may be clamped in place and drilled through, although it is an improvement if the necessary holes are jig drilled. This, however, requires a rather expensive jig, and is only justified when a large number of machines of the same type are to be made. A point to be noted in the erection of the various members is that all tie-rods should have an equal amount of thread in each forked end, and, further, that the threaded portion of the tie-rod inside the fork must run past the inspection hole. Fig. 9 shows two forms of wire bracing, the turnbuckle and steel wire type, and the swaged tie-rod, the latter being more generally used.

There are various methods in use for truing up the assembled fuselage, but whatever method is used the utmost accuracy is essential, as any deficiencies in the trueness of the fuselage will prevent the accurate alignment of the complete machine. One method is to set out on a boarded platform the complete side elevation and to adjust the wires or tie-rods until the various members are in agreement with the setting out. The plan, or horizontal struts, are then accurately centred and the two sides connected, and the plan and sectional, or cross-bracing wires, inserted. The plan wires are then adjusted until the centres of the plan struts are in agreement with a cord stretched from end to end. The sectional wires are finally tensioned until the body is square at all points. The fuselage can be checked by placing one straightedge transversely across the tail end and sighting through another straightedge placed at various points, preferably near the strut sockets. The fuselage can then be levelled longitudinally, and the straightness of the longerons checked. Points to which particular attention must be paid are : (1) the fittings for the attachment of the main planes, which must allow the latter to assume their correct angle of incidence ; (2) the engine supports, which must be level when the fuselage is level ; and (3) the position of attachment of the tail plane.

Another method of truing up is to support the body on two trestles, placed a short distance in from each end, the top longeron being uppermost. A line is then marked on each side strut a certain distance from the top longeron, the crossstruts being centred. The fuselage is then levelled up as far as possible in its untrued state, and a straightedge is lightly clamped at each end to the struts on each side, its top edge agreeing with the line previously marked on the struts. The tierods are then adjusted until all the marks on the vertical struts correspond with the tops of the straightedges, the struts at the same time being perfectly plumb. To ensure that the fuselage is square at all points the straightedges should be levelled up transversely. A line can then be stretched from end to end, and the plan bracing wires adjusted until the centre lines on the struts agree with the line. The final operation is the tensioning of the internal cross-bracing, each bay being checked for squareness.

Method for Rapid Truing-up of Fuselage.—A method which permits of rapid truing up is that in which a bench is constructed to take the fuselage in an inverted position, as shown in Fig. 10. The bench should only be boarded on its top surface at points coincident with the various struts, and the boards should be planed over until they are all perfectly straight and level, both longitudinally and transversely. A line may then be stretched from end to end, and each board marked across its width with a scribing point. In truing up, the fuselage is lightly clamped to the bench and the plan wires adjusted until the centre lines of the top plan struts are in line with the marks on the boards. The side wires are then tensioned until the side struts are vertical ; or locating points may be marked on the bottom longerons and the wires adjusted until these points agree with datum lines

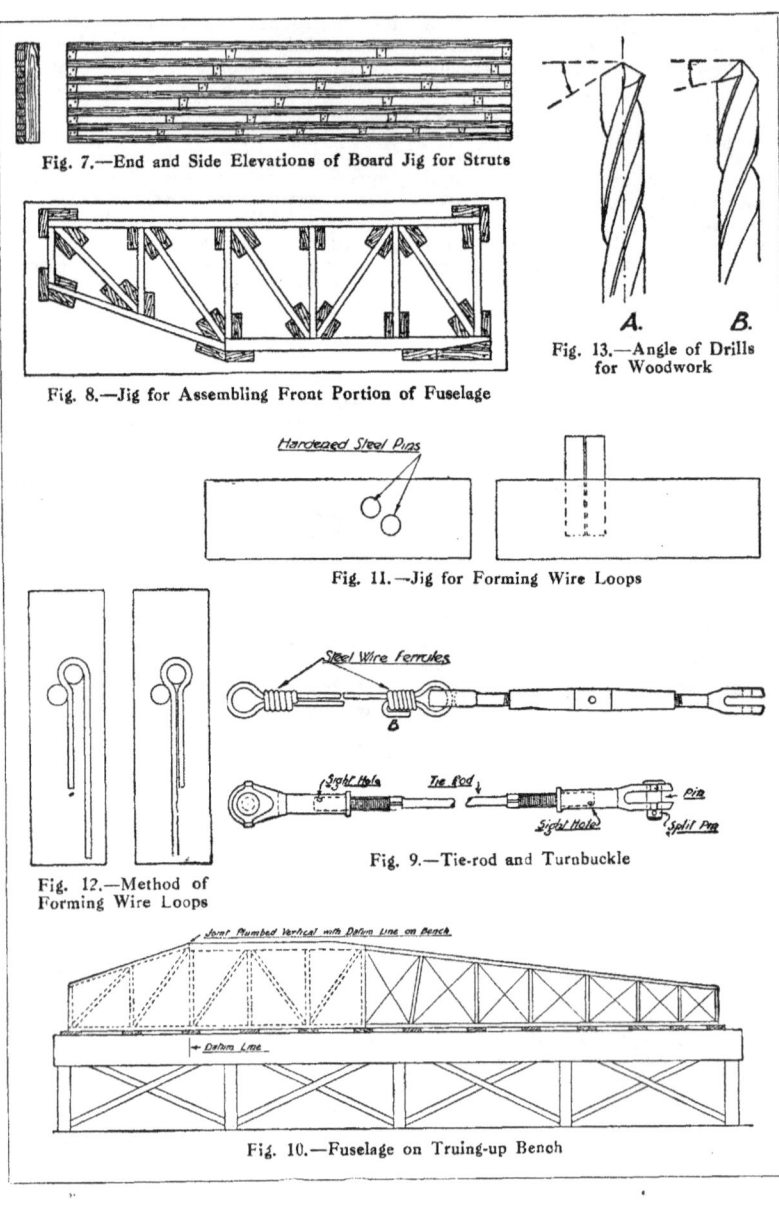

Fig. 7.—End and Side Elevations of Board Jig for Struts

Fig. 8.—Jig for Assembling Front Portion of Fuselage

Fig. 13.—Angle of Drills for Woodwork

Fig. 11.—Jig for Forming Wire Loops

Fig. 12.—Method of Forming Wire Loops

Fig. 9.—Tie-rod and Turnbuckle

Fig. 10.—Fuselage on Truing-up Bench

AEROPLANE WOODWORK

marked on the bench. The body can then be squared up by means of the internal cross-bracing or sectional wires, and the bottom cross-struts, which are now at the top, owing to the inverted position of the fuselage, can then be checked. If the previous operations have been carried out correctly, the centres of these struts should be in line, and the wires would only require tightening. Slight irregularities may be corrected; but it will be found that the correction of any serious discrepancy will involve the adjustment of both sectional and elevation wires, possibly right throughout the length of the body.

Tension of Wires.—An important point in truing up the fuselage, and in fact which also applies to all parts of the machine, is that all wires should be adjusted as near as possible to the same tension. It is possible by twanging the wires to obtain a fair idea as to their relative tensions, although, of course, the accuracy of this method is dependent upon practice. An overstrained wire tends to distort the framework. A further point to note is that over-tensioning of the wires generally will cause the various members to be initially stressed before the load for which they are designed is applied. When the bracing is of the steel wire and turnbuckle type, care must be taken to ensure that all bends are made in the form of easy curves. A sharp bend or kink is extremely detrimental to the strength of the wire. When making up these wires—a job which frequently falls to the woodworker—it is an advantage to mark the necessary lengths on a hardwood board, steel pins being driven into this to form locating points. The bends should be made with the special wire benders, supplied for the purpose, or an appliance as shown by Fig. 11 may be made. This is a hardwood block into which is driven or screwed steel pins of a diameter suitable to the size of the bend required. Fig. 12 shows the operation for forming the eye, the steel wire ferrules being slipped on before the last bend is made. When finally finishing off the wire in position, the ferrules are driven down until they abut against the shoulder formed by the loop, and the free end bent round, as shown at B (Fig. 9). A point to note in making up the wires to length is that the turnbuckle should show a thread or so outside the barrel. If the eye and fork ends are screwed too far into the barrel there is a possibility of insufficient adjustment being left for taking up subsequent slackness in the wire after use. It may be noted that with the steel wire stay there is always considerably more stretch than with the swaged tie-rods, this being due to the loops flattening out under tension. The turnbuckles are prevented from unscrewing when finally tensioned by means of soft iron or copper wire passed through the hole in the centre of the barrel and fastened off.

In the attachment of the various fittings to the fuselage care must be taken to ensure that all bolts are a good fit in the holes. They must not be driven in with force, as this is likely to start a split in the members; conversely, a slack fit may result in the loosening of the fitting. The proper drilling of the holes is dependent on the drill being of the correct size, and also on its correct grinding or sharpening. In sharpening a twist drill it is preferable to use a fine emery wheel than to sharpen it by hand on an oilstone. Whatever the method of sharpening used, it is important that the drill be given the proper clearance, and that the drill point be central, otherwise a hole larger than the drill will result and there will also be a tendency for the drill to draw away from the proper direction. For the best results when drilling in wood the angle of the cutting edge, shown at A (Fig. 13), should be about 30°. It must also be ground back, as at B. If this latter angle is too flat the drill will require considerable forcing, the same effect resulting if the cutting edge is ground down too much. Careful attention to drill sharpening is very necessary in aircraft woodwork, and, apart from its value in ensuring accuracy, it is more than repaid by the resultant ease of working. A further point of some importance when drilling is to drill from both sides of the member, this reducing the possibility of inaccuracy in direction. A hole badly out of truth, or over size, will necessitate the scrapping of the part in which it occurs. On no account should inaccurately drilled holes be plugged and redrilled.

Construction of Fuselage Fairing.

—A typical example of a fuselage fairing —the term applied to the superstructure fixed to the top of the fuselage—is shown by Figs. 14 and 15. It is usually made in two portions, the rear portion being composed of light fillets, or stringers, supported on plywood formers, and the front portion of formers covered with three-ply. The formers in the rear portion are generally composed of a spruce core, to each side of which is glued a stiffening layer of three-ply. In assembling it is necessary to prepare a board the full length of the fairing and to screw blocks at the various points at which formers occur, so that the latter can be held in place while the stringers and plywood covering are applied. In addition to the convenience in

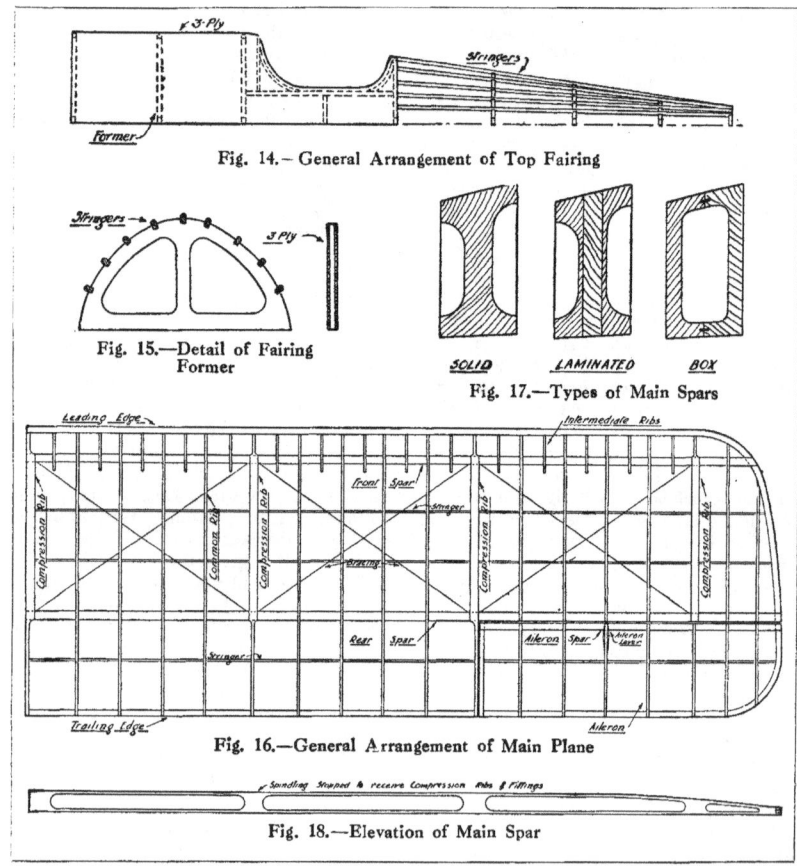

Fig. 14.—General Arrangement of Top Fairing

Fig. 15.—Detail of Fairing Former

Fig. 17.—Types of Main Spars

Fig. 16.—General Arrangement of Main Plane

Fig. 18.—Elevation of Main Spar

AEROPLANE WOODWORK

assembling, this also guarantees exactitude.

Main Plane Assembling.—The main planes of an aeroplane, as shown by Fig. 16, are composed of two main spars connected together by ribs. The spars may be spindled out from the solid, laminated or hollow in section, as shown by Fig. 17. In the preparation of the laminated type, the layers are machined in the mill to the required thickness plus an allowance for cleaning up by hand. The spar should be glued up in a warm room, and the greatest care taken to ensure that no portion of the glued surface becomes chilled. In clamping, consideration must be given to the straightness and trueness of the spars, as, with this form of construction, careless clamping may easily result in a warp, which will practically enforce its rejection. In gluing up the hollow-box type of spar the hand-screws must be applied to bear evenly across its width. An improperly applied hand-screw or clamp will result in the pressure being exerted on one edge only, and, possibly, in the weakening of the thin outside wall of the spar. At those points along the spar to which fittings are to be bolted, the bar may be left solid in the spindling process, as shown by Figs. 18 and 19, or it may be spindled right through and blocks glued in afterwards. In the latter case the blocks should be accurately planed to the inside size of the spar. An over-size block will cause a "bad joint" when gluing up, and one under size, a crushing in of the walls when the fitting is bolted up.

When the spars are planed to size and shape, with an allowance of about $\frac{1}{32}$ in. for shrinkage, they should be set out for rib and spar-plate positions. The holes necessary for the latter should be jig drilled. After this operation the spars should be allowed to stand for a few days to allow shrinkage to take place before the various fittings are bolted on. In stacking spars preparatory to assembling, care should be taken to ensure that they are laying true without twist or sag, and are separated by means of small fillets, so that the free circulation of air round each spar is possible.

Construction of Ribs.—In building up the ribs it is first necessary to make a template of the wing section, minus the thickness of the upper and lower flanges, unless the shop drawing applies only to the rib formers or webs. A dimensioned wing section of average proportions is indicated by Fig. 20. The template, which is shown by A (Fig. 21), should be cut from very dry material, and the positions of the spars, stringers, etc., indicated thereon, and from this the correct bevels of the top and bottom spar edges can be obtained. The templates B and C (Fig. 21) are useful for testing the rib contours during their assembly in the wing. By reference to Fig. 22 it will be seen that the actual details of the complete rib comprise light flanges, usually about $\frac{1}{2}$ in. by $\frac{3}{16}$ in., and fretted-out nose, main and trailing edge formers. Supplementary templates should be prepared for these, thus enabling a number to be marked out on boards of the required thickness and cut in a power-driven jig-saw. Allowance must be made for cleaning up to template, the outside curve being of most importance.

In the final cleaning up to shape, a form of jig which will enable six or more formers to be planed at once is a great advantage. A simple form of jig suitable for this purpose is composed of two hardwood sides cut accurately to shape, working upon two guides which are sufficiently large to ensure that when opened out the jig is true and square. Two long bolts with wing nuts form the clamping medium. A typical jig of this type is shown by Fig. 23. A matter of importance is that the ends of the formers which butt against the main spars must correspond very accurately with the lines on the main template, and must be at the correct angle relative to the chord line. The effect of discrepancies in this direction will be evident when the complete rib is attached to the spars, taking the form either of a bad fit or deformation of the wing curve. The flanges may be of the plain fillet type or may be grooved to fit over the formers, as shown by Fig. 24. In attaching the flanges to the formers they may be glued and tacked, or glued and screwed.

In some cases the flanges are attached to the main formers only, the nose and trailing-edge formers being inserted during the course of the building up. This pin the bolts when the ribs are attached first, although, of course, in the latter case they could be arranged on the spars and not fixed until the fittings are attached.

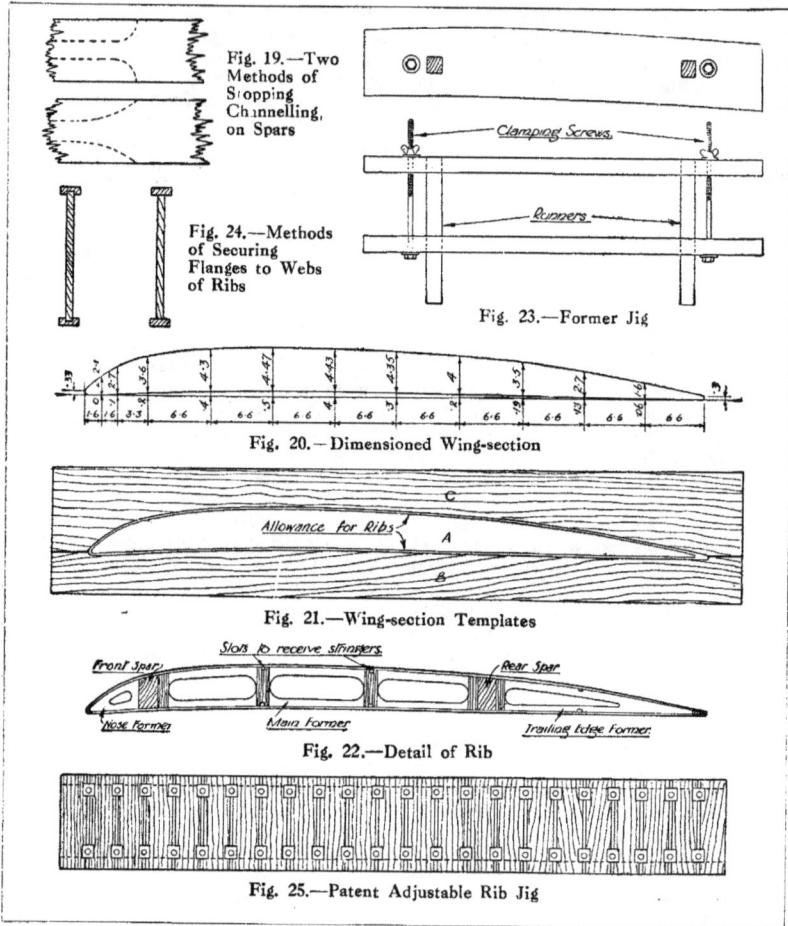

Fig. 19.—Two Methods of Stopping Channelling on Spars

Fig. 24.—Methods of Securing Flanges to Webs of Ribs

Fig. 23.—Former Jig

Fig. 20.—Dimensioned Wing-section

Fig. 21.—Wing-section Templates

Fig. 22.—Detail of Rib

Fig. 25.—Patent Adjustable Rib Jig

method enables the various fittings to be bolted to the main spars before the assembly of the wing is commenced, and this, in many cases, is a distinct advantage, as it is often very difficult to cut off and split-

When the method of works procedure necessitates the assembly of the complete rib beforehand, some form of jig, to ensure the continuity and accuracy of the wing curve. is necessary. There are several

AEROPLANE WOODWORK

types of jig in use for this purpose, of which Fig. 25 shows a good example, this being designed and patented by the Blackburn Aircraft Co. It is composed of a number of narrow boards, fixed to two rails, the space between each board being that necessary for the movement of the bolt through the hardwood stops. In use it would be necessary to make a template similar to that shown by A (Fig. 21), but in this case the full size of the section, it can be adjusted without trouble to any shape of rib.

Another type of rib-assembling jig, very similar in general principle to the one described, enables a number of ribs to be inserted at one time, and is so constructed that as each rib is pressed down in the jig the lower one falls clear. When the flanges are screwed to the formers care must be taken to countersink the holes for the screws just sufficient to enable

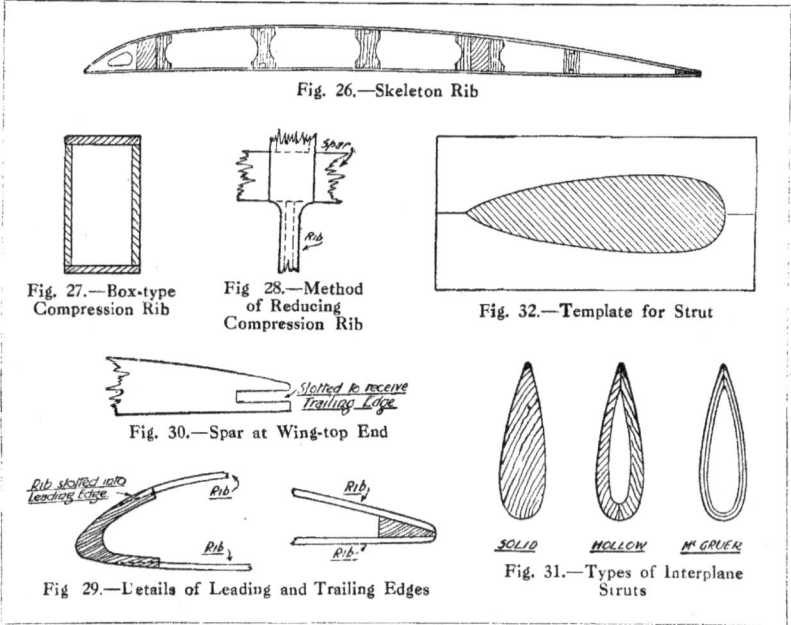

Fig. 26.—Skeleton Rib

Fig. 27.—Box-type Compression Rib

Fig 28.—Method of Reducing Compression Rib

Fig. 32.—Template for Strut

Fig. 30.—Spar at Wing-top End

Fig 29.—Details of Leading and Trailing Edges

Fig. 31.—Types of Interplane Struts

without reduction for flange thickness. This is temporarily fixed to the jig, and the stops adjusted accurately to it. It is then taken out and the flanges and former inserted, the glue having been previously applied, and the nails or screws inserted between the stops. The former would, of course, be packed up from the face of the jig, to enable it to lay central in relation to the width of the flange. The great advantage of a jig of this sort is that them to finish flush. Heavy countersinking will seriously weaken the flange. Sometimes a type of rib, shown by Fig. 26. is used alternately with ribs of the construction just described. This is generally known as a skeleton rib, and is usually built up during assembly of the wing. The box-rib (Fig. 27) is a much stronger rib, designed to take the compression between the spars due to the internal wire bracing; the usual method of diminishing its width from the back spar to the trailing edge is indicated by Fig. 28.

Considering the actual procedure for assembling the wing, and assuming that the fittings have been previously attached to the spars, and that the ribs have been assembled without the nose and trailing-edge formers, the first operation is to slide the necessary number of ribs on to the spars. These should then be spaced at approximately their correct positions, the internal tension wires inserted and lightly tensioned, the plane at the same time being roughly squared up. Starting from the root of the wing, the spars should be lightly clamped together, and each flange glued and bradded or screwed to the spars. It is usual to work right along the spar, fastening the flanges to the top edges of the spars only, and then to turn the wing over and proceed as before. The trailing-edge formers are now attached, and to ensure that these abut tightly against the spar, a piece of wood about 4 ft. long may be inserted through the fretted-out portion of the former next to the spar, this enabling six or more formers to be clamped up at the same time. As each flange is bradded down the curve should be tried with the templates previously described and shown by Fig. 21 (B and C).

In attaching the nose formers a slightly different method is adopted, these being placed in position and the leading edge applied and clamped to the spar. By reference to Fig. 29 it will be seen that the rib flanges are notched into the leading edge, and the latter should, of course, be prepared before the assembling is commenced, having been accurately marked off from a rod or setting-out board.

The usual joint between the wing-tip end and the main spars is shown by Fig. 30, the connection to the leading edge taking the form of a splice, glued and bound with tape. The longitudinal stringers are bradded through at each rib. The final operation, as far as the woodworker is concerned, is the squaring of the plane, each bay being tested with a squaring rod, and finally the complete wing from corner to corner, the spars at the same time being sighted for straightness.

With accurate construction a straightedge placed along the wing at any point across its width should touch every rib, and the trailing edge should show perfectly true with the spars. As previously noted, the straightness and trueness of the finished wing is dependent upon the accuracy with which the various details are prepared, and too much care cannot, therefore, be taken to ensure that all parts accurately correspond and are correct to drawings.

Preparation of Interplane Struts.
—The interplane and undercarriage struts are shaped to the sections shown by Fig. 31, and are either of the solid or hollow type. With the latter type the strut is spindled in two halves and glued together between moulds to ensure even pressure along the joint. The solid section strut may be spindled to shape and finished accurately to template by hand. The disadvantage of this method is that most struts vary in section along their length, so that it is necessary to construct spindling jigs, which require constant attention to ensure that the spindling machine cutters are not cutting too deeply. Another method is to use a copying lathe, this involving the construction of a pattern strut in hardwood. It is an improvement where a large number of struts of the same type are to be made, to have a casting made, this eliminating the wear, which is certain to occur with a pattern strut of wood. In finishing the struts by hand, whatever the method of machining, templates must be used. Where the strut tapers, it will be necessary to make two or three sizes, each different section requiring two templates so that they can be tried on together, as shown by Fig. 32. This will ensure the strut being correct for shape and size. An ingenious form of strut construction is that known as the McGruer bent-wood strut. This type of strut is formed by moulding layers of spruce to the required shape, the joints being effected by splicing.

When the struts have been worked to size, they are cut to length, and the strut sockets attached. To ensure that the bolt-hole centres are exactly to length, a board jig should be made. This, in its

AEROPLANE WOODWORK

simplest form, will consist of a flat board of spruce or whitewood into which steel pins are driven or screwed, these corresponding in size to the strut-socket holes. In cutting the struts a small allowance over the correct length may be made, this will permit slight errors in the fittings to be rectified.

Finding True Length and Bevels of Struts.—In some instances the woodworker may be required to set out and obtain the true lengths of the struts from a general-arrangement drawing. In the case of the undercarriage struts, and occasionally the interplane struts, which slope in two directions, the apparent lengths and angles are, of course, useless. Fig. 33 indicates a graphic method of determining the true lengths and bevels of the undercarriage or chassis struts, the method, of course, being applicable to any strut possessing a double angle. The front and side views are set out either full size or to scale with the trammels or beam compasses; the length of the strut on the front view, from the centre of the socket hole at the top to the joint with the vertical block at the bottom, is swung downwards to the horizontal and projected across, cutting verticals projected downwards from a line corresponding with the point of greatest thickness of the strut.

This line usually marks the position of the fork joint in relation to the width of the strut. The lengths A B and C D (Fig. 33) will then constitute the true length of the struts at their centre lines, the necessary allowance is then made for the increase in length due to bevels. The true angles of the front and rear struts in side elevation can then be found by measuring the angles E and F. The angle made by the struts with the base blocks in front elevation does not alter, and can, therefore, be measured off from the front view.

Airscrew Construction.—In the construction of the airscrew, what has previously been said concerning the need for accuracy of workmanship, the use of well-seasoned, straight-grained timber, and the preparation and use of glue is of intensified importance. From Fig. 34, which is a typical working drawing of an airscrew, it will be seen that the total thickness is made up of a number of layers, or laminations, each of which is different in shape. The first operation is to mark and cut out patterns of the various laminations, allowing about $\frac{1}{2}$ in. outside the finished outline. The boards having previously been reduced to the correct thickness are then marked out from these patterns, care being taken to ensure that the latter are laid parallel to the longitudinal grain of the

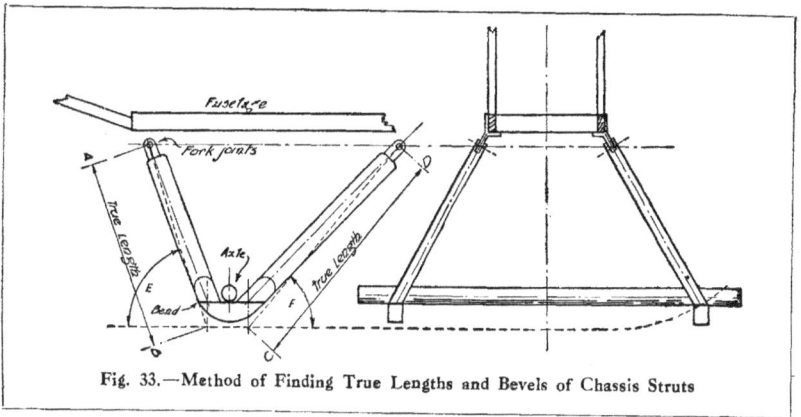

Fig. 33.—Method of Finding True Lengths and Bevels of Chassis Struts

wood. After the laminations have been cut out they must be balanced, and the heavy ends marked. In arranging the layers for gluing up, the heavy ends are placed alternately with light ends, this, of course, ensuring better balance than if the layers were glued-up indiscriminately. To obtain a better surface for gluing, each layer is grooved or toothed with a fine the layers are being placed together, and for this reason the second method is generally preferable. After gluing, the block is clamped to a bench or board, which must be perfectly rigid and true, as deficiencies in this direction will result in casting. The clamps are arranged as shown by Fig. 35, from which it will be seen that, to prevent tipping, the layers

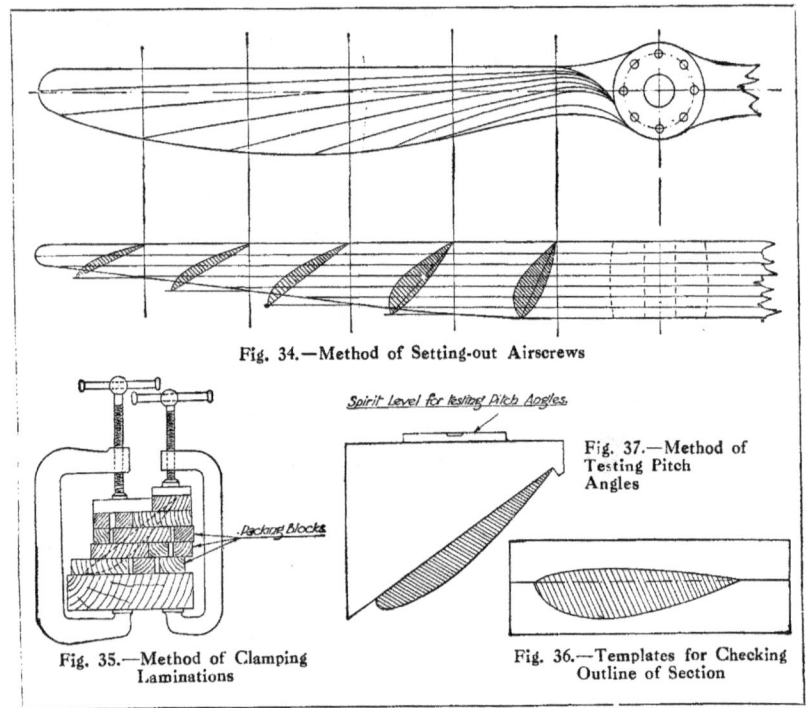

Fig. 34.—Method of Setting-out Airscrews

Fig. 35.—Method of Clamping Laminations

Fig. 36.—Templates for Checking Outline of Section

Fig. 37.—Method of Testing Pitch Angles

toothing plane. The gluing-up room must be kept at a temperature of approximately 70° F., and free from dust and draughts.

There are two methods in use for gluing up : The whole set of laminations may be glued up together, or they may be glued up successively in pairs. The disadvantage of the first method is the possibility of the glue becoming chilled while are packed up with small blocks, which correspond accurately to the thickness of the laminations. These packing blocks may be varnished, or dipped in linseed oil to prevent their adhesion to the block. The latter must remain under pressure for at least twenty-four hours before the operation of working up roughly to shape is commenced. In the construction of airscrews of a standardised type, the opera-

AEROPLANE WOODWORK

tion of rough shaping is usually carried out on a propeller-shaping machine. This machine is similar to a copying lathe, in that it works to a pattern. preferably of cast iron, which is made exactly to shape and size. This pattern need only consist of one blade and the boss portion, as in operation the machine works from the tip to the boss of the airscrew, when it is turned round on the mandrel supporting it, and the direction of travel of the cutters reversed.

In working up the airscrew to shape, whether the rough shaping is performed by hand or machine, it will be necessary to make metal templates for each different section of the blade indicated on the drawing. These templates, which may be of the form shown by Fig. 36, will enable the outline and thickness to be accurately checked. For testing the angle of each section, the template shown by Fig. 37 is used, or it can be made to form also one of the outline-testing templates shown by Fig. 36. The pitch angles, to which these templates must be accurately cut, are indicated on the general lay-out of the airscrew, and apply only to its flat side. In testing the pitch angle, the airscrew must be laid on a perfectly true table, which is preferably of slate, with a pin projecting to form a good fit in the shaft hole in the boss. For the angle to be correct, the spirit level should show dead centre.

Care must be taken to ensure that the shape of each blade is correct and also that the offsets of each blade from the centre line of the propeller, shown in the plan (Fig. 34), accurately correspond. In the latter respect a good deal is dependent upon the correct drilling of the shaft hole, and although it is possible to accomplish this with a hand brace and expanding bit, it is usually performed on a power-driven boring machine. In drilling the holes to take the propeller boss flanges a jig is necessary, or the actual propeller boss may be applied and the holes drilled through from each side, care being taken to ensure that the holes are not drawn out of shape.

The final operation is balancing the airscrew. For this purpose a spindle is inserted in the boss hole, this rotating either on friction wheels or hardened knife edges, mounted on a suitable stand. If the blades have been carved true to shape and section, the airscrew should be reasonably well balanced, and any small difference may be rectified by the removal of timber from the boss, or by scraping the face or flat side of the heaviest blade. Considerable difference cannot be rectified in this manner, and it will then be necessary to ascertain whether the corresponding sections of each blade are true to template and also if the blade profiles and the distances from the boss centre to the tips are correct. Very small differences can be corrected by the application of an extra coat of wood filler or varnish. The balancing must be carried out in a room free from draughts. When properly balanced the propeller should remain at rest in any position in which it is placed.

Throughout the various operations concerned with aircraft woodworking, accuracy is of primary importance. The individual fitting together of parts cannot be permitted, as this adversely affects their interchangeability. The close limits often demanded may appear to the woodworker to be unnecessarily fine ; they are, however, absolutely essential, if reasonable exactitude is to be obtained when the machine is finally erected. Throughout the different woodworking operations the utmost use should be made of jigs and fixtures, as their use not only ensures dimensional accuracy, but also results in a reduction of the operations necessary to produce the component.

Picture Framing

INGENIOUS inventors have devised a good number of appliances designed to assist in making mitre joints, but none of them will be found in use in the workshops of the professional picture-frame makers, who work for profit, and therefore may be supposed to have an open eye for any appliance which is cheaper to use. The truth is that these mitre cutters and mitre cramps are rarely satisfactory in use, and actually are not labour-savers. The only thing which can be said in their favour—and that is a doubtful advantage—is that they enable the unskilled to avoid the trouble of mastering the craftsmanship of the frame-maker, and to do work which he may think is creditable but, judged by the professional standard, usually is not so. Therefore at the outset it is advised that the would-be frame-maker should not invest his money in these more or less expensive devices, but to learn how to make picture frames in the manner in which it is done in the trade.

It is proposed to describe the whole process, which is simple enough, and once understood, the worker will be able to attain to expertness with a very moderate amount of practice and perseverance. The tools required are mostly those found in the workroom of a woodworker, and may be enumerated as : Tenon saw, *mitre block, trying plane, *shooting-board, hammer, and bradawls ; not a very formidable equipment. Those marked with an asterisk can be made by anyone sufficiently advanced in carpentry to aspire to frame-making. Illustrations of these two appliances are given for the benefit of those who do not possess them but may decide to make them.

The mitre block (Fig. 1) may be built of $\frac{3}{4}$-in. beech, oak, or other hardwood. The crossed saw-cuts must accurately make an angle of 45° with the sides of the block, and, of course, must be truly square with the base.

The shooting-board (Fig. 2) explains itself. It may be made of deal, excepting the two strips at the top, which are better made of hardwood ; they should be fixed into place with stout screws. These strips must stand at angles of 45° with the working face of the board, and should make a right angle with each other.

The raw material of the frame-maker is moulding, purchasable in an infinite number of patterns and sections, not all desirable. Mouldings may be of plain wood (usually oak), or of deal to which a composition has been applied on the front and one side. Also they may be of " compo." (to use the trade term) gilt or faced with metal leaf to imitate gold or silver.

Mouldings are enriched in various ways by the application of compo. designs in relief. There is no need to further describe them, as every room in every house holds a variety of patterns. Those referred to as undesirable have sections that involve special difficulties in the mitreing. Fig. 3 shows a selection. Also the

PICTURE FRAMING

beginner is warned against highly decorated mouldings, which, unless treated with the utmost care and skill, inevitably shed portions of the compo. ornament when the mitres are being planed, or when the nails are being driven. It should be explained that the sections illustrated as unsuitable are so by reason of the sides being under- slightly in excess of these dimensions, say, $18\frac{1}{8}$ in. by $12\frac{3}{32}$ in.

The mitre block should be supported firmly, preferably in the vice. Then with the left hand the length of moulding is held against the near side of the channel, the end of the former being adjusted to the right-hand cross-cut, the rebate edge

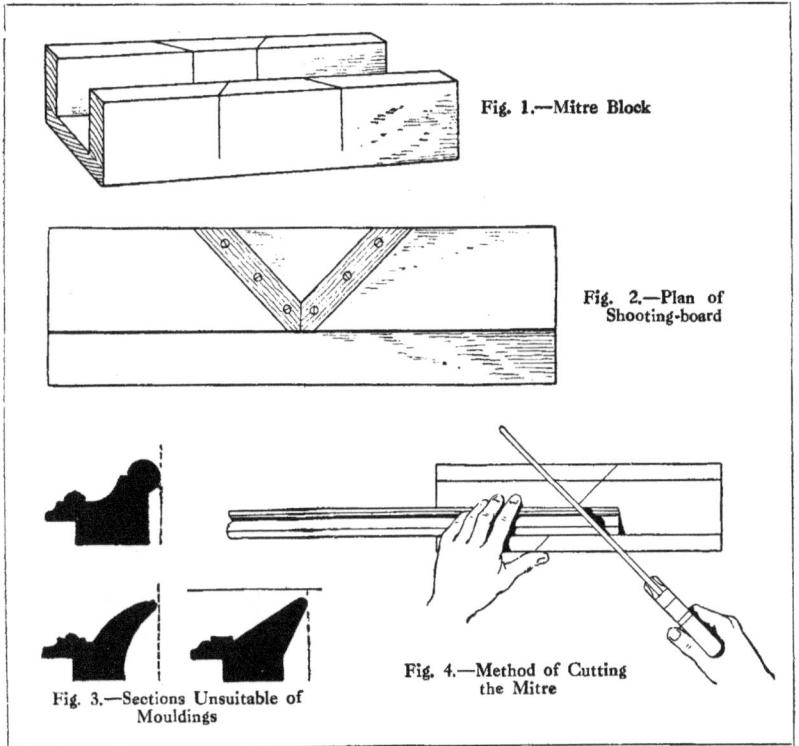

Fig. 1.—Mitre Block

Fig. 2.—Plan of Shooting-board

Fig. 3.—Sections Unsuitable of Mouldings

Fig. 4.—Method of Cutting the Mitre

cut, which makes it difficult to keep them firmly against the stops of the shooting-board when planing the mitres. Plain wood moulding is the best for a novice to start with.

It will be assumed that a picture measuring 18 in. by 12 in. has to be framed. The rebate measurement of the frame must be of the moulding facing away. The tenon saw is inserted and the moulding cut through (see Fig. 4).

The length, $18\frac{1}{8}$ in., is now measured in the rebate, and using the left-hand saw-cut is cut again through the moulding just beyond the mark to allow a trifle for planing. The only difficulty the beginner may encounter is the saw leaving the kerf at the far side of the block, which, if working quickly, might result in damage to the moulding. To prevent this, the saw should be worked with short strokes. Carefully-sawn mitres made with a sharp saw (all saws should be sharp) on a true block, when the moulding is of plain wood, need not be planed, but may there and then be glued up. There will be a slight burr on the face of the joint, which is easily removed with glasspaper after the glue is dry. Such joints are stronger than planed ones, because the roughness of the surfaces forms a key for the glue. In most cases, however, it will be desirable to shoot (to plane) the mitre surfaces true on the shooting-board. The plane should be long and heavy, the full-size trying plane serving very well. Cross-grain of hardwoods presents considerable resistance, which only the momentum of a heavy plane will overcome. Each stroke of the plane should pass over the moulding without pause, otherwise ridges will be formed.

The piece of moulding should be held firmly against the stop with the left hand, allowing its mitred end to sit against the base of the plane in advance of the iron. The plane is then drawn back and propelled sharply forward, care being taken to keep its base always in contact with the guiding face of the board.

The plane must be sharp and set finely. Three strokes should be sufficient to ensure a clean face to the mitre. Each pair of sides should be accurately matched in length. When this is done all are laid together, and examination made to see if they fit all round without gaping at any joint. If they do not close up accurately, each pair of faces should be tested with the square to detect which particular ones are faulty, and correction made on the shooting-board (see Fig. 5).

Assuming that all fit snugly, they may be glued up. One long side is gripped in the vice, as shown in Fig. 6, and one short side applied to it in the manner shown in Fig. 7, and the bradawl passed in. This is more easily done if the bradawl be driven nearly through the upper member before putting it into position. The relative positions of the two mitre faces should be noted, the upper one being displaced $\frac{1}{8}$ in. or so from its proper position. This is the whole secret of the frame-maker's craft. The bradawl is now removed and a suitable size brad substituted. Both faces are to be glued with fresh hot glue, and brought together with the brad point sitting in the hole in the lower piece, and the brad hammered home. As the head of the brad approaches the side of the moulding, it will be seen that the upper face of the mitre will begin to slide downwards. By the time the head is fair with the wood surface, the joint also should have become fair; but if still standing high, it may be adjusted accurately by continuing the hammer blows at the point where the brad-head lies. During the hammering the left hand should control the upper piece of the moulding to prevent it turning on the brad as a pivot.

The result of this method of nailing is to bend the brad within the body of the wood, in the manner illustrated in the right-hand part of Fig. 7; and this has the effect of forcing the glued surfaces into close contact and of keying the joint, so that made in this way a joint holds well even before the glue has set, and subsequently is stronger than a joint made with the help of clamping devices. Some little practice is needed to get all to go so well that the front faces of the two pieces of moulding come fair. If, however, the hole be driven with the faces held fair, and the hammer blows be directly downwards, there is little chance of a bad result.

The two other pieces of moulding are then joined, and afterwards the two halves of the frame, the procedure being the same as described.

When all mitres are closed, the frame is laid down on a flat surface, and if there is any "wind" in the frame it is set fair by a few light blows of the hammer on the joint or joints which stand up, a piece of wood being interposed between the joint and the hammer face to prevent marking the former.

Such is the whole art of frame-making as practised by the professional craftsman. It is worth some trouble to acquire it, as it is very expeditious, and the frames are stronger than if joined in any other way. Difficulties inevitably will be encountered by the novice, particularly when dealing with compo. and fancy mouldings. Pieces of ornament which may become detached may be restored to place by gluing on. Very heavy mouldings may require two method of joining involves risks, as, for instance, when the moulding is pierced, as in the so-called Florentine patterns, or when it is desirable that no brad-heads should be visible. In such cases the following method of gluing and clamping may be adopted. Four corner pieces, as shown in Fig. 7 on page 711, are made of

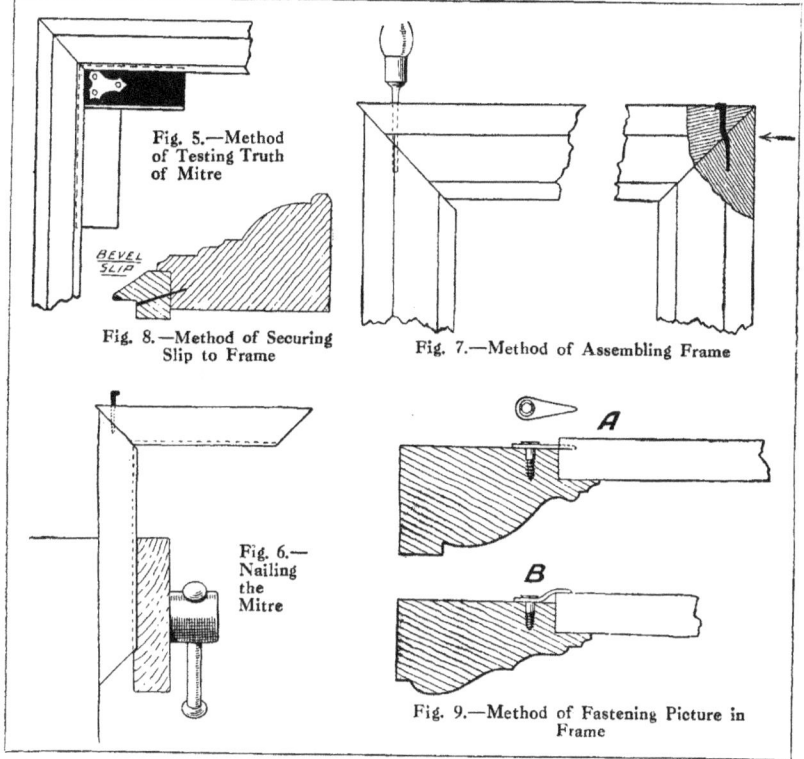

Fig. 5.—Method of Testing Truth of Mitre

Fig. 8.—Method of Securing Slip to Frame

Fig. 7.—Method of Assembling Frame

Fig. 6.—Nailing the Mitre

Fig. 9.—Method of Fastening Picture in Frame

or more brads to each joint. The additional ones may be driven in after the frame is joined up and the glue dry. Frame-makers usually punch in the brad-heads and fill the holes with a composition, afterwards colouring or gilding it to match the finish of the moulding.

Cases may occur in which the foregoing hardwood. A length of stout cord also is required. All the joints are glued and brought together on a flat surface, one of the corner pieces being placed at each outside angle, and the cord passed twice or four times round all, assurance being made that it rests in the groove cut in the outer angle of each corner piece. Strips of wood are then inserted between the strands of cord in the centre of their length on each side, and the cords tightened by twisting them, the tension being equalised by twisting a little at a time at each side.

In this way very considerable pressure may be brought to bear on the frame joints, and a close set of joints results. Subsequently, when the glue has set they may be bradded if desired. The whole outfit is simple, and is worth all the corner cramps ever put on the market. After closing the joints, by whatever method they are made, all exuded glue should be removed with a damp sponge.

Frame measurements are two—" rebate measurement " and " sight measurement," the latter being the dimensions of the picture as seen through the frame when the former is in place. If an inner gold-slip is desired, rebated slip should be used ; this form is easier to join up, and its bevelled surface looks better. The slip should be joined up in the same way as described for the frame, and then the frame measurements taken from the outside of the slip, making the rebate measurements of the frame just sufficient for the latter to enter. The slip should be bradded securely to the frame, as shown in Fig. 8.

Frames made without mitreing will not be dealt with here. Mostly they may be described as holes in pieces of flat wood, and are designed and ornamented according to the taste of their makers, who may be fret-sawyers, carvers, or what not. They call for no special description.

Apart from the construction of the frame itself, the subject of framing presents several problems. All pictures fall into two classes : (1) Oil paintings, usually on canvas, strained over a stretcher, but sometimes on wooden panel ; (2) water-colour paintings, engravings, and, in fact, every kind of picture on paper.

The first class is quite easy to deal with, since the problem of protecting the picture from damp does not exist. It is only necessary to secure it in its frame by a method which will hold it fast in the rebate, and leave no projecting nails to injure the walls. This method of securing can be done as shown at A in Fig. 9, using brass points cut from the sheet and drilled and countersunk at the large end. These are driven into the stretcher whilst it is pressed home in the rebate, and the screw is inserted. If the stretcher should be of less thickness than the depth of the rebate, the point is driven into the frame and the screw into the stretcher. This will make a very neat and strong job.

In the second class of pictures, a matter of prime importance is to guard them from the effects of damp. Mildews inevitably ruin them sooner or later, even in well-aired living-rooms. Therefore it is worth while to devise a method of sealing them up against damp. This can be done by papering the picture to the glass with gummed strip, afterwards pasting a sheet of thin Rexine or other waterproof material over the back, bringing its edges over the gummed strip. This makes for the picture a perfectly damp-proof case of a very permanent kind.

If the picture is mounted on stiff card there is no necessity for a backboard. It may be dropped into the rebate of the frame, and secured there with headless pins (gimp or upholstery pins are the trade descriptions).

If, however, the rebates are not deep enough to take the thickness of the picture with sufficient to spare to accommodate the pins, which is rarely the case, then brass points may be used as described above, screwing them to the frame back, and bending their points so that they clip the picture, as shown at B in Fig. 9. If a backboard be used, the points may be driven into it in the same way as described in connection with oil-paintings.

By these methods there are no projecting metal points likely to injure the wall surfaces. A strip of baize 1 in. wide may, with advantage, be glued across the back of the frame at top and bottom.

Wood Turning

THE production of circular shapes by revolving the wood in a lathe and operating on it with suitable cutting tools is termed wood turning. It differs from woodwork at the bench as widely as two crafts can differ which deal with the same material. Turned articles may vary extremely in shape and in size, and these variations require different methods of securing in the lathe, different speeds of rotation according to their weight, different arrangements of grain, and in many cases more or less complicated building up preparatory to turning.

In wood turning one of the first things to learn is how to avoid accidents. A revolving piece of wood demands precautions which are quite unnecessary in operating on a stationary piece. As the cutting tools are held and manipulated by hand, it is not always possible to hold them so firmly that centrifugal force cannot affect them. The alternative is to take care that they are caused to approach the work in a manner that avoids risk. Only experience can thoroughly teach this. The wood turner has often to work with tools extremely close to a dangerous position, and it is at such times that he needs to be cautious and to hold them with extreme firmness and steadiness. If the tool is forced out of position it may damage or even completely spoil the work, and in serious cases the operator himself may suffer some injury. Another point is that either with or without a tool accident the work may be thrown out of the lathe owing to it not having been adequately secured. Unlike a bench worker, a beginner at the lathe may have acquired considerable skill and then meet with an accident which causes him to lose confidence in his ability to use the turning tools safely. An experienced turner, however, never has mishaps, and while experience is being gained there are always some ways of working which are safer than others. The beginner should do more scraping and less actual cutting with gouge and side chisel, and he should reserve these latter for surfaces where they can be safely used with comparatively little skill.

Turning Tools.—Sharp tools are as necessary at the lathe as at the bench. A tool too dull to cut at the bench can be forced to scrape or tear at the lathe, but the result is a rough surface produced with difficulty. Time spent in properly grinding and sharpening tools is never wasted. The tools used at the lathe are very few compared with those required for bench work. Fig. 1 shows all the main forms of cutting tools, and nearly all the work can be done. if necessary, with the gouge and side chisel alone. It is desirable, however. to have at least two different sizes of these tools, large ones for large work and quick removal of material, and small ones for small work. For average work a gouge and side chisel $\frac{5}{8}$ in. wide are suitable. The sizes obtainable range from $\frac{1}{4}$ in. to 2 in. In Fig. 1, A is a turning gouge, B a side chisel. C a facing chisel, D a round-nose chisel, and E a diamond-point chisel. The gouge is ground on the outside, and is ground back at the sides more than an ordinary firmer gouge, so that viewed from the front and side it appears as in Fig. 2. The side chisel is ground as in Fig. 3, usually with some amount of slope, as

coachmaker's chisel, long and thick, with its end ground semicircular. The diamond point is used for right-hand and left-hand scraping where an ordinary chisel could not be held at right angles to the surface. Sometimes instead of a double edge, two separate tools, as in

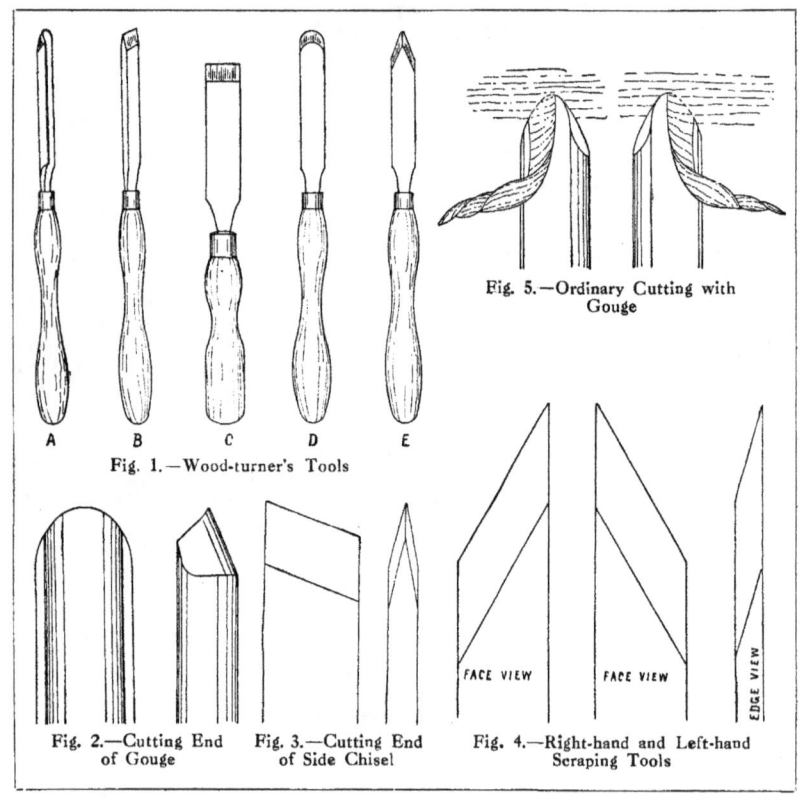

Fig. 1.—Wood-turner's Tools

Fig. 2.—Cutting End of Gouge

Fig. 3.—Cutting End of Side Chisel

Fig. 4.—Right-hand and Left-hand Scraping Tools

Fig. 5.—Ordinary Cutting with Gouge

shown in the face view, though some prefer an edge at right angles. so that both points can be used for parting. The firmer chisel is used for scraping, and does not differ in any way from an ordinary bench chisel, except that the angle of sharpening is often more obtuse. The round-nose is used for scraping concavities. It is a

Fig. 4, are employed, one for right-hand and one for left-hand scraping. The side chisel also may be used as a substitute.

All turning tools, with the exception of the firmer chisel, are long and stout with long handles, the latter being desirable to give plenty of leverage and power to resist varying stress at the cutting end. The

WOOD TURNING

gouge is the only tool used exclusively for cutting. The side chisel is occasionally used for scraping, and the other tools invariably for scraping, that is, they are approached in a horizontal position, and operate by a scraping action. The gouge

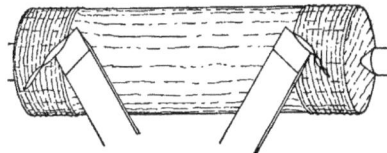

Fig. 6.—Method of Using Side Chisel

is held at a suitable angle to cut shavings. It is generally used with a lateral sliding movement to right or left so that it cuts, as in Fig. 5, the movement being towards the side on which the shaving is being cut. This is better than making a direct frontal cut with the point or middle portion of the cutting edge only, though the latter method is suitable occasionally. The side chisel is used similarly, as in Fig. 6, on cylindrical articles of small or moderate diameter, and produces a very smooth surface. On large diameters it is better to scrape with a firmer chisel, and on flat surfaces it is impossible to use the chisel as in Fig. 6, the reason being that the upper point must not be allowed to touch the surface or it will dig in with more or less disastrous results. The main use of the chisel, however, is for parting or for cutting incisions or ends, as in Fig. 7. The cuts have to be made so that the shavings are thin enough on one side of the chisel to be forced away by its wedge-like action. Thus in making a division at some distance from either end of a cylindrical piece as seen to the left in Fig. 7, a number of cuts are made side by side until there is sufficient clearance to allow the chisel to go as deeply as required. Similarly, if it is necessary to remove a considerable amount from an end to obtain the desired length, it must be done gradually by a number of shavings, each perhaps about $\frac{1}{16}$ in. thick, for no amount of force would remove a thick slice at one stroke of the chisel. The gouge is used in a position sloping up to the work, as in Fig. 8, and the side chisel also when used for the purpose shown in Fig. 6. The scraping tools are held horizontally or nearly so, as in Fig. 9. The exact position of the hands often varies somewhat with different workmen. A good practice adopted by many is to keep the forefinger of the left hand below the rest to clasp it and the tool together. Others use the left hand palm downwards on the tool instead of the reverse way as illustrated. In all cases the right hand grasps the end of the tool handle as shown.

Rest.—Turning tools cannot be used without a support or rest for them to bear on, for the downward pressure on the cutting edge is much more than could be resisted by the hands alone. The work, of course, revolves towards the operator, and the support should be as near the cutting edge as possible. If far back there is more leverage for the hands to resist, and varying thicknesses of shaving and varying stress make this dangerous. Therefore the rest must be kept as close to the surface of the work as convenient. The wood-turner's rest is quite different from that of the metal-turner. The usual design is shown in Fig. 10. It consists of two main parts—the rest itself and its base, which is clamped to the lathe bed. The rest itself, shown in the upper part of the figure, has a rounded top edge for the tool to rest on, and from there its surface

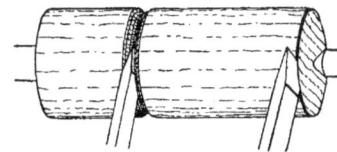

Fig. 7.—Method of Using Chisel for Cutting Ends and Divisions

slopes downwards away from the work. It is provided with a post which fits into a socket in the base, and when adjusted for height and for horizontal angle it is clamped by a set-screw. The base also can be adjusted to any angle on the lathe bed, and moved in or out to suit the diameter of the work. It has a slot, as shown, which receives a suitable bolt for clamping. Adjustments for height do not average work the fork is sufficient and it is quickly adjusted and quite reliable.

Centring Work for Turning.—In preparing a piece of hard wood for turning,

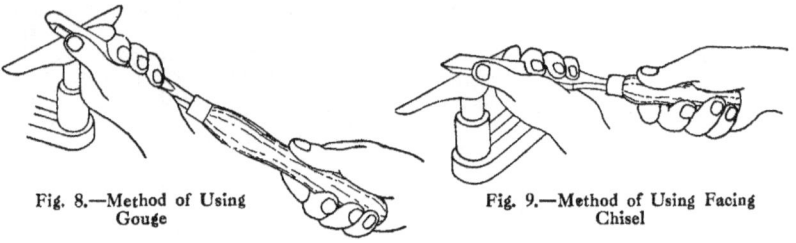

Fig. 8.—Method of Using Gouge

Fig. 9.—Method of Using Facing Chisel

vary much, but some amount of adjustment is necessary. On face-plate work, that is, flat disc-shaped articles, the top of the rest must usually coincide with, or be very slightly below, the lathe centre height, when the face of the work is being operated on. In turning the edges of such work, and in cylindrical articles between centres, the turner adjusts to any height he finds convenient, his own height in relation to the lathe having something to do with it. Usually the top of the rest is kept a little above the lathe centre height.

Fork Centre.—Another feature peculiar to the wood-turner's lathe is the fork centre (Fig. 11), which is screwed into the mandrel nose for turning articles between centres. Its forked end is forced into the

it is necessary to make a saw-cut to receive the fork centre, as in Fig. 12, or cut a recess with a chisel ; but in softwood this is not necessary. The piece of wood prepared for turning is, of course, sawn square in the first place and then its corners are generally removed, as shown in Figs. 12 and 13, sometimes by sawing, sometimes with a hatchet or pared off with a chisel. This saves the gouge some work in roughing down to diameter. A piece secured between centres in the lathe is shown in Fig. 13. It is driven by the fork centre at the left-hand end, and is supported at the other end by the fixed dead centre in the poppet. The point of this centre is forced into the end sufficiently to keep the wood securely between the centres. A little oil is necessary at the dead centre before the

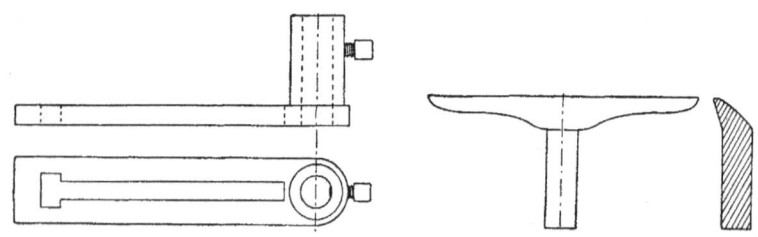

Fig. 10.—Details of Wood-turner's Tool Rest

end grain of the work and revolves the latter with the mandrel. For very heavy and large work something more secure is often necessary ; but for small and lathe is started. A small hole with a bradawl is often bored as a guide for the dead centre to enter, otherwise it may shift considerably to one side in screwing up. Sometimes a centre punch is used instead of a bradawl. The fork centre end of the wood is treated similarly when no saw-cut is made. It has the advantage of indicating the exact centre as well as providing a guide for the points. To guess the centre when putting the wood in the lathe may involve waste in turning, or may result in failure of the piece to hold up to diameter, a flat being left on one side after the piece is reduced to size. It is economical, therefore, to saw the wood just large enough to turn to the required size, and mark the exact centres on its ends. A simple way to do this without measurement is to rule pencil lines diagonally from corner to corner on the ends, so that their point of crossing gives the centre. This is done while the wood is square before its angles are removed.

Work between centres almost invariably has its grain running as shown in Fig. 13. All the simplest work in turning is done in this way, and the beginner should start with small work between centres. The

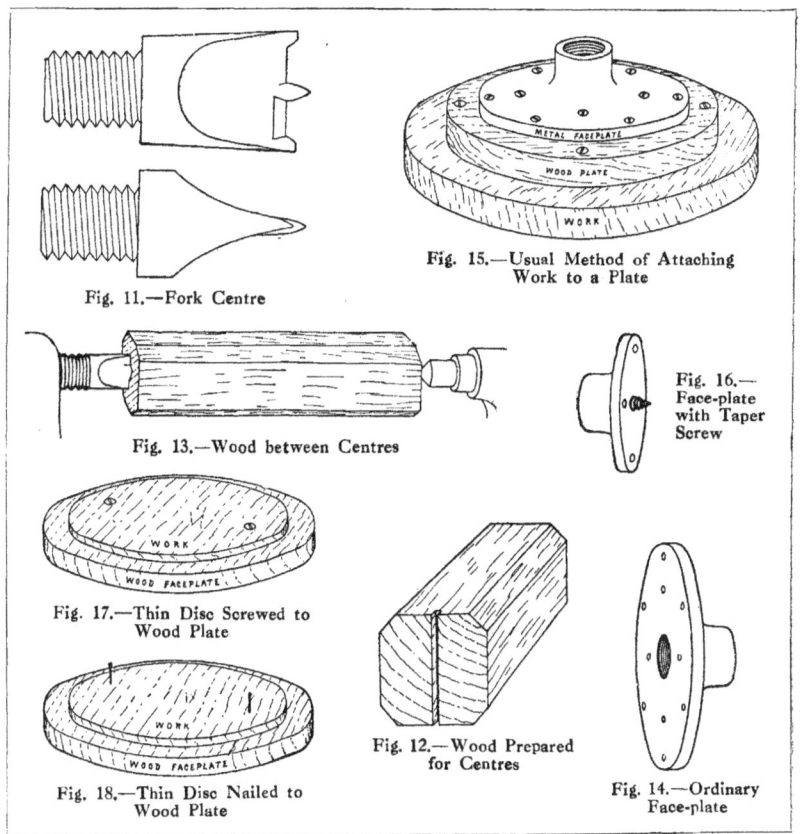

Fig. 11.—Fork Centre

Fig. 15.—Usual Method of Attaching Work to a Plate

Fig. 13.—Wood between Centres

Fig. 16.—Face-plate with Taper Screw

Fig. 17.—Thin Disc Screwed to Wood Plate

Fig. 12.—Wood Prepared for Centres

Fig. 18.—Thin Disc Nailed to Wood Plate

Fig. 14.—Ordinary Face-plate

fact that the length of the piece is much greater than its diameter does not necessarily mean that the finished article is similarly proportioned. In many cases a number of articles all alike are wanted which can be turned most expeditiously together in a stick and cut off in a number of comparatively short lengths. Such lengths, however, are usually greater than their diameter. If the diameter is greater than the length, it would as a rule be best to turn them with the grain running the other way. In such a case they would not be made between centres.

Face-plates.—When articles of a thin disc-like character have to be turned, the use of the sliding poppet with its dead centre is dispensed with. The work then is screwed, or otherwise secured, to a face-plate, which screws on to the mandrel nose, the fork centre also being dispensed with. The face-plate and work revolve with the mandrel, and as the overhang or extension outwards from the mandrel end is slight, no support in place of the dead centre is necessary. Moreover, the attachment of the work to the plate holds it in quite a different way from the between centre method shown in Fig. 13. In the latter, the fork centre has no hold at all independently of the pressure of the dead centre at the other end of the work. But a piece of wood screwed to a face-plate is secure without such pressure, and the absence of the dead centre support allows unobstructed turning of the flat front face as well as the edge or diameter of the work. Fig. 14 shows an ordinary face-plate, which is usually of cast-iron, though small ones are often of brass. It screws on in the mandrel nose up to the shoulder, and the direction in which the mandrel revolves tends to tighten it, so that there is no risk of it running off. It is provided with a number of screw holes, and the screws, which are put through from the back, must, of course, be short enough not to come through to the front face of the wood. The work may be screwed directly to the metal plate, but much more frequently a disc of wood, larger in diameter than the metal, is interposed, as in Fig. 15. This wood plate usually remains more or less permanently on the metal face, being changed only when worn out or of unsuitable diameter for the work in hand. Its advantages are that it can be refaced when out of truth, diameters can be marked on it, or recesses cut for chucking the work, and screws or nails can be put through the work into it if screwing from the back is undesirable. Moreover, a large diameter for the attachment of large work can be obtained in this way with less weight than a metal plate of similar diameter.

In Fig. 15 screws are shown put into the work outside the diameter of the metal plate. This is the usual way when a wood plate is used. In some cases the screws must be within the radius of the metal, but this does not involve removal of the wood plate. The metal plate is always provided with plenty of holes, and these need not all be used for the attachment of a wood plate. Pieces of work of small and moderate size do not need more than two screws to hold them to the plate, and in many cases a single screw in the centre is sufficient. Fig. 16 shows a plate provided with a central taper screw for small work, the screw being a part of the plate itself. This is sufficient to hold a block of wood of moderate size, and is quicker than putting an ordinary screw in with a screwdriver. It will be seen that the plate is provided with screw holes as well, which can be used if necessary. Plates of this kind sometimes have thin wood faces put on, though it is more usual to attach the work directly to the metal face. The thickness of the work must always be more than the length of the taper screw, and a considerable body of wood around is necessary to prevent splitting. Risk of the latter is minimised by boring a hole of suitable size before screwing the work on the plate. Very small and thin work cannot be put on the taper screw of a plate of the kind shown in Fig. 16, and neither can they be attached by screws put through from the back of the plate, because they could only penetrate for so short a distance that they would not hold the work securely enough. They must be put through from the front, as in Figs. 17 and 18, and their points

WOOD TURNING

must not penetrate far enough to reach the metal. When the methods of attachment shown in Figs. 17 and 18 are adopted, it is evident that little or nothing can be

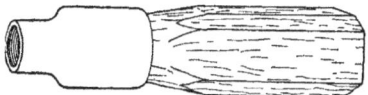

Fig. 19.—Wood in Cup Chuck

removed from the front face by turning, the work being usually planed to thickness before it is put on the plate. This, indeed, is often the quickest way, the face being merely glasspapered in the lathe and tools used only for turning to diameter.

In some cases the face is not a plain one, but may be recessed or dished or turned to any required contour across the face before the back face of the work with the tool. If the work is screwed direct to a metal plate, then it is always desirable to have the plate smaller in diameter, so that in turning the edges there shall be no risk of damage to the cutting tool through contact with the metal.

Cup Chucks.—The cup chuck, or bell chuck, is another variety, not so much used as the fork centre or face-plate, but often required for some kinds of work. It screws over the mandrel nose in the same way as the face-plate, but is shaped so that the end of a piece of wood can be driven a tight fit into it (see Fig. 19). The inside diameter of the chuck is usually about 2 in., and the wood to be turned must fit this whether the finished diameter beyond the chuck is smaller or larger. The cup chuck can be used in conjunction with the dead centre of the poppet, in which case it

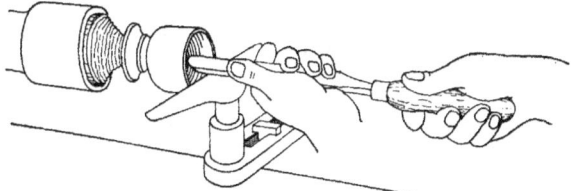

Fig. 20.—Example of Cup-chuck Work

sides having the edge turned. The screws then must be arranged to come in a zone where little or no material has to be faced off. The nails in Fig. 16 are shown only partly driven in. The turning can frequently be done with their heads standing out as shown, and it makes it easier to remove the work from the plate. They can be pulled out with pincers. If driven completely in, the work must be prised off. When a wood face-plate is used, it is usually of larger diameter than the work. In some cases it is convenient to have the plate smaller than the work, as when the edge of the latter is rounded or turned to a contour which would be difficult or impossible with a plate extending beyond the diameter of the work. Or sometimes, to avoid the trouble of re-chucking, it is an advantage to be able to get right round to

is merely a substitute for the fork centre; but usually the work is allowed to run without this support, for the advantage of the cup chuck is that the end of the work can

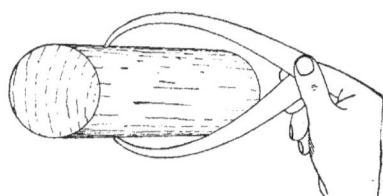

Fig. 21.—Measuring Diameter with Callipers

be got at, as in Fig. 20, which would not be possible if the poppet was used. As the wood is supported only at the end where the chuck is, its length must be limited, otherwise the outer end would not run truly under the pressure of the turning tool. The length permissible, however, is ample for the majority of small articles, and in many cases a number can be turned and cut off one at a time from a single piece of wood. The end of the wood is driven into the chuck with a hammer, and after the work is finished and cut off, the work in the lathe has to be turned to definite sizes, and measurement is necessary at frequent intervals during its reduction. In work between centres all diameters have to be calipered. The callipers may be set to the size required, and the work reduced until the callipers will just pass over it with light pressure, as

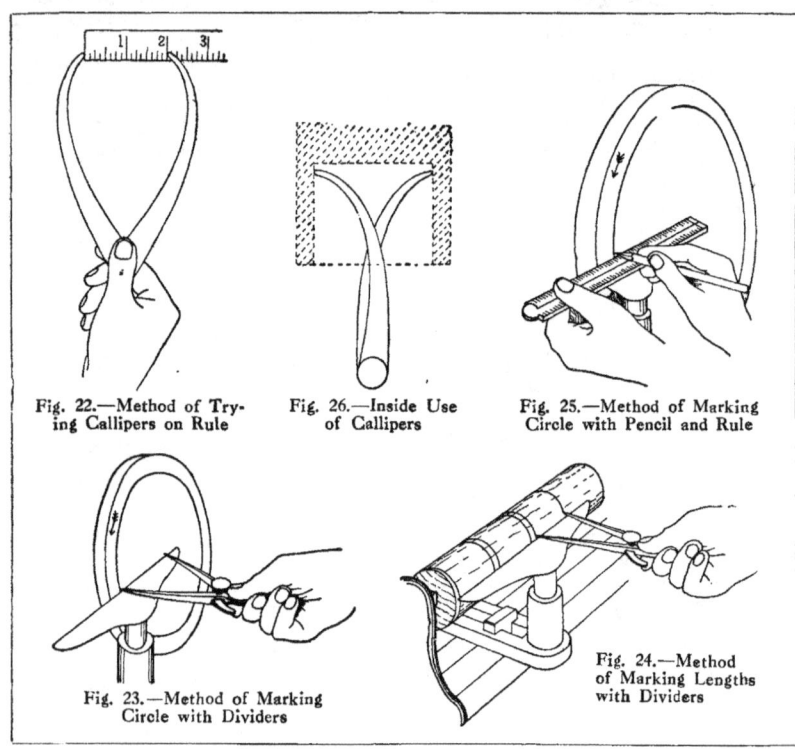

Fig. 22.—Method of Trying Callipers on Rule

Fig. 26.—Inside Use of Callipers

Fig. 25.—Method of Marking Circle with Pencil and Rule

Fig. 23.—Method of Marking Circle with Dividers

Fig. 24.—Method of Marking Lengths with Dividers

stump is forced out of the chuck by inserting the end of a suitable rod of iron behind it, through the screwed end of the chuck, and hammering it so that the wood is punched out. Before driving the wood in, it is pared roughly circular with a chisel to suit the chuck, or sometimes it is put between centres and turned.

Measurement and Testing.—Most in Fig. 21, or the callipers may be adjusted to the work and its size found by trying them on the rule, as in Fig. 22. The first method, of course, is the proper one to adopt when reduction must be made to an exact size. The callipers are set to that size on the rule, and the work is alternately reduced and tested until it is right. On small diameters tests can be made while the lathe is running, but as a rule it is best to stop the lathe for callipering the work. On the face-plate diameters can be measured direct with the rule across the front face, and if there is much thickness a small try-square can be used to see that the edge is at right angles with the face. But frequently the edge is not a simple one at right angles. It may have various diameters which must be tested, so that the callipers are sometimes necessary in measuring face-plate work. Next to the rule, therefore, callipers are the most important measuring instrument used in wood turning. As diameters vary greatly, more than one size of callipers is necessary, unless the lathe-centre height is so small that nothing above a very limited diameter can be turned in it. A pair of callipers of that capacity may then suffice for everything.

Lengths between centres or thicknesses on the face-plate can be measured direct with the rule, or where a number of similar measurements have to be made, it is sometimes preferable to set a pair of dividers to the size. Thus diameters on the face-plate may be struck with them, as in Fig. 23, or lengths between centres marked as in Fig. 24.

For large diameters on the face-plate, trammels are sometimes used. But rule and pencil, as in Fig. 25, are suitable for most of this work. A pencil circle can be put on and its full diameter measured, and then if it is slightly over or under size, an incised circle can be made correctly with the point of the side chisel. In any case, if the measurement is important, a rule is used across the full diameter before the work is finally passed. Its end is kept flush on one side with the forefinger of the left hand, and its further extremity is moved in a slight arc, so that it passes to and fro over the centre of the circle, and the full diameter can be noted. If measurement was made without this precaution, the rule might not be exactly across the centre, and the diameter would appear slightly less than it actually was.

A straightedge, or the edge of a steel-bladed square, is used a great deal in testing for straightness, both between centres and on the face-plate. Without this test a flat surface on the face-plate might be slightly concave, or convex, or variable. The same defects might not be possible lengthwise in a cylindrical article between centres, because calliper tests would show variations in diameter ; but it is much quicker to use callipers only at places some distance apart, and test for straightness between. A tapering article must necessarily be done in this way, the large and small diameters being turned at the ends and the work tested for straightness between those points, for calliper tests along a tapering body are out of the question. Instead of making repeated straightedge tests on large work between centres, a good method is to reduce to diameter at the ends, and at one or two intermediate points, if the length is very great, and then plane a flat along the whole length down to the level of the finished diameter. This flat can be seen while the work is revolving, and the turner has thus a guide to tell him when he has reduced to diameter at all parts of the length.

A great proportion of turned work, however, is not of the plain character that makes these methods possible. In most cases a number of different diameters have to be callipered, and measurements from one point to another lengthwise are necessary. The latter may be made direct with a rule ; but if a number of similar articles have to be turned, it is more convenient to mark the distances on a strip of wood, and transfer from this to the work. In some cases the first article turned can be used as a pattern for the others, being held close to the revolving wood, and pencil lines run round the latter at the important points. Curves and mouldings may be turned to the eye, or templates may be made for testing. A template may be of thin wood or cardboard or thick paper. The required contour is marked on it and cut so that the template can be tried against the work, and the latter turned until it fits. Calliper tests or other means of measurement are usually necessary in conjunction with the template, otherwise the latter would not give correct results.

A template does not necessarily represent the entire contour of a piece of work. It is often more convenient to make templates for small portions only perhaps two

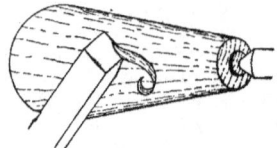

Fig. 27.—Method of Turning in Direction to Avoid Tearing Grain

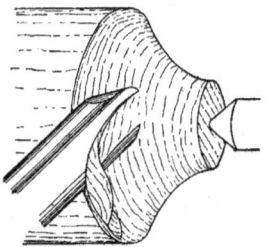

Fig. 28.—Method of Reducing Large to Small Diameter

or three separate ones for a contour which is continuous but has portions which do not require fitting to a template, and which would make the fitting slower and more tedious if they were included in the template. Templates are necessary for curves where the eye cannot be trusted, or where mechanical accuracy is demanded, as when the curve must be of definite radius.

Callipers have sometimes to be used for inside measurements as in Fig. 26. Ordinary callipers are reversed, being closed and the arms slid past each other, as shown, so that the points can enter a cavity and measure its interior diameter. The diameter at the entrance can be measured with a rule, but it may be necessary to ascertain the size at some distance farther in, and for this purpose inside callipers are required. The ordinary callipers, shown in Figs. 22 and 26, which are intended primarily for outside measurements, are not suitable for measuring small inside diameters unless in rather shallow recesses. This is because the curvature of their arms prevents them from penetrating when the points are set to only a short distance apart. In such cases, callipers intended specially for inside measurements are the only kind that can be used. These have straight arms with slightly hooked points. This makes them useless for ordinary outside measurements, because the inner edges of the arms come in contact with the work before the points have advanced far enough to reach to the full diameter. Another kind of calliper is made for both purposes. They are double in character, the pivot being midway instead of at the extremity. The arms in one direction are straight, and those on the other side of the pivot are curved, and they are constructed so that the inside and outside points are always identical in extension, which is useful when work is being done where inside and outside parts have to fit each other and must be alike in diameter. It is comparatively seldom, however, that inside callipering in wood turning is necessary.

General Work.— In turning, as in bench work, cutting against the grain must be avoided. Thus in the case of a tapering article, as in Fig. 27, the side chisel must move from the large towards the small end, and not in the reverse way. Similarly, in turning down from a large to a small diameter, as in Fig. 28, the gouge

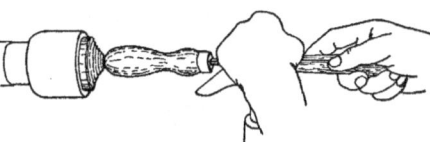

Fig. 29.—Method of Boring with Narrow Chisel

Fig. 30.—Handle between Centres

would cut best if held on its side as shown, the cut beginning at the large part and proceeding to the small diameter. This gives better results than holding the

WOOD TURNING

gouge on its back at right angles to the surface being cut, the reason being that the cutting edge. as illustrated, makes a clean slicing cut, the material moving past

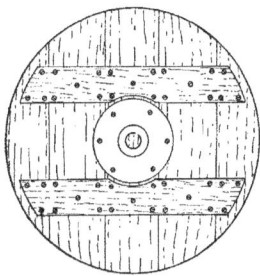

Fig. 31.—Large Plate with Cleats across Back

it diagonally and with the grain sloping in a direction which makes it impossible for it to tear up. In face-plate and in cup-chuck work central apertures of small diameter cannot be roughed out with a gouge, as the latter could not be held in a position to avoid risk of catching and severely jolting the work. Such apertures, therefore, must be sunk entirely by means of scraping tools, either a chisel of suitable width, or a round-nose if the recess is concave at the base. An instance of the latter has been already illustrated in Fig. 20. A tool handle turned in the cup chuck would be bored with a narrow chisel, as in Fig. 29, perhaps $\frac{1}{8}$ in. wide, and it would not be allowed to penetrate to the full depth required for the point of the tool tang to reach, but only as far as the diameter of the hole made by the chisel suited the tang. The remainder would be bored with a brace and small bit.

An alternative method of turning a tool handle is shown by Fig. 30, and this is the best way if the handle is a long one. It is turned between centres, and the hole bored with a brace and bit afterwards. Considerable skill is necessary then to bore the hole exactly parallel with the handle. If it slopes to either side, the tool and handle will not be in a line, which looks bad. The ferrule must be at the dead-centre end, as shown in Fig. 30, otherwise it could not be put on until after the handle was removed from the lathe and cut off. It is fitted by calliper measurement to drive on tight, and the handle is generally replaced in the lathe for finishing after the ferrule is on. Only a very slight amount, or nothing at all, is cut off the end beyond the ferrule, as it is usually not necessary, and the impression left by the dead centre is a guide for starting the boring.

Face-plate Work.—Work attached to the face-plate must generally be screwed, and screw holes in it are unavoidable. As the screws usually enter at the back of the work and do not go right through it, the holes made are seldom objectionable. If desired, they may be plugged after the work is finished. In some circumstances glue is used as a means of attaching work to the plate. It is not done by gluing direct, but by gluing paper to the plate, and then gluing the work on the paper. A very secure hold is obtained in this way, and a clean, easy removal of the finished work from the plate. The only objection is the interval of an hour or two for the glue to dry before the turning can begin. The method is suitable not only for small, light articles, but even for moderately large and heavy ones. One advantage of the absence of

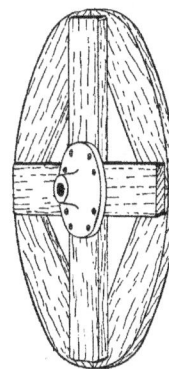

Fig. 32.—Skeleton-type Plate for Very Large Diameters

screws is that the risk of turning down on a screw and spoiling the edge of the tool is avoided. A piece of paper as large in area as the back of the work is used only when comparatively small blocks of wood are attached to the plate. For larger work the paper and glue are used only in places some distance apart.

Rings built up in segments are often attached by gluing, and in these it is sufficient to use a piece of paper under each end joint of the first layer. A ring built in six segments, for instance, would require six patches of paper glued to the plate in positions corresponding with the joints of the first layer of segments. Each piece of paper might be from 2 in. to 4 in. square, depending on the size of the work. The pieces would not be less in width than the segments, and would extend about an equal distance along them, the joint being midway on the paper. To obtain a close joint in gluing the paper to the plate, superfluous glue is squeezed out by pressing the edge of a steel square, or other suitable article, on the paper and drawing or pushing it from the centre out to the edges. The paper then is in close contact with the wood, and the gluing on of the work can proceed immediately after. When the turning is finished the work is prised off with a chisel. It is slightly lifted in this way all round before being finally forced completely off. The paper causes separation without splinters of wood from either the work or the plate adhering to the other, as would be the case if wood was glued directly to wood.

A simple disc of wood on a metal face-plate to facilitate attachment of work is only suitable for comparatively small diameters. If more than 10 in. or 12 in. in diameter, cleats would have to be screwed to the back to stiffen and keep it from warping. Plates much above that diameter, of course, are too large to be cut from a single piece of board. They must be made up of two or three pieces edge to edge to give the required width, as in Fig. 31, and cleats then may be the chief or only means of holding them together. But pieces edge to edge with cleats across the back are in the largest plates often superseded by the method shown in Fig. 32. This, it will be seen, does not give a continuous surface across the entire plate, but only a ring of variable width from the circumference inwards, and perhaps a small portion at the centre, the latter being usually necessary in order to have a centre from which to strike circles. This skeleton type of plate is sufficient for work of large diameter, for, apart from the fact that such work often consists of rings without central parts, it is not necessary for a solid piece of work of large diameter to fit against a plate over its entire area.

A plate with an outer ring of surface only is sufficient both for attachment and for providing a bearing surface for the work. Therefore very large plates are seldom made with surfaces continuous from centre to periphery. Work not large enough to be put on such a plate is better in any case on a smaller one. Sometimes large work requires a plate fully up to its own diameter, and sometimes a plate much smaller will do, or may even be desirable to permit of getting at the back of the work and so avoiding re-chucking. A plate made as in Fig. 32 is usually of the largest diameter that the lathe will take, but in some cases there may be others similarly built of smaller diameter.

In preparing pieces of wood for turning, suitable allowances in size must be made. They must be sufficient but not excessive. Discs of wood to go on the face-plate are generally sawn circular to a slightly larger diameter than the finished one. If a band-saw is not available they may be cut with a keyhole-saw or a bow-saw. Occasionally in small diameters with no band-saw the corners are cut off with a tenon-saw, and the roughly octagonal piece made circular by the turning; but this is rougher work for the gouge than turning a similarly octagonal piece between centres. One reason is that the diameter, and consequently the flats, are often greater, and another is that some of the angles present almost end grain to the tool, and this is harder to cut than grain running the other way. If a number of discs of small diameter are wanted, a piece of wood long enough from which to cut a number may be planed, and circles marked on it for sawing.

In work between centres and in cup-chuck work, the wood put in the lathe

WOOD TURNING

must be longer than the finished article. There are instances where pieces between centres can be cut to finished length before turning; but as a rule it is necessary to allow for cutting off at both ends. At the fork-centre end especially, an inch or two must nearly always be wasted, because the mark of the centre in the end is not wanted, and the turning tools cannot be allowed to go too near in cutting down the end of the work. At the dead-centre end the side chisel or other tools can go quite close to the stationary centre with no risk at all, and very little need be cut off at that end. In finishing the turned article it is usual to cut down to a very small fresh grain, which loses some of its moisture and shrinks. This, of course, occurs transversely to the fibres, shrinkage in length being negligible. Thus a large disc on the face-plate will become elliptical through shrinkage. In large work where dimensions are important, shrinkage must be guarded against, and warping also. More or less elaborate building up is necessary in such cases.

Shrinkage and warping are minimised by using well-seasoned wood, and by allowing intervals of time where possible between preparation for the lathe and final reduction to size. As soon as the turning is finished, the article should be

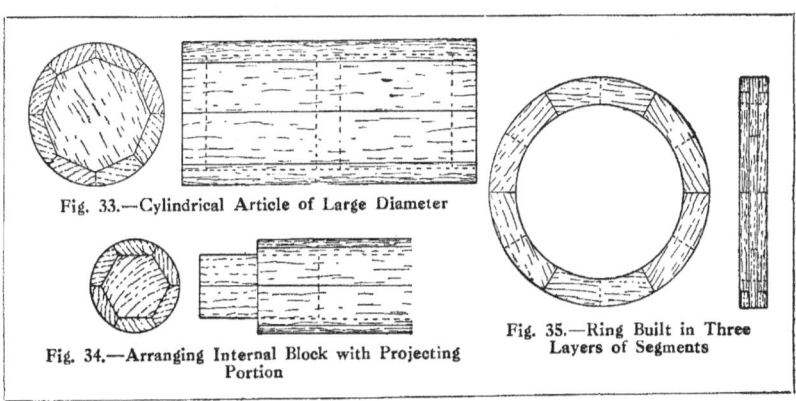

Fig. 33.—Cylindrical Article of Large Diameter

Fig. 34.—Arranging Internal Block with Projecting Portion

Fig. 35.—Ring Built in Three Layers of Segments

diameter with the point of the side chisel and the wood is then taken out of the lathe and the waste ends sawn off. When a number of small articles are turned on one length of wood between centres, the same method is adopted of cutting down between each to as small a diameter as possible without risk of breakage, and finishing with a saw after it is taken out of the lathe. In cup-chuck work the finished article can be cut completely off with the side chisel while the lathe is running, the article removed being enclosed in the left hand at the last moment.

Built-up Work.—Shrinkage of wood to be turned has to be considered, the same as in bench work. Turning exposes varnished or otherwise protected unless the work is of a rough class, in which no ultimate finish of this sort is intended. The character of the turned article also is a factor which may decide its treatment. Very small articles cannot shrink appreciably unless extreme accuracy in size is important. In most work between centres shrinkage need not be considered. Large diameters between centres are built up as much to reduce weight and material as to avoid shrinkage, warping, or splitting. The method of building up is shown in Fig. 33.

There is, of course, the alternative of solid building, often done because the diameter required is greater than the thickness of wood available. An advantage in the latter kind of building up is that the pieces are better seasoned throughout their thickness, and consequently cracks are not liable to occur on the exterior, as is the case with a very thick section of unbuilt-up wood. But for very large diameters a hollow interior, as in Fig. 33, is preferable to solid wood. Interior blocks are prepared, the number depending on the length of the article, and round these, staves or lags are nailed or screwed. The greater the diameter the greater should be the number of staves, and consequently of flats, on the blocks. Octagon blocks are shown in Fig. 33, but often more flats than this are desirable. The number is decided by marking out an end view on a board, and settling what thickness of wood to use for the staves and how thin they may be reduced at their edges. Fig. 34 shows a hexagon block with grain running the same way as that of the staves. This is suitable for a smaller diameter than that of Fig. 33. Fig. 34 shows the hexagon block projecting some way beyond the ends of the staves. This is often done when the article has to be turned to a smaller diameter there, and to reduce the staves sufficiently would necessitate making them extremely thick in other parts. The projecting block, therefore, is turned to the diameter. Work of this sort often occurs in making patterns for columns, cylinders, and large pipes. Flanges or mouldings of larger diameter than the main body are generally made as rings to fit over the latter, shallow grooves being turned to receive them. The rings may have to be fitted in halves, or sometimes they can slip over an end and bear against a shoulder on the body. In pattern-making the entire article is usually in halves for convenience of moulding. Cylindrical articles built in the way illustrated are not necessarily parallel. Taper can be provided for by cutting the blocks to suit.

In face-plate work segmental building up is common. A ring built of segments is shown in Fig. 35. Here also the number of segments to the circle varies according to diameter, six being generally the minimum, but six is exceeded only in very large diameters. Too few to the circle means short grain at their ends. Six is suitable for most work, and is very convenient for marking out, as dividers or trammels set to a radius are at the same time precisely a sixth of the circle. Segmental building up depends for its strength on layers with overlapping joints. The first layer with its six end joints must have these joints covered and held together, and the construction stiffened by bringing the end joints of the next layer midway between those of the first. In Fig. 35 three layers are shown. This is stronger than two only; but a much greater number than this is sometimes needed to build up to the depth of ring required. If the ring is attached to a solid plate, the latter, of course, holds the first layer, and in some cases where the depth is very shallow a single layer may make up the thickness required, though in good work more than one layer would be used. In an independent ring, as in Fig. 35, two layers are the minimum. Rings built in this way cannot become elliptical by shrinkage, and are as strong in one direction as in another, as the grain almost follows the circle. Only the principle of building up is shown in Fig. 35. A sectional view has to be marked out fullsize first of all, and then the number of layers and widths and radii of the segments can be obtained. They are usually glued together, nails being sometimes used as well; but nails must not be in places where there is any risk of turning down on them.

Re-chucking. — Re-chucking means the removal and replacement of a piece of work on the face-plate, in order to turn some part which cannot be got at with the work in its original position. Thus if opposite faces of a disc have to be operated on, the disc must be reversed on the plate after the first face is finished. It might be supposed that this would be necessary in nearly all work, but as a matter of fact the majority of articles can be turned without re-chucking. In metal turning re-chucking is very common, and is simpler than in wood turning. It is simpler because the metal-turner uses a variety of adjustable chucks which grip the work, and it is an easy matter to bore a central aperture, or turn an outer diameter, and use this as a means of reversing the work centrally on the plate. In wood turning the work is not held by a concentric grip, but almost always by screws. The jaws of a metal chuck would generally be in the way and the risk to the cutting tools would be considerable. Moreover, a grip tight enough to hold the work securely would generally leave its marks on the surface gripped, and this would be objectionable. Therefore the work must be rescrewed to the plate when reversed.

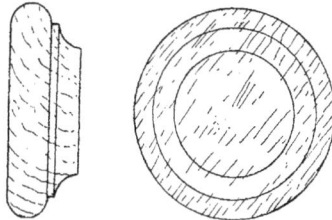

Fig. 36.—Example in which Back can be Turned without Re-chucking

As it is nearly always highly important that the re-chucked work should run true with the portion already turned, it would not do simply to set it to a circle on a plain plate and screw it there. It would inevitably get more or less out of centre during the screwing, and although with a great deal of care it could be readjusted until true, it would be a tedious and unsatisfactory method. Therefore the surface of the plate must be recessed to receive the work and keep it central while the screws are inserted; and this is also some guarantee that it cannot be accidentally forced out of centre during turning, as might happen if it depended on screws only to keep it in correct position. Most articles turned on the face-plate simply have to be flat on the back, and no turning need be done there, the surface being planed true before screwing to the plate. There are cases also where the back face need only be turned near the edge, an example of which is shown in Fig. 36, where the edge is rounded. In such cases re-chucking is generally avoided by using a face-plate of smaller diameter than the work, so that the edge of the latter stands out sufficiently for the tool to be used right round to the back as far as necessary. A rounded edge, as in Fig. 36, and all convex surfaces are finished by scraping with a chisel, the chisel being swung round to follow the curve.

Concave surfaces can be finished only with a round-nose. As it is desirable to make wood face-plates last as long as possible, they are never recessed deeper than can be avoided, and the larger the plate the stronger is the objection to turning a recess in it. When a plate has been recessed for re-chucking a piece of work, it generally has to be levelled down to the base of the recess before it can be used for other work, and this repeated a few times soon makes it so thin that it has to be discarded. Very large plates, therefore, are scarcely ever recessed, but work is chucked on them by putting on instead of reducing. The portion put on usually consists of blocks at intervals in a circle of the required diameter, perhaps three, four or six of them. They are screwed or nailed on and turned, just as a recess would be turned, the intervals between the blocks not making much difference, except that the tool must be approached carefully and held steady. Either the inner or outer diameter of a ring of blocks may be turned,

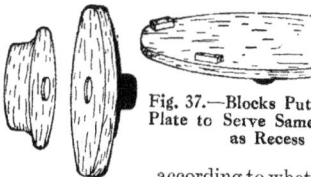

Fig. 37.—Blocks Put on Large Plate to Serve Same Purpose as Recess

Fig. 38.—Method of Centring Work by a Stud Fitting in Recess on Plate

according to whether they fit inside or outside the work. An example is shown in Fig. 37.

In some work re-chucking can be done by means of a small central hole, either in the work or the plate, and a corresponding stud to fit it on the other. In such a case, if the projecting stud was required on the face-plate, the latter would never be turned down to leave a stud standing out. The stud would be a nailed-on piece. On the other hand, a small hole, say, 1 in. or a little more in diameter, in the centre of the plate would not be so objectionable as a recess of large diameter. For a small hole would not interfere with the attachment of other work, all of which would be large enough to cover the hole and bear on the surface around. A disadvantage of the hole would be that the centre from which to strike circles would be lost, and the hole would have to be plugged in order to get a new centre. Central holes and studs of small diameter would be the best method of chucking work on the face-plate, except for the one objection that for large work they are not accurate enough. Where accurate chucking is important, it is best to fit the work to the plate at as large a diameter as possible, and the larger and heavier the work the more essential this becomes.

The stud of small diameter is very common in pattern-making. Large numbers of bosses, as in Fig. 38, are required, and these are almost always provided with studs for correct centring on the pattern. As the boss and stud must be concentric, the boss is chucked by its stud on the face-plate, as shown. Sometimes the block of wood for the boss is put on the plate and turned to provide the stud on the solid wood, and then re-chucked to turn the front of the boss; but a more expeditious way is to nail the stud on the block and attach to the plate without any need for actual re-chucking.

Glasspapering and Finishing.—Work is glasspapered in the lathe while revolving, but to avoid a scratched surface, the glasspaper should be constantly moved from side to side rather than held stationary. Glasspaper is used on flat rubbers the same as for bench work, when the shape of the work permits. For flat faces on the face-plate, the glasspaper would be wrapped on a flat rubber, and also for straight cylindrical surfaces between centres. Convex and concave outlines are generally done without a rubber. It might be supposed that varnishing and polishing could be done advantageously with the work revolving, but this is not the case. Small articles can be polished best while revolving, but large surfaces cannot, and the application of varnish with a brush, except on very small work, always has to be done with the lathe stopped. The reason is that a lathe, no matter how slowly it is running, brings fresh surface under the brush too rapidly for the varnish to be taken up by the wood, and the varnish in the brush is exhausted immediately. The result is a wet patch where contact begins, and a mere trace of varnish or none at all beyond that.

Turned work is comparatively free from tool marks, and very little glasspapering is necessary before varnishing. In rubbing down successive coats, the glasspapering should be very light. It is done with the lathe running, and is simpler and quicker, especially when the contour of the work is intricate, than glasspapering stationary work.

Tool Sharpening.—The sharpening of tools is dealt with specially in an earlier section, but a few notes dealing particularly with turners' tools may now be given. The wood-turner usually keeps an oilstone specially for sharpening the turning gouges. A stone used for the gouge as well as for other tools would soon get worn so concave by the gouge that it would not be suitable for chisels and other flat tools. The gouge soon wears a deep groove, and this is an advantage, because it can then be sharpened more quickly than on a flat surface, and the groove acts also as a guide, so that less attention is required to keep the gouge from moving too much to one side and slipping off the stone. In a stone of ordinary width, say, 1¾ in., there is room for at least two grooves side by side, and often three are formed, the first and largest in the middle and a smaller one on each side. It does not take long to start a groove if the gouge is kept constantly on the same line, and once very slightly started the gouge follows it easily afterwards. The groove, of course, begins and ends slightly short of full length of the

WOOD TURNING

stone, starting from the surface near the ends and going down to its full depth along the middle portion of its length, where the pressure is greatest. But no matter how deep the groove becomes, it is always necessary to give a rolling motion to the gouge as it travels backwards and forwards along the stone. It is necessary that the edge should be sharpened not only at the point, but equally all round its curve.

An oil-stone slip is used to remove burr from the inside, and, of course, must never be tilted, but lie flat in the channel and move parallel with it. This is analogous to the turning over of an ordinary chisel on the stone and rubbing the burr off. In both cases this operation, though it should be frequently repeated, requires only a few light strokes compared with the rubbing down on the other side where the grinding angle is. For rough turning some turners think the use of a slip unnecessary, and do not use it, holding that the burr becomes removed almost immediately by the turnings after the cut is begun.

The side chisel is ground and sharpened equally on both sides. The round-nose requires a rolling motion like the gouge, and is sharpened on the same stone as the gouge. Being flat it does not require the use of a slip, but is laid on a flat stone, the same as an ordinary chisel, for rubbing the face. In grinding, also, the gouge and round-nose must be given a constant rolling motion to grind uniformly and neatly to their curves. As grinding is not so often necessary as sharpening, the grindstone or emery-wheel is not usually allowed to become grooved. This can be prevented by moving the gouge constantly across the face of the grindstone from one side to another, so that it has no chance to wear a groove. This is not so easily done on an oilstone where the hands are employed in moving the tool backwards and forwards, and too close an approach to one side or one end results in its slipping off the stone.

Removal of Chucks, etc. — Face-plates, cup chucks, and fork centres screw on to the mandrel nose in the opposite direction to that in which the lathe runs, so that the tendency is for them to tighten rather than come off when the lathe is running. The way to remove a face-plate is to grasp the belt cone or the belt of the lathe with the left hand and unscrew the plate with the right hand, the latter being generally pulled by its upper edge and a pushing action exerted on the former, so that they are forced in opposite directions. As soon as the plate is loose enough to unscrew freely, it is supported beneath by the right hand, and the farther side of the belt is pulled downwards to revolve the mandrel in the reverse direction to its ordinary running. The plate then comes off in the right hand. A very heavy plate may have to be supported with both hands, while another person turns the lathe in its reverse direction.

In putting a plate on it should not be run up to the shoulder so that it stops with a jerk, or there may be trouble in getting it off again. Even without this a plate sometimes becomes jammed so tight on the mandrel that the hands cannot unscrew it. In such a case the usual method is to start it with a hammer, but this jars the lathe and should be avoided if possible. A short stout piece of rod to serve as a punch is used in conjunction with the hammer. In order to use it on the plate, there is generally a suitable hole drilled in the exterior of the boss of the plate, or a notch is cut in the edge of the plate. The end of the punch is inserted there at a suitable tangent to jar the plate in the direction of unscrewing. Occasionally, and especially in large lathes, a lever is inserted between the under edge of the belt pulley and the base of the headstock, and its projecting end pressed downwards to prevent the pulley and mandrel from turning while the plate is being loosened. But if the plate is very tight this is scarcely any more effective than holding the pulley with the left hand. The same lever is sometimes used in large lathes as a brake for stopping quickly. In small lathes the left hand is generally pressed on the belt cone to stop the lathe after the driving power has ceased.

Repetition Work. — In commercial work where very large numbers of similar articles are constantly required, both the lathes and the methods become modified. Knives of various shapes are attached to carriages, and take the place of the ordinary turning tools and the ordinary tool-rest. They automatically turn to diameters and lengths. Plain round rods are not turned in lathes at all, but are rounded to the required diameter by being pushed or drawn through special machines. Lathes are made intended only for face-plate work, the ordinary bed and sliding poppet being absent. On the other hand, two lathes may be fitted on a single long bed, the headstock and poppet of the smaller one being removable if the full length of the bed is wanted for the large one. The headstock of a lathe may have a screwed nose at each end of the mandrel so that a face-plate can be put on either end, the one at the back being intended for large plates and work. At the front the swing is limited to the height of the centre above the lathe bed. At the back the plate projects beyond the end of the lathe bed, and a radius from the centre down to the floor is available. The tool-rest, then, is on a stand separate from the bed.

In some ordinary lathes the headstock can be reversed if necessary, or turned at right angles for face-plate work too large to clear the bed.

Copying lathes are a highly specialised variety. They are used for turning irregular shapes, generally ovals which are not uniform in the longitudinal direction. The tool advances and retires automatically, its carriage being oscillated by a revolving metal pattern of the article to be produced. Articles of very irregular contours can thus be produced automatically in large numbers all alike, such as gunstocks, boot trees, wheel spokes, adze and hammer handles. Some of these machines are made to turn out two articles simultaneously from one pattern.

Spiral Turning.—Most cheap reproductions of antique spiral turned work are the product of automatic or semi-automatic lathes, but all the original specimens, and also the really high grade copies, are a combination of lathe work and carving.

An example of this is shown by the table leg (Fig. 39). Fig. 40 shows the leg turned preparatory to having the spiral formed on it. It will be observed that the necks are sunk to the same depth as it is intended to cut the twist, say, 1 in. Referring to Fig. 39, it will be seen that the twist begins and finishes on opposite sides of the cylinder. This is the usual practice, and in calculating the size and the number of the twists required to obtain this effect and to fill a given space, the workman does not reckon for so many complete twists, but so many twists and a half. Between A and B (Fig. 39) the neck of the twist is $\frac{3}{4}$ in. wide, and circumscribes the cylinder four and a half times.

To set out the spiral, divide the circumference of the cylinder by four equidistant longitudinal lines. Multiply the number of twists desired (four and a half) by four, and divide the length of the cylinder by the product (eighteen). Spin pencil lines round the cylinder at the points thus obtained (see the enlarged view of the cylinder, Fig. 41). A flexible straightedge is made by folding a piece of stout paper so as to obtain a firm edge to rule by, and by beginning at A (Fig. 41) and ruling a continuous line diagonally across the divisions until B is reached, a left-handed spiral may be developed. Now, if two lines are laid down parallel with this and $\frac{3}{8}$ in. on each side of it, the setting out will be complete. In the event of the job having no squares, it will not matter at what point the spiral begins, and the setting out of a twist of this description would be completed by ruling a single additional line $\frac{3}{4}$ in. away from the first. It is usual to cut twists in pairs, consequently for a set of table legs two would be required for each hand. To mark out a right-handed twist, a beginning may be made at the same point, and the line carried round in the opposite direction.

When a number of pieces have to be cut the spiral may be readily reproduced in the following way: Wind a perfectly straight strip of stout paper round that part of the cylinder which is set out to form the bead. The paper must be just wide enough to cover the bead part, and

WOOD TURNING

long enough to reach its entire length. Secure it with a couple of pins, and trim one end of it quite fair with the annular line at that part of the cylinder. This strip forms a template. To use it, spin a pencil line round one end of the cylinder to be marked out. Pin the trimmed end of the template securely quite fair by this line and revolve the job, when the strip will automatically take up the correct position on the cylinder, and the twist may be marked out by running a pencil along both sides of the strip. To reverse the hand of the twist, turn the paper over, pin and wind in the opposite direction.

For " setting in " the twist a saw fitted these the neck should be nicely hollowed. A chisel may now be taken to round up the bead, and i followed by a cabinet-maker's file (not a rasp).

If the work is being done on a treadle lathe glasspapering is effected in the following manner : The foot is worked so as to swing the flywheel backwards and forwards, the hand holding the glasspaper being carried to and fro along the twist. Should a power machine be employed it will nave to be run " dead slow," and after glasspapering the job in one direction, the belt will need to be crossed and the motion reversed to obtain a uniform finish.

Reeding.—Formerly this class of work

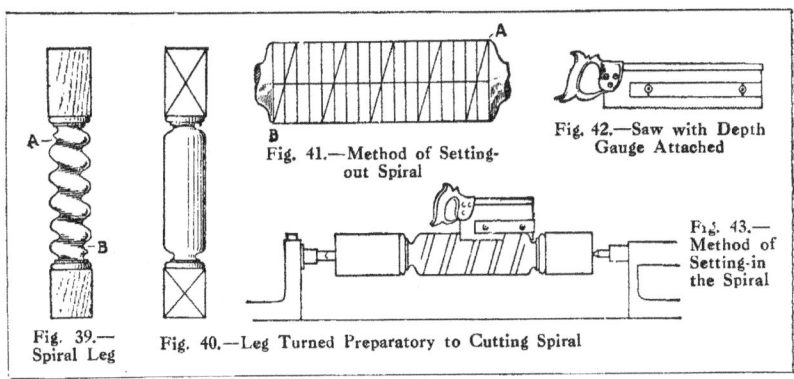

Fig. 39.—Spiral Leg
Fig. 40.—Leg Turned Preparatory to Cutting Spiral
Fig. 41.—Method of Setting-out Spiral
Fig. 42.—Saw with Depth Gauge Attached
Fig. 43.—Method of Setting-in the Spiral

with a depth-gauge is shown by Fig. 42, the method of fixing the gauge being that which is usually employed in the shops where spiral cutting is frequently done. The idea of punching holes through a tenon saw, however, may not commend itself to the occasional operator, in which case he will have to devise some temporary means of securing the gauge to the saw blade. The gauge in this instance will be set ¾ in. from the saw teeth. The operation of " setting in " the twist is shown by Fig. 43, constructional lines being omitted for the sake of clearness. Success with this is dependent on getting a perfectly fair start. A carver's gouge may be used to remove the surplus timber between the saw-cuts, and on reaching the bottom of was done entirely by hand. The turned material was longitudinally pencil-lined, dividing the job into equal width spacing, depending on the number of reedings, and the work finished with wood-carving tools, the principal tool used for the purpose being the ordinary carving **V** or parting tool.

A later and quicker way is to operate on the work with horizontal cutters whilst it is supported between the lathe centres. This method of course necessitates special attachments for the lathe.

Example of Wood Turning.—An outline of the usual procedure in making an article such as a wooden stool is shown by Figs. 44 to 47.

When the square for the seat is

mounted on the screw chuck, start the lathe, and with the compasses scribe a circle of the size required. The corners may then be removed by a single cut with bit. In " setting up " see that the end of the frame arrests the forward movement of the block before it reaches the point of the bit. A cardboard template may be

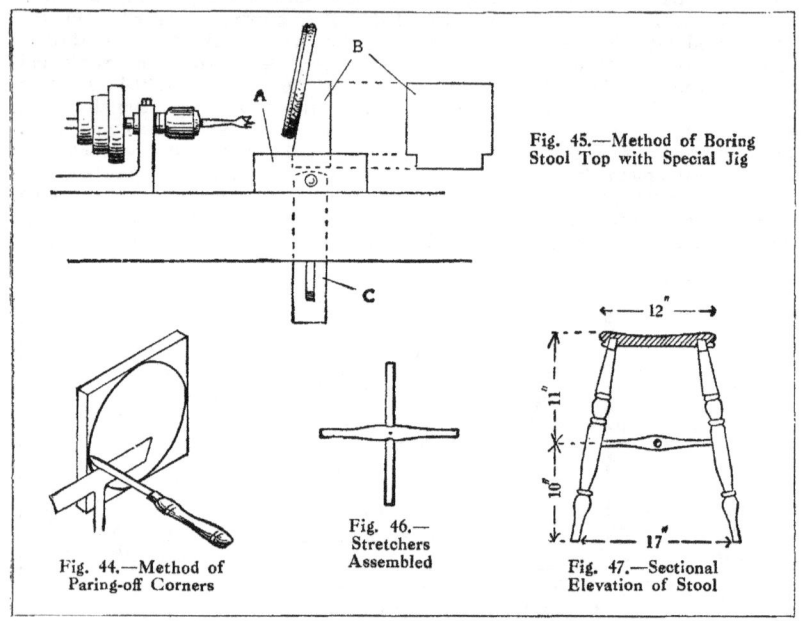

Fig. 45.—Method of Boring Stool Top with Special Jig

Fig. 44.—Method of Paring-off Corners

Fig. 46.—Stretchers Assembled

Fig. 47.—Sectional Elevation of Stool

the parting tool (Fig. 44). The point of the parting tool should be spread a little to give clearance, or the tool will become unduly hot and the temper may be drawn. As the corners of the square will fly off with considerable force, care should be taken to keep out of the "line of fire," and to protect any windows that may be in the vicinity.

Fig. 45 illustrates a fit-up for boring the stool top. A is a square frame, put together like the four sides of a box, and is held in position by a wedge passing through the leg C. The wooden block shown by B slides in this frame, and determines the angle and depth to which the holes are bored. The stool top is held by the hands in the position shown, and together with the block is fed towards the

used for marking the positions of the holes. The boring of the legs and stretchers presents no special difficulty. They may be bored in the lathe or by hand, whichever is preferred. The hole in the stretcher should be bored from both sides to prevent breaking through.

In fitting up, the glue should be used very hot, and special attention should be paid to the holes. The stretchers are put together as shown by Fig. 46. These are not glued, but are secured with a brad. The legs are next assembled round the stretchers, the brad in which is placed towards the bottom. The legs are then driven into the holes in the top, and the stool is ready to be stained and varnished.

A part sectional elevation of the stool with dimensions is shown by Fig. 47.

Veneering

THE process of veneering has been very unjustly condemned at times, and is frequently referred to in terms of contempt, it being believed in some quarters that veneering is synonymous with cheap and shoddy work. These impressions, in some cases, have doubtless arisen because of the abuse of veneering, and in others from a wrong impression of its particular purpose. In these circumstances it may be advisable to deal with the proper uses of veneering before dealing with the particular processes involved.

When veneering was in vogue a good deal more than it is to-day, much cheap and shoddy work was produced with inferior wood groundworks and bad veneer. Instances are common where orange-box and egg-box wood has been sold to cabinet-makers, who used it instead of the more expensive pine or American whitewood for groundworks, and then veneered it with cheap knife-cut veneer worth about ½d. a square foot. It was work of this kind that was largely responsible for the suspicion with which veneered work was viewed, and it may be said here that when veneering is used to conceal bad wood and poor construction, it is being used in a wrong way, and the resultant work may properly be termed "shoddy." In this connection reference should be made to the shoddy inlaid mahogany bureaux, of which many thousands exist. Instead of mortising the carcases together, the drawer rails are simply butted between the carcase ends, with 3-in. French nails driven through the ends into the rails. The nails were punched in, and the holes stopped with plaster-of-paris before knife-cut veneer was laid over the ends, concealing the holes and also the imperfections of the wood always found in cheap timber. Veneering of this kind is always unsatisfactory, as it "blisters" very easily, and when this occurs it cannot be easily remedied. Cheap wood frequently contains a lot of resin, and knots shrink away from the veneer with disastrous results.

In the proper use of veneering good, sound wood is used for the groundwork, with good figured veneer. In some cases Honduras mahogany is veneered with wood of another kind, and the work generally when properly done is superior to, and more costly than, ordinary solid wood. This leads naturally to an excellent reason for veneering. If "curl" timber is to be used in panels, for example, the cost of the wood would be prohibitive, and it would not last nearly as long as the same "curl" timber cut into veneer and used in conjunction with plain panel boards. It may be said, generally, that the more richly figured woods cannot be used in the solid because the contrasting grains and erratic growth—which give such a beautiful effect—are conducive to twisting and warping. This timber, however, when cut into very thin layers and properly treated and glued or veneered on panel boards, gives the rich effect desired, and "stands" far better than the solid curl or figured wood. Satinwood, for example, can only be used "in the solid" for thin facings or mouldings owing to its poor standing power. The more richly figured it is the more it costs, and for this reason even mouldings in satinwood work are frequently made with mahogany groundworks and thin satinwood facings. Economy in working on material is not the particular object aimed at, but rather increased durability.

Another "proper" use of veneering is in connection with curved work, such as circular and elliptical tables and cabinets. With such work, the rails of a circular table, for instance, or even a complete rim, it will be understood that "building up" in layers is far better than cutting solid rails, which are fitted between the legs. The latter method, if employed, causes weakness due to the inevitable short grain in parts, and the end grain is objectionable in appearance, as it has no figure and will not polish and look well. In both of these cases veneering is resorted to for decorative purposes, and as in the case of a built-up rim, the construction may be seen inside the rim. The veneering is obviously employed to enhance the appearance of the table. There is no attempt to deceive, and the maximum strength is obtained. This point also applies to quartered veneering, which may frequently be seen to advantage in old-fashioned piano cases and bedsteads of burr walnut. These, obviously, could not be made from solid wood, and if they were, it would only be at the expense of much labour and wood, and additionally, the wood would twist so much as to make the work valueless in a very short time. It will thus be seen that veneering is quite legitimate when used for "quartering" or for geometrically arranged units of contrasting woods in panels, drawer fronts, etc.

The durability of veneering is sometimes questioned; but the best test of this factor is the examination of old work, particularly that of the eighteenth century and the Victorian era. There are few who have not at some time admired the fine veneers and veneering of that typical piece of Victorian furniture, the parlour table, either circular or elliptical, even though at the same time it may be regretted that the design was not so good as the workmanship.

At this stage it may be advisable to mention briefly the methods employed in cutting veneers. The old cabinet-makers evidently cut them by hand, as the examination of old work shows much of the veneer to be almost $\frac{1}{8}$ in. thick, with a very rough back caused by large-toothed saws. The advent of very large circular saws brought about the introduction of saw-cut veneers of moderate thickness, whilst the improved circular saw is really a very flat cone or drum with small sections of saw bolted all round. The flat cone gives the necessary rigidity and prevents buckling, and thus enables saw-cut veneers of twenty or more to the inch to be produced. A later development was the introduction of knife-cut veneer. The log is simply fixed in a large lathe, and is made to rotate against a large firmly-set knife, which takes off the veneer in one long roll. For purposes of convenience the sheet is cut into smaller ones 2 ft. or 3ft. wide, which are known generally as sheets. The wood used for veneer is, of course, chiefly in logs or balks, and bone-dry seasoning is not essential. With knife-cut veneer cutting, very dry wood is too brittle, and it is therefore the practice to first cut the veneer and then to dry the sheets in specially constructed drying rooms.

The advantages attaching to "saw-cut" and "knife-cut" veneers are not generally appreciated. It may be said of the former that a finer finished surface may be obtained by the use of saw-cut veneer than is the case when knife-cut veneer is used. Against this must be set the extra cost of saw-cut veneer, and the fact that extra labour is entailed, as saw-cut veneer cannot usually be laid by hand. The extra thickness of saw-cut veneer is its chief advantage, which prevents undue absorption of glue. With thin veneer, and particularly with figured veneer, the glue will penetrate right through the leaf. It will be understood that a "gluey" surface is undesirable for polishing, as the stain—bichromate of potash, for instance—only takes readily to a really clean wood surface. This drawback is not very apparent when the work is finished; but the penetration of glue in the case of thin veneers undoubtedly reduces the lustrous qualities of the wood,

The absorption of glue leads up to an important process which is very necessary when dealing with veneers with very open grains. Among the latter are included bird's-eye maple, Hungarian ash, and occasionally pollard oak. The first-named wood being marked with small

Fig. 1.—French Cabinet with Veneered and Marqueteried Decoration

consequently producing a flat, uninteresting effect. If a piece of figured wood were used for both knife-cut and saw-cut veneers, and then laid, cleaned up and polished, one would have no difficulty in picking out the knife-cut piece, it being so much less "deep" and lustrous in appearance.

"eyes," the glue penetrates right through the wood, and as is usually the case with very light-coloured woods, the glue shows unsightly in the grain when the work is polished. To obviate this tendency, light-coloured open grained woods are specially treated. The underside of the veneer is first toothed level, and then it is carefully covered with a thin layer of glue-size and whiting. When this dries it forms a thin skin which usually effectually prevents the glue soaking through the veneer when it is laid. Some cabinet-makers prefer to mix whiting and ochre, for instance, with the glue, matching the finished colour of the surface, so that if some should penetrate it will not show in contrast to the natural wood. The first is probably the better method, because, as indicated previously, more lustre is obtained if the veneered surface is kept perfectly free from glue.

Before proceeding to describe the actual methods and tools used in veneering, it may be well to mention that veneering is divided into two distinct processes, namely, " hand " and " caul " veneering. The first is done with a veneering hammer, a very simple tool which can easily be made by a woodworker; the second method briefly consists in the application of pressure applied by means of hand-screws or cramps, and " cauls." Both methods will be described in detail later.

Hammer veneering is generally used for knife-cut veneer, and it may be success-fully employed in practically all cases where only a single piece is to be laid. Built-up patterns such as those to be described and illustrated later cannot be laid with a veneering hammer, as the mois-ture in the glue causes the pieces to swell quickly, thus causing the built-up pattern to " cockle up " and smash when the hammer is applied. For this reason " marqueteried " patterns cannot be laid with a veneering hammer, although they are frequently cut in knife-cut veneer. The illustration (Fig. 1) shows a fine cabinet with a " marqueteried " panel, and it will readily be understood that when the pattern leaves the marquetry cutter, with all the various pieces glued on to a sheet of paper, any dampness would cause the groundwork veneer to stretch unduly, with disastrous results to the insets. The marqueteried panels sold by various firms are glued down on paper, and for the reasons indicated they have to be laid with cauls and the application of pressure. The cabinet illustrated belongs to the early Louis XVI. period. Later Louis XVI. work is characterised by fine " diaper " ornament, some of which is cut as mar-quetry, whilst other diaper patterns are made up with small lozenge- or diamond-shaped pieces of veneers with intersecting lines of ebony, boxwood, etc., the whole forming a charming surface decoration.

Probably the most important part of veneered work is that in connection with the groundwork, as the proper selection and treatment of this part determine the durability of the veneering when the latter is properly done. The two woods most chiefly used are American yellow pine and Honduras mahogany. It is essential that groundworks should be free from sap and imperfections such as shakes and knots. The best wood is that gener-ally termed " panel wood." Panel boards do not shrink or warp to any great extent, as the " medullary rays " practically run parallel to the surfaces and act as stiffening agents. Fig. 2 shows the panel boards in a log, and as the boards are cut nearer the outside there is a tendency for the boards to " cast," which is due to the oblique medullary rays and the tendency of the boards to go " round " on the heart side. Panel boards cannot, of course, always be used, and therefore steps must be taken to counteract the natural ten-dency of the boards to curve.

Fig. 3 shows an ideal arrangement for a groundwork. This is built up with narrow strips of wood, with the heart side alternating all through. One pulls against the other, and no distinct " casting " takes place. It is usual when a groundwork of this kind is utilised to veneer the ground-work on both sides. When a plain single board is used, the veneer should be placed on the heart side, as the boards have a natural tendency to go round on the heart side (*see* Fig. 4). An additional reason is that if veneer is laid with a hammer it expands somewhat after being glued and damped, and shrinks somewhat during the drying. This causes the wood to go hollow on the face side, and if the ground-work is already round it pulls the surface almost straight.

Three-ply wood has come into vogue,

VENEERING

and this material may be used to advantage. It can be obtained in almost any thickness and also with from three to seven layers. The principle is to place each layer with the grain running at right angles to the layer below. Shrinkage and warpage are thus counteracted. Old French bed panels were made in a similar way.

up, if necessary, and planed to thickness; the toothing plane is brought into use. This tool has a body similar to a smoothing plane, and a single-toothed iron is set upright in the stock. The iron is made with a series of serrations on the face side, so that when ground and sharpened, the cutting edge resembles that shown by

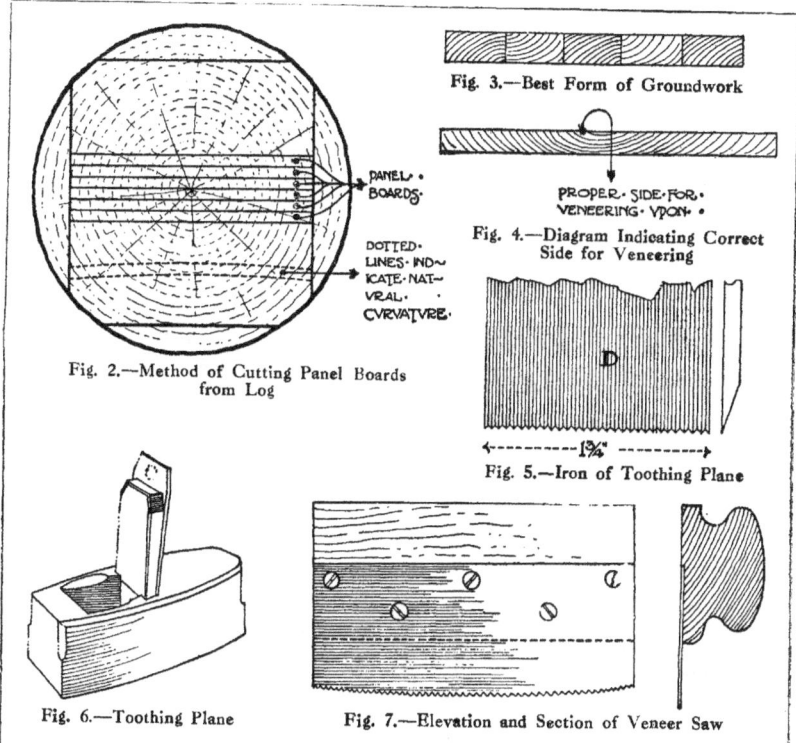

Fig. 2.—Method of Cutting Panel Boards from Log

Fig. 3.—Best Form of Groundwork

Fig. 4.—Diagram Indicating Correct Side for Veneering

Fig. 5.—Iron of Toothing Plane

Fig. 6.—Toothing Plane

Fig. 7.—Elevation and Section of Veneer Saw

The groundwork was first prepared, and then veneered each side, with the veneer grain placed across the grain of the groundwork. An outside layer was then put on each side in the same direction as the groundwork, thus forming a five-ply panel, which would keep flat and sound for generations.

The groundwork having been jointed

Fig. 5. Various degrees of coarseness can be obtained in these irons, a fairly coarse one being the best for groundworks. The fine ones are used for levelling down saw-cut veneers before they are scraped and glasspapered. The toothing plane (Fig. 6) should first be used diagonally on the groundwork, that is, from opposite corners; then it is toothed in the direction of the other diagonal before it is completed by toothing from end to end of the wood, in the same direction as the grain. Whether the veneer is to be laid with a veneering hammer or cauls, proper toothing is essential, and the groundwork is then ready for sizing.

It should be mentioned here that all groundworks, and particularly soft ones, such as pine or American whitewood, should be sized after toothing. It is usual to prepare the size with a small quantity of liquid glue mixed with water. This should be well rubbed into the toothed groundwork with a brush, and then allowed to dry. A little experience is necessary before one can do this really first step. The leaf to be laid should be free from shakes, and it may be cut from the sheet by using the edge of the toothing plane-iron (like a saw) against a straightedge. Chisels are sometimes used ; but unless great care is taken they will cause the veneer to shatter and break when cutting across the grain. A veneer saw such as is shown in Fig. 7 is the tool generally used by expert cabinet-makers.

It should be distinctly understood that there is a right and a wrong side to veneer, and particularly knife-cut veneer. If both sides of the leaf are carefully examined, it will be noticed that the " pores " of the wood are slightly depressed on one side, with corresponding projections on

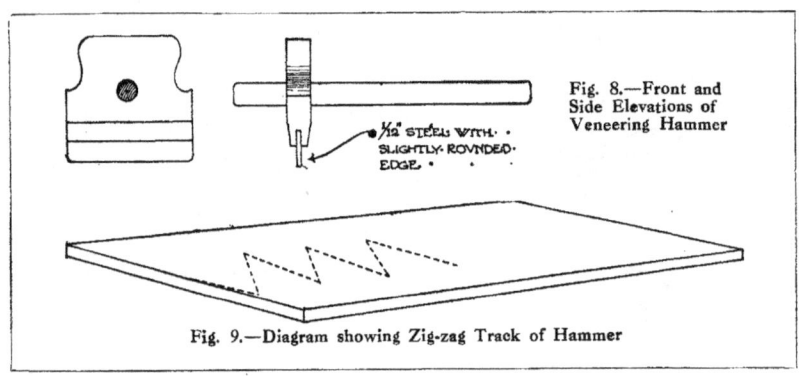

Fig. 8.—Front and Side Elevations of Veneering Hammer

Fig. 9.—Diagram showing Zig-zag Track of Hammer

well, as occasionally the size is made too strong, which prevents it sinking properly into the wood, with the result that it can be distinctly seen as a layer when dry. Should this occur, a fine toothing plane should be used to roughen the surface again before the veneer is laid.

When circular or curved groundworks are employed, a certain amount of end grain is inevitable. Sizing in such instances is imperative, as otherwise the glue for veneering would be absorbed by the groundwork, and peeling and blistering would result.

Assuming that knife-cut veneer is to be laid with a veneering hammer on a flat surface, the selection of the veneer is the the other side. The leaf should be laid with the depressions downwards, so that the slightly raised parts can be removed when the surface is cleaned up.

The proper side having been selected, the groundwork should next be well covered with glue. The knife-cut veneer is then pressed flat with the hands, and the outer surface damped with a cloth. A little glue is then dabbed on with a brush here and there, and a hot flat-iron is then passed all over the surface until the glue underneath runs freely. A veneering hammer such as shown by Fig. 8 is then brought into play, the veneer being squeezed down with the steel edge. It should be remembered that it is necessary to rub out as much glue as possible from underneath the veneer, and this can best be effected by rubbing away from the centre of the veneer with a "zig-zag" motion, such as is indicated in Fig. 9. The glue should first be pushed from the centre towards one end, and then from the centre to the other end, until as much as possible is rubbed out. If this is done properly the veneer will then be laid flat and without blisters.

During the whole process of laying, it is essential that the outside of the veneer should be kept moist. A frequent cause of failure is that the surface is kept too wet. To obviate this, the outer surface should be kept moistened with size, as after the ironing is effected and rubbing takes place, the size dries slightly and practically closes the pores of the wood, thus preventing blisters. These latter are more frequently caused by air underneath the wood than the absence of glue, as is generally supposed, and, as has been previously indicated, can best be obviated by the application of size rather than water as a dampening agent during the ironing and laying. Of course, blisters may occur, and for the reasons indicated above, a blister should be carefully slit with a thin-bladed knife in the direction of the grain, and a little glue inserted. The whole is then rubbed, the glue and air being rubbed out simultaneously.

When the veneer is laid and stood aside to dry, the air should be kept away from the surface. If a single piece only is being handled, the veneered side can be laid flat on the bench or floor ; or if two are handled, the surfaces can be placed together with a sheet of paper in between and cramped or hand-screwed.

The hammer-veneering practice in connection with knife-cut veneers varies but little when curved work is required to be veneered. Examples of the latter frequently occur in cabinet work, such as, for example, bowed fronts in chests of drawers and dressing-tables, writing-tables, and sideboards. On the smaller side there are clock cases with curved heads, jewel boxes, and caskets. With work which is only slightly curved, such

as bow drawer-fronts, the veneer will bend quite easily, and lay without blisters if the surface is damped with size instead of water. With the small work, however, involving " quicker " curves, it sometimes happens that fractures in the veneer occur whilst bending. To avoid difficulties of this sort the usual plan is to use the veneer with the grain of the groundwork, which enables the veneer to be laid with comparative ease.

The next type of veneering to be dealt with is that generally termed " caul " veneering, and, as has already been indicated, it is employed in all cases where marqueteried patterns or built-up designs are employed. Its use is general also in connection with saw-cut as distinct from knife-cut veneer. The former kind is usually too " strong " for treatment by the hammer method, and chiefly for this reason caul veneering is almost inevitable when the veneers are laid in large pieces. The narrow cross-bandings used round drawers and panels, or very small pieces of saw-cut veneer, can, of course, be laid with a veneering hammer or even the thin side of an ordinary hammer ; but if the veneer is at all buckled, hammering is quite unsuitable. The chief requirement for caul veneering is a fairly good number of hand-screws, and if there are not sufficient of these, large and small cramps can with a little ingenuity be pressed into the service.

Veneering on a large scale simply consists of labour-saving appliances, by the use of which many surfaces can be veneered at one time. In the large firms a gluing machine, which quickly spreads the glue quite evenly over the groundwork, is usual, and then quite elaborate systems are adopted for heating the cauls and applying the necessary pressure. These are, it will be readily understood, quite simple operations in themselves ; and, as a matter of fact, the use of the above-mentioned plant is not justified unless working on a large scale.

For simple caul veneering a good example is a pair of bureau ends. It is presumed that these have been prepared and sized as already described. The underside of the veneer is then slightly toothed and the following apparatus prepared: say twelve bearers about 2 in. square, and a "caul" slightly larger than the surfaces to be veneered, made of ¾-in. pine or whitewood accurately planed and gauged to thickness. It will be seen (Fig. 10) pressure is first applied to the middle, and as the hand-screws are tightened up at each side, pressure is brought to bear over the whole area. The bearers should be placed in pairs at intervals of 6 in. or 7 in. (see Fig. 12). It is well to test the whole bearers, caul, and ends before the actual

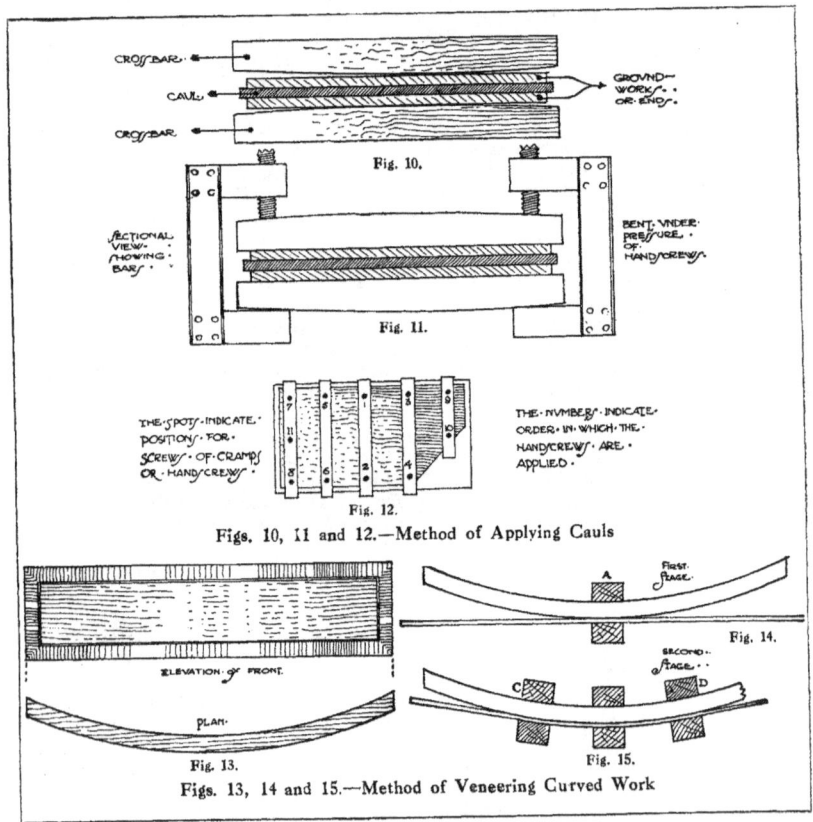

Figs. 10, 11 and 12.—Method of Applying Cauls

Figs. 13, 14 and 15.—Method of Veneering Curved Work

that the bearers are "round" on the underside. The amount of curvature is rather exaggerated in the diagram, but ¼ in. should be sufficient in a 21-in. length. It will be seen by referring to Fig. 11 that when pressure is applied by means of hand-screws to the bearers or cross-bars, the veneering is done, so that the bearer faces can be planed flatter or rounder as occasion requires. The hand-screws should always be "set" near the proper size, so that time should not be lost after the caul has been heated. Probably the chief mistake made by beginners is in connection with the glue. Both surfaces should be well covered with glue, and then set aside until it is quite "chilled." When a spread surface is really "chilled," the hand can be laid quite flat on the glue, and then taken off without sticking in any way. If this is not done the glue will at once grip the veneer, and any alteration of position is almost impossible without splitting the sheet. Even supposing the veneer could be dropped into the exact position, it would at once cause the veneer to swell rapidly, and cause buckles. A bad after-effect is also occasioned, as after the glue dries the veneer contracts to its original size, thus causing the surface to go hollow.

The caul is heated on both sides, preferably over a blaze of shavings in a fireplace, until the hand cannot comfortably be placed on both sides. The procedure generally is as follows : (1) Cover the groundworks with glue and allow to chill. (2) Place the veneers in position, and pin down each sheet with two fine veneer pins. (3) Cover each sheet of veneer with a sheet of newspaper. (4) Thoroughly heat the caul on both sides and place between as indicated in Fig. 10. (5) Place two cross-bars in position at the middle of the ends, and hand-screw together until the glue runs out at each side. (6) Place a second and third set about 6 in. from the centre bar, and hand-screw similarly. (7) Place the remainder of the bars in position, and hand-screw. (8) When all is properly hand-screwed, test all the hand-screws and tighten wherever possible. (9) Add hand-screws at each end on the middle parts of the cross-bar.

The work having been completed in the manner indicated above, it may be stood aside to dry, twelve to twenty-four hours elapsing before the hand-screws are removed. Should any glue have penetrated the veneer, the paper prevents it sticking to the caul. With very "figury" veneers a good deal of glue penetrates, causing the paper to stick to the surface. This can, however, be easily removed by toothing it down with a toothing plane. Should blisters be suspected, the parts may be tapped with the knuckle, when the sound will indicate their position. As in the case of hammer veneering, they can be rectified by slitting the veneer with a thin knife and inserting glue, afterwards applying a very small caul or square piece of wood with hand-screw, in preference to rubbing down with hammer.

The second example of caul veneering is that where a curved surface has to be

Fig. 16.—Example of Built-up Veneer

negotiated, such as illustrated in the drawer front shown in Fig. 13. The practice is very similar, a thin wooden caul of $\frac{1}{4}$-in. or even $\frac{3}{16}$-in. whitewood being used in conjunction with a few cross-pieces of $\frac{7}{8}$-in. wood about $1\frac{1}{4}$ in. wide. The method employed is as follows : (1) Cover the groundwork with glue, and allow to chill.

(2) Place and pin the veneer in position, and heat the caul. (3) Cover with paper, and place on the caul. (4) Put blocks A (Fig. 14) in position, and hand-screw as indicated in diagram. (5) Put blocks c and D (Fig. 15) in position, and hand-screw. (6) Follow with the succeeding blocks, and hand-screw. (7) Carefully examine the edges, and adjust the hand-screws as necessary. (8) Set aside to dry for twelve to twenty-four hours.

In cases where the drawer is made prior to veneering the front, it is advisable to cramp the ends of the caul down by cramping over the back and front. Care must be taken to ensure that the pressure is along the drawer sides, as otherwise the dovetails may be strained and weakened. With an example such as is illustrated, decorated with mosaic stringing and cross-banding, a cutting gauge should be set to the margin required, and the veneer cut by working off the edges of the front. The surplus veneer can be easily removed if it is heated with an old file to soften the glue. The stringing is then cut a little longer than the finished length on one side and glued against the veneer by rubbing with a hammer. One end is then mitred with a chisel and the second length fitted, the process being continued all round. Cross-bands of saw-cut veneer are next prepared, and the long sides are then rubbed down in two or three short lengths with a hammer. All four mitres are now cut with a very sharp chisel, and the end pieces may then be fitted and glued down between them.

A very popular and effective method of decoration consists of building up geometrical patterns in veneer, with mosaic lines or stringing between the various pieces of veneer. Such an example is the top of a portable dressing case now in the Victoria and Albert Museum, a corner being shown by Fig. 16. This dates from the eighteenth century, and the figuring and lustre of the wood is actually improved by the natural toning effected by age. A few simple examples of similar veneering are illustrated by Figs. 17, 18 and 19. These could well be utilised with but slight alteration for drawer fronts, door panels, tops of writing-cases, and other small work of a similar character. The more decorative side of veneering is dealt with in the next section. The practice in most examples is very similar. Fig. 19 can be taken as a specimen to be executed in well-figured saw-cut mahogany veneer.

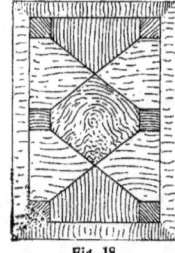
Fig. 17. Fig. 18.
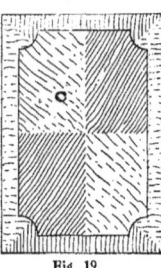
Fig. 19.
Figs. 17, 18 and 19.—Examples of Decorative Veneer Work

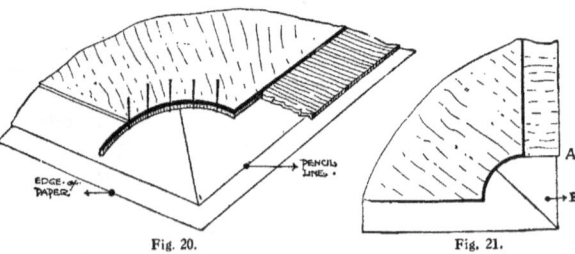
Fig. 20. Fig. 21.
Figs. 20 and 21.—Method of Fitting Curved Corners

VENEERING

The design is first to be drawn on a piece of strong cartridge paper that has been damp-stretched on a plain piece of wood or an old drawing-board. Four pieces of veneer are then cut with the grain running from corner to corner, and the two inside edges planed true and square on a small shooting-board, with either a small metal block plane or a shoulder plane. This piece is then planed to width and length. The next step is to cut the hollow corner. This may be marked with a pair of compasses, and then cut banding and the quartered part; these may be purchased in small quantities, and are about $\frac{1}{16}$ in. square. A short length should be cut for one side, and then glued down to the paper by rubbing with the flat end of a small hammer. One end is then mitred ready for the hollow corner. As these lines are rather brittle, a small piece should be put into hot water for a couple of minutes to render bending easier. One end is then mitred to fit the straight length, and pressed round the curve with a hammer. In the case of a

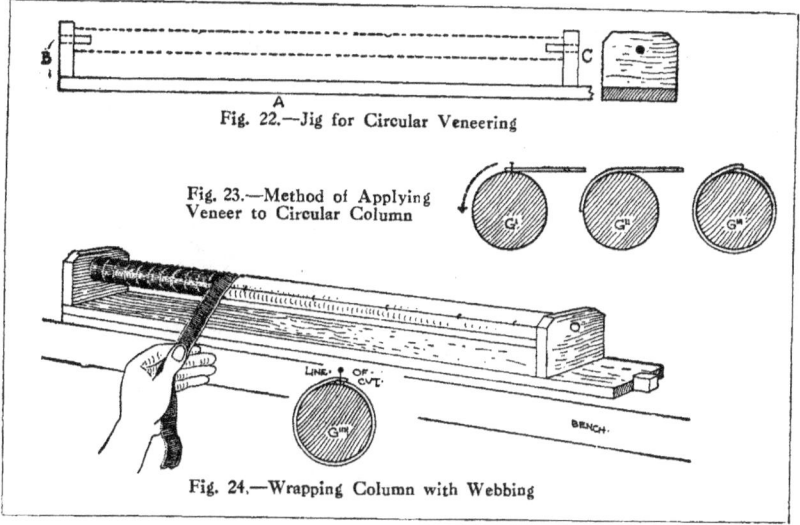

Fig. 22.—Jig for Circular Veneering

Fig. 23.—Method of Applying Veneer to Circular Column

Fig. 24.—Wrapping Column with Webbing

very carefully just outside the line with a fine fret-saw. To finish the edge cleanly a half-round file should be used; or alternately, a strip of rounded wood with fine glasspaper wound round. This piece of veneer when finished to shape is then glued down to the paper, and the other quarters cut and glued in the same way.

If great care is exercised, it is sometimes quicker to fasten the four veneers together with two fine veneer pins, and then plane the edge and hollow out the corners, afterwards separating them and gluing down. The design shows a line between the cross-banding very small or "quick" curve, veneer pins should be inserted occasionally as indicated by Fig. 20. A straight length is then laid, and so on until the line is laid all round. The cross-banding is next dealt with. This should be cut from the end of a leaf with a sharp cutting gauge in lengths which should have one edge shot true on the shooting-board. It is then glued on the underside, and rubbed down with a hammer. The straight piece should be cut square at A (see Fig. 21), and then the piece marked B is cut and fitted. Repeat for the other parts.

So far only ordinary hammer and "caul" veneering have been dealt with. The fine possibilities of veneering in cabinet-work, however, are so many, particularly in small work, that it may be well to deal with one or two special processes of veneering, which, with but little adaptation, may be applied to a large number of varied jobs.

As an example, the method of veneering a circular column or pillar will be taken, and this is identical with the method of veneering a circular pedestal, say 18 in. in diameter. The only difference is one of size, this applying also to the stand used for revolving the work, which is described and illustrated later. Supposing a column 4 ft. long by 2 in. in diameter is required to be veneered, the first essential is to prepare a satisfactory groundwork. Good straight-grained timber must be used for this purpose in order to prevent casting later, and the rounding of the material should preferably be done on a lathe. Failing the use of the latter, the groundwork can be rounded up with planes. If this procedure is adopted, a circle should be set out with dividers at each end of the piece, and then planed an octagonal shape before being finally rounded to the circle lines. It should now be carefully toothed all round, taking care to remove all slight ridges, which may be detected by simply feeling the surface with the hand. It is next sized as previously described, and stood aside to dry.

The next step is to prepare a simple apparatus which will enable the column to be easily revolved. This is shown by Fig. 22. The piece A represents a length of deal or whitewood rather longer than the column to be veneered. Piece B is a square piece firmly fastened with screws or nails to one end, with a $\frac{3}{8}$-in. dowel glued in the position indicated. Piece C is to act practically as a sliding head-piece, and is secured to the bottom part by means of two screws. The dowel in piece C is left dry. The column is inserted as indicated by simply withdrawing the right-hand dowel and then pushing it into a hole bored into the column. This allows the column to revolve freely.

It should here be mentioned that columns and circular pedestals are usually veneered with either thick knife-cut veneer or thin saw-cut veneer in order to prevent splitting. Thick veneer can be used, even when marqueteried; but special precautions must be taken, which will be briefly mentioned later. Knife-cut veneer having been selected, it should be damped slightly to prevent splitting. The groundwork or column is then well covered with glue, and set aside to thoroughly chill. This should be tested before the veneer is placed on it, and when the hand can be put on any part and removed without the glue adhering, the fixing of the veneer can be proceeded with. The diagram G^1 (Fig. 23) shows one edge of the veneer secured with pins, the latter being driven in every 6 in. or so. It is then slowly revolved in the direction of the arrow indicated, the hands being rubbed along to press the veneer down as the column is revolved. A sectional view would then be as indicated in diagram G^{11}, and the process continued until the veneer is rolled all round as in diagram G^{111}, overlapping the edge as indicated. The overlapping part is then pinned down. Strong webbing is the next essential, one end of which is tacked to the left-hand end of the column. The latter is now slowly revolved, and the webbing bound firmly tight down the column. This is indicated in Fig. 24, and when it is bound completely in its length the end is tacked at the right-hand end, and the column removed from the stand.

A shaving blaze is then made, and the column carefully revolved in the flames until it is well heated all over to melt the glue. The webbing is thoroughly wetted, causing it to shrink, which causes the glue to be pressed out. It is then heated again and damped, and set aside to dry. The necessary pressure is, of course, executed by the dampened webbing, and the action will be better understood if one notices the varying degrees of tautness in a clothes-line. In dry weather it hangs limply, but when thoroughly wetted in a shower of rain it becomes taut. Diagram G^{1111}, (Fig. 24) shows the section of the column

VENEERING

after the webbing has been removed after an interval of eight to ten hours. The overlapping of the veneer has been purposely enlarged. A clean joint is formed by cutting through the two thicknesses at one time with a keen-edged knife against a straightedge. The glue is then softened by ironing and damping, when the surplus outside veneer can easily be removed. It is necessary to lift one edge all along to remove the inside surplus piece, and when this has been taken out, a little glue is inserted all along and the veneer rubbed down with a hammer. If this is carefully done, the joint will be scarcely perceptible when the column is scraped and glasspapered.

It will be understood that the process described can be applied with a little adaptation to other veneering problems.

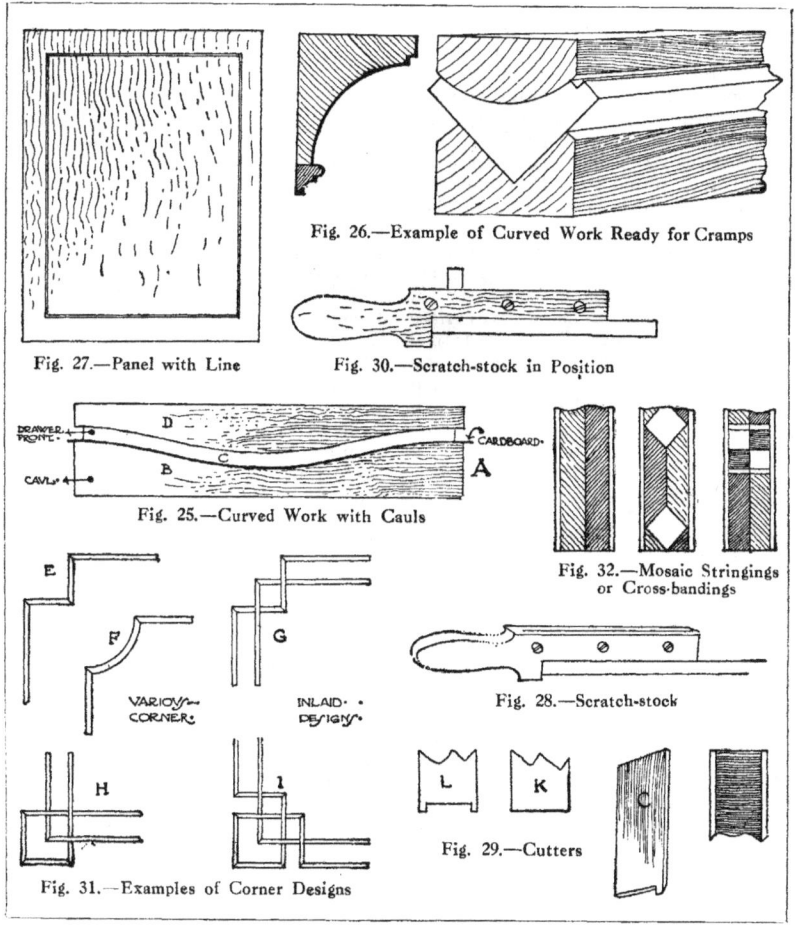

Fig. 26.—Example of Curved Work Ready for Cramps

Fig. 27.—Panel with Line

Fig. 30.—Scratch-stock in Position

Fig. 25.—Curved Work with Cauls

Fig. 32.—Mosaic Stringings or Cross-bandings

Fig. 28.—Scratch-stock

Fig. 29.—Cutters

Fig. 31.—Examples of Corner Designs

The semi-circular lid of a casket could, for instance, be veneered in this way; and, as has been previously indicated, a large cylinder or pedestal would only need a larger stand for revolving the groundwork, the other operations and their sequence being identical with those described and illustrated.

The next practical process of veneering to be dealt with is that necessitating the use of a curved caul. This process is particularly useful when one has to veneer curved drawer-fronts, table-rails, and work of a similar character. Fig. 25 shows a drawer-front ogee in shape, which would be about 4 in. or 5 in. wide. Curved drawer-fronts of this type are usually bandsawn from thick timber, and if a number are sawn from a thick block, waste pieces—indicated by B and D—will be obtained. The drawer-front is first rasped and filed perfectly true, and then the curved surface of B is filed exactly to fit the drawer-front. The usual steps, namely, sizing, gluing, and pinning down the veneer, are then proceeded with, when the curved surface of B is made very hot. The veneer is then covered with a piece of newspaper, and the whole placed together as indicated in Fig. 26 and firmly hand-screwed. In some cases a thin piece of cardboard can be utilised with advantage. It is inserted between the newspaper and the piece B (Fig. 25), and because of its relative softness a better pressure is exerted all over the drawer-front. Whenever veneering of this type is to be done in the manner described, the whole should be tested first by hand-screwing together and carefully observing the edges to see that the uniformity of pressure aforementioned is obtained. Any defects should be remedied by filing away the high parts of the groundwork, and again testing.

It will be seen that practically any shape can be dealt with in the manner described, whether for drawers, rails, or small panels. It cannot be said that this process is more effective than the one where a thin caul is used, such as was described earlier; but, as already indicated, if one has the waste wood for the curved cauls it is a more convenient way.

Most cabinet-makers, be they amateurs or journeymen, at an early stage wish to become proficient in inlaying lines, bandings and stringings. These materials are very much used in inlaid cabinet-work, used with discretion and with proper regard to proportion, they much enhance the appearance of furniture, particularly that made of mahogany and satinwood. The materials may be purchased from most cabinet-makers, timber and veneer merchants. Square lines of ebony, box, holly, and other stained woods can be obtained in lengths of about 3 ft., ranging from $\frac{1}{16}$ in. to $\frac{1}{8}$ in. square. The mosaic stringings are in similar lengths up to $\frac{3}{8}$ in. to $\frac{1}{2}$ in. wide with various designs, such as chain, loop, herring-bone, and various geometrical devices. The cross-bandings are made from $\frac{1}{8}$ in. to 1 in. wide, with one or two lines on each side. Mosaic stringings and cross-bandings are always made a bare $\frac{1}{16}$ in. thick, which is equal to the average thickness of saw-cut veneer. This thickness is very useful when inlaying veneered work, it only being necessary to remove just the thickness of the veneer, so that the stringing or cross-banding can be laid in level with the surface.

Fig. 27 represents a small panel which is to be inlaid with a single boxwood line about $\frac{3}{4}$ in. from the edges. Fig. 28 shows a scratch-stock used for inlaying. It is simply made from a piece of $\frac{7}{8}$-in. mahogany or beech, cut to the shape shown, with a saw-cut through the stem as illustrated. One or two screws are then put in, so that the cut part can be pressed together in order to secure the steel cutter. The steel cutter for a small line is illustrated by C (Fig. 29). This is made from $\frac{1}{16}$-in. steel filed to the shape shown, the projecting piece exactly equalling in size the line to be inlaid. To obtain a proper cutting-edge, the small piece is filed like a chisel bevel, and then secured in the scratch-stock with the screws. Fig. 30 shows the scratch-stock in position, the groove being cut by working the stock backwards and forwards to scrape away the groove. This action is repeated until all four grooves are cut, when the corners are finished off neatly with a chisel, and picked out clean with a marking awl or sharp point.

Various designs can be made on drawer-fronts, panels, etc., by varying the corner. The simplest one is shown at E (Fig. 31), and this is known as a broken corner. F is known as the " hollow " corner, the groove being cut with a gauge, and the wood picked out with an awl. G is an elaboration of E, and, as will be seen, it is effected by the introduction of a second line. H is an effective treatment with double lines, and I indicates an elaboration of the one shown in H.

The best procedure is to " set out " the lines and corners with a sharp pencil, and then to work out the grooves with the scratch-stock before finishing the corners with a chisel. In order to prevent the wood tearing where the lines cross, these grooves running across the grain should be cut first. It is then a comparatively simple matter to scratch the remaining grooves in the same direction as the grain of the wood or veneer, as the case may be. The grooves having been completed, the lines are carefully cut with butt or mitre joints, and glued into their respective grooves. The practice necessary to inlay mosaic stringings or cross-bandings such as are illustrated in Fig. 32 is almost identical to that previously described. If solid wood is to be inlaid, a cutter should be made as shown by K (Fig. 29), which cuts away the whole groove in one operation. Should, however, the surface to be inlaid be veneered, a cutter is made with two teeth as shown by L. Two narrow channels are then scratched, and the strip of veneer remaining in the middle is removed by heating it with a file to soften the glue, when it can be easily removed with a chisel.

Some little practice is required to get the groove exactly the size required, and it is advisable to make the cutter slightly smaller than the groove required. Should the stock not be worked exactly square, the groove will be made slightly larger than the size of the cutter. The groove when properly made should just grip the sides of the cross-banding, when it can be mitred, glued, and rubbed down easily with a hammer.

It should be mentioned that a scratch-stock can be improvised by making a cut in the end of a marking gauge, to receive a cutter which is secured as before with screws. The stock illustrated is, however, very easily made, and better than an improvised gauge.

Inlay and Marquetry Work

Inlaying.—Inlaying consists of recessing a design in wood, ivory, etc., and laying in another shade or kind of wood for decorative purposes.

Inlaying dates back to the times of the early Egyptians, who practised the art several centuries before the Christian era. They were particularly skilful in the use of gold and ivory. Amber also was employed, being brought from the North Sea by the Phœnicians. Specimens of Egyptian inlaid work may be seen in the British Museum, and also in the Louvre in Paris, that have survived the centuries, and prove most interesting records of an ancient art. Ebony and ivory were favourite media, used in chairs and thrones. There are numerous Biblical references to inlaying, including the description of King Solomon's throne, which was, we read, "a great throne of ivory, and overlaid with the best gold." The Greeks also devised ornaments consisting of small particles of stone pieced together to form conventional representations of animal and human figures.

Its execution is by no means easy, and it requires considerable skill, especially in more advanced work. Yet in the ordinary inlaying which concerns woodworkers generally, and cabinet-makers especially, the work does not present such great difficulties as some workers believe. Some of the more difficult inlaid work, in which very intricate designs are introduced, is quite beyond the ordinary woodworker, as the whole surface which is being treated is covered with a thin veneer, in which the design is worked out. This form of inlaying requires very expensive tools, and often many coloured woods, so that the general worker is deterred from undertaking such work himself, and passes it on to expert inlayers. In such cases a piece of veneer of the same size as the surface which is to be treated is sent to the inlayers, and is returned with the inlaid design inserted, the various pieces being held together by a piece of paper glued on the outer face. The sheet of veneer is then glued to the groundwork, and when the glue is dry, the paper is removed and the surface cleaned off.

There is no reason, however, why the woodworker should not decorate his work by the aid of simple inlaid designs. Such inlaying might be applied in almost any kind of furniture or fittings, and would greatly enhance both the value and appearance.

The woods used for inlaying may vary from $\frac{1}{16}$ in. to $\frac{3}{16}$ in. in thickness, but that about $\frac{1}{8}$ in. thick will be found very suitable. The woods employed should be selected with a view to forming a contrast with the groundwork which is being inlaid, and the choice will, of course, to a great extent be governed by the wood in the groundwork.

The colour treatment is an important matter, and should, if possible, be obtained through the use of natural-coloured woods.

INLAY AND MARQUETRY WORK

for those artificially stained often give very unsightly effects. The natural coloured woods most suitable for the purpose may be classed as follows: White tints are obtained with white holly, sycamore, and maple; yellow with satinwood, lancewood, canary, and light oak; red with rosewood, mahogany, and padouk; brown with dark oak, satin walnut, and birch; and for black tints ebony should be used.

Having set out the design full size on a piece of paper, the pieces of wood to make up the design are cut out to the shape required. A very fine fret-saw would be found very useful in this operation, and the shapes may be transferred from the paper pattern by means of carbon paper. The pieces are then fitted together to form the complete design, care being taken that good joints are obtained. The pieces to form the complete design are then glued directly to the paper pattern, and the edges are also glued together. Another piece of paper is then glued over the top, and the whole is cramped between two pieces of board until the glue is dry. The inlay is then removed, and the piece of paper at the back on which the design was originally marked is stripped off. The inlay is then placed in position on the groundwork, and is scribed round the edges with a marking or scribing point. The wood in the groundwork must next be cut away to a sufficient depth to receive the inlay, care being taken to work exactly to the scribed lines. The cutting is accomplished with chisels and gouges, and a router would also be found most useful in removing the surplus wood. The inlay is now glued in position, and cramped until the glue is set, when the surface is cleaned off by scraping and glasspapering.

Any straight joints could be easily shot on an ordinary shooting board. An iron plane should be used, and in some cases several pieces of veneer could be worked at the same time. If, however, only one piece is planed at a time, it might be found desirable to cover it with a thin piece of wood while working the plane. A pattern is also found very useful when cutting several veneers to a certain shape and size.

The pattern should take the form of an aperture in a sheet of cardboard, as when made in this manner it enables the worker to examine the grains of the veneers without removing the pattern.

Another item is that all end grain veneers should be protected round the edges with small stringings, in which the grain runs lengthwise. This is very important, especially in drawer fronts and similar positions, as the end grain veneers would be very liable to split.

Figs. 1, 2 and 3 show three inlaid designs which would be simple to execute and would be very suitable for panels or large flat surfaces. Other simple forms of inlaying are given in Figs. 4, 5 and 6, which show the application of inlaid stringings and bandings.

Fig. 4 shows a form of stringing inlay suitable for a panel, tea-tray, or any flat surface to which such a form of decoration might be suitably applied. The outer edge in this design is inlaid with a banding about $\frac{1}{2}$ in. wide; inside this is a narrower banding about $\frac{1}{4}$ in. wide, and a simple geometrical design is inlaid directly in the centre.

A simple inlaid stringing for applying to the front of a drawer is shown in Fig. 5. The stringing in this case might vary in width from $\frac{1}{4}$ in. to $\frac{1}{2}$ in., and should be set from $\frac{1}{2}$ in. to $\frac{3}{4}$ in. in from the outer edge. Another case in which good effects are created with inlaid stringings and bandings is illustrated by Fig. 6, which shows the top portion of a cabinet in which inlaid bandings have been introduced.

In the application of such inlaid designs as those illustrated by Figs. 1, 2 and 3, the designs are first set out full size on a piece of paper. The size to which the designs are set out must, of course, be governed by the size of the surface which is being treated; but the inlay should not appear to be too large or over-done. The design (Fig. 1), shown enlarged by Fig. 7, would be most suitable for a long vertical rail or panel. The enlarged design which is shown by Fig. 8 would also be very suitable for application in a similar position. Both designs are very flexible, and may be increased or diminished in length to meet

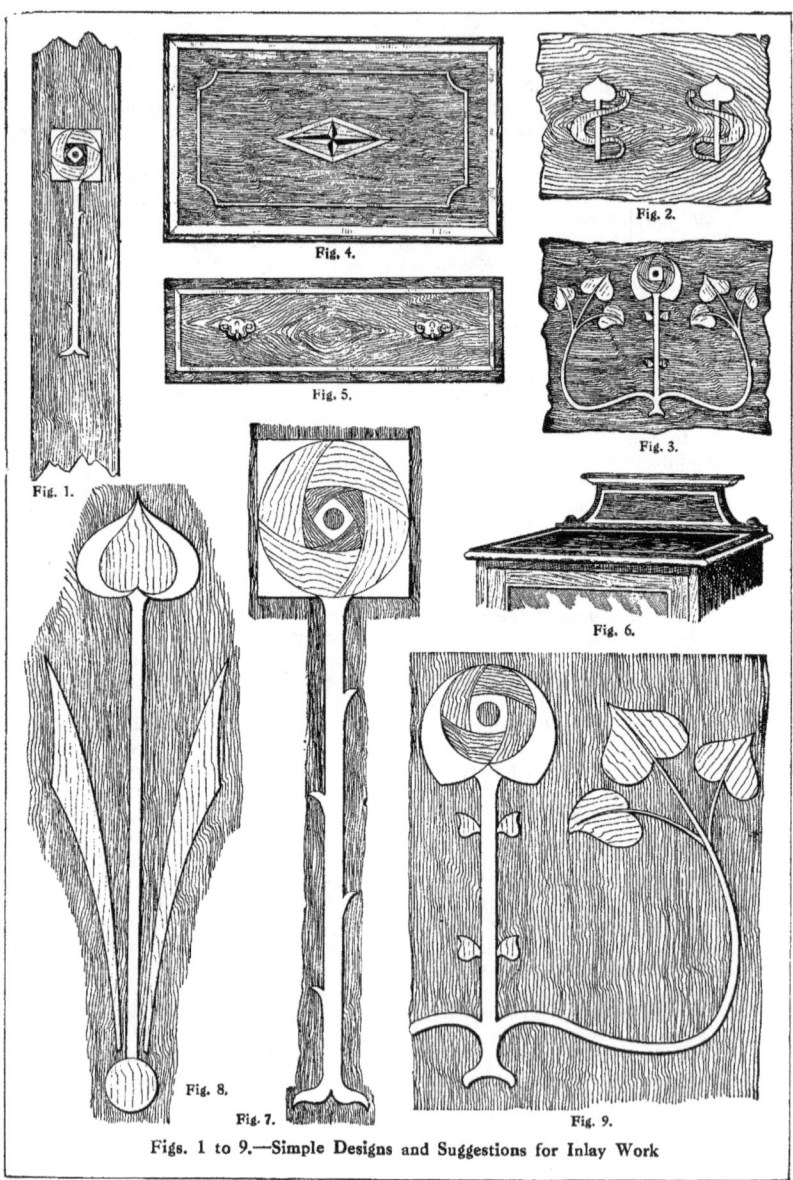

Figs. 1 to 9.—Simple Designs and Suggestions for Inlay Work

INLAY AND MARQUETRY WORK

almost any requirements. In the design (Fig. 7) three kinds of wood are introduced, while in that shown by Fig. 8 only two kinds are used. The designs shown (Figs. 2 and 3) are most suitable for square

Fig. 10.—Method of Making Bandings of Two Kinds of Wood

or oblong panels or surfaces. In that shown by Fig. 2 only two kinds of wood are used. A part of the design which is shown by Fig. 3 is shown again to an enlarged scale by Fig. 9. Three kinds of wood are employed to execute this design.

Various forms of inlaid stringings and bandings are often used ; but that most commonly met with simply consists of a strip of one kind of wood. Other kinds of bandings consist of two, or even three, kinds of wood made up in geometrical patterns. The method employed to make up these kinds of bandings is illustrated in Fig. 10, which shows a banding composed of a number of oblong pieces of two kinds of wood. A number of strips are first cut and glued up edge to edge, a dark and light strip being used alternately. When the glue is dry, one edge is planed straight and square, and strips of the width required for the banding are cut from the edge as shown. To allow for the insertion of the stringings and bandings, the wood is routered away to the required depth, and they are glued into the groove and well pressed in position.

In inlaying a small geometrical design, similar to that shown by Fig. 4, to the centre of a panel, the inlay should first be built up on a piece of paper as already described for the other designs ; the outer edges should then be scribed round, and the wood routered away in a similar manner.

A router suitable for the purpose might be purchased from any tool merchant, but a very simple home-made tool is shown by Fig. 11. It consists of a wood stock to which a cutter and iron fence are fitted. The stock should be of beech, about 11 in. long by 2 in. wide and 1 in. deep in the centre, handles being formed at each end as shown. The iron fence is shown by Fig. 12. A slot is formed in the centre, and it is secured and adjusted on the stock by means of a bolt and fly-nut. It will be found advisable to provide a number of cutters of various widths as shown by Fig. 13. The cutter passes through a slot cut in the middle of the stock, and is held in position with a wedge as shown in Fig. 11.

Marquetry Cutting.—The method of inlaying by cutting the pattern in several veneers at one operation, and afterwards letting one into the other, is one that allows much greater freedom and elaboration of design than can be obtained by inlaying in the solid. The wonderful work of the French craftsmen during the periods of Louis XIV. and XV. affords striking evidence of the possibilities of the craft in the hands of a capable worker. The furniture of this period reached a degree of richness and beauty that has never been surpassed, the work of known craftsmen such as Riesener being preserved as national treasures in both the London Wallace collection and the Jones collection at the Victoria and Albert Museum. The designs are chiefly floral forms worked

Fig. 11.—Simple Router

Fig. 12.—Fence for Router   Fig. 13.—Cutters

up by means of shading and the introduction of grained pieces to produce a highly shaded effect, although in the later work the patterns partake frequently of a more conventional character. Of this later style, Figs. 14 and 15 are illustrations of the top and front of a lace-box in French marquetry, which gives very clearly an idea of the possibilities of the process. One ordinary length of time; while in the process under consideration, to the careful fret-worker, the work presents nothing out of the way to accomplish.

Fig. 14.

Fig. 15.

Figs. 14 and 15.—Top and Front of Box with Marquetry Decoration

will readily perceive that to inlay such a pattern as this in the solid would be an undertaking that would require an extra- Veneers employed for marquetry are either saw-cut or knife-cut, the former being the thicker, and usually the better

INLAY AND MARQUETRY WORK

to employ, though for a design in which many woods are employed the thinner veneers can be more conveniently used. In commercial work, marquetry sawing is 8 in. wide, the seat being 1 ft. 8 in. from the ground.

In carrying out a design in marquetry a full-size drawing requires to be made

Fig. 16.—Marquetry-cutter's Stock

Fig. 17.—Method of Sawing

done on a long stool that is commonly called a "donkey." This is illustrated by Fig. 16, the worker sitting astride it, the wood being gripped in the vice at the end, which can be tightened at will by the pressure of the foot on the treadle underneath. The chief advantage of such an appliance lies in the fact that the work can be released for turning about, for convenience of cutting, by just relaxing first with the woods that are going to be employed marked clearly thereon for reference. The sheets of veneer that represent the different varieties of wood in the design are then glued together, with a sheet of brown paper interposed between each, to allow of easy separation afterwards. Thin glue only should be employed, and it will be found best to arrange to set the grain of each piece alternately in

Fig. 18.—Detail Design of Front of Box (Fig. 15)

the pressure of the foot. The stool, as will be seen, is of such simple construction that the home-worker could easily put it together. It is 2 ft. 4 in. long and opposite directions, so as to minimise curling when dry. Some form of press is necessary in marquetry at this stage, and also for later operations. An old-fashioned linen or similar form of press serves admirably; but failing the possession of such an article, a couple of hand-screws will be necessary. The work is set between two pieces of hardwood, technically termed cauls, that are gripped together by two or more of these screws. One-inch mahogany is best for the purpose, as this wood is less liable to warp than others. A simple method of clamping up, dispensing with the hand-screws, is by means of two battened pieces of hardwood that are tightened up with four stout bolts and nuts.

The sheets of veneer, after gluing together, require to be screwed up tightly by one or other of these means, so that every portion of each sheet shall come in actual contact with the next one, otherwise the woods will be liable to split in the sawing. After drying, a tracing of the pattern is pasted to the uppermost sheet, to serve as a guide in the sawing. An ordinary fret-saw frame is sufficient for the amateur worker's requirements, one with sufficient sweep being necessary to cover the whole sheet. In commercial work a fixed saw is often used, the work being moved about so that it cuts along the lines of the pattern required. The fewest possible number of holes should be made for the reception of the saw, which requires to be very fine. Fig. 17 shows the normal position of the worker's hands during the sawing. The design that is being cut is a reproduction of that on the front of the box (Fig. 15), an enlarged outline of which is given by Fig. 18. In this particular design there are a few pieces only that will become detached before the sawing out is completed; but whatever sections are required, these need to be carefully placed on one side.

When all the sawing is completed, the next thing is to separate the sections. This can usually be done by inserting the thin blade of a knife at the edges where they join, and so split the paper. In case of any difficulty, as in the instance of fragile delicate shapes, the best plan is to put the work in the press for some hours, between several thicknesses of damp blotting or old newspaper, when they can very easily be separated. The portions in the woods required are retained and fitted into the other parts; then the next process is to glue down to a solid ground.

It will be found by far the best plan to employ a good wood for the foundation, for which purpose Honduras mahogany is considered the most suitable. Whitewood and yellow pine is sometimes used for common work; but it is liable to give trouble when gluing hardwoods to it, as the softer material absorbs most of the glue. Resinous woods, such as yellow deal and pitch-pine, must never be used.

When the pattern is somewhat intricate and in many sections, the different portions are frequently placed over the working design and secured with very fine pins in their correct position. The upper surface of the whole is then given a coating of thin glue, and a sheet of paper pressed down over the pins, in actual contact everywhere with the veneers, and allowed to dry. After this the pins may be removed, and the complete design can then be very readily glued to the foundation wood. In doing this the veneer as well as the ground should be glued, and when laid in place be covered with a few sheets of newspaper to prevent it sticking in the press. Care must be taken to obtain an even pressure all round, to ensure all the superfluous glue being squeezed out, the work being left in the press until quite dry. In cases where white or very light-coloured woods are employed in a design the glue should be whitened with powdered flake white, so that it does not show a very conspicuous mark round the edges of the forms.

When dry the work should be taken from the press, and the paper that covers the surface of the pattern removed with a steel cabinet-scraper. A smoothing plane, the iron of which has been very finely set, can be employed for a start in the case of the thicker veneers; but where they are very thin the scraper alone should be used. The direction of stroke of the scraper should, of course, be varied to suit the direction of grain of the inlay.

INLAY AND MARQUETRY WORK

EXAMPLES OF INLAID AND MARQUETRY WORK

Inlaid Photograph Frame.— As an elementary piece of veneering and inlaying the photograph frame shown by Fig. 19 will be found to be an instructive as well as an interesting piece of work. As the execution. The method of solid inlaying may be adopted, or veneers may be used. If veneers are used the worker has a wider choice of colours, and three or four or even a greater number could be introduced. If three colours are used, one should be used for the flower and bamboos, one for the stems, leaves, etc., and the remaining

Fig. 19.—Inlaid Pnotograph Frame

surfaces to be covered are quite small, little difficulty will be experienced in laying the veneers ; but at the same time several processes are involved which may be applied to larger work. It will be observed that the frame outline is very simple.

The design allows for much variety in

85—N.E.

one for the background. If four colours are used, the leaves could be separated from the stems, and the centre of the flower could be a different colour from the petals.

The most appropriate wood for the background would be rosewood, padouk, or dark walnut. Oak or satinwood could be used for the stems and leaves, and holly for the flower and bamboos. The veneers used should be about $\frac{1}{16}$ in. thick, and they must be glued to a $\frac{3}{16}$-in. background, which should, preferably, be of mahogany. The background may be cut from a piece of wood 8 in. by 6½ in., and should be marked out as shown in Fig. 20. When the veneers have been cut and fitted they are glued in position on the background, and the work should be cramped between two boards until the glue is dry. It would be a good plan to leave the shaping of the background until after the veneers are glued in position.

In the case of solid inlaying, the light wood for the inlay is cut directly into the dark background. Wood $\frac{1}{16}$ in. thick should be used, and the cutting, which is done with a fret-saw, should be on the bevel, as shown in Fig. 21. The two boards are cut together, and great care must be taken to work the bevel in the right direction. The piece which is going to be inserted must be undercut, so that it is wedge-shape with the thickest part of the wedge upwards. The whole of the inner portion of the frame should be cut and glued up first, the cutting of the opening and the outer shape being left until last.

Another method would be to simply overlay the ornament. In this case the ornamental parts are cut from $\frac{1}{16}$-in. wood, and are glued to a $\frac{3}{16}$-in. background.

The back of the frame is made up as shown in Fig. 22. Small fillets, to allow the photograph and glass to be inserted, and a wood back are fitted behind the opening, being fixed in position with screws, as shown in Fig. 23. A strut or leg is hinged to the wood back to support the frame, and a piece of tape is arranged between the back and strut.

Inlaid Finger-plates. — The photographic reproductions (Figs. 24 to 29) show a series of inlaid finger-plates. Figs. 24, 25 and 26 are of mahogany, inlaid with a satinwood line, and a centre of green sycamore with a conventional ornament in satinwood. Figs. 27, 28 and 29 are of ebony.

For making the groove for the satinwood line a scratch-tool gauge is used. A level piece of board is fixed on the bench to work on and the plate is put on with two small screws through the holes. Although this method is suitable for straight lines,

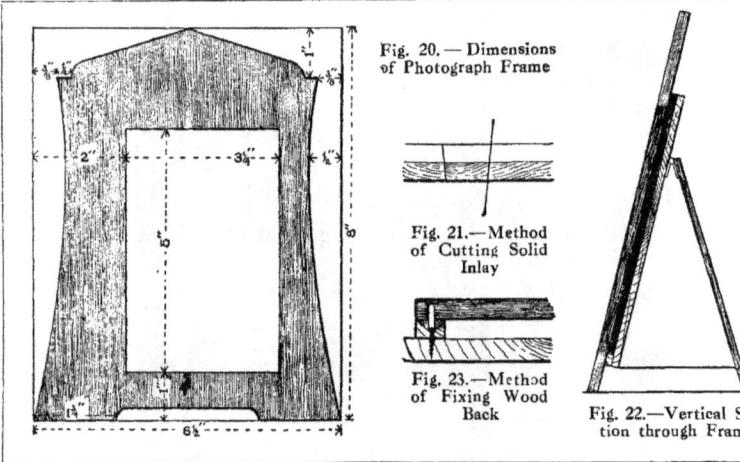

Fig. 20. — Dimensions of Photograph Frame

Fig. 21.—Method of Cutting Solid Inlay

Fig. 23.—Method of Fixing Wood Back

Fig. 22.—Vertical Section through Frame

INLAY AND MARQUETRY WORK

Figs. 24, 25 and 26.—Inlaid Finger-plates with Rounded Ends

it is hardly practicable for completing the grooves across the grain round the circular ends; but it will scribe an impression if used carefully. To do this, one of the screws must be taken out to allow the end to overhang, and the impression is made the required depth by scraping out with a $\frac{1}{8}$-in. chisel. When the groove is completed, the centre oval is to be put in. These when bought are always glued on paper to keep them from getting broken in handling. They are inlaid with the paper side out, to be cleaned off. To get the oval in true position, a pencil line is marked lengthwise through the centre to correspond with a similar line on the plate. The mark is cut to the required depth with the sharp point of a knife, and the waste pared away with a chisel. It can be made quite level by reversing the chisel and scraping. The inlay should lie in nearly level; just a shade high to allow for scraping to a clean surface. The plate is shown at this stage by Fig. 30, ready for gluing in the inlay.

The glue must be quite hot, sufficiently strong, but not thick, and the work should be done quickly in a warm place. In the case of the curved satinwood line, a length of the satinwood is necessary about 1 in. longer than will go right round. There will have to be one join where the two ends meet, which must be on the straight. The line is well-brushed over with glue, and worked round into the groove as quickly as possible, pressing it in with a hammer, the end being nipped off with the point of a knife to make the join.

To glue in the "oval centre," the paper side must be wetted with a rag dipped in hot water and the other side glued, also the sunk place on the plate, and it is put in immediately and pressed over with the hammer to force out the surplus glue. It must be fully assured that no part is inclined to rise before it is put away in a dry place to set.

A rub over with linseed oil will greatly improve the colours of the woods, and show up to advantage the varying shades in the grain of the mahogany. When there is time, it is best to leave them a few days after being oiled, before polishing.

Inlaid Trays.—Figs. 31 and 32 show two modern trays of French manufacture

Figs. 27, 28 and 29.—Inlaid Finger-plates with Shaped Ends

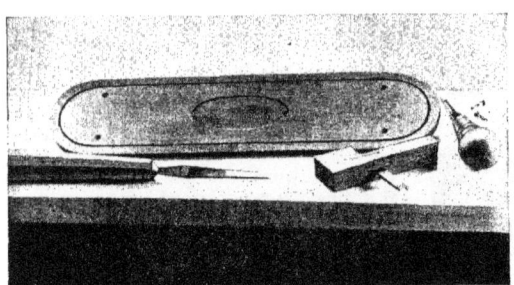

Fig. 30.—Finger-plate Ready for Inlay

in the South Kensington Museum, which are considered quite the finest in this style of work that has been produced, not only in the beauty of their inlays, but in the general design and construction, which is of the simplest. The superb inlays are such, of course, that would need a practised hand to undertake; but the construction, as will be described, is such that even an ordinary worker could produce an article on similar lines.

The inlaid tray shown by Fig. 31 is of quite simple construction. Two sides are cut with a short tenon at each extremity that fits into the ends of tray which are set slightly slanting. Then a narrow strip is fixed (by means of small screws) at the bottom of this framing all round, for the bottom to rest on. One face of the strip for the ends will require to be planed at a slight slant. The ends of the tray bottom require to be finished off similarly, so as to obtain a good fit.

A tray that would probably stand wear better than the foregoing would be obtained by carrying the tenons right through the ends, and then securing with hardwood pegs, in which case the bottom could very well be grooved into the sides and ends.

The rim of the tray shown by Fig. 32 is obtained by preparing a curved moulding in four parts, the moulding being of any suitable section and being grooved for fitting round the bottom of the tray.

Should a difficulty arise in obtaining the wood of a suitable width for the bottom, two boards will require to be butted together with the greatest care, so that the joining line is practically imperceptible. Three channels should be cut in the under side of the bottom across the grain for

Fig. 31.—Inlaid Tray with Plant Design

INLAY AND MARQUETRY WORK

the purpose of letting in three hardwood strips; these are to prevent the material warping. On drying, the bottom is planed quite level, and then the inlaying on the face of the work is proceeded with.

Chessboard in Marquetry. — For the art of marquetry, perhaps no more suitable object could be found for decoration than a chessboard, which is in itself a decorative object, since the checkers of the board represent the very simplest form of contrast. Moreover, wood is the most natural material to employ for this purpose, and is, as a matter of fact,

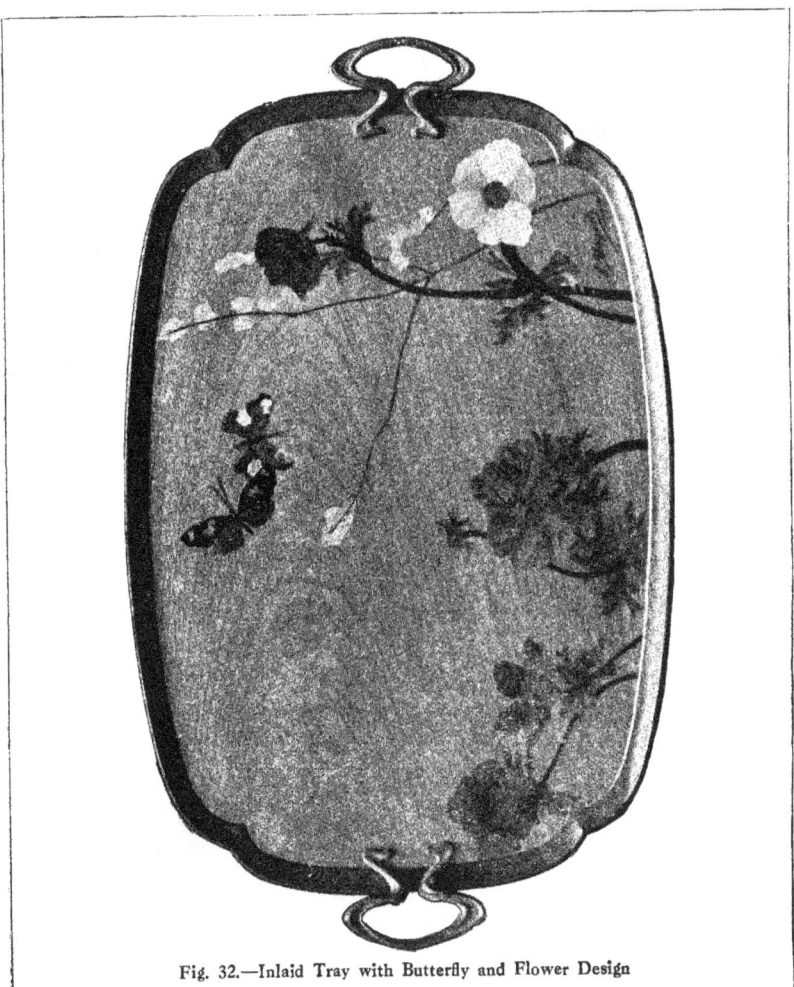

Fig. 32.—Inlaid Tray with Butterfly and Flower Design

Fig. 33.—Chessboard in Marquetry Inlay

generally employed, though other substances have been used.

The "game and playe of the chesse" is so ancient that any association with it and the ultra-modern developments of decorative art seems out of place. A suggestion is therefore given for a border treatment of the board in Italian arabesque of the simpler kind, fairly easy to cut, and to be worked in some lighter coloured wood than the checkers, so that the play may not be confused by any extraneous ornament asserting itself too strongly (see Fig. 33). It would be possible, of course, to decorate the checkers also without destroying the contrast between the black and white. Indeed, this has been done by means of inlay in the blacks and engraving in the whites, forming an extremely rich effect. This, however, would necessitate a considerable degree of skill, while the present decorative scheme is fairly easy of attainment.

As regard material, the whole board with its border may be done in ebony and ivory, though this would be expensive. An alternative treatment would be ebony and whitewood, with some wood of medium strength of colour, such as mahogany, canary, or box, for the background of the ornament. The range of wood veneers is, however, a wide one. There is also an almost endless variety of dyed veneers.

The veneers must be fastened firmly together for the process of cutting. This may be done by means of placing glued paper between them; but it is sometimes difficult to separate the pieces afterwards. A better way, in certain circumstances, is to fasten them with small wire nails, placing sheets of greased paper between each veneer.

It will be obvious that in a design of this character the ornament and groundwork will be cut at one operation, the two pieces afterwards fitting exactly. Therefore in fastening the veneers together place the coloured woods alternately.

Box in Marquetry.—The box illustrated by Fig. 34 is of the simplest possible construction, as perfectly plain spaces are the most suited to marquetry ornamentation. The opening of the lid is at the line immediately above the keyhole. The feet may be attached either by means of glue or small screws. In this instance also, as in the case of the

Fig. 34.—Box in Marquetry Inlay

INLAY AND MARQUETRY WORK

chessboard, the principal ornamental *motif* is made to repeat, thereby effecting a saving of labour. There are, therefore, six panels of the same design for the back and sides, with two others for the top.

Letter-case in Marquetry.—A letter-case, or cover for a blotter decorated with a marquetry panel in the centre, is shown by Fig. 35. The cover which would look very well in oak or walnut, $\frac{1}{4}$ in. or $\frac{3}{8}$ in. thick, has a canvas or leather bag, and also a simple inlaid border along the top and bottom. It is closed, when not in use, by means of a simple metal clasp.

The centre panel of the cover is intended to be executed in veneers the separate pattern for which is given by Fig. 36, a key to the woods employed being given underneath; these are ebony, box, mahogany whitewood, and canary, the material employed being very thin, not more than $\frac{1}{32}$ in., which is the usual thickness of veneer.

All the veneers are cut out at the one sawing, so that the sections forming the mosaic exactly fit one another. It will be found the best to saw away the outside

Fig. 35.—Letter-case Decorated with Marquetry

Although it may seldom happen that practical workers discover much aptitude for original design, yet it may be pointed out that this art of marquetry inlay offers many opportunities to the craftsman for the carrying out of his own ideas and the exercise of his own individuality. Especially is this so in the case of the simpler geometrical patternings which form a distinctive feature of the art. The box illustrated has therefore been designed with the idea of combining the more simple geometrical forms with some foliated ornamental device almost equally simple.

- CANARY
- WHITEWOOD
- MAHOGANY
- BOX
- EBONY

Fig. 36.—Pattern of Centre Panel of Letter-case

sections first, consisting of the background, lower part of the blotter, and sleeve, before proceeding with the inner details. It is unnecessary to drill any holes for the reception of the saw, as in all cases, with the exception of the features which will be dealt with later, all the cutting can be started from the sides. In this connection, it may be noted that in cutting out the letters on the background, a saw-cut may be made connecting them, as this will not be perceptible in the finished work. As each section is sawn out it is placed on the working drawing in its proper position ; then, when all the sawing is done, proceed to separate the layers.

Next prepare the boards forming the back and front covers, the shape of the centre part being marked out in the centre of the one forming the front. This space has next to be sunk very slightly to receive the veneers. Make a chisel or knife-cut all round, then break the grain inside with the chisel and remove the waste, making the depression an equal depth throughout, that is the thickness of the veneer, and then make level all over.

In inlaying spaces so large as this, after the ground has been levelled all over, it is sometimes pricked with a pointed tool at intervals, to form a better attachment for the glued veneers, which are now fitted, and then glued in and placed under a weight to harden.

In the execution of the features, the thin dark parts shown in the working pattern are carefully cut away in the sawing, the very fine grooves left in the work being filled in with dark wax after the sections have been glued in their place, and then scraped flat.

The top and bottom borders are now proceeded with, careful cutting of the alternate light and dark triangles, with the underneath sections, being indispensable, together with the accurate marking and chiselling out of the recesses to receive them. When they have been glued in and have hardened go over the whole with a smoothing-plane, the iron of which has been very finely set, then finish with a cabinet scraper.

There now remain the corners to be rounded off and the canvas back to be cut and secured with small round-headed brass nails the shanks of which have been cut short ; or another way would be to thin the edges of the leather with a knife, making a slight cut down the covers where they are glued on, and a thin shaving off all the way down, so that the edge of the leather is on a level with the wood and then does not easily become caught and torn up.

The brass clasp is of very simple design, and includes a catch bent up of wire that hooks on a brass pin inserted in the back of the cover. The inside of the letter-case is lined with a suitably coloured leather paper, and pockets or straps are included to hold the stationery according to requirements.

Woodcarving

WOODCARVING is classed as one of the arts, but it is an art in the exercise of which a more than usual amount of manipulative skill is called for in addition to the possession of artistic feeling.

The object of this section is to teach the craftsmanship side of the subject only, and for this purpose the whole of the progressive processes employed in carving a panel will be detailed, and later examples of incised and pierced carving.

As a preliminary, a brief consideration of the woods used and the tools employed in carving will be made.

Woods Used for Carving.—There are dozens of varieties of wood that can be carved, but it will be found that in ordinary woodcarving use is not made of more than about sixteen different kinds. These sixteen are favourites because their structure is such that the carver's tools leave a clean, sharp cut, or because their grain is so straight as to enable the wood to be worked with the least amount of trouble and risk of splitting. All woods used for carving must be thoroughly seasoned, and where time and convenience allow it is desirable for the carver himself to stock the wood for a year or two, so that when using it he can be sure that it is thoroughly dry. The woods in most general use are oak, Italian and American walnut, lime, holly, pearwood, chestnut and mahogany. Bog-oak is often used for carving, and in Ireland the carving of this wood is one of the peasant industries, the work produced being small but of good quality. Bog-oak is so called from the fact that it is found embedded in the decaying vegetable matter of the bogs, and the oak itself has often entered on the first stage of putrefaction. Other suitable woods are sycamore, satinwood, sandalwood, boxwood and ebony, but these are not used to the same extent as those mentioned first.

Tools.—Woodcarving tools are varied in shape, both in length and in section, but they can be classified into various types.

The classification here adopted is as follows: The tools are divided into four types, referable to the shape of their stems, namely (*a*) straight tools, (*b*) curved or bent tools, (*c*) spoon-bit tools, and (*d*) tools of special shape. Types *a*, *b*, and *c* are shown by Figs. 1 to 4, and type *d* by Figs. 5 and 6.

Type *a* consists of those tools which are, viewed from the edge, quite straight. They are, of course, of various sections, and are used for all ordinary work. Indeed, it is only necessary to supplement this type when doing special work, such as under-cutting, pierced work, carving that is in high relief, or work which requires to be deeply sunk from the surface. These tools can be obtained either of the ordinary shape as regards their width, as in Fig. 7, or as spade tools (Fig. 8). They also can be had shouldered (Fig. 9) or unshouldered (Fig. 10).

Type *b* consists of tools so shaped (*see*

THE PRACTICAL WOODWORKER

Fig. 2) as to enable them to flow easily along internal or concave curves. It is obvious that a tool quite straight in its length would always have the line of pressure at too acute an angle with the grain; and if the tool made any progress at all, it would move in a series of jumps, which would leave a rough and uneven surface. But by bending the tool the line of force is directed in such a manner that it leaves the tool free to move along the surface in a way that allows the edge to cut evenly.

The above description also applies to tools of type c (Figs. 3 and 4), which, however are so shaped that they can cut curves of greater depth and less radius, thus working in less space.

Type d (Figs. 5 and 6) are tools which are of quite a special nature, and can be used only for a specific purpose. All these types can be had either shouldered or unshouldered, and type a can b had as spade tools, in addition to the ordinary shape (see Fig. 8). It is recommended that only shouldered tools should be used. They are stronger and far more serviceable than the others (see Figs. 9 and 10). An objection to unshouldered tools is that the tang drives into the handle without any check, and almost invariably splits it.

The various sections of carving tools are shown in Fig. 11. The tools are made in widths varying from $\tfrac{1}{32}$ in. to $1\tfrac{1}{2}$ in. and 2 in. The choice of tools suitable for general work or to any particular class of work is a matter needing much judgment and care.

Tool handles vary in size, in shape, and in the kind of wood from which they are made. They are known and regulated by the size of the ferrule, and vary from $\tfrac{3}{8}$ in. outside diameter of the ferrule to $\tfrac{7}{8}$ in. The woods most generally used for tool handles are box, rosewood, beech, hornbeam, and mahogany. Of these, box and beech are the most lasting. All handles should be ferruled, and the handle itself should be about $\tfrac{3}{8}$ in. thicker than the ferrule. The length of a handle should be $4\tfrac{1}{2}$ in. or 5 in. If longer, they are, except for the very large tools, clumsy and awkward to use. If shorter, there is much loss of power in using them. A good plan in selecting handles for a set of tools is to have them in various woods, and marked distinctively with respect to the position and number of the rings that are often turned on them. If all are of the same wood, they can be stained in different colours; the object being to enable the

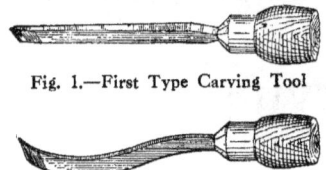

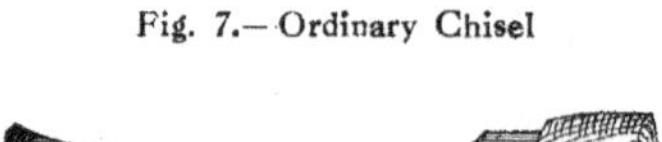

Fig. 1.—First Type Carving Tool

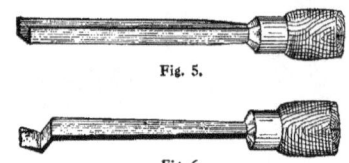

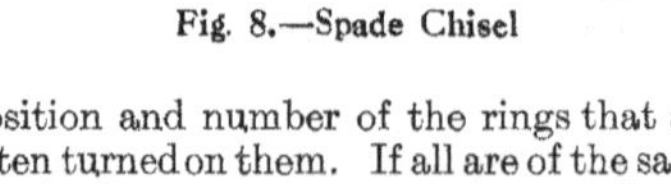

Fig. 5.

Fig. 6.

Figs. 5 and 6.—Fourth Type Carving Tools

Fig. 2.—Second Type Carving Tool

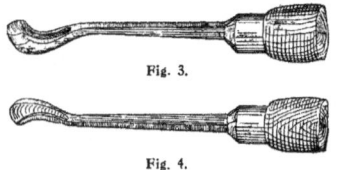

Fig. 3.

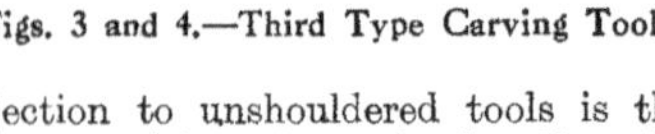

Fig. 4.

Figs. 3 and 4.—Third Type Carving Tools

Fig. 7.—Ordinary Chisel

Fig. 8.—Spade Chisel

WOODCARVING

worker to distinguish the tools easily when they lie grouped together.

Fig. 9. Fig. 10.
Figs. 9 and 10.—Shouldered and Unshouldered Tools

Fig. 11.—Cutting Edges and Sections of Carving Tools

It is important to have the handle fixed to the blade in a proper manner. The tools are generally bought with the handle fixed. But even then it is advisable to know when the tool is handled in a business-like manner. To begin with, in most cases the blade should be in perfect alignment with the handle. Especially is this the case with the setting-in tools. It is not so much a necessity with V-tools and fluters, because the force transmitted through these tools does not, as a rule, proceed in a perfectly straight line, but moves in the direction of a curve. A tool whose blade is so fixed in the handle that it forms a concave curve on its face side is often of greater advantage in getting round a concave curve than one in which the blade is in perfect alignment with the handle. But in all tools to which force has to be applied by other means than mere hand pressure, the blade must be fixed quite straight. To retain all the force given by the mallet, it is necessary that it should be directed by the shortest possible route, which is a straight line.

Other necessary tools are mallets and cramps. All roughing out should be done with the mallet, and bosses, cornices, and other work intended to be fixed at a height from the eye should invariably be finished with the mallet. When the carver is engaged on these classes of work the mallet should never leave his hand; for the cut left by the chisel with the mallet behind it is always the most effective when looked up at from the ground. Further, by the free and continuous use of the mallet the work is got over in half the time it would otherwise take.

It is a general practice of wood-carvers to use the half-closed palm of the hand as a sort of mallet, and for light work this is a good custom, although its continued practice eventually results in a deformation of the hand.

Supplementary tools are punches, files,

LIST OF WOOD-CARVERS' ESSENTIAL TOOLS

No. on Sheffield Tool List.
No. 1.—Straight Chisel, ½ in. wide, chiefly used for setting in.
No. 3.—Straight Gouge, $\tfrac{1}{16}$ in., ⅛ in., and ¼ in. wide, for grounding small spaces.
No. 3.— ,,   ,, ⅜ in. wide.
No. 4.— ,,   ,, ⅜ in. wide, for setting in, grounding, and modelling.
No. 5.— ,,   ,, $\tfrac{3}{16}$ in. and $\tfrac{5}{16}$ in. wide, for setting in and grounding.
No. 5.— ,,   ,, ½ in. wide, for setting in, grounding and modelling.
No. 7.— ,,   ,, ⅜ in. wide, for grounding and modelling.
No. 8.— ,,   ,, ⅛ in. and ¼ in. wide, for modelling.
No. 8.— ,,   ,, ¾ in. wide, for grounding and modelling.
No. 11.— ,,   ,, $\tfrac{5}{16}$ in. wide, for modelling.
No. 21.—Spoon-bit Chisel, Square, ⅛ in., $\tfrac{3}{16}$ in., and ⅜ in. wide for grounding.
No. 28.—Spoon-bit Gouge, or Front-bent Gouge, ¼ in. and ½ in. wide, for modelling.
No. 39.—Straight V-Parting Tool, $\tfrac{5}{16}$ in. wide, for outlining and modelling.

rasps, rifflers, and a few other tools which ordinarily have a place in the woodworker's kit.

Preliminary Work.—The first procedure is to select the piece of wood, cut it to a suitable size and plane it up. Next the design is traced on tracing (transparent) paper, pinned to the panel at one end, and the carbon paper placed underneath. It is then pinned at the other end, and the outline of the design traced over with a style or a hard pencil; the shading may be ignored. The work, which for the purpose of the present example is a panel design as shown by Fig. 12, is now ready to be tooled. The cut-out portions on each edge require taking out first. Fix the panel in the bench screw, and cut but a good wood-carver does as much work as is possible with his carving tools, and relies as little as he possibly can on tools that may be termed artificial aids.

The work is now secured to the carving

Fig. 12.—Design for Carved Panel *(see also Fig. 36, p. 1357)*

out the pieces with a bow saw close to the line *(see* Fig. 13). They will be rough from the saw, and this roughness will be removed by means of the carving tools. It may be thought that a spokeshave or a bull-nose plane would do this work better; bench, three methods being here mentioned. The first, and the one employed with this panel, is with carver's cramps. A piece of cardboard, thick leather, or paper should be used to prevent the cramp marking the surface of the wood. A

WOODCARVING

second method, and one that has the advantage of leaving the whole surface of the panel quite clear and unencumbered, is the use of a carver's screw, which is screwed through a hole in the bench from the underside into the panel, and tightened with a wing-nut. A third method is by means of clips and screws which grip the edge of the panel, and are screwed into the bench top.

which represents a section of the finished carving. Thus along the edge of the panel will be drawn two lines, B representing the depth of the ground, and A the depth of the chamfer (*see* Fig. 15).

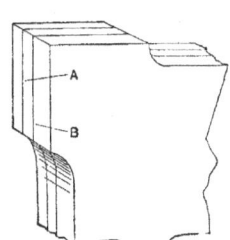

Fig. 15.—Panel Marked for Depth of Ground, etc.

Fig. 13.—Photograph showing Preparatory and "Bosting in" Stages

Wasting Away.—The next process is known as "wasting away," "bosting in," "roughing out," etc. "Bosting in" consists in cutting away that part of the wood on which there is no design, and which when finished is known as the "ground." On this ground the design stands in relief.

First, the depth to which the ground is to be taken is decided upon. In this case the depth has been fixed at ⅜ in. It will be noticed that the margin is not raised, but consists of a chamfer taken from the level of the ground, as shown in Fig. 14,

Fig. 14.— Chamfered Edge of Panel

Now proceed to cut away the ground with the two gouges, taking short quick strokes, beginning so that each succeeding cut is with the grain. In this panel the first cut inside the design was made at the lower end, and the work proceeded upwards. This work of roughing out should be well done, each cut being made as though it were the final one, avoiding the temptation to permit slipshod work merely because it will be subject to further tooling.

Fig. 13 shows the "bosting in" carried out from one side only; the other part of the panel will be done from the other side when the panel is turned round. The uncut half shows the design traced on in outline only. It will be seen that the cuts are made obliquely across the grain. Do not cut with the grain if it can possibly

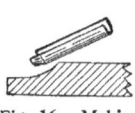 

Fig. 16.—Making Sloping Cut   Fig. 17.—Beginning the Cut

be avoided; a uniform depth is more easily maintained by cutting across. Make all the cuts a uniform depth as far up to the design as possible. When the tool is used at an ordinary angle, as in

Fig. 16, a sloping cut is made. To make the cut that is necessary, hold the tool nearly perpendicular at the beginning of the stroke, as in Fig. 17.

The value of the photographic illustrations is enhanced because of the way

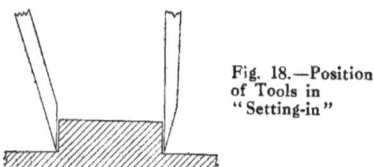

Fig. 18.—Position of Tools in "Setting-in"

in which the various stages are linked together. Thus in Fig. 13 two stages are shown : the preparatory stage and the " bosting in." Next is shown the " bosting in " and the " setting in."

The following are the materials and tools used to get the panel up to the stage shown in Fig. 13 : Panel in oak, $16\frac{7}{8}$ in. by $12\frac{3}{16}$ in. by $\frac{3}{4}$ in., and to plane and square up this panel, a jackplane, tryplane, rule and square. For tracing the design : Tracing paper, carbon paper, H pencil or style, drawing pins, and straightedge. For cutting out : Bow saw, carving tools No. 5 by $\frac{3}{8}$ in., and No 4 by $\frac{3}{8}$ in. Cramps, screw, or slips, and carving tools No. 8 by $\frac{1}{4}$ in. and No. 7 by $\frac{3}{8}$ in. are also wanted.

Setting In.—The " roughing out " may now be continued over the whole panel, to get it ready for " setting in." This consists of cutting along the edge of the design vertically, down to the depth required for the groundwork.

The tools required, in addition to those specified for the first stage of the work, are a mallet and the following carving tools : No. 3 by $\frac{1}{8}$ in. ; No. 3 by $\frac{3}{8}$ in. ; No. 4 by $\frac{1}{4}$ in. ; No. 4 by $\frac{5}{8}$ in. ; No. 5 by $\frac{3}{16}$ in., and No. 6 by $\frac{3}{8}$ in.

In " setting in " the definite form of outline is given to the design. Hitherto it has been more or less vague and shadowy, suggestive only ; now it is being carried a step farther, giving it definition and clearness.

The tools used may be applied either side to the outline, the chief requirement being that of fitting the curve accurately. Much care must be exercised on this part of the work.

In cutting a concave curve, such as the inside edge of the stalk, a tool slightly " quicker " in curve than the curve of the stalk should be used. This is to prevent the corners of the tool cutting into the stalk. One object that should be kept in view is to use as few tools as possible, within reason, of course. A multiplication of tools is confusing and inconvenient, and time is wasted in trying to find a tool that exactly fits any particular curve. A narrow tool is preferable to a wide one, and many light, continuous blows to one heavy " dead " blow.

The value of the " wasting away "

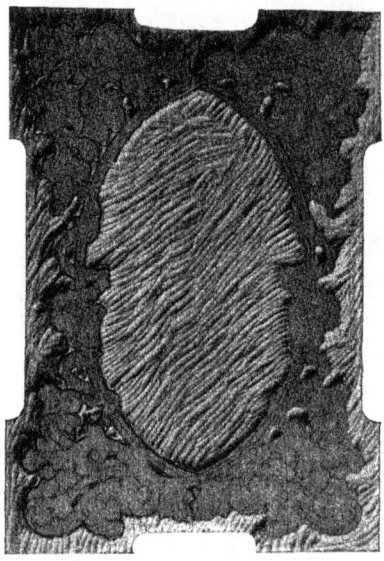

Fig. 19.—Photograph showing Panel after " Setting-in "

process will be evident by the ease with which the " setting in " is done, and the manner in which the chips fall away from the design, showing that the lateral pressure is proceeding in that direction, and not through the design itself, where it

WOODCARVING

would tend to damage that portion through which it passed. Some of the smaller indentations on the design may be passed by, and a major cut made including these, and this arrangement will stand until all the surplus wood has been taken away to form the ground. This procedure saves the outstanding and thinner parts of the design whilst the heavy work of cutting the ground is proceeding.

In " setting in " hold the tool so that the face nearest the design is inclined slightly towards the design, as in Fig. 18. In one case is shown the tool with its front face to the design, and in the other the back face (the ground surface) to the design. Note that it is the face of the tool, and

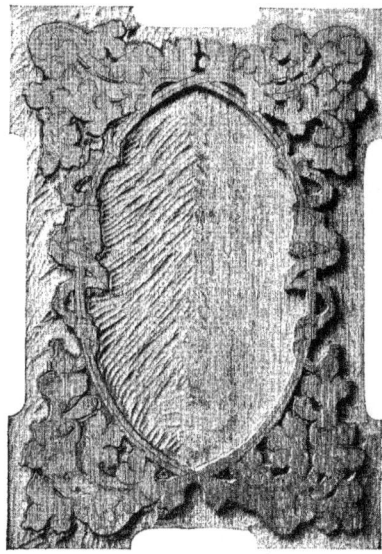

Fig. 20.—Photograph showing Panel " Set in " and " Ground Out "

not the tool itself, that should be slightly inclined towards the design. Set in to a uniform depth, and with a continuous cut, not in separate attempts, which produce a ragged edge. Connect all the cuts made into a continuous whole by inserting the corner of the tool into each preceding cut.

Throughout the whole work make those cuts which lie across the grain before those cuts are taken with the grain. This is to prevent undue splitting, especially of the corners. Fig. 19 shows the panel after the " setting in " has been done.

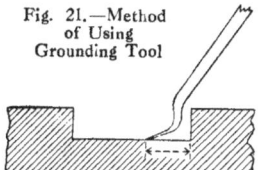

Fig. 21.—Method of Using Grounding Tool

The next stage is that of " grounding."

Grounding.—As shown in the photograph (Fig. 19) the panel is shown with one half " set in," the other half being " wasted away." In Fig. 20 the whole of the panel is shown " set in " and one-half " grounded out." This grounding is shown in various stages. The lower part of the panel is shown with the ridges left by the " wasting away " process, just taken off with a No. 5 gouge. The upper part shows the groundwork taken to a level surface. This is also shown well in the centre part of the panel. Six tools are used to cut the ground. Their sizes and the number of curve are: No. 3 by $\tfrac{1}{16}$ in.; No. 3 by $\tfrac{1}{8}$ in.; No. 4 by $\tfrac{1}{4}$ in.; No. 3 by $\tfrac{3}{8}$ in.; No. 5 by $\tfrac{3}{8}$ in., and a $\tfrac{1}{8}$-in. tool known as a " grounding tool." It is curved near the cutting edge to enable it to cut a larger surface than a straight-bladed tool can; and to do this it has to be held more perpendicularly than the ordinary tool. Fig. 21 shows the angle at which it should be held. Notice the respective distances of the cutting edge from the wall of the carving lying immediately behind when the tools are placed in their cutting position.

Special attention is called to the fact of the tools being flat in section. For " wasting away " the tools used were quick gouges. These made deep cuts with sharp ridges between. The tools now used have to flatten the ground by reducing these ridges. The first tool used is the quickest of the six—the No. 5 curve by $\tfrac{3}{8}$ in. wide. This speedily brings the ridges down to a more or less level surface. Judgment as well as skill in tool manipulation are here necessary, because a stronger cut than usual will make the tool dip below the general ground level.

Some carvers use a router at this stage. It consists of a flat piece of wood, through which is fixed a cutting iron nearly at right angles to the wood, and projecting under to the depth it is proposed to take the ground. This tool, well used, ensures a perfectly level surface. It is certainly a saver of time and labour. If a router is used a little depth should be left to cut down with the carving tools, to get a tooled surface finish.

There are only three curved tools : the one already mentioned (No. 5) and a flatter one (No. 3), and one between. a No. 4. Of No. 3 curve there are three tools of varying widths, from $\frac{1}{16}$ in. to $\frac{3}{8}$ in. ; this is to fit the varying spaces. The No. 4 curve tool is for use in some of the smaller spaces ; being a little more curved, its corners do not catch in the wood and make a nasty cut. It is a mistake to suppose that a quite flat tool (No. 1 on a tool list) is necessary to finish off the ground. It is not necessary to get a surface that is as flat and smooth as a surface finished with a plane, and, moreover, a No. 1 tool is much too difficult a tool to use to get such a surface, because of its corners catching in the wood. A wide surface such as in this panel is a good test of a carver's ability, because it is rather difficult to keep uniformly level. The general tendency is to leave it raised in the centre.

In cutting the centre, begin at the edges and work the wood down towards the centre. It is possible that the " setting in " has not been done deeply enough, and the chips do not come off quite clean, a ragged edge being left where the horizontal cut is deeper than the vertical incision. This must be re-set in ; in fact it is rather a good plan to go over the outline with the setting-in tools again very lightly, so that a sufficient depth is obtained for cleaning off to a smooth surface. It is as well not to put the final finish to the surface of the ground now, as in the course of modelling the tools at some points cut up the surface, and this can be better dealt with by leaving a little depth for the final finishing.

Modelling.—" Modelling " is the term applied to the process of treating the hitherto flat surface of the design so that the variation of surface may produce effect. So far the work has been entirely mechanical. Anyone possessed of an average manual dexterity may do the " wasting away." " setting in " and the " grounding " quite successfully and without trouble or difficulty. But for " modelling " higher faculties than mere manual skill are brought into operation. Successful modelling is only possible to a mind ripened and cultivated by an art training.

Every carver must understand what is meant by the term " modelling." and what the real object is, in so treating the plain surface of the design. It is, as previously stated, to produce an effect ; but the real question is, " What kind of an effect is it good to produce ? " An answer to this can be made in a general manner ; much must be left to each individual operator. But a few words of advice are possible and, always bearing in mind their general and not too close and particular application, they are now given. It will be noticed that the design, although obviously based on a natural form, is yet only approximately like it. In using this natural form as material for the building of the design, the type has been altered in shape according to the laws governing convention in the art. These laws require, most of all, that the type chosen as the motif must be altered to conform (1) to the requirements of the material, and (2) to the necessities of the space available for the ornament. It is obviously impossible for a spray of leaves to be taken from the tree on which it grows to fit a space of the shape of panel with symmetry, order and fitness ; hence requirement No. 2.

It is equally impossible, although perhaps not so generally recognised, that a natural form can be faithfully reproduced in such a material as wood in its entirety ; hence requirement No. 1. Therefore, as

WOODCARVING

nature cannot be followed in the treatment of the design, the carver's own ideas must necessarily be followed. It is here that infinite possibilities of good work and of bad work open up. The artistic mind will recognise that something more than clean,

Fig. 22.—Photograph showing Beginning of Modelling

clever, smooth cutting is required. The mechanical type of mind can see the necessities of the form only, and produces a work that is altogether lacking in life and nervous vigour. The consideration of this leads to the knowledge that to model work correctly there must be some perception of what are the leading features or characteristics of the natural form used in the design and emphasise them. As already mentioned, each mind differs in its interpretation of design; and it is therefore obvious that varied results can be obtained from the same design. The treatment given here is a suggestion only. Keen observation, close comparison, and the use of intelligent thought will keep the work within the limits of reason and fitness.

The tools necessary for getting the modelling of this panel up to the stage shown in Fig. 22 are a $\frac{3}{16}$ in. No. 5; $\frac{1}{8}$ in. No. 6; $\frac{1}{4}$ in. No. 8; $\frac{1}{8}$ in. No. 4; $\frac{1}{4}$ in. No. 4, and a $\frac{1}{4}$ in. No. 39. First go over the design very carefully for any correction that may be necessary in its outlines. Then carefully consider those parts that must be lower than the remainder, such as the stalks, the underlying parts of the leaves, where a part of the leaf turns over. This should be done with judgment, to get all these lower parts to their approximate ultimate level. Approximate is stated because these levels will have to be varied from the first result, because of the effect produced by the treatment of the leaves. This latter causes a different value to be given to the underlying parts as the work proceeds. The top right-hand corner of the panel shows the work at this stage.

In treating the stalk, take note of the tendency to dip it too suddenly where it disappears under a fold of the ribbon or a leaf, producing an effect, when looked at in side elevation, as shown in Fig. 23, and avoid it. The true treatment should be as in Fig. 24; the stalk almost level, or with the slightest perceptible rise. Always

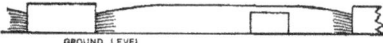

Fig. 23.—Section of Incorrect Method of Carving Underlying Stalk or Leaf

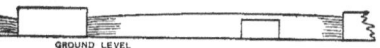

Fig. 24.—Section of Correct Method

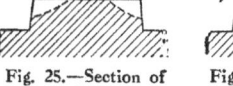

Fig. 25.—Section of Lobe in First Stage in Modelling

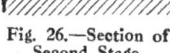

Fig. 26.—Section of Second Stage

throughout the modelling process look at the work from all possible points of view, what appears to be in good proportion and direction from some points may be quite wrong from others.

The next stage is to take the leaves

approximately to their ultimate shape. The lower right-hand corner shows this stage. The ¼ in. No. 4 tool is used first to lower the edges, then ¼ in. No. 8 to give the central prominences or bumps existence by cutting a hollow channel along the edges of the leaves and across the neck of each lobe. Fig. 25 shows a section of a lobe, with one side cut down with tool *e*. Fig. 26 shows this section still further reduced, this giving the centre of each lobe prominence. Fig. 27 gives a plan of one leaf, showing by dotted lines what is meant by cutting down the neck of each lobe. The panel should be treated up to this stage in all its parts before anything further is attempted. It will always be found better and more economical, as far as time is concerned, to work each stage in its entirety before proceeding to

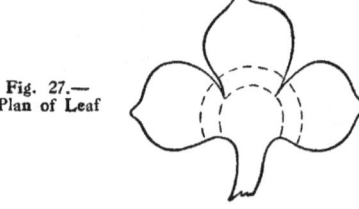

Fig. 27.—Plan of Leaf

the next. Thus even if half a dozen panels were being carved at the same time, and providing there was sufficient bench room, it would be well to have them all cramped down and work the whole of them through each stage before proceeding to the next.

Fig. 28 shows a full-size detail of the entwined ribbon.

Fig. 29 shows the work carried much farther. This figure is, perhaps, the most valuable, as well as the most interesting, of the series. It shows in the top left corner the design " set in " ready for surface variation. In the top right corner this is advanced a stage and much of the lowering has been done. The lower left corner shows this taken farther still, and the lower right corner gives an illustration of the finished design. The ribbon work is taken to a stage just short of the finishing point. Thus in this illustration are included all the stages relative to the process of " modelling." Such illustrations show much more clearly how the ultimate result is arrived at than any description possibly could. In fact, short of an actual demonstration, such an illustration shows the best possible methods that are employed in " modelling."

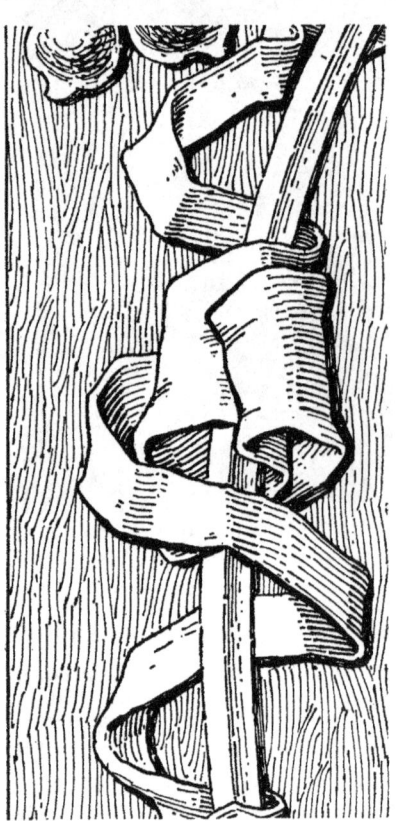

Fig. 28.—Full-size Detail of Entwined Ribbon Work

The tools actually used are a ¼ in. No. 4; ³⁄₁₆ in. No. 7; ⅛ in. No. 7; ⅜ in. No. 5; ⅛ in. No. 3; ³⁄₁₆ in. No. 5; ⁵⁄₁₆ in. No. 3; ¼ in. No. 8; ¼ in. No. 39; ¼ in. No. 28. Most of them are small tools, that is, small

WOODCARVING

in width. There is one type of tool introduced that is somewhat new; that is the spoon-bit tool. This type has been used for grounding (No. 21 by $\frac{1}{8}$ in.); but

Fig. 29.—Photograph showing Portion Fully Modelled

that was flat in section. This tool for modelling is curved in section. Its use is necessitated by the deep and sudden cutting round and between the lobes of the leaves, to get the sudden contrasts between height and depression, between high light and deep shadow, necessary to good work.

The sudden dippings and equally sudden but graceful swellings give the life and vigour to the work. It is a very difficult matter to get the "bossiness" characteristic of Gothic work, which permanently influences this design, without thinness and mere "knobbiness." The elevations should swell gradually and broadly, not quickly and suddenly; or they look thin and scraggy. They should be fat rather than lean. In modelling, the surface contour should be looked at from all points of view, so that it shall be as perfect as possible. Not, bear in mind, perfect in finish, although this is desirable, but, rather, perfect in proportion of mass and grace of curve. Another point is that the elevations should not be thin and sudden, as shown in Fig. 30, which is a section of one of the lobes. The better section is given by Fig. 31, which shows a much fuller centre and much narrower channels cut on each side.

Another hint is to vary the contour so that a continuously varying play of light and shade is possible. Take the edge of a leaf, let it swell up from its source to its highest point, and sink again to its lowest point, with lesser variations, twists, and curls between. Subordinate the stalks,

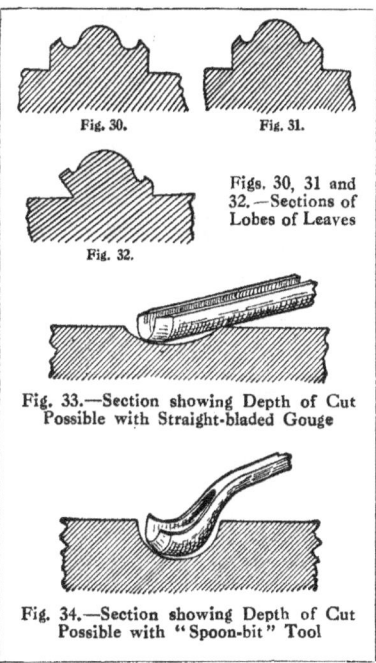

Figs. 30, 31 and 32.—Sections of Lobes of Leaves

Fig. 33.—Section showing Depth of Cut Possible with Straight-bladed Gouge

Fig. 34.—Section showing Depth of Cut Possible with "Spoon-bit" Tool

but make them clear and distinct and firm in outline and direction. Do not have all the leaves the same height, and do not give them equal values of light and shade.

Some may have their centres left high and their edges low, leaving a greater comparative height of centre lobe. Others may have only a slight difference between the highest point in the centre lobe and the lowest point in the edge, showing a slightly

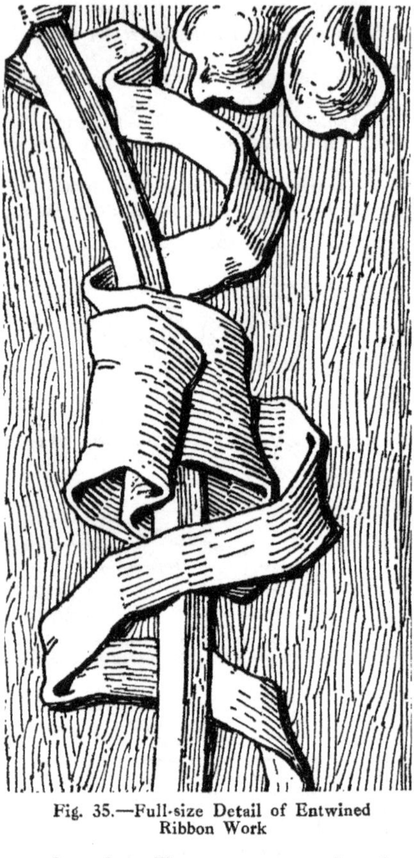

Fig. 35.—Full-size Detail of Entwined Ribbon Work

graduated swelling curve connecting the edge and the centre. The edges of many of the leaves, notably those edges that stand high, are slightly undercut. This gives a deeper shadow, which emphasises the value of the leaf, and by cutting away the visible " wall " of the leaf makes it look lighter because now only the edge is plainly visible, and not the whole of the wood constituting the wall of the leaf. Fig. 32 shows how much undercutting is done.

In the whole of the modelling a clean, neat, light touch will be found to be absolutely essential. In the earlier portion of the work the hand and arm had a good deal of free play; a fair amount of force could be used. In the modelling portion, the hand, arm, and fingers are not allowed any free play. Their actions are restrained by reason of their short-stroke, and by reason of the great variation of contour.

The spoon-bit gouges can work to a greater depth within a shorter distance than the ordinary straight-bladed gouge, as shown by Figs. 33 and 34. Fig. 33 shows the ordinary gouge working, and illustrates the depth that can be got with a definite length of stroke. Fig. 34 shows the same with regard to the spoon-bit gouge, and it can be seen that, because of the bend in the tool, the ratio of the depth of the cut to the length of the stroke is increased considerably. These tools are more difficult to use at first than are the straight-bladed tools, but practice will overcome this difficulty. A full-size detail of the entwined ribbon on the right-hand side of the panel is shown by Fig. 35.

The reproduction of a photograph (Fig. 36) shows the panel finished.

The tools required to finish the panel are just the same as already mentioned. Mention may be made of the spoon-bit tools and their scope and use. They are necessary in getting the hollows in the carving deep enough without extending the width of the cut. This cannot be done with the ordinary straight-bladed tool without so extending the width of the cut, and in addition cutting the surface roughly. This design has many deep depressions of small plan measurement, and their presence makes the spoon-bit tool a necessity. The object of these depressions is to get an effective play of light and shade. The depth gives blackness of shadow, and the high lights of the resulting prominences, contrasted with these, and combined with secondary shadows and half-tones, give an effect that is characteristic of fourteenth- and fifteenth-century Gothic carving.

A note of warning may be given here. Some students have a tendency to be done with a skilful use of the straight-bladed tool. To get the leaves to lie over effectively and produce good, strong curves and flowing surfaces, most of the edges are reduced nearly to the ground level.

Fig. 36.—Photograph showing Panel Completed

carried away with the value of the spoon-bit tool, and get many more tools of this kind than they will ever find a use for; some even get sets of these tools. Really only very few of these tools are necessary, and very much work of this kind may be But, necessarily, some of the leaf edges are raised, and if not otherwise treated, would show a comparatively high wall; this tends to a clumsy effect if left. To remedy this, the leaf edge is cut away far enough under to put it behind the line of vision or to just coincide with it. This lightens the edge of the leaf, intensifies the depth of shadow, and "lifts" the leaf off the ground.

In modelling the panel no part should be quite finished off before the rest is taken up to nearly finishing point. That is to say, the whole surface should be worked up in stages, these stages being applicable to the whole panel, one stage after another. This ensures a harmony and unity in the ultimate appearance that cannot be obtained by the treatment of finishing one part before the other portions are brought up to nearly finishing point. The degree of finish that is considered necessary differs in the opinion of different people naturally. Perfection of form is what should be aimed at rather than perfection of surface finish. Thus, in finishing the surface of the leaves, the eye should be on the level of the leaf, to see how nearly the surface curve fits the carver's idea of a good, sweeping, flowing curve. Test the curves of the raised "boss" in each lobe from all points of view, and note how the convex curves fit the concave curves and flow into them.

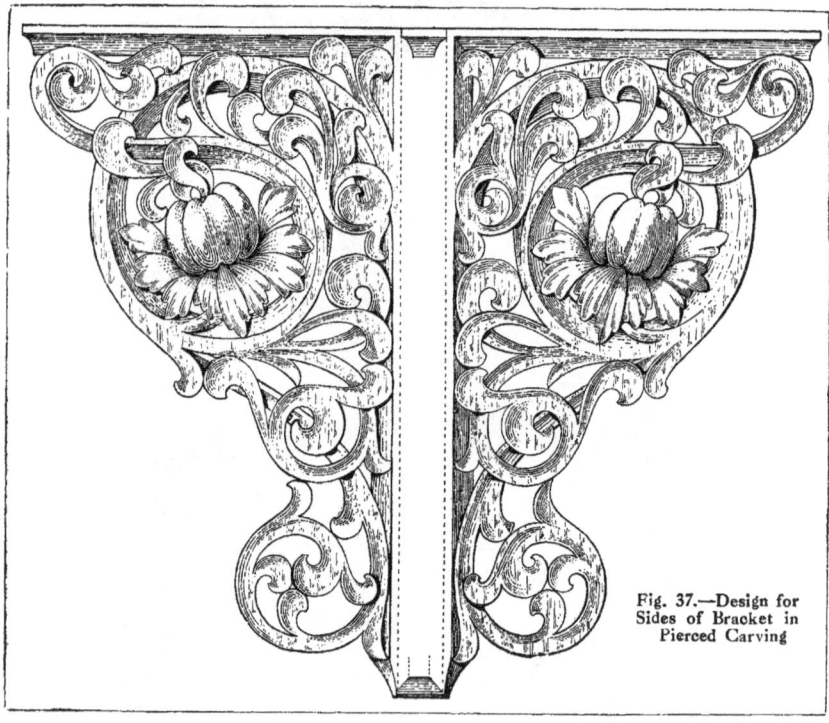

Fig. 37.—Design for Sides of Bracket in Pierced Carving

A surface of this kind may have the tool marks left on it, only they are not so evident as to interfere with the perfection of form already mentioned. Without this perfection no amount of smooth surface finish can make a good job of the carving.

Before finally finishing the panel, place it at a distance of 5 ft. or 6 ft., in a good side light, and carefully note any lack of

WOODCARVING

balance in the lights and shadows. There may be a little latitude allowed in the symmetry of the lights and shadows, providing this does not produce bad balance. But balance is the most important, and any transgressions of this essential principle of ornament should be rectified at once. The finish of the surface may then be proceeded with. When the carving is

Fig. 38.—Design for Centre Piece of Bracket in Pierced Carving

finished, no treatment other than waxing, or fuming and waxing, is necessary.

PIERCED CARVING

Pierced carving is well explained by its name. It is that form of carving which, instead of having a definite groundwork, has what would normally be the groundwork completely cut away with a saw. What is left is the design, and this is modelled in the usual way.

Now, as wood is a material that is not equally strong across its width and along its length, it follows that this form of carving, which must necessitate the complete removal of much of the wood, needs to be employed with much judgment and restraint, or a result will follow that is weak both constructionally and artistically.

Some of the considerations that operate in deciding what are suitable designs, and what is the suitable treatment for pierced work, are as follows :

The pierced portions (which in ordinary relief carving is the ground) must not be too large in extent. As a precaution, and to see whether the ground spaces are too great, it is advisable to blacken them in with the pencil, and the design will give a better idea as to the suitability of these spaces as regards their size. The reason for this is that the pierced portions always give a blacker shadow than ordinary groundwork, and thus tend to bring themselves under notice, and, in consequence, appear to be bigger than they really are.

The amount of wood cut away need not necessarily be as large as the space shown on the design. A stalk, for instance, may for reasons of strength be quite thick at the back, and just thinned down to its normal thickness at the front edge.

The thickness of the wood makes for a greater appearance of relief in pierced work than in flat relief carving. This has to be kept in mind in conceiving the design, in respect, especially, to the balance and proportion that should exist between the various parts.

Figs. 37 and 38 show the design for a bracket. Later illustrations show photographs of a bracket in the various stages of the carving, and they will present a series of lessons only slightly less valuable than an actual demonstration of the work.

The first thing that has to be decided is the wood to use. Oak would be a very suitable wood for the execution of this particular example. The dimensions of the various pieces are : Two pieces for the back, 1 ft. 3½ in. by 9½ in. by ¾ in., one piece for the support, 1 ft. 3½ in. by 8 in. by ¾ in.; also one piece for the top (which is not carved), 2 ft. by 1 ft. by ¾ in. It will be seen that the back piece is made in two parts. This is because the wood is the more easily obtained in narrower than wider widths, and because it is much more easily worked in a narrow width. The two pieces are jointed together with a groove-and-tongue joint glued when the carving is finally completed. These pieces may, for economy, be cut one out of another, the actual marking out for the brackets and back piece being a simple matter. The thickness (¾ in. finished) will be found quite sufficient; the thickness of wood when pierced and carved tends to appear to be much thicker than it really is.

First prepare the wood by planing it to thickness and shooting one edge. This operation may be done whilst the board is in one piece, and it can be cut into smaller pieces afterwards. Then put on the square lines of the top end, and trace the design.

Tracing the Design —Take a tracing of the design on ordinary tracing (transparent) paper. Do this carefully as regards the outlines; but there is no need to put in the shading lines. To fix the tracing, make the top square line coincide with the one already drawn on the wood, and the upright line copied from the design with the back edge or with the line drawn on the wood, which represents this back edge. Then pin this tracing along the back edge, and, inserting the carbon paper black side downwards, pin along the top and front edges, and begin to trace.

Students will do well to spend some time in earnestly and seriously studying the design to understand it thoroughly well. No amount of subsequent good work will atone for a wrong interpretation of a design. Keep to the lines so far as possible, and do not fall into the mistake of supposing that any kind of work will do now, or that this part of the work is not of so much consequence in the later stages. Work as carefully now as if finishing the bracket. Bad work at this stage makes bad results follow at every subsequent stage.

Fig. 39 shows the separate pieces, two of them with the design already traced on, and the other piece with the design on tracing-paper fixed with pins, and the carbon paper inserted ready for tracing the design. In tracing this bracket design, it must be remembered that it is to be carved on both sides. Therefore great accuracy will have to be exercised in fixing the design, so that both sides will coincide when the piercing has been done. After the outline has been traced, it is as well to pencil the parts that are to be cut out with the saw. This prevents subsequent confusion as to which is design and which is groundwork.

The bracket is now ready for actual work on it to be done with brace and bits, saws, and carving tools.

Boring Holes.—The first step to be taken in pierced carving is to bore holes so that the saw may be inserted to cut away the surplus wood, and for this suitable tools and a bench are required. For pierced carving tools, which may properly be called supplementary tools, are necessary. The ordinary tools are chisels, gouges, V-tools, veiners, etc. But to execute some forms of wood carving many other tools are necessary. Thus in pierced carving the following tools are also required: a ratchet brace; several bits, namely, ⅛ in. shell bit, ¼ in. shell bit, $\tfrac{5}{16}$ in. shell bit, ⅜ in. shell bit, ½ in. centre bit, ¾ in. centre bit; a bow saw (a 10 in. will do), and the keyhole saw.

The wood may be bored on a saw stool or wooden packing box; but a much better way is to have it held in a joiner's bench screw, and hold the brace and bits horizontally when boring the holes. The work should be fixed high enough to get the chest in use so that it may support the brace.

Fig. 40 shows the pieces of wood partially bored. One of the pieces is shown just traced; the second shows those parts bored that necessitate the use of the smallest bits, in this case the ⅛ in. and ¼ in. shell bits. These are as small bits as it is desirable to use, as with a smaller

WOODCARVING

bit the saw could not be threaded through. It is desirable that all the holes should be bored with one bit that can possibly be done at one time whilst it is in the brace. This is to save the continual changing of bits that would otherwise take place.

This procedure also encourages the use of system in executing the work. It must be laid down, as an almost invariable rule, that each stage of the work should be finished before the next is begun. Even if several panels or pieces of work have to

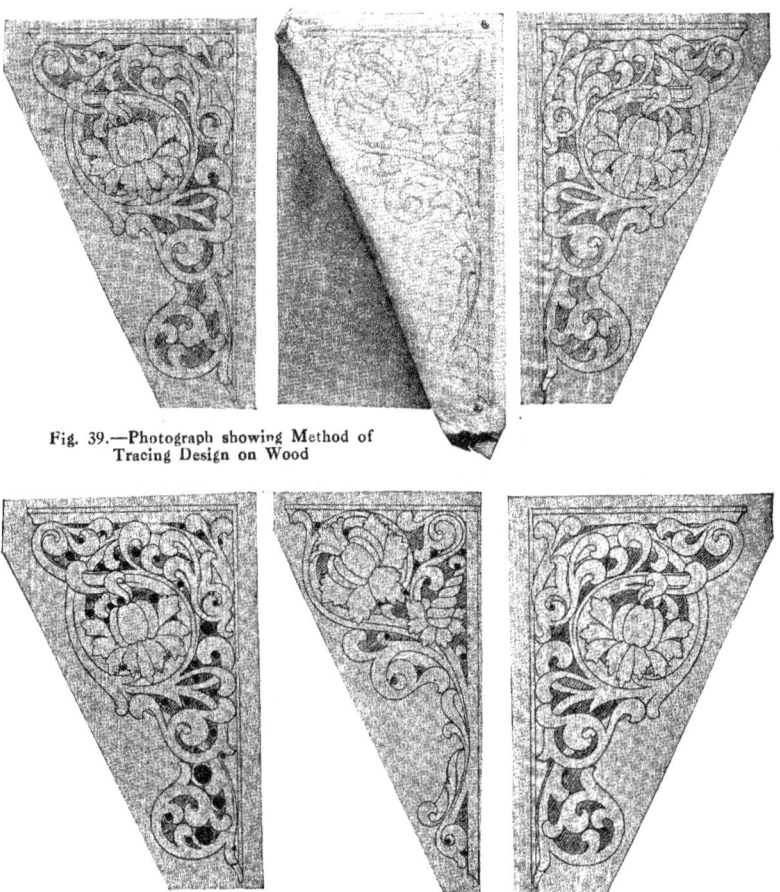

Fig. 39.—Photograph showing Method of Tracing Design on Wood

Fig. 40.—Photograph showing One Piece Traced, One Piece Partially Bored, and the Third Piece Wholly Bored, Ready for Sawing

be done, it is always best to do the work of one stage on all the panels before proceeding to the work of the next stage.

The $\frac{1}{4}$ in. shell bit is the smallest to make holes through which the saw (whether bow saw or keyhole) can be threaded. Nevertheless, some of the spaces are too small to get the $\frac{1}{4}$ in. bit into. This can be obviated by using a smaller bit, say $\frac{1}{8}$ in. bit, and then cutting away the wood that lies between with the carving tools.

But another method may be pursued. It may be said that the result of, and, indeed, the reason for, pierced carving lies in the fact that the pierced portions give deeper shadows than if the ground had been there, although even it might have been taken for a great depth. In a small space, however, if the ground is taken a good depth, the whole of the cut-out space is in shadow, and therefore the necessity for cutting right through may be avoided. The holes may be or may not be bored as desired, but the space need not necessarily be cut right through.

In Fig. 40 the work of the smaller bit may be noted, and to facilitate the further work of the carving tool, the holes are bored in pairs. The third piece in the photograph shows where the other bits have been used. It may be stated that the largest bit that the space will allow should be used. Thus it is possible to use many bits of varying size up to $\frac{3}{4}$ in. in this case. The two largest bits used in this piece of work are centre bits, $\frac{1}{2}$ in. and $\frac{3}{4}$ in., and the spaces vary sufficiently to necessitate the use of all the sizes of bits between the two extremes of $\frac{1}{8}$ in. and $\frac{3}{4}$ in. Sometimes in a small space a succession of bit-holes may save much labour with the saw. The bits can take out the greater amount of the wood, leaving only a few corners to be cut out with a carving tool. Where the design has thin stalks, which does sometimes occur, then the bits used should be smaller than the available space, so that additional strength may be given to the stalks by leaving a greater thickness of wood at the back, the front edge being thinned down to make the requisite size of stalk. In boring the holes, it is most essential that the brace and bit are kept level and at right angles to the face of the wood. Otherwise the line of the hole will pierce the stalk or leaf or other member of the design, and produce inequalities of line that will damage the appearance of the work when finished.

Another point that should be noted is that in boring there is a tendency on the part of the bits to break the wood away at the back of the panel. With centre bits, this tendency may be made non-existent by boring from the face until nearly through, when the point of the centre bit will pierce through to the back; the wood can then be turned round and the holes bored from the back. But with shell bits this cannot be done. The best way to get over the difficulty is to have a piece of deal firmly fixed to the work at its back, and keep it there until all the boring is completed. The result is that the deal gets broken, and the oak pieces remain intact. Twist bits and screw bits may also be used.

Respecting the outline of the edges of the brackets, the boring for them may be done now; but they are, as a rule, left until the pierced design has been carved and the pieces are ready to be made up.

Sawing.—The next stage of the work is that of sawing. There is a choice of a keyhole saw, a fret saw, and a bow saw (already illustrated on earlier pages of this work). The cutting shown in Fig. 41 has been done with a keyhole saw, which is thicker and stronger than a fret saw, and makes a coarser cut, but possesses the advantage of quickness in use, there being no threading and unthreading of the blade, as there is with both the fret saw and the bow saw. To a fretworker, the fret saw will naturally appeal; it is clean in its action, and there is a less amount of cutting with the chisel afterwards.

For sawing, fix the wood firmly in the bench screw. Now insert the saw in the larger spaces, and cut towards the angles, keeping as close to the line as possible, and having the saw at right angles to the face.

In using a keyhole saw, do not take too

long a stroke, or the point will catch either in the wood or on its face, by reason of being pulled too far through.

The centre piece in Fig. 41 shows the beginning of the sawing, and the piece to the right hand the sawing completed. There are some small portions which, although they are bored, are not, necessarily, cut through with the saw. They may be cut down to about half the depth, just as if they were ordinary groundwork, still with the hole quite through. The advantage of the hole is that it helps with the dark shadow. A hole cut right through a piece of wood gives a darker shadow, when placed under ordinary conditions, than if it was only cut down as groundwork.

Make the saw cuts as continuous as possible, and take great care where they meet, in angles, so that there is no overstepping of the cut on the design. The back edge may possibly appear to be quite too ragged and untidy, caused by the saw pushing its way through. This really does not matter, as in the case of the centre bracket it is carved both sides, and consequently any tearing that occurs will quite easily be cut away in the modelling.

Respecting the two other pieces, the back is generally trimmed off, and, in fact, this trimming is really a necessity in most cases, as the members of the design need thinning to show thin edges only. If, however, it is thought necessary not to have any tearing of the back edges, use the board that was employed during the boring operations, and tack it, or cramp it, firmly to the bracket pieces, and cut it along with the oak. A clean edge will show itself when the board is removed. In going round a quick corner, the saw often sticks. In such a case use a touch of oil to reduce the friction, and so make the saw run more easily.

Modelling.—The first thing to be done after the sawing is to clean up the edges. Cut well into the angles, which in the case of the very acute angles will be rough, and perhaps will be found awkward to do. If it is found impossible to cut them clean for the whole of the depth, cut them for as far as may be found possible. In the case of stalks, as already mentioned, it may not be necessary to thin them down to their surface thickness; but it may be advisable to leave them thicker, and only thin them on their front edges. The wood should lie on a flat, smooth board whilst

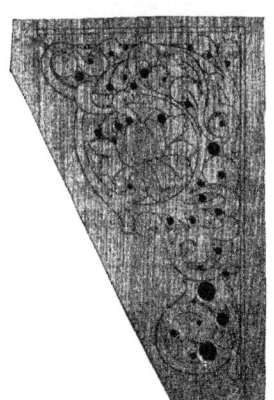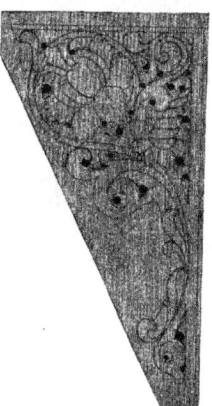

Fig. 41.—Photograph showing Boring and Sawing of Bracket

cleaning off, and all should be securely cramped down to the bench. This only will prevent splintering at the back.

It will be noticed on glancing at the photograph of the work in this stage (Fig. 42) that the front edge has been sawn. This is necessary, inasmuch as the design comes over the outline, and requires lowering in various places along it. This sawn outline, too, requires cleaning off in the same way as already described.

The surface is now ready to begin modelling. First of all, study the design proportion, it may be necessary that some portions of the design will have to be taken lower than others. This part of the work may be called "arranging the masses," and is of greater importance than the later work of finishing the surface, because the effect produced by the carving depends more on its general contour and perfect proportion of parts than on any pleasing surface treatment. A glance at Fig. 42 will show where the lowest parts are.

Stalks, as a rule, are subordinate members, and require sinking to greater depths

Fig. 42.—Photograph showing Partial Sawing, Complete Sawing, and Two Stages in Modelling of Bracket

and get to know its plan, general arrangement, and intention. Then wherever any portion of the design passes under any other portion, set this in with whatever tool will fit the curve of this particular member. Generally it will be found necessary to use the mallet to do this, although, as a rule, no member should be taken to a great depth. Take particular care that in thus setting in, the " line " of the design is not broken. That is to say, the member that goes under another should have its disappearing and reappearing points in line.

For the purposes of good balance and than other members. The flower is the chief point of interest in the design, and should be placed in considerable prominence. The stalks, which, although subordinate, yet are of value, giving the lines of direction, should be carefully cut to keep their curves intact and shapely. A large part of the foliage ends on the outlines or the borders of the design. These will have to be very carefully " set in," graduating the depth of the setting in to the fall of the curve, remembering that the margins are curved in section, the curve falling inwards. In getting this curve, take special care to get it good in

WOODCARVING

direction as regards its length. Where the ends of petals fall on this hollowed edge, some cutting against the grain will inevitably take place, and sufficient time should be spent to cut these places clean and make them workmanlike. Do not slur them over, and depend on the surface carving to produce the necessary effect.

In cutting the masses to their respective shapes, opportunity will be provided, by the lowering of the surface in parts, to still further correct any deviations from a good curve of outline. In blocking out in which the masses are arranged. Another part shows the sawing of the outer edge done, and the "setting in" only of the design, ready for the modelling. The other portion of the illustration shows a part of the work only sawn on its interior, thus connecting the work at this stage with that at the immediately preceding stage. Having got the work to this stage, correct all inequalities of curve in the outline. As some of these may not have been reached, and probably cannot be reached by the carving tools, files may be

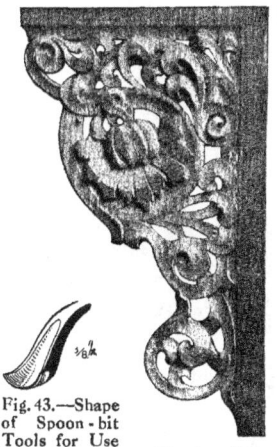
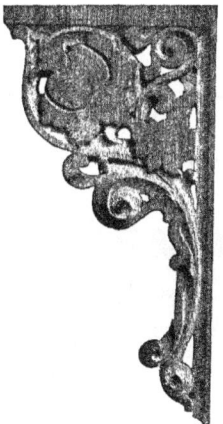

Fig. 43.—Shape of Spoon-bit Tools for Use in Quick and Deep Curves

Fig. 44.—Photograph showing the Parts of Bracket entirely Sawn, some Parts Partially Modelled, and One Part with Modelling nearly Finished

the centre bracket, which is carved on both sides, it must be remembered that in cutting from both sides there is a danger of cutting some of the members too thin. Thus some modification of the cutting must be resorted to, and the relief in this centre bracket will not be so great as on the back, unless a piece of wood of thicker dimension is used; and this is subject to the probability of appearing too bulky to look well.

Fig. 42 shows clearly the work up to this stage, including part of the work done in the preceding stage. One part of the illustration shows the beginnings of modelling, used to correct them. The use of the files in this connection should be rigidly limited to the edges, and should not in any circumstances be applied to the surface carving.

The carving tools proper will now be required. To get into the corners formed by the overlaying of the design on the edges or margins, right- and left-hand skew gouges will be necessary, or, at any rate, desirable; and it will be an added convenience if these are what are known as spoon-bit tools of the shape shown by Fig. 43.

The modelling of all three pieces being

by now much farther advanced, what now remains to be done is just surface work.

The piece in the middle is now partially "set in" and cut down, the piece on the any up to the present, and it represents the last step but one in the work of modelling. It is at this stage that the ability of a wood-carver is the most severely

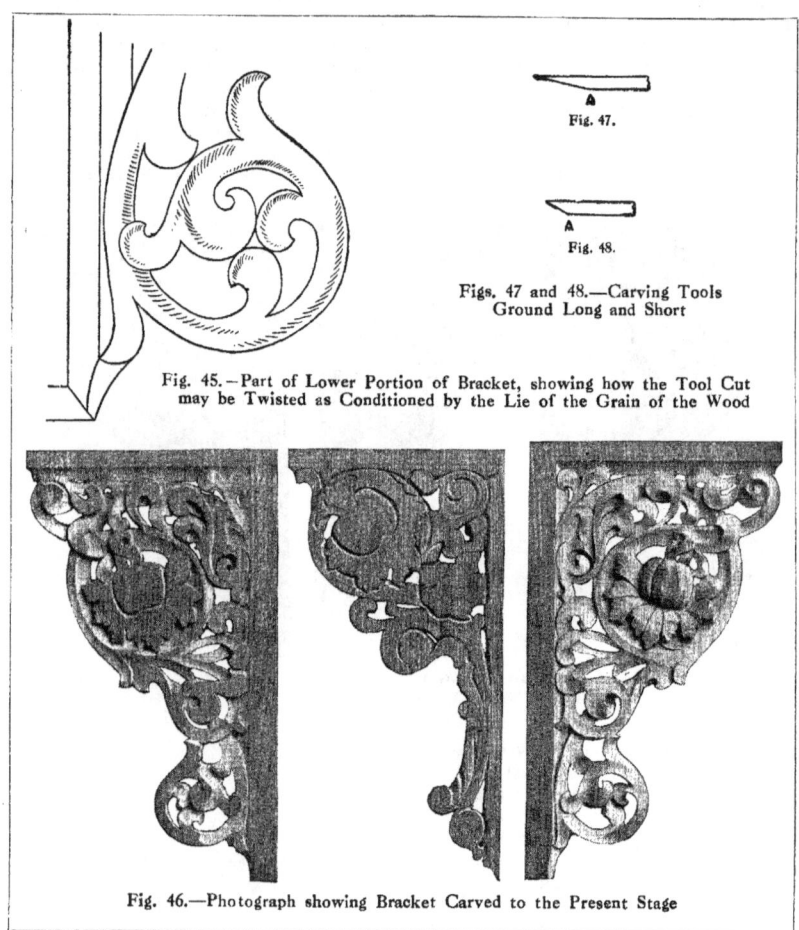

Fig. 47.

Fig. 48.

Figs. 47 and 48.—Carving Tools Ground Long and Short

Fig. 45.—Part of Lower Portion of Bracket, showing how the Tool Cut may be Twisted as Conditioned by the Lie of the Grain of the Wood

Fig. 46.—Photograph showing Bracket Carved to the Present Stage

left is roughly massed, and the right-hand piece is taken to that point when all that remains to be done is to supply the surface work. In Fig. 44 the third piece is the one that has been taken the farthest of tested. No attempt should be made to hide, by entire removal, the means whereby the members have been modelled. It should be seen that the carving has been done by the carving tool, and not by a

WOODCARVING

smoothing machine. What should be counted as the essential ideal is to produce a perfection of form, a perfect balance of mass, an effective comparison of elevation and depression, a judicious contrast of light and shade, rather than a perfect technique, and an accurate rendering of the form.

The tools used to get the work up to the point shown by Fig. 44 are (as per Sheffield tool list, $\frac{3}{8}$ in. by 3 in. $\frac{3}{8}$ in. by 4 in., $\frac{1}{4}$ in. by 4 in. $\frac{3}{8}$ in. by 5 in., $\frac{1}{4}$ in. by 5 in., $\frac{1}{4}$ in. by 5 in., $\frac{3}{8}$ in. by 7 in. $\frac{1}{4}$ in. by 7 in. $\frac{5}{16}$ in. by 25 in., $\frac{1}{4}$ in. by 21 in., $\frac{5}{16}$ in. by 39 in., $\frac{1}{8}$ in. by 4 in. One of these tools is a spoon-bit tool necessary to cut the hollow on the larger curved stalk at those points where the smaller leaves lie on it.

Compare, first of all the right-hand portion of the bracket with that part which is at the left hand in the photographic reproduction (Fig. 44). The first operation is to emphasise the depressed parts, and take them down to their lowest point. First set them in with tools of suitable curve. Thus, to take the most prominent member, the centre flower take suitable tools and set in along the line that has already been cut in with a V-tool. Reduce the inner end of the petals to the depth of the setting in. This particular part will need to be rather deeply cut to give the contrast necessary to the balance of the whole thing. In thus sinking the inner ends of the petals opportunity will be provided to give effective twists to the petals.

In sinking the various depressions to their ultimate depth, take care that they are not sunk too far to render it impossible to get a good curve. This warning is necessary, as it sometimes does happen that a depth is reached which makes it impossible to cut the member to a good curve. Especially is this the case with the upper part of the large stalk, where the small leaves are lying on it. If this is not particularly seen to, a lumpy and irregular surface is produced that gives a very bad effect. This stalk needs to be lowered in all its length, besides the hollow that is contained in it.

It is desirable to take the work from the bench from time to time, and hold it up in the position it is to occupy when finished, so that no mistake will be made in shaping the masses the wrong way, giving thereby ill-balanced effects of light and shade. Note particularly how the little curves of the leaves hold a deep shadow, and try to cultivate the ability to see these shadows and the high lights that lie close to them. It is an ability that can be cultivated by concentration. The twisting of the stalks and the leaves and, in fact, any member is often determined by the lie of the grain. For example, note the curled ending to the scroll at the bottom of the bracket. Taking the cut of the tool as from the top (*see* Fig. 45) in the direction of the curve then the twist leans towards the outside on the outer part, and towards the inside when the inner part is reached.

Finishing the Surface.—A stage when the finishing of the surface has been done has now been reached. This is shown in Fig. 46. The right-hand piece is now finished as regards its surface. The left-hand piece is taken up to that point where only the surface finishing is needed, whilst the centre piece is taken up to that stage already mentioned as the "arranging of the masses."

One very important point is the selection of the right tools for finishing, and a rigid adherence to the use of these particular tools. The best tools to use are the spade tools shown by Fig. 8. (p. 1346). These are lighter, and are capable of being used in places that the ordinary tool cannot reach. Some workers keep complete sets of spade tools for the sole purpose of "modelling." When this is done, a point that might be mentioned is, that the tools have what may be described as a "long" grind. This is shown in Fig. 47 in contradistinction to a "short" grind, shown in Fig. 48. The advantage of a "short" grind is that it gives strength, and the position of the edge A near to the cutting edge is useful in giving leverage to the tool when doing heavier work. But for finishing the surface, no heavy work is needed, and thus a lighter tool and a lighter and thinner cutting edge is made possible. This is especially useful in cleaning off the edges. A thicker tool would not easily get in

The extreme edge or arris should be cut off with a flat tool. This not only gives

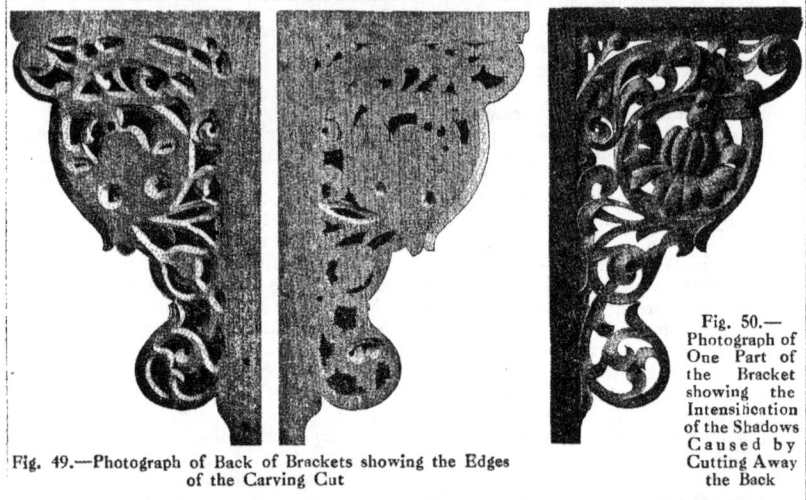

Fig. 49.—Photograph of Back of Brackets showing the Edges of the Carving Cut

Fig. 50.—Photograph of One Part of the Bracket showing the Intensification of the Shadows Caused by Cutting Away the Back

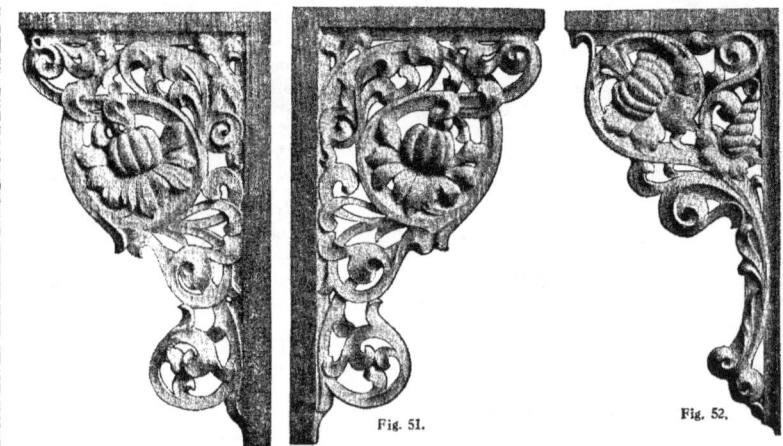

Fig. 51.

Fig. 52.

Figs. 51 and 52.—Photographs showing Carved Parts of Bracket Finished and Ready for Putting Together

without leaving bruises. But a thin tool can be more easily manipulated, and cleaner work may result from their use.

a smooth appearance, but makes the direction good, and gives an opportunity for correcting any slight inequality of outline that has crept into the work. Take care in doing this to get the angles well cut; a slight deviation at an angle will often produce awkward effects. Where the leaves are lying on the stalk, or on the hollow edge, great care has to be taken to get the angles cleanly done and well cut. Here the tools will necessarily have to be taken against the grain, and consequently sharp tools are essential. Moreover, the vertical setting-in cut must be deep enough, and the horizontal cut must never be cut below the level of the deepest part of the vertical cut.

Carving the Back of the Work.—Owing to the fact that the relief extends the full depth, or rather, the thickness of the wood, some of the members of the design must present at some point in their contour a thick and clumsy edge if not treated in some way that will remove this awkward appearance. There is a way in which this can be done, by cutting the superfluous wood away from the back. Fig. 49 shows a view of the back thus treated. The right-hand side piece shows it just begun, and the left-hand piece shows it finished. The treatment adopted in this case is quite simple and quite easy of accomplishment. It only involves the use of three tools, viz., ⅜ in. by 4 in., ½ in. by 5 in., and ⅜ in. by 6 in.

If the carved pieces were seen at both sides, then the style of treatment would be much more full of work. But as they go against a wall, all that is necessary is to cut them, so that from the front they help in making the appearance lighter. The difference in appearance is seen in Fig. 50, which should be compared with Fig. 46. The shadows at the back are intensified, and a greater contrast is; therefore, possible. The edges, too, are lightened, and this also helps to make the work look lighter. Much care is required in dealing with the stalks, because of their lightness. They require thinning down, but not so much that their strength is materially diminished. It would be better to cut away the wood at the sides only, in the case of any part of the work that would, by cutting all the wood away at the back, interfere with the strength.

In actually cutting the back, repeatedly take up the wood and look at it whilst in its intended ultimate position.

The whole of the carved parts of the bracket, finished and ready for putting together, are shown in Figs. 51 and 52. The backs of both side brackets will be finished at the back, whilst the centre bracket will be carved both sides. The front edge of this centre bracket will be carved, and some judgment will be required in carving it, so that it does not look thin and insignificant.

Making Up and Finishing.—In making up, the first step is to join the two

Fig. 53.—Photograph of Bracket Complete

side brackets together. This is best done by making a groove-and-tongue joint. The top edge of the joined pieces should now be planed true and square, and likewise that of the central bracket. Smooth up the sides with a finely set smoothing or panel plane. In fixing the bracket, the underside of the shelf should be trenched with a stop-tapered dovetail trench. To fit this, a tapered dovetail will be cut on the top of the central bracket, and it will be glued in from the back. The back edge of the shelf should be rebated to receive the back top edge, and this will be screwed up with brass screws in cups. The back edge of the shelf will require stop-rebating.

1370 THE PRACTICAL WOODWORKER

The completed bracket is shown by Fig. 53.

CHIP CARVING

Chip carving, as the name implies, consists of the formation of design by the siderable use of, providing as it does a simple method of decorative treatment. To the carver experienced in ordinary woodcarving chip carving will be a very simple operation, but to the novice, apart from its utility, its practice will be found

Fig. 54.—Design for Chip Carving Based on the Decagon

Fig. 55.—Pattern Incised

Fig. 56.—Pattern with Ground Removed

Fig. 57.—Pattern with Ground Stamped

removal of chips which are cut away from the wood in straight lines. From time immemorial it has formed the chief ornamental decorative art of primitive peoples, but even so it is still made considerable to be of great educational value for the development of accuracy and precision, and the acquirement of the necessary knowledge of wood cutting.

The practice of chip carving may be

WOODCARVING

carried out entirely with a knife, and many workers use this tool only, but the use of a small selection of ordinary carving tools not only considerably facilitates the work but increases its scope.

The knives used are of the short-bladed variety with either straight, curved, or angular blades. When knives alone are used, the actual process of carving consists of merely two operations—setting-in and cutting-out. The wood is removed by first setting the limit and then cutting it away by a slicing action of the tool. The first cut is made with the knife almost straight, and the second cut with the knife inclined at an angle of about 45°. With each successive cut, the angle between the knife and the work is reduced, until the correct face of the part being cut is obtained.

The principal hand tools of the chisel variety that are used for chip carving are the V-tool and the skew chisel. Compared with the knife the V-tool saves a vast amount of work, for one stroke of this tool is the equivalent of three of the knife.

Fig. 58.—Sideboard Ornamented with Incised Work

The chief objection to its use is the danger of splitting the corners when cutting across the grain. Other useful tools are the straight spade chisel and the veiner.

The designs for chip carving are mostly of a geometrical character, and a fair knowledge of geometry is essential for their proper setting out. Much of it appears of a complicated nature in the complete design, but mostly it will be found, upon study, to resolve itself into elementary geometry and may easily be produced by means of compasses and rule. Fig. 54 shows a design of this nature which is based on the setting out of the ten-sided figure or decagon. For such a design as this, if desired, instead of the decagon having plain bands, a rim could be run along the centre of each band.

Floral designs which are not of a geometrical nature also lend themselves to the art of the chip carver, but there is by no means the latitude with this class of design allowable as with ordinary carving.

A carver's **V**-tool is the most suitable for the first stage in the actual incising; a $\frac{1}{4}$-in. tool is a most convenient size to use. Besides this will be required a couple of carver's gouges, a $\frac{1}{8}$-in. and a very small one being convenient sizes for general work. An admirable stamp for matting the ground after it has been cut away can be made by cutting the point off a large French nail, then filing crosslines across the flat end. Of course, a large variety of matting punches that give various textures can be purchased; but the simplest are generally the most effective, and the one suggested is to be recommended.

The wood employed for incising requires to be of close grain, and not too soft. Material like pine and deal is wholly unsuitable, it being wellnigh impossible to obtain absolute clean incisions. Among the woods that can be thoroughly recommended are sycamore and satin walnut, the latter especially giving little trouble with well-sharpened tools.

The piece of wood to be incised must

Fig. 59.—Hall-stand Ornamented with Relief Carving

WOOD INCISING

Wood incising is a simple means of enriching flat surfaces in wood to produce a general effect of carving, though very much easier to execute. It is of such a nature that after a few trials to enable one to manage the tool, good results may be produced from the start.

WOODCARVING

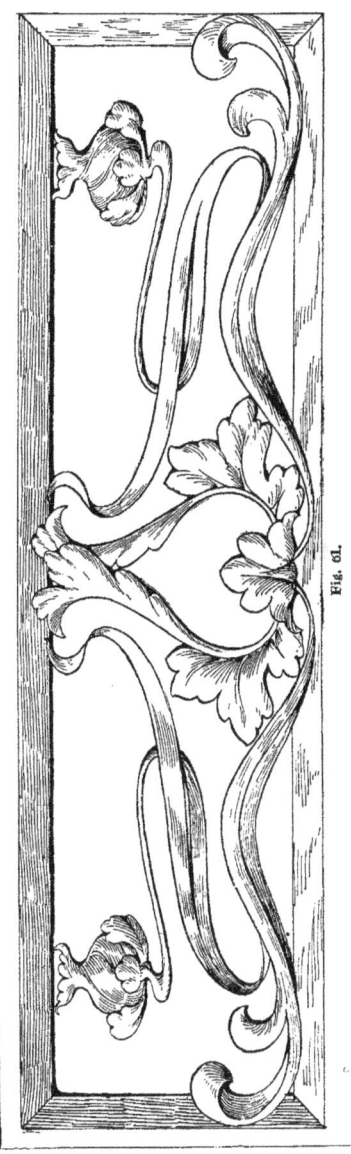

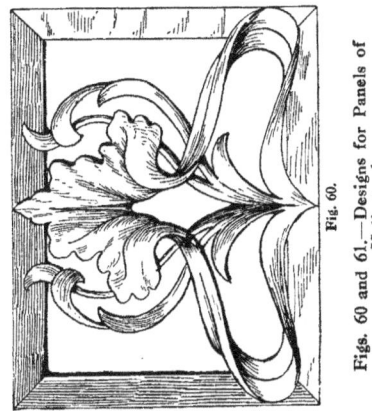

Figs. 60 and 61.—Designs for Panels of Hall-stand

have the design clearly drawn out on its surface, and needs to be rigidly fixed during the working. A small board can, of course, be conveniently held in the vice, or cramps may be used; but whatever method is adopted, the work must be rendered perfectly immovable, and in such a position, if possible, that it may be got at from all sides.

Figs. 55, 56 and 57 show the three stages in the production of the ordinary variety of incised work, each of which can be adopted as a complete method, though the third is the most effective.

Before beginning on the actual work, it is wise to practise a few strokes on a waste piece of the same wood that is to be incised so as to be able to gauge the amount of pressure necessary and obtain a little facility in the use of the tool. A deep cut is not necessary, and will make it difficult to obtain uniformity in the line; a shallow cut that is continuous throughout is what should be striven for. After all the outlines have been gone over in this way, veins and inner lines being delineated in thinner strokes, the next stage in the work is to cut away the ground with the gouge right up to the incised lines. With just ordinary care, this will be found quite a simple operation. In the case of very

Fig. 62.—Carved Overmantel

Fig. 63.—Corner Cabinet with Carved Doors

WOODCARVING

small spaces, if one does not possess a carving tool small enough, a makeshift may be made by rubbing a stout knitting needle flat at one end on a stone, then finishing off on an oilstone. Such a tool set in a handle will be found extremely useful for very small work; but the greater part will be done with the gouges.

While it is not essential to obtain an absolutely smooth ground, it should be of regular depth throughout; a few gouge markings, however, even in the case of work that is not to be stamped, will be found rather to improve the appearance, contrasting with the smooth raised portions. When the ground has been gone over as described, the design will, of course, stand out in relief. If it is desired to "matt" the ground, the stamp is next brought into use, the end being stamped in rows round the pattern, close up to it, until the markings meet in the middle of the spaces. Naturally this operation will, of course, lower the ground still

Fig. 64.—Design for One Panel of Corner Cabinet

further and impart a greater appearance of relief, while affording striking contrast.

Fig. 58 is an example of a piece of furniture to which this class of decoration has been applied.

to any piece of furniture previously designed for the purpose, it may be welcome to the handicraftsman, who will, of course, understand that neither the lines of construction nor the identical ornament depicted need be slavishly

Fig. 65.—Design for Second Panel of Corner Cabinet

EXAMPLES OF CARVED FURNITURE

Hall-stand Ornamented with Carving.—The half-tone reproduction (Fig. 59) shows a well-designed hall-stand with carved panels. Because of its unlikeness

followed. The sticks, etc., pass through a well, their lower ends being received by a metal tray which drops flush into the bottom shelf. The panels should be carved to some simple designs, those shown (see Figs. 60 and 61) being very suitable and, if thought desirable, the small ones may form the fronts of drawers, which will contain gloves, brushes, etc.

Carved Overmantel.—Fig. 62 shows an overmantel that, although plain, is yet pleasing in effect, and will harmonise with most schemes of modern house decoration. The framing is square without mouldings, except the moulded caps to the stiles. It is rebated for the panels and the mirror. The mirror is 30 in. by 21 in., bevelled 1 in. The two upright panels are 21 in. by 8 in. by ½ in.; and the top panel 48 in. by 6 in. by ½ in. The framing is of 3-in. by 1-in. stuff, with 2-in. by 1-in. muntins. The base is of 4½-in. by 1-in. stuff, quite plain and square. There is no shelf, the only elaboration is in the carving of the panels, and even this is as plain as possible. The carving is flat and simple in character, and the groundwork is unpunched.

Corner Cabinet with Carved Doors. —The carved ornament of the cabinet shown by Fig. 63 is based on a style that had its vogue about three centuries ago. The majority of readers will probably be pleased with the quaint effect which its employment and the general lines of the cabinet have produced. Half-scale drawings of the carved panels, which measure 10 in. square, are shown by Figs. 64 and 65. Grotesque animals have long been a favourite with the wood carver.

KNIFE CARVING

All the essential tools and appliances for knife-carving are a suitable knife and a stone for keeping it in good order, no special work bench being necessary. The curved form of knife shown by Fig. 66 will be found the most generally useful. With regard to the material to use, any close-grained stuff is suitable, that is, a wood that will not easily split. A beginner should preferably select a wood that is not too hard, pear being an excellent variety, it having the advantage that it is soft, and therefore easy to work.

The Swiss peasant carvers are the most facile wielders of the knife, as most of their carving displays much character and extreme skill of execution. One of the knife-carved articles that originated from this source is the wooden nut-crackers in the form of a bear, shown by Fig. 67, carved in walnut. The article stands by itself and forms, in addition to its useful qualities, an interesting ornament.

A more modern design for nut-crackers that works on the same principle is shown by Fig. 68. These are intended to be used in connection with a nut-bowl shown by Fig. 69, which will be found to form a quaint and interesting table ornament. The front view of these crackers is shown by Fig. 70, though, if it is intended to employ them in connection with the bowl, it will be necessary to bring the feet together, as in Fig. 69, and insert two short dowels for standing in position on the raised edge of the bowl.

In starting to carve such a subject as this, a full-size drawing of both front and side views should be made, afterwards proceeding to plane up a piece of wood in width and breadth sufficient to take the design. The general outline of the front view should be set out on the wood, as shown by Fig. 71. Then saw round the out-lines with a fret-saw which will result in a block of wood shaped as shown by Fig. 72, the first stage in the actual carving being to form the general shape, as seen from the side, and indicated by the dotted lines. The general shape having thus been obtained, it will be found a comparatively straightforward operation to proceed to the working up of the forms by sinking parts here and there to throw others into relief, etc. Those workers who may prefer to execute the work without the aid of a saw must strive for a good general shape first, without concentrating their attention on details, going at the work boldly at the start, removing as large chips as one can safely do rather than to chip off small fragments, as a bolder effect is thus obtained. Fig. 73 gives some idea of the general form to aim for in a very early stage of the carving, before proceeding to the details, care being taken at this stage not to cut away too much of the wood, so as to have plenty for finishing off. The hole A into which the movable jaw is

Fig. 67.—Swiss Nut-crackers, Knife-carved

Fig. 70.—Front Elevation of Crackers

Fig. 69.—Carved Bowl with Nut-crackers

Fig. 71.—Outline Set Out on Wood

Fig. 66.—Knives for Carving

Fig. 68.—Nut-crackers for Bowl

WOODCARVING

inserted is pierced straight through, the inside being smoothed with glasspaper. Even in the early stages of the work a beginner should pay particular attention should be kept sharp by frequent recourse to the oilstone. Finally, all finishing should be done with the knife alone, without the aid of files or glasspaper,

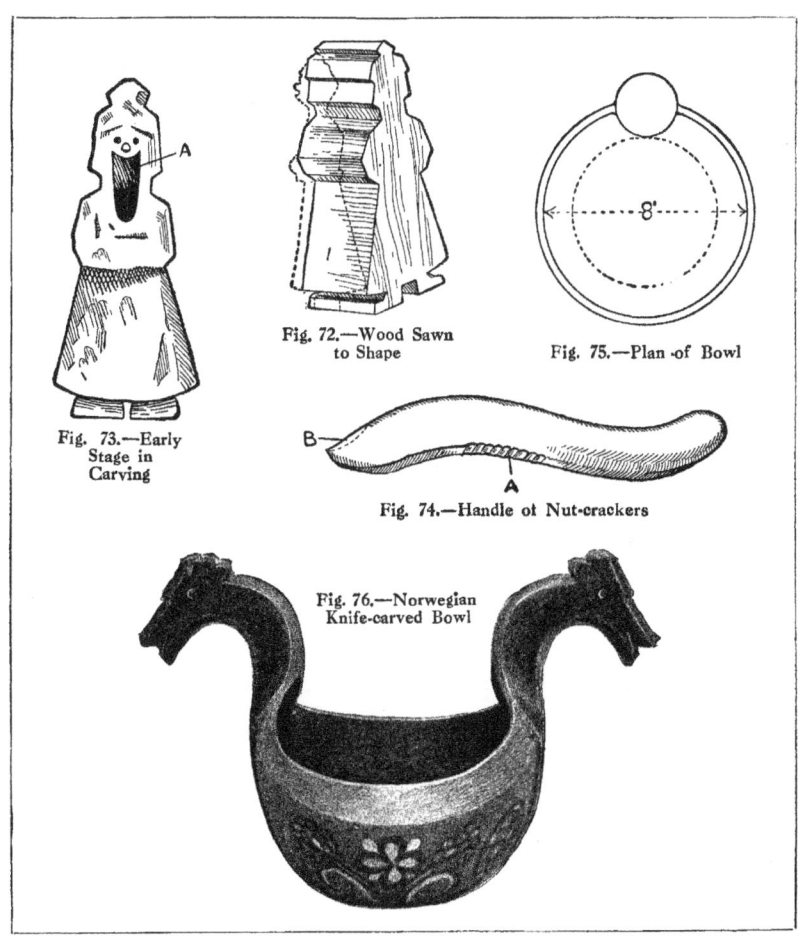

Fig. 72.—Wood Sawn to Shape

Fig. 75.—Plan of Bowl

Fig. 73.—Early Stage in Carving

Fig. 74.—Handle of Nut-crackers

Fig. 76.—Norwegian Knife-carved Bowl

to keep the work clean—that is, clean cut —without any appearance of raggedness, which is rather difficult to eliminate in the afterwork. To this end the knife which are apt to produce a rounded uninteresting surface.

The handle of the crackers is shown by Fig. 74. The shape shown should be accurately sawn out, and the small amount of carving of the jaw neatly executed to coincide with the upper part. The series of cuts, shown by A, are intended to form a surface for gripping the nuts. Also the hollowed-out part at B is to serve the same purpose. The handle portion should be nicely rounded off so as to be comfortable to hold, then it is slipped through the slot in its correct position, and drilled almost through, the handle being then removed and the hole in this slightly enlarged, so that a wooden peg, when slipped through, while fitting tightly into the other holes, will allow the handle to move easily.

Referring again to the bowl shown by Fig. 69, a suitable size for this would be 8 in. in diameter, the plan being given by Fig. 75. As the raised portion, where the figure is stood, will prevent the bowl being wholly turned in a lathe, the depression is hollowed by carving, though if a worker possesses a lathe it will be found of great assistance to turn out the wood up to the dotted line, then removing the rest with a gouge. This bowl, to present a good appearance, should be nicely smoothed up. making it of regular thickness as far as possible throughout.

Fig. 76, the original of which is in the South Kensington Museum, shows an old Norwegian bowl carved wholly in one piece of wood, which imparts an excellent suggestion for a similar treatment on more modern lines for a nut-bowl of quaint form.

Fretcutting and Pyrography

FRETCUTTING

FRETCUTTING is the practice of producing open woodwork in ornamental patterns.

The tools necessary for its execution by hand are comparatively few, the principal one, for light work, being a light iron frame with saw-blade. For heavier work the key-hole saw or bow saw are used. A 14-in. saw-frame (iron) is a suitable size. Tension may be secured in two ways—by the top clamp or by a screw in the handle operated by a turn of the wrist after the saw is threaded up. A suitable cutting-board and cramp are also necessary. A wood cutting-board with a V-shaped opening will be found quite adequate. Metal cutting-tables are liable to injure saw blades. For boring holes in the wood an archimedean drill is required. A bradawl or other pointed instrument should not be used as it is likely to split the wood. The best kind of drill stock is that which has a spring in the handle because it assists in the withdrawal of the bit and prevents side-jerking, a common cause of broken drill bits. A small screwdriver hammer. small brads or nails, a tube of liquid glue, a dozen or more saws. glasspaper, and the outfit is complete.

Saw-blades can be had at extremely low prices; but if the worker is desirous of turning out really good work, a good saw-blade is absolutely necessary. For turning sharp corners a medium blade with sharp, well-defined teeth is recommended. Saw-blades having short, closely-set teeth, are much too slow for general work. Those saws with rounded backs, which enable corners to be turned without leaving behind them any visible trace, are to be recommended.

To begin the actual work the design is pasted on the wood, and it is necessary to note that the grain must run lengthwise of the pattern, not across it. The paste must be applied thinly and evenly on the design (not on the wood), and the design deftly laid on the wood, the pattern being smoothed down with the palm of the hand or a soft rag so as to exclude all air and force out wrinkles. A paste made of starch boiled to a thick jelly, in which a small piece of gum arabic has been dissolved, is the best adhesive. It adheres to the wood firmly, but can be removed easily by the finest glasspaper. A few drops of oil of cloves added to the paste will preserve it.

The holes are drilled in the waste portions of the design—if possible opposite some projecting point, and the saw threaded up. The work is then firmly held down to the cutting-table with the left hand, and the fingers spreading over the work at the back of the saw. The cutting is then proceeded with, the hand-frame being held perfectly upright with a firm grip, so as to completely control its movements. Use a steady, regular stroke, feeding the work gradually to the saw, otherwise the edges of the fret will be irregular. Some workers move both the saw-frame and the wood; but to the beginner this is a dangerous operation, as

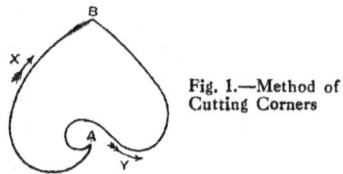

Fig. 1.—Method of Cutting Corners

it requires skill, only acquired by practice, to perform the double action perfectly. The worker quickly learns to keep the saw upright, and the left hand soon accustoms itself to holding down and feeding the work to the saw. If the worker possesses a treadle fretsaw, he has the advantage of having both hands free to guide the work, and the saw is always in an upright position, consequently there is only the guiding of the wood to the saw with which he has to contend. One important point is that in all cases the saw teeth must be placed downwards, otherwise the upward stroke brings the dust up through the saw line, and if the pattern is pasted to the wood, it raises it, and, naturally, the effect of this deters the most experienced cutters from following the line of the pattern.

There is no doubt that the beginner's first difficulty lies in the turning of corners accurately. There are two methods given here which will help. Suppose that in cutting a hole the saw begins at A (Fig. 1) and cuts to the corner B, by way of the

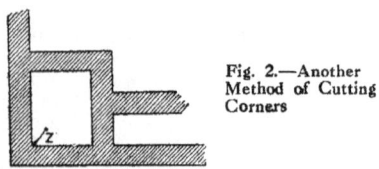

Fig. 2.—Another Method of Cutting Corners

arrow X. The saw may then be drawn back, beginning again at A sawing to B in the direction indicated by the arrow Y. Another method, and a much quicker one, is when the saw reaches the corner Z (Fig. 2), to withdraw it a little and cut its own width in the waste portion towards the line. The small hole thus formed allows the saw to be turned without any breakage, the corner being cut clean and perfect. The beginner, however, after a little practice, will be able to turn corners without the use of these two artifices; but, of course, much depends on the quality of the saw-blade.

The cutting of the outside of the design is usually left until all the inside of the design has been finished. The only exception to this is when most of the inside is to be cut away, as is the case with overlay borders. In these circumstances it is always advisable to cut the outside

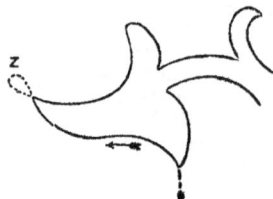

Fig. 3.—Method of Sawing Delicate Points

first, because if the inside were cut away it would leave the work weak across the grain, and it would require exceptionally gentle handling afterwards.

Outside the points are in some respects more difficult to turn than corners. However, the beginner may easily overcome the difficulty by making a round turn in the waste wood opposite, and, keeping well on the outside of the line, proceed to cut again. This is shown in Fig. 3 by the dotted line Z. Long, tapering points require care in cutting, otherwise they are liable to snap off. To do this successfully the work must be drawn to the corner of the V-slot in the table, and the wood pressed well down and fed up only as little as possible.

When the work has been cut out it is ready for finishing off. If there are slots and tenons for the fixing of a shelf or support these should be measured previously, as it is desirable to have a perfect fit without relying too much on nails and glue. Tenons might be made a shade longer, and taken off afterwards with a small plane or chisel.

The outside edges of shelves and other work having a continuous straight cut are often left uneven, and if these cannot be altered or made correct by using the saw they are best left alone. A small plane might be sometimes used with advantage ; but the worker is not advised to use metal templates which are either screwed or fixed with pin-points to the wood. The saw, when travelling along the side of a template, is liable to be pushed out of truth, thus sawing out of the vertical, and its edge is either dulled or broken by constant friction. A better method in place of templates is to draw a sharp knife-blade along the line, making a groove for the saw to run in. These methods, however, are never used by those experienced in fretcutting.

The glasspapering must be done thoroughly on both sides of the work, whether it is to be seen or not. The swarf or roughness round the frets is first removed, and then the design, if it has been pasted on. Water should not be used, as it warps the wood ; glasspapering is the only effective method to be employed. At this stage the worker will probably see his work much clearer, and any small diversions from the line of the pattern will be easily noticed, and in all probability he will attempt to remedy this with files. Such an attempt will most likely result in making it worse, because files are not adaptable to woodwork, especially when they are used across the end grain of delicate frets. Strips of glasspaper glued on shaped pieces of thin wood are more suitable, but not to be altogether recommended.

Straight sawing requires practice, and if the beginner has mastered the earlier stages of sawing straight lines and curves it should not be difficult for him to turn out fair work by his first attempts.

So far it has been assumed that the fret has been of a plain character, such as a bracket, in which case the shelf and support would, of course, require to be fixed.

If nails are used in any piece of fretted work it should be remembered that all hammering must be reduced to a minimum. Holes should be drilled with a fine bit in the back of the work, and the nails gently driven through into the shelf or other portion which is desired to be fixed. All joints, except those intended to be taken apart for cleaning, should have a touch of glue given them as an extra security. Screws also are more serviceable than nails, and have the advantage of making the work more superior, besides allowing for the work to be taken to pieces when required. Clock cases should invariably be screwed, so as to allow for the regulating or repairing of the timepiece. A wooden vice is a handy tool for assisting the worker to fit up his work, because all parts may be securely held in position while being nailed or screwed.

Overlays, such as those which form rebates for photo frames, mirrors, etc., should be cut from woods not more than $\frac{1}{16}$ in. thick, otherwise a heavy and clumsy appearance is given to the article. These thin woods should always be cut between two waste pieces and nailed together with fine nails, the design being pasted on the uppermost piece. Any holes which are to be pierced should be drilled with a sharp bit, using only sufficient pressure to force it through the wood. The outside is then sawn with a No. 1 saw-blade, and the inside, which is secured with the nails, is sawn last.

If the overlay is an ornament with interior fretting, this should be cut first, and the outside left until the last. Afterwards it should have the swarf cleaned away from the bottom edges with No. 1 glasspaper, and without further attempting to clean it, it should be glued into position under pressure.

PYROGRAPHY

Pyrography or poker-work is a method of decorating wood by charring or carbonising the surface by means of hot tools.

The process is one that is absolutely permanent, and extremely useful for the decoration of small articles in wood. It has the advantage of not necessitating the manual labour required for carving

Fig. 4.—Shield Design for Panel

and similar processes. Poker-work can be greatly improved by the addition of wood stains that may be applied with a brush. Perhaps one of the chief characteristics which contribute to the effect of the work is the softness of line resulting, for the poker point not only makes a black line where it touches the wood, but darkens it slightly on each side. The line forms an effective definition to stained surfaces, and prevents the stain from spreading.

The outfit necessary for the work consists of a hollow metal point, attached by a screw to a cork handle, through the middle of which runs a metal tube, communicating at one end with the interior of the point, and at the other with a length of rubber piping, leading to one of the two openings in the cork of a glass bottle containing benzoline. Another length of tube goes from the second of these holes to a pair of hand bellows fitted with a rubber reservoir. A small spirit lamp is also provided.

Some outfits are constructed to dispense with the spirit lamp, by means of an arrangement to burn the benzoline gas, and others have the liquid contained in a metal receiver in the tubing, with an appliance of the same kind fitted to it; but these are not recommended. It is convenient to have one or two extra points which cost about seven shillings each.

The method of working the poker is as follows : When the point has been heated in the flame of the lamp for a few moments, and the bellows kept in action, the vapour of the benzoline is forced through the tube into the hollow in its interior, and a glowing heat is thus maintained, when the design can be burnt into the wood as easily as drawing it with a pencil.

The best woods for poker-work are holly, sycamore, and pure white chestnut. If desired, made-up articles, such as photograph frames, boxes, mirrors, chessboards, brushes, panels, letter and newspaper racks, trays, tables, etc., can be obtained with patterns ready traced on them. On no account should wood that has been previously polished or varnished be used.

The illustrations (Figs. 4 to 9) show the very wide range of effect which it is possible

Fig. 5.—Tree Design for Panel

to produce by burning an outline to the design and afterwards filling in certain parts with stain.

Fig. 4 shows a shield design for exhibiting the owner's monogram or initials on

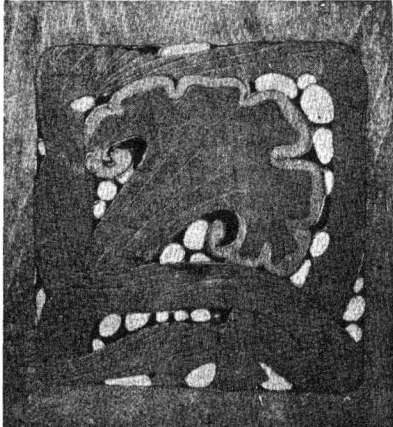

Fig. 6.—Panel Design with Strong Contrasts

a chest-front or top. It has the recommendation of being simple but effective; the background in the original was stained a light green, the shield in pale mauve, and the leaves scorched a brownish black by means of a blowpipe, which will be referred to later. This scheme is thoroughly harmonious; care must be exercised to introduce only those colours which harmonise with the velvety brown of the scorched wood. The tree design (Fig. 5) is intensely rich in effect, the foliage being burnt a jet black, and the ground colour a dark green. The ribbon, which greatly assists the decorative composition, is left the natural colour of the wood, a straw colour. Fig. 6 is somewhat more complex in design, but shows well the capability of the process for producing strong portions of light.

Large surfaces of jet black may be produced in the following manner: Obtain two blowpipes, one with a nipple and one from which the nipple has been removed. Connect the one without the nipple to a gas supply by means of an indiarubber tube, which will give, when lit, a very small gas-flame. The other blowpipe is held in the left hand, the small flame being directed on the work by means of a blast of air from the mouth. The small tongue of flame will be found manageable enough to work in the smallest surfaces as well as the large ones, and will produce a rich velvety black, which cannot be obtained really satisfactorily by means of the poker point alone.

The stains for filling in the design may be the ordinary water-colour ones, although for bright effects aniline dyes are better, taking care only to select those of known permanence. Ready-made greens and violets usually are not; but many colours are. Transparent oil colours thinned out with turpentine may also be used, as long as they are used thinly, and do not obliterate the poker outline.

The design (Fig. 7) is stained all over a deep brown, with the exception of the shield, which is dark green, and the eyes of the dolphins, which are white. The stork design (Fig. 8) would make an interesting cabinet detail.

For the production of a panel such as that shown by Fig 9, the work should be commenced by drawing a careful outline of the design on the panel, taking great

Fig. 7.—Another Design with Strong Contrasts

pains to get the main forms correct and the essential details; but not necessarily adding all the small shading lines such as those of the hair and the tail feathers of the bird. Much of this by a fairly proficient worker can be put in direct. When the pencilling is satisfactory, start by putting the outline of the face and features in boldly, with the poker point, in a telling line that will readily assert itself. It is best to try the point first on a piece of spare wood, to see that it is working properly. The hand holding the mirror and lines of the hair are done in a similar manner, taking special pains in this latter to obtain an even effect, while thickening the line out in certain places to produce the effect of shading. The peacock is executed in finer lines throughout, the "eyes" of the tail feathers being put in before the lines of the feathers are indicated, and in working them, keep well outside the pencil lines so that the light portions are not lost when the lines behind are put in. Put in the neck and upper wing feathers dark, a flat point being the best for large surfaces.

This design is one that would colour admirably; a harmonious combination of peacock green, blue and red-brown is one that would look particularly well. The light parts can be left the natural colour of the wood, or toned down slightly with very pale warm brown tone should the white colour of the wood be too glaring and necessitate it.

Fig. 8.—Stork Design for Panel

Fig. 9.—Design for Panel for Mirror Frame

The Fixing of Metal Fittings

In very many cases the proper way of fitting brasswork and ironwork is obvious from the shape of the article. In this section attention will be directed to a few practical points which may not be apparent at first sight, but only a few of the fittings—those generally met with—will be mentioned, there being no room in it to treat of the many scores, even hundreds, of attachments shown in the cabinet brass-ware catalogues.

pilaster are level, the effect not being considered so good if half is sunk in the pilaster and half in the door stile; besides, time is saved in fitting. Having decided the position of the hinge as regards the distance from the top or the bottom of the door, place it on the edge of the door stile, and with a pointed steel marker mark each end. Close the hinge as in Fig. 3, set the point of the gauge to the bare thickness of the knuckle B (Fig. 3), and mark a

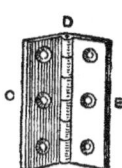

Fig. 1.—Butt Hinge (Open)

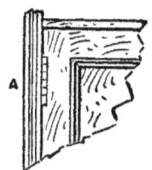

Fig. 2.—Part of Door and Pilaster

Fig. 3.—Butt Hinge (Closed)

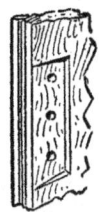

Fig. 4.—Method of Half-sinking Hinge

Hingeing a Small Door.—Brass butt hinges are generally employed for doors of furniture, the size varying according to the height of the door, say 1¾ in. long for a door 1 ft. 9 in. by 1 ft. 3 in. Fig. 1 shows a butt hinge open. When the outer face of the door stands inwards a little from the face of the pilaster or post A (see Fig. 2, which shows part of the left-hand corner of a door), the hinge is sunk its entire thickness when closed into the door stile, as shown in Fig. 2. This is the favourite way, even if the face of the door and the

gauge line on the face of the door stile. If the hinge is sunk too deep in the stile the door will be what is termed hinge-bound; that is it will not remain closed, but will spring open.

Next take another gauge. It is best to have two or more in use, so as not to disturb one when going about another part of the operation. From the side of the hinge C (Fig. 1) set the point of the gauge to the centre of the knuckle D, and mark on the edge of the door stile. Then cut away the wood for the hinge, and fix with screws. When all the hinges are fixed to the door or doors, extend the first gauge used to the extra distance that the pilaster A (Fig. 2) stands forward from the face of the door, and mark a line on the inner edge of the pilaster. This gives the limit inwards of the hinge. It is common simply to fix with screws, but for good work a tapering recess, as in Fig. 4, is made in the post for the back part of the hinge. This recess prevents the door from dropping by taking the weight of the door off the screws.

Fitting Hinges to Box.—The same kind of hinge is used as for the door, but the plate C (Fig. 1) is sunk into the back of the box, and the plate E into the lid (*see* Fig. 5). The gauge is set from the side of the hinge C (Fig. 1) to the centre of the knuckle D, and marked on the back of the box and of the lid. A gauge is set to bare

Fig. 5.—Butt Hinge Fixed to Box

half thickness of the folded hinge, as in Fig. 3, and the back edge of the lid marked. The hinges on the lid may be first fixed with screws, and then by resting them on the back of the box the position of the flanges may be marked with the steel marker.

Some boxes with moulded-edge lids project at the back as well as at the ends and front. In such a case the portion of the hinge in the lid must be taperingly sunk as for the door (*see* Fig. 4), and the thickness of the hinge when closed into the back of the box, as for the door in Fig. 2.

Fitting a Drawer Lock.—With a set-square draw a vertical pencil line at half the length of the drawer front, this giving the position of the keyhole. Set the marking gauge from the plate A (Fig. 6) to the centre of the pin B in the keyhole, and press the gauge point on the pencil line. Next, with a small centre-bit, bore a hole right through the drawer front, and cut the lower part C so as to allow the key to be pushed through the drawer front. If a brass escutcheon is to surround the key, this must be considered when pro-

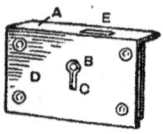

Fig. 6.—Drawer Lock

ceeding as above. Pass the key through the hole and into the lock, held into position reverse to Fig. 6, and mark the portion of the lock containing the mechanism. Next sink the top plate A, and afterwards the back plate D. When the lock is finally fixed with screws, and the key works smoothly in the escutcheon and the lock, place the drawer in the job and push it home. The mortise to receive the bolt E may now be made. To do this, turn the bolt up—the drawer withdrawn—and smear it with the discoloured oil from the oilstone. Sink the bolt, push the drawer home, turn up the bolt with pressure on the key, when a black impression on the underside of the rail above the drawer front will be seen. In the case of shallow drawers, say about 3 in. deep, it is difficult to make the mortise with ordinary chisels, so a special tool can be bought with an L-shaped end to do the job.

Fitting a Cupboard Lock.—This is somewhat the same as fitting a drawer lock, only upright instead of horizontal, the lock bolt shooting into the pilaster. But an important difference is to be considered; that is, what is termed the measurement " to pin." This means that the lock must be of such a size that the pin in the keyhole will be central with the door stile. For example, most door handles have a keyhole cut in the plate, and presuming the door stile to be 1½ in. wide, the lock would have to measure ¾ in. " to pin "

Fig. 7.—Intersecting Door Stiles with Rebate

to bring the handle in the middle. Also in case of double doors, there are two ways of the stiles meeting, one with a rebate as

THE FIXING OF METAL FITTINGS

in Fig. 7, and the other flush as in Fig. 8. In the former the "to pin" would measure from the quirk A (Fig. 7), while the latter

Fig. 8.—Door Stiles without Rebate

would have to include the bead B (Fig. 8). In Fig. 7 the left-hand door is prevented from opening by the rebate ; but in Fig. 8 each door can be opened independently of the other when the lock is not in use. A flush bolt is fixed on the left-hand door to secure it.

In ordering door locks, both joiners' and cabinetmakers', the "hand" must generally be stated; that is, whether they are intended for doors that bolt to the left or the right, looking at them from the outside. If the "hand" is not stated, there is the risk that when the locks are received, it will be found that the bevels (if any) of the bolts face the wrong direction. The rule for determining the "hand" is simple. In which direction must the bolt shoot, regarding the door from outside ? To the left ? Then the lock is "left-handed." To the right ? Then "right-handed."

Fixing a Bullet Catch.—If a door does not need a lock, it is usual to fit a spring-bullet catch, as shown by Fig. 9, instead of the old-fashioned turn-button. When the door is pushed to, the bullet A recedes like a latch lock until it springs back into a hole in the striking plate, which is fixed to a pilaster. The striking plate prevents the bullet from bruising the wood as the door is pushed to and pulled out. In fixing, a centre-bit hole is bored in the edge of the door stile to receive the spring

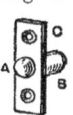

Fig. 9.—Bullet Catch

casing B (Fig. 9), and the plate c is sunk level with the door edge. To get the true position of the striking plate, make a line central with the plate c and across, each cutting through the bullet, and transfer to the pilaster. Place the striking plate with the hole over the crossing lines, and then mark the position with a steel pointer. Possibly some portion will project beyond the face of the pilaster ; this must be cut off and filed to a slight bevelled edge, so that the bullet will slide easily.

Flush Bolt for Double Doors.—This is fixed in the left-hand door when there is no rebate, as in Fig. 8. Long doors, such as in bookcases, require one at the top and another at the bottom. For small doors, such as in cabinets or sideboards, one is sufficient, being fixed at the top, as in Fig. 10 ; or the reverse way at the bottom. In fitting, the wood is cut away to receive the end plate A, and then the groove for the mechanism behind the plate B. The latter will then rest on the edge of the door, and its position can be marked with a steel marker. A smear of discoloured oil, from the oilstone, put on the end of the bolt c will mark the position of the hole. The latter may be bored with a twist-bit. If there is no room for a brace to turn, fit a crosspiece of wood to the bit, and use as a gimlet or auger. In cheap work to save the trouble of flush fitting, bolts can be bought for simply fixing with screws to the back of the door stiles.

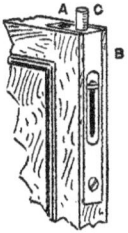

Fig. 10.—Flush Bolt in Door

Fitting Toilet-glass Movements.—With large plate-glass mirrors the positions of these are most important, as should they be fixed too low, the glass will be top heavy and have a tendency to turn over. If fixed too high, the weight tends to drag the glass to a vertical position, thus causing a heavy strain on the movement. Hence to get a really satisfactory balance, the mirror should be temporarily fitted up with the pediment, glass, and back all complete. Experimental screws may be fixed ½ in. above the centre, and the balance tested. To avoid damaging the sides of the frame with the screws, stick with thin glue a piece of brown paper on the sides of the glass frame, and over the paper, blocks of ¾-in. pine. These can be stripped off later by inserting a knife between the paper joint.

The movement shown in perspective in Fig. 11 is about the oldest, and is really the most dependable on account of the regulating thumbscrew. Note that the latter is at the bottom, as being less liable to fall off the ball centres (Fig. 12) when taking the mirror away from the supporting standards. To avoid fracturing the glass, it is safest to fit the movement to the frame before finally fixing the mirror; and to ensure a good fit, take a paper pattern of the side A (Fig. 11), and transfer it to the side of the frame. For the back plate B adjust the marking gauge to the width. When fixing the ball centre to the supporting standards, the relative positions of the faces of the frame and standards must be considered. Besides the foregoing movement, there are several on the market which do not require sinking into the wood, being simply fixed with screws, and having no thumbscrew, hold the mirror at the desired angle by friction. They cannot, however, be recommended to last any length of time.

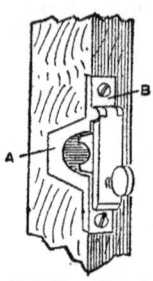

Fig. 11.—Hinged Glass Movement

Another kind needing no sinking into the wood is Dovey's patent. The perspective view A (Fig. 13) shows the left-hand plate fixed to the standard. Fig. 14 is an end elevation showing the plate A and the companion plate B. The latter is shown in perspective by Fig. 15. The stud centre C drops in the fork D (Fig. 13). The lower part of the plate E (Figs. 14 and 15) rests on the projecting flange F (Fig. 13), the latter taking all the weight of the frame and mirror; the stud C only restrains the mirror laterally. A slight push forwards or backwards adjusts the frame at any desired angle. If there is a weak point, it lies in the ease in which the centre studs might be accidentally jolted out of the forks D.

Fig. 12.—Ball Centre for Glass Movement

Fixing Rule-joint Stays.—These are so named on account of their resemblance to a folding two-foot rule. They are used for propping up a box or desk lid; also for supporting fall-down flaps in writing cabinets. The general form of stay (see Fig. 16) has plates at each end for fixing, which are at right angles to each other. The end A is fixed to the box lid or writing-flap, and B is fixed to the side of the box or writing cabinet. The stays are made in pairs measuring from centres 3 in. long when folded to about 8 in. long at $\frac{1}{2}$-in. intervals.

The first thing to decide is a suitable size for the job. A 3-in. is strong enough to hold up most lids, but the appearance must be considered. To avoid botching by haphazard fitting, first make a full-size drawing of the end of the article with the

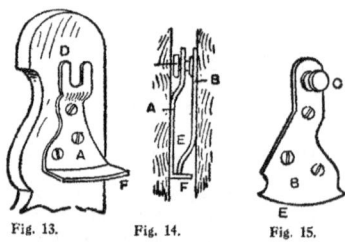

Figs. 13, 14 and 15.—Parts of Glass Movement

lid open as in Fig. 17 (see the scale below it). Draw a line D about 2 in. from the top edge, and from this a line E representing the proposed stay. On measuring, it is found to be about 13 in. long. Hence the nearest stock size of stay is a 6-in. one. To avoid confusion erase lines D and E (Fig. 17), open the stay to full length, and divide the centres A and B (Fig. 16) into eight parts. Take five and describe the radius from the box hinge F (Fig. 18), which is enlarged to double the scale of Fig. 17 for clearness; (see the scale of inches) producing the arc G. Note that the plate A travels along this line until it lies at rest at H. With the stay in position as in Fig. 18, mark the centre C. Next with radius C to B produce arc J.

THE FIXING OF METAL FITTINGS

From the centre A with full length radius produce arc K, and where J and K intersect is the position for the side plate B. If necessary the stay may be reversed as at L. In the case of a box, if while fixing the stay the bottom of the box could be taken out, all that is then needed is to measure the distance of five parts from

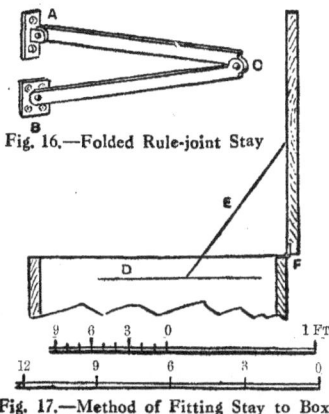

Fig. 16.—Folded Rule-joint Stay

Fig. 17.—Method of Fitting Stay to Box

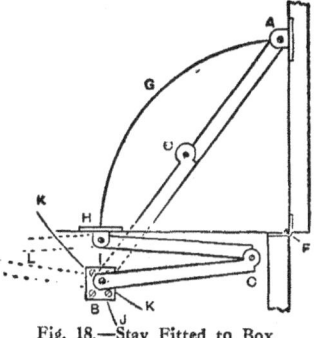

Fig. 18.—Stay Fitted to Box

the hinge F to A, and fix the latter plate to the box lid. Then close the lid, turn the box over, and place the stay in position as shown and fix the side plate B.

Fixing Fall-down Flap Stay.—If Figs. 17 and 18 are turned on their sides they illustrate a writing cabinet flap in principle. Always remember that the centre of the hinge F is the starting point; also that the nearer the end of the stay A to the front edge of the flap when open, the greater the support. However, the rough-and-ready method as described had better not be adopted for a flap, as the slight moving of the plate B to the right or left would result in the flap not being exactly level when open.

Strap Hinge for Writing-desk.—Strap hinges are used where the surface for fixing is limited, the remaining space being covered with leather or cloth; for example, in writing-desks and card tables. Fig. 19 is the simplest form of hinge, and is fixed to the edges of box and lid parts as at A and B (Fig. 20). The dotted lines show the lid folded down when in use for writing. Another pattern of strap hinge is shown in Fig. 21, the plate near the knuckle being extended. This is practical owing to the show-wood strips C on the writing falls. D indicates the leather which passes over the inner sides of the desk, and being pasted to the latter forms a hinge to the two falls D. By using the simple hinge, as in Fig. 19, the marginal strips C (Fig. 21) can be discarded, and the whole surface can be covered with leather, etc. When fixing the hinges, place the two parts of the desk open as in Fig. 20. Next put the hinges in the correct position, mark round them with a steel pointer, and sink to the required depth, taking care not to sink the plates too deep, or the desk will be hinge-bound.

Back-flap Hinge for Table.—Fig. 22 is a perspective view of a back-flap hinge as used for kitchen tables with fall-down leaves. The holes for the screws are countersunk in the opposite side to an ordinary butt hinge (see the end section, Fig. 23), and the flanges are not sunk into the top or leaves for the reason that the centre A (Fig. 23) of the knuckle must be exactly level with the under-faces of the top and the leaves, thus preventing a gap between the latter when in the position as in Fig. 23. When fixing the hinges cut away the wood neatly to receive the knuckles, and with the top and leaves in alignment put in the screws.

Rule Joint.—While in common work the joint between a flap and a table-top or between a hinged flap and a fixed rail is often a simple butt joint, in better work it is customary to employ what is known

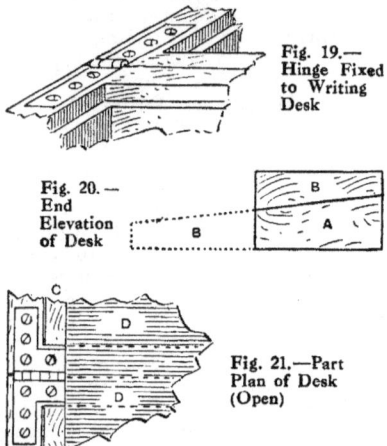

Fig. 19.—Hinge Fixed to Writing Desk

Fig. 20.—End Elevation of Desk

Fig. 21.—Part Plan of Desk (Open)

as the rule joint, which resembles, but is not identical with, the joint in a folding rule. The rule joint has an excellent appearance and marked advantages when fitted to the flaps of tables, bureaux, etc., the hinges being invisible from the front in either the down or up position of the flap. When open, all that can be seen is the moulded edge of the table-top or fixed rail, and a part of the rebate formed on the flap. The hinge is much as usual, save that one flap is longer than the other, and the quality needs to be good.

A rule joint in cabinetwork is shown in the up and down positions by Fig. 24,

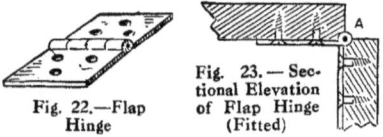

Fig. 22.—Flap Hinge

Fig. 23.—Sectional Elevation of Flap Hinge (Fitted)

A indicating the table-top or fixed rail, and B the hinged movable flap. Any difficulty there may be in understanding and setting out the work arises from doubt as to what is the proper centre from which are struck the arcs that define the moulded surfaces. Fig. 25 is a diagram of the joint. The dot and dash lines C C and D D indicate at their intersection E the centre of the hinge pin and also the centre from which the quarter-circle must be struck, C C being the joint line which determines the wall of the rebate, and D D representing the inner surface of the let-in hinge.

Fig. 26 shows the gauging of the work. Note that the flaps or flanges are of unequal length, and that the two or more hinges used in making a joint must be identical in thickness and position of centre pin. The rebate and convex and concave mouldings are formed with rebate plane and pair of hollows and rounds; more easily and accurately with a pair of special planes, which only a professional would ever think of buying; or with a universal plane, etc., the arcs having first been scratched on the sides—from templates if it is found awkward to use dividers; but there will be no difficulty in using these instruments on the fixed part, and the same will apply to the other part if the work is left a trifle full, as suggested at G (Fig. 26), and the rule joint set out before shooting the edge true.

In setting out the fixed part, lines should be squared across top, under-side, and side edges. Then the thickness line of the hinge should be added on each edge, thus giving the centre for the arc. The radius may be the thickness of the stuff minus two-and-a-half to three times the thickness of the hinge flange, but is variable. The line on the underneath side will give the centre of the recesses for the knuckles of the hinges, which recesses may be cut with chisel and small gouge. Let in for the hinge flanges on the fixed part, cramp up the table flap into position, square across, complete the letting-in, and attach the hinges with reasonably short but well-fitting screws accurately inserted, taking great care that the pins are in exact alignment with the squared line on the underside of the work. To facilitate the alignment, the hinges should have been marked with a fine line indicating their pin centres.

THE FIXING OF METAL FITTINGS

In a special pattern of rule-joint hinge obtainable, the longer flange is bent to avoid recessing the quarter-cylinder portion of the fixed part, and its employment reduces any tendency for the joint to show open when the flap is down. This hinge is shown by Fig. 27, the bent part being indicated by the letter A. The sweet working of the rule joint is simply a question of very careful measurements and fitting.

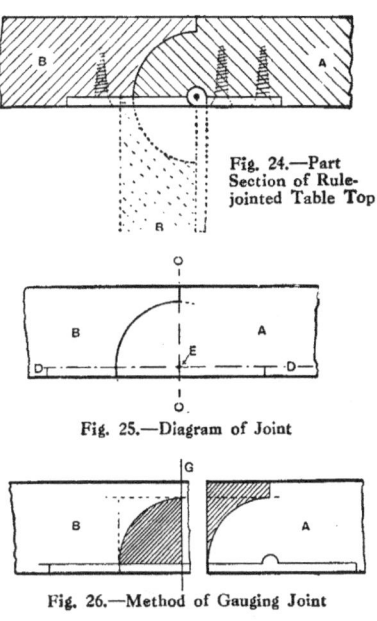

Fig. 24.—Part Section of Rule-jointed Table Top

Fig. 25.—Diagram of Joint

Fig. 26.—Method of Gauging Joint

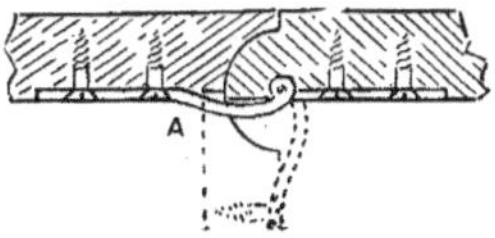

Fig. 27.—Section of Improved Hinge (Fitted)

Stopped Butt Hinge for Box.—This is for keeping a box lid open while the contents are under examination. Fig. 28 is a perspective view of a cheap form of hinge where the flanges are simply doubled back, meeting at A, thus preventing the lid from opening beyond the perpendicular.

The hinge, however, does not look so well when fitted, owing to the rounded edges, as the cast stop butt shown in Fig. 29, which is a sectional end view of the hinge when fitted to a box and lid. The method of fitting and fixing is the same as for an ordinary butt hinge.

Dolphin Hinge for Secretaire.—The dolphin hinge (Fig. 30) is generally used in secretaire bookcases and large chests of drawers. In these, what appears to be a drawer is a fall-down flap with a compartment fitted for writing purposes and materials. The bevelled ends A (Fig. 30) limit the movement of the hinge, and support the fall in a horizontal position for writing. Fig. 31 shows the fall as a drawer front with the hinge fitted to the latter and the side of the writing compartment. Fig. 32 is a sectional view showing the method of rebating the fall and the bottom of the sliding compartment, the hinge being indicated by dotted lines. When the fall is raised as in position B (Fig. 31) it engages with the latch movement, which prevents B from falling when being pulled out like a drawer. In fixing the hinges, the fall B (Fig. 32) should be laid perfectly level with the bottom C. With the hinge opened to full extent, place it as shown by dotted lines, taking care that the working centre of the hinge is exactly where the surfaces of B and C meet. Mark round the hinge with a steel pointer, and sink flush so that it will slide inside the outer ends of the bookcase or chest of drawers. The principle of the dolphin hinge is a very strong one, as the working strain comes on the sides of the screws instead of drawing them out as in butt hinges.

Fig. 28.—Stopped Butt Hinge

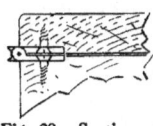

Fig. 29.—Section of Stop Butt Hinge (Fitted)

Quadrant for Writing Fall.—A quadrant with stop plate as shown in Fig. 33 can be had in various stock sizes. It is suitable for falls where the weight placed on them is not too great, and hinges as shown in Fig. 34 may be used. As a change from the sliding compartment,

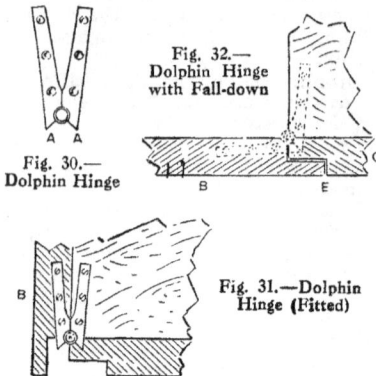

Fig. 30.—Dolphin Hinge

Fig. 32.—Dolphin Hinge with Fall-down

Fig. 31.—Dolphin Hinge (Fitted)

Fig. 34 is a part plan of a fixed one. By reference to Fig. 32, it will be seen that if the sliding system were pushed home with the fall B down, the latter could not be raised, as the edge E of the fall would catch against the fixed bearer of the bookcase on which C slides. To overcome this, note the hollow channel F (Fig. 35) provided for the radius of the fall G. Fig. 36 is a sectional elevation with the fall down and the quadrant in position. The plate H is fixed to the inside of the compartment C (Figs. 34 and 36). The end plate J of the quadrant is sunk flush with the end of the fall. Presuming that a suitable-size stock quadrant is bought, the next thing is to ascertain the diameter of the circle of which it is a part. To do this, place it on a piece of paper, and mark the outline with a fine pencil (see Fig. 37). Then mark three points A, B and C at equal distances apart. Set the pencil compasses from A to B, and from B describe the arcs D, E and F. Next from A draw arcs G and H. Repeat the same from C, making J and K. Draw the converging lines as shown, and where they meet is the centre of the circle of which the quadrant is a part. A full-size drawing of Fig. 36 should be made, and with the knuckle of the hinge K as centre, describe

the arc L, this representing the outer circumference of the quadrant. Place the latter to this line, and mark the position of the plate J on the end of the fall, and then that for the plate H resting against the stop on the end of the quadrant. It will be seen that the quadrant must exceed the quarter circle by the width of the plate H and stop M. Consequently when the fall is up, a hole will have to be made at N to receive the end of the quadrant.

Link-joint Hinges for Card Tables.—These are made in various forms to suit different kinds of tables; the principal feature in them is that there is no knuckle to stand up and interrupt the level surface of the table when opened out for playing. Fig. 38 is a plan of one form, of which Fig. 39 is a sectional side elevation showing the oblong link A with two centres. Fig. 40 is a perspective view showing it fitted. B indicates the show-wood ends of the top, and C the green baize playing surface.

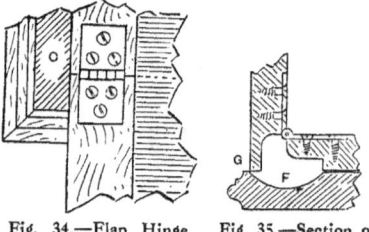

Fig. 34.—Flap Hinge Fitted to Writing Fall

Fig. 35.—Section of Flap Hinge (Fitted)

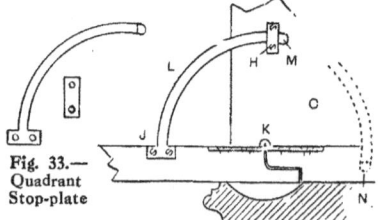

Fig. 33.—Quadrant Stop-plate

Fig. 36.—Quadrant Fitted to Secretaire

The same kind of hinge is also suitable for an envelope card table (see Fig. 41), which is a part plan. The construction of

THE FIXING OF METAL FITTINGS

the top does not lend itself to complete covering with baize owing to the hinges and the tapering corners of the leaves;

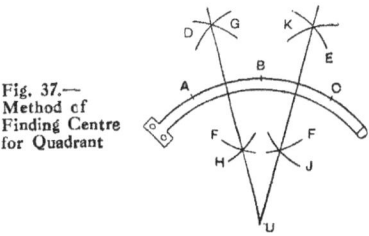

Fig. 37.—Method of Finding Centre for Quadrant

hence D is the polished surface and E the baize. When the leaves are closed, the hinges appear as in Fig. 42. Another pattern of hinge suitable for an envelope table is shown in plan by Fig. 43, the hinge showing the same as in Fig. 42, when the leaves are folded.

For a circular card table, which is half circular when the leaves are folded, the usual pattern of hinge is as shown in Fig. 44, F being the show-wood margin on top, G the green baize, and H the edges of the leaves. This pattern is also used for squared tables when open for playing, and

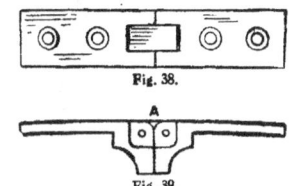

Fig. 38.

Fig. 39.

Figs. 38 and 39.—Plan and Elevation of Link-plate Hinge

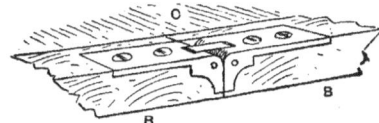

Fig. 40.—Link-plate Hinge Fitted to Table

oblong when closed, with the difference that the hinge flanges J are straight instead of curved as for the circular table.

In fitting Fig. 40 a gauge may be used for marking the width of the top plate; but for the sides the measurements and shape can be transferred to the table by the aid of paper templates and compasses, taking care to keep inside the lines when cutting away the wood. The latter instructions may be applied to all the hinges illustrated in Figs. 39 to 44.

Fitting Link-plate Locks.—Link-plate locks are used for the old-fashioned writing desks, or for boxes with lids. They are somewhat like a drawer lock, but with the addition of a link-plate (see Fig. 45, which shows a plate upside down). This is fixed to the underside of the lid, the links A dropping in holes B

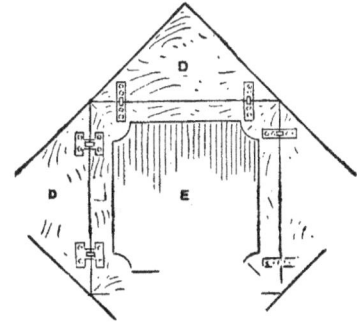

Fig. 41.—Part Plan of Envelope-type Card Table

(Fig. 46). The latter is fixed as described for a drawer, next the link-plate is placed in the lock, and the key turned as in locking. On the upper face of the plate two spikes (see Fig. 47) are provided; these are simply to assist in getting the plate exactly in the right position on the underside of the box lid. The latter is lowered (being hinged, of course) on to the spikes, and a tap with a hammer presses the spikes into the lid. The key is turned as for unlocking, and when the lid is lifted the plate comes with it. The position of the plate is then marked with the steel marker, and sunk flush with the underside of the box lid and fixed with screws.

Fig. 48 shows the same principle of lock,

but vertical. This pattern is used for sideboards with pedestals, or for cupboard doors or show-cases, when the doors lie

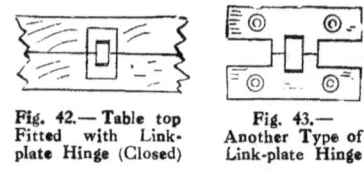

Fig. 42.— Table top Fitted with Link-plate Hinge (Closed)

Fig. 43.— Another Type of Link-plate Hinge

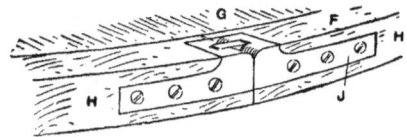

Fig. 44.—Curved Hinge Fitted to Round Table

on the edges of the carcase ends as in the sectional plan (Fig. 49). A is the door stile, on which is fixed the link-plate, and B the carcase end, in which is fitted the lock. Another pattern of lock used for the same purpose as Fig. 49 is shown in Fig. 50. This allows the keyhole to be on the face of the door. E is the link and F the link-plate, which is fixed on the ends of the cupboard. The central position required for the keyhole will determine the size of the lock. The fitting is practically the same as already described.

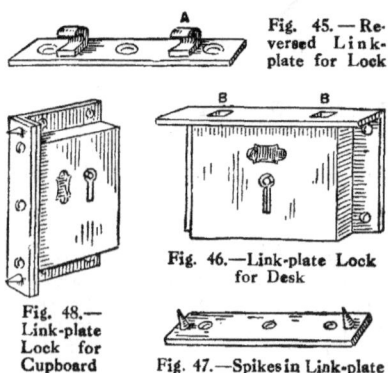

Fig. 45.—Reversed Link-plate for Lock

Fig. 46.—Link-plate Lock for Desk

Fig. 48.—Link-plate Lock for Cupboard

Fig. 47.—Spikes in Link-plate

Fitting a Wardrobe Centre Hinge.

—In large wardrobes the doors with full-length mirrors are so heavy that centre hinges as A (Fig. 51) are considered more satisfactory than large butt hinges. Also the doors are more easily handled when taken to pieces for removal. Fig. 51 is a part plan of, say, a wardrobe with three carcases and three doors. B is the left-hand door, C the centre one, D the left-hand end of the middle carcase, and E the right-hand end of the left-hand ditto. These parts rest on a plinth or base extending the whole length of the job. Above all is a movable cornice. A hinge plate A is fixed into the plinth and another in the under face of the cornice. The centre of the hinge fixed on the bottom of the door is dropped into a corresponding hole in the plinth, and the cornice is dropped over

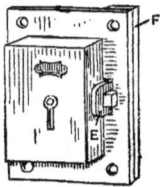

Fig 50.—Another Link-plate Lock for Cupboard

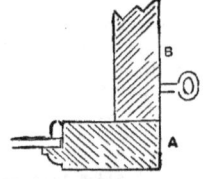

Fig. 49.—Detail showing Fitting of Link-plate Lock

the centre of the hinge fixed in the top of the door. Thus when the carcases are fixed to the plinth and the cornice the door is securely in position. Fig. 52 is a view of a hinge with a straight plate ; these are just as good as the angle-ended ones. Note the drop in the lower plate at F. This prevents the plates rubbing together.

The main point of consideration is the position of the centre G (Figs. 51 and 52). To find this, make a full-size sketch as Fig. 51, but without the hollow channel and the rounded edge of the door. In place of these draw a rebate $\frac{1}{4}$ in. deep in the end D (Fig. 51)—see part plan (Fig. 53) —and also extend the door into the rebate. From the point J project an angle of 45° or mitre ; next from the corner of the door K another one downwards at the same angle. Where the two intersect is

THE FIXING OF METAL FITTINGS

the position for the centre of the hinge G (Figs. 51 and 53). With G as centre draw an arc on the edge of the door, and another

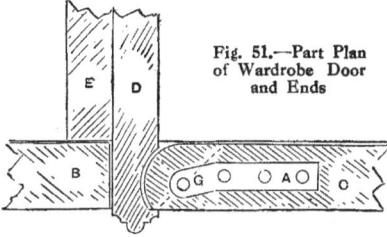

Fig. 51.—Part Plan of Wardrobe Door and Ends

arc giving ample clearance for the working of the door. To test these, get a piece of tracing paper, and draw the outline of the door; fix an ordinary pin at G, move the tracing paper, and see if it clears the channel. When this is found correct transfer to the door, and mark the position of the plate with the steel marker, and sink the plate flush. The same should be done to the opposite end of the door, the plinth, and the cornice. The door should open outwards until it stops at a right angle against the fillet of moulding. To prevent the door from accidentally crashing against the moulding, a chain or slotted elongated plate is fixed near to the top of the door, and to the under-face of the carcase top to limit the movement.

Skew Hinges.—Skew or rising butts are fixed on doors when some obstacle,

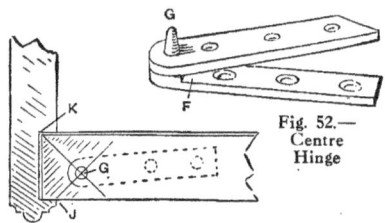

Fig. 53.—Method of Finding Centre of Hinge

such as a carpet, etc., lies in the path of opening; doors so fitted also close of themselves. The butt hinge is constructed with a spiral joint working on a centre pin,

as shown in Fig. 54, in which the hinge (a right-handed one) is shown on the edge of the door and casing, ready for letting in. The inside of the knuckle should stand out $\frac{1}{16}$ in. beyond the edge; otherwise the hinge is fixed in the ordinary way.

Procedure.—The usual procedure in finishing better-class woodwork is to fit all the metalwork previous to polishing. It is then removed, the article polished, and the metalwork refitted with new screws. A type of screw that lends itself to neat and rapid fitting is shown in Fig. 55. The insertion of these screws entails the use of a special type of screwdriver with

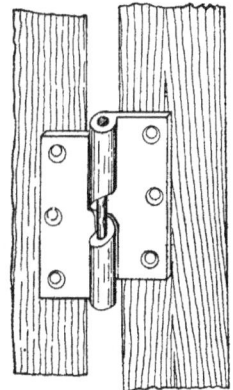

Fig. 54.—Method of Fitting Skew Hinges

an end of square section as shown in the figure. Both screw and driver were introduced in the spring of 1921.

Allowances in the Fit of Movable Parts.—Woodwork exposed to the weather sometimes requires rectification in order to make doors, fastenings, windows, etc., work properly. A door which fits close in the dry atmosphere of summer will be much too tight in winter. This is because the wood absorbs moisture and swells. Even indoors there are some variations of this kind. Drawers which slide easily in summer may be tight in winter or in rainy weather. An article near a fire-grate will be drier and more uniform all the year round than one in the same room but at some distance away. Therefore all doors and other working parts should fit correctly in damp weather, and open joints or slack fastenings be tolerated in dry weather.

Doors may become tight for another reason than that just mentioned. Woodwork in common with all structural work, settles and becomes slightly readjusted in the course of time. When first put together there are severe strains in some parts which exert a permanent force, not yielding slightly to the strain, and this makes it impossible for the joints to remain permanently as they are when the door is first put up.

This sagging or sinking of the door may also affect the position of the lock, which may have to be readjusted after a time if sufficient allowance is not made in the first place. Also, if the door swells or warps, the lock, though correct for height, may become too tight in the horizontal direction, so that even if the door is pressed

Fig. 55.—Improved Type of Screw and Screwdriver

sufficient to make any immediate change in the structure, but as time passes they have some effect, both on the material and on the joints. A hinged door may be screwed tightly at first, but it will sag more or less of its own weight in the course of time. This should always be remembered when a door is being hinged. If it is made merely an easy fit at the bottom, with little or no clearance, it will soon be scraping there and become unworkable. On the top edge it can never become tight, but will tend to open. Therefore no allowance is made there ; but at the bottom there must be ample allowance. In the vertical joints the door will tend to open on the hinged edge near the top, but will remain constant at the bottom hinge. In the lock joint of the door the tendency will be to remain constant near the bottom, and become closer and tighter near the top as the weight of the door strains it away from its attachment to the upper hinge. For this reason it is desirable to screw the upper hinge extra tight. Screws which are tight when first put in can often be tightened still more after they have been in place a few days. But it is not the hinges alone which are affected by the weight of the door and tightly screwed hinges will not prevent sagging. The door itself and the post to which it is hinged are always capable of tightly against its frame the catch will not quite enter. A slight amount of slackness here also should be allowed in fitting the lock, unless it is done in damp weather and the wood may be expected to shrink afterwards.

In the case of sliding parts, such as drawers and windows, a suitable lubricant applied to the sliding surface will make a great improvement, and sometimes result in quite satisfactory working where before they seemed hopelessly tight. Too much slackness in sliding parts causes them to jam, owing to the parts getting out of parallel unless operated very carefully. Therefore a moderately close fit, with lubricant if necessary, ensures the most perfect working.

If a drawer or window works tightly it should not be assumed that uniform reduction all over the sliding surface is wanted. It may be only a very small portion of the surface which is to blame due to the frame or the part which fits within it not being parallel. Measurement may disclose this, but as a rule a close examination will show where reduction is needed. If serious friction is occurring it always leaves perceptible marks on the surfaces in contact. The sense of touch as well as sight will tell an experienced workman a great deal, and by it he may discover where there is contact and

THE FIXING OF METAL FITTINGS

where slackness in parts which he cannot see, for where there is slackness it can generally be found by testing whether there is any play between the parts. The front of a drawer should be a close fit at top, bottom, and sides. This can be seen, but the closeness of fit throughout the length behind the front cannot be directly seen. When the drawer is pulled nearly out, it can be seen whether its back part fits the front of the opening, or the same thing can be determined by measuring the drawer to see if it is parallel in width and depth.

The other possibility of inaccuracy is in the parallelism of the opening into which the drawer slides. If it is closer at the back than at the front, the drawer will get tighter as it goes farther in. If it is wider open at the back, slackness there will be apparent when the drawer is in. This is less serious than tightness, its chief disadvantage being that the front of the drawer will not always be flush and parallel with the front of the case. Accurate work in preparing and putting together the parts makes want of parallelism less likely.

Ordinary window frames are sometimes slightly out of parallel, making a sash which perhaps is already a close fit in one part much too tight when the sash is raised or lowered to one of the extremes. It is obvious that the frame and not the sash is the cause of this.

Besides the effects of sag, and of swelling and shrinking, warping may interfere with the proper and original fit of parts. Doors sometimes warp so that they do not close properly against their stops but come into contact at top or bottom first and require pressure to do so at the other part. This usually means that some pressure against the door must be exerted to cause the lock to catch. As it is practically impossible to straighten the door, the remedy is to take off and replace the stop to suit the altered condition of the door.

A peculiarity about hinged doors, gates, etc., is that unless perfectly upright they will, when free to do so, open or close automatically to a certain position. If a bookcase or wardrobe leans forward, the doors, when unfastened, will open of themselves, or if it leans back they will close themselves. A slight tilt to one side as well as forward means that, where a pair of doors is concerned, they will not come to rest in similar positions. A case with a single door could easily be adjusted so that the door would open or close automatically to any position. With the post and hinges perfectly vertical a door will remain in the position it is opened or closed to. The explanation of the foregoing is that a door naturally swings by gravity to the lowest position it can find, and if the hinge post leans in a certain direction the door swings automatically in the same direction.

Fitting Castors.—When castors are to be fitted to articles of furniture, it is important in the first place to see that they are of the correct size and type for each particular case. They should turn freely on the swivel, and the bowls should run smoothly.

It is usual to put good quality castors on good class furniture, and cheap castors on common furniture ; and in both cases it can be done to give satisfaction, that is, to run well and wear well for many years without giving any trouble. The better kind of castors are usually of cast brass, well made and finished, being fairly reliable and free from faults, smooth running, durable, and of good appearance. Moderately cheap castors may be of brass ; but they are not very substantial, being only suitable for light wear. The very cheap ones are of iron, often brassed over. These should be examined before putting on, for very likely the bowl pin or the swivel pin may need a little extra riveting.

The ordinary screw-castor is the most generally adopted and extensively used ; but the screw does not go into the wood very well (especially the common ones), and too often there is no attempt to screw it in. A hole is made so that it can drop in, then a nail is inserted through one of the small screw-holes in the plate to retain it ; but it is soon off again, and sometimes causes damage to the wood.

The right way to fix such a castor is to bore a hole with a gimlet, slightly less in diameter than the screw, then to insert the screw by the aid of some tool such as a nail punch, the point being placed through one of the screw-holes, gripping the castor and punch to turn the screw in until the plate is quite close to the wood. Screws (about 1 in. No. 4) should be inserted in each hole; but these may not hold in the end grain of soft wood, so wire nails will do instead. Perhaps they may need to be about $1\frac{1}{2}$ in. long. If the plate is not firm up against the wood, nor supported by the screws or nails, undue strain may cause the castor-screw to break in the leg, which often happens.

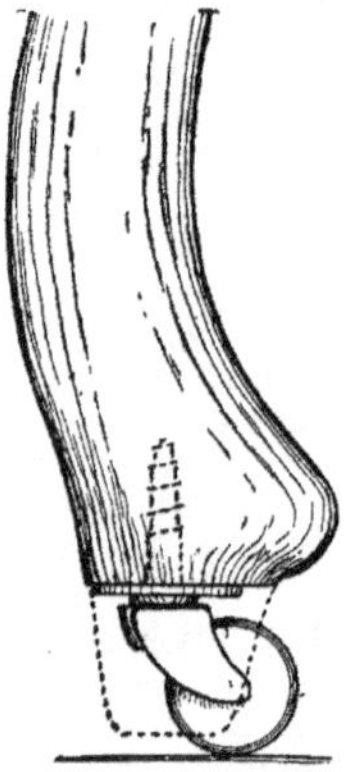

In the case of a turned chair leg, a tight-fitting castor ring should be put on to prevent splitting. These are too often regarded as ornament only, and put on altogether too loosely.

Fig. 56.—Method of Fitting Castor to Cabriole Chair Leg

The pin-castor is the same as the screw-castor, except that instead of the screw there is a solid iron pin to drive into a tight-fitting hole. The pin is not likely to break. It is useful for replacing a screw-castor that has been put in too loose a hole, which otherwise would need to be plugged with wood.

When fitting castors to "cabriole" legs. it is important to be very particular to judge the exact point for the insertion of the screw. It must be sufficiently back from the toe to avoid strain being on the short grain of the wood. Breakages frequently occur through misjudgment in this connection.

The fitting of a castor to a cabriole chair leg is shown by Fig. 56.

It must be ascertained that the legs are quite level and this can be done by holding a straightedge on two castors both turned the same way and glancing to see that the other two are exactly in line with the edge. This being correct, the screws can be put in to retain the castors. Should it happen that the left back leg is apparently $\frac{1}{8}$ in. higher than the other, it should be measured, and if too long must be cut. But it may be the front right leg that is $\frac{1}{8}$ in. too long; or perhaps both require reducing $\frac{1}{16}$ in.

Another useful castor is the "socket" or "cup" castor. In fitting these, the wood pin on the leg should fit the cup fairly tight and the full depth. It is well to countersink the end on account of the rivet at the bottom of the cup. When the wood pin is too thick for the socket it can be pared or rasped down; but when a little too loose, a common method is to glue a piece of black linen round it. The correct size screws (average $\frac{5}{8}$ in. No. 5) should be used for fixing these castors.

Gliders are simply knocked on to the legs, but this should be done with care, as if struck too hard with the hammer they will shatter to pieces. They must be alternately tapped directly over the points to enter the wood. Should the wood be very hard, it is well to pierce holes with a small bradawl.

Wood Finishing, Painting and Enamelling

FRENCH POLISHING

Of the many different processes of wood finishing the most general is that known as french polishing, which imparts to domestic furniture and interior fitments a bright, level, finished surface, through which, in the case of good-quality woods, is reflected the colour and beauty of their figure; and in the case of inferior woods staining either before or during the process of finishing, so that the appearance will convey an impression that the woods are of better quality than they really are. Another feature is the production of surfaces that will replenish easily and, moreover, that will improve in lustre with subsequent treatment.

This method of finishing was introduced into Great Britain from France, where in 1730 the Brothers Martin were granted a four years' monopoly of their finish called Vernis Martin or Martins' Varnish. The varnish was apparently of the spirit or quick-drying class, one of the earliest known recipes of which is as follows: Alcohol 1 pt., gum shellac 2 oz., gum sandarach 2 oz., gum mastic 1 oz., and many applications must have been needed to bring about the fine results obtained on specimens of their handicraft. The above proportions give a rather thin varnish, and although drying quickly, the work would have to stand aside several times to harden sufficiently to allow of each coating being smoothed down to a level face before the next was applied, especially so when the woodwork was of a coarse, open-grain character. No record has been found of the wood being prepared for the reception of the varnish by the use of anything to seal up the open grain.

The present-day method in the case of hardwoods, and those that are veneer-faced, is to wipe the work over first with linseed oil, which removes its rawness, and at the same time causes the figure to stand out more clearly, and then to seal up the pores with a grain filler.

Fillers.—There are several well-known brands of grain fillers on the market which are much superior to home-made preparations. An efficient substitute in general use is made of finely-crushed whiting to which some dry colour pigment has been added in order to prevent the filler showing white in the grain. For a filler for mahogany, sufficient venetian red should be added to give it a fairly red tint; for walnut, brown umber powder would be added, ar 1 for oak, some yellow ochre. Sufficient turpentine is added to the whiting and colouring matter to form a stiffish paste. The addition of a little fine pumice powder adds to the efficiency of this filler, but it is not absolutely necessary. The paste is applied to the oiled surface of the wood with coarse rag, being spread about well and forced into the pores. It should be borne in mind that a filler is not only cheaper than polish but that it will save much of the labour required in the application of the polish. In no circumstances should plaster-of-paris and tallow be used—a mixture one occasionally finds recommended ; its disadvantages lie in the liability of the plaster to ooze out again when the tallow softens up in hot weather, and in its eating the colour out of any aniline dye that may be used in the polish or varnish.

After filling, the surplus filler is wiped off quite clean, special attention being given to the corners and quirks of mouldings, and a polish (made by steeping about 6 oz. shellac in 1 pt. methylated spirit) is applied in such a manner that it is forced into the wood till it will absorb no more, then still more polish applied until a film possible by the hand-rubbing process alone. It also has the decided advantage that it enables the colour to be much more evenly distributed in cases where any alteration, other than that gained by staining the wood before it is oiled and grain-filled, is desired.

Similarly, this practice of using spirit varnish in conjunction with polish is the method usually adopted for common wood that has been stained to imitate a better kind. In this connection it is rarely that goods made of deal, pine and canary woods are paste-filled, the omission being made good by a free use of varnish instead. Occasionally jelly-size is added to the staining medium with the same object in view, that is, to save the excessive use of

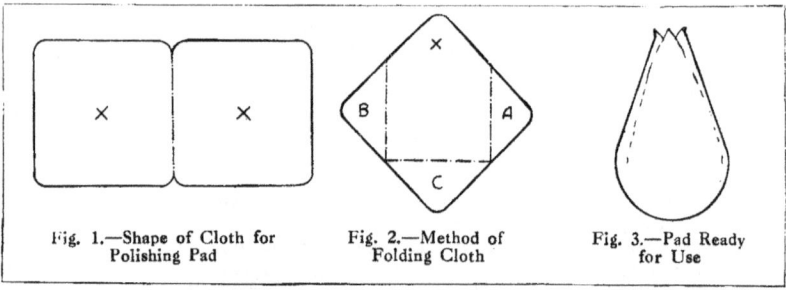

Fig. 1.—Shape of Cloth for Polishing Pad   Fig. 2.—Method of Folding Cloth   Fig. 3.—Pad Ready for Use

of lac is formed on the surface that will burnish up to a bright lustre. There are many variations in the methods and the ingredients used, mainly to adapt the process to suit the varying class of work.

On the cheaper class of goods part of the hand rubbing is eliminated, and a surface built up more quickly and cheaply by the aid of several applications of spirit varnish applied with a camel-hair brush. This does not imply that varnish only is used—on the contrary, polish is applied until the grain appears filled up and the surface is smooth. One or more coats of varnish are then applied, and, when these are hard, more polish is applied and worked out to a finish. On turned work and other irregular surfaces the above procedure allows of a more even finish than is the more expensive polish and varnish. Some stain makers advise the application of one or two coats of jelly-size after the stain is dry.

Method of Applying the Polish.—From a sheet of ordinary grey or white wadding tear off a piece about 6 in. by 4 in., double it across once, x to x (Fig. 1), and then from one corner to another, c to x (Fig. 2) ; finally fold the other two corners, A and B to meet midway. Saturate the face side with polish and spirit in about equal parts till it feels quite damp ; a slight crushing in the hand should then cause it to assume the shape of a pear cut in half (*see* Fig. 3). This should be enclosed in a soft piece of rag in order to prevent any loose portions of wadding adhering to the work. The pad should now be worked over the wood with a circular

WOOD FINISHING, PAINTING AND ENAMELLING

and figure-eight sort of movement, gradually traversing the whole surface.

An occasional spot of linseed oil applied to the face of the pad acts as a lubricant and ensures freedom. More polish is added to the rubber as it is required, the rag being removed for this purpose. When spirit (which is used as an aid to assist the polish working more freely and thereby ensuring an even distribution over all portions alike) is being added, the removal of the rag is not necessary.

The first rubbing completed, the work should be set aside for a few hours, to harden, and the polish-rubber meantime put away in an air-tight tin.

On taking up the work again, remove any apparent roughness with fine glasspaper, and then apply more polish until there appear no signs of open grain. At this stage, the polish is used thinner by diluting it in the rubber when recharging —a suitable proportion is one part spirit to each three parts of polish. Later about equal parts of polish and spirit should be used, and still later, spirit only when it is found that there is a sufficient body of polish on the surface to burnish up to a lustre. The lustre is obtained by working up the rubber straight from end to end, rather than by the small circular motion as when applying the polish finally clearing off any smeariness or traces of oil by means of a swab of clean soft rag folded to a smooth face and made damp but not wet, with methylated spirit. A light swinging motion should be given at first so as not to soften up the film of lac. Slightly more pressure may be applied as the pad becomes drier.

When the use of varnish is deemed advisable as an aid in getting the work through more quickly a suitable one may be made as follows . Methylated spirit 1 pt., orange shellac 4 oz., gum sandarach 2 oz., pale resin 2 oz. ; when dissolved strain through muslin or open mesh rag ; apply with a camel-hair brush.

Brush Polish.—Ordinary french polish in itself contains little brightness—it is the friction during and after its application that produces the lustre—and it is hopeless to expect to be able to obtain the grain-filled, glass-like polish on any medium which, when applied with a brush, leaves something behind that merely lies on the surface of the wood. Recognising this, it is obvious that there are many articles that could be greatly improved in appearance if they were to be coated with french polish in the first instance by means of the polish rubber, and afterwards coated with a spirit varnish made from the recipe as given above.

WOOD STAINING AND FUMING

The staining of wood is divided into two distinct types of work, namely—improving the colour of good-quality woods or entirely altering their colour so that the articles when finished are in accordance with the prevailing styles or periods which they represent, and staining inferior woods in order that they may imitate those of a better quality. Of the former case mahogany and oak may be mentioned as typical examples. Mahogany is rarely finished out in its natural colour ; the alteration may be nothing more than a wipe over with red oil (made by steeping 2 oz. alkanet root in 1 pt. linseed oil).

In well-equipped workshops an aged or Chippendale colour is obtained by subjecting the work to the action of the fumes arising from liquid ammonia in an airtight chamber. The length of time of the treatment varies from twelve to forty-eight hours according to the density of the colour desired. A pint-and-a-half of ammonia divided into six equal portions, and placed in shallow dishes on the floor of a chamber of dimensions of about 9 ft. long 4 ft. wide, and 6 ft. high, will produce the desired effect. Care must be taken to first remove any mirrors or brass fittings from the articles. As the fumes do their work by acting on the tannic acid which the wood contains, it will readily be seen how important it is that the surface of the wood should be perfectly clean, and the pieces so arranged that the fumes may play freely around them. Oak is rarely finished out self-colour. a more or less aged appearance being preferred. The lighter tones can be obtained by submission to ammonia fumes—hence the common term "fumed oak finish." Apart from this there are at least ten other distinct colour finishes peculiar to oak which are known respectively as Jacobean, Flemish, Austrian, Weathered, Maltese Grey, Cloister Brown, Forest Green, Verde Green, Golden Oak and Mission-room oak.

English stain makers are not particularly desirous of supplying stains that give this wide range of colour finishes, and consequently polishers have to get the desired result as best they can. The majority of them manage very well by the aid of aniline dyes, though the results, particularly in the matter of wear, by no means equal those that are obtained by the use of good penetrating stains in the first instance.

For oak the home-worker is generally content with an antique, or Jacobean, colour finish—a colour which may range from a light nut brown to one which is nearly black, a characteristic feature, in most cases, being a worn-off appearance on portions which it would appear were most likely to be subject to friction. This effect may be obtained by waiting until the stain is dry, wiping the work over with linseed oil and rubbing with a piece of wadding saturated with oil and dipped into medium-grade pumice powder. An effort is made with this rubber to rub the stain off again from those parts where the friction effect is desired. Some of the powder will enter the grain, a matter which is all to the good as it helps to impart a burnished appearance. No grain-filler is required, as the open grain showing improves the appearance. It may be pointed out that to impart an antique finish to articles of modern design does not show good taste. A suitable stain consists of 2 oz. vandyke crystals dissolved in ½ pt. liquid ammonia, the mixture being then diluted with water so that it will give the desired colour by two applications. For the faded light brown appearance, vandyke, even when thus diluted, will not always bring about the desired tone. In such cases it is advisable to add brown umber powder, or even yellow ochre, to the stain, adding more ammonia to sharpen it up if already weakened with water.

Oak, like mahogany, is amenable to the darkening influence of bichromate of potash (1 oz. to 1 pt. water). By varying the strength of the solution many useful colour effects may be obtained.

Water stains are only effective when applied direct to clean wood free from polish, varnish or greasiness ; mention of the last item directs attention to the folly of stopping up nail holes and other defects with putty before staining. Where this method of dealing with defects is adopted it should be done after the stain is dry, the work grain-filled and a rubber of polish applied. After this treatment it can then the more readily be seen what colour the putty should be to ensure that it does not show up different from the background ; generally the same colour pigment added to the grain-filler will suffice. Used at this stage it ensures the avoidance of greasiness around the defects through which a water stain would not penetrate. Water stains may be used hot or cold and should be liberally applied by means of a brush, the stain being dabbed well into the corners and quirks of mouldings. The work should be allowed to stand until it is nearly dry and then a piece of soft rag used to wipe up the surplus. The final wiping should always be in the direction of the grain of the wood.

It should be noted that a surface left direct from the plane does not come up rough on the application of water stains, whereas a surface that has been levelled with coarse glasspaper, even if followed up by a finer grade, swells and comes up rough directly stain or polish is applied. The reason of this is that the fibres of the wood have, by this treatment, been bruised and bent, whereas the plane cuts them off level. If trial of the stain on odd pieces of wood produces this result, the trouble can be mitigated, to a great extent, by sponging the work over with clean water, and when dry smoothing down with fine glasspaper.

Staining Inferior Woods.—The practice of imparting colour to wood as practised by the old craftsmen is wellnigh a

WOOD FINISHING, PAINTING AND ENAMELLING

lost art. Liberal use was made of dyes extracted from shrubs and roots; hence in many of the old recipes such dyes as logwood, fustic, turmeric, Persian berries, walnut shells, nut-galls, red sanders, madder root and alkanet root are mentioned. Modern practice with its chemicals and aniline dyes has resulted in most of these vegetable dyes having become obselete, and nowadays some of them are exceedingly difficult to obtain. Few think of using logwood chips now that it is possible to obtain the dye in the form of a logwood extract which, used in conjunction with copperas, is a foundation stain for a black finish.

The quantity of furniture which is not made of the hardwood that its colour represents is surprising. In some instances—notably kitchen furniture—the wood finisher makes no attempt to show the figure of the wood. Take the table as an instance. The wood is simply coated with venetian red mixed with jelly-size to form a thin paint which is applied with a brush. No grain filler is used. This surface, when smoothed down with worn glasspaper, is then given just a rubber of red polish with a pad without a covering, but one that has previously been used. The object of this is merely to prevent the surface coming up rough. Several applications of red spirit varnish make a finish. Occasionally this varnish finish is improved upon at this stage by working the same polish rubber, with its cover made fairly wet with polish and spirit in about equal proportions, over the varnished surface in order to work down any lumpiness. The rubbing should not be worked out to dryness, for the warmth of the room will generally cause the varnish to dry out bright.

Should it be desired to make use of any figure the wood may possess, instead of entirely hiding it, the work should first be coated with a weak walnut stain and then a polish coloured with bismarck used. This procedure does away with the objectionable redness, by imparting a more or less brownish groundwork which shows up from underneath, instead of merely on the surface, as is the case when the redness is toned down by the addition of spirit walnut dye to the bismarck-dyed polish.

Another useful method is to procure some burnt sienna (ground in water) and to mix this with water to which common brown vinegar—$\frac{1}{4}$ pt. vinegar to 1 pt. water—has been added. Stale beer may be used instead. The sugar the beer contains acts as a binder. If the article is made of canary wood and presents a reasonably flat face it may be grain-filled to advantage.

Walnut Finish.—With this finish it is invariably desired to show the figure of the wood, consequently a stain that will penetrate well into the wood answers the purpose better than the jelly-size mixtures. As there are different varieties of walnut, so will it be necessary to vary the stains to imitate them. For general purposes, 2 oz. vandyke crystals dissolved in $\frac{1}{4}$ pt. liquid ammonia and the solution then diluted with water until it gives the desired tint by two applications will meet most requirements where a fairly dark colour is desired. If ammonia is objected to and a variation of colour is desired, take common brown vinegar 1 qt. and dissolve in it burnt umber powder $\frac{1}{4}$ lb., rose pink 1 oz. This yields a lighter colour than the vandyke, and may be lighter still by using raw umber of the burnt variety.

Ebony Finish.—Black or an ebony colour can generally be readily obtained by mixing lampblack in ordinary polish until it forms a creamy paste, which is then diluted with spirit until it can be easily applied with a camel-hair brush. This should be followed up by a polish made from bleached shellac to which some black aniline spirit dye has been added. If a particularly fine finish is desired, it is best to finally finish off with the bleached shellac polish free from dye.

Rosewood Finish.—A rosewood finish can be obtained on the same lines, using the foundation black less intense and polishing with a red dye polish. Oak cannot be imitated on soft woods by means of stain, except so far as its colour is concerned. There are many cases in which, if the colour only is imparted, it will effect a decided improvement. Chippendale is merely an intermediate colour between mahogany and rosewood—generally it is supposed to be a good class mahogany that has become darkened with age. Brown merging into a faded red is characteristic of genuine Chippendale goods. Modern practice, however, calls a rosewood colour, even to the extent of showing no figure, a Chippendale finish. It will be seen, therefore, that the matter resolves itself into individual ideas as to what the exact colour should be. By the use of the dyes indicated for mahogany and rosewood there should be little difficulty in hitting upon an ideal representative colour.

Combined Stain and Varnish.—Work treated with combined stain and varnish does not possess the same good wearing qualities as work that has been stained first and varnished afterwards, though this can be obviated to a great extent by using only so much varnish-stain as will produce the desired colour, and then using a clear varnish for finishing. A mahogany red colour may be imparted to varnish by dissolving ½ oz. bismarck aniline dye in ⅛th pt. methylated spirit; sufficient of this should be added to the varnish to obtain the desired colour on the work by two applications. Similarly for walnut, use an aniline dye sold as spirit walnut, or a rosewood dye where that colour is desired. It may also on occasion prove advantageous to blend several dyes; for instance, the bismarck dye yields a more or less strong red colour, the addition of a few drops of the walnut dye to this may easily make all the difference between success or failure in obtaining the particular mahogany colour desired. There is a Chippendale dye sold, which, when first dissolved out, presents quite a strong purple colour which is apt to be misleading, but, as the other colours of which the dye is blended in their turn dissolve out, this apparent strong purple colour becomes less intense, and produces what some polishers call a plum colour. Black dyes are sold under several names, spirit black being the most familiar one. This is useful for converting spirit varnish into a black lacquer. When used for french polishing purposes, it is better to use it with a polish made from bleached shellac, known as white polish.

Transfer Imitation of Inlaid Woods.—This was a popular feature a few years ago when real inlaid woods had a great vogue. It has the merit of imparting to articles a more decorative appearance at a much lower cost than when real inlaid woods are used. It has another decided advantage, inasmuch as that by this means articles already made could, in the course of their renovation, be given an entirely changed appearance without the removal of the original polish.

Suitable designs are obtainable, which, if fixed during the polishing in the first instance, and finished out with a bleached shellac polish, will impart an appearance only distinguishable from the real inlaid woods by an expert. Being printed on a specially prepared paper which is afterwards entirely removed, their application requires no particular skill and involves no more trouble than that of affixing a freshly gummed label in a clearly defined position. The designs may be had in floral or geometrical patterns suitable for either centres or borders. The number of separate designs varies according to the sizes. When cutting up the sheets of designs it is not necessary to cut them out in outline, in fact as much of the plain paper should be left around the designs as circumstances will permit. If there should be no outline design on the back of the paper pencil marks may be put on the back at such points as will serve as guides to ensure the designs being fixed correctly. If necessary similar tally marks on the partly polished surface of the work may be made. Once the transfers are pressed down they cannot be moved, therefore they should not be placed by guess work.

The transfer adhesive (which may be a thin, clear spirit varnish, or even french polish so long as it is free from dye) should be applied to the design whilst the latter is laid face upwards on a sheet of paper. It is not necessary to cut it in over the design, though it should not reach the edge of the paper if it can be avoided.

WOOD FINISHING, PAINTING AND ENAMELLING

The design is next placed face downwards in its intended position and pressed well down, the pressure being commenced from the centre and worked outwards. After being set aside for about half an hour the paper should be slightly damped with clean water and pressed down again. After another slight wetting the paper should then peel off quite easily. The surplus moisture should then be carefully wiped off and the work set aside for about one hour when it may be finished off with a bleached shellac polish or clear varnish.

In the case of large designs, it is advisable to do the pressing down with the aid of a squeegee rubber roller such as is used by photographers. When it is desired to fix a design to an article that has already been polished, the method of application is identical, but care must be taken that the surface is quite clean and free from any wax preparation that may have been used for cleansing purposes. A drawback to the application of transfers to finished work lies in the fact that when polish or varnish has been applied for the purpose of preservation or renovation of the article, the designs do not appear to be very deep, and the effect is not so good as that which would be obtained on partly polished surfaces. In no circumstances should attempt be made to fix transfers direct to bare wood, as the open grain would spoil the effect that is aimed at and the adhesive would also fail to do its work.

Occasionally one may meet with designs that are printed on duplex paper, that is, a thin rice paper backed by a stouter paper that is non-porous. The method of using this type of design is exactly the same with the exception of the damping, which in this case would be non-effective. With this paper it is necessary to remove the top layer of paper first by lifting it at one corner with the point of a knife and carefully peeling it, leaving the tissue with its design firmly fixed. The tissue is removed with water in the usual way. Designs of this description may be the more easily affixed to round or other irregular surfaces.

REPOLISHING

The repolishing of an article generally calls for a greater knowledge of the underlying principles of the craft than does the polishing of new wood, as the latter is all straightforward work. In the former case there is an ever-present risk that there are bruises to contend with, pieces of veneer missing, the existence of repaired parts on which some of the old polish has been entirely removed, and more or less deep scratches which must be drawn up level. The original polish may in some places be so much faded or perished that nothing short of its entire removal will lead to satisfaction.

The first essential is cleanliness; the articles may have been frequently freshened up with furniture cream which has accumulated in the corners or failed to remove grime and marks of long usage. It is hopeless to expect to be able to repolish such a surface with the materials used for polishing new wood. Time is gained and more satisfaction assured if all brass fittings and similar furnishings are first removed, and the dirt-begrimed article is washed down with water in which a small quantity of common washing soda has been dissolved. In bad cases, it may even be advisable to use an abrasive, such as pumice powder, bath brick, or knife-cleaning powder to assist in the removal of past accumulations of dirt. On some woods, particularly rosewood veneer, there is a roughness to contend with caused by the shrinking or swelling of the veneer having forced the grain-filling preparation out. If the surface is removed with dry glasspaper it often creates a smooth face showing a more pronounced and open grain than when it was first polished. This contingency can be avoided to a great extent by first wiping the surface over with linseed oil, for then the surface instead of being removed in the shape of fine dust, becomes mingled with the oil, and is forced back again into the open grain.

In cases where the original polish is perished, or must be entirely removed for the purpose of changing the colour finish, its removal may be accomplished in several ways. Probably the best tool for this purpose is the steel scraper. Solvents are obtainable that will soften up the old polish and varnish at a lower cost than by the use of methylated spirit. Liquid ammonia is also an effective solvent. Occasionally articles which have been originally polished and later covered with paint and varnish, are met with. For the removal of such a coating as this the following will prove effective : One bucketful of freshly-made lime-wash, 2 lb. common washing soda, 1 lb. soft soap, ¼ pt. liquid ammonia. The solution should be applied with an old fibre brush. Shortly after its application the paint will soften and can then be scraped off with a putty knife or scraper. For carved work such as old oak chests, it is a good plan to mix fine sawdust with the mixture in order to thicken it sufficiently so that it will lie on the surface and retain its moisture for some considerable time. Lime mixtures have the disadvantage of turning such woods as oak and mahogany a darker colour than is desirable. This effect may easily be corrected by bleaching the article with a solution of oxalic acid (½ oz. oxalic acid dissolved in 1 pt. water are suitable proportions). After treatment the article should be well swilled in water and finally washed with common brown vinegar in order to neutralise the action of any lime or acid that may remain in the open grain. The article should receive this treatment whether oxalic acid has been used or not.

The foregoing are extreme cases ; those of a lesser degree may arise from the polish having sunk in to such an extent that, though there is no roughness, reviving preparations will not impart a durable brightness, and nothing short of applying more polish will ensure satisfaction. In such cases the cleansing with water and abrasives is generally dispensed with and the surface is wiped over with wadding saturated with linseed oil and spirit in about equal parts. The oil has the effect of disguising slight scratches and assisting the new polish to take more easily to the old, which the spirit mingled with the oil has partly softened. Should this treatment, however, fail to remove any excessive greasiness, a wipe over with common vinegar will do much towards removing it.

French polish for old work is now applied in a very much thinner state than that generally required on new woods ; and as most old work is faded to a slight extent, it is usual to enrich its appearance by using just a trace of dye in the polish. Assuming that repairs, resulting in the removal of the old polish around them, are carried out, these places, so far as the application of fresh polish is concerned, should be dealt with first, as in most cases it leads to a process of colouring-up, rather than the bringing about of the desired result by water stains. Owing to the ever-present risk that a suitable colour water stain is not at hand, experienced polishers simply ignore their aid, and apply polish over the defects till there are no signs of open grain. By the aid of spirit dyes and perchance a trace of a suitable colour pigment the mixture is applied until an even colour is secured. For instance, supposing it to be a walnut job, either of real or stained wood, in all probability it will show up light in colour where the old polish was removed, even after polish has been applied as advised. To bring about a perfect match, a general practice is to pour a few drops of spirit walnut dye into an old tin lid, with about an equal quantity of polish to act as a binder. If on trial this is found to be too dark when applied with a pencil brush, spirit is added. If not dark enough, and more dye will not render it so, a pinch of dry brown umber powder may easily make all the difference. It is not necessary to aim at getting the exact tint by one application : several may be made at different points, thereby allowing of figure being put in if it is wanted to agree with its surroundings. This colouring dries very rapidly and by means of the polish acting as a binder it should not rub off when applying more polish with the rubber ; nor should it break up under the application of spirit varnish. With mahogany goods, the bismarck dye may require the assistance of a trace of walnut

WOOD FINISHING, PAINTING AND ENAMELLING

dye to bring about a brownish tone, or a trace of venetian red powder to ensure a more solid colour ; in fact, it is a matter of ringing the changes frequently, without stopping to ask the reason why. The main thing is to obtain an even colour without showing any signs of patchiness, and in most cases a more perfect blending is brought about by using the merest trace of dye in the polish. After securing the correct colour, the polishing of the whole article may be proceeded with to a finish. Mouldings and turned or carved work should be given an even coat of rather thin spirit varnish, either clear or slightly coloured.

OTHER METHODS OF POLISHING

American Methods of Wood Finishing.—The methods used in America differ from those adopted in England and France chiefly on account of climatic influences. Shellac has the property of softening up at a prolonged heat that is beyond the normal, such as a heat wave, or long, dry, hot summer. Under such conditions it is a common experience to find that previously high polished surfaces soon become quite dull owing to the heat having softened up the film of shellac. Experience has taught that successive coatings of an elastic varnish, each ground down and reduced in thickness by the aid of pumice powder and water, until four, six, or, in the case of high-grade articles, even eight coatings have been applied, will give far and away better wearing results. This does not imply that when thus finished the articles will appear to be simply coated with a thick, glarish-looking varnish, for even on the cheaper class of goods this brightness is generally removed by means of pumice powder applied with an oil-soaked brush worked over the surface with sufficient force to entirely remove the brightness. The same process is applicable to articles which are made of choice hardwoods or veneer-faced woods, but in this case the dulling-down is carried on to a greater depth, so as to ensure freedom from brush marks, and so that the surface presents a perfectly level face. Rottenstone, applied with woollen cloths, is used with water at a later stage to remove any slight scratches or marks left by the pumice. This is followed up by a finer grade of rottenstone applied briskly with the palm of the hand until a beautiful polished surface is produced. The work is finally finished by one of the processes known respectively as " oiled-off " or " vapoured-up " with the following materials : three pieces of cotton material, such as old linen or frequently washed cheese cloth, a piece of wadding as large as the hand, and a bottle containing one part sweet oil and two parts turpentine.

The surface of the work is slightly moistened with the oil and turpentine with the object of picking up any of the rottenstone that may linger on the surface. The mixture is wiped off with a piece of rag folded as a swab presenting a face free from creases, followed up if need be by a second piece of rag similarly folded, in each case working in the direction of the grain. The third piece of rag is used with a slight sprinkling of domestic flour, which will remove any trace of greasiness the previous swabs have failed to remove. In skilful hands the second piece of rag may even be moistened with grain alcohol to advantage, though some operatives prefer to use the grain alcohol in conjunction with the oil and turpentine. As the alcohol passes away rapidly in the form of vapour, the term " vapoured-up " becomes quite understandable.

From the foregoing it will be seen that it is a process that is hardly likely to appeal strongly to the small worker owing to the length of time that elapses between the start and the finish. Mass production of pianos, American organs, roll-top desks, sewing-machine covers, etc., allows the goods to be constantly on the move through one or other of the various stages.

German Finish.—German or vitriol finish of cabinet furniture differs from the ordinary french polish lustre mainly in its freedom from finger marking and transparency with a high gloss finish. Shellac alone, when dissolved in methylated spirit, possesses very little brightness in itself: it is the friction of its application that burnishes it up to a lustre. If other gums are added to the shellac in proportions sufficient to impart elasticity and brightness, this burnishing up to a lustre is, by the German method, replaced by a method of polishing it up to a gloss. Incidentally it is a method of finishing that can only be economically adopted when the goods are handled on commercial lines.

The process is as follows: The wood is grain-filled in the usual way, and then coated with a shellac varnish free from other gums or resins; alternatively a shellac solution may be sprayed on, followed up by five or six applications of varnish, each of which is allowed to stand aside long enough to harden, and permit of its being ground down to a dead level face with pumice powder and water. When there are no signs of open grain showing, the polishing commences, this being done with a bleached shellac polish and the use of a trifle more oil than most french polishers generally use. The work is brought up to that stage when it is usual to clean the oil off with spirits but instead, the surface is pounced over with vienna chalk. Having at hand a suitable vessel containing diluted sulphuric acid (one part of acid to about ten parts of water) the operator dips the palm of his perfectly clean hand into the dilute acid and proceeds to rub the chalk with a circular motion until it becomes a creamy paste, continuing the rubbing and using his finger-tips to get it well into the corners and mouldings until the chalk become a fine powder again. The effect of this procedure is that the acid hardens the film of shellac and the chalk brings away all trace of the oil that has been used to assist in its even distribution. From the foregoing it will be seen that no oil comes into contact with the bare wood and that no dye has been used in the polish. Should any alteration in the colour of the wood be desired, this is done before using the grain-filler or by means of coloured varnish in the earlier stages—a proceeding that accounts largely for the transparent finish that is such a noticeable feature in this work. The composition of the varnish used is not common property, and it does not follow that it is always necessary; its advantage lies in building up a surface which, when rubbed down, presents a face free from open grain. Provided an ordinary french polished surface shows no open grain the acid finish is equally applicable.

Japanese Lac Finish.—This finish differs from the ordinary finish on account of the colouring and quaint decoration. On some of the choicest specimens there is no attempt to utilise the original figure of the woods of which the articles are made. The background may be an intense black, or broken up into several colours, with the leading portions of the designs standing up above the surface; in others the ornamentation is so thin as to present a practically flat face. Unlike the majority of English lacquers, that used by the Japanese contains no shellac or lac of any kind as we know it, but use is made of a kind of gum, which, as it oozes from certain trees, is milky white. On exposure to the air this turns nearly brown, and with a still longer exposure turns nearly black. The blackness can be intensified by the addition of water strongly impregnated with iron, or iron and tannic acid. It will be understood that by the use of only one kind of acquer it is possible to obtain three distinct variations in the colour. Unlike the lacquers familiar to us, this lacquer does not dry in the open air; on the contrary the articles, after each application, must be set aside in a damp air-tight room for periods varying from six to fifty hours. Many applications must be made before a surface is built up of sufficient thickness to enable it to be ground down to a sufficiently level face to take the final lustre. This final lustre is imparted by means of a powder made from calcined horn. The raised decorations are obtained by means of stone dust, clay, or other earthy substance mixed with the crude lacquer. The English adaptation of the process in its crudest form is called japanning. This simply consists of the application of a spirit varnish composed of methylated spirit,

WOOD FINISHING, PAINTING AND ENAMELLING

shellac, gum sandarach and gum mastic. The decorations are put on afterwards by the aid of transfers.

MISCELLANEOUS

Polishing Inlaid Woodwork. — In workshop practice it is usual for the articles to be quite finished so far as the cabinet-maker is concerned before it is passed on to the polishing department, and where inlaid woods form part of the decorative scheme the choice of woods is generally so arranged that staining is rarely required. Where these conditions do not apply, and the groundwork must be stained, the polisher, with a small camel-hair pencil-brush, gives the inlays one or more applications of rather thick bleached shellac polish or thin, clear spirit varnish. When this is quite dry, the work can be oiled and grain-filled without any discoloration of the inlays. Should it happen that the groundwork must be stained a darker colour, this should be done before the work is oiled, using a water stain if it is at all possible to get the desired result by this means. Thus, should it be a mahogany groundwork an application of a weak solution of bichromate of potash—$\frac{1}{2}$ oz. to 1 pt. of water—followed up when dry with red oil, will meet the requirements of most cases. If, instead of a water stain, the desired result is to be obtained by means of dyed polish, it leaves one with no alternative but to scrape the dye off the inlays afterwards, and then finish off the work with a bleached shellac polish. This procedure, though, has the disadvantage that the finished surface conveys the impression that the inlays are sunk in instead of standing up level as when water stains are used.

Bleached Shellac Polish. — This polish—commonly called white polish—to distinguish it from that made from orange, lemon or garnet shellacs—is better bought ready made. The lac from which it is made—commonly called white shellac—is sold in the form of thick, twisted sticks, and as the bleaching process has the effect of causing it to perish if left long exposed to the air, it should be kept under water until such time as it is required for use. To prepare it for use it must be broken up into a fine powder and spread out on paper in a warm atmosphere in order to dry out all the moisture. It is then put into a bottle and covered with methylated spirit in the proportions of about 6 oz. lac to 1 pt. methylated spirit; frequent agitation is required before it will all dissolve out and form a cream-like mixture. Its solution will be assisted by heat provided by a water bath. The warming should not be done by direct heat, nor should the bottle be kept tightly corked during the process, as there is a risk that as the spirit becomes warm the cork might fly out, carrying with it a fine spray of vapour that will readily ignite on contact with a naked light. In no circumstances should the drying of the broken-up lac be by direct heat, as such a procedure will have the effect of causing it to mass together again and thereby become most difficult to dissolve. This polish, being free from colouring matter, s used for finishing inlaid woods or their transfer imitations, and the lighter coloured woods, such as sycamore, ash, maple and light oak, when it is desired that they be finished out with a particularly clear finish. It is also used for the finishing stages of ebony or black-finished articles. It is also possible to buy transparent shellac, free from the milky-white appearance, but for general purposes the bleached shellac meets most requirements as when worked out it becomes practically transparent. For light oak goods, on which the slightly yellow tinge imparted by the ordinary lemon or orange shellac polish is likely to be objected to, a mixture of white and lemon shellac polish in about equal proportions will assist in gaining a finish free from the colour objection, and present a harder face than when white polish only is used.

White Hard Spirit Varnish.—This is useful for most general purposes and can easily be made from a similar solution to the above by adding to it 1 oz. gum sandarach and 1 oz. pale resin. Another recipe is : Methylated spirit 1 pt., gum sandarach 4 oz., Venice turpentine 2 oz. The latter is claimed to be a useful varnish for violins. Both kinds should be carefully strained before use and applied with a camel-hair brush.

French Polish Blooming.—Under certain atmospheric conditions polish will dull or bloom—a kind of whitish film appearing on the surface. As a general rule this can easily be removed by carefully washing the part with a solution made of one part paraffin to three parts water, drying with a soft cloth, and afterwards rubbing with another soft, dry cloth.

French Polish Sweating.—The sweating of a polished surface is a fault incidental to the necessity of having to use some kind of lubricant to assist in the even distribution of the shellac solution by means of a pad. Long custom has hitherto favoured raw linseed oil for this purpose; modern practice, however, prompts the use of a white oil, by the use of which it is claimed the annoyance of sweating is greatly reduced. Linseed oil also occasionally becomes oxidised on the surface and becomes difficult to remove if it is left too long before attempting to clear it off. Some kinds of wood—particularly rosewood—are naturally oily in themselves. Climatic influences cause the grain-filler to swell and eventually break the film of polish to a degree of roughness. Whatever kind of oil may have been used, sweating is generally the result of the inability of the operator to keep the lubricant from getting underneath the polish, or to effectively clear off the excess during the process of burnishing up to a lustre. It should be understood that the aim should be to use as little oil as the nature of the polishing solution will permit. Its use is not altogether avoidable. The commercial quality of the spirit also varies; with a mild brand much less oil may be suitable than when using a spirit that has been sharpened up by the addition of wood naphtha. Many are the devices to aid in the removal of this oil, or at least to check it from asserting itself quickly. Some operators wipe the recently polished surface over with glaze before attempting to burnish it up.

Continental practice favours burnishing it up first, then hardening the surface by applying, with a clean swab of soft rag, a clarified ox-gall solution made by filtering ox-gall through bone charcoal. The resultant solution should be quite clear, and be kept tightly corked when not in use.

French Polisher's Glaze.—This is very much in the nature of a bright lacquer. Its excessive use is not advisable on high-class articles owing to its poor wearing qualities. Chiefly, its use is confined to mouldings and other irregular surfaces that are somewhat difficult to burnish. Made by steeping about 8 oz. gum benzoin in 1 pt. methylated spirit and straining, it is applied by means of a pliable wadding pad enclosed in soft rag. A straight, end-to-end motion with a rather light pressure should be used. The first soaking of the benzoin in the spirit does not extract all the goodness out of it. It improves by keeping; that which is used directly it is made may not always prove a success. If it is required for immediate use it is better to buy it ready made.

The Use of Revivers.—If anything in the nature of furniture cream, which generally contains some kind of wax, is used as a reviver, the original shellac finish is not being restored to its original brightness, but wax is being deposited upon the surface. When this treatment has been tried and failed to give satisfaction, it is hopeless to expect that some other preparation, that is free from wax, will give better results owing to the inability of the latter to come into direct contact with the original polish. In such cases the preliminary treatment should be a washing of the surface with common brown vinegar, or water in which a little washing soda has been dissolved. Workshop practice in the use of revivers has an advantage in that the operator is able to clear off any apparent greasiness after their use by means of a swab of clean rag made slightly damp with spirit. Also, details such as wiping a glaze rubber over the mouldings, applying a coating of thin spirit varnish to turned portions, and making good parts from which the colour

WOOD FINISHING, PAINTING AND ENAMELLING

has worn off, make a great deal of difference. An old-time recipe for a reviver much used by wood finishers is as follows : ½ pt. brown vinegar, ½ pt. methylated spirit in which 1 oz. camphor has been dissolved, 1 oz. linseed oil, and ½ oz. butter of antimony. A more simple recipe consists of equal parts of spirits of camphor and camphorated oil. With the latter any excess of greasiness is finally removed by means of a swab of clean rag, made fairly damp, not wet, with spirit of camphor only. This mixture of oil and spirit containing camphor will prove useful in the removal of white marks caused by water and hot glasses.

Floor Polishing.—For the hardwood floors with their closely fitting joints, and block floorings to be met with in public buildings and mansions, polishing is an ideal finish on account of its easy application and subsequent freshening up with preparations claiming to have good sanitary as well as cleansing properties. Preparations containing wax require the aid of heavy brushes, whilst those of the oil class require soft polishing mops.

It is a common experience to find medium-sized floors with a border about 15 in. or 18 in. wide adjoining the skirting boards stained and varnished or polished a more or less brown colour. There is no apparent reason why other colours should not prove equally effective and fit in better with the decorative scheme. Nor does it follow that staining is the only method that can be usefully adopted ; paint followed up with a good quality hard-drying oil varnish would give far better wearing qualities than some of the cheap brands of the combined stain and spirit varnishes which are often used. The preparation of the boards before applying stain, paint, varnish or polish, rarely concerns the wood finisher, except to see that it is quite clean and free from the greasiness incidental to the frequent cleansing with soap. The interstices created by shrinkage of the boards are best dealt with by inserting wedge-shaped slips of wood glued in. Nail holes and such-like defects are better left to be dealt with after the staining is dry. They should be filled up with putty, coloured to match the stain.

Wax-polish finish is imparted by the friction of heavy brushes, and if special long-arm swinging brushes are not available some other simple means of imparting the necessary weight and friction must be devised, such as a fairly strong box about 2 ft. long by 18 in. wide, on the bottom of which can be screwed a number of new laundry brushes, bricks or other heavy material being placed in the box to impart the necessary weight. Woollen material should be fastened around its sides or damage is likely to result to the skirting boards. With some of the brushes referred to this contingency is guarded against by means of rubber pads. In a general way excellent results may be obtained by beeswax dissolved in turpentine so that it can be easily applied with flannel. The subsequent treatment is equivalent to that of cleaning a pair of boots—the more they are brushed the greater the shine. It follows that if the wax is very liquid in order to allow of its easy application, the subsequent heavy work may be eased by allowing it to dry off a little before starting to use the brushes, and that a final rub up with dry flannel or rag will greatly assist in bringing up a good gloss.

PAINTING AND ENAMELLING

Painting.—Many painting and enamelling jobs are spoiled by using a new, blunt-shaped brush instead of a flat, wedge-shaped brush. When new wood is to be paint-finished, the main pitfalls to guard against are the knots and nail holes. The former should be coated with knotting before applying the paint, and the latter dealt with after the first coat of paint is dry. The knotting should be spread over the knots and about 1 in. around. Work that it is desired to repaint should be thoroughly cleansed first by washing with water in which common washing soda has been dissolved–a small teacupful of soda to a gallon of water should suffice. Very dirty articles may sometimes with advantage be brushed over with water in which a lump of builder's lime has been slaked. Assuming the paint to be bought in tins ready for use—and a 4-lb. tin be deemed ample for the job—sufficient should be put into another vessel for the first coat, this being thinned out well with turpentine only. The first coat will dry out dull looking. The second and subsequent coatings may be applied a trifle thicker. Any thinning out that is required in the case of light paints should be done with linseed oil and turpentine in about equal proportions ; for dark paints use boiled linseed oil with the turpentine. The work will then dry out brighter and wear better than when turpentine only is used. The method of working is of prime importance where more than one colour is being used on one job, such as a door, for instance. The panels, being lighter in colour than the framing, would be done first, mouldings included if they are to be left the same as the panels, or left untouched if they are to be the same as the framing, or if intended to stand out a distinctive colour. When applying the paint to the framing the procedure is generally to coat the stiles between the panels first, and the top, middle and bottom rails last. A small brush with a fairly sharp point should be used for the mouldings as an aid to getting the paint well into the mouldings. By this method of working, in the event of any of the lighter colour paint having extended beyond its limits, the darker colours used afterwards would cover it up.

Painting and Graining Furniture.— Painted furniture is generally only suitable for bedroom use. Its lighter colour tones with fine line decorations, and imparts a pleasing, distinctive change to highly polished finishes. Such furniture always looks well against walls that have been distempered. For articles that are not grained, grey produces a good effect, brightness being imparted by more or less decorative lines and touches of orange, blue or green, either alone or in combination. Grained furniture is quite out of date as regards bedroom furnishings, though it still applies to the homely kitchen dresser, which is generally finished to resemble oak. This finish is obtained by means of oil paints and graining as practised by house-painters, a method which is very different from the old-time finish of bedroom furniture on which the oil paints were replaced with a foundation of whiting and jelly size. On very cheap goods the graining was done direct by a process of spirit graining and soft colour crayons, a procedure which enabled the goods to be grained, over-grained and varnished the same day. Medium-priced goods were given a coat of suitable oil paint over the whiting mixture, and the work finished out more on the lines adopted by house-painters. The art of imparting the figure has been much simplified since then by the use of embossed rollers or metal rollers furnished with uneven notches. Graining papers can also be had in a variety of designs. Each piece of graining paper can be used eight or ten times, and, after a cleaning with turpentine, an additional four or five times.

Enamelling.—In the process of enamelling no attempt is made to make use of the original or natural figure of the wood. Though, singularly, the cheaper class of bedroom furniture is grained to represent maple or birch, the better class of goods is finished out in self colours—generally white—which may be a bright porcelain finish, or a semi-dull, resembling eggshell. In the former case the woodwork, generally deal or cheap pine, is given several coats of whiting. The whiting is first soaked in water until it is quite soft, the surplus water poured off, and then made into a paint-like mixture by adding a double-jelly painter's size, in proportions of about $1\frac{1}{2}$ pt. water to each 1 lb. of size. A portion of the thicker mixture is reserved for the purpose of stopping nail holes and other defects. Putty should not be used for this purpose as it is apt to create an oily patch through which the whiting mixture will not strike. The article should be glasspapered to a smooth face and then a coat of the size mixture applied.

For a cheap, white enamel finish, a good foundation is thus prepared, but if the

WOOD FINISHING, PAINTING AND ENAMELLING

work is intended to be grained and varnished instead, suitable colour pigments should be added to the mixture in order to ensure a suitable colour background being given. Generally a little yellow ochre powder will suffice. On the other hand, some grainers prefer a coat of tinted paint applied on the top of the whiting mixture to grain on, rather than on the coating of clear size. For the better-class goods whiting is used as advised, but the enamel is not applied direct to such a surface—one or more coats of paint of practically the same colour as the enamel are interposed between the two. The paint is made sharp, that is, to dry dull, a result generally obtained by thinning out with good quality turpentine only. Makers of enamel supply, and advise the use of, a special flatting preparation.

Varnishing Painted Surfaces.—The varnishing of painted surfaces has the merit of preserving the surface and colour, as well as improving its general appearance. There are oil varnishes made for indoor use only, and also another kind specially prepared to withstand the vagaries of the weather. In the application of varnish the same conditions apply as for painting. An entirely new brush will not ensure a first-class finish. It requires some practice before one gleans how a varnish will behave. The aim should be to lay it on with confidence, and of just sufficient thickness that, as left from the brush, it will not run. The brush should not be overloaded, and as far as possible the varnish should be laid off with the tip of the brush only.

Stove Enamelling.—Enamelling by heat can only be successfully carried out on articles that will not shrink or split when subjected to more than normal heat. The advantage lies in the fact that the application of the enamel calls for no particular skilled labour in the putting of it on with a brush and laying it off level. Small articles may be dipped into the enamel or it may be sprayed on. The heat to which the goods are then subjected causes the enamel to become thinner and settle down to all inequalities of the surface and finally vitrify to a hard, bright finish. Provided that steps have been taken to first prepare the groundwork with something that acts as a grain filler and checks undue absorption, one application of the latter will generally suffice. Heat enamels cannot be made on a small scale. They should be bought ready made. Makers generally supply a first-coating preparation that is preferable to the whiting and jelly-siz, mixture.

Upholstery

Tools. — The tools necessary for upholstery work are very few, consisting in the main of hammers, needles, trimming knives, and web strainers.

The hammers are, of course, a very necessary part of the upholsterer's tool kit. The one known as a "cabriole," and illustrated by Fig. 1, has a fine head, its use being for driving in gimp pins and for tacks in awkward corners. It is a most useful hammer and is quite indispensable, although practice is required before it can be used with ease, owing to the smallness of the head. What is termed an "upholsterer's" hammer is shown by Fig. 2. This is of a similar style to the cabriole; but the head is larger and heavier, and its use is for driving in tacks in all-round work. For driving in studs, brass edging nails, etc., an ordinary hammer can be used.

Several different patterns of needles are required. The buttoning needle (Fig. 3) is pointed at both ends and round in its entire length, with an eye on one end for the twine. It is made in lengths varying from 8 in. to 18 in., according to the size of the work for which it is required; and,

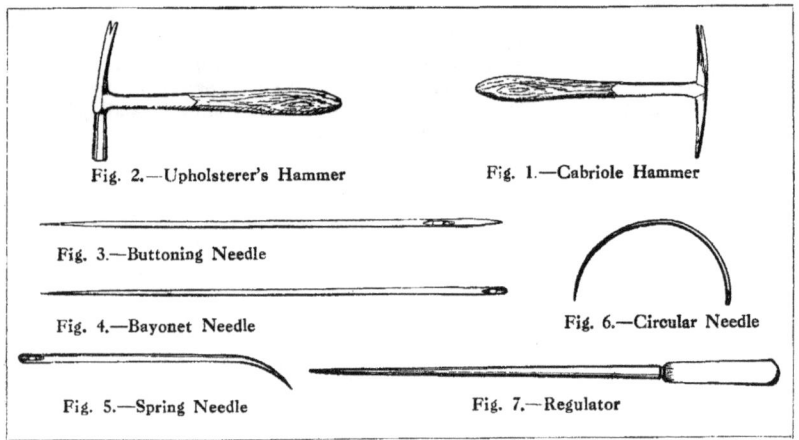

Fig. 2.—Upholsterer's Hammer
Fig. 1.—Cabriole Hammer
Fig. 3.—Buttoning Needle
Fig. 4.—Bayonet Needle
Fig. 6.—Circular Needle
Fig. 5.—Spring Needle
Fig. 7.—Regulator

UPHOLSTERY

as its name implies, its use is for putting in buttons, and also for making long stitches of twine on seats, etc. The " bayonet " needle (Fig. 4) is also pointed on both ends ; but unlike the stitching needle, one end of the bayonet is triangular in section, while the opposite end, which also contains the eye, is round. This needle is used for stitching edges, etc. and is made in a number of lengths, about 10 in. being a most useful size for all-round work. The spring needle (Fig. 5) is bent at one end, the curved portion being triangular in section, while the straight part, which contains the eye at the extreme end, is round. A useful length for sewing in springs, stitching hessian, etc., is 4 in. The circular needle (Fig. 6) is almost semicircular in shape, and is made in a large range of sizes, the smaller of which are used for putting on cord, seaming material in " surround " work, etc., while the larger sizes are sometimes used for sewing in springs, instead of the spring needle. A selection of ordinary sewing needles are also wanted for sewing covers, etc., while one or two packing needles of various sizes for seaming hessians, etc., will be wanted.

In working up edges during stitching, and also for getting stuffing material into position in buttoned work, laying creases, etc., regulators are required. Of these there are two kinds, one which is flat on one end and pointed on the other, being used in stitching, creasing, and for general purposes ; while the long-handled type of regulator (Fig. 7) is used for working stuffing material in buttoned work.

For straining the webbing one or other of the patterns of web strainers will be wanted, one kind is a sort of wide-mouthed pair of pliers, which is also found useful at times for straining spring canvas, etc. ; while another is made of wood, and has spikes on each end for holding the webbing and keeping the tool rigid on the frame while in use. There are also a number of other patterns of web strainers on the market.

In upholstery, the stuffing materials have to be torn asunder before use, and for this purpose one of two things will be required, namely, a pair of hand " cards " or a " carding " machine. Where only a small quantity of work is done, a pair of cards will suffice ; but in large shops where quantities of work are handled a machine is a necessity. Hand cards consist of two pieces of hardwood, each of which is covered with spikes, the bottom piece being fixed to the bench, while the top one is held in the hands of the operator. The stuffing material is placed on the bottom card while the top card is worked backwards and forwards, the spikes tearing the stuffing materials asunder. A willowing or carding machine is worked by hand, treadle, or power, the stuffing materials being fed into one end to a revolving drum having spikes on its surface, which, in conjunction with a spiked top board, tears the stuffing asunder quickly and efficiently, the carded material being thrown out on the opposite end of the machine.

There is a goodly quantity of sewing to be done from time to time in upholstery, and, although not an absolute necessity, a sewing machine will be found a decided advantage, as by its use a great deal of time is saved.

Materials for Stuffing and Sundries.—The shapes seen worked up on upholstered furniture require the use of certain stuffing materials, and although in the best class of work horsehair is used throughout, cheapness necessitates the substitution of inferior materials. Stuffing, as the term is applied to the actual work, is divided into two distinct operations, namely, first and second, the first stuffing comprising the working up of the edges with the assistance of canvas and twine. As a first stuffing, a firm material is required, and nothing really excels horsehair for the purpose ; as a substitute, however, there are a number of materials in use, which are described below.

Alva is a seaweed from the Baltic. This material is in long thin strands, and should be used perfectly dry, as when wet it is liable to breed vermin of an objectionable character. Alva which has become broken up by continual use is not nearly so good for stuffing, and therefore care should be taken in tearing it asunder, the hands only being used for the purpose, and on no account should cards or machining be resorted to.

Coir, as it is termed in the trade, is in reality coconut fibre, and can be recommended for first stuffing work. It should be of the long stapled variety and free from dust.

Algerian grass is another substitute for horsehair, for which latter material it is often used as an adulterant. When long stapled it works up well for edges, and it may be counted among the best of the substitutes for hair.

In the cheapest classes of work anything is considered good enough for first stuffings, wood-wool, shavings, hay, and straw each finding a place in stitched edges. Where good work is required good materials should be used, and it will be found that the best stuffs prove the cheapest in the long run.

For second stuffing horsehair is the best material to use; but here again the worker is hampered by the question of cost. As a substitute for hair one or other of the wool fillings can be used, care being taken that they are pure and clean. Medium-grade work often has wool as a base in the second stuffing with a top dressing of hair, this lending a softness to the seat unobtainable with the use of wool alone. Wool flocks are of various qualities, the cheapest being known in the trade as "shoddy," while the quality of the material rises by steps until the pure white wool is reached, intermediate qualities being unwashed and washed ruggings, linseys, mixtures, etc. Cotton flocks are entirely unsuited to chair upholstery, as they are hard and unyielding, and in the cheaper qualities contain a quantity of husks.

Wadding is a largely used material, and is obtainable in two kinds, "sheet" and "bundle." The former is used principally on seat backs, etc., which are upholstered plain (that is, unbuttoned), while the latter plays an important part in buttoned work, fancy surrounds, etc. Sheet wadding should be bought in the piece of 12 yd.

Webbing forms an important part in upholstery work, as the whole of the weight is practically supported by this material. There are two kinds of webbing in use, English and German. The former is the best and dearest, and is known for size by numbers, each width having a particular number, such as 10, 12, etc., which all manufacturers observe. English webbing is put up in pieces of 18 yd. German web is a far commoner material than English, and cannot be relied on for lasting work. The sizes are known by the number of strips of colour contained in its length, such as four blue, three red, etc., the greater the number of strips the wider the material. Whole pieces contain 36 yd.

Springs are used in the seats, backs, etc., of furniture, and are made from steel wire having a coating of copper to prevent them rusting. There is a large difference in the quality of springs, some being made from better-tempered wire than others, the cheaper kinds being stiff and unyielding, while the best kinds yield evenly to pressure. They are made in a number of sizes to meet the requirements of the trade.

Upholsterer's twine plays an important part in the work, for which it is specially made. It is very strong, and has a well-finished surface, in order that it may not unravel with the continual pulling through the stuffing material to which it has to be subjected. It is sold in balls weighing ½ lb., and is of various thicknesses according to the work for which it is required.

Laid cord is used for lashing springs together in order that they may not work out of position. It is in reality a thick string of good quality, and is sold in balls of 1 lb. upwards.

Hessian is a canvas made in various qualities for the upholstering and allied trades. The cheaper hessians are coarse in texture, and the thread from which they are woven is shaggy, and where strength is required they cannot be recommended. Good-quality hessians are fine in texture, light in colour, and very strong. These latter kinds should be used for the bottoms of chairs, etc., spring canvas, and in any work requiring durability. Cheap hessians are often used as a substitute for scrim, to which they are inferior.

UPHOLSTERY

Scrim is a fine canvas of open mesh made from a fine thread, its use being in first stuffings, to hold the filling material. It is superior to coarse hessian for the purpose as it answers well to the action of the regulator in working up edges for stitching. Both scrim and hessian are made in a variety of widths; but usually in multiples of ¼ yd. The two most useful widths for upholsterers are 6/4 (called six-quarter in the trade and representing 1½ yd.) and 8/4 (2 yd.).

Black linen is a closely woven material generally of 4/4 width, and used as a substitute for hessian for the underneath of chair seats, etc. Its cost is rather more than that of hessian.

Upholsterer's unbleached calico is sold in 70-in. width, and is rather finer and softer than the ordinary household calico. In good-class furniture, excepting in the case of buttoned work, a covering of calico is always run underneath the final covering material; and although calico is sometimes used in conjunction with buttoning, it is questionable whether it is possible to obtain such good results with the creasing as when the covering is run direct on to bundle wadding.

Upholsterers' tacks are of two kinds, "fine" and "improved;" the former, of which two sizes are used, ⅜ in. and ½ in., is for tacking on covers, hessians, etc., while the latter kind, which for ordinary work should be ⅝ in. long, is used for putting on spring canvas, webbing, etc. Improved tacks are thicker in the body and larger in the head than fine. Both varieties are put up in large packets containing ten small packets of 1,000 tacks in each.

Materials for Covering.—The number of materials for covering furniture is naturally very large, and the assortment of patterns consequently very varied. Under the heading of stiff coverings, which, correctly speaking, belong to the dining-room and library, may be mentioned the following :—

Roan is a real leather obtained from the skins of sheep, which is tanned, dressed and dyed and stamped with a grain and sometimes with a pattern.

Morocco is a goat skin, prepared in the same way as roan, but is softer than the latter and costs more than double the price of roan. These two coverings are, of course, sold by the skin, which varies in price according to the quantity of usable material required. In ordering, measurements should be taken of the actual material required without blemish, especially where plain work is in hand, but in buttoning, little imperfections can often be worked out in the creases.

Pigskin possesses fine wearing properties, but is very dear, and consequently is not in very great demand. The toughness of this leather necessitates its being softened with water and put on wet.

Much of the trade which was at one time done in furniture leathers has been usurped by the various imitation leathers now on the market. Pegamoid, roanoid, thannette, pantasote, and rexine are the best-known varieties of imitation leathers which really have a close resemblance to the real article. These cloths consist of a linen or duck base, on which is spread a composition. They are stamped in a variety of grains, and in some instances are hard to detect, when new, from the real thing. Being obtainable in running lengths, and in widths varying from 45 in. to 50 in., they are economical in use, and on account of the comparative lowness of price are in great favour with the public.

American cloth, called A. C. in the trade, was the origin of imitation leathers, although there is a great difference in appearance between this and real leather. Crockett's is a well-known make of A. C. and the first, second and even third qualities are to be relied on to stand hard wear. Widths are the same as pegamoid, etc., but prices are considerably less.

Tapestries may be said to be of three kinds, wool, silk, and mercerised. The mercerised description is composed largely of cotton, and goes through certain finishing processes in order to give it a lustre resembling that of silk, although when put to hard wear the covering quickly loses its attraction and becomes dead in appearance. Wool tapestries may be counted among the best of the soft coverings for withstanding hard wear, and, as they are obtainable in a large number of patterns and prices, are in good demand.

Real silk tapestries are not generally manufactured entirely from silk; but are backed up with cotton, the actual silk being on the face. The price of silk tapestries naturally depends on the quantity of silk used in their manufacture, which in the cheapest kinds is just about sufficient to enable it to be called silk. Tapestries are generally supposed to be six-quarter wide; but they generally finish about 50 in.

Among the velvets the following are in most general demand :—

Utrecht is self coloured, and has a stiff cropped pile, which varies in length of staple with the price paid for it. Cotton wool, and mohair are the materials from which the pile is woven. As a variation from the solid effects rendered by plain velvet there is moquette, a 50-in. material with a velvet pile and having a figuring in the form of colourings worked in the weaving. Cheap moquettes are made from a stock groundwork, the patterns being printed in after the material is made. There is, besides velvet moquette, one with an uncut pile, which resembles Brussels carpet. The trimmings of railway carriages are largely done in this material, which has excellent wearing qualities.

Stamped velvets are those in which the pile is depressed in places to form a figuring, the stamping being done by passing the material through heated rollers.

Genoa velvet has a raised velvet figuring with a flat groundwork, which latter often contains, in the better qualities, a certain amount of silk. Good-quality Genoa velvets are very rich in tone, and are high in price.

Plush is, or should be, a material with a silk pile, which yields various effects according to the light in which it is held. Whole suites are sometimes entirely covered with this material, although it is comparatively seldom that this is done, a more common practice being to use it in conjunction with silk tapestry, the plush forming the surrounds of the seats, etc.

By judicious selection of colourings some very fine effects are obtainable in silk tapestry and plush work, which is particularly suited to the covering of drawing-room furniture.

Plushette, as its name implies, is a sort of imitation of plush. It is a woollen material with a longish, rather shaggy pile, and is but seldom used as an entire covering for furniture, being more suitable as an outside backing for velvet and saddlebag suites, in cases where cost of material has to be cut down. Plushette is mostly 45 in. wide, while velvets and plushes, although obtainable in a variety of widths, are most commonly 24 in. wide.

Art serge is a cheap material of various colours. It cannot be recommended for wear, although the low price at which it can be obtained induces people to use it as a covering material. It is, in reality, more suitable for draperies than for upholstery. The width is mostly 45 in.

Repps are not much in favour nowadays, although at one time they were in great demand. They are rather expensive coverings; but are good wearing, and usually 45 in. wide.

Carriage cloth is in reality more applicable to coach trimming than to upholstery; but one occasionally has to use it for some particular purpose. It is a sort of low quality billiard cloth, made in the West of England, and runs about 60 in. wide.

Hair seating is another kind of old-fashioned material, for which there is but little demand, excepting for the upholstering of smoking compartments of railway carriages. The stuff is woven from horsehair, and is consequently very strong, although it is rather sombre in effect, that used for furniture covering being black in colour. It is quite unsuited for buttoning with creases, and if buttons have to be used, they should be but lightly pulled in. Hair-seating can only be cut in the length, each width required being obtainable. There is an imitation of hair-seating which should not be used for anything but outside backing. The width of this material is 50 in., and the price at which it can be obtained corresponds with its quality.

UPHOLSTERY

Sateens, of various colourings and qualities, and measuring 30 in. wide, are often used for outside-backs of easy chairs, couches, etc., in order to keep down the cost of coverings. They are a cotton fabric having a semi-lustrous surface.

Trimmings.—Among the trimmings used by the upholsterer are: Bandings, for use with real and imitation leathers, these being put on round the framework where the covering finishes off, and studs having heads covered with the same material as the banding and used to keep the latter in position. For surrounding the edges of tapestry and other soft coverings, gimps of various patterns and colourings are most commonly used, these being fixed by means of pins made specially for the purpose, or with small-headed studs. Edging nails, having round heads and made of brass, sold either natural colour or plated copper, silver, or antique, are also used as a finish for the edges of covering materials, more especially in conjunction with the thin flat solid seats known as pin-cushion. These nails are made in a number of sizes and are packed in boxes of 1,000. Rouch is a kind of fluffy gimp, and is used for edging heavy coverings such as moquette, saddlebags, etc. Cord is a silk-covered material used for stitching to the edges of upholstered furniture, in order to give a finish to the article. It is particularly useful in hiding the joins in combined tapestry and plush work. Rope is a kind of thick cord, and finds a place where the upholstery is carried out with rolls. Cord, gimp, rouch, and banding are each put up in pieces of 36 yd., but cut lengths can be obtained if required.

Methods of Working.—The manner in which a "spring" stuffed "standard" or small chair is upholstered from the bare frame will now be described.

The webbing is the first matter to receive attention, and to put this on, the chair has to be turned upside down on the bench, as webbing in spring work is fixed to the underneath of the seat framing. Fig. 8 is a plan of the underneath of a seat frame, and shows correct positions of webbing and also the places occupied by the springs. Begin webbing the frame by running one strand in the centre of the frame from the front to the back, turning the end of the web underneath before tacking, in order that it may not break away when the strainers are sed. No. 11 or No. 12 web should be used, this being put on with ⅝-in. "improved" tacks. The web having been tacked on the front rail, pull it over to the back; then with the strainers pull it taut and tack off, cutting the webbing away to within about 1 in. of the tacks, and, turning this surplus piece over, fasten it down with a couple of tacks. The first or centre strand of web is shown at A (Fig. 8). The strands B and C can be put in in the same way as A. From the illustration it will be seen that

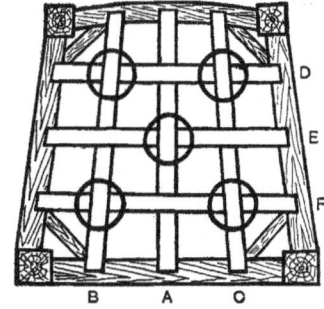

Fig. 8.—Standard Chair Seat Inverted, showing Positions of Webs and Springs

B and C are not run in straight, but incline inwards to meet the shape of the side rails. The cross strands D, E, and F are laced as shown.

All the web having been put in, the chair can now be turned right side up, and five 8-in. chair springs put in in the positions shown in Fig. 8. The spring needle should be filled with a length of twine, and each spring sewn in at four points, the twine being worked from the underneath in order that it may not get mixed up with the springs, and so cause waste of time in disentangling it. As each spring has received its four stitches, the twine should be cut off and a fresh start made in order that if one spring happens to break loose the whole lot will not necessarily do so.

The novice will no doubt find a little difficulty at first in accustoming himself to making the upholsterer's locking knot, which is used throughout the stitching-in of springs, working up of edges, etc. In putting in the springs the needle is pushed through the webbing from the underneath, and re-inserted on the opposite side of the last coil of the spring, after which the twine is pulled through and a double slip-knot made, and the twine pulled off tight and tied off, thus finishing the first stitch.

In the second and subsequent stitches the "locking" knot has to be used, this being made as follows : The twine is inserted on one side of the spring, and partly brought through on the other, the needle being held with the left hand. The fixed end of the twine at the last finished stitch is then held at a sufficient distance away from the knot to admit of it being wound twice round the pointed end of the needle, which is now drawn out and the free end of the twine drawn tight. It will be seen that by this means the twine is locked on the underneath of the web, and the stitch in the spring made firm, the two remaining stitches being put in and the end of the twine tied off on the last one.

All the springs having been put in, they have now to be covered with stout hessian termed "spring canvas" in the trade. The hessian is tacked to the top of the chair rails, and in taking measurements for cutting off the piece it should be remembered that the springs have to be depressed about one-third of their height, and they will consequently project above the level of the rails. A further allowance of 1 in. all round should be made for turning the hessian over in tacking. There is a right and a wrong way of putting on spring canvas, and any attempt to tack it right along one or other of the rails first is certain to end in failure. Get the canvas central, and drive a $\frac{3}{8}$-in. "improved" tack in the centre of the back; follow this with one in the centre of the front, and then put one in the middle of each of the sides. The four corners can now be pulled over, and a tack temporarily driven in each, when, if everything is in order, the tacks can be finally driven home ; or if the canvas appears to be unevenly pulled over, those at fault can be knocked out and the error rectified. The remainder of the tacks which run between those in the centres and corners of the chair rails can be inserted, and the raw ends of the hessian turned over on the top and kept in position with $\frac{1}{2}$-in. "fine" tacks.

The springs have now to be set in the positions they are to occupy, the centre one being set upright, while the four corner ones must incline outwards a little, so that when the chair is sat on the springs become level by reason of the depression acting more in the centre of the seat than it does at the sides. Were the springs set in upright, the chair seat would sink in the middle, and consequently prove uncomfortable in use. Previous to stitching the springs to the canvas, they have a natural tendency to work out of their correct position, and here skewers will be required, their use being to stick into the hessian and so prevent the springs jumping out of position while being sewn in. Four stitches are required to each spring as was done when stitching to the webbing, and each spring has, of course, to be run in independently of its neighbour, the locking stitch already described being used in all but the first stitches to each spring. In sewing the springs to the canvas the advantage of having a curved needle will be seen, as by this means the needle can be run in on one side of the spring and out on the other without the necessity of making two insertions of the needle.

The next step to be taken is to make a number of loops of twine all round the framework, this being done by partly driving in a $\frac{3}{8}$-in. improved tack at each of the corners, one in the centre of the back, and two at equal distances apart on the front and two sides. The twine for these loops can be tied to the tacks, which can then be driven right home. The reason for making the loops of twine is to provide a support for the stuffing on the edges, and the loops have therefore to be made large enough to admit of a moderate amount of stuffing being wound round them.

UPHOLSTERY

The first stuffing can be carried out with alva, hair, coir or grass, as desired, for each of which materials the working up is the same. After having got a goodly amount of stuffing in the loops of twine, fill in the centre of the seat, and measure it for the scrim, which is the next thing to be put on. The material should not be scrimped, as a goodly quantity is taken up in the stitching, and it is better to cut the stuff too large than too small. Temporarily tack the scrim all round, after the manner described for putting on the spring canvas, using $\frac{1}{2}$-in. fine tacks, which should on no account be driven right home. See that the scrim is put on evenly, and then, using the buttoning needle and thick twine, run a stitch in one of the corners of the seat, about 4 in. from the outside edge of the chair frame. If the corner chosen for the first stitch was a back one, take the needle to about the centre of the back, still keeping it about 4 in. in from the edge of the wood framing, push it through the scrim, stuffing and spring canvas, but not through the webbing, and bring it back again about $\frac{1}{2}$ in. nearer the last stitch, and, before pulling it right out, get hold of that part of the twine which is nearest the last stitch, and wind it twice round the needle, which on being pulled right out and the twine drawn tight, again forms the "locked" stitch. Now take the needle to the next corner, make another stitch, and continue these long stitches all round the seat.

Attention must now be directed to the stuffing up of the actual edges in readiness for the stitching, and here will be seen the advantage of stitching the scrim down in the centre, one important point being that it is possible to knock out the temporary tacks without the risk of its shifting from its correct position. If the back corners of the scrim have not already been cut, in order to allow them to run down each side where the back legs are, give them a slit with the scissors, and also cut off any superfluous scrim. Now knock a few tacks out of the back and insert, if necessary, sufficient additional stuffing material to make the edge about $1\frac{1}{2}$ in. high, and comparatively firm, allowing the edge to project over the level of the seat rail as in Fig. 9, which is a section of a chair seat with scrim finally tacked, but before stitching is begun. As the edge is filled up and got to a correct shape, the scrim is turned under and finally tacked with $\frac{1}{2}$-in. "fine" tacks, the tacks being run on the edge of the chair frame, which should be rasped down to receive them.

When the back is tacked down, take the front in hand, leaving the actual corners until the two sides are finished. Stuff up the two sides and then work up the corners, allowing them to project over the front edge of the seat rail as before. It is of the greatest importance that the

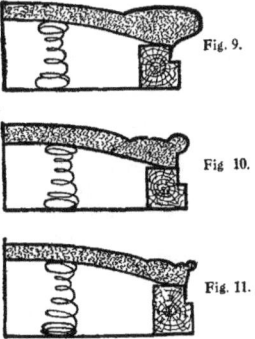

Figs. 9, 10 and 11.—Sections of Chair Seats, showing Shapes, with Blind-stitching, First Through-stitching, and Second Through-stitching

edge should be evenly stuffed up all round, and it should also project the same distance over the wooden framework, otherwise the finished stitching is certain to be irregular. The edge has now to be given a row of "blind-stitching" which pulls the stuffing material to the front. All the stitching, whether "blind" or otherwise, is started on the left-hand and worked towards the right. To put in the blind row proceed as follows. Fill the buttoning needle with about a couple of yards of thin twine and insert the needle (keeping the eye end towards you) within about $\frac{1}{2}$ in. of the back leg, and close to the top of the seat rail. Pull the needle out on top of the scrim to about three parts of its length, and, shifting the point of the needle about so that the stuffing material goes between the loop of twine made by the stitch, push it out again about 1½ in. from the point where it is inserted on the edge of the chair seat, making a double slip-knot, and pulling the twine tight. This is the first stitch, and the slip-knot ensures the twine being held fast.

The next and subsequent stitches are carried out as follows : Insert the needle about 2 in. to the right of the last stitch, bring it out about three-quarters of its length on the top of the scrim, and return it again to the front, bringing it out about ¾ in. to the left of the point at which it was inserted, and before pulling it right out take a couple of turns round it with the twine, which can then be pulled tight, and the same process repeated until the whole of the chair seat has received its row of blind-stitching.

At this point the services of a flat regulator will be required, its use being to draw the stuffing material towards the front. The pointed end of the regulator is inserted just above the blind-stitching, and by working the regulator about the stuffing material is worked forwards in order to bring the shape of the edge up to that shown by Fig. 9.

The work is now ready for putting in two or three rows of what is called "through-stitching," which, unlike the "blind-stitch," comes right out on the top of the scrim. For putting in the through-stitching, the bayonet needle should be used on account of its point being stronger than that of the buttoning needle, and consequently the point can be used for regulating as the stitching is proceeded with. For a moderately high edge, say 1½ in. from the top of the seat rails, two rows of through-stitching will be quite sufficient for ordinary soft coverings ; but for leather it is as well to put in another row, especially in plain work. The first row of through-stitching makes a roll on he edge of the chair of the shape shown in Fig. 10. The locking-stitch is employed as was done in the case of the "blind" row but the stitches should be closer together than in the last-named row. It is of the greatest importance that the stitching be kept even, as if this is not done the finished edge is certain to be faulty. A little practice will soon accustom the worker to running his rows in evenly. The point where the first "through" row comes out on the front edge of the chair-seat should be about ½ in. from the blind row, and where three rows of "through" are used, the first should be a trifle closer to the blind row.

The first row having been got in all round the chair seat, get the regulator at work again in order to pull the stuffing material well up to the top of the roll just formed, in readiness for the next row of stitching, the putting in of which gives the shape of the edge shown in Fig. 11. In a seat in which three rows are run, the top or last row can be a trifle smaller in diameter than in a two-row edge, and this, coupled with lowering the first row a trifle, gives room for putting in the extra row. It will be observed that in carrying out the stitching, the edge is always kept forward over the level of the wood framing. Had the edge been kept upright, it would be found that the straining on of the cover would have drawn the edge inwards, and consequently marred the appearance of the finished article by reason of the upholstered seat being smaller at the top than the frame of the seat. By allowing the stitching to project over the frame when the covering is put on, the edge finishes level, with the result that a perfectly level edge is obtained, instead of a receding one. The first stuffing of the chair is now completed.

The chair frame which is intended to have its back upholstered contains a rebate round the part to be upholstered for the reception of the tacks required to hold the upholstery, and if the outside back of the chair has to be run on the outside of the frame, a second rebate is required ; but in some cases the outside back is run in from the front, this being put on before the stuffing materials, etc., are put on. If the back is a large one, two strands of webbing may be run each way, using No. 10 web, which should be put on with ¼-in. "fine" tacks so as not to split the framing; but if the work in hand is moderately small, the webbing can be left out. Whether the back is webbed or not, the inside of the back will require to be covered with stout hessian, using ⅜-in. "fine" tacks to hold it.

For a back with a stitched edge a similar process to that done in working up the seat is necessary excepting that in this case no springs will be required. It is as well to put a few long loops of twine in to hold the stuffing round the edge, and after the scrim has been temporarily tacked, the long stitches can be put in as was done in the working up of the seat, and the edge, which, when finished, should be about 1 in. high from the framing, stuffed up ready for stitching. One row of blind-stitching is wanted, this being followed by one of "through," which is all the stitching necessary to complete the first stuffing of the back. An important point to remember is the keeping of the edge in proper line in the stitching as any irregularity in this direction is certain to be apparent when the covering is put on.

The final stuffing and covering can now be undertaken.

If horsehair is to be used for the second stuffing, some more loops of twine will be wanted on the top of the seat, in order that the filling may not move about when the chairs are used, and so spoil the shape, which it has a tendency to do unless secured by twisting some of it round the twine. If hair proves too expensive, wool flock may be used as a substitute; but this latter material will not require to be held in position with loops of twine. Although a very good seat can be worked up with a wool second stuffing, it cannot be compared with a hair-stuffed seat, as the latter retains its shape longer, and is also softer than the former. In gauging the quantity of stuffing necessary to form a correctly shaped seat, a certain amount of practice is required. The experienced upholsterer can tell at once, by lightly pressing his hand over the work, whether enough stuffing has been put on, and the worker should accustom himself to detect inequalities in the stuffing material before he starts the covering.

Shape is a great point in upholstery, and if this is not well looked after the finished work is spoilt. A correctly formed seat should be moderately high in the centre and gradually worked off to the edges, which latter should stand out firm and be well defined. Fig. 12 is a section of a correctly shaped standard chair seat. The stuffing material should be put on evenly and free from lumps, and it will have to be considerably higher than the finished seat, as the putting on of the covers depresses it considerably. In a second stuffing, which has wool flock as a base and has a top dressing only of hair, the shape of the seat should be worked up with wool, and an even layer of hair spread over this. Owing to the springy nature of horsehair, it should be compressed with the hands before it is put on.

Fig. 12.—Section of Standard Chair Seat Finished

In all good-class work a first covering of calico is run on the top of the stuffing material. It is not sufficient that the calico be put on and tacked down whichever way it pulls over, method and care being necessary in order that the seat may be shaped correctly for putting on the covering material. The calico having been cut to size, lay it on the top of the stuffing with the threads running from back to front and side to side. This is important, as if the material is put on diagonally, the shape of the seat may suffer from unequal pulling. Pull the material over to the back of the chair first, and temporarily drive in one tack in the centre, using ½-in. "fine" for the purpose. Follow this up with one in the centre of the front, passing the hand across the calico two or three times from back to front, in order to flatten the stuffing material and level it up. It is not sufficient that the stuffing be merely knocked down; the hand should pass right over the seat, and care must be taken that the shape is maintained. Now get one tack in the centre of each side, again using the hand to stretch the calico and equalise the height of the stuffing material. Run one tack in temporarily on each side of the four just put in, and about 1½ in. away, starting at the back, then doing the front and following up with the sides, keeping the hand going over the surface.

The back corners of the calico can now be cut out in order that it may run down on each side of the legs. To make the first cut, the calico should be pulled forward from the corner until it can be doubled over with the crease just touching the back leg. Then with the scissors start cutting from the point of the calico, and continue to within ⅛ in. of the crease. The ends can now be pulled over, one to the back and the other to the side, the surplus calico at the sides being cut away and the ends temporarily tacked. The front and sides are next tacked off, but the front corners are not cut away yet.

As the calico is now, it may require a little more stretching to equalise the surface of the seat and work it up to good shape; and it will be seen that by driving the tacks half-way in only on the first laying of the material, any irregularities, such as under- or over-stuffing, can be easily set right, which would not be the case had the work been finally tacked off in the first instance. Put right anything which is wrong, and, until practice is acquired, put the tacks in temporarily again, so that it can be ascertained for certain that the work is a correct shape.

Start finally tacking the calico at the back of the chair, knocking out two or three of the old tacks at a time, and leaving the corner tacks until the front and sides have been dealt with. During the whole of the tacking the hand should be continually used to stretch the calico, which must not be turned under when tacked, as it would prove too bulky, and would in all probability show when the final cover was put on. The tacks which hold the calico must not be run close to the polished woodwork, as they would be in the way when the covers are put on. A rule which should invariably be followed throughout upholstering work is the starting of the tacking in the centre of the seat or other part being dealt with, as by this means alone can the covers be got on evenly.

After the calico has been tacked all round, do the back and side corners, and follow up with those at the front, cutting away any surplus material, and avoiding bulky folds, which are certain to show up when the final cover is on.

It sometimes happens that in stitching up the front corners, the woodwork of which is higher than the sides and front, that the edge has a tendency to pull down too far; and although, properly speaking, this should not be the case, emergencies have sometimes to be dealt with. If the irregularity is but trifling, a little wadding or stuffing material carefully wedged in under the calico will often overcome the difficulty; but where this method is not sufficient to rectify the error, a piece of stiff but thin cardboard may be tacked to the front and side of the corner, the card being bent in order that it may run round the corner and hold the edge.

The beginning of the upholstery work for a settee and divan chairs is to web the back of the settee, on the inner side, three webs lengthwise, then twelve woven in across. Then the arms may be webbed, one lengthwise and three across. This is shown in Figs. 13 and 14; also the positions of the springs, which must be stitched to the webbing with twine, and fixed to the wood with staples. They are next lashed down to a convenient level judging for a stuffing over them of from 1½ to 3 in. in thickness, according to the part. The spring canvas is to be stretched and tacked over, and may be stitched to the top coils of the springs. The back is then ready for "first stuffing"; but it is as well to do the arms up to this stage, and it will be found necessary to untack the spring canvas of the back a little at each end to pull through the arm spring canvas for tacking to the back of the upright. These two openings must be left available for pulling through other covers of the arms and back, which

UPHOLSTERY

may then be "first stuffed" and covered with scrim. The scroll front edges of the arms will require forming firm with three or four rows of stitching. The seat frame is webbed on the underside, and the springs placed as shown in Fig. 15. Those on the webbing may be lashed down with the spring twine. Those on the front rail must have a length of tough cane lashed firmly along the front of the top coils; then they may be lashed to the other springs.

The spring canvas must be stretched over and tacked to the four lower rails.

wrinkles or fullness, by removing the partly driven tacks and inserting them as required. Undue pulling or stretching of the material should be avoided. In fixing the back and end edges of the seat cover, they should be tacked, not to the seat rails as were the scrim and calico, but turned up and tacked to the back rails the same as the back and arm covers, to effectually close the opening. It may be necessary to stuff in some wadding between the rails after the tacking is done. The front of the seat and arms can next be padded with wadding and covered

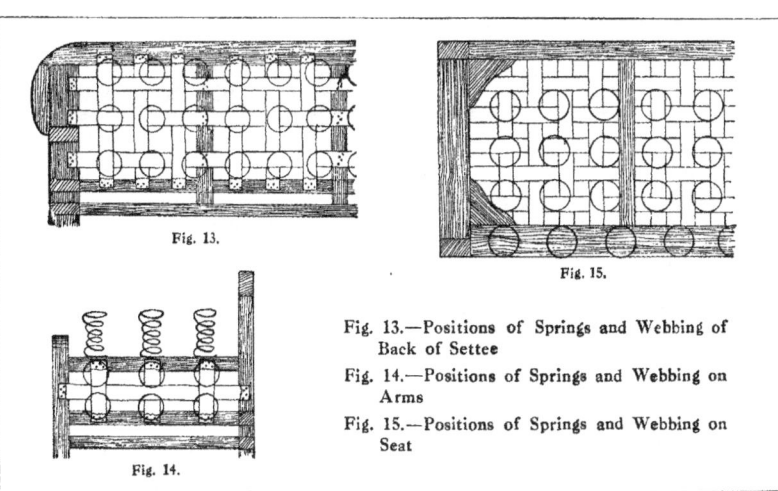

Fig. 13.—Positions of Springs and Webbing of Back of Settee

Fig. 14.—Positions of Springs and Webbing on Arms

Fig. 15.—Positions of Springs and Webbing on Seat

It may then be "first stuffed," and a round firm-stitched edge formed along the front. The back and arms can then be "second stuffed" and covered with calico; also the seat. It is then ready for the final covers, which must be cut and fitted approximately to the shape, to be put on, back first, arms, and seat. When they are ready, sheets of wadding are laid over the stuffing, and if the covers are of Pegamoid or other leather material, a double thickness of the wadding will be an improvement. The covers should first be tacked in place temporarily, to be carefully drawn into correct position free from

with calico, then with the material. The outside ends and back may be covered with canvas and the finished material.

The treatment of the divan chairs is very similar; but the arms require six springs each, three on the rail and three on the webbing. The nine springs in the back must be in three rows and not higher than 10 in. from the top.

For the covering of the underneath of seats, either stout hessian or black linen is used, the former being cheaper than the latter. Here, again, certain principles should be followed in putting on the canvas or linen, as the case may be. The canvas is cut off to the required size, and laid on the underneath of the chair or couch seat, with the thread running from back to front and side to side, the reason for this being that if the threads are run on diagonally it is difficult to make the canvas lie flat and free from wrinkles. The tacking is carried out after the method followed in putting on covers, that is, one tack is driven in the front, back, and two sides for the start, in order to ensure the hessian being put on correctly. The remaining tacks, which should be about 1 in. apart, are put in, and finally the corners which run round the legs are cut out and tacked off. The edge of the canvas or linen should, of course, be turned in underneath, and kept about ⅛ in. away from the polished edge of the frames.

There now remains the gimping or banding to be put on round the edges of the covers.

Start putting on the gimp on the right-hand side close up to the back leg. Make it fast in one corner, and then stretch it across as far as possible in a direct straight line ; and if there is no rise in the polished work where the front legs come, strain the gimp right round to the opposite back leg, and tack it off to within 1½ in. of the leg. Then cut the main piece of gimp off, so that the piece can be doubled under and fastened off close up to the back leg. By putting on as much of the gimp as possible, without tacking it along, it is more easily kept straight when the intermediate tacks are inserted, the two hands being free to put in the gimp pins, which is not the case if the gimp has to be held in one hand and the pins inserted and driven with the other.

In shaped work it will not always be found possible to run the gimp very far without pinning it ; but the pins in these cases should be kept as far apart as possible before the intermediate spaces are filled in, as the tension is more equal and the gimp consequently lies flatter. The same method of procedure applies also to putting on leather and other banding as to gimping, excepting, of course, that studs are used to hold the banding instead of gimp pins.

In best-class upholstering gimp is stuck instead of being fixed with gimp pins. Paste and glue mixed together in about equal parts form a good adhesive, which should be evenly and thinly spread with a flat stiff brush on the back of the gimp, care being taken that none comes through to the front. No more gimp should be treated at a time than will allow the adhesive to remain tacky, and there must not be enough put on to come through on the front or spread over the cover. Sticking gimp may be a little difficult at first, but it is worth the trouble.

Buttoning Upholstered Furniture. —Buttoned work is usually set out in diamond shapes, or a row of diamonds top and bottom connected with runners as in chair-back work, etc. Certain well-defined proportions are observed in the size of the diamonds, and in setting out diamonds on a scroll or easy-chair swell, an allowance must be made for the curved sweep, otherwise the diamonds will be out of proportion to those marked out on a flat surface, even although all have been set out to one size. To set out a chair-back, draw a line exactly down the centre, then mark off other lines as required equidistant apart. Set out the diamonds 7 in. long by 5 in. wide, and snip with the scissors at each corner through the scrim ; this will allow the buttons to sink deeply. The marking of the covering material can now be done. Allowance must be made on this for the " fullness " of the diamonds, and may vary from 1½ in. to 2 in. each way. If a very bold outstanding diamond is required, allow, say, 2 in. each way. Therefore set out the diamonds on the skin 9 in. by 7 in. Begin laying and buttoning in the centre line of chair-back and work to the edges, setting up each diamond with filling and tying down the buttons as evenly as possible.

Toys

ROCKING ELEPHANT

THE rocking-elephant toy shown by Fig. 1 is of a class of toy which is always in favour, and the idea of substituting an elephant for the usual horse will add much to its popularity. A soft wood is quite suitable, and the toy has been designed so that most of the parts may be economically cut from 6-in. by 1-in. deal boards.

The construction is of a simple character, and will require but brief explanation, as the parts are fully set out in the illustrations. There are two rockers, particulars of which may be gathered from Figs. 2, 3 and 4. The front and back (Fig. 5) are identical in size and shape, and are notched $\frac{1}{4}$ in. into the rockers, as shown by Figs. 4 and 10. The seat (Fig. 6) is tenoned into the front and back, and the belly-piece (Fig. 7) is similarly fixed. It should be noticed, however, that the mortises for the seat are cut right through, but those for the belly-piece only go half-way, yet in the front the same mortise may be continued through to take the lower tenon on the head.

The scale patterns for the head and tail (Figs. 8 and 9) are ruled into 1-in. squares to facilitate the preparation of the full-size patterns. The head is mortised into

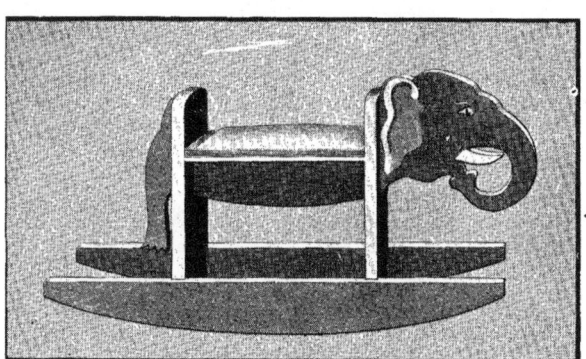

Fig. 1.—Rocking-elephant Toy

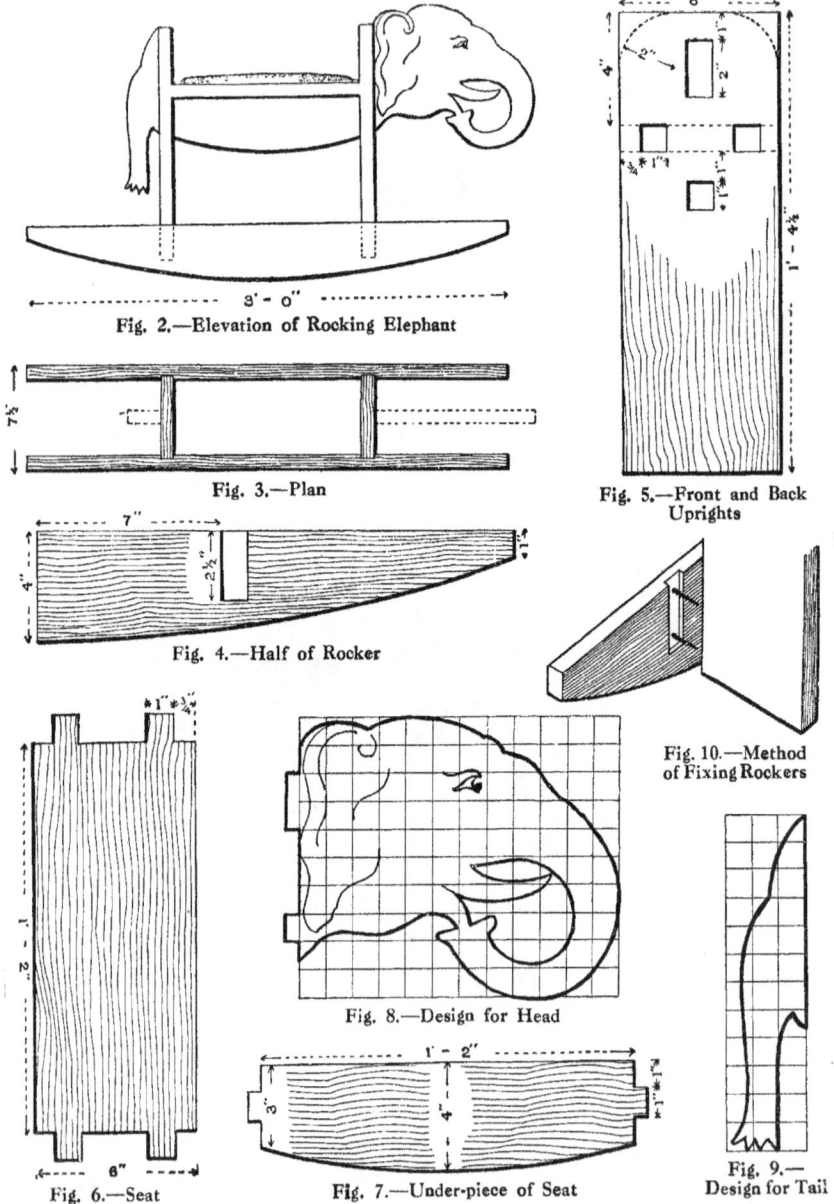

the front, and the tail is fixed to the back with screws or nails. The best method of fixing the parts together is to fix the seat, belly-piece, head and tail to the front and back first, and then to screw on the rockers, all the joints being glued. The seat should be comfortably stuffed and covered with suitable material. The toy could be finished a dark grey, but the rockers might be of a bright colour.

HOBBY-HORSE

ORDINARY deal may be used in making the hobby-horse shown by Fig. 11, but if a hard wood such as elm could be obtained the horse would be much stronger.

The design shows quite a distinct improvement on the older types of such horses. It runs on two back wheels, and at the front is fitted with a single leg, to the bottom of which an ordinary castor is fitted. There is a saddle, which can be adjusted at three heights, varying from $9\frac{1}{2}$ in. to 12 in. An elevation and a plan are shown by Figs. 12 and 13.

The design for the head is shown by Fig. 14, and this could be very easily enlarged to full size with the help of the lines which are ruled across this illustration, increasing these to 1-in. squares. It will take a piece of wood 1 ft. 1 in. long by 1 ft. 2 in. wide by $\frac{3}{4}$ in. thick to cut the head. The wood should be smoothed up first, and the cutting may be done with a bow-saw. The axle (Fig. 15) is 9 in. long by $1\frac{1}{4}$ in. square, and it is connected with the head by the cross-piece (Fig. 16), which is 1 ft. $10\frac{1}{4}$ in. long by $2\frac{1}{4}$ in. wide by $1\frac{1}{4}$ in. deep. A slot $\frac{3}{4}$ in. wide is cut down in the cross-piece as shown, and a tenon $1\frac{1}{4}$ in. long is formed at the bottom end; this is mortised into the axle, and the joint is secured with glue and a wood pin. Angle-pieces (Fig. 17) are fitted between the axle and the cross-piece. They are cut from wood $\frac{3}{4}$ in. thick, and are simply glued and nailed in position. The head is attached to the cross-piece with a couple of $\frac{1}{4}$-in. bolts, or with screws driven from each side of the cross-piece.

The leg (Fig. 18) is 9 in. long by $2\frac{1}{4}$ in. wide by $1\frac{1}{4}$ in. thick. A notch is cut in the top end so that it may fit over the head, to which it is attached with either bolts or screws. A castor of the ordinary type, but preferably with a metal wheel, is fitted to the bottom end of the leg, and metal wheels are fitted to the ends of the axle.

The saddle is shown in detail by Figs. 19 to 22. The top (Fig. 19) is cut from wood $\frac{3}{4}$ in. thick; a mortise 2 in. long by $\frac{3}{4}$ in. wide by $\frac{1}{2}$ in. deep is cut in the underneath side. The saddle support is shown complete by Fig. 20, and consists of a centre-piece (Fig. 21) and two filling pieces (Fig. 22), which are fixed on each side of the centre-piece. The end of the centre-piece, which projects below the filling pieces, fits in the slot in the cross-piece connecting the head of the horse and the axle, and it is attached with a bolt and fly-nut. The centre-piece of the saddle support is tenoned into the top of the saddle and fixed with glue, while the top of the saddle could be rounded around the edges to form a comfortable seat.

In painting the horse, grey would be a suitable colour. For the bridle, strips of thin patent leather could be used; but the reins should be of stout leather.

TOY MOTORS

Motor Wagon.—The reproduced photograph (Fig. 23) shows a toy tipping motor wagon, and details of the construction are given in Figs. 24, 25 and 26. It consists of an under-carriage to which is hinged the wagon body. A small wire hasp on the front of the body engages with a screw-eye in the seat to keep the body from tipping when not required to do so.

The following gives the principal measurements, the same letter being used to indicate the same part throughout the illustrations: The carriage base A is 10 in. long, 4 in. wide, and $\frac{3}{8}$ in. thick; the axles B and C are 5 in. long, $1\frac{1}{4}$ in. wide, and 1 in. thick; the bonnet D is 2 in. long, 2 in. wide, and 1 in. thick; the footboard E is 3 in. long, $1\frac{1}{2}$ in. wide, and $\frac{1}{4}$ in. thick; the seat F is 4 in. long, $1\frac{1}{4}$ in. wide, and 1 in. thick; the packing piece G is 3 in.

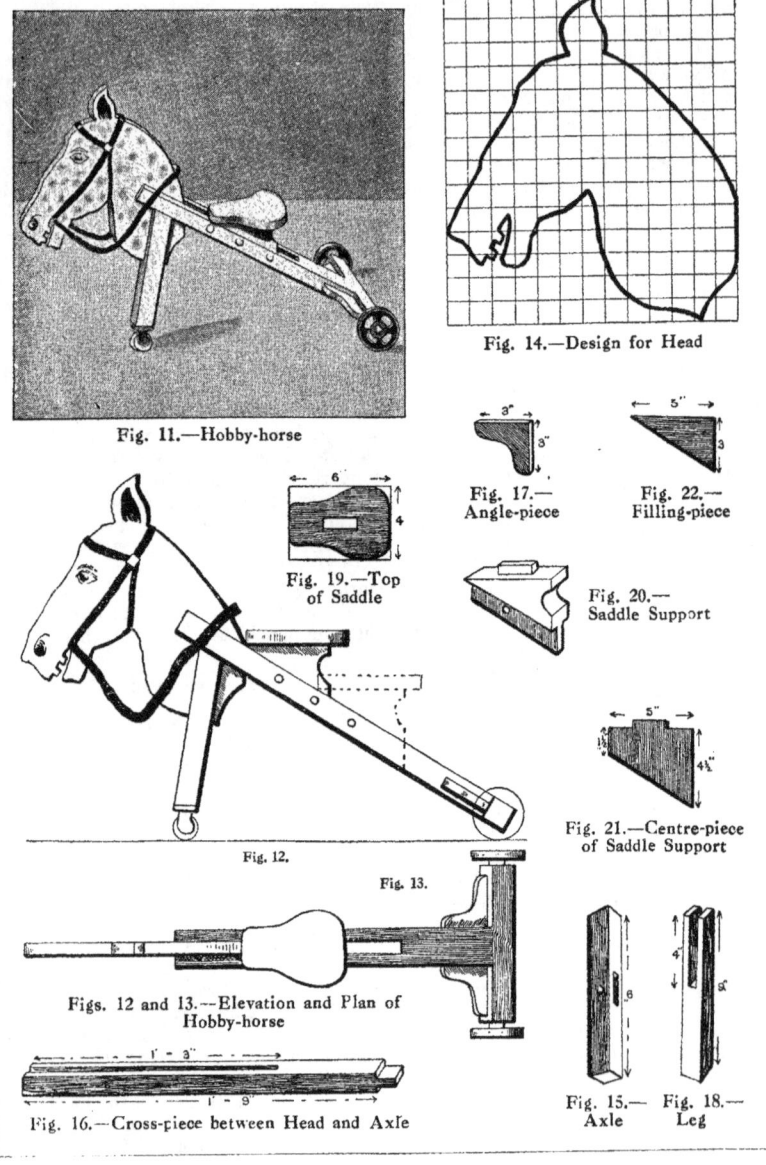

Fig. 11.—Hobby-horse

Fig. 14.—Design for Head

Fig. 17.—Angle-piece

Fig. 22.—Filling-piece

Fig. 19.—Top of Saddle

Fig. 20.—Saddle Support

Fig. 21.—Centre-piece of Saddle Support

Figs. 12 and 13.—Elevation and Plan of Hobby-horse

Fig. 16.—Cross-piece between Head and Axle

Fig. 15.—Axle

Fig. 18.—Leg

TOYS

long, 1½ in. wide and ½ in. thick; the body H is 9 in. long, 5 in. wide, and 2¼ in. deep; the sides J are 9 in. long, 2¼ in. wide, and ¼ in. thick; the ends K are 4½ in. long, 1⅞ in. wide, and ½ in. thick; the bottom L is 9 in. long, 4½ in. wide, and ⅜ in. thick; and the hinge M is 2½ in. long.

position of the sides shown in dotted lines, Fig. 30 a front elevation, and Fig. 31 gives the setting-out of a side and shows how the two sides can be set out to save wood.

The following are the principal measurements of the various parts, each part bearing the same letter throughout the illustrations: The base A is 9 in. long, 3 in. wide, and ⅜ in. thick; the back B is 4 in. long, 3 in. wide, and ⅜ in. thick; the sides C are of 6¾ in. long, 4⅜ in. wide, and ⅜ in. thick; the axles D and D^1 are 4 in. long, 1 in. wide, and ¾ in. thick; the bonnet E is 1¼ in. long, 2 in. wide, and 1 in. thick; the footboard F is 2½ in. long, 1½ in. wide, and ¼ in. thick; the seat back G is 3 in. long, 2 in. wide, and ⅜ in. thick; the seats H and J are 3 in. long, 1⅜ in. wide, and 1 in. thick;

Fig. 23.—Motor Wagon

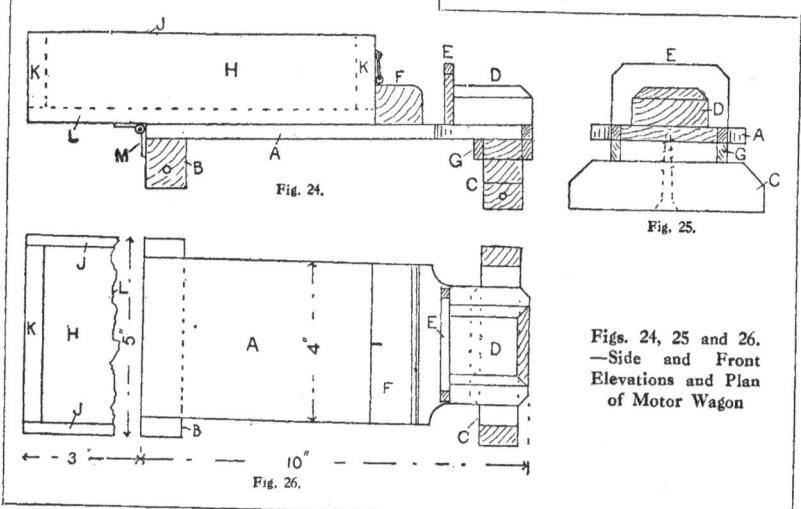

Figs. 24, 25 and 26.—Side and Front Elevations and Plan of Motor Wagon

The rear wheels are 2½ in. and the front wheels 1¾ in. in diameter.

Motor Cab.—A toy motor cab is shown by Fig. 27, and the details of construction are given in the following figures, where Fig. 28 shows the side elevation with the front side of the cab removed, Fig. 29 a plan with the top removed and the

and the roof K is 4 in. long, 3¼ in. wide, and 3/16 in. or ¼ in. thick.

The rear wheels are 2½ in. and the front wheels 1¾ in. in diameter. The front axle is pivoted.

Motor Van.—A general idea of the construction of a toy motor van can be obtained from Figs. 32 to 35. The principal measurements are given on the first three figures; any others may be obtained by means of the scale of inches.

The bottom A and the front B may be planed up in one piece, 4 in. wide and ⅜ in. thick (B is drawn ¼ in. thick; but this is no advantage unless a number are being made). Shape the base, make the seat, nail the front B to the back of the seat, and nail the pair to the base. The axles are planed up in one piece, and the rear axle is nailed to the base. The front axle can be fixed with a stout screw, to act as a pivot, after all the other parts are fixed.

The sides can now be shaped, and after nailing the pieces C to them, fixed in place. Three-ply wood is recommended for the sides, but any thin wood will do so long as the grain runs horizontal; the strips C and front B will prevent splitting. Three-ply is recommended for the top, but ordinary thin wood will do, the grain being placed cross-wise, and glue blocks fitted in the angle between the sides and top, as the sides will be too thin for secure nailing. The dash-board D is nailed to the bonnet E, and both nailed on the base. The wheels might be attached by means of round-headed screws, and a door fitted in the opening at the back.

It will readily be seen that, with a few modifications, this toy might be made up as a motor wagon or a motor lorry, or some other kind of motor vehicle.

A bright varnish colour of green, with red band-lining, makes a suitable finish.

Fig. 27.—Motor Cab

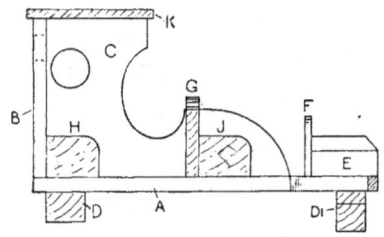

Fig 28.—Side Elevation

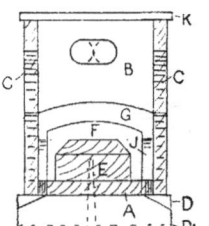

Fig. 30.—Front Elevation

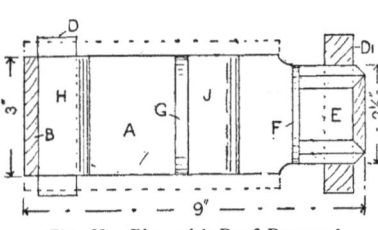

Fig. 29.—Plan with Roof Removed

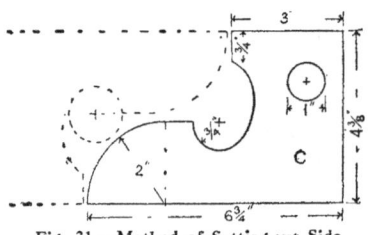

Fig 31.—Method of Setting-out Side

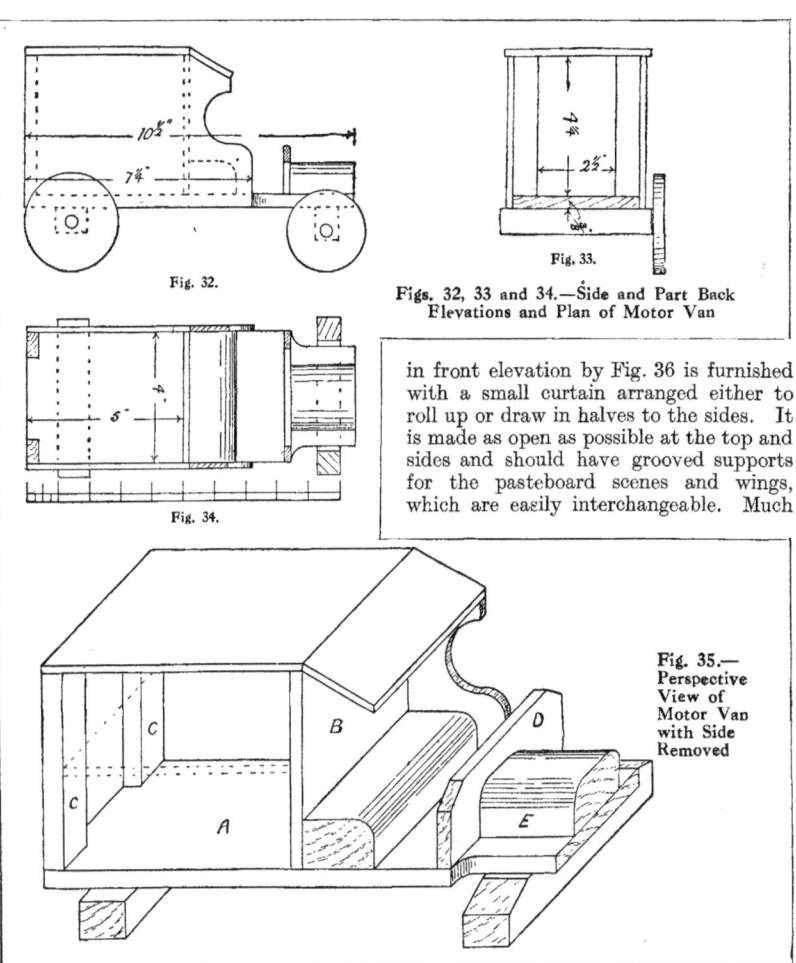

Figs. 32, 33 and 34.—Side and Part Back Elevations and Plan of Motor Van

Fig. 35.—Perspective View of Motor Van with Side Removed

in front elevation by Fig. 36 is furnished with a small curtain arranged either to roll up or draw in halves to the sides. It is made as open as possible at the top and sides and should have grooved supports for the pasteboard scenes and wings, which are easily interchangeable. Much ingenuity can be expended upon the scenery and little properties, coloured illustrations being often adaptable for the former.

The very small toy theatres hardly afford any scope at all, but the one illustrated by Figs. 36 to 42 would be quite workable without being too bulky. The main framing is explained by Fig. 41.

MODEL STAGE

THE miniature stage is always a popular plaything, not without educational value. Its main requirements are a frame or proscenium, with or without footlights, and capable of being surrounded by curtains to screen those directing operations from the back or wings. The stage shown

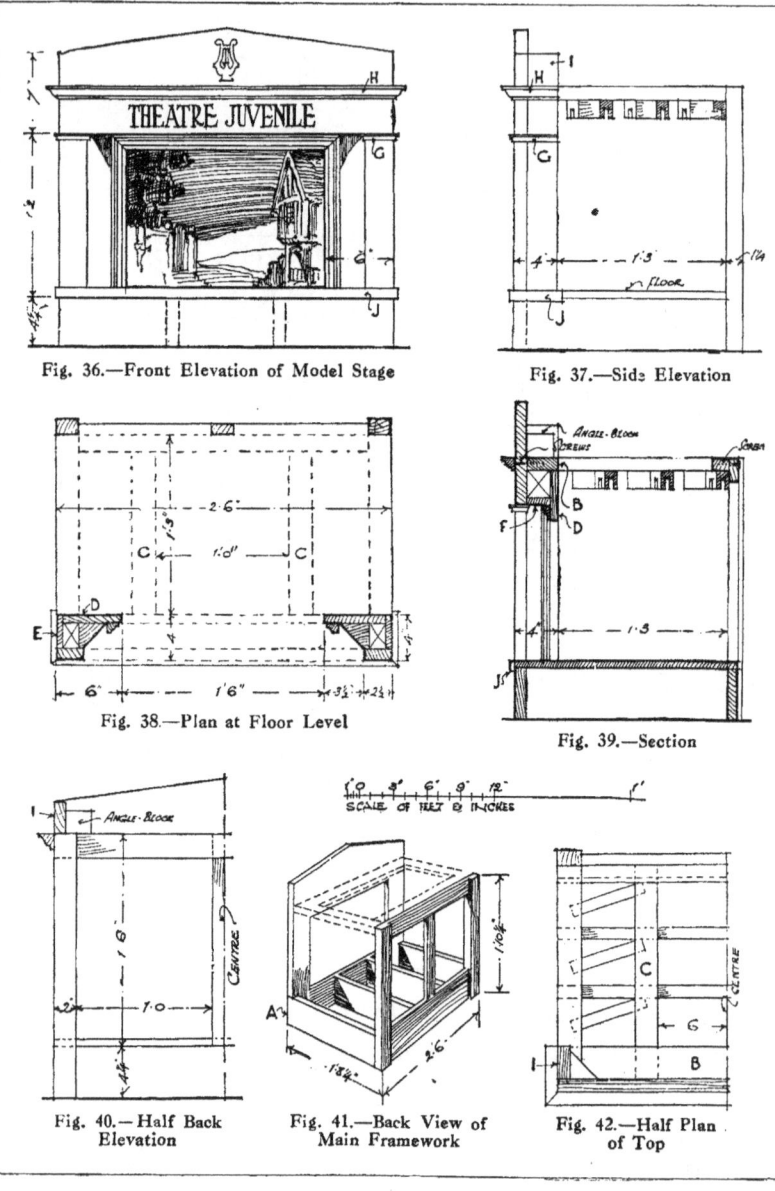

Fig. 36.—Front Elevation of Model Stage
Fig. 37.—Side Elevation
Fig. 38.—Plan at Floor Level
Fig. 39.—Section
Fig. 40.—Half Back Elevation
Fig. 41.—Back View of Main Framework
Fig. 42.—Half Plan of Top

The front (turned away from the spectator) might be $\frac{3}{4}$ in. thick, and measures 2 ft. 6 in. wide by 2 ft. $1\frac{1}{4}$ in., rising to 2 ft. 3 in. in the centre; the stiles are $2\frac{1}{2}$ in. and the bottom rail $4\frac{1}{4}$ in. wide, while the height of the opening in the middle of them is 1 ft. 2 in. This part of the work should be halved together. The back framing should also be halved, and consists, as shown, of 2-in. by $\frac{3}{4}$-in. top rail, 4-in. by $\frac{3}{4}$-in. bottom rail, a small centre stile, and two $1\frac{1}{4}$-in. by 2 in. corner ones. Front and back are connected at the bottom by means of four 4-in. by $\frac{3}{4}$-in. rails spaced out equally; the end ones can be mitred at A and slightly housed elsewhere, the whole being strengthened with angle blocks. A piece of $\frac{3}{4}$-in. framing with halved joints will be required where dotted at the top of Fig. 41, and can consist of $1\frac{1}{4}$-in. by $\frac{3}{4}$-in. stuff, with the exception of the front rail, which should be $3\frac{1}{4}$ in. wide, as shown at B in Figs. 39 and 42, which also show how this top part should be secured with screws through the front and back framings. Extra bars in the top framing will be required as at C in Figs. 38 and 42, 12 in. apart, but have been omitted from Fig. 41 for clearness.

Having produced the skeleton of the work, it will be a simple matter to box up the front as explained by Figs. 38 and 39. An inner facing about $\frac{3}{8}$-in. thick is shown at D in both these figures, together with an outer lining E and a splayed upright at either side as in Fig. 38, these being built up on small blocks in the centre where marked with diagonal crosses. A small soffit F (Fig. 39), together with a moulding mitred round the opening (Fig. 36, etc.), a necking G, and a small cornice H are shown in Figs. 36, 37 and 39. It will be noted that the cornice covers the screws connecting the front and top (Fig. 39). A small return piece as at I in Figs. 37, 40 and 42 can be fixed by means of an angle block at the back.

The floor can next be inserted, cut to fit round the back uprights as in Fig. 38. It can be of three-ply, and should be finished at the front with a narrow fillet, as at J in Figs. 36, 37 and 39. The last pieces of woodwork required will be some rails to hold the scenes, wings and skypieces. These are seen in Figs. 37, 39 and 42, and can be $1\frac{1}{4}$ in. by $\frac{3}{4}$ in., grooved $\frac{1}{4}$ in. by $\frac{3}{4}$ in. deep, and fixed to the underside of the top framing in the position shown.

As regards the decoration, this should really serve as a foil to the scenes, but a gaily painted finish will probably be preferred by the youthful owners. White and gold or dull blue would look well, and ornament can be added to any extent. If footlights are desired, they can be made out of sheet tin.

Easy Patternmaking

PATTERNMAKING differs from other woodwork in the necessity for knowing the requirements of moulding. A carpenter or joiner or cabinetmaker, if he knew precisely the form of the casting required, could make a wood pattern of the same shape; but this would not do at all. Even the simplest casting usually requires a pattern more or less modified to enable the mould to be made from it; and even if it appears the same as the casting, it is always desirable that it should be made by a man who knows how it is going to be moulded. A slight amount of taper or draught for withdrawal from the sand is necessary, and in many cases openings or holes are cored instead of cut in the pattern. In more complicated work patterns have to be made in halves or in several pieces, core boxes are wanted, and the best way of moulding requires much consideration, and must be decided before the work is begun; but really complicated patternmaking is not within the province of the present chapter.

The patternmaker works from drawings, and he must be able to understand them readily and have a reasonably clear idea of what the most complicated piece of work will be like before he begins to construct it. The woodwork in other trades is generally simpler, and always the same things are being repeated. In pattern work precisely the same things are never repeated, unless more than one similar pattern is made, because a very large number of castings all alike are required, and one pattern would not be sufficient to make so many moulds. The patternmaker therefore depends on drawings to give him particulars and dimensions of everything he does. The only exceptions are in some very simple work which can be described verbally, or which has to replace a worn-out or broken casting, the original pattern for which is not available.

Dimensions usually have to be exact in pattern work, and geometrical accuracy is always important, true surfaces and correct angles being nearly always essential. Besides this, allowances must be made for machine work on the casting, and for shrinkage of the metal in cooling after it has been poured into the mould. These allowances are variable, and some experience is necessary to know how much to allow on the various measurements. Distortion of the casting in cooling is another thing which occurs in some circumstances, and allowance has to be made for that also.

The construction of a pattern is often different from that which would be adopted by a woodworker with no knowledge of patternmaking. It must be made so that shrinkage or warping of the wood will not affect important dimensions or surfaces in relation to each other. This is important, while mere appearance is of no importance at all. The mortice-and-tenon joints so common in ordinary woodwork

EASY PATTERNMAKING

are rarely seen in patterns, the reason being that half-lap joints screwed together are easier to make, and quite as good, if not slightly better, for the prevention of warping.

The shapes of patterns also are often so different from other articles of wood, that methods of building up seldom seen in the latter are constantly employed for patterns. Rings and other circular work are built up in segments. Cylindrical work, except in very small diameters, is lagged or staved up, being hollow in the interior. In rectangular and other shapes boxing up is commonly adopted to avoid the use of great thicknesses of wood. The advantages of this are not only economy of material and lightness; but primarily because it permits of building to prevent shrinkage of the wood from affecting important measurements of the pattern.

There is so much lathe work in the construction of patterns that a patternmaker cannot pretend to have much experience at his trade unless he is as skilful at the lathe as at the bench. There are few patterns which have not some turned parts fitted to them, perhaps only prints, while others are worked to shape entirely in the lathe, the only bench work about them being the preliminary preparation of the wood.

The patternmaker's knowledge therefore differs considerably from that of other woodworkers, and is more extensive. It is a branch of engineering, and he must know something of other branches that affect his own. He must know what allowances the machinist wants and where they are wanted. He must know a great deal about moulding, or he will give the moulder trouble, besides being in frequent difficulties himself about how to proceed. Besides being able to work from mechanical drawings, he frequently has to draw portions of his work full-size before he can begin the construction; and in addition to this, there is continual marking-out and testing for accuracy while the work is proceeding, all of which in a modern shop demands more technical knowledge than physical strength or even manual skill.

Yellow pine is used for patterns in most cases. Mahogany and other hard woods are often used for small patterns, because they are more durable than pine. The objections to hard wood for all patterns are expense, weight, and greater trouble in working it. Yellow pine is light, straight-grained, not very liable to warp, and is easy to work.

The patternmaker has benefited as much as other woodworkers in the improvements in saws and planing machines. He now has lathes specially designed for pattern work, and he has the trimmer, which has proved more useful in pattern construction than in any other woodworking trade. In the hand tools used at the bench, improvements and additions have been made, and also in ready-made fittings, parts and accessories, things which save time and give better results.

Moulding.—Without a knowledge of moulding it would be impossible to make patterns. The sand used by the moulder differs in character from what might be supposed by people who know nothing of foundry work. It is a cohesive kind of sand, which keeps its shape when the pattern, with reasonable care, is withdrawn from it. Sand is used because it is the most suitable material for standing the intense heat of the melted metal which is poured into the mould. There are limits to what can be done in the withdrawal of patterns from sand, even when there are no undercut or projecting parts on the pattern, which necessarily drag the sand along with them in withdrawal. As much taper as possible is always allowed by the patternmaker, and in addition to this the moulder takes precautions of his own to prevent damage to the mould in withdrawal of the pattern.

Sand, enclosed in a moulding box, has to be lifted away from the top of a pattern, and if there are projecting portions in the top this is a much more delicate operation than lifting the pattern out of the sand, and extra taper is wanted in such parts. For this reason it is generally advisable to have the plainest surface in the top of the mould, and the irregular in the bottom. If a pattern is divided in halves, or if parts in the top are left loose, then the withdrawal of the upper part is done after the mould halves have been taken apart, and the top one turned over and laid joint

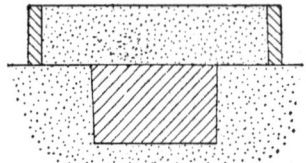

Fig. 1.—Simple Mould Closed by Putting Box of Sand on Top

surface uppermost. A pattern is not made in halves unless there is some advantage in doing so. All moulds must be jointed; but it is not always necessary to joint the pattern to correspond with the joints in the mould. In some cases the moulder prefers an unjointed pattern. In others, a pattern for a ball, for instance, it would not be made in halves, although the mould would have to be jointed through the centre. But if the ball had parts attached to it, which would make it difficult to lift the top half of the mould away without injury, then the pattern would be made in halves.

Moulders' joints are made at any plane where they are required, and not always through the centre, and patterns also are jointed wherever joints are necessary.

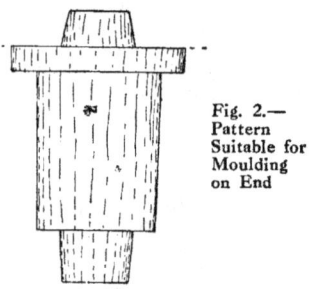

Fig. 2.—Pattern Suitable for Moulding on End

As in ordinary castings the mould must be completely closed, there is always at least one joint in a mould. An example of this in a simple mould is shown in Fig. 1.

The article is a plain square block, on the vertical sides of which a slight amount of taper would be planed for easy withdrawal. The top of the mould could be left open, but the top surface of the casting would be rough, irregular, spongy, and its edges would not be sharp. Therefore in all ordinary work it is the practice to put a top box of sand as in Fig. 1, a hole being provided for pouring in the metal. The upper sand simply provides a flat surface and this is the case in a great many moulds even where the casting is much more complex than the simple block shown. The lower sand is usually enclosed in a box also, because for convenience in ramming the sand round the pattern and then withdrawing the latter, it is necessary to turn the mould over. A box for the upper sand is essential, because there

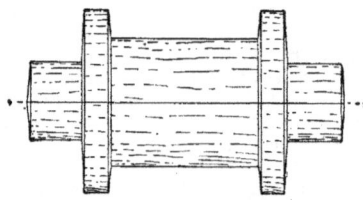

Fig. 3.—Pattern Made in Halves for Moulding on Side

would otherwise be no means of keeping the mass of sand together and closing the mould. The upper and lower boxes also are made to fit each other, so that in closing the mould the top can be replaced accurately on the one below, a very important matter when portions of the mould extend into the upper box, and must match the lower without overlapping edges, for it is impossible to examine or do anything to the interior after a mould is closed.

There is nearly always more than one way of moulding a pattern. In simple forms this is a matter which is easily decided, and often of two or more ways it makes no difference which way it is done. The patternmaker may suppose it will be done one way, while the moulder will decide differently, and all moulders will

EASY PATTERNMAKING

not treat it in the same way. But, as a rule, some one way has obvious advantages apparent both to patternmaker and moulder. For a simple shape like Fig. 2, which may be a bush with a flange or collar at one end, the best way to mould it would be on end with the flange on top, the mould joint occurring across the top as dotted. But with a flange at both ends, as in Fig. 3, it would be best to mould it on its side, and make the pattern in halves. In Fig. 2 there would be taper lengthwise on the body, on the edge of the flange, and on the prints, the top print being tapered much more than the bottom. In Fig. 3 everything would be parallel in the horizontal direction ; but the flanges and print ends would be tapered as shown.

As prints have been mentioned, it may be as well to say before going farther, that

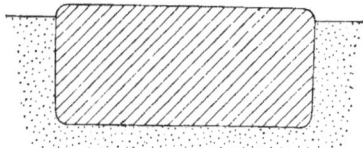

Fig. 4.—Example in which Joint cannot be made Flush with Top Surface of Pattern

they are used on almost all patterns for the purpose of coring holes and interior cavities, which would give trouble if cut in the pattern. Thus in Figs. 2 and 3 prints are put on the ends, because a hole is required through the middle of the casting, and the casting itself ends at the flanges. If a hole with a considerable amount of taper was cut through the pattern in Fig. 2, it might be moulded without coring, though an interior column of sand of comparatively small diameter would be weak and liable to tear up. A sand core made separately and inserted after the pattern is withdrawn is much stronger. The impressions left by the prints support and centre the core, making its insertion a very simple matter. With the pattern moulded as in Fig. 3 coring is unavoidable. In the example illustrated

the patternmaker would simply put prints on instead of cutting the hole ; but in other instances, he would have to make a core-box in addition to the pattern.

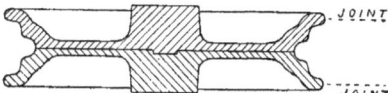

Fig. 5.—Example of Pattern requiring Two Joints in Mould

Departures from simplicity in the outline of the pattern may necessitate modification of the joint plane. A pattern with rounded corners, as in Fig. 4, would require a mould joint in the position shown so that the upper sand can be lifted to include the rounded angle, for it is obvious that if the mould was rammed flush with the top surface of the pattern, the latter could not be withdrawn without destroying the rounded angle in the mould. This is an instance where the pattern itself would not be jointed.

It is not always possible to make a mould with one joint only. Patterns often occur of a shape which could not be withdrawn from a mould with a single joint. An example is shown in Fig. 5, in which two joints are necessary. It is a sheave pulley that can only be moulded on its side, to do which the pattern must be divided through the centre, so that the halves can be drawn opposite ways to leave the sand which forms the recess between the

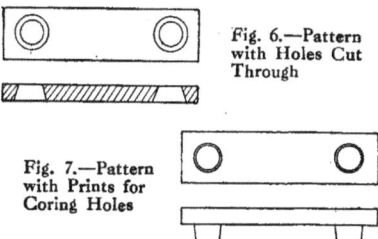

Fig. 6.—Pattern with Holes Cut Through

Fig. 7.—Pattern with Prints for Coring Holes

flanges. In some cases where only a small groove was wanted it might be omitted in the pattern, and turned in the machine shop. In a case like Fig. 5 it is not necessary to make a central mould joint corresponding with the pattern joint. The mould joints occur in the central plane of the rounded edges of the flanges, and

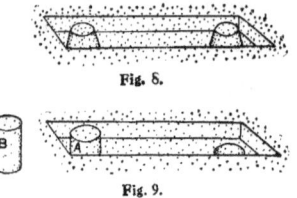

Figs. 8 and 9.—Moulds for Patterns Figs. 6 and 7

pattern joints here are unnecessary. A detail not shown in the illustration is that the bosses of the pulley would, as a rule, be left loose, fitting only by a central stud to keep them in position. Shallow bosses with a large amount of taper might be solid with the central plate. If in making the pattern there was any distinction between top and bottom, the boss in the lower half would be screwed on, and that in the upper half left loose.

Prints and Cores.—As prints and cores continually occur, it will be best to deal with them before going farther into the subject of patternmaking. The reasons for their use have already been mentioned. Where cores might or might not be used the procedure in both cases and the difference it makes will be taken as an example. Figs. 6 and 7 show a thin plate through which it will be supposed that holes have to be cast. If they are cut through the pattern, as in Fig. 6, a great deal of taper is essential, or the pattern would leave the mould with its holes choked with the sand that ought to have remained behind. This taper is cut with a gouge, circles being struck with dividers for cutting. In some rough work, where a large number of holes is wanted, they are burnt out to the correct taper with a suitable iron heated to a dull red. In each case the holes are bored first with a bit. The large amount of taper is often objectionable in the casting, and cutting gives the patternmaker more trouble than

putting prints on, as in Fig. 10, while it makes little difference to the moulder. Therefore it is unusual to cut such holes through the pattern, and the method is only suitable for plates not exceeding about $\frac{1}{2}$ in. thick. If the holes are cored, prints are put on the pattern as in Fig. 7. Circles are struck at the centres and the prints adjusted one at a time and nailed on.

Figs. 8 and 9 show the moulds resulting from the patterns (Figs. 6 and 7) respectively. In Fig. 8 the mould is correct for casting. In Fig. 9 the holes left by the prints must be filled by cores which stand up to the correct height to touch the top sand when the mould is closed. One of these cores is shown inserted at A, and at B a core is shown separately.

These cores are made in boxes and afterwards baked dry and hard. A large stock of plain core boxes is kept in every foundry, so that beyond putting suitable prints on the pattern the patternmaker is not concerned in the production of the cores unless they are of unusual size, in which case he has to make a core-box for them. Simple cores of this kind are kept in stock in foundries, and the moulder finds some of the diameter he wants and cuts them to the length required. As the prints are tapered he would generally rasp a little taper on the cores to make them fit the print impressions. Cores

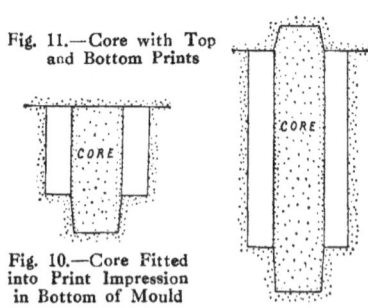

Fig. 11.—Core with Top and Bottom Prints

Fig. 10.—Core Fitted into Print Impression in Bottom of Mould

are not necessarily cylindrical as in the example shown, though the cylindrical form is the commonest. Cores are used not only for small round or square holes,

EASY PATTERNMAKING

but for hollowing out interior parts of all imaginable outlines.

A core may rest simply in a print impression in the bottom of the mould as in Fig. 9 and as shown in section in Fig. 10; or, owing to its length, it may require a top print as in Fig. 11; or it may rest horizontally in print impressions at each end as in Fig. 12.

Top prints are shallower than bottom ones and have more taper, as shown in Fig. 14, the top end of the core being tapered to fit them. This extra taper in the top is partly for convenience in lifting the top part of the mould off the pattern; but a more important reason is that in closing the mould the upper part has to be lowered on to the top end of the core, and if there was little or no taper the core, instead of entering the print impression properly might go to one side and break the sand away.

Prints on the sides of patterns are almost as common as prints on the bottom, though the latter position is preferable if the method of moulding allows it. In many cases, of course, prints occur both on the bottom and the sides.

In patterns turned between lathe centres, and having prints at the ends, the prints are turned solid with the pattern; but in most other cases prints have to be made separately and put on the pattern

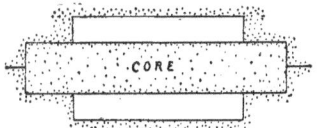

Fig. 12.—Core in Horizontal Position requiring Print at Each End

Fig. 13.—Small Round Prints Turned in a Stick

after. Small prints are turned in a stick, as in Fig. 13, and sawn off, and their ends pared with a chisel. Usually they are varnished before removal from the lathe.

Prints exceeding about 1 in. or 1½ in. in diameter are turned with studs to fit holes in the pattern, the holes being bored deeper than the studs so that there shall

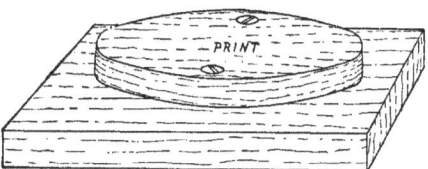

Fig. 14.—Large Thin Print Screwed On

be no trouble in making the prints a close fit on the pattern. Generally these studholes have to be bored with a centre-bit; but when they occur in the centre of a boss or other turned part they are bored with a narrow chisel in the lathe, which is more accurate than trying to bore exactly on a centre with a bit. The studs are made a moderately tight fit in the holes, and this is sufficient to keep the prints in place on the pattern without the use of nails or screws. The majority of prints are fitted in this way, and it is convenient because prints sometimes have to be changed for others of different size when a pattern is frequently used.

Large prints, above about 3 in. or 4 in. in diameter, are usually thin, as in Fig. 14, and are turned with the grain as shown instead of as in the smaller prints. They are generally screwed on the pattern. They are planed to thickness, sawn round, and put on the faceplate for turning to diameter. Occasionally they are pared round with a chisel instead of turned. Those turned between centres are undercut or concave at their large end so that they will bed properly on a flat surface. The taper in prints is rather more than is usually allowed on the pattern itself, though there are great variations in the latter. A print at its large end is slightly larger than the size of the core, while at the small end it is less.

Core-boxes.—Core-boxes must be specially made for a pattern whenever there is a departure from the ordinary sizes likely to be kept in the foundry, or whenever there is any detail about the core which makes it other than a plain round one of uniform diameter The average box is made as shown by Fig. 15. In small sizes the cleats shown on the back will be omitted. The box must be in halves for removal of the core. The halves are kept in correct relation to each other by dowels as shown, two generally being sufficient, though more would be used in a large box.

slackness sidewise when the box is closed. The dowels may be of metal or wood. Patterns in halves are dowelled similarly to core-boxes. In both cases the rough halves are dowelled first and worked to shape after. A box is gouged out roughly and finished with a plane of suitable curvature, the circle to work to being struck on each end of the box, with dividers.

When a box is not absolutely plain, but

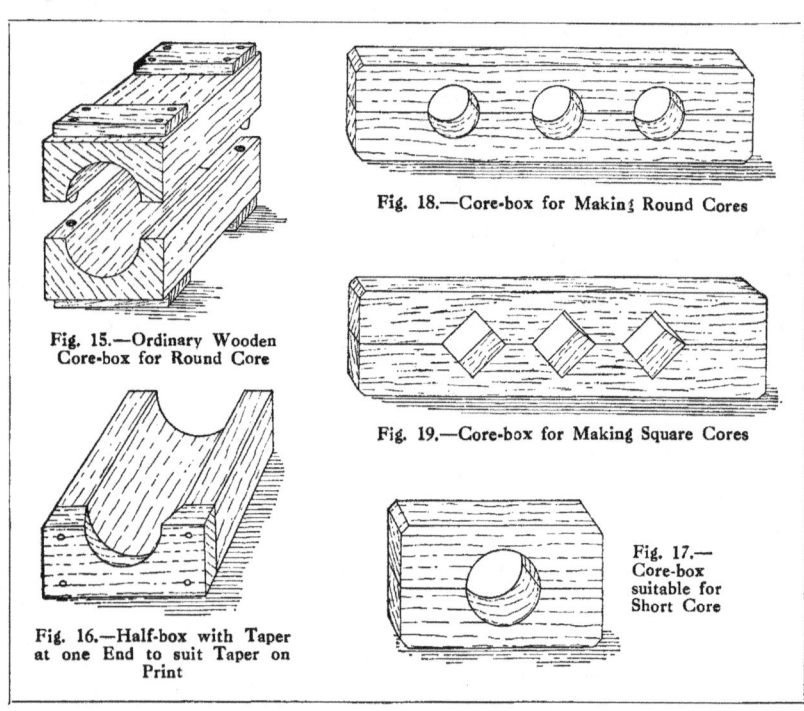

Fig. 15.—Ordinary Wooden Core-box for Round Core

Fig. 16.—Half-box with Taper at one End to suit Taper on Print

Fig. 18.—Core-box for Making Round Cores

Fig. 19.—Core-box for Making Square Cores

Fig. 17.—Core-box suitable for Short Core

Sometimes for the sake of economy in the pattern shop only a single half of a box is made, where both halves would be alike, and the core-maker makes two halves and sticks them together. It is necessary then to nail ends on the half box to enclose the sand. But generally two halves are made and dowelled together as shown, the dowel pins in one half being an easy fit in the holes in the other. but with no

has varying diameters, it cannot be planed through, and must either be done entirely with gouges and chisels, or it is built up. A simple instance is shown by Fig. 16, where a piece is put on the end because of taper in a top print. This taper must be exact, and it is much easier to make the box in two pieces, as shown, than in a single one. The parallel part can have its diameter marked on both ends and be

EASY PATTERNMAKING

planed through, and the tapering part also can have both its diameters marked and be cut straight through with a gouge. Fig. 16 shows only one half of the box.

Fig. 17 shows another way of making a plain round box when the length of the core is not very great. The grain of the wood runs transversely instead of parallel with the core. Fig. 18 shows how a number of holes may be cut through such a box. This is done when a large number of small cores are wanted, because it saves time in making them, and the extra work for the patternmaker is hardly worth considering when the holes to be cut are so small and simple. Fig. 19 shows a box

if required for another pattern. Larger boxes are made as in Fig. 21 and screwed together. The ends fit in rebates and cannot be forced out of position in ramming the core.

In making any of these boxes the patternmaker has first to consider the proportions of the core required and decide which shall be the open part of the box, for it will be seen that in all the examples so far shown the boxes are open on two opposite faces or at the ends and closed on all the others. In making the cores the box is laid on a flat surface, which makes it equivalent to having a bottom, with only the upper face of the box open

Fig. 20.—Core-box that can be Varied in Length

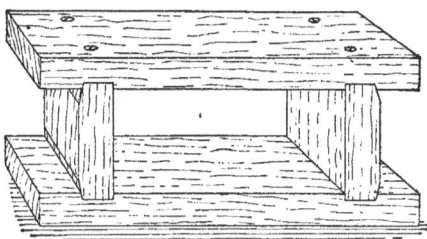

Fig. 21.—Ordinary Core-box for Large Square Cores

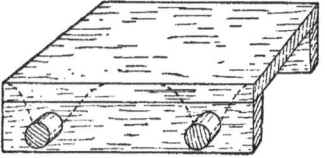

Fig. 22.—Pattern to Mould with Flanges Downwards

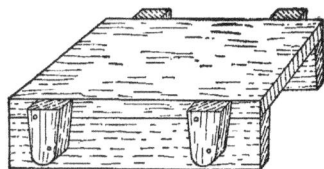

Fig. 23.—Method of Using Pocket Prints

for small square cores made similarly. It will be noticed that they are set diagonally in relation to the box-joint, which makes it much easier for drawing the box halves away from the finished cores. In all these the box halves are dowelled together first and then the shapes of the holes marked out correctly in relation to the joint. Fig. 20 shows the same kind of box not dowelled but with its halves kept at the required position by nails with their heads standing out as shown. This is quicker than dowelling, and an advantage about it is that the box can be set to make cores slightly longer or shorter

for putting in and ramming the sand. The longest way of the core is usually the long way of the box, the grain of its main parts running in this direction. This, however, is often not the case in boxes like those shown by Figs. 17, 18 and 19. But the length of such cores is never very much in excess of their transverse measurements, or they would be made in boxes like those in Figs. 15, 16, 20 and 21.

The kind of box and the long direction of the core being settled, it then remains to decide, in cores which are rectangular in cross section, which shall be the open and which the closed sides in the box. If the core measures the same each way, this matter settles itself; but very often the core measures more in one direction than in the other. In large boxes it is economy of wood to make the broadest surface the open one; but this gives the coremaker a little more trouble in ramming and levelling the sand in the box. In many cases it is of little or no importance which way is decided on. In cores of more complex shape it often requires a good deal of thought.

Core-boxes are left comparatively rough on the outside except at the open ends or other faces where the core surface is levelled with the exterior of the box. Only such faces and the interior are varnished. The joint surfaces, either in boxes or patterns, are usually not varnished. Sharp angles and corners on the outsides of boxes are generally roughly chamfered with plane or chisel.

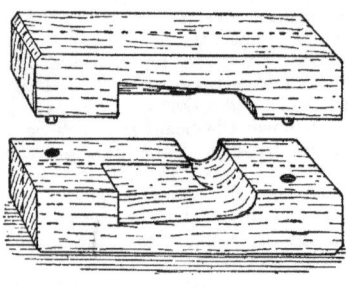

Fig. 24.—Special Box for Pocket-print Cores

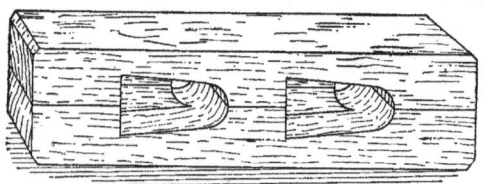

Fig. 25.—Box for Making Two Cores Simultaneously

Another class of prints, which, though they may be used for simple round or square holes like those that have been dealt with, are not so simple themselves.

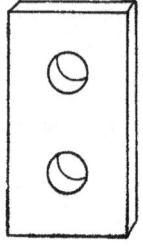

Fig. 26.—Pattern with Holes One above the Other

They are called pocket prints or tail prints, because besides providing an impression of the core, they include an additional part to allow for withdrawal from the sand and insertion of the core. As an example, it will be supposed that a pattern as shown in Fig. 22, which must mould with its flanges downwards, requires holes through the flanges, as indicated by the round prints. Round prints could be put on as shown; but as they would not mould when covered with sand up to the level of the top of the pattern, the only thing the moulder could do would be to joint the sand down to

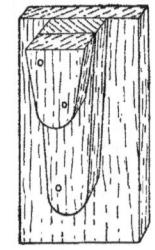

Fig. 27.—Pocket Prints to suit Holes in Fig. 26

their centres, as dotted, and lift those portions off in the top before drawing the pattern. In some cases this method would be adopted, not only for prints, but

EASY PATTERNMAKING

for parts of the pattern itself; but not in such a case as that illustrated.

Instead of round prints, pocket prints would be put on as in Fig. 23. Only the

be cut out of the solid, or it may be made in two parts, as indicated by the dotted line in Fig. 24. The procedure in the latter case would be to mark out and cut the

Fig. 28.—Box that makes Two Rounded Cores to be Carried by One Print

lower portion of these represents the shape of the cores and of the holes required in the casting, the part above the centre line being carried up to the top of the pattern with plenty of taper as shown. The mould joint then can be a plain one flush with the upper surface of the pattern and prints, and there is no difficulty in moulding from it. Round cores can then be put into the print impressions, and will rest at the bottoms of these, in the semicircular part, leaving a print impression above, which must be filled with sand to complete the mould and secure the cores. The patternmaker makes a stopping-over piece of thin wood cut out to fit over the core. When the core is placed in position, the moulder uses this to fit down over the core and press against the vertical face of sand while the space above the core is being filled.

When a large number of pocket prints occur on a pattern it is often considered better to make a special core-box than to let the moulder stop them over. Figs. 24

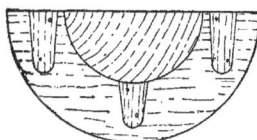

Fig. 29.—Prints for Coring Bolt-holes through Flange

and 25 show such boxes, the first a single one, the second to include two cores, as is often done when a large number of small cores of any kind is wanted. The box may

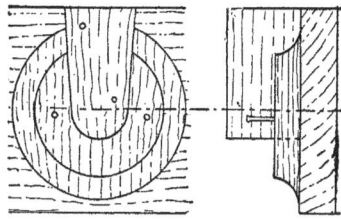

Fig. 30.—Loose Boss Fitted round Fixed Pocket Print

pocket portions of the core, the halves of the box being dowelled together first. This portion, of course, can then be cut completely through, and the thickness of the box at this stage only represents that of the pocket print. Then pieces representing the length of round core are nailed on, marked out in place, and the round hole cut through them. The boxes are always made in halves as shown.

Instances often occur where two, or even more, holes are required, one above the other, on the side of a pattern, as in Fig. 26, with no other way of moulding. The difficulty is overcome either by putting two pocket prints on, as in Fig. 27, or one print only with a special box, as in Fig. 28.

How pocket prints are used for coring bolt holes through the flange of a pipe or

Fig. 31.—Core with Variations not indicated by Prints

column is shown by Fig. 29. A new feature here is that the lower print does not come up to the joint surface, but only to the under surface of the pattern; and this, of course, is as far as it can come, and is all that is wanted for moulding.

An arrangement which often has to be adopted is shown in Fig. 30. A loose boss occurs on the side of a pattern, and a fixed pocket print is attached to core a hole through. The print is nailed on the pattern first, and is made thick enough to stand out sufficiently beyond the face of the boss. The latter is cut out to fit round the print. In some cases it would be possible to put a round print on the boss and draw them in together, and this, of course, would be simplest and best if practicable. But always when parts are left loose to be drawn out after the pattern has left the mould, it is essential to have sufficient space to draw them into.

The shape and size of a print does not necessarily indicate that a core of that section runs right through the mould. There may be a lot of variations in the core after it leaves the print, and the latter does not always coincide with the size of the core at the entrance, though core and print must coincide. Fig. 31 shows an example which may be supposed to be circular in cross section. The interior of the casting contains a much larger diameter than the ends and prints. The diameters at the ends are not alike, and in that to the left the print is made still larger to include a rounded angle. All this comes from the core-box, the pattern simply having plain prints as dotted. If the pattern is made in halves, the outline of the core would generally be marked out on the joint surface ; but otherwise the moulder depends on the core-box to show him the shape of the core. Cores do not always cut through a casting at two places only, as in the previous examples. In the casting there may be a number of openings at various points, all of which are formed by one core, or perhaps by two or more cores fitted together, and wherever there is a core opening there is usually a print on the pattern. Exceptions to this may occur when cores cut through at top of a mould, as in the case of cylindrical and other cores in the vertical position, a top print not being used if it can be avoided.

Joints.—As far as the jointing of wood is concerned, patternmaking is simple. The patternmaker relies chiefly on screws, nails, glue, and the plainest joints possible. He uses a much greater quantity of screws than other woodworkers—that is, he uses screws where others would use nails, or would make more elaborate joints and glue them. Patterns often have to be taken apart and altered, and sometimes the requirements of moulding make it necessary to unscrew parts in the foundry. Therefore, in the main structural work of a pattern nails are seldom used, though small, fine varieties of them are used a great deal for the attachment of small details, parts that can easily be prised off with a chisel if necessary.

Glue is used chiefly for the building up of thick parts. Even in small patterns some of the thicknesses may be so great that it is necessary to glue up, not because thick metal is wanted in the casting, but because portions of the pattern must be made solid and cored out. It is mainly in such cases that patternmaker's glue joints occur, and seldom in the ordinary constructional joints where a joiner or cabinetmaker would use glue. It is more frequently used alone than as a reinforcement to screws or nails. Pattern contours are often so peculiar that patternmakers are sometimes afraid to use nails because of the possibility of damage to the edges of the cutting tools in subsequent working of the pattern to shape. Waiting for glue joints to dry before the work can proceed is sometimes an objection to the use of glue.

Although pattern joints are simple, experience is required to know how to proceed in building up a pattern of any given shape, especially when shapes vary so much, and there is usually only a drawing from which to work.

First, there is the rule, to which there are few exceptions, that in each individual piece the grain of the wood should run the way of the longest measurement. Next, the strength of the construction and provisions against warping and shrinking require the crossing of grain in putting

EASY PATTERNMAKING

the parts together. The area of the joint surfaces and the means of uniting them must be sufficient to guarantee rigidity and ample strength in the pattern. Sometimes this cannot be done without making additions to the pattern which are not would not be made. It is assumed that each of the examples, A, B, C and D, mould in the position shown, the vertical part of each being tapered accordingly. The argument might be put forward that if the vertical pieces were attached to the end instead of beneath the horizontal ones, there could be no possibility of an over-lapping edge on the outer vertical face, and therefore the withdrawal of the pattern would be less likely to tear up sand. This is true, but, nevertheless, with rare exceptions, the pattern will stand rougher usage and the joint be more secure if made as shown. In this way rapping on the upper face to loosen the pattern in the sand cannot break the joint or split the wood. At A the piece below crosses the grain of the upper one and prevents it from curving. At B it will be sup-

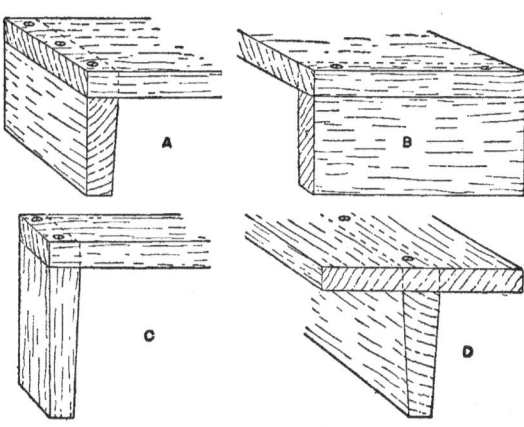

Fig. 32.—Examples of Plain Joints Uniting Pieces at Right Angles

wanted on the casting. A stronger pattern is often possible by coring instead of cutting parts out of the pattern, although the pattern would mould without coring. But in the majority of cases a pattern can be made like the casting, except where cores are necessary for moulding. When the way of moulding has been settled, the best method to build up the pattern soon becomes clear.

Edge joints uniting pieces at right angles, as in Fig. 32, constantly occur in patterns. These are almost invariably screwed. In extremely small patterns fine nails might be used. Such joints are scarcely ever glued. The feature illustrated in Fig. 32 is that pieces should be fitted with the joint beneath the upper piece, and not at the side of it. The dotted lines in each case show how it

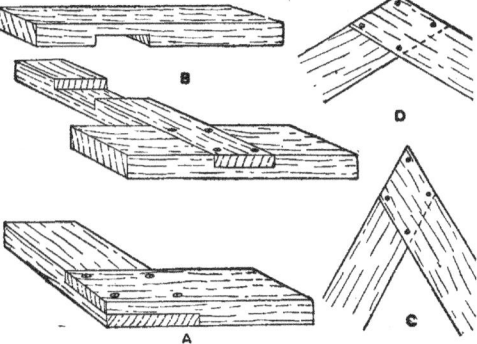

Fig. 33.—Examples of Half-lap Joints

posed that it is necessary to run the grain of each the same way. There is no objection to this; but the stiffness of the upper piece across the grain must then depend on other attachments. If the pieces are narrow and comparatively thick no crossing of grain is necessary. The cause of the difference between A and B would usually be that the direction of the grain has been determined by the length and width of the horizontal piece, the grain running the longest way, and parts attached to this must conform to the requirements of the casting. At C the grain of the piece beneath runs in an awkward direction for making a strong joint, though the piece itself is stronger than it would be with short transverse grain. The reason for running the grain in the direction shown is, of course, that the piece is narrow compared with its length, and if the grain ran the short way it might get broken. Usually pieces at right angles, as shown in these examples, are stiffened by internal brackets or ribs or fillets, which are as necessary in the design of the casting as in the pattern. Without them it would be difficult in some cases to guarantee a permanent and exact right angle in the pattern. D shows a central rib beneath a flange at right angles, the latter being in a single piece rather than divided, and attached to each side of the rib.

It is generally a rule that the larger and more important parts should as far as convenient be made in single pieces, and minor parts attached to them with as many joints as necessary, the result being greater strength than when the main part is divided to allow subsidiary parts to continue without joints.

Short grain is objectionable in all woodwork, and though instances sometimes occur where it is tolerated, the usual practice is to join pieces together so that the direction of the grain is charged to suit the shape and proportions of the construction. The shapes in Fig. 33 might be cut from single pieces of wood with the grain running in any convenient direction, but such a thing would never be done in ordinary work. They are built up so that the direction of the grain changes in accordance with the rule already mentioned. If either of the projecting parts in any of the examples in Fig. 33 were shorter than their width, a joint might be avoided and a single piece used with the grain running all one way, though even then, if the over-all width was great, it would be liable to curve, or perhaps split, if not strengthened by a piece with grain running crosswise.

In patternmaking the usual joints are half-lap or halved joints, as shown in Fig. 33. Half of each piece is cut away so that they can be screwed together as shown. This method is suitable for uniting pieces at any angle, and also where pieces cross each other and continue beyond the joint in each direction. A is a corner joint at right angles. B shows two joints, one crossing and the other where the end of one piece is united to an intermediate part of another. C is an acute angle and D an obtuse one, both formed by pieces halved together at the joint. Accuracy in all these cases depends on the accurate marking-out and cutting of the angles at the shoulders of the joints. The pieces are generally screwed together with ends rough and slightly overlapping to be trimmed flush with a chisel after. A gauge is set to half the thickness for marking the halving lines.

Fig. 34 is a typical example of construction which frequently occurs in patterns. First a portion has to be halved together, as at A and B in Fig. 33, and then ribs or flanges are screwed to its edges as in Fig. 34. These ribs are not halved, but are nearly always fitted as shown, one extending the full length and the other butting against its inner face, just as the sides and ends of an ordinary rough box are fitted.

Rebated joints (Fig. 35) are often used in pattern construction, chiefly as a precaution against the possibility of parts being knocked slightly out of place sidewise, which easily happens where there is only a narrow butt-joint with two or three screws to hold it. In patterns which are formed by boxing up rebated joints are always used, because if a side or end gets slightly forced in, it is not easy to get at the inner face for forcing it back again, and the overlap at the joint is bad for moulding. In simple brackets and other work, as in Fig. 32, the joints are seldom rebated.

EASY PATTERNMAKING

Built-up Work.—With a good proportion of pattern work building up is necessary when it is large or when it would involve short grain if not built up. Rings

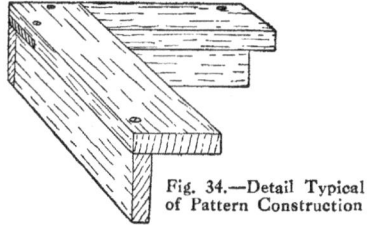

Fig. 34.—Detail Typical of Pattern Construction

of various cross sections and of all sizes are often required, and are always built up in segments, even if small.

A plain ring built in three layers of segments is shown by Fig. 36. If turned from a solid piece it would be weak, and shrinkage across the grain would make it more or less elliptical. A number of layers of segments are used for strength and permanence of form, the joints in each layer alternating with those in the next as shown. If only a single layer was used it would be difficult to unite the ends securely. Therefore at least two layers are used, no matter how shallow the ring may be, and it is better to have not less than three layers. A greater

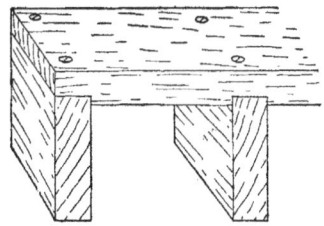

Fig. 35.—Rebated Joints

number than three is often necessary on account of the depth to be built up.

Some cross sections are shown in Fig. 37, A being the rim of a gear-wheel with its arms and boss, B the same for a bevel-wheel, C a half section of a flywheel, and D a worm wheel without its teeth. In all these the segmental rim is only a part of the pattern, arms or a plated centre being fitted to the rim for carrying the central boss. This fitting is done in any way that happens to suit the shape of the pattern. In A the rim would be turned first, and the arms fitted into it after, recesses being cut in the rim for them. At B, where, the diameter being comparatively small, a plate or web is generally used instead of arms, the first layer of segments would be glued on the web and the whole be turned together, the boss, of course, being made separately and fitted with a stud. At C the arms come mid-way in the depth of the

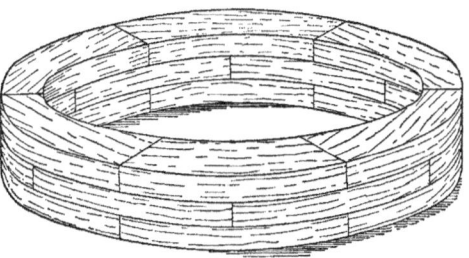

Fig. 36.—Ring Built in Segments

rim, and would be fitted in at that stage of the building up, half the number of layers being built up first on a face-plate, then the arms fitted in, or in some cases segments fitted between the arms, and the remaining layers put on, after which the rim is turned to shape. At D the pattern has to be divided through the centre of its web for moulding, and the halves would be made separately, the procedure for each being the same as in making the pattern at B.

In building up in segments, material is economised by varying the widths of the segments in the rough, and the inner and outer diameters of the layers to suit the cross section required. At A (Fig. 37), for instance, the segments at the arms are wide, and those above are narrow. It would be a waste of material, and give more trouble in making the glue joints, if the entire depth was built up uniformly to suit the widest part of the rim, and the narrow part reduced from this in turning. Therefore variations are made in the widths of the layers in the rough, just enough for turning being allowed everywhere, perhaps $\tfrac{3}{16}$ in. on the internal and external diameters. The larger the diameter the more should be allowed for glued on correspondingly farther out from the centre. This is simpler work than might be supposed, a full-size cross section being drawn first, and the thicknesses and radii of the layers marked on it. The building up is done on a face-plate which is put in the lathe for facing off each layer in turn, and marking circles for setting the next layer to.

Fig. 37.—Cross Sections of Circular Patterns Built in Segments

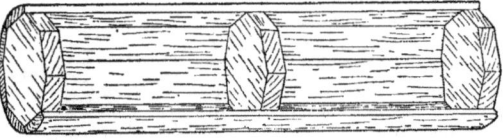

Fig. 38.—Cylindrical Pattern Built up of Lags on Interior Blocks

Figs. 38 and 39 show another kind of building up in lathe work. Most cylindrical-shaped patterns are small enough to be turned from solid wood; but sometimes the diameter is too great, involving

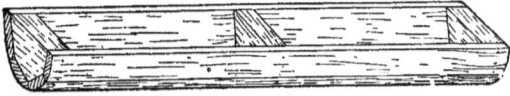

Fig. 39.—Half Pattern Lagged Up

turning, because of the likelihood of greater untruth in the rough. At B the layers vary almost negligibly in width, but considerably in diameter, so that the rim built up in the rough would be stepped, each succeeding layer being of larger radius than the preceding one, and

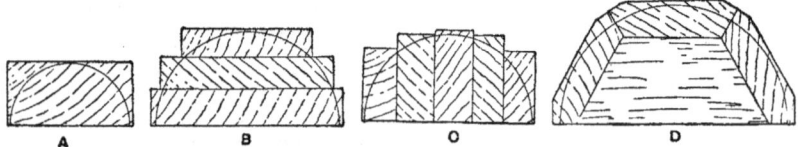

Fig. 40.—Methods of Preparing Halves of Cylindrical Patterns for Turning

not only a large amount of material, but making a heavy pattern for handling in the foundry, and one which is liable to

EASY PATTERNMAKING

shrink considerably owing to its bulk. Such a pattern is staved or lagged up as shown, thick internal blocks being prepared with a suitable number of flats, to which the lags are fitted and usually glued and nailed, glue being used in the edge joints of the lags. Such a pattern may be completely closed in, as in Fig. 38, but more frequently it is in halves, as in Fig. 39.

the more flats are required on the internal blocks. Halves are dowelled together before the pattern is turned; in fact, the

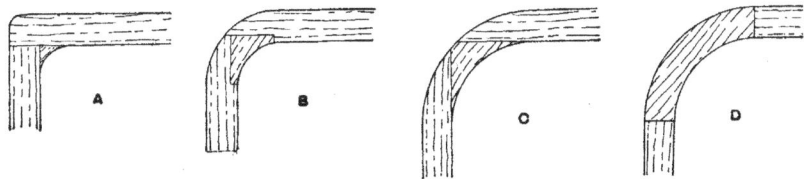

Fig. 41.—Examples of Rounded Corners

Some cross sections of cylindrical patterns in halves as they would be prepared for turning are shown by Fig. 40. If small, say less than 6 in. in diameter, a solid piece could be used for each half, as at A. If larger, two, or in some cases three, pieces, as at B, would be glued together. An alternative and slightly better but more troublesome way of building is shown at C. At D the lagging-up method, as in Fig. 39, is shown. The larger the diameter

blocks are usually dowelled before the lags are put on; but if the blocks are numerous it is not necessary to have dowels in all of them. The number of blocks required in any given case is a matter about which the patternmaker uses his judgment.

External angles are often rounded in patterns and internal angles filleted, as this strengthens and improves the appearance of a casting. Unless the curves are very small, it is usual to make them to a definite radius, which is decided by the draughtsman and not by the patternmaker. Outer angles are often rounded in cases where there is no corresponding inner angle to receive a hollow or fillet, and sometimes the latter are used where

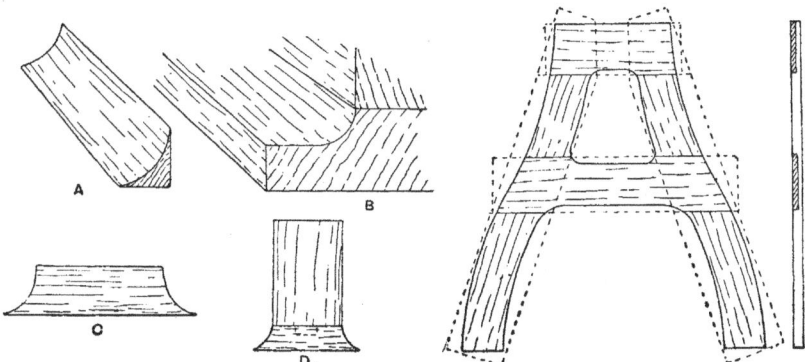

Fig. 42.—Examples of Fillets

Fig. 43.—Frame Built of Pieces Halved Together

there is no outer angle to be rounded, or where the purpose the casting is designed for does not permit it to be rounded.

The commonest method of treating an angle is shown at A (Fig. 41). The interior fillet is small and of no definite radius, and with it the outer angle is often left square. B shows a corner where the inner and outer curves would be struck to a radius, the thickness of metal round the curve being the same as along the straight. The fillet would not necessarily be let into the straight pieces as shown. It might have feather edges as at A, but they are less likely to break if made as at B. At C the radius is larger, and the piece inserted as a fillet cuts through the outer curve. Here the fillet is shown with feather edges, but sometimes it would be let in as at B. To do so would have the effect of shortening the straight pieces, and perhaps slightly weakening the corner. At D the radius is so large that a segment is fitted in. This does not imply that it is built up in a number of thicknesses, as in previous illustrations of segments. In the best work it would be built up, joints of intermediate segments coming midway, and perhaps the ends of the straight pieces cut to allow overlap in the joint there. But often a single segment only is put in, although its depth may be considerable, for it is only a quarter-circle, and a sufficiently strong joint can be made by inserting fine nails at an angle to hold the curved piece to the straight ones, and in such work there is almost invariably a base to which the straight and curved pieces are screwed.

The direction of grain in curves of this sort depends on circumstances. At D it would usually run as shown, the same way as the straight pieces, except that it must cross the corner at about 45°. At A it would be at right angles to that of the straight pieces, so that it would show end grain as indicated. In the two others, B and C, its direction would depend on the depth of the fillet in relation to its measurement in the other direction. If its depth is much in excess of the measurement across its feather edges, it would be best to make it the same way as at A; but otherwise it would be better to make it the same way as that of the straight pieces, so that shrinkage of the latter will not leave the end grain of the fillet standing above their top edges.

Feather edges in wood are weak, and in the case of fillets, glue is often used to hold the fillet and prevent its edges from breaking. The shellac used on patterns also helps to secure the thin edges. Small fillets are planed in lengths as at A (Fig. 42), and are nailed in place with or without glue. In many pattern-shops leather fillet is bought instead of wood fillet being made, the chief advantage of the former being that it can be used in curves. Its edges, of course, will not break. Putty, beeswax, or plaster-of-paris are sometimes used for fillets, chiefly on curves; and a patternmaker accustomed to the work can insert such fillets very quickly, uniformity in size being obtained by means of a firmer gouge drawn along the angle, so that it presses the material in and forms the fillet. In the most substantial work, fillets which follow curves are cut in the solid as at B, and this method is the best for straight fillets also. It takes longer and is rather wasteful of material. In work turned in the lathe this is the usual way. C shows a turned boss with fillet. Although such bosses are often studded loosely on the pattern so that they can be taken off by the moulder, the thin edges do not, as a rule, suffer much damage. With short grain, however, it would be impossible to make a thin edge, and even one $\frac{1}{16}$ in. thick would soon get broken. Therefore long bosses must be made in two parts as at D.

Fig. 43 is an example of framed work which includes fillets and curves. Patterns of this class are very common, and are framed together with half-lap joints. The framework generally forms a base for the attachment of ribs, lugs, bosses, bearing blocks, feet, and other details. The frame, as seen in the edge view, is thin, usually less than 1 in. even in the largest patterns, and is almost invariably stiffened with ribs fitted round the edges, sometimes on both faces of the pattern,

EASY PATTERNMAKING

sometimes on one only, sometimes only round an outer edge, sometimes on all edges. These ribs are fitted in short lengths joined end to end, as happens to

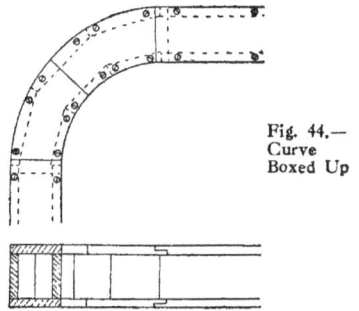

Fig. 44.—Curve Boxed Up

be most convenient to suit the curves. They are generally screwed to the frame, being screwed on first in the rough, and removed for working to curvature.

The pattern is first marked out full-size on a drawing-board, and then the pieces prepared and halved together, the frame at this stage appearing as indicated by the dotted lines in Fig. 43. The pieces are wide enough to include the small inner curves or fillets. Then the finished outline is marked on the pattern, and it is worked to shape and the other details fitted.

Large curves sometimes have to be built up, their cross sectional measurement perhaps being too great to allow of the use of solid material; that is, they have great thickness or depth as well as width. Fig. 44 is an example. It is a case where some parts can be left quite rough, just as the exteriors of core-boxes are left rough. Therefore the segments which form the curve need not be worked to curvature on the interior, which is boxed in, and, of course, would be cored out in the casting. It is not pattern surface which has anything to do with the formation of the mould, and therefore the patternmaker does not spend time in producing the curved outlines there. The pattern, in fact, is slightly stronger if the pieces are left straight as dotted.

General.—Boxed-up patterns of rectangular form are generally made with rebated joints. The advantage of this is that rough usage cannot force any of the pieces inwards, and so cause overlap at the joint. Here also the inside faces can be left unplaned and the thickness need not be uniform as long as the edges are gauged and planed to the lines at the rebates. These last represent a heavy class of work in which interior cross-bars or ribs or battens sometimes have to be fitted, and have nothing to do with the casting; but are wanted for strength in the pattern.

In pattern work it is important to prepare the pieces with their faces and edges at correct angles in relation to each other before putting the parts together. Fig. 45 illustrates the importance of this.

One of the commonest features in pattern work is the attachment of pieces edgewise to the face of another piece as shown, and in doing this it is often necessary, as at A, to keep one side practically at right angles, and allow considerable draught on the other. In other cases, as at B, the draught is equally divided on each side. Other pieces fitting against or between these, as at C, must have their joint edges cut to the correct angle before insertion. Slight inaccuracies of angle in any of these joint edges will affect the truth of the pattern so fundamentally that it will be difficult or impossible to correct it after it is put together.

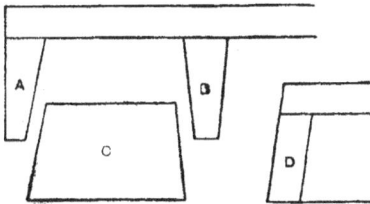

Fig. 45.—Diagram showing Importance of Exact Angle

To a beginner the extreme accuracy required and the slight variations of angle for draught seem tiresome and sometimes confusing. A piece like C, for instance, will have its ends tapering one way to fit the taper on the piece it goes between, and will have its faces tapered the opposite way for moulding, and all this must be done before the piece is fixed in place. A try-square is used for testing ordinary allowances of taper as well as for exact right angles. If the taper is considerable a bevel may be used.

In preparing pieces like A and B they would first be planed parallel in thickness with the edges at right angles, and then a gauge would be used to mark the amount to be planed off for taper, A having it gauged off on one face only, B on both faces. Or if the taper is only slight, it might be planed off at a guess. The angle of the ends of C would either be marked off direct, or a bevel would be set for transferring the angle. Taper may occur opposite ways, as at D, and then the amount would be gauged off opposite edges, or a bevel used.

As the grain of the wood usually runs

short and weak grain at one part, though strong at another.

Fig. 47 illustrates a constructional method often followed. A boss is required with a fillet only round part of its circumference, the other portion being flush with the edge of the part to which the boss is attached. In such cases the boss is turned in the usual way with a fillet and screwed in place, and the portion of the fillet not wanted is then pared off. The part to which the boss is screwed is cut to outline first, and is a guide for paring the boss. The boss may be centred by a stud or by a circle struck with compasses.

The patternmaker sometimes has to use battens to stiffen his work and keep it true; or sometimes also to hold boards together. These battens, not being wanted on the casting, must be stopped off by the moulder, that is, their impressions must be filled with sand. The moulder understands that this is required

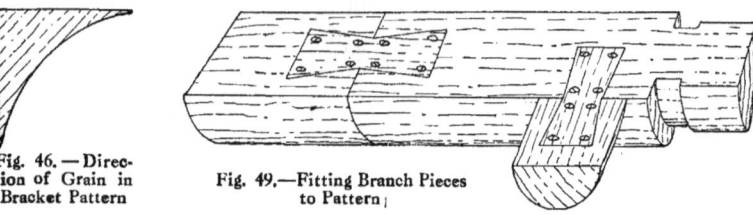

Fig. 46.—Direction of Grain in Bracket Pattern

Fig. 49.—Fitting Branch Pieces to Pattern

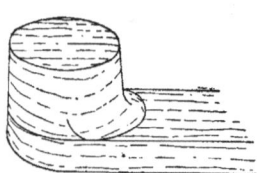

Fig. 47.—Turned Boss with Part of Fillet Pared Off

Fig. 48.—Half Cylindrical Pattern with Flanges

the longest way of each separate piece, it sometimes has to take a diagonal direction, as in the case of brackets shown by Fig. 46, otherwise it would leave extremely

but to call his attention to it, it is usual to cross-hatch battens with chalk or pencil marks all over their surfaces.

To prevent risk of mistakes in the

EASY PATTERNMAKING

foundry it is sometimes necessary to make cores so that there is only one way in which they will fit into the mould, for otherwise the casting may be spoiled

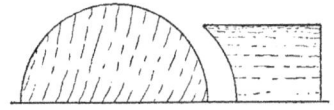

Fig. 50.—Branch to Fit Side of Cylindrical Body

through the core being put in wrong. Such mistakes are possible when the core has some peculiarity which makes it non-reversible, while at the same time it is reversible in its print impressions. that is, it can be put in the wrong way without the mistake being obvious to the moulder. The usual remedy is to modify one of the prints and the end of the core-box which fits that print. If the prints are round ones a flat portion is generally cut on one of them. and a similar flat made in the core-box.

Patterns of cylindrical shape in halves are very common and usually have flanges which are turned separately and fitted on as in Fig. 48. The body of the pattern is turned between centres, and the flanges are turned on a face-plate. Grooves to receive the flanges are turned in the body, the diameter across the grooves being a little less than the print diameter. Flanges are generally made with a fillet as shown. Flanges can, if necessary be fitted round the body of the pattern without grooves,

or round the print and against the end of the body, or sometimes it is convenient to put them on the end of the body and put a print on after. But fitting into a groove is

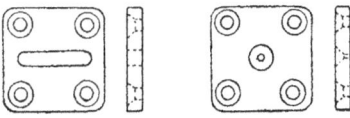

Fig. 52.—Metal Centre Plates

the best way, because it makes it easy to put the flanges on correctly and securely. Flanges are made separately. because it would be a waste of material to turn down from their diameter to that of the body and because they are stronger with their grain as shown.

Sometimes branches have to be fitted at right angles, as shown in Fig. 49, or an existing pattern has to be lengthened. Unless these attached pieces are very short the only way to unite them is by cutting recesses in the joint surface and fitting in dovetail pieces as shown. These are about 1 in. thick, depending on the diameter of the pieces united. A dovetail is preferred to parallel sides, because it is scarcely any more trouble to cut, and if fitted properly it pulls and keeps the joint close. Such pieces need not be carefully marked out to any particular size or angle; but

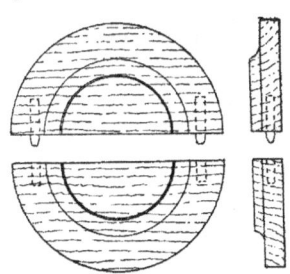

Fig. 53.—Turned Flange with Centre not Cut

when made can be laid on the joint surface, and a line scribed round them to which to cut the recess. Another arrangement, occasionally practised, is to

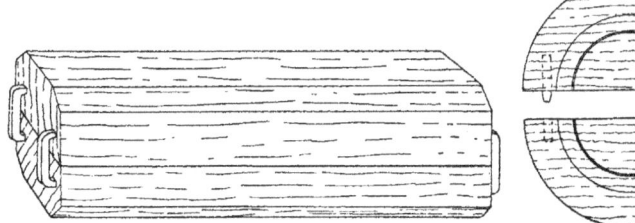

Fig. 51.—Halves Held by Staples

cut the dovetail solid on the end of one part and fit and screw it into the other. This, however, is not always practicable, and a separate dovetail, as shown, is as good if done properly.

A branch at right angles is gouged to fit the curve, as in Fig. 50. The branch would usually have a print and flange on its end. The exact length of the branch piece would be obtained from a full-size view, and a line would be scribed across the joint of the branch to indicate how far to cut back for the diameter of the main body. The parts are then laid joint downwards on a flat surface, and the concave part gouged until close contact is made. If the branch is very short, diagonal screws or nails might be used instead of a dovetail piece.

In work of this kind it frequently happens that old patterns are altered instead of new ones being made. Only in such a case would it be necessary to fit a piece to the end to make up a required length, as in Fig. 49. Such a piece, if made specially, would, as a rule, have a print turned solid with it and be grooved for a flange. If the length to be added is very short it would simply be screwed on the end, and flange and print screwed to it. In other cases, to avoid cutting the print off a pattern which has to be temporarily lengthened, the piece to be put on would be cut to fit over the print.

As it is impossible, except in very rough work, to turn a pattern solid and saw it in halves after, and still retain a sufficiently circular shape accurate to size, the halves must be held together securely for turning. For this purpose the staples or dogs used for glue joints and for other temporary purposes are generally employed in the lathe. They are placed either where they will not be in the way of the tool, or else their positions are changed as the work proceeds. Fig. 51 shows halves held together by staples and ready for turning between centres.

Another way of holding the halves together is to screw them, the heads of the screws being sunk sufficiently to allow for turning down to diameter. At the ends this is generally done by sawing out pieces, but at intermediate places the holes are countersunk with a centre-bit. When the diameter is large, it is sometimes desirable to use staples as well as screws, as the latter are only along the centre.

Centre plates (Fig. 52) are also commonly used, alone in small work, in conjunction with the other methods when it is large. These plates are of metal, and are screwed to the end of the wood. The plate for the fork centre has a slot and that for the dead centre a countersunk hole. Their advantage is not so much that the centring is more correct, but that there is less risk of the work being forced out of centre or thrown out of the lathe. Therefore they are invariably used for heavy work, and staples are used in addition. Work in halves on the faceplate, such as flanges, simply require each half screwed to the plate the joint being across the centre of the plate.

When a flange is cut to fit over a pattern as in some of the preceding instances, the diameter of the hole is nicked with the turning chisel, and the central part sawn out after removal from the face-plate. With a band-saw this is quicker than boring it out in the lathe, besides which the pieces sawn out are often useful for other purposes. Trimming with a paring gouge is generally necessary after sawing. Fig. 53 shows a flange which has been turned but has not yet had its central part cut out.

Dowelling.—Dowels fulfil a different purpose from those in joinery. In patterns they are almost always used not to hold parts together, but to allow them to be brought together correctly in relation to each other, and separated again when necessary during the process of moulding. The dowels are fitted securely to one half or one portion of the pattern, and their short projecting ends slip easily into holes bored in the other part. In principle they are the same as the studs, already described as used on prints and bosses, the difference being that a dowel is longer and smaller in diameter, and tapered so that it only becomes a close fit when the joint surfaces of the opposite parts are in contact.

EASY PATTERNMAKING

Fig. 54 shows how an ordinary wooden dowel appears when in position with the dowelled parts together. In the upper piece it is a tight fit. It does not neces-

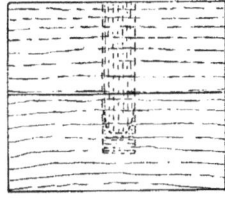

Fig. 54.—Parts Kept in Position by Wooden Dowels

sarily go through as shown, but the moulder sometimes finds it convenient to be able to knock the dowel back temporarily flush with the joint surface, and therefore where the thickness of wood is not great it is generally best to bore right through. For the same reason it is better not to glue the dowel in, as dowels used in joinery are. The ready-made birch dowel-rod is commonly used, and a bit must be found for boring holes into which the rod will drive rather tightly. The diameter of rod used depends on the size of the work; but the range is not very great, being usually ⅜ in. or ½ in.

The positions of dowel holes may be marked on the joint face of the pattern or core-box, the number and their locations being decided by the size and shape, and the centres decided on must be transferred to the opposite half. The simplest way to do this is to lay ordinary pins or fine wire nails with their heads on the desired centres, and to press the upper half down on this to leave corresponding impressions on both, as in Fig. 55. Then the holes are bored with a centre-bit. If the hole is to go right through one of the pieces, as shown in Fig. 54, the parts can be clamped together and the holes bored from the outer surface of one, through the joint, and sufficiently far into the other piece. After the holes are bored, the dowel rod is driven in and cut off, with the necessary projection. This latter is then tapered and rounded slightly with knife and file, care being taken not to reduce the diameter at the base.

Metal dowels are also commonly used for small work. They require holes bored to fit the cup and peg, which are driven in with a hammer. Another is the plate kind used for larger work, and made in iron. The plates are let flush into the surface of the wood and held by two or four screws, according to the size. One plate has a hole through it, and the other a pin of corresponding diameter. These are very easily fitted except for the slight extra trouble of cutting the recesses for the plates. A hole is bored first at any suitable place, not the size of the pin, but larger. The plate is placed on this, and a line scribed round its outer edges as a guide for cutting the recess. This plate is screwed in place, and then the one with the pin put on it as it will be when the halves of the pattern are together. Then the other half of the pattern is laid on top, and a little pressure causes points on the back of the pin-plate to leave their impression in the wood. This shows the exact position for the plate, and it only remains to scribe round its edges, and cut the recess to these lines and screw the plate in.

Although each individual dowel may be

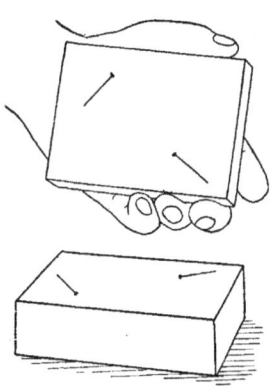

Fig. 55.—Dowel Centres marked on Opposite Halves by Pins

an easy fit in its hole, the halves of the pattern often fit too tightly when first tried together. This is due to more or less inaccuracy of position of the dowels in relation to others in another part of the joint surface. It can generally be rectified by putting the pattern halves together, and hammering one or the other endwise and sidewise until they will go together and come apart easily. Wood dowels, if badly out of position, may be filed when it has been determined where they want filing ; but generally they can be corrected in the same way as the metal ones. Always, if possible, the parts are dowelled together before their exterior is worked to shape. In cases where this cannot be done, extra care must be taken to get the edges of the parts flush when fitting the dowels.

The number of dowels used in the joint of a pattern depends on its size and shape. In many cases two are sufficient. If a part, such as a boss or print, can be allowed to swivel on its centre, then a central stud is better than two dowels, as the latter needlessly fix its position circumferentially, and involve the risk of its being put on the wrong way ; for it is a practical impossibility to dowel a part so that it fits equally correctly in either of the two possible ways of putting it on. To avoid this risk of misplacement, it is a good plan when possible to use a central stud and a dowel at some distance away from it, or to place the dowels so unsymmetrically that if the parts are put together wrong it will be obvious. It is a common practice also to cut corresponding marks in each half of the pattern to indicate to the moulder that these marks must come together when the dowelled parts are correctly placed. In a large pattern two dowels are not enough. A long cylinder or pipe pattern, for instance, would have three or four or more large dowels on its centre line, and its flanges, if large, would have dowels also. In some cases flanges in halves are dowelled when made, and in others it is decided that the dowels in the body of the pattern will be sufficient. The essential thing is to keep the edges of the halves flush. If a great number of dowels are used it is difficult to make the fit so good that the halves will separate easily.

When a loam pattern is large and only one casting is required from it, a separate core is not made if it is possible to modify the pattern to serve as a core after the mould has been made from the pattern. To do this the core is made first and its surface blackwashed. Then a thickness of loam representing the thickness of metal in the casting is put on to convert the core into a temporary pattern. After it has been moulded the pattern layer of loam can be stripped off, leaving the core as originally made.

Woodworking by Machinery

In the commercial production of woodwork, machinery plays an important part; in fact, it would scarcely be an exaggeration to say that machinery exists, nowadays, for the performance of most, if not all of the preparatory operations connected therewith. The use of machinery in woodworking usually effects a considerable saving in time as compared with hand-work, and should also appreciably decrease the cost of production, in spite of the somewhat heavy running and maintenance costs attending the use of power. Further, some machines (the "surface planer" for example) tend to raise the standard of the output, inasmuch as they will turn out far truer work than could be expected by hand under similar circumstances.

THE MORTISING MACHINE

This is not always a power machine; being in most cases operated by hand, the running and maintenance costs (excepting for the wages of the operator) may be described as negligible. It further possesses an advantage not previously mentioned: little or no skill is required to turn out correct work on it. In fact, in a small joinery establishment, the youngest apprentice usually attends to the mortising machine.

Fig. 1 is a typical mortising machine, and although the patterns of different makers vary somewhat, the actuating principles are precisely the same. In passing, it may be well to mention that this will be found the case with most, if not quite all, woodworking machines.

Operating the Mortising Machine.—Fig. 2 shows the machine in operation. The material to be mortised is "set out," and "gauged" on both edges, the same as previously described for hand-mortising. The job A is placed with its "face-side" towards the fence B and is secured in the carriage of the machine by the screw-wheel C. A transverse motion is given to the carriage by turning the hand-wheel D; this locates the gauge marks in their correct position with regard to the chisel E.

The shank of the chisel (*see also* Fig. 3) is tapered to fit a similar hole in the "chisel box" of the machine. A reciprocating motion is given to the chisel by the lever F. Turning the large hand-wheel H moves the carriage along, and with it the timber, thus determining the length of the mortise. The rotary handle J is for adjusting the stroke of the machine to the depth of the mortise required; the full depth in the case of a "blind" mortise, or rather more than half depth if the mortise is to be made right through the timber.

Making the Mortise.—The job having been secured in the machine and the necessary adjustments made, the lever is gripped in the right hand and the large hand-wheel in the left, as shown. A commencement is made about midway

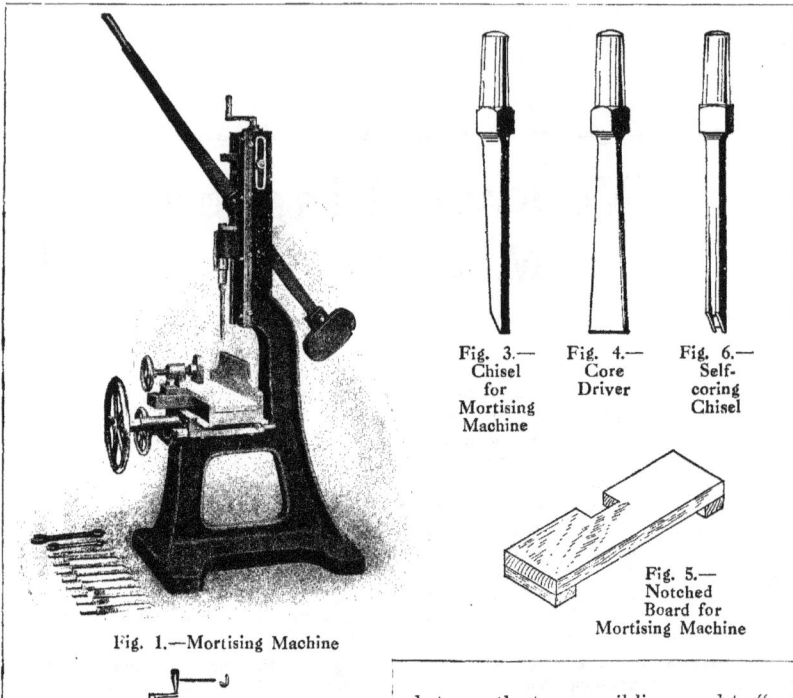

Fig. 1.—Mortising Machine

Fig. 3.—Chisel for Mortising Machine

Fig. 4.—Core Driver

Fig. 6.—Self-coring Chisel

Fig. 5.—Notched Board for Mortising Machine

Fig. 2.—Operation of Mortising Machine

between the two pencil lines used to "set out" the length of the mortise, or in making a short mortise, rather nearer to the line which is towards the back of the chisel. Move the lever downwards, pressing the chisel as far as possible into the timber. The lever is now raised, so as to lift the chisel just clear of the job, and the hand-wheel is turned so as to move the timber forward $\frac{1}{16}$ in. or so towards the face of the chisel, which is again depressed. These movements are repeated alternately, the timber being moved forward a little each time the chisel is raised, till one end of the mortise is reached. If the mortise is a deep one, three or four strokes will probably have to be made before the required depth is reached, and under such circumstances, the part just mortised would be gone over again, with the chisel reversed, when working towards the other end of the hole. The chisel is reversed,

WOODWORKING BY MACHINERY

that is, made to face in the opposite direction, by giving half a turn to the handle K, and the other end of the mortise is finished in a similar manner to the first, excepting,

Fig. 7.—Trimmer

of course, that the hand-wheel is rotated in the opposite direction. If the mortise is " blind " it is now ready to be cleaned out, but if a " through " one, the hole just made, being only about half-way through, will have to be met by mortising from the other edge. In turning the lower edge to the top for this purpose, take care that the face side of the work is directed towards the fence of the machine. Complete the second half of the hole in the same way as the first, making sure that the one is mortised right through to the other.

Cleaning the Mortise.—A " blind " mortise may be cleaned out by placing the job on the bench or in the bench-screw, and removing the loose material with a mallet and chisel. For cleaning out a through mortise, a core driver (Fig. 4) may be used in the machine. The chisel is removed, and the core driver substituted.

A piece of board (see Fig. 5) notched out as shown, to receive the core, is placed on the carriage of the machine. The core to be driven is laid directly over the notch, and the job is secured in the machine the same as for mortising. Depressing the lever pushes the core out of the mortise.

A self-coring chisel, as it is called, is shown by Fig. 6. This tool may perhaps not be quite all that its name would imply, but it certainly reduces the labour of cleaning out mortises to a minimum. Each chip of wood as it is cut passes into the groove in the back of the chisel. This groove should retain one chip until it is pushed out by the next. If this cycle of operation does not always synchronise the tool is even so a good one, and a set of self-coring chisels are at least worthy of consideration when installing a new mortising machine. It may interest some readers to know that a punch and die, for punching the holes in venetian blind laths, may be obtained to fit the mortising machine.

THE TRIMMER

The Scope of the Machine.—The trimmer (see Fig. 7) is also a hand-operated machine. It is similar in principle to the old mitre-cutting machine, which latter, owing to its lack of accuracy, never became popular with professional woodworkers. If the trimmer is a development of the mitre-cutting machine, it has been improved almost out of recognition, the result being a tool almost indispensable for certain classes of woodwork. A good trimmer will, at a single stroke, " shoot " a mitre in a heavy moulding, whilst light mouldings, after being roughly cross-cut

Fig. 8.—Operation of Trimmer

to length, may be " mitred " directly on the machine.

Truing up end-grain timber either square or at an angle, and cleaning up pieces of stuff to exact lengths (cutting to " dead length ") are also jobs that come within the special province of the trimmer. A stroke or two of some of the larger machines will clean up the ends of a table, or a sideboard top, in almost less time than it would take to secure the job in the bench-screw, preparatory to hand-planing.

Components of the Trimmer.—On referring to Fig. 7, which is a back view of the machine, it will be seen that two fences, A and A, and also two knives, B and B, are provided. This is so as to enable mitres to be cut left-handed as well as right-handed.

The fences are adjustable and may be set at any angle between 45 degrees (a mitre) and 90 degrees (right-angle) with the knives. The fences of some of the more capacious machines will give all angles between 30 degrees and 135 degrees.

Mitring on the Trimmer.—Fig. 8 shows the method of mitring a moulding on the trimmer. The moulding is held to the fence, which has been previously set to an angle of 45 degrees, and the knife, actuated by the lever, is drawn through the job. In mitring the components of a square picture frame, one end of each piece of moulding would be treated as shown. They would then be "marked off" to the required lengths, and the remaining mitres would be cut from the other fence by moving the lever in the opposite direction.

The removal of too great a thickness of timber at a single cut should not be attempted on a trimmer. The lever should always be capable of being removed across without undue effort on the part of the operator. In "truing" up a job, whenever it is necessary to move much stuff, better work will result if the surplus material is taken off in several thin slices, and besides, the machine will not be likely to suffer from overstrain.

Sharpening Trimmer Knives.—It is a common practice to sharpen the knives of trimmers by rubbing them with an oil-stone, without removing them from the machine; it is, however, better practice to take them out occasionally properly to sharpen them.

When the knives need grinding, they may be treated in a similar manner to the straight cutters of a surface planer (*see* remarks on the Surface Planer).

THE CIRCULAR SAW

Its Parts Described.—A circular saw-bench is usually the first power machine that the aforetime hand-worker contemplates installing. Its advantages are many. As well as doing ordinary sawing expeditiously and well, bevel cutting, tenoning, ploughing, rebating, and even light moulding may be executed on an up-to-date machine. In fact, the number of uses to which such a machine can be applied are largely dependent upon the resource of the operator. The various "shifts" and adjustments needed are easily and quickly made; there is little in the machine to get out of order, excepting the saw itself; whilst the actual operation of sawing could not well be simplified. Against the above must be set the facts, that considerable practice and experience is essential to the keeping of circular saws in good order, and also that they require a good deal of power to drive them.

Figs. 9 and 10 show up-to-date types of jobbing saw-benches, the principal difference between them being that of size. Fig. 11 is another view of the machine shown by Fig. 10 and is included here to show the bevelling or canting arrangement at the back of the fence A.

Operating the Circular Saw.—The fence is merely a gauge to determine the size of the piece of timber being cut, and in use is set to that size from the inner side of the saw teeth, the timber of the size required passing between the fence and the saw. The operation of cutting a short piece of timber into boards is shown by Fig. 12. Note the "feed stick" used in the right hand, to pass the end of the board between the fence and the saw.

When it is required to cut "feather-edged" boards, window sills, and similar jobs, where one edge is required to be thicker than the other, the fence of the saw-bench may be canted as shown by

Fig. 9.—Circular Saw Bench

Fig. 13. Some form of fence-canting arrangement is now provided on most jobbing benches, and though not absolutely essential, it is a great convenience. A sill is shown being cut to bevel by Fig. 14.

The Rising and Falling Table.—Both the saw-benches illustrated by Figs. 9 and 10 are provided with a rising and falling table, a necessary movement when cuts of limited depth are needed and it is desired to shroud a part of the saw as in ploughing and in the sawing out of rebates. The rising and falling movement is actuated by the hand-wheel A (Fig. 15), where the solid lines indicate the normal appearance of the machine, and the dotted lines show the table raised and the fence pushed forward as required for rebating.

Rebating.—A small saw, of a stout gauge, so that it will stand up to its work without packing, is most suitable for sawing rebates. The operation is performed in two cuts, as will be gathered from Fig. 16, which shows the first cut already made and being met by the second one.

Fig. 10.—Another Pattern of Circular Saw Bench (Front)

Packing, Packing-boxes, etc.—To keep circular saws steady and up to their work their front part must be supported with packing, which is accommodated in boxes either formed in, or attached to, the underside of the top of the saw-bench, on each side of the saw opening.

In the case of a home-made bench, having a wooden top of sufficient thickness, the boxes may be merely rebates cutting the top itself, but a properly constructed machine will require wooden packing-boxes fitted, and screwed or bolted to the underpart of the table. Lining or beating pieces are also fitted on either side of the rear half of the saw opening so as

Fig. 11.—Rear View of Saw Bench showing Canting Device

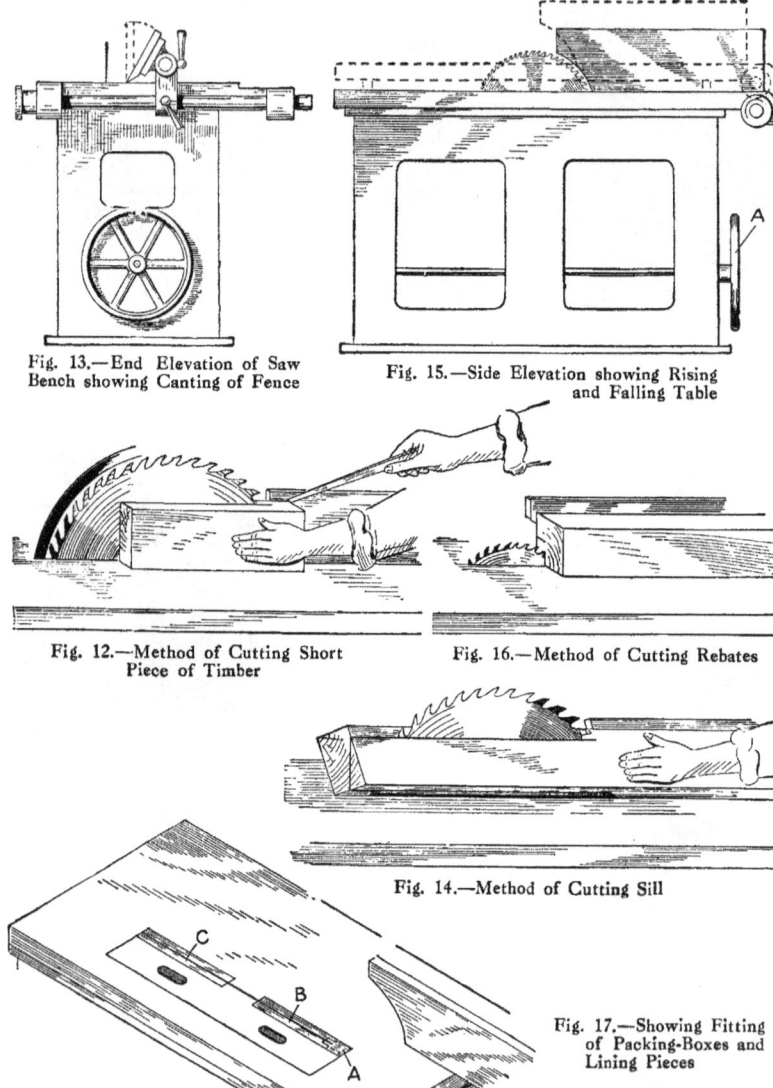

Fig. 13.—End Elevation of Saw Bench showing Canting of Fence

Fig. 15.—Side Elevation showing Rising and Falling Table

Fig. 12.—Method of Cutting Short Piece of Timber

Fig. 16.—Method of Cutting Rebates

Fig. 14.—Method of Cutting Sill

Fig. 17.—Showing Fitting of Packing-Boxes and Lining Pieces

to preclude the possibility of the teeth of the saw, when running, coming into contact with the metal of the bench. the mouthpiece, B the packing-boxes, and C the beating or lining pieces.

Fig. 18 shows the packing-boxes in

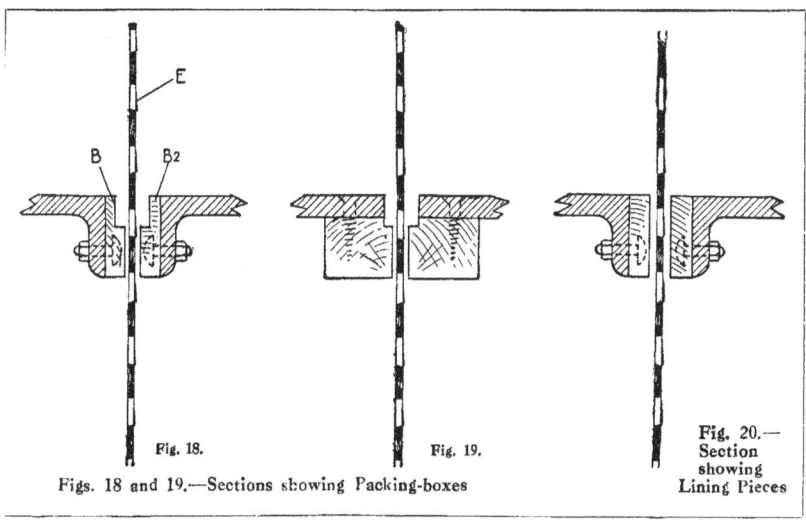

Figs. 18 and 19.—Sections showing Packing-boxes

Fig. 20.—Section showing Lining Pieces

To hold the packing in position, and to fill up any unoccupied space at this part, a mouthpiece is fitted to the front of the section and one way in which they may be secured to the underpart of the bench top, E being the saw, and B and

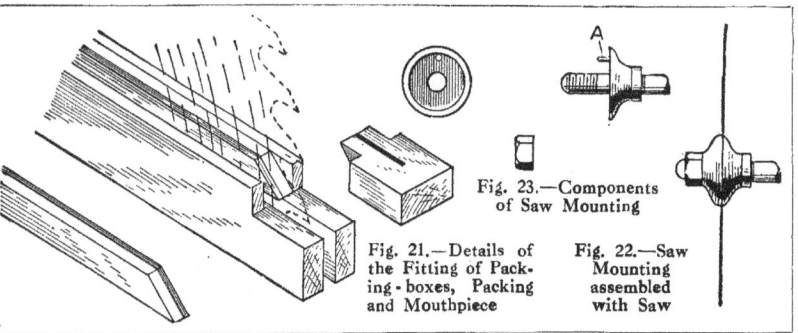

Fig. 21.—Details of the Fitting of Packing-boxes, Packing and Mouthpiece

Fig. 22.—Saw Mounting assembled with Saw

Fig. 23.—Components of Saw Mounting

saw opening. These fittings should be made of hardwood; mahogany or beech is suitable. The arrangement of the fittings is shown by Fig. 17, which is a view of the top of the saw-bench. A shows B2 the packing-boxes. In the case of a small machine there may be insufficient room to admit of packing-boxes being fitted in the manner indicated, and Fig. 19 shows how such a restricted space may be treated. The lining or beating pieces are shown in section by Fig. 20. Note that none of these fittings should come in contact with the saw; there should be a space of about $\frac{1}{16}$ in. between the saw and the packing-boxes, and at least twice that amount between the saw and the lining pieces.

How the packing-boxes, the packing and the mouthpiece fit together will be gathered from Fig. 21, where the far-side packing is seen in position. The packing should just extend to the gullets of the saw, as shown.

Saw-packing may be prepared in several ways; some sawyers use plaited hemp, others wind hemp round thin strips of wood, whilst some use ready-made engine-packing of size sufficient to fill the packing-boxes. The packing-pieces shown in Fig. 21 are intended to be made by gluing carpet felt on to a piece of board of suitable thickness. When the glue is set, strips of sufficient width to make the required packing-pieces are sawn from the board and planed to fit the packing-boxes. The felt of the packings should be oiled before inserting them in the packing-boxes, the felt side being disposed towards the saw. The packing should be sufficiently tight to support the saw, but not so tight as to prevent its being revolved easily by hand.

The Saw Mounting.—The construction of that end of the saw-bench spindle on which the saw is mounted is shown by Figs. 22 and 23. The centre hole of the saw (Fig. 24) should be a sliding fit on the spindle. The smaller hole in the saw passes over the driving-pin A (Fig. 23), and should show a little clearance, say a bare $\frac{1}{16}$ in., all round it. This is important, because it allows the saw to expand freely when warmed up by its work. To minimise the danger of its working loose with the running of the machine, the large nut which screws on to the end of the saw spindle and secures the saw thereon usually tightens left-handed.

When putting a saw on to the spindle and tightening the nut, make it a rule to have the driving-pin A to the top. The saw will then always take up the sam position relative to the spindle, and wi run true irrespective of whether the centr hole is a good fit or not.

The Sizes of Circular Saws.—Ci cular saws as used for woodworking ar procurable in various diameters, fror a few inches to several feet. As the diameter increases saws have, generall speaking, to be made stouter. Thic saws waste more material than those tha are of thinner gauge; moreover, sma saws are much more easily worked an take less power to drive than do large ones. Whilst, therefore, a saw of th maximum size that it will take may be necessary adjunct to the saw-bench, sav of smaller diameter may often be advar tageously used thereon, and for some job: such as rebating, are absolutely essentia

Grinding and Sharpening the Teetl —The teeth of a new circular saw shoul invariably be ground true before it i sharpened and put to work. The grinc ing is effected whilst the saw is runnin by applying a piece of hard flag-ston lightly to the teeth, as shown by Fig. 2! Hold the stone in position for a secon or two, then stop the machine and examin the teeth. The extreme points of som of them will have been ground off, whilɛ others will not have been touched. Cor tinue the grinding, a little at a time so a not to burn them, until the points of a the teeth have been reached. This proces assumes that the saw is correctly mountɛ on its spindle.

Now run the saw into a piece of wooc and note whether the teeth are squar across. If they are not, they should b made so by grinding a little more off th long side. Dull saws also should b similarly treated; they should be lightl stoned before being removed from th saw-bench for sharpening. If the stonin or " breasting " operation is neglected, th teeth will become uneven in length, whe all the work will fall on the longer ones.

A home-made vice for holding circula saws while being sharpened is shown b Fig. 26. This may be made from harc wood, if that is available, though for hold ing small saws a vice made frcm floor

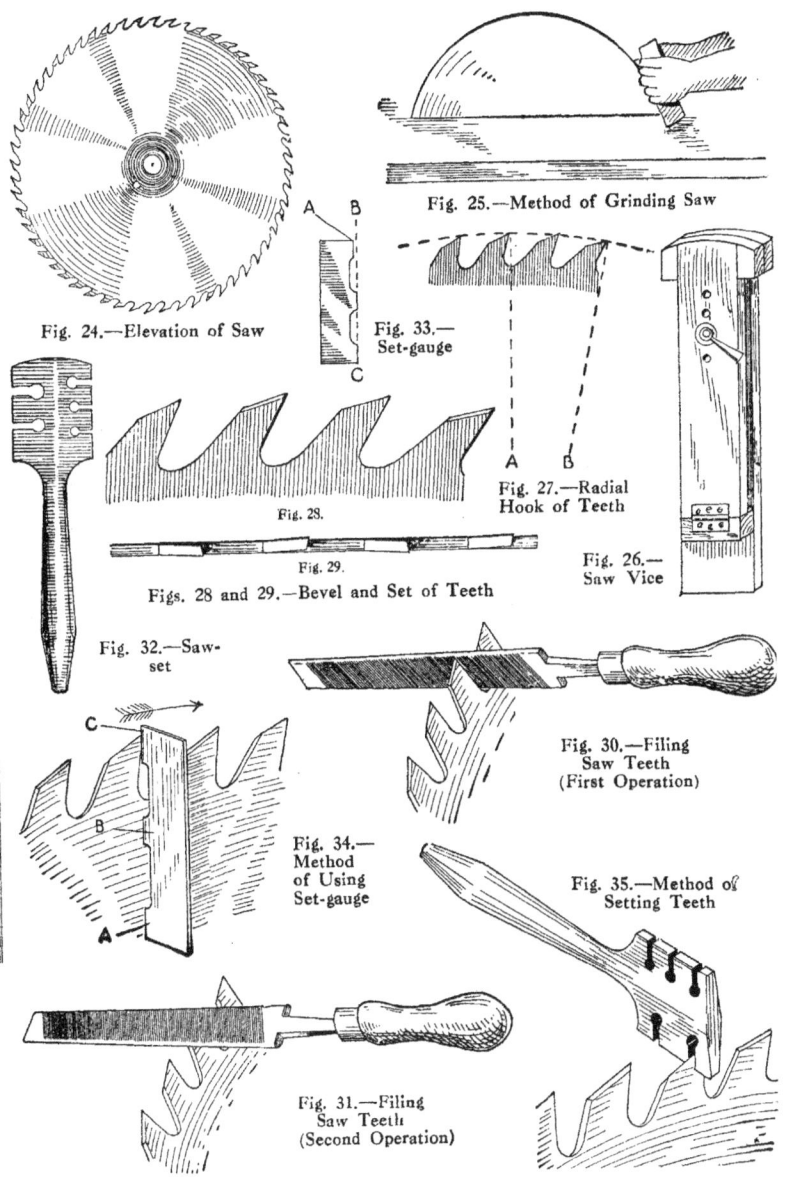

Fig. 24.—Elevation of Saw
Fig. 25.—Method of Grinding Saw
Fig. 33.—Set-gauge
Fig. 27.—Radial Hook of Teeth
Fig. 26.—Saw Vice
Fig. 28.
Fig. 29.
Figs. 28 and 29.—Bevel and Set of Teeth
Fig. 32.—Saw-set
Fig. 30.—Filing Saw Teeth (First Operation)
Fig. 34.—Method of Using Set-gauge
Fig. 35.—Method of Setting Teeth
Fig. 31.—Filing Saw Teeth (Second Operation)

board or shelving will answer quite well. The vice should be firmly screwed to the sharpening bench. A mill saw file will also be needed. This is a single-cut flat file, and should be procured with two rounded edges.

On consulting a saw makers' illustrated catalogue, it will be noticed that the number and size of the teeth in different saws varies considerably and this quite irrespective of the size of the saws themselves. This is arranged so that saws of a given diameter may be chosen for various classes of work. For instance, a circular saw used in a mill for the rapid " breaking down " of heavy timber, would require fewer, and larger teeth, than might advantageously be employed in a joiners' or cabinet makers' shop for cutting tenons or rebates. There are, however, certain conditions to which all saws must conform, and these conditions must be kept in mind when saw-sharpening. Consider Fig. 27. It will be seen that the dotted lines A and B, passing from the centre of the saw to its circumference, only touch the fronts of the saw teeth at their extreme points. The " rake " of the front of the teeth away from these lines is termed " hook." Such radial hook is essential to the satisfactory working of the saw and must be preserved when filing the teeth. It may be well to mention that whilst, as previously stated, the spacing of the teeth of a saw is governed by the purpose for which it is required, the amount of " hook " which may advantageously be given to the teeth depends upon their spacing. Briefly, the more " hook " that can be given to the teeth of a circular saw without unduly weakening them, the better the saw will work.

Filing the Teeth.—Notice from Fig. 27 that the dotted circumferential line, also, only touches the extreme points of the teeth. It is necessary that the teeth be " backed off " as shown, so as to enable them to enter the timber, but at the same time a good stiff point should always be retained. Both the tops and also the fronts of the teeth require filing, and it does not much matter which is done first, some operators working one way and some the other. If, however, the fronts are first attended to, the saw may perhaps more easily be kept circular. The fronts of the teeth may be filed square across, though if the handle of the file is sloped slightly towards the back of the tooth, filing will be " sweeter," but no appreciable bevel should be given to the fronts of the teeth.

In filing the tops of the teeth the handle of the file is kept down a trifle, so as to impart a slight bevel to the teeth at this part, and to bring them to a point (*see* Figs. 28 and 29, which show a front and side view of the teeth respectively).

The grinding previously done to the teeth should just be filed out. The bevel should be such as to cause the outer part of the cutting edge to enter the timber well in advance of the inner (*again see* Fig. 29). If it did not do so the work would be rough. Too much bevel should not be given; what is required is a chisel point and not a needle point. Excessive bevelling of the teeth will cause shavings to come from the saw in place of sawdust, which is an inefficient combined operation. The two operations of saw filing are shown by Figs. 30 and 31. File each alternate tooth, those whose points are set to lean away from the operator. Then reverse the saw in the vice and file the intermediate teeth.

Setting a Circular Saw.—The saw will now require " setting," and for this purpose a saw-set (Fig. 32), and a set-gauge (Fig. 33). will be required. The saw-set may be purchased, but the set-gauge will probably have to be made. A strip of thin steel about 3 in. long by ⅜ in. wide will be needed. A piece of a broken bandsaw, or the blade of an old table knife answers admirably. File or grind to the shape shown. The distance that A (Fig. 33) is filed back from the line B C represents the amount of " set " to be given to the teeth. The set may vary from about $\frac{1}{64}$ in. in a saw used for fine work to $\frac{1}{32}$ in. or more in a large saw used for cutting heavier material. If two gauges are made, one to each of the above sizes, one of them will probably be found satisfactory for any saw up to 30 in. diameter.

WOODWORKING BY MACHINERY

The saw to be set is held in the vice the same as for sharpening. Put a chalk mark on the tooth at the top of the saw where a beginning is to be made. The operator should stand with the teeth of the saw facing him, in the same position with regard to the saw as when sawing. Hold the saw-set in the right hand and the set-gauge in the left, and proceed to set each tooth that turns towards the left. Teeth that are bevelled on the right are set to the left and *vice versa*. First apply the gauge just behind the point of the tooth as shown by Fig. 34, and keeping A and B in contact with the saw, slide C over the point of the tooth and note whether it touches it or not. If it does, that tooth may be passed as being suffi-

parallel first, and if the job will not stay up to the fence, set the tail back a shade. The other end of the plate should not quite reach to the teeth of the saw. Set-screws for making the necessary adjustments are provided at the back of the fence.

Circular Saw Speeds.—A suitable speed for circular saws is 8,000 ft. per minute. On a jobbing bench, however, where a great part of the work is done with saws of less diameter than the maximum that the bench will take, it becomes necessary to run the larger saws at a circumferential or edge speed in excess of this, so as to give a better speed to the smaller saws. Under such circumstances 9,000 ft. per minute may be taken as a basis, and if

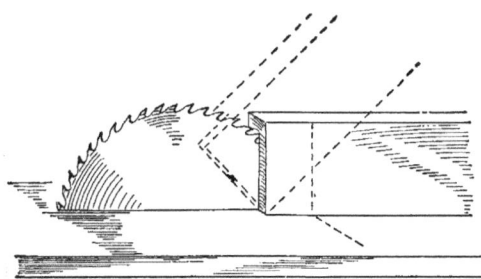

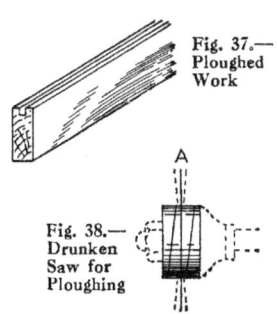

Fig. 37.—Ploughed Work

Fig. 36.—Method of Cutting Tenons

Fig. 38.—Drunken Saw for Ploughing

ciently set and the gauge applied to the next but one. If C clears the point, apply the saw-set as shown by Fig. 35, pull it gently towards you, and gauge again. C should just stroke the point of a correctly set tooth. Set the teeth round on one side of the saw, working on the top, and rotating the saw in the vice, as required. Then take the saw-set in the left hand and the set-gauge in the right, and proceed to set the teeth which are bevelled on the left.

Position of Saw Relative to Fence. —The front plate of the fence of the saw-bench should be parallel with the saw, both horizontally and vertically, or it may be found necessary to work with the tail of the plate—the end that is farthest from the saw—set back a trifle. Try it

this is divided by the circumference in feet of the largest saw that it is intended to use, the quotient will represent the revolutions per minute of the saw spindle.

Cutting Tenons on the Circular Saw.—It takes considerable time and some practice to cut tenons on wide rails accurately by hand, but with a circular saw in good condition the job may be speedily and easily accomplished. The shoulders of the tenons should be set out the same as for hand work, and one or two tenons should be gauged with the mortise gauge. Make a line across the saw-bench at right angles to the fence and immediately under the points of the teeth of the saw. Put the face side of a gauged rail to the fence, and set it so that the saw will cut one side of the tenon. Saw this tenon in till its shoulder line and the line on the bench coincide. Then raise the farther end of the rail, as shown dotted by Fig. 36, till the saw reaches the shoulder line at the top. When a number of tenons require cutting, treat all on one side first, and then alter the fence and cut their other sides.

Ploughing with a Circular Saw.—Ploughing (*see* Fig. 37) may be effected on the saw bench by various means. Sometimes a small and very thick saw, that cuts a kerf of just the size groove required, is used. The disadvantage of such saws is that, owing to their thickness, they cannot be set, and consequently have to be dished—made thinner towards the centre so as to obtain the necessary clearance, with the result that, as they wear down, they become thinner, and the groove they make becomes correspondingly narrower. Another way is to use a drunken saw. This is a saw specially fitted with bevelled collars so that it can be set obliquely to the saw spindle on the swashplate principle. Its construction will be gathered from Fig. 38. The saw A is permanently fixed to the inner pair of collars, but may be turned on a sleeve which holds the outer collars in position. As it is moved round from the position shown it leaves the perpendicular, the width of the groove it will cut being determined by the amount that the saw is "staggered." Such saws are very efficient if run at a fairly high speed, but they are rather awkward to set to size. There are, also, several patented appliances on the market for which special advantages are claimed. When using ploughing saws, it becomes necessary to substitute a wooden "gate plate" for the metal one in the table, so as to obtain a larger saw opening.

The "Tension" of the Saw.—A peculiarity of circular saws, and one that sooner or later is bound to give trouble to the operator, is their tension. If a circular saw were merely a disc of steel of even tension with regard to the molecules of metal, it would not stand up to its work. The heat generated in running, together with a further stretching effect brought about by its velocity, causes the rim or periphery of the saw to expand, and if its tension were uniform, the rim would become too large for the centre.

A saw in such condition would be termed "centre bound." To compensate for this effect, the saw maker stretches the centre of the saw by hammering it. In other words, he makes the centre too large for the rim,. so that the two may coincide when the saw is at work. As it is impossible to strike an exact balance, and also because the rim is constantly stretching, the practice is to over-compensate, that is to stretch the centre a little too much, leaving it to the sawyer to adjust matters by tightening his packing near the teeth of his saw, so as to cause a slight excess of heat and consequent expansion at this part. A new saw will usually need packing more tightly in the vicinity of its rim than one that has been in use for some time. After a considerable period of working, the compensation will become neutralised by the stretching of the rim. Such a saw will refuse to stand up to its work, will probably show a tendency to "gather," or cut thicker towards the top; it may, however, be put into condition again by re-hammering. It should be sent to a saw maker, or a professional saw doctor, for this purpose.

What to Avoid in Sawing.—Properly handled, the circular saw is not dangerous. Certain precautions, however, are necessary if accidents are to be avoided. Of course, a sawyer may cut himself rather badly, but accidents of this description do not, as a rule, happen to the novice, but to the older hand who has become careless through over-confidence. What should be guarded against is timber coming into contact with, or closing in on, the back of the saw, and being thrown by it, with considerable force, in the direction of the worker. To minimise the danger of such happenings, several excellent saw guards have been devised and placed on the market. The user of circular saws should certainly acquaint himself with the various types of guards and obtain the one best suited to his particular work.

WOODWORKING BY MACHINERY

Fig. 39.—Bandsaw

THE BANDSAW

The Utility and Components of the Bandsaw.—The bandsaw as shown by Fig. 39 is primarily intended for cutting curves. It may be described as an endless steel belt with saw teeth cut in one edge, running over a pair of light wheels or pulleys. In some cases three wheels are employed, but this pattern is nearly obsolete for power machines. The pulleys where the saw passes over them are covered with resilient material, usually vulcanised rubber, to prevent damage being done to the teeth of the saw. Motion is imparted to the lower saw pulley through a short shaft by the ordinary belt and pulley drive, the saw itself actuating the upper pulley, which is generally "bushed" and runs free on a short axle. The upper pulley may be raised and lowered by turning the hand-wheel seen immediately beneath it, so as to accommodate saws of different lengths, and in the machine here illustrated a spiral spring is introduced into this adjusting gear, the object being to render the tension on the saw elastic and to compensate for any expansion or contraction that may take place in the saw blade. In some patterns of machine compensation is effected by a weighted lever.

To support the saw when working, guides are fitted both above and below the table. The upper saw-guide is

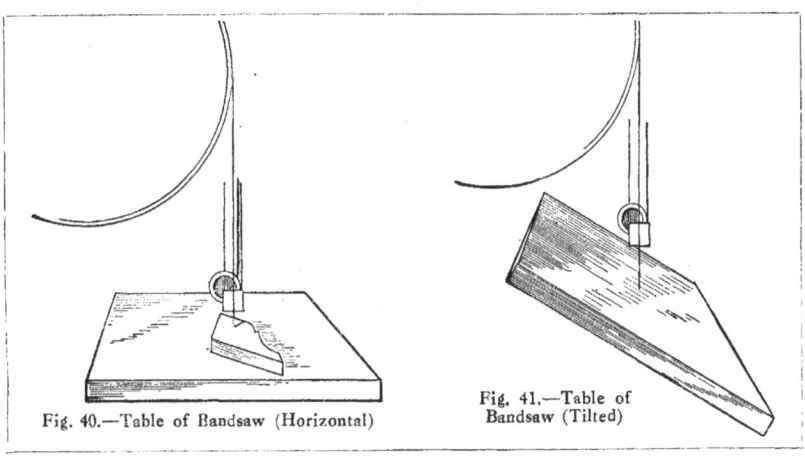

Fig. 40.—Table of Bandsaw (Horizontal)

Fig. 41.—Table of Bandsaw (Tilted)

adjustable vertically, and in use should be as close as is convenient to the timber that is being cut. The table may be canted to an angle with the saw for cutting bevels. The top saw-guide is clearly shown immediately above the table in Fig. 39, and again in Figs. 40 and 41. The back thrust of the saw is taken on the flat of a revolving disc, and the side, or turning strain (torsion), sometimes by hardened steel guides and sometimes by wooden guides. The lower saw-guide, which may be seen below the table in Fig. 39, may be similar to the upper one, but is often of much simpler construction, frequently consisting of only a piece of wood or metal on each side of the saw to take the twisting or torsional strain. Probably the simpler form of bottom saw-guide will, in practice, be found the more satisfactory.

Bandsaw blades may be purchased set and sharpened ready for use. They are obtainable in various widths from $\frac{1}{16}$ in. upwards, $\frac{1}{4}$ in. and $\frac{3}{8}$ in. being the most useful sizes for light joinery and cabinet work, and $\frac{5}{8}$ in. to $\frac{7}{8}$ in. for the cutting of shallower and heavier sweeps, and also for wheelwrights' work.

Bandsaws require to be carefully used to prevent frequent breakage. Instances are in evidence where 1-in. bandsaws have been worn down to $\frac{3}{8}$ in. without fracture. Properly used, bandsaws are a paying proposition, their output, for the power absorbed, being probably higher than that of any other form of saw; they are, however, fragile, and should be treated accordingly. Another brand should be tried if the user feels that the one he is using is not doing so well as he has a right to expect.

Fitting the Saw.—Before proceeding to put a saw on to the machine, note that the top pulley, in addition to being adjustable in a vertical direction, is also arranged to cant. This has the effect of throwing it out of line with the lower pulley, which is necessary to enable the saw to be run in any desired path on the pulleys. See that the points of the teeth, on the cutting side of the saw, point downwards towards the table. If they point upwards, turn the saw's inner side out. Lower the top pulley, if necessary, to enable the saw to be passed over both saw pulleys, then turn the hand-wheel in the opposite direction, so as to tighten the saw. After the saw is felt to grip the pulleys, a further turn or two should be given to the hand-wheel, so as to compress the spring and impart the necessary elasticity.

The Tension Required for Bandsaw.—With regard to the tension needed, no hard-and-fast rule can be laid down, but wide saws may be worked tighter than narrower ones. With $\frac{3}{16}$-in. and $\frac{1}{4}$-in. saws, the lighter the tension they can be worked with, the less should be the risk of breakage. If the tension is sufficient to preclude any possibility of the saw slipping on the bottom pulley (the top pulley dancing on the spring, or the spring becoming slackened out through the expansion of the saw blade when it is warmed by work), there does not appear to be any advantage to be gained by pulling the saw tighter, excepting for heavy work.

The saw now being approximately in the position in which it is desired it should run on the pulleys, proceed to adjust the top saw-guide in such a manner as not to deflect the line of the saw. The revolving disc should be brought into contact with the back of the saw, which should run quite freely between the two side guides. If the side guides are of metal, take care that they only enclose the untoothed part of the blade; they must on no account come in contact with any part of the teeth. Should they do so, this may usually be remedied by adjusting the disc a little farther forward.

Testing and Adjusting.—Now revolve the machine slowly by hand and watch the saw. If it should begin to creep to the outer edge of the top saw pulley, do not allow it to creep off. Its forward movement may be arrested by turning the set-screw which tilts the top pulley. Similarly, should the saw try to creep to the back of the pulley, it may be stopped by turning the set-screw the other way. Adjust the set-screw till the back of the saw bears upon the flat disc of the saw-guide only just sufficiently to revolve it. If it is desired to use the lower saw-guide, this may now be adjusted to the saw,

WOODWORKING BY MACHINERY

For light work, however, the bottom guide may usually be dispensed with. Before starting the machine, see that it is well lubricated, paying special attention to the saw-guides.

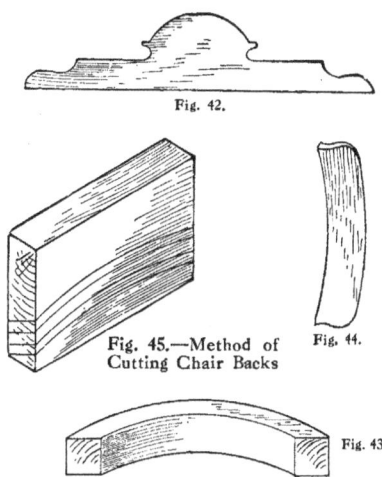

Figs. 42 to 44.—Examples of Work Executed with Bandsaw

Points Relating to Cutting.—Thin wooden or cardboard templates are usually employed when pencilling out the shapes that are to be sawn by the bandsaw. If the shapes are at all intricate, or the timber to be sawn is rough or dirty, it will usually pay to "jack" or machine it over before marking it out. Wide saws do better work than narrower ones when cutting flat curves, but the saw employed should always be sufficiently narrow, so as to turn quite freely any curve that may occur in the job being cut. Beyond this, no particular instructions need be given for executing the shapes shown by Figs. 42 and 43.

The beginner will need to exercise care in following the lines, facility being only acquired by practice.

Fig. 44 shows rather an interesting example of bevel cutting. It is the back of a common Windsor chair, such as is to be found in most households, and is well worth a little study. Actually, by cutting it on the bevel, and fixing it in a more upright position than that at which it was cut, not only is a considerable saving of timber effected, but also a curve in two directions is obtained at one operation. Fig. 41 shows how the table of the bandsaw may be canted for work of this description, and Fig. 45 illustrates how the cuts would be made in the timber.

Sharpening and Setting.—Bandsaws should be kept sharp and sufficiently, though not coarsely, set. Without considerable practice, setting by hand is a tedious operation, and unless time for practice is ample the owner of a bandsaw should purchase a setting machine, of which there are several efficient and comparatively inexpensive types on the market. Bandsaws may be set by hand with a plier saw-set of the Morrell type, and the novice, having only an occasional saw to set by hand, is advised to use this method.

Sharpening should follow the setting of bandsaws, and not, as in the case of circular saws, precede it. Where many bandsaws have to be sharpened by hand, a proper vice for holding them should be

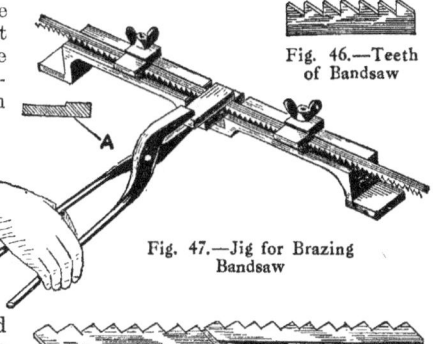

Fig. 46.—Teeth of Bandsaw

Fig. 47.—Jig for Brazing Bandsaw

Fig. 48.—Shape of Joint of Bandsaw

obtained. There are several good types of sharpening vices for bandsaws on the market. For occasional use, wooden chops may answer, but it is difficult to hold narrow saws securely in them, and therefore they are only recommended as a makeshift. Three-cornered, single-cut files are used for sharpening bandsaws. A special bandsaw file with rounded corners is preferred by some workmen.

The Shape of the Teeth.—The shape of bandsaw teeth will be gathered from Fig. 46. There is no need to sharpen a bandsaw from both sides, in the manner that hand and circular saws are treated. The file may be held quite level, and the teeth sharpened consecutively, straight across them, from one side only. If a good brand of saw is procured, the teeth will, no doubt, be correctly shaped to begin with. An endeavour should be made to retain this shape, at the same time sharpening each tooth with a similar number of strokes of the file, and these as few as possible. With practice, one stroke should suffice to sharpen a tooth.

Repairing Bandsaws.—When bandsaws break they have to be repaired by brazing them. This is supposed to be a difficult task, but such is not the case where proper appliances are available. If they are not, it is scarcely worth while attempting the job.

A " jig " of some sort, for holding the ends of the saw to be brazed in perfect line, is essential. A suitable form of jig is shown by Fig. 47. A sufficient source of heat for melting brass must also be at hand. This may take the form of a smith's fire, a gas blow-pipe, or a benzoline or paraffin blow-lamp. The ends of the saw to be brazed are prepared by filing them to the form shown by Fig. 48, and are secured in the jig so as to overlap each other in the manner indicated. Note the section of the platform of the jig (A, Fig. 47). The saw is aligned by pressing it up against the projection shown. A little spelter and powdered borax mixed may be damped and placed on the saw, just over the joint. When brazing in the manner indicated by Fig. 47 a smith's fire is sufficient to supply the necessary heat. Two pieces of iron are brought to a good red heat. One is placed beneath the saw and the other is held over the top as shown. When the spelter melts, drop the piece of iron held in the tongs, draw out the lower piece, and grip the joint with the tongs for a few seconds, or till the surrounding saw turns black. Remove the surplus borax and spelter surrounding the joint by filing. See that the thickness of the joined parts is uniform with the rest of the saw, and that the run of the back of the saw is regular. Lightly draw-file the joint, and finish it off with emery-cloth. A machine of the type illustrated, having 30-in. saw-pulleys, is intended to be run at a speed of 500 revolutions per minute. This gives a speed of about 3,750 ft. per minute to the saw. Such a speed in the case of the machine under notice is advised, but care should be exercised in using the correct surface speed for bandsaw machines by unknown makers. There are some badly designed machines on the market, generally sold through factors, and sometimes to be picked up at a low price second-hand. Such machines need not, perhaps, be altogether avoided where cost is the deciding factor, but when no actual speed data can be obtained it will be advisable to have the opinion of a qualified man.

THE POWER FRET-SAW

Its Principle Described.—There is a certain similarity between the work of the power fret-saw (Fig. 49) and that of the bandsaw just described, inasmuch as they are both of them " turning " saws, that is, saws for turning curves. Most of the work that the bandsaw will perform may be executed equally well on the fret-saw, but at a much reduced rate of speed ; in the class of work, however, for which it is suitable, such as inside cutting or piercing, there is no other machine that can compete with it.

Unlike the bandsaw, in which the cutting is continuous, the fret-saw is a reciprocating machine and cuts on the down stroke only. Motion is imparted by belt to the pulleys seen in the lower left-hand corner of Fig. 49, and from these through a short shaft to the disc shown. A crank pin in the disc translates the circular motion to a reciprocating one, and actuates

WOODWORKING BY MACHINERY

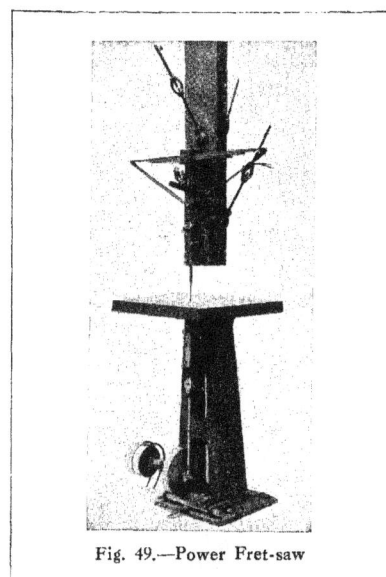

Fig. 49.—Power Fret-saw

the saw through a connecting rod. The laminated spring, seen above the table, is usually made of lancewood, and is connected to the upper saw plunger by a leather strap, keeping the saw in a continual state of tension throughout its stroke. The entire top fitting of the machine is fixed to a wooden pendant, which hangs from the roof of the workshop. By this means an unrestricted sweep is obtained for the work being cut, which would otherwise be limited in size by the frame of the machine. The saw blades are provided with pins which enable them to be instantly attached to, and just as readily detached from, hooks formed in the saw plungers (see Fig. 50).

Blade and Blade Speed.—The fret-saw blades most commonly used are either 7 in. or 8 in. long, and may be obtained of widths varying from $\frac{1}{8}$ in. to $\frac{1}{4}$ in. Some brands of saws are rolled from steel wire. These are tougher and consequently less liable to fracture than saws cut from sheet steel. A suitable speed for fret-saws is about 1,000 strokes per minute.

Examples and Scope of Power Fret-Saw.—Fig. 51 shows frets used in a chair back; Fig. 52 how holes are bored in the work for the insertion of the saw, and Fig. 53 shows the saw threaded through one of the holes and ready to begin work.

Properly executed, fret-sawing should come from the machine perfectly clean. In an up-to-date cabinet works a good fret-sawyer is an important individual, but a man whose work required cleaning

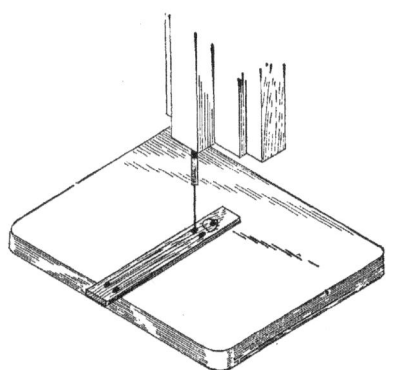

Fig. 53.—Method of Cutting Frets

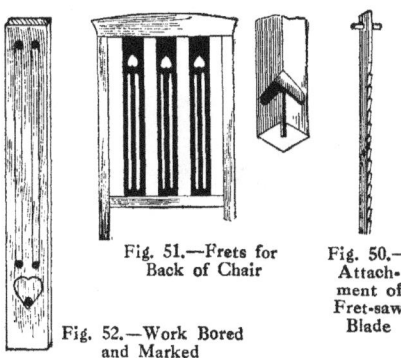

Fig. 51.—Frets for Back of Chair

Fig. 52.—Work Bored and Marked

Fig. 50.—Attachment of Fret-saw Blade

up by hand would hardly be tolerated. Little more that is helpful can be written about fret-sawing; what is essential to the efficient working of the fret-saw is

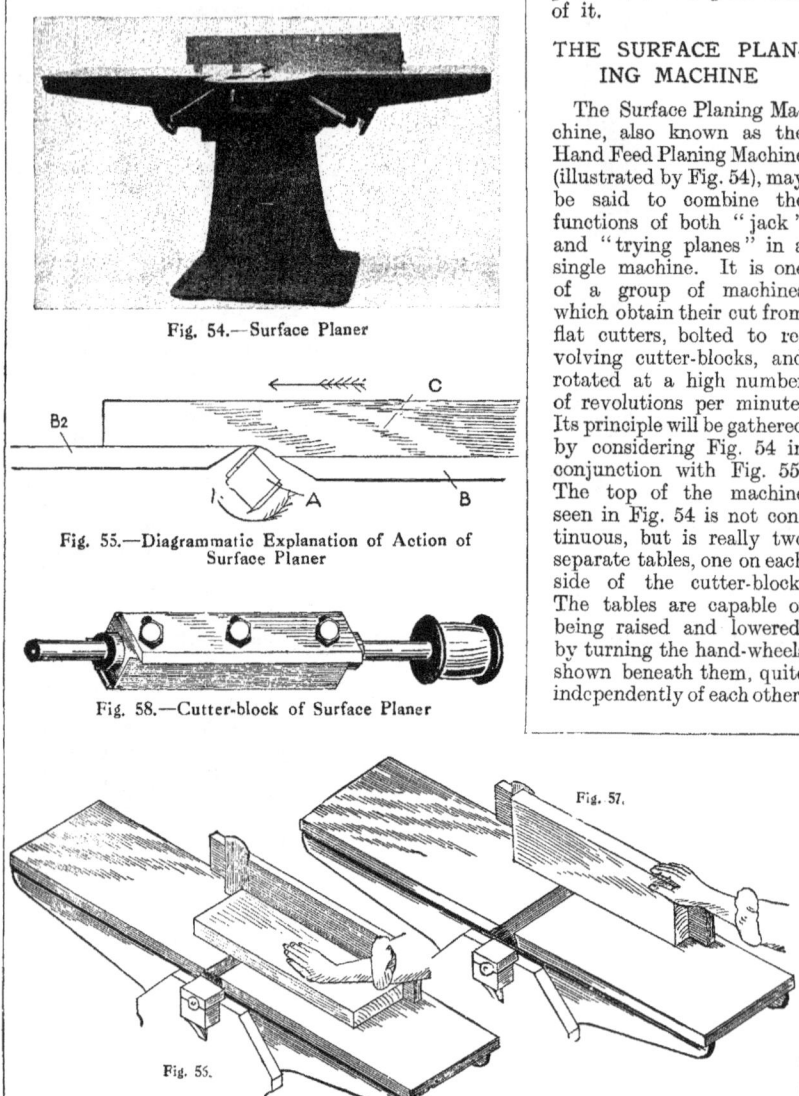

Fig. 54.—Surface Planer

Fig. 55.—Diagrammatic Explanation of Action of Surface Planer

Fig. 58.—Cutter-block of Surface Planer

Figs. 56 and 57.—Two Operations with Surface Planer

THE SURFACE PLANING MACHINE

The Surface Planing Machine, also known as the Hand Feed Planing Machine (illustrated by Fig. 54), may be said to combine the functions of both "jack" and "trying planes" in a single machine. It is one of a group of machines which obtain their cut from flat cutters, bolted to revolving cutter-blocks, and rotated at a high number of revolutions per minute. Its principle will be gathered by considering Fig. 54 in conjunction with Fig. 55. The top of the machine seen in Fig. 54 is not continuous, but is really two separate tables, one on each side of the cutter-block. The tables are capable of being raised and lowered, by turning the hand-wheels shown beneath them, quite independently of each other.

WOODWORKING BY MACHINERY

Reference to Fig. 55 will make this clear; A is the cutter-block with cutters attached, revolving in the direction shown, and B and B2 are the tables. It will be seen that B, which is the front table, is adjusted considerably lower than the back table B2.

The Operation of the Surface Planer.—The operation of the machine is as follows: B2 is adjusted level with the highest point reached by the cutters; B is adjusted sufficiently below to give the amount cut it is desired to remove from the timber. The timber C passes from the table B, over the top of the cutter-block, to the table B2. Now, bearing in mind that the table B2 is perfectly disposed across its width, and in line with the top of the cutters, the timber as it is operated on by the cutters passes immediately from the cutters and is supported by B2, the result being that the forward movement of the timber is continued in the same plane throughout its entire length, and that it is planed straight (planed *out-of-wind*). It must not be assumed that this result is always to be attained by passing work once over the machine; newly sawn and fairly straight timber may often be planed up true with a single cut, but rough, or twisted material, has usually to be passed several times over the cutters.

After the face of the timber has been planed true, one edge has to be shot straight and square, just the same as in planing by hand, and for this purpose a fence is provided, the normal position of which is square with the tables. Fig. 56 illustrates the planing out-of-wind, and Fig. 57 the operation of shooting the edge of a short piece of stuff. Should the edge require bevelling, or chamfering, the fence may be set to an angle with the tables, in a similar manner to the fence of the circular saw (previously described).

How the Cutters are Secured.— Fig. 58 shows the cutter-block of the surface planer removed from the machine, the method of fastening the cutters (in this instance with studs) being clearly shown. Studs are not invariably, but are generally used for securing the cutters of surface planing machines. The alternative method is to use slotted cutter-blocks and dovetailed bolts. These latter are always employed for securing moulding cutters when cutter-blocks are used for moulding; this will be referred to later.

Grinding the Cutters.—When the cutters of a surface planer require grinding either an ordinary grindstone may be used, or a grinding machine similar to that illustrated and described at the end of this section. Fig. 59 shows the operation being performed on an ordinary grindstone. A bevelled fence, which may be of wood, is fixed to the frame in front of the stone, which revolves in the direction shown. The cutters, being narrow and difficult otherwise to hold, are fixed in a wooden holder so as to obtain the necessary purchase. An enlarged detail of the holder attached to the cutter is shown by Fig. 60.

Surface planing machines may be obtained as small as 8 in. wide, but machines are made that will plane up to 24 in. The maximum width that a machine will plane is represented by the width of the table, and also by the length of the cutters. Care is essential to the keeping of these long cutters straight when grinding them, and frequent applications of a wooden straightedge should be made. Previous to fixing them in the machine the cutters are sharpened, usually by rubbing with an oilstone, and the same precaution should be taken to keep them straight. After being secured in the machine any further sharpening of the cutters that may be necessary is done without removing them, the tables drawing out longitudinally to enable this to be effected. The longitudinal adjustment of the tables is also necessary when a larger opening is needed between them, as when using moulding cutters.

The Cutter-block.—Fig. 61 is the cutter-block of a surface planer partly shown in section. It will be observed that it is provided with projecting lips on which the cutting edges of the cutters rest. These lips answer the same purpose with regard to the surface planer as does the cover iron to an ordinary plane. That is, to some extent they prevent the grain of the timber being torn up and also knots being displayed. In adjusting the cutters of a surface planer, first fasten each of them by its two outer studs to the cutter-block, allowing the cutting edges to overhang the lips of the block about $\frac{1}{16}$ in. Only tighten the studs sufficiently to hold the cutters in position. The method of adjusting them accurately with each other and with the back table is shown by Fig. 62. A piece of planed wood,

Moulding Cutters, etc.—Referring back to Fig. 61, two dovetail slots will be seen in the cutter-block. It is usual to slot the cutter-block of a surface planer, either along the whole or some part of its length, so that moulding cutters may be affixed, and the machine used for moulding without removing the straight, or planing cutters. Dovetail bolts (Fig. 63) are used for securing moulding cutters to

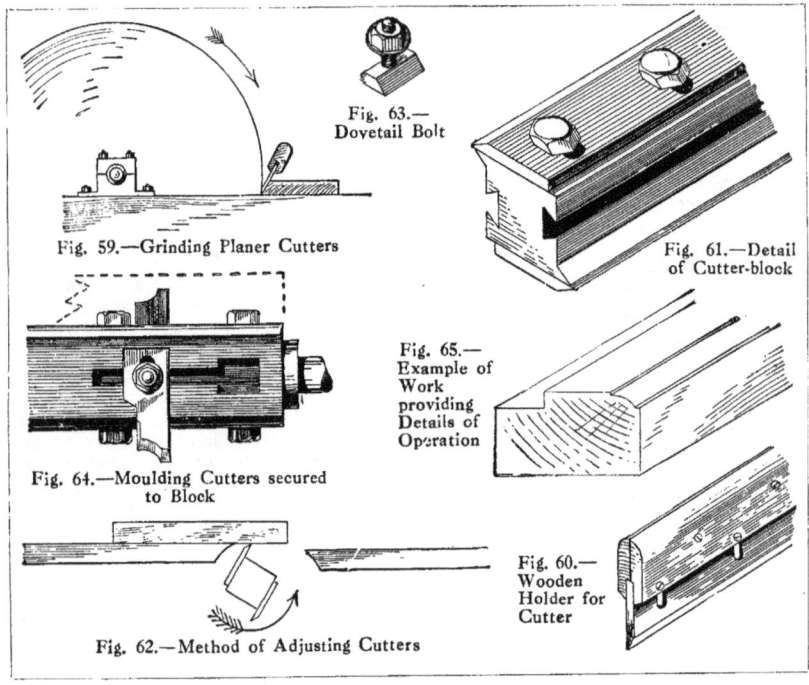

Fig. 63.—Dovetail Bolt

Fig. 59.—Grinding Planer Cutters

Fig. 61.—Detail of Cutter-block

Fig. 65.—Example of Work providing Details of Operation

Fig. 64.—Moulding Cutters secured to Block

Fig. 60.—Wooden Holder for Cutter

Fig. 62.—Method of Adjusting Cutters

say about 1½ in. square, is held on the back table towards one end of the cutters. These are revolved slowly by hand in the direction shown (the opposite to that in which they work). They are adjusted by tapping with a hammer till each of them, in passing, just touches the piece of wood. Trials should be made on each end of the cutters, and when both are correct, the inner studs may be tightened up hard, then the outer ones made secure.

the cutter-block. Fig. 64 shows a pair of moulding cutters so secured.

In machining a piece of frame similar to that shown by Fig. 65 a side and an edge would first be planed, and the job made of a uniform width, either by passing it through the thicknessing machine or between the fence and the saw of the circular saw-bench. By drawing the fence of the surface planer forward to within the width of rebate from the front edge

WOODWORKING BY MACHINERY

of the tables and lowering the front table below the back one to the depth of the rebate, the rebate may be taken out at a single cut.

In affixing moulding cutters to a cutter-block, it is necessary to do so in such a manner as not to upset its balance. That is to say, whatever amount of effective weight is fastened to one side of the block, a similar weight must be added to the other. Now, the effective weight of a cutter on a cutter-block varies with the projection of the cutter, similar to the weight on the end of a lever, consequently the simplest way to machine a moulding is to use a pair of cutters of similar weight and profile. If this is done, their effective weight should be sufficiently equal for all practical purposes. A pair of such cutters suitable for moulding the frame under consideration is shown secured to the cutter-block in Fig. 64.

Adjustments for Cutting Mouldings —When the tables of the machine are adjusted to the correct height for moulding they should be sufficiently high to enable the work to pass over the straight, or planing, cutters without touching them. Adjust the front table first, then with a straightedge set the back table in line with the front one. Adjust the tables of the machine longitudinally so that the cutters, when revolving, will just clear them. Make the tables fast by tightening up the star wheels, or whatever else is provided. Fix the fence in the required position. The machine may now be started, and the work moulded by passing it steadily over the cutters.

Moulding cutters may be adjusted in the machine to a short length of the required moulding, if this is available. Another way, when working to a drawing, is to set one of the cutters in the machine by measurements taken from the drawing. A lath, as indicated by dotted lines in Fig. 64, may then be placed on the cutter-block in front of the cutter, one end of the lath being held tightly against the frame of the machine ; by passing a pencil line round the cutter, its position on the cutter-block may be marked on the lath, and the second of the pair of cutters may be set by the pencil line ; perhaps the most usual way of setting up, however, when only a drawing is available, is to transfer the pattern on to the end of one of the pieces of timber to be moulded, when the cutters may easily be adjusted by laying this in the desired position on the front table of the machine, adjusting the fence to the timber and the cutters to the pattern marked on the end of it.

When mouldings are too long or too springy to be adequately held by hand, springs are sometimes used for the purpose. For keeping the mouldings to the tables, the springs are secured to the fence of the machine, while those holding the mouldings to the fence are affixed to the table. In Fig. 66, which is a somewhat different type of machine than that previously illustrated, springs are shown fixed to the fence. They are, of course, removable when they are not required. A suitable speed for the surface planer is 3,000 revolutions per minute.

MOULDINGS AND MOULDING CUTTERS

Mouldings are composed of more or less conventional curves, used singly or in combination. These shapes are known as members, their appearance in what may be termed their basic form or counterpart being shown by Figs. 67 to 71. In woodwork, however, their forms are usually modified by the designer to suit his requirements. Fig. 67 is the bead, Fig. 68 the ogee, Fig. 69 the ovolo, Fig. 70 the cavetto or hollow (frequently called the scotia), and Fig. 71 the scotia (sometimes called the hollow). There are one or two other conventional members, but those shown are the ones most frequently used in woodwork. To the left of the diagrams are shown the members themselves, the machine cutters which work them being depicted by the right sketches. In Fig. 68 two cutters are shown, illustrating how certain of the mouldings may be worked from an alternative direction. This applies to Figs. 68 to 70. The direction of rotation of the cutters, of course, cannot be altered ; it is the position of

Fig. 66.—Another Type of Surface Planer

the timber with regard to them that is changed.

The fact of there being an alternative position in which a job may be moulded is frequently a great convenience to the woodworking machinist. For example consider Fig. 72. If this moulding were being worked on the surface planer it might be placed on the tables of the machine in the position shown, and the similar in shape to that shown at the bottom of Fig. 68, difficulty would be encountered. The operation of working the ogee would leave insufficient timber on the underside of the job to support it solidly on the tables. This difficulty would be immediately overcome by turning that edge of the timber which is now on the right to lie on the table, and the present top side will then be towards the fence, using a cutter similar to that shown on the right of Fig. 68.

In the working of mouldings composed of several members, it is the usual practice to work with cutters each of which is shaped to a single member. They may be used in single pairs, working a member at a time, or in combination, by bolting several different pairs to the cutter-block and working the entire moulding at one operation. It might be imagined that the work would be simplified by grinding the entire profile of a complex moulding

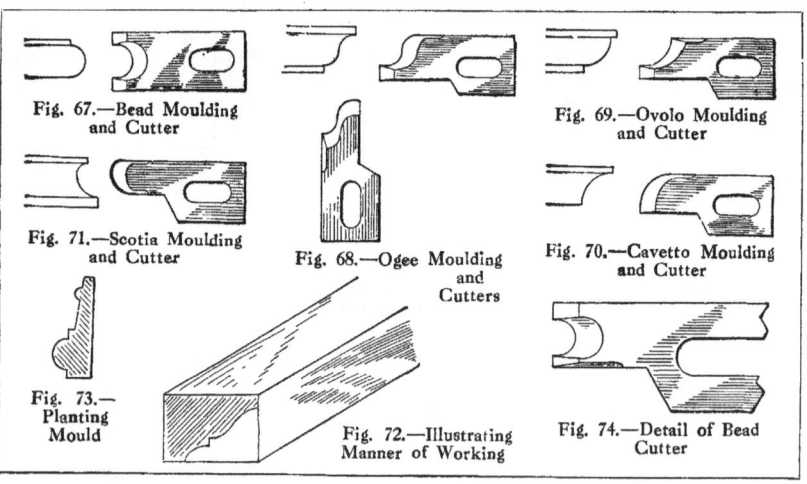

Fig. 67.—Bead Moulding and Cutter

Fig. 69.—Ovolo Moulding and Cutter

Fig. 71.—Scotia Moulding and Cutter

Fig. 68.—Ogee Moulding and Cutters

Fig. 70.—Cavetto Moulding and Cutter

Fig. 73.—Planting Mould

Fig. 72.—Illustrating Manner of Working

Fig. 74.—Detail of Bead Cutter

hollow might be worked with a cutter similar to that shown in Fig. 71; but if an attempt were made to work the ogee from the same position, using a cutter on a single pair of cutters; this, however, is not the case. Besides being difficult to make and keep in shape, such cutters will not produce the same sharpness of profile that is obtained by combining single-member cutters; moreover, a cutter carrying the entire profile of a moulding can be used to work that moulding only, whereas a few single-member cutters, judiciously selected, may be combined in a variety of ways. Those illustrated by Figs. 67 to 71 are what are known as slotted cutters, and, as stated, are intended to be bolted to a cutter-block. Mention may also be made of another type of cutter in general use in woodworking machine shops. This cutter is not slotted. It is used in the collar head of the spindle moulding machine, and will be illustrated in conjunction therewith. The development of the shape of moulding irons has been described in a previous chapter.

In an ordinary cutter-block four slots are provided, but the cutter-block of the surface planer has two of its sides permanently occupied by the straight planing cutters; it has, therefore, only two unoccupied sides available for moulding. Working under such conditions it is not always convenient to use a pair of cutters for each single member, and a small planting mould, as Fig. 73, might well be a case in point. This moulding could be worked with two single bead cutters of different size, which might easily be of similar weight. Where, as in the example shown, two small cutters of similar weight can be set almost opposite to each other, and whose circle of rotation (projection beyond the cutter-block) does not greatly vary, it is quite permissible to use only one cutter for each member. In fact, some machinists when moulding on the surface planer rarely use more than one cutter per member, even when moulding one member at a time. They roughly counterbalance the other side of the cutter-block with an idle cutter, which they bolt lengthways on the block, and then adjust the balance to a nicety by adding washers as needed. Employed by a practised machinist, the method answers quite well, but it is not recommended to the inexperienced operator.

Now refer to the illustration of a bead cutter (Fig. 74). It will be seen that the lower edge is bevelled back so as to form a cutting edge. It is necessary to bevel in this manner all edges that are required to cut. Blanks for shaping into moulding cutters may be procured ready tempered. An emery-wheel may be used for grinding blanks to shape, but to commence with it will be advisable for a beginner to purchase one or two finished cutters, and particularly to notice the manner in which they are ground, before attempting to make his own.

Owing to the angle at which they work, moulding cutters working on a cutter-block, or in the collars of a spindle moulder, do not retain their true profile, but lose a little in depth. That is to say, the profile of the mouldings worked will be somewhat shallower than that of the cutters they are worked with. If the several diagrams of cutters in operation are studied, the point should be sufficiently clear. Allowance for this characteristic of moulding cutters should be made when grinding them, so that mouldings do not come from the machines shallower than is anticipated.

Whilst on the subject of mouldings it is as well to point out that they may be successfully made on a light circular-saw bench by obtaining a cutter-block to fit the end of the saw spindle and substituting for the metal gate piece a wooden one having an aperture sufficiently large to allow of the cutters passing through. The speed will probably be rather slow, and the rate of feed will have to be regulated accordingly.

THE VERTICAL SPINDLE MOULDING MACHINE

The Utility and Action of the Vertical Spindle Moulding Machine.— Primarily, the spindle moulding machine is intended for the cleaning up and moulding of shapes having straight, circular or irregular outlines, but with its many accessories and attachments it may be put to a variety of other uses as well. Such is the diversity of work that can be dealt with on the machine that it would be difficult to fix a limit to its capacity;

THE PRACTICAL WOODWORKER

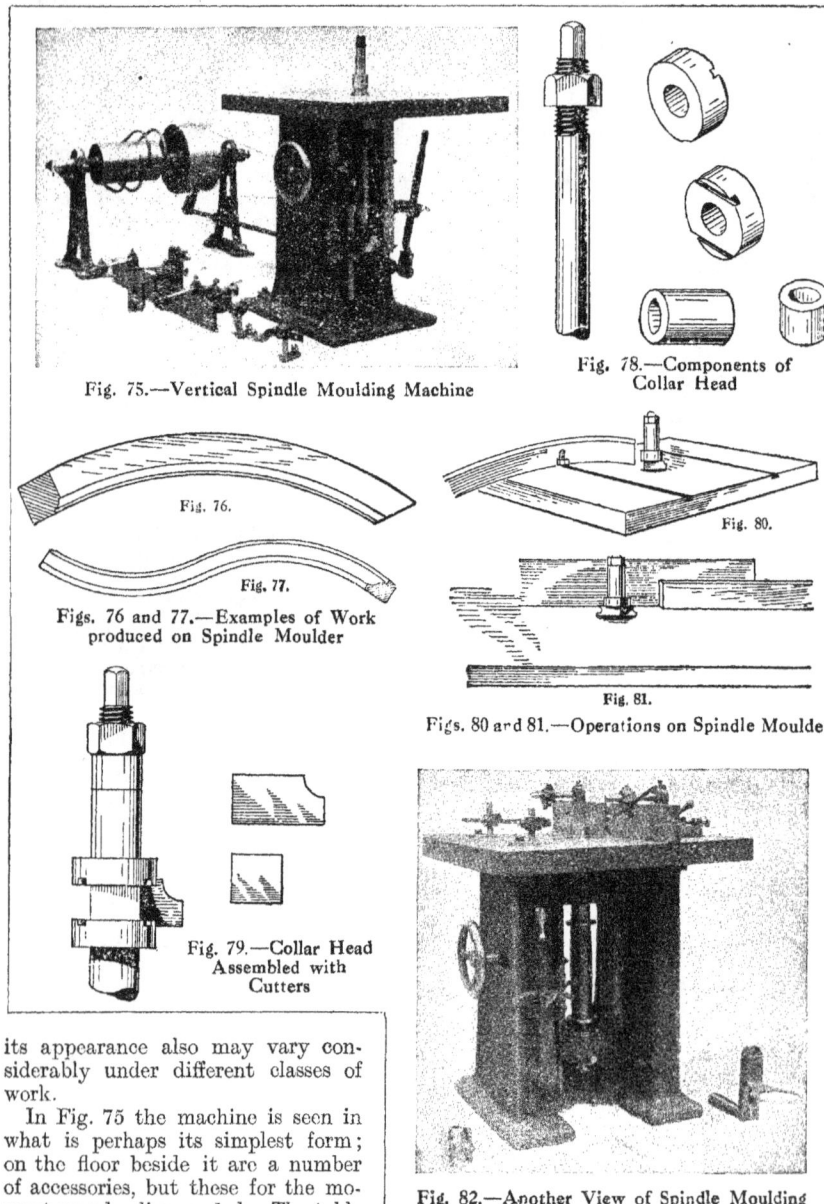

Fig. 75.—Vertical Spindle Moulding Machine

Fig. 78.—Components of Collar Head

Figs. 76 and 77.—Examples of Work produced on Spindle Moulder

Figs. 80 and 81.—Operations on Spindle Moulder

Fig. 79.—Collar Head Assembled with Cutters

Fig. 82.—Another View of Spindle Moulding Machine

its appearance also may vary considerably under different classes of work.

In Fig. 75 the machine is seen in what is perhaps its simplest form; on the floor beside it are a number of accessories, but these for the moment may be disregarded. The table is seen cleared, as would be the

WOODWORKING BY MACHINERY

case were the machine about to be used for the moulding of light shapes, say similar to Fig. 76 or 77. The spindle seen projecting above the table is the operative part of the machine, and carries at present what is known as a collar head. The collars may be adjusted to various heights above the table by turning the hand-wheel seen on the left of the machine. The several loose pieces that go to make up the collar head are shown by Fig. 78. In Fig. 79 these pieces are seen assembled and with a cutter in position, the method of holding the cutters securely being clearly shown. Only one cutter is depicted in Fig. 79, the other side of the collars being made up with a blank. This is the usual method of working when cutters are light in weight and their projection is only trifling, but should the vibration set up be sufficient to affect the quality of the work, or to cause overheating of the bearings of the machine. a second cutter should be substituted for the blank.

The shapes to be moulded are moved forward against the collars always in an opposite direction to that in which the cutters revolve, the collars themselves forming the fence or guide for the work. The distance to which the cutters project in a radial direction beyond the collars represents the depth to which the work will be moulded.

There is some difficulty, not to say danger, to a beginner in starting a moulding when working against the collars; the cutters, projecting as they do beyond the collars, reach the timber first, that is before it receives the support of the collars, and till experience is acquired a smash may easily occur. Those inexperienced in collar work should adopt the plan shown by Fig. 80. One of the dovetail bolts, used to secure the fences of the machine to the table, is nutted down in the position shown. The job is pressed up against the bolt, which acts as a fulcrum, round which the work may be swung towards the cutters. When the cutters have entered the timber to their predetermined depth, and the collars engage the work, it is pressed tightly against them and moved clear of the bolt. The forward movement to complete the moulding is then easy and safe. Sweeps that are fragile, or of area insufficient to be otherwise safely worked, may be moulded previous to their severance from the board from which they are to be sawn (*see* Fig. 87). This also applies to straight mouldings of a fragile nature.

For heavy work on the spindle moulder, or when it is necessary to use several cutters, so as to work a more or less complex moulding at one operation, a cutter-block with slotted cutters is employed, the cutter-block replacing the collars on the machine spindle. When using a cutter-block for moulding swept or irregular shapes. an eccentric or ring fence is used in conjunction with it. In the lower left-hand corner of Fig. 82 will be seen the cutter-block.

The appliance shown to the right of the machine is the ring fence. The principle of the working of this combination will be gathered from Fig. 83, which represents a view, looking downwards, of the table of the spindle moulder, with cutter-block and ring fence in position. The path of the cutters is represented by the dotted circle, and this is shown concentric with the inner diameter of the ring, but not with the outer. It will be seen that the cutters attain their maximum projection (point of full-moulding) at a point corresponding with the thinnest part of the ring. Now, if a piece of timber is put to the fence in the position shown and moved forward, it will gradually engage the cutters, which will penetrate deeper and deeper till the point of full-moulding is reached. By continuing the forward movement of the timber, and keeping it in contact with the ring at this point, a moulding of uniform depth may be worked to the extent needed. Straight as well as swept mouldings may be worked against either the collars, or the ring fence of the spindle, but where a number of straight lengths require moulding, it will usually be found more convenient to use the straight fences supplied with the machine. Straight "returns" similar to the corner shown by Fig. 84 are readily worked against the collars. In moulding this class of job, the end-grain should invariably be treated first. Then, should a chip or two of timber be splintered off by the cutters as they emerge from the material, on the completion of the moulding of this part, the breakage will be moulded out in the "sticking" of the straight.

It is sometimes essential, in the moulding of swept shapes, to work from each end, so that the cutting may be with, and not against, the grain of the timber. Keeping the cutters thin and sharpening them frequently, will go a long way towards obviating the necessity for adopting this method of working. There are, however, times when it has to be resorted to. When this is the case, two sets of cutters (right and left handed), which duplicate each other when laid face to face, will be needed, and the direction of rotation of the spindle will have to be reversed when changing from one set of cutters to the other. The reversal may be effected in more than one way, but the simplest is to cross the belt driving the spindle from the countershaft (see Notes on Driving later on) in an opposite direction.

In the making of straight mouldings on the spindle moulder, either the cutterblock or the collars may be employed. The choice may depend upon the nature of the job, the method of working that the operator adopts, or the suitability of the cutters for the work required. There are, however, two distinct ways of working with either appliance: before the cutters or behind them, the method to adopt being governed by the exigencies of the job in hand. In Fig. 85, the former, more usual, and, generally speaking, the safer way is shown. The cutters work between and behind a pair of fences, the timber to be moulded passing in front of both fences and cutters.

Most straight, moulded work can be executed in this way, the exception being where thin material has to be moulded over the whole or the greater part of its wider surface, as in making a moulding similar to Fig. 86. The two convex members (beads) not having the same projection, would not lie solidly against

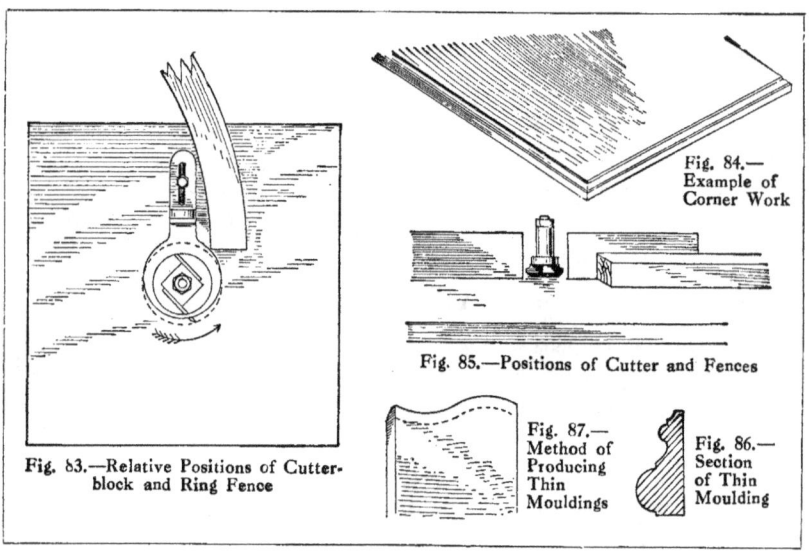

Fig. 83.—Relative Positions of Cutterblock and Ring Fence

Fig. 84.—Example of Corner Work

Fig. 85.—Positions of Cutter and Fences

Fig. 87.—Method of Producing Thin Mouldings

Fig. 86.—Section of Thin Moulding

WOODWORKING BY MACHINERY

the farther of the two fences, and a drop would occur when the material was deprived of the support of the front fence. This might be dangerous, and in any case would spoil the last few inches of each length of moulding so treated. The method to adopt under these circumstances is shown by Fig. 81. The fences are pushed together till they become continuous, and they are then secured behind the spindle. The back of the timber to be moulded is placed against the fence and is passed through between the fence and the cutters.

When moulding between the cutters and the fence, side springs must always

Fig. 88.—Dovetailing Machine

be used. These are flat, steel springs for holding the work up to the fences; otherwise it would be drawn from them and into the cutters. The springs are not shown in Fig. 81, but may be seen affixed to the table of the machine in Fig. 82. Top springs are also shown secured to the fences. These are for holding the timber down to the table, and are generally used along with the side springs. In adjusting the springs, make them sufficiently tight to preclude any possibility of the timber "chattering" or being drawn away from the fences, but not so tight as to make feeding jerky or difficult. For general work, the speed of the spindle moulder should be the same as that of the surface planer; about 3,000 revolutions per minute.

MACHINE DOVETAILING

Its Principles Described.—Several totally different types of machine have been tried for the making of dovetail joints by machinery. Perhaps the perfect dovetailer is yet to come, but it is thought that the most successful and popular machine is one constructed on spindle-moulder lines. This may take the form of a modified spindle moulder, fitted up for the automatic making of dovetail joints only, or, as in the illustration (Fig. 88), an attachment to an ordinary spindle moulding machine, enabling it to be turned into a semi-automatic dovetailer and back again into a spindle moulder at will.

Before describing this machine, or attachment, there is a peculiarity regarding the dovetails made by it, that must of necessity be made clear. For the saving of labour in dovetailing by hand, the spaces between the pins are usually made considerably wider than the pins themselves. In dovetails made by the method about to be considered, the pins and the spaces are of equal width. This simplifies considerably the machining of dovetails, and a few pins, more or less, make little or no difference to the machine; also, by cramping two pieces of wood to be dovetailed in the machine at the same time, one horizontally and the other vertically, and adjusting one piece the width of a dovetail to one side of the other, the two pieces, say the side and front of a drawer, may be dovetailed at one operation.

Now consider Fig. 88. A small rotary cutter of the shape of a dovetail is inserted in the end of the spindle of the spindle moulder. The dovetailing appliance consists of a compound slide and cramps for holding the wood to be dovetailed. Two pieces of wood are cramped in the positions shown. The slide is actuated in one direction by turning the handle seen to the left of the machine. This handle in conjunction with a form of dividing-plate, or spacing-wheel, determines the spacing of the dovetails. The work is moved forward to the cutter, by the hand lever seen above, and behind the spacing handle. Suitable stops are provided for the correct placing of the

Fig. 89.—Panel Planing and Thicknessing Machine

pieces of wood relative to each other in the machine, and also for stopping the work when the cutter has reached the correct depth.

It will be readily understood that in dovetails made entirely by this method, the mortises will be imperfect, their extreme ends being semicircular owing to the rotary action of the cutter. The obvious and perhaps the best way of overcoming this defect is to clean out the corners of the mortises by hand. This would always be done in good work, and seeing that the job may be very easily and quickly accomplished, it is a matter for wonder that the practice is not more general; in the manufacture of cheap drawers, however, a usual method is to round the entering sides of the pins slightly. This appears to be rather a slovenly system, but it cannot be detected in the finished article without taking the drawers right out and examining their backs.

The automatic dovetailer, previously mentioned, is very similar in action to the machine just described, with the exception that, after the pieces of wood to be dovetailed have been cramped in position, the operation of dovetailing them is automatic. This is a specialised machine for the obtaining of a large output of work. The speed of the dovetailing spindle may be 10,000 revolutions per minute. For cheap work, there is an arrangement that automatically chamfers the pins of the dovetails on their inner or entering sides. This makes for easy assembling of parts, and also ensures that the rounded ends of the mortises are hidden. The machine will cut over thirty complete dovetails per minute.

THE PANEL PLANING AND THICKNESSING MACHINE

The Scope of the Machine.—This machine is made in various sizes and is readily obtainable to plane up to 30 in. wide, whilst larger machines are made to order. It will plane timber, one side at a time, of any width and thickness up to the full capacity of the machine, and at a speed that may be varied from about 10 ft. to 40 ft. per minute. It is also used for planing the back of timber that has been previously faced up or straightened on the surface planer, reducing the work to a uniform thickness and effecting a

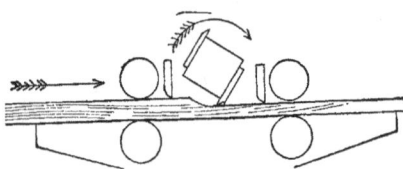

Fig. 90.—Action of Panel Planer

considerable saving of time in the subsequent operation of cleaning off.

The Action of the Panel Planer. —A fairly representative type of panel planing and thicknessing machine is shown by Fig. 89. The wood to be treated is fed into the machine by the grooved roller seen in the illustration, the work passing between the platform of the machine and a revolving cutter-block similar to that of the surface planer. The distance between the platform and the cutters may be regulated by turning the hand-wheel seen on the left of the machine, and the thickness of the timber that will pass under the cutters is indicated on the rule fixed high up on the left, enabling work to be planed to any predetermined thickness. A smooth roller, to carry the finished work away from the cutters, is provided at the far end of the machine. Pressure is applied to the feed rollers by the outer pair of spiral springs seen in the illustration. The inner springs operate two pressure bars, one of which is disposed on each side of the cutter-block. These are to prevent panels and other thin stuff from "dithering" when passing under the cutters. A further pair of rollers is fixed in the platform of the machine. These are actuated frictionally by the work passing over them. They should be adjusted just flush with the top of the platform. The arrangement and working of the principal parts of the machine will be gathered from diagram (Fig. 90).

As in the case of most high-speed woodworking machinery, driving is effected through a countershaft. Separate belts are used for driving the cutters and the feed. This simplifies the machine considerably, and it also enables the feed to be arrested without stopping the cutters, a necessary provision when the cutters lag, and there is a danger of their being drawn up and perhaps becoming jammed when making a heavy cut.

Operating the Machine.—The actual operation of the machine is perfectly simple, and the treatment of the cutters, so far as keeping them in order is concerned, is similar to that already described for the cutters of the surface planer. The procedure for setting the cutters (adjusting them in the machine) is slightly different. A short piece of planed wood of known thickness, say $1\frac{1}{2}$ in. by $1\frac{1}{2}$ in., is laid along the platform of the machine, under and towards one end of the cutter-block. The platform is raised till the indicator on the rule of the machine registers the thickness of the piece of wood, $1\frac{1}{2}$ in. in this case. One end of the cutters may now be adjusted to the wood by revolving them backwards by hand and tapping them with a hammer, as described for the regulating of surface planer cutters. To adjust the other end of the cutters, lower the platform, move the piece of wood to the other end of the cutter-block and repeat the former operation.

Make sure that all the studs are secure before starting the machine. Go over them a second time with the spanner. A loose cutter may wreck an entire machine.

THE TENONING MACHINE

As well as cutting plain tenons, the tenoning machine illustrated by Fig. 91 will tenon and scribe moulded framing at one operation, make tenons having one shoulder in advance of the other, as required for the framing up of rebated stuff, and also by substituting a grooving head on the top spindle of the machine, may be employed to cut the housing for shelves and similar work. Further, a circular saw may be fitted in the place of the top cutter-block, making the machine very convenient for cross-cutting and dimension sawing. As seen in the illustration, the tenoning machine appears to be somewhat complicated, but its operation should be readily understood if Fig. 91 is considered along with the diagram (Fig. 92).

Operating the Tenoning Machine. —The work to be tenoned is laid on a sliding table and is held in position by a lever, or by a screw cramp. The end of the work A overhangs the table B, as shown. Two horizontal spindles C and D, fitted with cutter-blocks each carrying straight cutters, revolve, one above and one below the tenon to be made. By sliding the table forward, the work is passed between the two sets of cutters, and the distance that they are adjusted apart determines the thickness of the tenon.

Working immediately behind the two horizontal spindles are two vertical ones,

Fig. 91.—Tenoning Machine

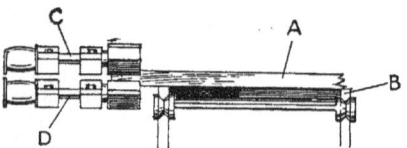

Fig. 92.—Operation of Tenoning Machine

Over and above the facility with which the actual operations of tenoning, scribing, etc., may be accomplished, the tenoning machine possesses a further advantage over tenoning by hand, in that no preliminary setting out of the work is needed. Stops are provided on all up-to-date machines, and once these stops are correctly adjusted, the reproduction of tenon and shoulder lengths becomes almost automatic.

The tenoning cutter-blocks are of skew shape, so as to give a shearing cut, and at first sight the cutters might seem to call for special treatment. This, however, is not the case. The cutters are quite straight, the shearing cut being the effect of the shape of the cutter-block. The cutter-blocks of most woodworking machines. intended principally for use with straight cutters, which are also provided with cutter-blocks and cutters. They are for dealing with moulded framing, the shoulders of which have to be scribed. The scribing cutters differ from moulding cutters in that they cut a recess to fit each projection of the moulding and leave a projection to fit each recess. After the work has been passed between the tenoning cutters by continuing the forward movement of the table, one or both shoulders may be scribed, either through their entire width or only partly through, as may be desired.

So that the shoulders of tenons may be cut clean and smooth, the tenoning cutter-blocks each carry a further set of cutters called shouldering cutters. These are provided with teeth, like a saw, and are fixed to the inner or shoulder ends of the blocks. Their action is to sever the wood cleanly across the grain.

Fig. 93.—Sand-papering Machine

WOODWORKING BY MACHINERY

are skewed to some extent. The skew may be more noticeable in the case of the tenoning machine than in that of some of the others. The feature makes no difference whatever to the grinding of the cutter.

The Drive.—Driving is effected by belts from a countershaft, which is usually an integral part of the machine, and as the gear ratios of machines by different makers may vary considerably, the countershaft speed recommended by the makers should be adhered to as nearly as possible.

THE SAND-PAPERING MACHINE

Mechanical sanders, or sand-papering machines, are now available for the finishing of most, if not all, woodwork requiring a sand-papered surface. The abrasive material (so-called sandpaper, in reality glasspaper) may be attached to a travelling belt, a revolving cylinder, a cone or a disc, according to the class of work that the machine is required to perform. Combination machines, made to suit some special requirement, are frequently met with. Perhaps the most useful type is the disc sander (Fig. 93). Not only may this machine be comparatively inexpensive —a little disc sander may be fitted to a lathe spindle at the cost of a pound or two —but it is more useful than some of the others, which may be said to be merely smoothing machines. The disc sander, as well as smoothing or finishing flat wooden surfaces, such as those of drawers, jewel boxes, etc., will true up certain classes of work with extreme accuracy, whilst newly sawn timber may often be finished without preliminary planing.

The machine shown by Fig. 93 has two discs, enabling two workers to sand at the same time; it is also of an improved pattern, having hoods fitted over the discs, and pipes for exhausting the dust; a very necessary provision where much sanding is done. On the actual machine of which Fig. 93 is a photograph, each disc has a sanding surface measuring 30 in. in diameter, but much smaller machines may be equally as useful. In the one under notice, the glass paper is secured to the discs by metal rings, and in practice half a dozen sheets may be fastened to a disc at the same time, so that when the outer sheet becomes worn it may be torn off, exposing a fresh sanding surface.

In the case of small discs, often fitted up in the workshop, glue will be found to answer very well for securing the paper to the discs. The tables, which support the work whilst being sanded, may be canted to any desired angle for edge-bevelling, and they may be moved up close to the discs so that thin material may be safely treated. On the top of each table is an adjustable fence, this also may be set to any required angle with the sanding surface.

Speeds (as given by different makers) at which disc sanders should be run vary considerably, and it is thought that some of them are higher than is necessary or desirable. There is no doubt that a good deal of latitude is permissible, but if the edge of a disc sander is run at a speed of about 4,500 ft. per minute, it will be found satisfactory.

Perhaps the best abrasive material for use with mechanical sanders is American garnet paper. This is obtainable in 50-yd. rolls, and widths up to 48 in.

THE EMERY GRINDING MACHINE

For performing the grinding operations inseparable from the use of woodworking machinery, many patterns of emery grinding machines are obtainable; emery machines of several types are available for every class of grinding connected with woodworking. Gulleting and sharpening saws, making moulding cutters, and grinding the straight cutters of planing machines are but a few of the uses to which emery machines may be put. The advantage of automatic and what may be termed semi-automatic machines, as used for saw sharpening, probably reposes more in the number of saws that can be dealt with than in any superiority machine sharpening may have over hand filing. The small user will have little or no need of such machines. With cutter grinding machines, the situation is different. Some machinists still prefer the old-fashioned wet and dirty grindstone, and were time of no account, and the grinding skill always available, there would probably be no cheaper, and certainly no better, way of grinding machine cutters. The saw-mill machinist is usually an excellent grinder and generally prefers grit stones for the grinding of both planing and moulding cutters. But planing, and moulding machines, as used in a saw-mill, are automatic in their action, and once

Fig. 94.—Emery Grinding Machine

the cutters are adjusted and the machine started, only require the timber feeding to them. This is usually done by an assistant, giving the machinist plenty of opportunity to prepare his cutters for the following job. The conditions under which the joinery or the cabinet machinist works are not the same. In his case, the manipulation of the timber on the machines may require even more skill than the setting of the cutters; in consequence, if there is access to an automatic or a semi-automatic emery machine and an assistant is provided, a great part of the grinding may be left to him.

A Typical Emery Grinder Described.—The grinding machine shown by Fig. 94 is of comparatively simple form. When straight cutters are being ground, its action may be termed semi-automatic. It is provided with a couple of emery wheels for the shaping of moulding cutters. As seen in the illustration, these are on the left-hand end of the spindle. On the other end is mounted a cup-shaped emery wheel. This is shown partially enclosed in a sheet metal guard or hood. In front of the cup wheel is a swing frame, which is attached to a base plate or table, sliding on planed rails. The straight cutter to be ground is secured by bolts to the inner side of the swing frame, the bevel of the cutter bearing against the rim of the cup. The bevel is adjusted by turning the small hand-wheel seen on the extreme right of the machine. The thumb-screw, passing through the frame, determines the amount to be ground off the cutter. Now if the machine is started, one of the two handles seen projecting above the table taken in either hand, and the frame with the cutter attached is moved backwards and forwards, across the face of the revolving wheel (the movement being continued so long as metal is being removed, that is, until the end of the thumb-screw, bearing against the base plate, arrests the forward movement of the frame), in theory, a perfectly straight cutter should result. There are one or two reasons why this may not happen in practice, but with moderate care, and the occasional application of a straightedge to the cutter under treatment very satisfactory work may be done on a machine of this description. The speed at which emery wheels should be run depends, to some extent, on their diameter, and also on the degree of hardness imparted to them in process of manufacture. Wheels 9 in. to 10 in. diameter are suitable for the grinding of moulding cutters, and if such are obtained of a degree of hardness adapted to working at a speed of 1,500 revolutions per minute they may be found to give greater satisfaction than wheels requiring a higher rate of speed. The surface speed of emery wheels is decided by the grit and grade the makers usually stating the surface speed. When grinding on an ordinary grindstone, water is needed, but with emery wheels the operation is usually performed dry. The process generates a considerable amount of heat, a large

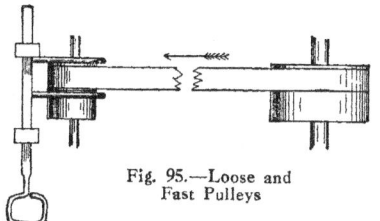

Fig. 95.—Loose and Fast Pulleys

percentage of which passes into the cutter under treatment, and care is needed so as not to " draw " the temper. This applies more particularly to the grinding of moulding cutters. If straight cutters are kept moving, no part of them will be in contact with the wheel sufficiently long to draw their temper (soften them); in shaping moulding cutters, however, the space to be treated is restricted. The grinder should work with a pail of water beside him, and he should hold the cutter with his fingers as close as possible to the part under treatment. As soon as the cutter feels uncomfortably warm, it should be cooled in water before proceeding further with the grinding.

POWER AND TRANSMISSION

Prime Movers Discussed.—The decision as to the best form of motive power to adopt for the driving of woodworking machinery will, most likely, be governed by local conditions. Water-power may be ruled out, it being so seldom available in this country. Amongst prime movers that remain, electricity, where available, will probably be found most convenient and under certain conditions the most economical. Electric motors need no special foundations and very little attention beyond an occasional inspection by an expert, also a separate motor, of only the power needed to drive it, may be harnessed to each machine. This system not only eliminates the necessity of using open belts, it also cuts off all current consumption except that required to drive machines that are in actual use. The steam engine is still a very popular prime mover with large power users, perhaps not so much because of its efficiency, as owing to the fact that wood waste may be used for boiler firing; a steam plant, however, needs almost constant skilled attention, which may form a considerable item in wages alone. A suction gas plant will consume wood waste, requires practically no skilled attention, and should certainly be taken into account by those installing medium or even large sized plants. The small man will probably choose between an engine consuming town's gas, and an oil engine, and here, again, his selection may depend upon local conditions. It is difficult to decide which of the two would be likely to prove the cheaper, but town's gas, where obtainable, would certainly be found the most convenient.

The Transmission of Power.—Motion is usually transmitted from the engine to a line of shafting, which may be fixed to the roof of the workshop, to the walls, or under the floor, power being taken from this shaft by a separate belt, either through a countershaft, or direct to each machine that has to be driven.

Whatever faults belts may possess (and these are certainly not insignificant), there does not appear to be any adequate substitute for belt driving, at least, so far as woodworking machinery is concerned. Both leather and fabric belts are used, some makers of the latter answering very well in situations where they are not

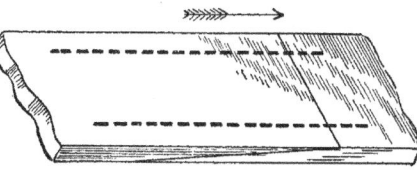

Fig. 96.—Scarfed Joint for Belt

required to run between forks, the friction of the latter soon fraying their edges; generally speaking, however, it is thought that the best leather belts obtainable will be found the most satisfactory and economical.

Any allusion made to forks and to loose and fast pulleys, would probably be quite intelligible to most readers ; for the benefit of those to whom it is not, it may be explained that these constitute the gear usually employed for the starting and stopping of belt-driven machines. The driven spindle is provided with two pulleys of equal size, fixed side by side. One of these is " fast " (secured to the spindle so that it cannot rotate on it). The other pulley is loose and revolves freely on the spindle. The belt, driving the pulleys, runs between the prongs of a fork, which should be arranged as close to the pulleys as possible, and must only operate on the advancing side of the belt. Provision is made for moving the fork across the face of the pulleys, and the belt running between the prongs of the fork is moved along with it from loose to fast, or from fast to loose pulleys, thus starting or stopping the machine as required. The gear in its simplest form is shown by Fig. 95, from which it will be seen that the face of the driving pulley should equal in width the combined faces of the two others—the loose and fast pulleys. The faces of loose and fast pulleys are usually crowned, that is to say, the pulleys themselves are rather larger in diameter in the middle than at their edges. The tendency of a running belt is to seek the highest part of the pulley, so that the crowning has the effect of retaining the belt in position on one pulley until it is forced over on to the other one by means of the fork or striking arm.

Machine belting is readily obtainable in widths of from 1 in. upwards, and in lengths sufficient for almost any drive. Fabric and composition belting is practically continuous ; leather belts are, of necessity, made with joins every few feet. These joins are " scarfed " (see Fig. 96). They are usually cemented and afterwards sewn. Some makers reinforce the sewing by the insertion of copper rivets. When fitting leather belts, they should be so placed on the machines that the ends of the under part of the joints point in the opposite direction to that in which the belts are to be run (see Fig. 96).

Belt fasteners, of which there are several different types on the market are used for, joining the ends of belts together. Only some of them are suitable for use with woodworking machinery. The fastener employed should make a joint sufficiently flexible to pass easily and smoothly over the smallest-sized pulley in use. If, on revolving a machine by hand, any stiffness or obstruction is noticeable when the joint of the belt is passing over the pulleys, the probability is that the fastener in use is at fault.

The width of belts is proportioned according to the power that they are required to transmit ; the point is taken into consideration by makers when fitting pulleys to their machines so that, on a well-designed machine, the width of the belt to use may be determined by the pulley accommodation. Briefly, if the makers of a machine have provided it with pulleys measuring $4\frac{1}{2}$ in., say, across to their faces, then a 4 in. wide belt is what they have considered to be needed to drive that machine.

The efficiency of a belt is frictional, and therefore affected by the tension of the belt itself. But a belt should not, if it can possibly be avoided, have to depend upon tension for its efficiency. Particularly does this apply to belts used for driving high speed woodworking machinery, where an over-tight belt may ruin the journals of a machine. Not only is over tension bad for the belts themselves, but it is sure to cause over heating and excessive wear in the bearings of machinery. Whilst high speed belts should not be too slack, they should depend for their efficiency on weight rather than tension ; consequently, a long drive is usually preferable to a short one, and a horizontal to a vertical one.

A belt's effective area, and consequent efficiency, may be augmented or decreased by the situation of the machine required to be driven. Fig. 97 will explain this. It is merely a question of on which side of the main or driving shaft (relative to the direction of its rotation) the machine is placed. The larger circle at the top of the diagram represents the driving pulley, and on the left is seen the effect, when the belt is under load, of having its working or pulling side towards the bottom of the pulleys. The working side of the belt is drawn tight, causing a corresponding slackness on the top, or idle side, which sags down between the two of a machine shop, it is rarely, if ever, possible to get every machine so placed as to be in the best possible position for driving, but an attempt should be made to allot the most favourable situations to the belts which, in proportion to their width, incur the heaviest loads.

When it becomes necessary to reverse the direction of rotation between two

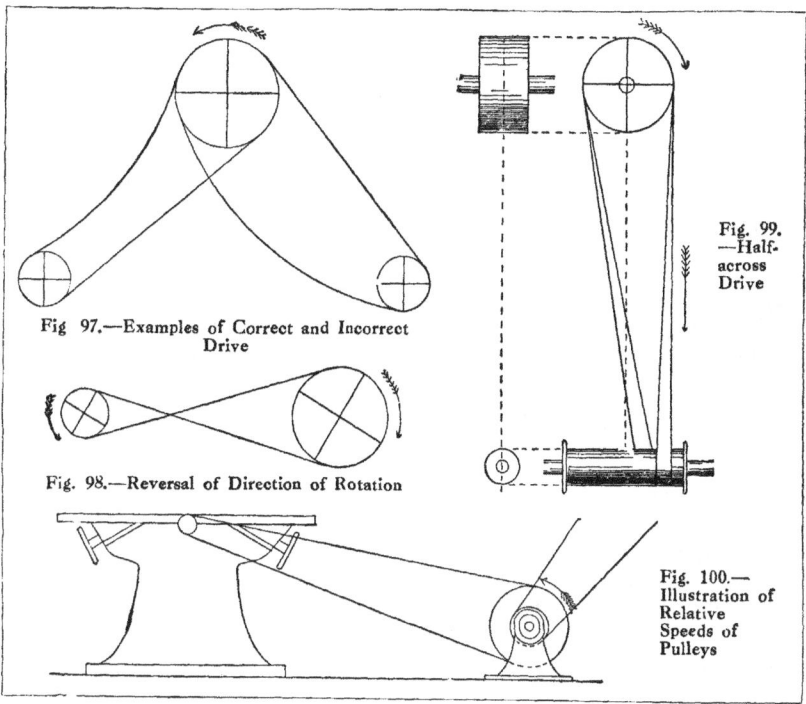

Fig 97.—Examples of Correct and Incorrect Drive

Fig. 98.—Reversal of Direction of Rotation

Fig. 99.—Half-across Drive

Fig. 100.—Illustration of Relative Speeds of Pulleys

pulleys and thus increases the area of belt surface in contact with them (known as "arc of contact"). It will be readily understood that an arrangement of this sort, which causes the efficiency of the belt to increase under load, is an ideal one. To the right is shown the effect of having the pulling side of the belt towards the top, the loading of the machine causing the idle side of the belt to fall away from the pulleys. Of course, in the arrangement pulleys, this may be effected by crossing the belt (see Fig. 98).

One of the essentials to success in belt driving is the alignment of shafting and spindles. These, with one exception to be described presently, should be perfectly horizontal, and must be parallel with each other. Each driving pulley, also, has to be adjusted in alignment with its corresponding driven pulley or pulleys. In other words, a belt transmitting power from one horizontal shaft to another, should be square with both of them.

The exception to the foregoing is the drive from the horizontal countershaft to the vertical spindle of the spindle moulder. This is known as a "half-cross" drive, and its arrangement is illustrated by Fig. 99. In the case of the machine under notice, no difficulty should be experienced in arranging the half-cross drive; the countershaft, as sent out by the makers of the machine, will be of the correct height, and the faces of both driving and driven pulleys of ample width. Presuming that the countershaft is level and in line with the main shaft, the centre of the vertical spindle should fall on a line square with the countershaft and passing through the middle of the driving pulley's face (see Fig. 99). If the table of the machine is adjusted level in each direction, the spindle may be considered vertical.

Pulley Speeds.—The subject of "gearing," that is, so arranging pulley diameters that the several machines may be run at their proper speeds, must now be considered. In the driving of woodworking machinery, the gearing is usually upward; the shafting travels faster than the engine, and the machines revolve more quickly than the shafting. Suppose the crankshaft of the engine is running at 100 revolutions per minute and is fitted with a pulley 24 in. in diameter; this to be driving a 12-in. pulley on the main line of shafting. The main shaft will then turn at a speed of 200 revolutions per minute (twice the speed of the engine), because the engine (driving) pulley is twice the diameter of the pulley on the shaft (the driven pulley). The method of determining the speed of a driven shaft is to multiply the speed of the driver by the diameter of the driving pulley and to divide by the diameter of the driven, thus:

$$\frac{100 \times 24}{12} = 200.$$

A suitable speed for the main shaft is 300 revolutions per minute, and this speed should not be greatly exceeded. The faster the main shafting is run, the more power will be needed to drive it when the machinery is running light (without load), also the greater the attention that will have to be given to it in the way of lubrication. Further, should the shafting be fixed to a floor above, there is the question of vibration to be considered. The uninitiated may feel tempted to increase the speed of the main line of shafting, so as to decrease the size, and consequent cost, of the pulleys required to drive the machines at the necessary speed. For the reasons stated, the method is not to be commended.

Presuming the main shafting to be running at 300 revolutions per minute, and the pulley on the surface planer to be 4 in. diameter, then, to obtain the necessary speed for the surface planer (3,000 revolutions per minute), if it were driven directly from the main shaft, a pulley 40 in. in diameter would be needed, the speed of the shafting having to be multiplied by ten. Where the speed at which a machine is required to run is very high, as in this case and that of all cutter-block machines, the size of the pulley on the main shaft is kept within reasonable limits by the introduction of a countershaft (see Fig. 100). The arrangement might be as follows: a 20-in. pulley on the main shaft, driving 8-in. loose and fast pulleys on the countershaft, would give it a speed of 750 revolutions per minute, then a 16-in. pulley on the countershaft would drive the 4-in. pulley of the machine at the required speed of 3,000 revolutions per minute. These speeds may be verified as shown in the preceding paragraph.

To obtain the diameter of a pulley needed on the main shaft, to drive another pulley at a given speed, multiply the speed required by the diameter of the pulley to be driven, and divide by the speed of the main shaft. For example, supposing the speed required to be 750 revolutions per minute, the diameter of the pulley to be driven to be 8 in. and that the speed of the main shaft is 300 revolutions per minute, then 750 multiplied by 8, and divided by 300 gives 20. $\frac{750 \times 8}{300} = 20$

Therefore 20 in. is the diameter required.

Drawing for Woodworkers

PRACTICAL woodworkers should have training in draughtsmanship to enable them to prepare the drawings and details of the work which their hands will eventually create, and also to enable them to read the drawings and details prepared by designers.

There are ways of reading—a lack of spirit, punctuation, and tone may alter the gist or meaning of an author's endeavours; similarly a proper appreciation and capability of reading a drawing or detail not only causes a woodworker to understand fully what is required, and his mind and work to harmonise with those of the designer, but assures a much better result in the object to be formed and enables the woodworker to prepare drawings, details and sketches which are necessary for his work, and which may be, in a practical commercial sense, of great advantage when it is necessary to submit ideas to clients.

This section will illustrate and explain simple principles of drawing, and the reading of drawings, and will start at the beginning, so as to provide a course of training for woodworkers who are totally inexperienced in what should be an essential part of their training, and thereby enhance their value to themselves or to their employers, who greatly appreciate an employee who is qualified to use both tools and designing instruments with ability.

Practical draughtsmanship embraces the capability to draw in a manner that fully illustrates what is intended and required, but succinctly and without being laboured. This must not be taken to infer that a drawing should be rough, carelessly drawn or thought out, or inaccurate, or that many of the freedoms that a good draughtsman indulges in after much practice are to be sought by a beginner who for a considerable time must be slow, sure, accurate and neat and may need to take three or four times longer with a drawing than will be necessary after drawing principles and instruments are mastered. A good draughtsman should be capable of preparing a detail drawing in the shortest possible time with simple quickly-formed lettering for the purpose of showing what is required to say to a worker who is proficient in reading and working from a drawing. Also, when needs require a good draughtsman should be able to prepare an illustration of an article of woodwork that will represent to a lay mind what such article will truly look like when completed.

DESCRIPTION, PURCHASE AND USE OF DRAWING IMPLEMENTS

There are only a few very necessary items, and, if convenient, it is advisable to obtain the best of them by purchasing a few at first, then one by one, until the lot are obtained. An immediate collection of a lot of shoddy instruments is not recommended, but the same amount of money expended on a lesser quantity of best quality is much more satisfactory. It is often possible, but not quite so easy as formerly, to purchase good quality instruments at cheap rates at a pawn-brokers.

In the following descriptions of the or what may be termed consumable articles.

The Drawing Board and its Support and Position.—There are a few sizes and types of drawing boards on the market, and it is necessary to consider

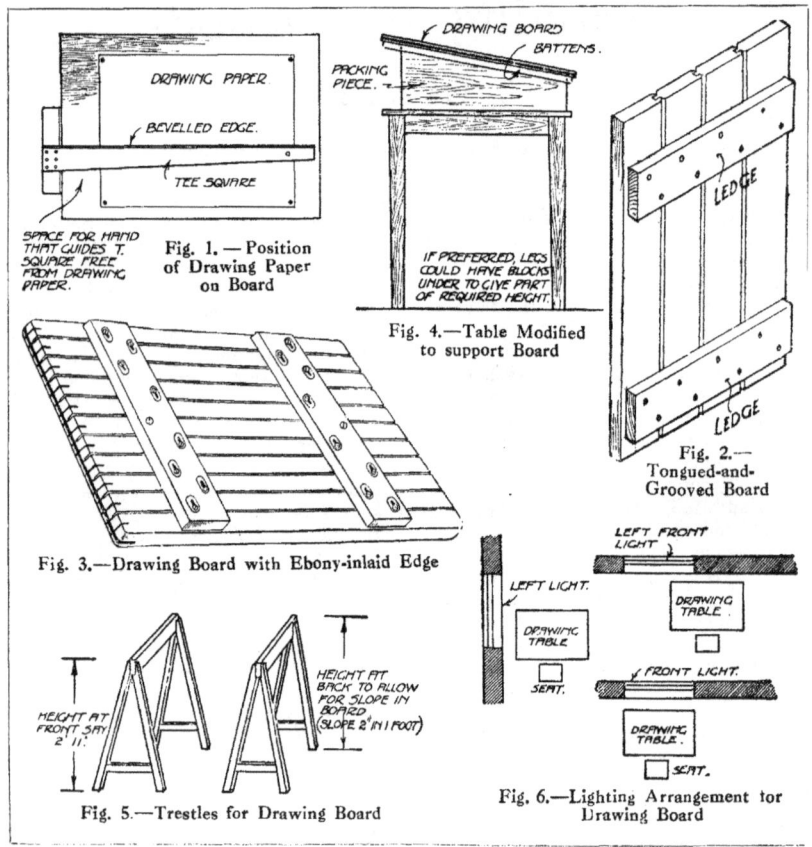

Fig. 1. — Position of Drawing Paper on Board

Fig. 4.—Table Modified to support Board

Fig. 2.—Tongued-and-Grooved Board

Fig. 3.—Drawing Board with Ebony-inlaid Edge

Fig. 5.—Trestles for Drawing Board

Fig. 6.—Lighting Arrangement for Drawing Board

various items, the order in which they should be purchased and are necessary is consecutive from the first described article, the first few, of course, being of equal importance as regards acquisition. In the later pages will be described drawing materials such as paper, pencils, etc., these to enable a draughtsman to choose the type best suited to his requirements.

The usual sizes are :—
Half Imperial . 23 in. × 16 in.
Imperial . . 31 in. × 23 in.
Double Elephant . 41 in. × 28 in.
Antiquarian . 54 in. × 32 in.

DRAWING FOR WOODWORKERS

Many students are advised to, or do, purchase the half-imperial size, which although suitable for most elementary work does not permit of much scope as regards the size of the drawing. The writer recommends that nothing smaller than imperial size be obtained, and preferably double-elephant, which will be found to be the most convenient size, especially at a later date when large detail drawings have to be prepared. Of course, a small drawing can be prepared on a large board. For all ordinary purposes it is seldom that a larger sized drawing than imperial is required, or that a greater width of paper than 30 in. is necessary, and a drawing board 41 in. long allows plenty of room, firstly, to allow the paper to be placed a few inches away from the running edge of the board, as shown by Fig. 1. This permits the left or T-square guiding hand to be kept clear of the paper, and so avoids rubbing it by the fingers, which however clean at starting of drawing become a little dirty later by sharpening pencils; and, secondly, allows a little space at the right-hand side of board for placing rubbers, pencils, note paper, inkstand, if these articles are not kept elsewhere, such as on a shelf under the drawing board or on a table or support of the board. (See 'T-square' for practical hints as to length to use.)

The type of drawing board is the tongued-and-grooved board shown by Fig. 2, which should be made of dry best quality pinewood, and provided that a good quality board be purchased this type will be suitable to begin with, although the class and quality of board shown by Fig. 3 is to be preferred and would last practically a lifetime, but its cost is twice or 2½ times that of the former board. Fig. 3 depicts a drawing board of best quality, well seasoned pine boards, with the running edge inlaid with ebony, mahogany battens at back fixed to the boards with brass slots and screws which allows for the expansion and contraction of the wood, and prevents the board getting out of shape or square, or splitting. This type of board is best, and great care should be exercised in its selection. A too hard or dense wood should not be chosen, otherwise there will be difficulty in inserting by a fair pressure of the thumb, and easily withdrawing, drawing pins.

A rigid support for a drawing board is essential. For many beginners an ordinary firm four-legged table would be most convenient, and would save an outlay on a special drawing table or trestles. The height of an ordinary table is usually not sufficient for drawing purposes as, except for small drawings, all parts of which could be comfortably reached without standing up, it is necessary to have such a height as will allow the draughtsman to sit down as much as possible, and when standing is needed, which is often, there will be no necessity to cramp the body as would be the case if drawing had to be done at a low level while standing. The correct height depends upon the draughtsman's height. A comfortable working height must be assured, the board should slope upwards from front to back, and generally the height at front may be assumed to be correct if it is half the draughtsman's height plus 1 in. to 2 in., e.g. the writer is 5 ft. 10½ in. and his board is 3 ft. 0½ in. off the floor at the front edge. The board should be sloped about 2 in. in every foot, or 1 in 6. The above are rules for guidance, and a comfortable height and slope should be arranged by the user. A table sometimes carries with it the necessity of taking the drawing board off it, and consequently stopping work at meal or other times, which is a drawback, but if an old table can be solely used for drawing it is very suitable; otherwise it is better to make or purchase a bench or trestles, the former being preferable as it permits of a space at the sides and underneath for instruments and many other things. Fig. 4 shows a table or bench with packing pieces to give proper height and slope, and Fig. 5 a pair of trestles.

The position of a drawing board should be such that it would be lighted both naturally and artificially from the left, front, or left and front, probably either of the two last positions being better than

THE PRACTICAL WOODWORKER

the former. Fig. 6 illustrates various lighting arrangements.

The Tee Square.—T-squares are purchasable in lengths equal to the lengths of boards, and are made in two shapes,

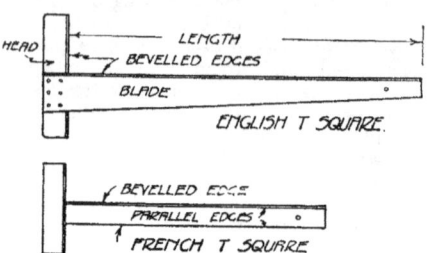

Fig. 7.—Two Types of T-squares

English and French, as shown by Fig. 7, the English being preferred by the majority. They are made in pearwood and mahogany. A pearwood T-square is quite suitable to commence with, but a mahogany one with an ebony running edge will last much longer. A thick heavy T-square should not be used, as a light thin one is more easy to handle. The head runs along the left-hand side or running edge of the drawing board. The use of a T-square is not quite so simple as might be thought, and it is essential

what is most comfortable to a draughtsman, and which will be least tiring to the fingers. Different draughtsmen vary the method of using, but there is a right and wrong way. The correct method of using a T-square should assure a slight pressure downwards on it, a slight pressure at the side of the head to keep it fairly tight against the running edge of the drawing board, and at the same time allow for a quick and accurate movement to the extent of from a small fraction of an inch to a greater distance. It should be carefully noted that the writer advises that the blade be lightly gripped along the top edge by two fingers, and sometimes it is convenient to use the little finger as well, and the bottom edge by the thumb with the forefinger lightly pressing on the blade. The position of the arm is such that there may be always a slight pressure in a direction away from the head of the T-square which will keep the head against the running edge of the drawing board. After a time it will be found that all the positions and actions will become automatic and that the square may be easily moved in any required direction either up or down the board, and stopped at the point required. When it is required to move the T-square just a little, say to draw a horizontal line $\frac{1}{16}$ in.

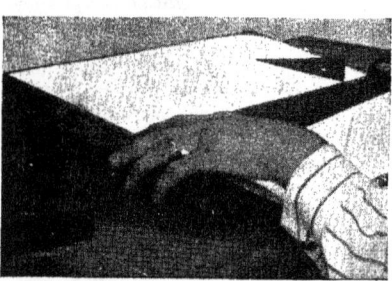

Fig. 8.—Usual Method of Holding T-square

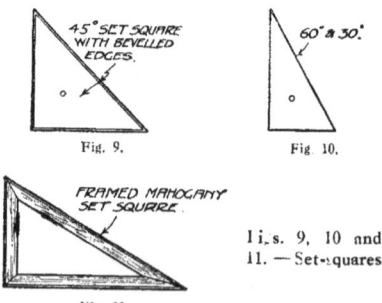

Fig. 9. Fig. 10.

Fig. 11.

Figs. 9, 10 and 11.—Set-squares

thoroughly to master its use, as a wrong beginning, although it may feel and seem perfectly right, may create a habit which will be difficult to overcome later. The proper method depends a little upon

or $\frac{1}{8}$ in. above or below another line, a little practice will soon make this quite easy by moving the fingers slightly in such a manner that the T-square is levered in the direction required by the

DRAWING FOR WOODWORKERS

tips of the fingers; for instance, if it be needed to move the square down the board just a little it will be found that if the two or three fingers that grip the running edge of the blade are held in a vertical position, and if they are slightly pulled towards the bottom edge of the board, that such action will make the T-square move as required. The width of the blade near the head should not be more than the fingers can comfortably span. A usual method, but one not recommended by the writer, is shown in Fig. 8.

In using the pencil or drawing pen—which latter will be fully described later—against the T-square, the action should be with pencil or pen held quite perpendicular to the width of the blade and at an angle of about 70° from the drawing board in the direction from side to side.

The Set-squares (or angles).—These are made in various sizes and of various substances, and 45° and combined 30° and 60°. They are made in sizes measured along their longest edge containing the right angle in the case of 30° and 60° and along either of the sides containing the right angle in the case of 45° set-squares, from 4 in. by 1 in. stages to about 10 in. and then by 2 in. stages to about 18 in. Set-squares are made (cheapest first) of plain pearwood, framed pearwood, vulcanite, transparent celluloid, and framed mahogany. The wood kinds, except sometimes the plain pearwood, have bevelled edges; the vulcanite and celluloid being thin are not always bevelled. Figs. 9, 10 and 11 show three squares. Transparent celluloid is the best, as it is possible to see through this material, and consequently the work underneath being visible more readily makes it possible to move the square to the position needed. For general use and for small work about 8 in. or 9 in. set-squares are useful; for large detail work about 10 in. or 12 in. set-squares should be used with the T-square in the manner depicted by Fig. 12, when lines at right angles or perpendicular to the running edge of the T-square have to be drawn (and also lines at 45° in the direction as shown by the position of the set-square). Fig. 13 shows similar positions for 30°—60° set-squares. In all the positions it will be noted that as regards lines to be drawn at right angles to the T-square, or what are commonly called vertical lines in drawing, that the action edge of the set-square faces the head of the T-square and also the light. A wrong position is shown by Fig. 14. The movements and methods should be thoroughly mastered, and woodworkers will find that in a short time correct and comfortable drawing positions will be attained. Once a wrong method is started and persisted in, later it will be found to be difficult to overcome the incorrect habit.

The Drawing or Ruling Pen is used for drawing lines in ink, and three types are shown by Fig. 15. The pen is constructed with two nibs, the back and fore nib the former being the one that travels along the edge of T-square, set-square or other edge. The better class of pens have the fore nibs hinged so as to allow them to be opened for cleaning and setting purposes. The ink must be "fed" into the space between the two nibs so that it will be separated from the running edges and therefore prevent it running under and consequently being smudged by the T-square, etc. The ink will flow through the space between the points of the nibs to the paper, and the screw depicted is to regulate the thickness of line by varying the distance between the points of the nibs. A good pen should have a thick or stout back nib so as to provide sufficient stiffness to prevent such nib slightly bending when pressed against the edge of the squares, and thereby affecting the thickness of lines. Many users prefer a thin back nib, but it is doubtful whether a good draughtsman really requires it, as an expert is very light in action with instruments—a heavy pressure should be avoided, but a pressure that is light, sure, and yet firm enough for the purpose. The weight of a pen is almost sufficient to draw a line. For general work a fairly substantial pen is best as it can be gripped more firmly than a small thin pen. Draughtsmen should purchase a pen about 6 inches long from a reputable maker.

For small fine lined work a 4½-in. pen is handy, but if the larger pen is kept in good order it will be found that very fine lines can be drawn with it. The pen should be used in the same manner as a pencil—that is, vertical in one direction and slightly inclined in the other—with the back nib against the running edge of the T-square, set-square or other ruling edge.

Some prefer to hold the pen with the forefinger on the screw (if a hinged nib pen is used), which is usually quite tight enough to prevent it being rotated by such finger, and others prefer to keep the finger a little above the screw. The writer finds greater comfort and control by the former method. The nibs must exactly coincide as regard length and shape at their points, which should be obvious to the eye, and to test perhaps the simplest thing to do is to open the nibs about $\tfrac{1}{32}$ in., press the pen perpendicularly to the surface of a piece of paper and note whether the imprints are identical. Another test is to use a dry pen—i.e. with no ink in it—and use it as if a line is to be drawn, with a little more pressure than ordinarily used, and two impressed lines should show on the paper, both lines of the same depth. A pen that is not set correctly causes an uneven line and

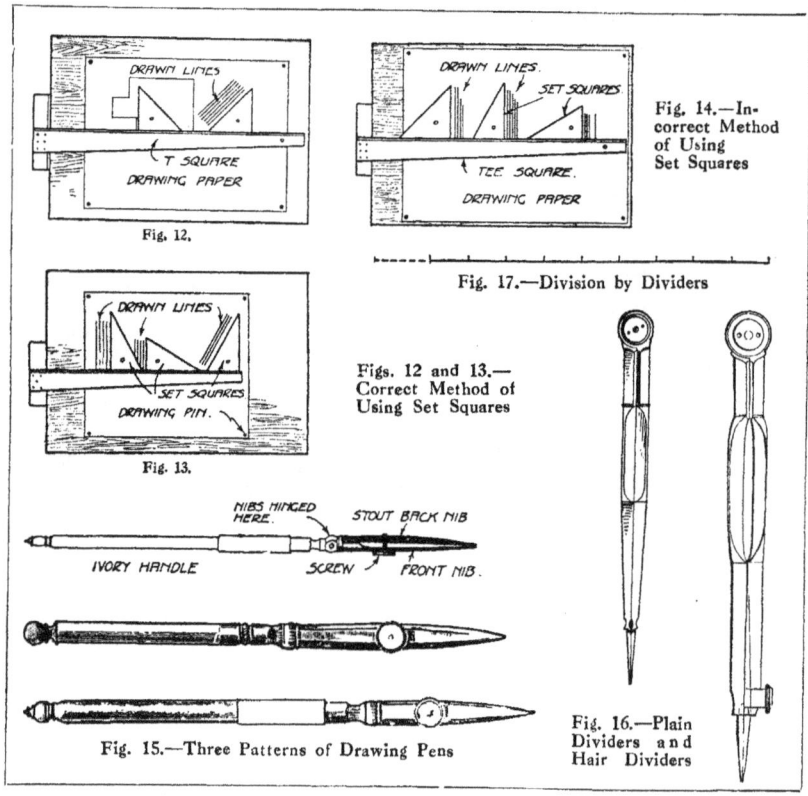

Fig. 12.

Fig. 13.

Fig. 14.—Incorrect Method of Using Set Squares

Figs. 12 and 13.—Correct Method of Using Set Squares

Fig. 15.—Three Patterns of Drawing Pens

Fig. 16.—Plain Dividers and Hair Dividers

Fig. 17.—Division by Dividers

retards the proper flow of the ink, and should be sent to the makers for resetting. If resetting or sharpening is attempted by the owner great care must be taken in grinding the nibs down on a very fine oilstone, only grinding the outside of the nibs and not the surface against which the ink is held, except to take off any little burr that will be caused by grinding one side only. The nibs must be so ground that both the nibs wi l be of the same length, etc., as mentioned above; it will be found that the sharpening process by means of a slip of folded paper, or cloth, or if the ink has become hard then by means of dipping the nibs in water, and then wiping them, or very carefully scraping them with a penknife.

The Dividers—Plain and hair dividers are depicted by Fig. 16 made of electrum. Dividers are used for dividing a line into equal parts, or to measure one length or distance for the purpose of representation elsewhere. As an instance, if the line shown by Fig. 17 is to be divided into 9 equal parts, the points of the

Fig. 18.—Method of "Stepping-out" with Dividers

will necessitate grinding each nib separately for a little time and then together.

Enough ink should be inserted in the drawing pen by means of an ordinary nib or with the filler which will be found attached to the cork of most bottles of drawing ink. The amount of ink should not exceed in height ⅜ in. from point or otherwise there will be a likelihood of the ink running. If the charged pen be not used for a time, such as during a few minutes when it may be set down to enable attention to be paid to other work, it may be found that the ink has congealed or hardened in the pen, when it will be necessary to clean the pen of such ink dividers should be set at a distance apart to what is thought to be one ninth of the length of the line, and starting at one end of the line with one of the points of the dividers very lightly resting on the end of the line, the dividers should be "stepped-out" and probably it will happen that nine divisions will not result, but either more or less, and this will necessitate reducing or increasing the distance apart of the points and stepping-out again, and perhaps again, until the proper division is obtained. In course of time a good degree of accuracy should be attained. As an example, if the first stepping-out results that the ninth step is too much by the distance shown dotted in Fig. 17, then the points of the dividers should be set at a reduced distance apart, equal as near as possible to one ninth of the length of the dotted line; this will be easier than re-gauging one ninth of the whole line. The points of the dividers should not be pressed too much into the paper or large holes will be made; if the points are sharp and the dividers lightly handled the imprints will be hardly perceptible, but after the points are set to the distance apart required, the final "stepping-out" should be made with sufficient power to assure that a hole is formed that can be seen for purposes of marking.

There is a knack in using dividers which is rather difficult to explain and illustrate, and once the knack is acquired "stepping-out" can be done with a rate of movement equal to a person's sharp walk. Fig. 18 will, it is thought, show the movements in "stepping-out" along the line indicated. In the first case particular note should be made of the correct method of holding the top or head of the dividers. Place the one point at the end of the line and hold the dividers vertically with the thumb and forefinger as near as possible in the manner illustrated, which shows the tip of the thumb at the top of the dividers and the tip of the forefinger about half an inch over the top. This position will allow with ease for the rotation required for the first step, which after it is made will cause the top of the dividers to be held in the way shown with the tips of the thumb and forefinger reversed as regards their position to the top of the dividers. It is important to note that the dividers must be stepped-out by turning or rotating them so that the point describes imaginary semi-circles as shown by Fig. 18, and not in such a manner that would result in finger and thumb being twisted into confusion at the top of the dividers. Plain dividers about 5 in. long are suitable for most purposes. Hair dividers which have one of the points adjusted with a screw by which the points can be set or varied to a very small extent apart, are very useful.

Compasses with Pencil Point.—Bow pencils are depicted by Fig. 19, where A represents a cheap compass suitable for students, and B and C the best types with solid and needle points. B has knee joints which allow the lower sections to be set so that the point and pencil may be either approximately vertical or at such an angle to the drawing paper that will assure an even pressure on the paper without a tendency to move the points. The solid or needle point should be as nearly vertical as convenient, as otherwise during the rotation of the compass it is apt to slip out of the very small indentation in the paper and also to cause a too large hole. Compasses should be so held that, while they are firmly gripped, there is only the slightest pressure on the paper. Generally, circles, or parts thereof, should be described clockwise.

Compasses with Pen Point.—A bow pen is shown by Fig. 20. It is used in the same manner as a bow pencil, but it is more essential to keep the pen point in a vertical position so that both of the nibs bear equally on the paper.

Half Sets.—A useful set of instruments is that known as a "half set" and shown by Fig. 21, where A represents a cheap set, and B a superior set. A half set comprises a pair of dividers, one leg of which is removable to allow the fixing of either pencil or pen points, and in addition a lengthening bar may be fixed so as to permit of the drawing of circles or arcs of large radius. This would be often necessary for woodworkers in setting out details of large work or drawing to a large scale.

Spring Bows.—These are shown by Fig. 22, and are used for small work. The screw allows for fine adjustment to various radii. They are used with more of a spinning action than bow pens, etc., and it is possible to make circles either in pencil or ink of such a small diameter as $\tfrac{1}{16}$ in. A combination set of spring bows is shown by Fig. 23.

Cases of Drawing Instruments.— Various cases are shown by Figs. 24, 25 and 26; a set such as Fig. 25 would be quite suitable for most woodworkers. If

DRAWING FOR WOODWORKERS

instruments are bought one or two at a time they may be kept in roll-up pocket cases, which may be bought ready-made, or made at home. Fig. 27 shows such a case.

Drawing Pins.—There are a few matters about drawing pins which are worth mentioning. They should be about $\frac{3}{4}$ in. to $\frac{7}{8}$ in. diameter across head, should have either flat heads with bevelled edges, or be mushroom headed so as to allow a **T**-square or set-square to ride over them

drawn is shown among the various pins in Fig. 28.

French Curves.—These are shown by Fig. 29, and are used for drawing curved lines which cannot be drawn by compasses. By careful arrangement it will be found that a curved line containing curves of different radii may be drawn in sections with various edges of the curve. When ink curves are to be drawn it is important that the drawing pen should be held so that the width of the nib is tangen-

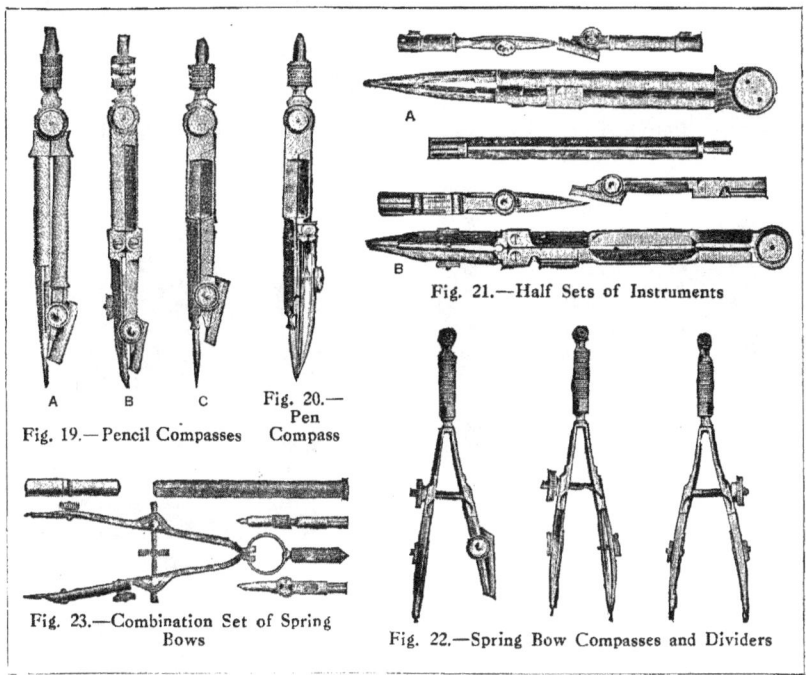

Fig. 19.—Pencil Compasses
Fig. 20.—Pen Compass
Fig. 21.—Half Sets of Instruments
Fig. 22.—Spring Bow Compasses and Dividers
Fig. 23.—Combination Set of Spring Bows

easily, and preferably the points should not be screwed or fixed through the entire thickness of head, as after a time it may be found that the thread may strip when the pin is being pressed into the drawing board, with a painful result. A large drawing pin is perhaps a little more easily withdrawn than a small one, as there is more leverage. A pin that is easily with-

tial to the edge of the French curve, otherwise the pen may work broadside on and cause a line to be formed of varying thickness.

DRAWING MATERIALS

Drawing Papers.—There are many kinds of drawing paper, and the most suitable to use depends upon the use for which a drawing is required. For making preliminary or sketch drawings, the following is a list of some drawing papers :—

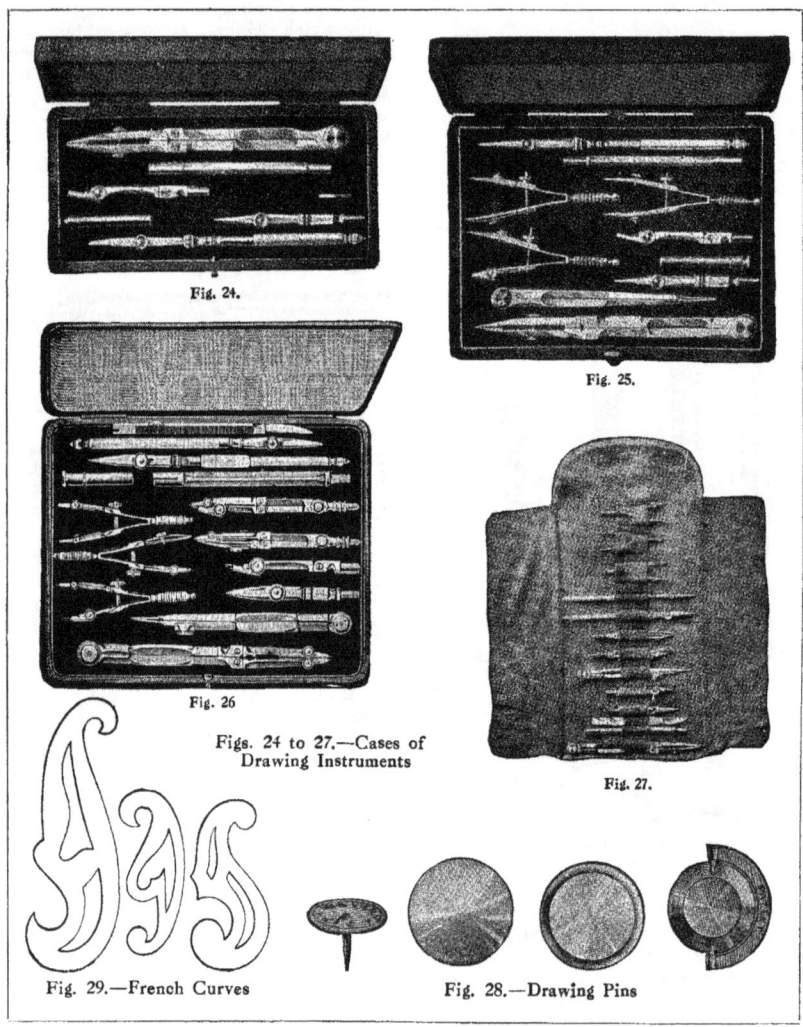

Fig. 24.
Fig. 25.
Fig. 26.
Figs. 24 to 27.—Cases of Drawing Instruments
Fig. 27.
Fig. 29.—French Curves
Fig. 28.—Drawing Pins

full-size working details, or drawings from which tracings are to be taken, the cheaper kinds of paper should be used.

(a) Pure white cartridge, medium, stout and extra stout thicknesses.
(b) Thin and thick tough cartridge.

DRAWING FOR WOODWORKERS

(c) Thin common detail paper, and thicker grades.
(d) Thin tracing detail paper, and thicker grades.
(e) Parchment detail paper.
(f) Smooth extra tough parchment detail paper.

These are usually supplied in rolls of 22, 25, or 50 yds. and in width of 30 in. upwards, but many of them can be obtained in sheets. The following better classes of papers are supplied in sheets :—

(g) Whatman's hand-made drawing papers, in rough, medium rough (not pressed) and smooth (hot pressed). For fine work and for drawings to be lithographed, etc., the smooth surface is preferable; for general drawings the medium rough is usually used. The rough is most used for art and colour work where a grained effect is desired.

(h) Joynson's machine-made drawing paper of rough and smooth surfaces.

Qualities g and h are obtainable in Imperial (30 in. × 22 in.), Double Elephant (40 in × 27 in.), and Antiquarian (53 in. × 31 in.), although h is not usually obtainable in the last size.

A roll (22 yds.) of thin tough cartridge paper, and a roll of thin or medium detail paper will be found suitable to start with. Both of these papers should have a fine hard and smooth surface, especially for ink work. It is difficult to describe the exact texture of paper, and woodworkers should send for samples of such papers from drawing office material shops. The samples of papers should be roughly tested by drawing a few lines with a drawing pen and an ordinary pen, with Indian ink, and carefully noting whether a clear line results without tearing up the surface of paper or "flashing" of the ink into the grains of the paper.

Rolls of paper will be found more economical than sheets, as the rolls cost proportionately less than sheets and the exact length required can be cut. 30-in.-wide paper will be found most useful. This advice also applies to tracing paper.

Tracing Paper.—This is a thin transparent paper used for making a copy of another drawing by means of placing the tracing paper over the drawing to be traced, and then by either pencil or pen tracing the lines, etc.. of the drawing underneath, which is plainly visible through the tracing paper. Tracing paper is also useful to prepare original details or drawings on when it is required to make several copies by the blue-printing process, the tracing forming the negative. Tracing paper is obtainable in rolls the same size as drawing or detail papers, and is made with glazed and unglazed surfaces. Probably many woodworkers would prefer a tough thin glazed paper. Generally ink will flow quite freely on tracing papers, but should it be found that it does not do so a little french chalk rubbed over the paper will remove any greasiness which retards the flow of ink.

Tracing Cloth.—This is transparent like tracing paper, and, as its name implies, is a cloth and not a paper. It would be seldom required by woodworkers, unless a drawing is required which would be subjected to much usage and consequently calls for a material that would not easily tear. It is much more expensive than paper. One surface is glazed and the other unglazed, and generally the unglazed surface is worked upon, and if to be inked upon—it is seldom used with pencil—it must be carefully wiped over with french or prepared chalk, otherwise it will be very difficult to make clean sharp lines.

Pencils.—Three lead pencils will be sufficient for all ordinary work—HB, H, and HH, the former being softer than the others. HB pencils should be used for notes and sketches and for drawing freehand curves, etc.; H will be found quite hard enough for general drawings, and HH for fine accurate work. Hexagon-shaped pencils are preferable to round, as they are not so apt to roll off the drawing board when placed down. The points of pencils used by woodworkers for marking on wood are often formed as at A in Fig. 30, which is a strong point and useful where pressure has to be exerted to make lines on hard wood, but for drawing purposes, where a light pressure only must be made so as to avoid tearing the paper, a longer point is more convenient, as shown at B, C, and D in Fig. 30. Although the formation of a pencil point may appear to be a

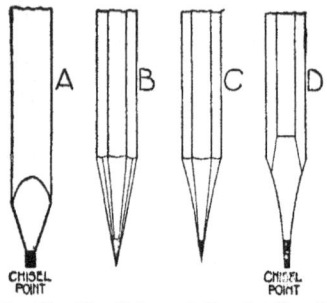

Fig. 30.—The Points of Drawing Pencils

very simple thing, it is difficult at first to form this long point after the habit of the stump point has been acquired. The point of the pencil should be about 1 in. long and the exposed lead nearly ¼ in. If a woodworker finds it difficult to use a pencil lightly for drawing purposes—he being probably used to pressing hard on wood—then a good way to overcome hard pressing is to make the lead point about ⅜ in. long with a HB grade pencil and start drawing. Oft-broken points and waste of pencils will soon overcome the habit. At D is shown a chisel point, which may be made on hard pencils when they are to be used for drawing straight lines. Such a point retains its sharpness longer than round points, as B and C. When a pencil is used against a T-square or set-square it should be held and used in the manner as previously described, i.e. vertical in one direction and slightly inclined towards the direction in which the pencil will travel. A strip of very fine glasspaper pinned or glued to a piece of wood is useful for keeping the points sharp.

Drawing Inks.—The ink mostly used by draughtsmen is liquid Indian ink, jet black in colour. It is waterproof and may be coloured over or wetted without causing it to run. It may be obtained in stick form and " rubbed up " in water, but this is a tedious process, which makes it preferable to purchase the ink in liquid form. The stick form is not waterproof and consequently must not be used if the ink is required for drawings to be coloured. There are several good brands of Indian ink on the market, which cost about 1s. 6d. per bottle. These last a considerable time with an ordinary amount of work. The corks usually have pen fillers attached, and the drawing pen, etc., should be charged with this filler and the cork placed back in the bottle after every filling of the pen. The cork should not be left out of the bottle longer than is necessary as this class of ink rapidly dries up and becomes thick. The smallest admixture of common ink with Indian ink, such as the use of an ordinary pen upon which is dried-up common ink, will at once thicken Indian ink.

Drawing inks may be obtained in a variety of colours, which are also waterproof.

Colours and Brushes—Sometimes it will be found convenient to use watercolours for the purpose of colouring drawings to indicate various materials or different woods to be used, such as rough frameworks or backings of a common wood, and the more expensive woods, as oak, teak, mahogany, etc., that are

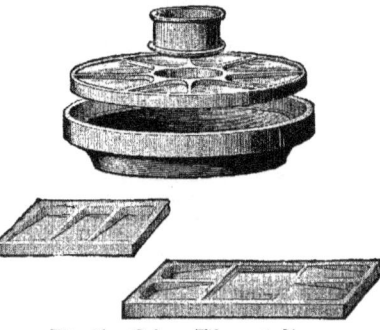

Fig. 31.—Colour Tiles and Slants

required for the parts of the work that would be exposed to view; and also to differentiate on a drawing the parts that are in section and elevation. Wood-

DRAWING FOR WOODWORKERS

workers would require the following colours: Sepia, burnt sienna, crimson lake, raw sienna, gamboge, Payne's grey and Prussian blue. With these colours many others can be made by mixing. All work shown on a drawing in section should be coloured with a much darker tone than work in elevation. It is a good principle to use one colour for one material, with variation in the tones as just stated. For instance. unwrought fir or red pine could be coloured in elevation with a light wash of raw sienna, and in sections with a dark wash. Wrought fir or red pine should be coloured with burnt sienna; oak with sepia with a little yellow; mahogany with a mixture of sepia, burnt sienna and crimson lake, and walnut with burnt sienna and sepia. Woodworkers should experiment with these colours. and it will soon be found that a satisfactory colour may be obtained by correct proportioning of the colours, for which no hard and fast rules can be given.

Colours are sold in hard cakes, in pans with the colour of a fairly hard nature, and in tubes with the colour quite soft. For practical use the writer recommends tube colours, as the required quantity can be quickly squeezed out and mixed with the proper amount of water.

Water-colour brushes are made in many sizes, with two kinds of brushes (red sable and camel hair), and with either wood or quill handles. A camel-hair brush is certainly much cheaper than a sable one, but the superiority of the latter over the former is only too evident after a trial of the two types. A sable brush is full of life, and the point of the brush can be easily worked into corners and to a line, whereas a camel-hair brush is apt to be listless and more difficult to work. A sable brush may cost six times as much as a camel-hair one, but the former should be purchased. Two sizes will be enough, " small goose " size, which has a brush length of about ⅝ in., and " middle swan," with 1¼ in. brush. The smaller size will be suitable for small work, and the larger size for colouring large surfaces. The colours should be mixed with clean water and the saucers or " slants " must also be kept clean. Fig. 31 depicts several types of tiles and slants, which are not costly. The round slant and water basin is useful, but for ordinary purposes a couple of plain slants and a cup of water will do.

With regard to the application of colour washes to drawings a little advice is necessary, as there is a right and wrong method of colouring. Never apply colour dry, or with a brush that is so devoid of colour that the hairs do not hang together with good cohesion. Keep the brush well laden and apply the colour to the paper fully (tracing cloth demands a little different treatment). Surplus colour can easily be drained off with a " dry " brush later. When small areas have to be coloured the brush may be kept a little " drier," so as to enable one to work more easily into corners.

When colouring tracing cloth which has a slightly greasy surface retarding the free flow of colouring, a little ox gall added to the colour will overcome the difficulty. It is usual to colour on the glazed side of cloth, or the opposite side on which the drawing is done.

Erasers.— Pencil erasers should be carefully chosen and should have the following qualities: Rapid erasing power, they should erase soft or hard pencil lines, and not get hard or brittle. They should not " rag " or " crumble " to a wasteful extent. As all pencil lines made for guiding or constructional purposes should be lightly made and not made with hard pencils, a soft eraser will very easily take out such lines. Guiding lines, which are afterwards pencilled over with a hard pencil, may be erased by a very soft rubber without damaging the sharpness of the final pencil lines, if great care be taken.

Ink erasers are of a different nature to pencil erasers and are hard, and partly composed of a very fine gritty substance, which makes it possible to erase ink lines by abrasion. Care should be taken in choosing a fine grained rubber, so that the surface of the paper, tracing cloth, etc., will not be damaged; care should also be taken in applying the rubber as lightly as possible, as erasure will thus be made very much more effectively than by hard pressure with the rubber.

DESCRIPTION AND USE OF SCALES

Scales are used for the purpose of representing on paper full-size articles in miniature. For instance, in preparing working drawings of any article of woodwork, it would not always be convenient to draw such articles full size, and consequently the articles are represented to a smaller size. The reduced size may be half or quarter full size, or any convenient smaller size. If, for example, a line 12 in. long is required to be shown to a quarter full size, it is manifest that the line required to be drawn will be 3 in. long, and, therefore a scale so divided and marked, indicating that every 3 in. represents 12 in., would be used.

Fig. 32 shows a very common type of scale with, at one side, what are usually known as $\frac{1}{8}$-in., $\frac{1}{4}$-in., $\frac{1}{2}$-in., and 1-in. scales, and on the other side $\frac{3}{8}$-in., $\frac{3}{4}$-in., $1\frac{1}{2}$-in. and 3-in. scales. The meaning of these figures is that, for instance, $\frac{1}{8}$ in. shown will represent one foot; or, in other words, one ninety-sixth full size; $\frac{1}{2}$ in. on the scale will mean 12 in. or one twenty-fourth full size; and $1\frac{1}{2}$ in. equals one foot or one-eighth full size, and so on.

Using the Scale.—It will be noted that the scales are marked with 0, or zero, at a certain point and the divisions then advance with equal divisions, such as 1, 2, 3, 4, and so on, in one direction, and in the other direction one division is subdivided into one-twelfth parts. Each of these one-twelfth parts equals one-twelfth of a foot, i.e. 1 in. The use of the scales is simple and is best illustrated by Fig. 33, which shows a simple line, on which it is required to find a length, assuming that the scale is $\frac{1}{2}$ in. to 1 ft. Upon placing the scale on the line with 0 at B it will be found that the line is more than 5 ft. long, and by so placing 0 at B, which is the wrong method, the end of the line at A falls at a point between 5 and 6 on the scale, where no definite division is shown. To correctly use the scale, the 5 should be

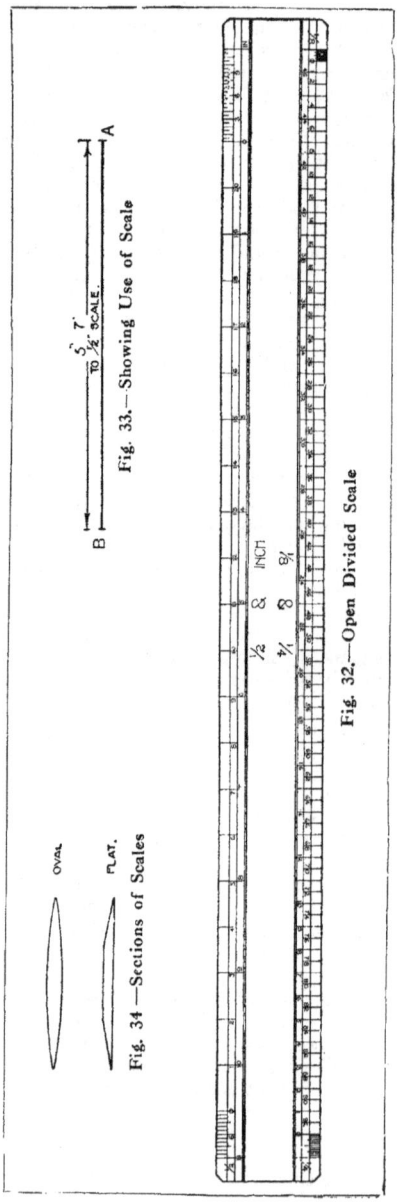

Fig. 33.—Showing Use of Scale

Fig. 34.—Sections of Scales

Fig. 32.—Open Divided Scale

DRAWING FOR WOODWORKERS

placed at A, and it will then be found that 5 ft. 7 in. is correctly read.

Open Divided Scale.—The type of scale shown by Fig. 32 is what is known as an open divided scale; that is to say, all the divisions, such as from 0 to 1 and 1 to 2 and so on, are not subdivided into twelfths, as before explained. If the scale is so divided, it is known as close divided. In the writer's opinion, an open divided scale is to be preferred, as it is not so confusing.

Scales may be purchased in cheap cardboard sets, or of boxwood or ivory. Boxwood scales are to be preferred to cardboard scales, the edges of which soon wear out. The edges of scales should not be used for cutting or ripping paper, as by so doing the divisions are quickly eradicated. A useful section of boxwood or ivory scale is oval, as shown by Fig. 34. In some cases the scales are on one side only, in which case the section is flat on one side and flat and bevelled on the other, the scales being on the latter side.

EXAMPLES OF DRAWING

Figs. 35 and 36 indicate methods of drawing plane figures. The correct methods of using the various instruments, etc., have been previously described. After settling upon the scale most suitable for drawing these articles, the next matter is the correct way to set out the work. On Figs. 35 and 36 are shown small numerals, and if the various lines are drawn out in sequence of these numerals the correct method of setting up the articles illustrated will be obtained, although the principles of practical draughtsmanship may deem necessary, in certain cases,

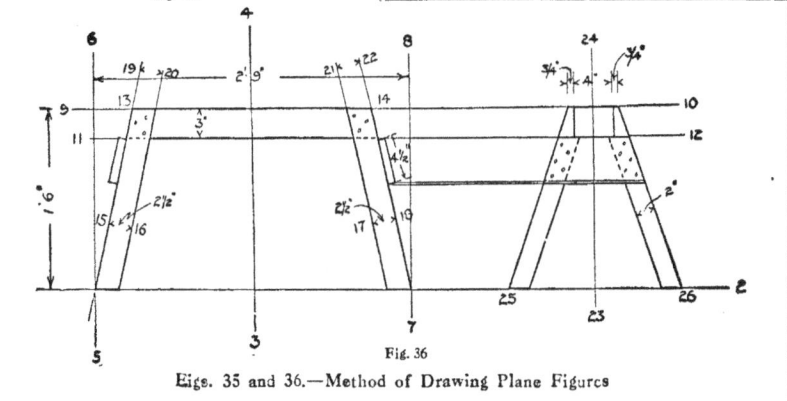

Figs. 35 and 36.—Method of Drawing Plane Figures

slight modifications. The chief thing to aim at, especially in symmetrical figures, is first to draw a base line and then a main centre line. It is assumed that it is the intention first to pencil the drawing and afterwards to line in, either in pencil or ink. For this purpose a soft pencil should be lightly used, and it is not necessary, in the preliminary setting up, to confine the length of the lines to any definite point, but to run them through in what may be termed a fearless manner. By so doing a certain practical advantage will be obtained, as, for example, when the horizontal lines are being completed, either in pencil or ink, any vertical lines that are " run through " will act as guides to indicate the correct points where such finished lines are to stop. After the drawing is lined in the superfluous lines may be erased—this demands care where the lining in is done in pencil, but in the case of ink lines they may be erased all over to eradicate the pencil lines.

Freehand Drawing of Mouldings, etc. — Whilst in connection with the ancient Grecian and Roman buildings the mouldings were definitely characteristic of each class, and (with the Grecian) all profiles or contours consisted of conic sections or (with the Romans) were formed of portions of true circles, a strict adherence to the proportions of these ancient prototypes is not usual in modern practice. The original custom was undoubtedly to develop all mouldings upon strictly geometrical and mathematical lines, a process especially called for in connection with Grecian sections, but not now usually adopted except with buildings of monumental character.

As each " period " in architecture has been remarkable for its mouldings as well as general massing, proportions and general features, so our present time is remarkable for the extreme diversity and freedom from application of any strict rules or restraints in the design of mouldings, a careful study of our best modern examples undoubtedly revealing the fact that nearly all sections are those of evolution, the outcome of a process of freehand sketching and development.

For the reason that the satisfactory appearance of mouldings chiefly consists in a wise distribution of lights and shadows and in gradations thereof by the formation of curves, it is suggested that, in view of the present need for extreme economy in all directions, a reliance be placed almost solely upon such aggregation of moulding members as are of a rectangular or square form on section, the curves, owing to expense, being very sparingly introduced, and particularly that all be *evolved* or developed upon *freehand* principles.

A few examples of mouldings as Fig. 37 are suggested as explanatory of this suggestion, and, as such are intended chiefly for execution in wood, attention is drawn to the expediency of making all curved members as hollow as possible so as to economise in material, such preferably being worked out of minimum thickness boards or scantlings. Attention may be drawn to the frequent advisability of designing the members of rectangular form with the upright and horizontal lines slightly " out of the true " as being an easy and cheap means of giving character to a combination, more particularly in connection, as shown, with the frieze member of an entablature combination.

In the process of the advised freehand principle of evolution or development it is well to use the cross-ruled or sectional paper as indicated, any slight deviation from the true verticals or horizontals being immediately apparent and any enlargement or reduction of the moulded group of members being then quite easy by means of redrawing on paper or setting-out board ruled into equal number of squares or divisions of larger or smaller size.

Other types of mouldings are shown by Figs. 38 and 39, and more are illustrated later on.

GENERAL ARRANGEMENT OF DRAWINGS

There is a certain knack in arranging a drawing on a sheet of paper and also in preventing waste likely to accrue by using either a larger sheet than is required

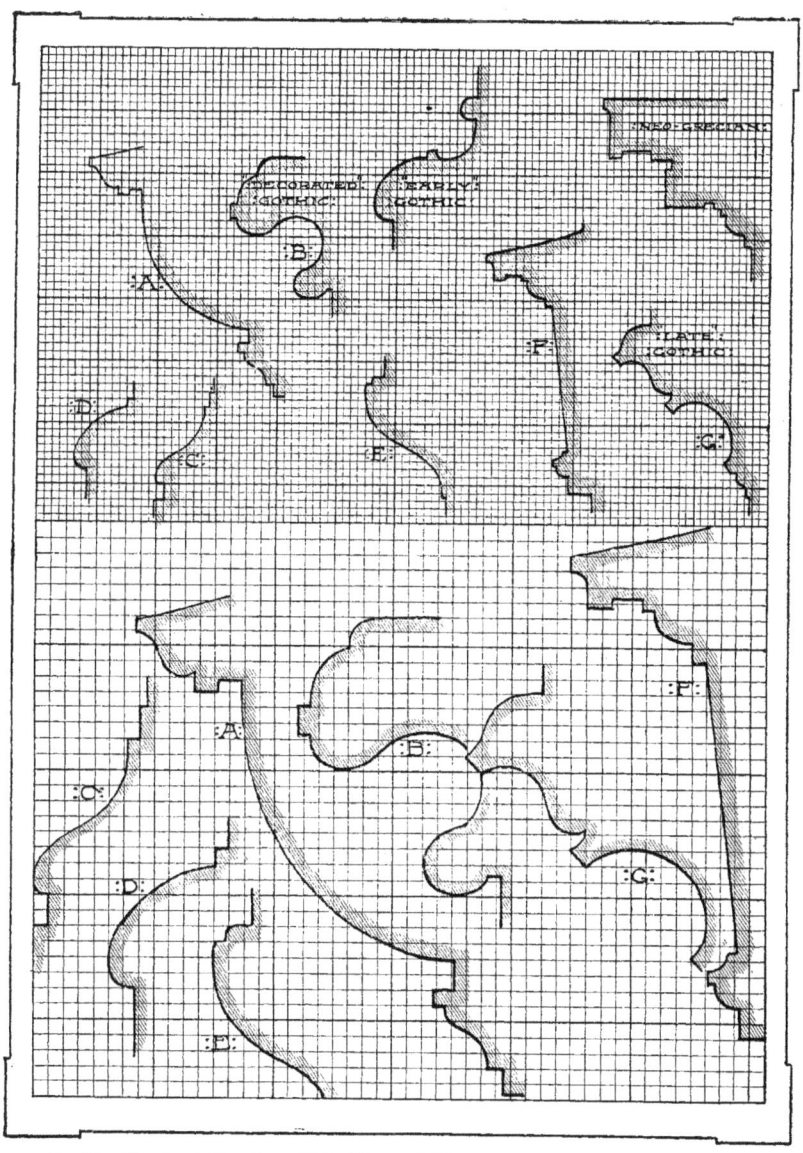

Fig. 37.—Freehand Drawing of Moulding and Method of Doubling or Halving Sizes

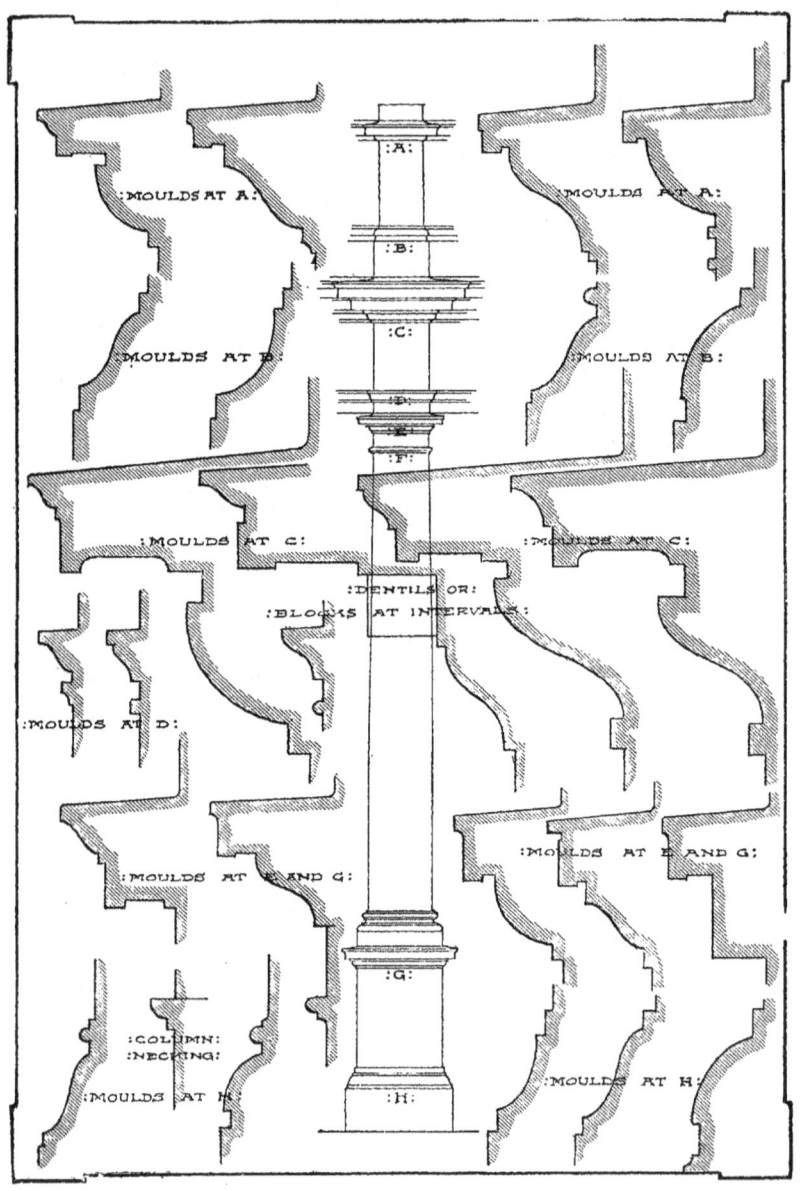

Fig. 38.—Examples of Mouldings for Execution in Wood

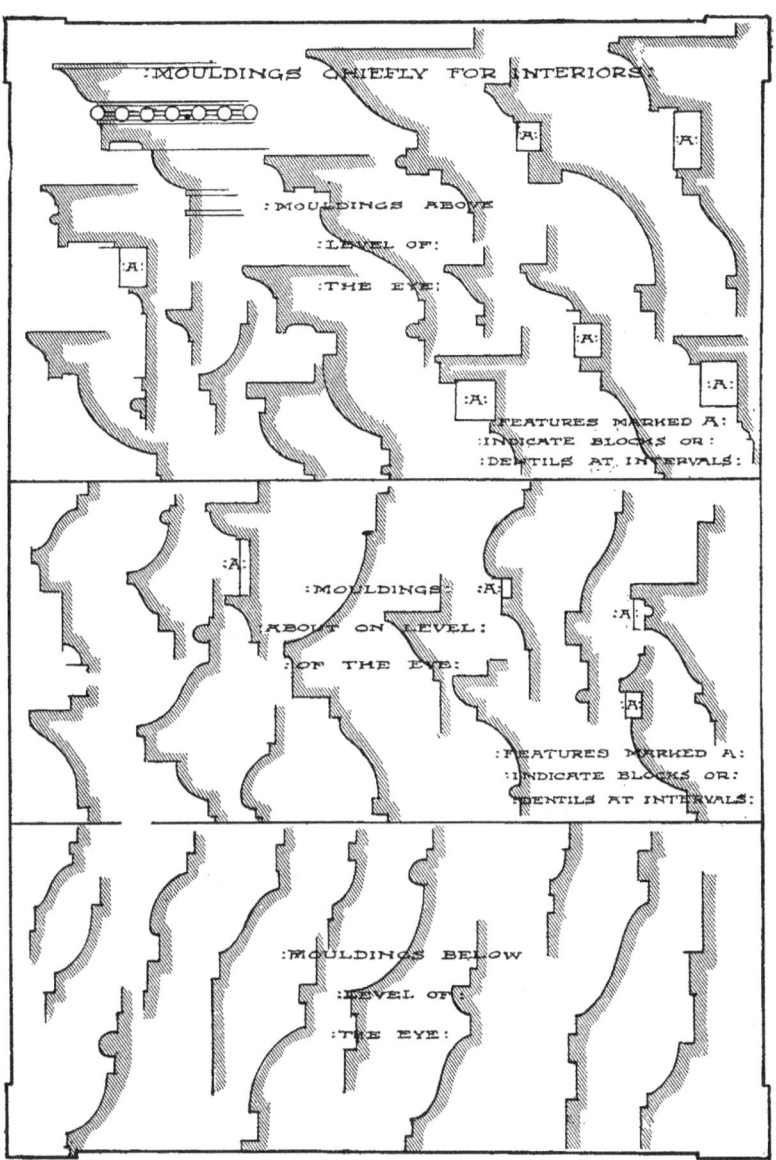

Fig. 39.—Examples of Mouldings for Execution in Wood

or a sheet too small—which may be found so after the drawing is well under way—due to some miscalculation as to the number of items to be shown on such drawing. For these reasons, before paper is cut off from a roll, or, say, whole sheets cut up for use, it is essential that practical consideration be given as to what size sheet will be found that this can be done in a few minutes, and it often saves time and paper.

An Arranged Example.—Fig. 40 depicts an easy arrangement of a drawing indicating designs for a simple larder shelf. It will be noted that the elevation is on the left-hand top portion of the sheet, with the plan immediately underneath, by

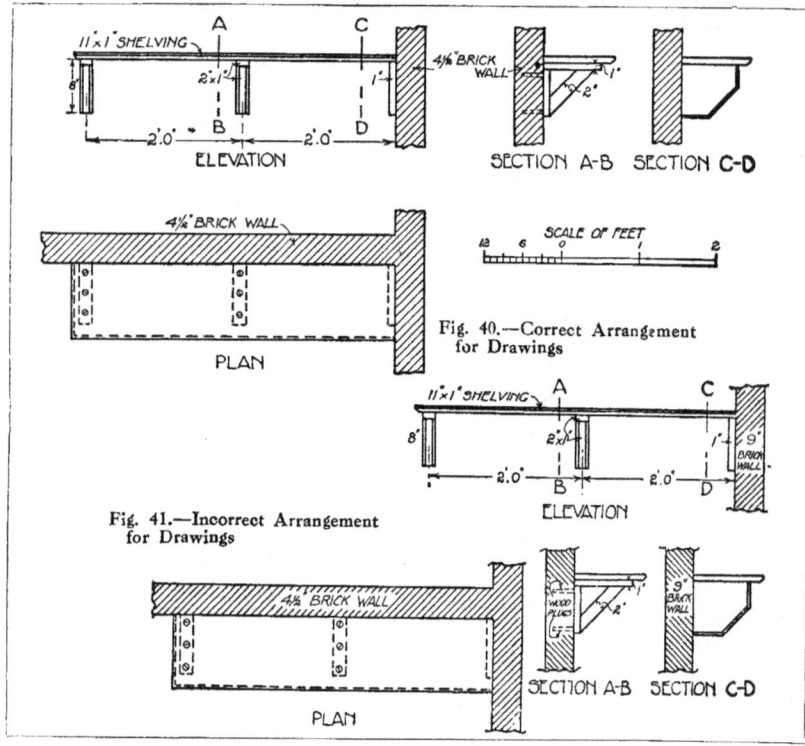

Fig. 40.—Correct Arrangement for Drawings

Fig. 41.—Incorrect Arrangement for Drawings

necessary. At the commencement of the drawing it is, of course, known what is required to be drawn, and the scale to which it is to be drawn must be considered. A good principle, which many draughtsmen adopt, is to take a scrap of wastepaper and roughly set out on it the position of the various items to be drawn and very approximately calculate their area. After a little experience it will be which arrangement the vertical lines of the elevation can be transferred to the plan, or vice versa; and vertical sections are shown on the right-hand top portion of the drawing, which arrangement allows for the horizontal lines of the elevation to be transferred across to such sections. The title, sub-heading, and any other particulars of the drawing may be placed in the right-hand bottom corner, as shown.

Fig. 41 depicts a bad arrangement of the drawings of the same article as Fig. 40.

Large Drawings.—The drawing shown by Fig. 40 may be termed a general drawing. In addition, practical woodworking draughtsmen would probably be called upon to prepare large-scale or full-size details, in which case a little modification of the principle of setting out general drawings will be necessary. A general drawing is often required to be filed after use, for future reference; but the detail drawings, although it is best, if possible, to keep a copy, are often only required for a short time and may be afterwards destroyed. Under these circumstances such details could be prepared on cheap rough paper, such as a very cheap detail paper, the backs of old discarded drawings or blue prints, etc., or even on lining or odd ends of wall-paper. Consequently, the question of the general arrangements of these drawings is not so important as in the case of general drawings, or those to be kept for reference. Again, practice often calls for mere sketches, such as would be prepared to illustrate any particular point in the workshop or during conversation with a craftsman who is preparing the article of woodwork for which such sketch may be required. These sketches may be prepared on any scrap paper.

OAK MEMORIAL TABLET AT SAINT PETERS

THE PRACTICAL WOODWORKER

TITLES FOR LETTERING

Fig. 42.—Types of Lettering for Drawings

ABCDEFGHIJKLMNOPQRSTUVWXYZ.

PLAN - SECTION - ELEVATION :

: ABCDEFGHIJKLMNOPQRSTUVWXYZ :

THE TYPES & SIZES OF LETTERING SHOWN ABOVE ARE SUITABLE FOR SUB HEADINGS, AND ALSO MAY BE USED FOR HEADINGS ON SMALL DRAWINGS. THE SINGLE LINE LETTERING IS SIMPLE & SHOULD BE USED FOR ALL PRACTICAL DRAWINGS & PURPOSES. THE OTHER TYPE FOR IMPORTANT DRAWINGS, ETC. IT IS IMPORTANT TO CONFORM WITH THE PRINCIPALS STATED BELOW ABOUT SLOPING & VERTICAL PRINTING

Fig. 43.

ABCDEFGHIJKLMNOPQRSTUVWXYZ   1234567890
ABCDEFGHIJKLMNOPQRSTUVWXYZ   1234567890
ABCDEFGHIJKLMNOPQRSTUVWXYZ   1234567890
abcdefghijklmnopqrstuvwxyz

THIS TYPE OF LETTERING IS SIMPLE AND QUICKLY FORMED AFTER A LITTLE PRACTICE ~ THE SLOPING LINES SHOULD BE MADE WITH A UNIFORM SLOPE & THE HORIZONTAL LINES MADE TO FOLLOW THE GUIDING LINES THUS. FOR PRACTICE PURPOSES SLOPING GUIDING LINES IN PENCIL MAY BE MADE THUS: ////////

Fi 44.

THIS VERTICAL LETTERING IS NOT QUITE SO EASY TO FORM AS THE SLOPING TYPE AND TO LOOK EFFECTIVE THE VERTICAL LINES MUST BE VERTICAL. NOT CARELESSLY FORMED AS SHOWN IN THIS LINE

THIS TYPE TAKES LONGER TO FORM THAN THE ABOVE, BUT EFFECTIVE. IN ALL THE ABOVE TYPES CAPITAL LETTERS MAY BE MADE LARGER AS SHOWN IN THESE TWO LINES OF LETTERING
EXAMPLES OF FIGURING DIMENSIONS –   2.½"   5'.6¾"   8'.0¼"   ETC

Fig. 45.

Figs. 43, 44 and 45.—Types of Smaller Lettering for Drawings

DRAWING FOR WOODWORKERS

LETTERING OR PRINTING FOR DRAWINGS

Fig. 42 to 45 indicate types of printing suitable for woodworkers. Fig. 42 shows various types suitable for headings and sub-headings of important drawings. Fig. 44 shows types of printing or lettering suitable for less important drawings, and printing which may be quickly done after a little practice, and Fig. 45 shows various types of single-line printing which may be done very quickly, and which may be used for headings, sub-headings and annotations on practical drawings where academical printing is not necessary.

The size of the lettering depends generally upon the size and scale to which the drawing is executed, and as a general rule there should only be three or four sizes of printing, i.e. one size for headings, another for sub-headings, a small type for general annotations, and, possibly, a fourth size for small printing, such as may be necessary in the description of the drawing number, etc.

ACADEMIC OR EXACT DRAUGHTSMANSHIP

Remarks have been made regarding principles of drawing that depend upon the use to which the drawing is to be put. Assuming that the woodworker has no knowledge whatever of drawing, but has fully studied the descriptions and practised the use of the T-square, etc., and various instruments and other mechanical aids to drawing, it is then necessary to impress the fact that it is best to be "slow and sure" and to be accurate and neat with the elementary studies of draughtsmanship. Students should not start away with the impression that drawing is very simple, there being many knacks and good habits to be cultivated, the advantage of which will be manifested at a later stage. The drawing of very simple figures should be commenced, after simple horizontal, vertical and diagonal lines have been drawn, in accordance with the descriptions given previously. It is far better to commence with a simple drawing, as of a few geometrical figures, and obtain a pleasing result than to start on some elaborate and complicated drawing which may be troublesome to the beginner and cause discouragement at the start. If simple drawing has been mastered and perfection attained, more elaborate drawings, and probably a few details, may be attempted, such as, for instance, a drawing showing details of a plain table, then, say, a plain cabinet, with a few mouldings. After such things have been drawn out successfully, the student may then be assured that he is in a position efficiently to make almost any drawing, excepting perhaps those entailing much curved, or what may be termed artistic or figure, work. The first few months of study should be devoted to neat and correct work, and then (after all the principles are well understood and mastered) little liberties may be taken, in such a manner that although the drawing may not be exact, as in scale, it would at the same time give a correct description of what is required. There are many draughtsmen who can or will only work to one standard. There are others, who may be termed practical draughtsmen, who are capable of "getting out" a drawing in a very short time, which may be all that is needed, and are capable, at the same time, of preparing highly finished drawings when such are essential. Practical draughtsmanship should be sought.

HOW TO READ DRAWINGS

There is quite as much art in preparing drawings so as to make them easily readable or comprehensible to others, and also in reading drawings, as there is in reading letterpress. The fundamental principle in the preparation of any drawing is to bear in mind that it is to be read and understood by others, and also that while all, or certain parts of it, may be quite obvious to the draughtsman who draws it, it may not be so to the person who has to read or work from it. Therefore, it is essential to make a drawing as clear and concise as possible.

The general arrangement of drawings on paper has been previously dealt with, from which it should be understood that all the parts of the drawing should be relative to each other. For instance, the plans, elevations and section or sections should be so drawn as to allow them to be contiguous, so that there will be no more necessity than is essential of jumping from one point of the drawing to another to understand the full meanings indicated by such drawings.

The general drawings should be nicely grouped together if possible on one sheet, and also, if it is possible and convenient, the large-scale details that may be required should be placed on the same sheet, or as many of them as possible, and such details should be clearly marked with corresponding marks or section lines on the general drawings, so as to allow for speedy reference. When preparing detail drawings many draughtsmen are apt to run one detail into another. This should be avoided as a general rule, as, although it may save a little paper, it may cause confusion to the woodworker who has to work from such drawing.

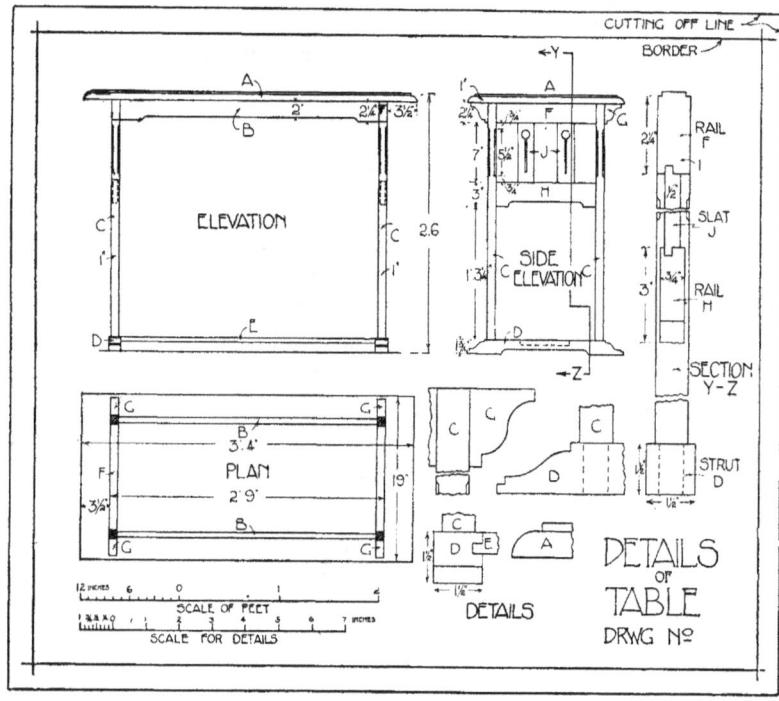

Fig. 46.—Typical Set of General Drawings Correctly Arranged

Fig. 46 illustrates a set of general drawings and details of a table arranged properly on the drawing paper, and a careful perusal of the general arrangement of the drawings and details on the sheet will make manifest the principles given above. Fig. 47 illustrates what may be termed a muddled drawing of the general drawings and full-size details of a veranda for a bungalow.

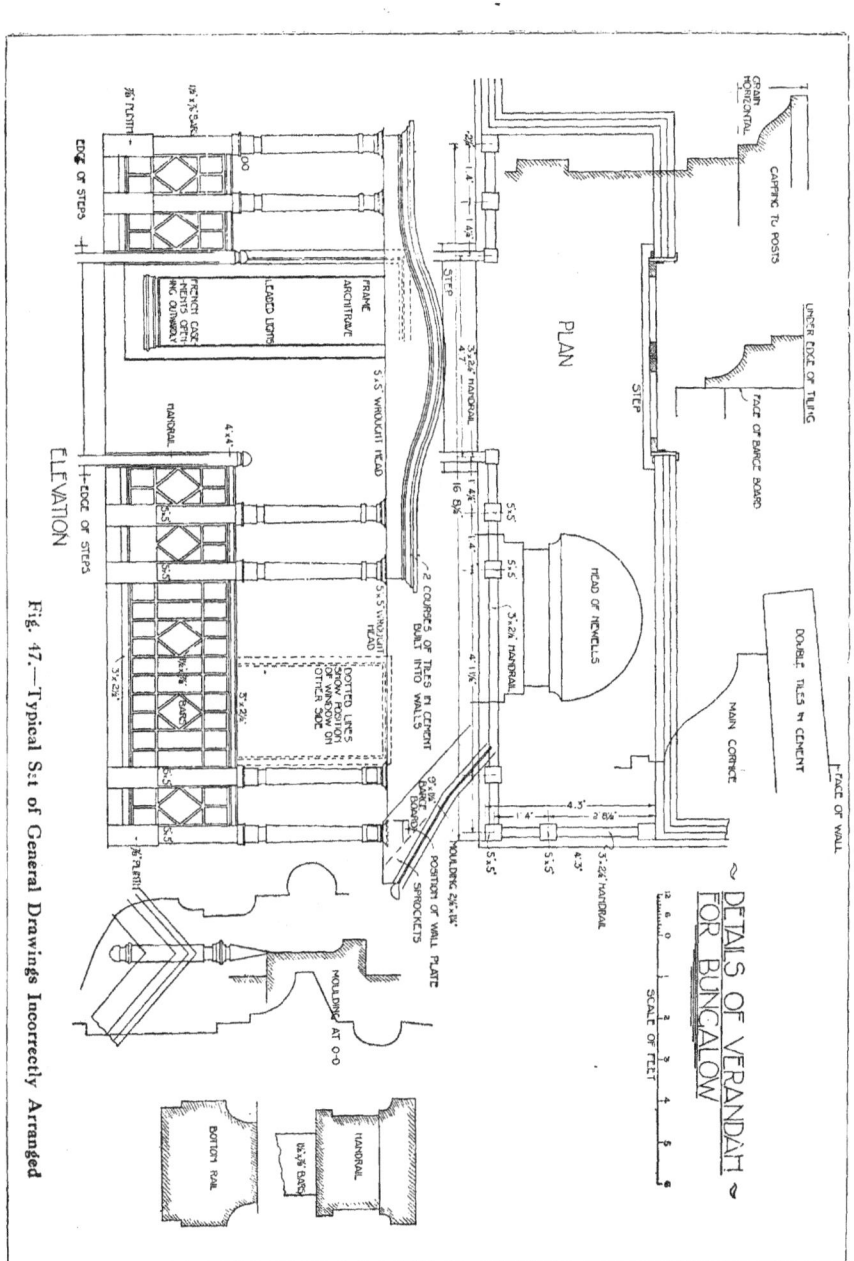

Fig. 47.—Typical Set of General Drawings Incorrectly Arranged

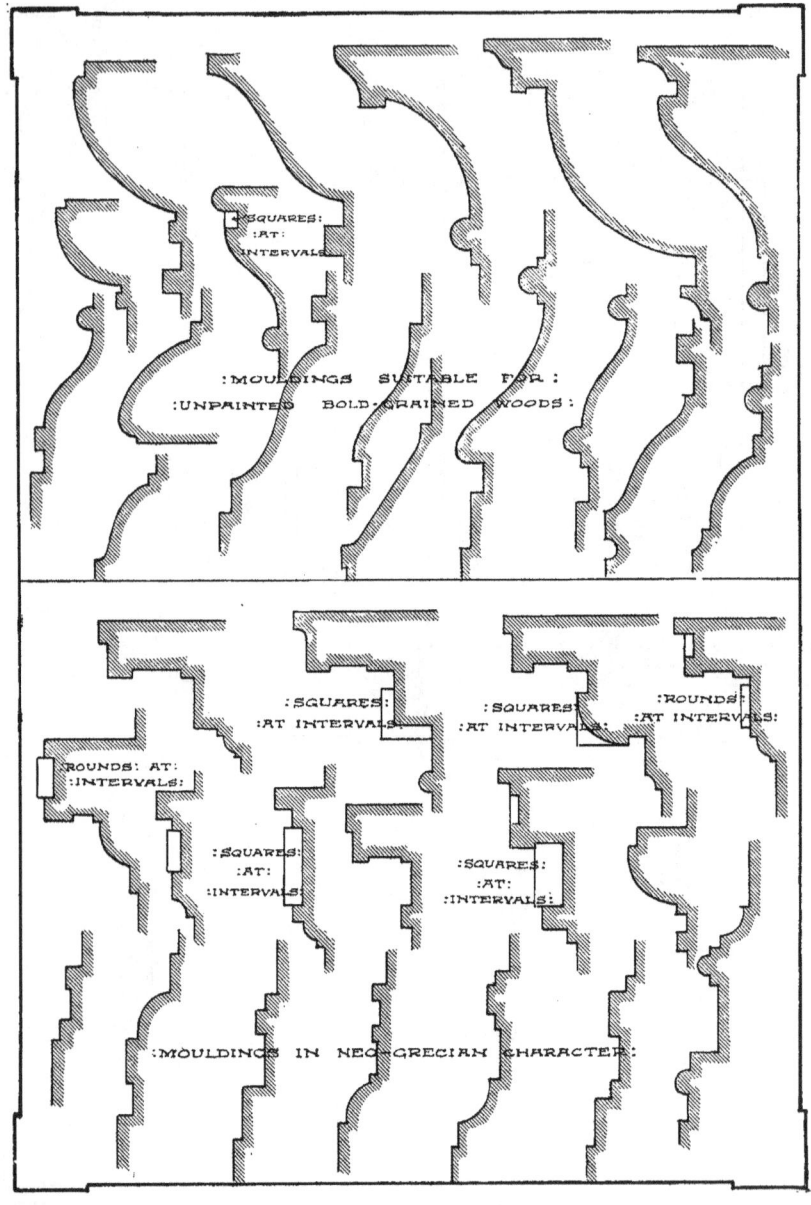

Fig. 48.—Examples of Mouldings for Execution in Wood

DRAWING FOR WOODWORKERS

A perusal of Figs. 46 and 47 will make quite clear the difference between the two methods of draughtsmanship.

Further examples of mouldings are shown by Fig. 48, and still more on page 1541.

ELEMENTARY PLANE GEOMETRY

Plane geometry is that connected with surfaces only, and not solid figures, such as, for instance, cubes, which come under the heading of solid geometry. An elementary knowledge of plane geometry is necessary for woodworkers, as it embraces the setting out of angles, polygons, circles, ellipses and various other figures. Only simple plane geometry will be described in this section, but sufficient will be given to meet the ordinary requirements of the practical woodworker.

Bisection of Lines.—Fig. 49 shows a line AB, which is required to be divided into two equal parts. Place the steel point of the compass at A; open the compass until the distance between the points is considerably more than half the length of the line AB, such as to point a. Then form part of the circle CD, with the steel point still in A. Similarly form another part circle EF with the steel point in B. Draw a line from G to H, which will bisect the line AB.

To Erect a Perpendicular Line.—To erect a line at right angles to another line at the end of the line as AB in Fig. 50. Place the steel point of the compass at C at any point above the line; extend the pencil point of the compass until it reaches B and strike a part circle cutting the line AB in the point D. Then a line drawn from D and passing through C until it meets the arc at E will give, if the line be drawn from B to E, the required perpendicular line.

To Draw a Line Perpendicular to AB from a Point such as at C lying away from the Line.—From C (Fig. 51) with a radius rather shorter than from C to B, draw an arc cutting AB in the points D and E. From D and E, with any radius, draw arcs cutting each other in F. A line drawn from C to F will be perpendicular to AB.

Perpendiculars by the 3, 4 and 5 Method.—Taking Fig. 52 it is required to form the line CB perpendicular to AB. AB is to be made equal to three units, and the compass placed with the steel point in A, and the points extended so that they are spaced apart equal to five units, and a short arc described at C; then take the steel point of the compass, place in B and extend to four units, striking an arc at C. A line drawn from B to the intersection of such arcs will be perpendicular to AB.

Measurement of Angles.—An angle is formed when two straight lines meet, as shown by Fig. 53, which depicts O as the corner, or apex, and OA and OB the arms, or bounding lines, of the angle. The angle is usually indicated by labelling the angular space, as at C. Any angle possesses magnitude, and is measured in degrees. It is usual to adopt, as the unit angle, not a whole revolution, but a one-three hundred and sixtieth part of a revolution, which is called "one degree," and written thus, 1°. One complete revolution contains 360 degrees. Fig. 54 shows a circular protractor, which is used for the measurement and setting out of angles, the protractor being transparent. For instance, if it is required to find what angle the dotted line marked B at Fig. 54 is to the dotted line marked A, the centre of the protractor would be placed at the apex, with the horizontal line of the protractor set on, and exactly coinciding with, the dotted line A, and the angle would then be measured, and which is, in this case, 45° as shown.

The protractor shown by Fig. 54 is one of the simplest, and is marked from zero to 90° from both ends. This type of protractor is figured in a similar manner as the rectangular protractor shown by Fig. 55, on which it will be noted that angles from zero to 180° from either end may be measured. The rectangular protractor is used in a similar manner to the circular protractor, the centre being as shown. In addition to angles, this protractor contains several scales.

Obtuse and Acute Angles, etc., are shown by Fig. 56.

Complementary angles are such as

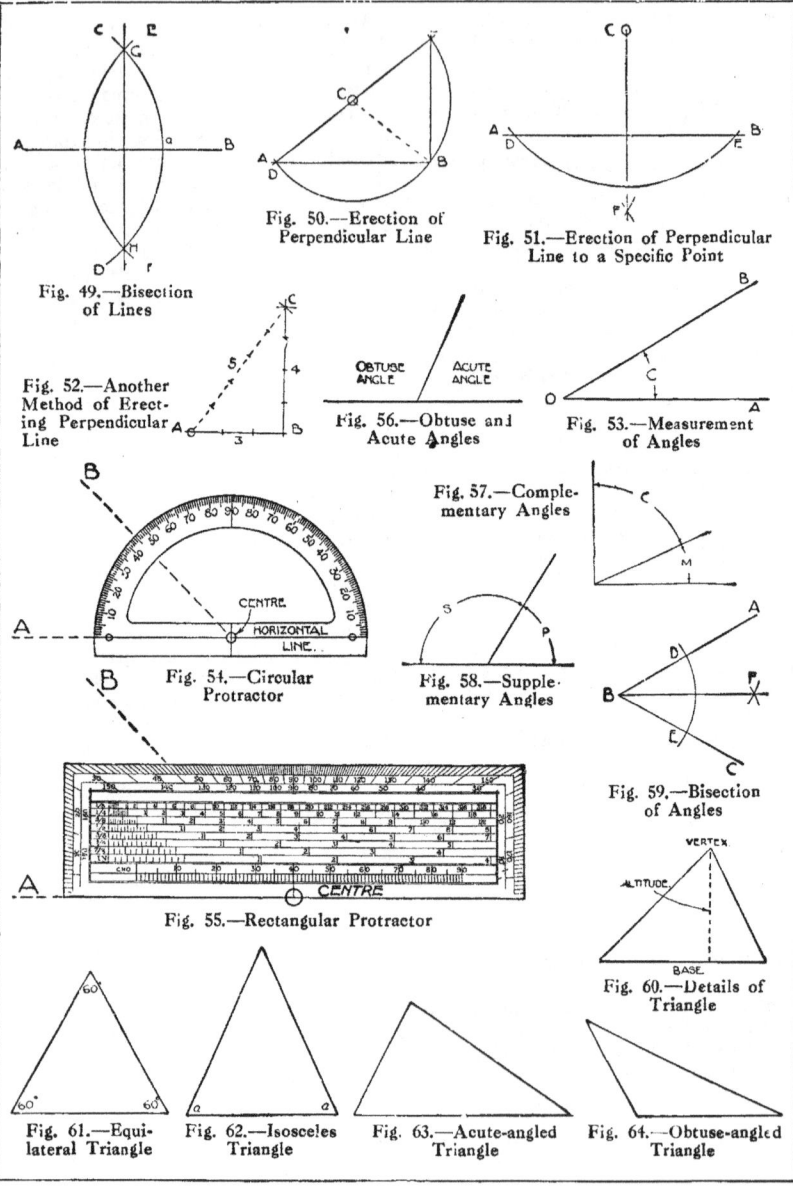

Fig. 49.—Bisection of Lines

Fig. 50.—Erection of Perpendicular Line

Fig. 51.—Erection of Perpendicular Line to a Specific Point

Fig. 52.—Another Method of Erecting Perpendicular Line

Fig. 56.—Obtuse and Acute Angles

Fig. 53.—Measurement of Angles

Fig. 54.—Circular Protractor

Fig. 57.—Complementary Angles

Fig. 58.—Supplementary Angles

Fig. 59.—Bisection of Angles

Fig. 55.—Rectangular Protractor

Fig. 60.—Details of Triangle

Fig. 61.—Equilateral Triangle

Fig. 62.—Isosceles Triangle

Fig. 63.—Acute-angled Triangle

Fig. 64.—Obtuse-angled Triangle

DRAWING FOR WOODWORKERS

shown by Fig. 57. Angles are complementary when their sum is 90° and one angle is the complement of the other. In the figure, C + M = 90°, C = 90° − M, and M = 90° − C.

Supplementary angles are such as shown by Fig. 58, where their sum equals 180° and either angle is the supplement of the other. S + P = 180°, S = 180° − P, and P = 180° − S.

Bisection of Angles as ABC.—From B (Fig. 59) describe an arc with any radius cutting the lines BA and BC at D and E. From D and E describe arcs of any radius cutting each other at E. A line drawn from B to F will bisect the angle.

Triangles.—Fig. 60 illustrates a triangle, which is a plane figure bounded by three straight lines, called its sides, meeting at three points, each of which is a vertex, or corner. In a triangle there are three angles, formed by the sides when taken in pairs. Any side of the triangle may be its base, in which case the opposite corner is called the vertex, and a perpendicular from the vertex to the base is called the altitude. These parts are shown by Fig. 60. Various triangles are as follows:

Equilateral triangles have all their sides and angles equal, as Fig. 61.

An isosceles triangle has two sides equal, as shown by Fig. 62.

An acute-angled triangle has three acute angles, as Fig. 63.

An obtuse-angled triangle has one obtuse angle, as Fig. 64.

Right-angled triangles have one right angle, as Fig. 65. The side opposite the right angle is the hypotenuse.

One of the most important theorems in elementary geometry is that "the square of the hypotenuse of a right-angled triangle is equal to the sum of the squares on the two sides containing the right angle," this being illustrated by Fig. 66. Mathematically, this theorem may be given as follows, the numerals being those as shown by Fig. 66:—

$$3^2 + 4^2 = 5^2$$
$$= 9 + 16 = 25.$$

or—

$$3^2 = 5^2 - 4^2$$
$$= 9 = 25 - 16.$$

or—

$$4^2 = 5^2 - 3^2$$
$$= 16 = 25 - 9.$$

Constructing Right-angled Triangles.—In the construction of right-angled triangles there are nine cases of how to draw or solve them if any two independent elements are given. There are five elements, exclusive of the right angle, viz., the base a; the altitude or height b; the hypotenuse c; the base angle B, and the vertical angle A, all of which are shown by Fig. 67.

Case 1.—Given the base and height (Fig. 68), make the base BC = $4\frac{1}{2}$ in. and the perpendicular CA $2\frac{3}{4}$ in. Join AB.

Case 2.—Given the base and hypotenuse (Fig. 69), make the base BC $1\frac{3}{4}$ in. and draw a perpendicular from C. With the centre at B, with the compasses set to a radius of 2 in. cut this perpendicular at A, then join AB.

Case 3.—Given the height and hypotenuse (Fig. 70), draw a base line and then a perpendicular CA 3 in. long. With centre A, radius 5 in., cut base at B. Join AB.

Case 4.—Given the base and base angle (Fig. 71), draw base BC $3\frac{1}{2}$ in. long and a perpendicular from C. Draw BA, making 40° with BC.

Case 5.—Given the height and base angle (Fig. 72), draw the base line and the line parallel to it at a distance of $1\frac{3}{4}$ in. Draw the hypotenuse at an angle of 30° with the base, and cutting the parallel at A. Draw the perpendicular AC.

Case 6.—Given the hypotenuse and base angle (Fig. 73), draw the base line, then the hypotenuse BA at an angle of 35° with the base and 4 in. long. Draw the perpendicular AC.

Case 7.—Given the base and vertical angle (Fig. 74), draw the base BC $4\frac{1}{4}$ in. long and draw a perpendicular at C. Draw the hypotenuse BA, making 90° − 60° = 30° with BC.

Case 8.—Given the height and vertical angle (Fig. 75), draw the base line and

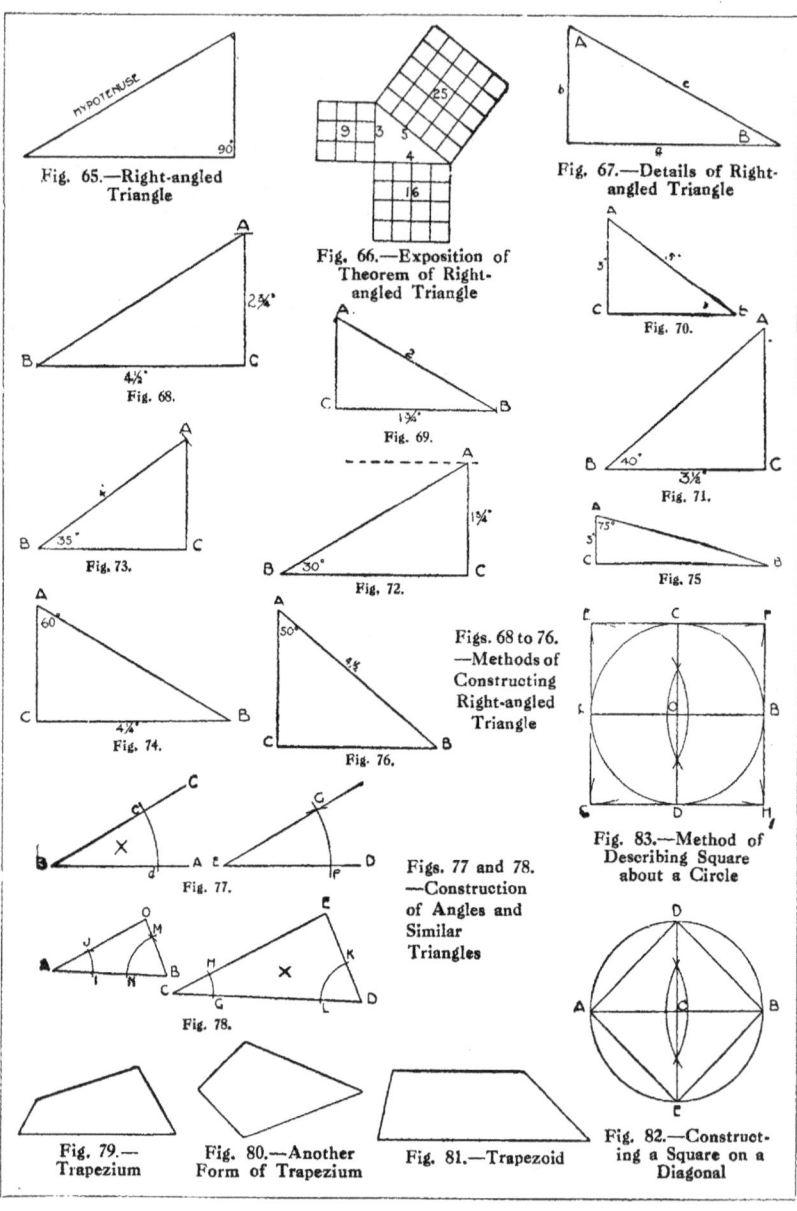

Fig. 65.—Right-angled Triangle

Fig. 66.—Exposition of Theorem of Right-angled Triangle

Fig. 67.—Details of Right-angled Triangle

Figs. 68 to 76.—Methods of Constructing Right-angled Triangle

Figs. 77 and 78.—Construction of Angles and Similar Triangles

Fig. 79.—Trapezium

Fig. 80.—Another Form of Trapezium

Fig. 81.—Trapezoid

Fig. 82.—Constructing a Square on a Diagonal

Fig. 83.—Method of Describing Square about a Circle

DRAWING FOR WOODWORKERS

perpendicular CA 3 in. long. Then draw the hypotenuse AB, making 75° with AC.

Case 9.—Given the hypotenuse and vertical angle (Fig. 76), draw a vertical line and then a line AB, making 50° with it and 4½ in. long. Draw the base BC.

Construction of Angles and similar Triangles.—Fig. 77 depicts at X an angle which it is required to reproduce. From B, with any radius, describe an arc cutting the sides of the angle in cd. From E, with the same radius, describe an arc cutting ED at F. Then measure the length from the point c to d. Then mark off the same length on the arc from F to point G, and the angle FEG will be equal to ABC.

At X (Fig. 78) is shown a triangle which is required to be reproduced to, say, a smaller scale. At A construct an angle similar to the angle HCG at JAI, in the same manner as described above. At B construct an angle similar to the angle KDL at MBN. Then produce the lines AJ and BM until they meet at O, which will complete the required triangle.

Four-sided Figures.—A *Trapezium* is a four-sided figure, of which none of the sides are equal or parallel to each other, as shown by Fig. 79. The trapezium may have two of its adjacent sides equal to each other, provided that they are not parallel to the opposite sides, as Fig. 80.

A *Trapezoid* is a four-sided figure with two of its sides parallel to each other, as Fig. 81.

A *Square* has four equal sides and all its angles are right angles.

To Construct a Square on a Given Diagonal.—Bisect the diagonal line AB (Fig. 82) and obtain the point c. Then from c, with radius CA, describe a circle cutting the bisecting line in D and E. Draw AD, DB, BE, EA, which will construct the square required.

To Describe a Square about a Circle.—Draw two diameters (which are lines drawn across the circle and passing through its centre), AB and CD (Fig. 83), at right angles to each other. From A and C, with radius equal to the radius of the circle (radius equals the distance from the centre of a circle to its periphery), describe arcs cutting each other at E. From C and B, with the same radius, describe arcs cutting each other in F, and then from A and D, with the same radius, describe arcs cutting each other in G. From D and B, describe arcs cutting each other in H. To complete the square, draw EF, FH, HG and GE.

Quadrilaterals are any figures with four straight sides.

A *Parallelogram* (Fig. 84) is a quadrilateral in which the opposite sides are parallel.

A *Rhombus* (Fig. 85) has all its sides of equal length, and is different from a rectangle inasmuch that its angles are not right angles.

A *Rectangle* (Fig. 86) has all its angles equal, and each is 90°, or a right angle. It differs from a square, which has all its sides and angles equal.

Polygons.—Polygons are figures which have more than four sides, and are distinguished and constructed as follows :—

A *Pentagon* is a five-sided polygon (Fig. 87) which indicates a regular pentagon, that is, one having its sides of equal length. It may be constructed as follows : Form base AB, equal in length to one of the sides of the pentagon, and produce AB on each side. From A, with radius AB, describe a semicircle cutting AB produced at C. Divide the semicircle into five equal parts. From A draw AD to the second division, and from B, with radius BA, describe a semicircle cutting AB, produced in E. From E mark on this semicircle the same length of arc as CD, obtaining F. With radius AB, and from D and F, describe arcs cutting each other at G. Draw DG and FG, which will complete a pentagon.

To Inscribe a Regular Pentagon in a Given Circle.—Draw diameter AB (Fig. 88) and divide it into five equal parts. From A and B, with radius AB, describe arcs cutting each other at C, and from C draw a line passing through the second division, cutting the circle at D. Draw DB, which will form one side of the pentagon. Set off the length DB round the circle to EFG, and complete the pentagon by joining these points.

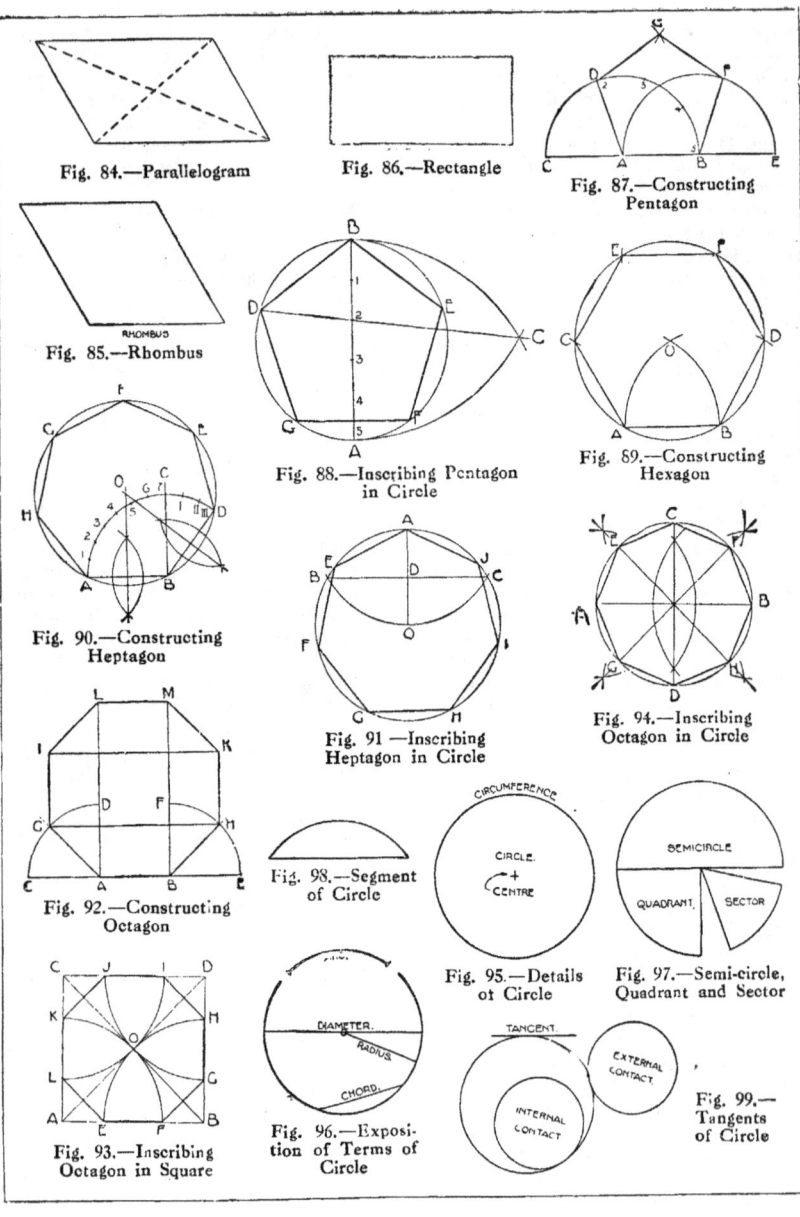

DRAWING FOR WOODWORKERS

Any polygon, other than the pentagon, may be formed by dividing the diameter into a number of parts corresponding with the sides in the required polygon, but in such cases CD must be drawn from the second division in every case.

A *Hexagon* is a six-sided polygon (Fig. 89) which indicates a regular hexagon, and may be constructed as follows: With A and B as centres describe arcs cutting each other at O. With the same radius O A) describe a circle and divide it into six equal parts around the circle, using radius A, as from A to C, C to E, E to F, F to D, and to B, and the hexagon may be completed by joining these points with straight lines.

A *Heptagon* is a seven-sided polygon Fig. 90), and may be constructed as follows: Draw a line AB and erect a perpendicular at B; draw the quadrant AC, and divide it into seven equal parts. Continue the arc AC to about D, and set off on it from C three divisions equal to the divisions in AC, and form the point D. Then draw BD and bisect AB and BD. and from the intersection O of the bisecting line describe a circle with radius OA. From A and B set off the length AB around the circle, that is EFGH, and join the various points to complete the heptagon.

To Inscribe a Regular Heptagon in a Given Circle.—With the radius of the circle, and from any point, A (Fig. 91), describe arcs cutting the circumference in B and C. Draw the line BC, which will be bisected by the radius AO at D. From A set off the length DB round the circle, and join the points AEFGHIJ, which will complete the heptagon.

An *Octagon* is an eight-sided polygon Fig. 92), and may be constructed as follows: Produce AB on each side and erect perpendiculars at A and B. From A and B, with radius AB, describe quadrants CD and EF. Bisect these quadrants, which will give AG and BH as two more sides of the octagon. At H and G draw perpendiculars GI and HK, equal to AB, and then draw GH and IK. Make the perpendiculars A and B equal to GH or IK, viz., IL and BM. The octagon may be completed by drawing IL, LM and MK.

To Inscribe an Octagon in a Square.—
97—N.E.

First draw diagonals AD and CB (Fig. 93), intersecting each other at O. From A, B, C and D, with radius equal to AO, describe the quadrant, cutting the sides of the square in E, F, G, H, I, J, K, L, and by joining these points the octagon will be inscribed in the square.

To Inscribe an Octagon in a Given Circle.—Draw the diameter AB (Fig. 94) and bisect it by CD. Bisect the quadrants AC, CB, AD and BD at points E, F, G, H. The octagon may be completed by drawing lines cutting all the eight points.

Circles.—A circle, with its centre and circumference, is as Fig. 95. It is a plane figure bounded by a curve, called its circumference, all points of which are equidistant from its centre. Diameter, radius, chord and arc are shown by Fig. 96. The diameter is a chord which passes through the centre, and the radius is a line from the centre to the circumference. A chord is a straight line joining two points in the circumference, and an arc is any portion of the circumference.

A *semicircle*, quadrant and sector are shown by Fig. 97. A semicircle is half a circle, a quadrant is a quarter, and a sector is any portion of the circle bounded by an arc and two radii.

A *segment* of a circle is indicated by Fig. 98, and is any portion of a circle bounded by an arc and chord.

Tangents with external and internal contacts are depicted by Fig. 99. Circles which touch one another are known as tangential, and they have two points on each circumference at the same spot, and the contact may be either internal or external as shown.

Concentric circles are illustrated by Fig. 100, and all have the same centre.

Eccentric circles are circles within circles, but the centres of them are at different positions.

To Inscribe a Circle in a Triangle.—Bisect any two of the angles, and produce the bisecting lines until they meet at the point D (Fig. 101). With the steel point of the compass at D, and with radius DE, describe a circle, which will be the inscribed circle required.

To Draw a Circle through Three Points.

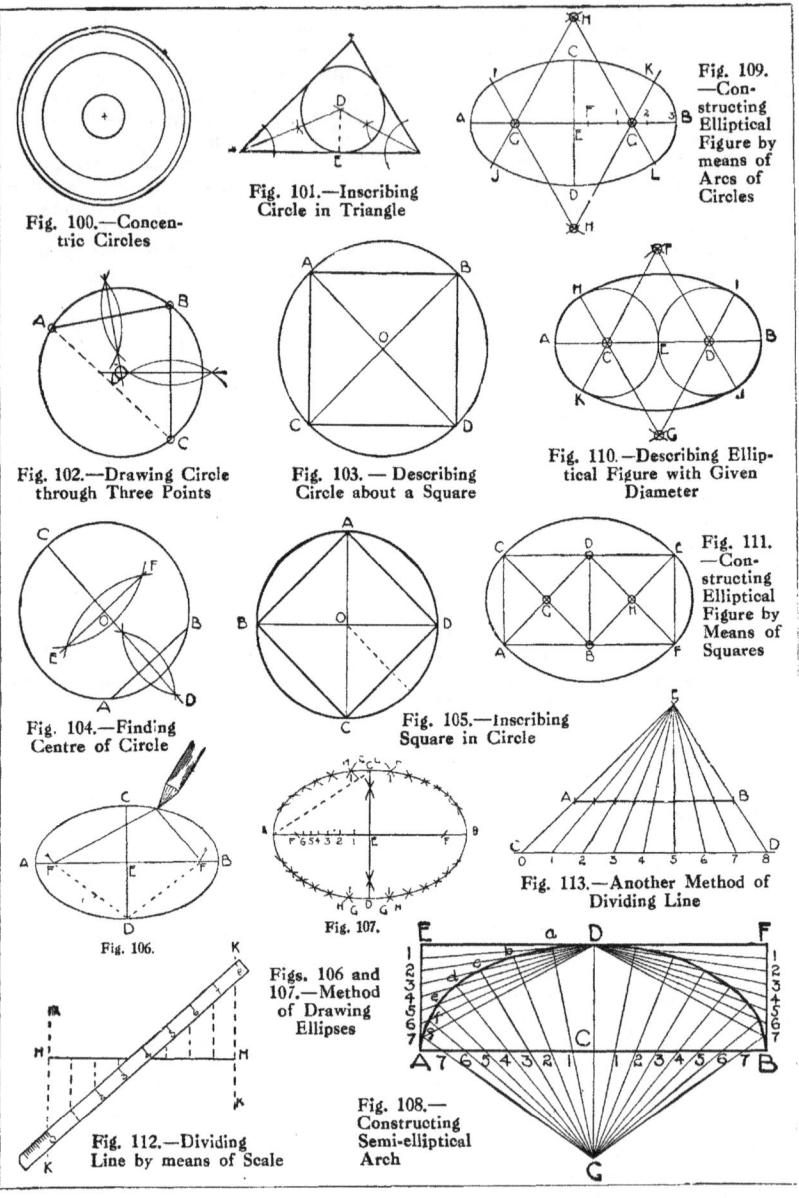

DRAWING FOR WOODWORKERS

—In this case the points must not be in a straight line. A, B and C (Fig. 102) are the three points. Join AB and BC, bisect AB and BC and produce the bisecting lines until they meet and pass each other at the point D. This will make point D of equal distance from each of the three points A, B and C. With radius DA (or DB or DC) describe a circle from the point D, which will pass through the points A, B and C.

To Describe a Circle about a Square (Fig. 103). Draw the diagonals AD and BC, and from the point O, which is the intersection of such diagonals, and with radius OA, or OB, etc., describe a circle which will touch the four angles of the square.

To Find the Centre of a Circle (Fig. 104). —First draw a chord, AB, and bisect it by a line which extends so that it cuts the circle at C and D. Bisect CD by the line EF, and the intersection O is the centre of the circle.

To Inscribe a Square in a Circle (Fig. 105).—Find the centre of the circle by the method last described, and draw two diameters at right angles to each other, and from their extremities draw lines A, B, C and D, which will form the required square.

Ellipses.—*To Form an Ellipse by means of Pins and a Piece of String* (Fig. 106).— Draw the given diameters AB and CD, at right angles to each other, so that the centres of the diameters form the point E. With radius EA, and from the point D, cut the long diameter in FF, which are called the foci of the ellipses. Place a pin in each of these points and another in D, and then pass a string round the three pins and tie it securely, thus forming a triangle of string FFD. Take out the pin at D and place a pencil in its stead, which may be drawn along and moved within the loop, the point of the pencil tracing a perfect ellipse.

To Draw an Ellipse where the Major and Minor Diameters are given (Fig. 107).— Place the diameters AB and CD at right angles to each other, as shown, and find the foci, as last described. Between E and F mark off any number of points, such as those shown at 1, 2, 3, 4, 5 and 6, making them nearer together as they approach F.

With radius IB and from FF, describe arcs GGGG. With radius IA and from FF, describe arcs HHHH, and these will intersect the arcs GGGG in IIII, and these will give four points in the curve. Proceed similarly to strike arcs from FF and 2B, and then with 2A, which will give four more intersecting points. When arcs have been struck with lengths from all the points to A and B, the curve of the ellipse may be traced by freehand through the intersections.

To Construct a Semi-elliptical Arch (Fig. 108), the span being AB and the height CD. Divide CA and CB into a number of equal parts, and divide AE and BF into a corresponding number of equal parts, and number the parts as shown. Produce DC, and make CG equal to CD, and from point D draw a line to the points 1, 2, 3, 4, 5, 6 and 7 in the lines EA and FB. From G draw a line through the points 1, 2, 3, 4, 5, 6 and 7 in the line AB, and similarly through the points in the line CB until they cut those of the corresponding lines drawn from D to the point in the lines EA and FB, and the intersection of these points will give the points of the ellipse, which may be drawn by freehand.

To Construct an Elliptical Figure by means of Arcs of Circles (Fig. 109).—Place the two given diameters AB and CD at right angles to each other, as shown. From A, set off AF, equal to CD and divide FB into three equal parts. Next, set off two of these parts at each side of E (such as GG), and from GG, with radius GG, describe arcs cutting each other in HH. Then from HH draw lines through GG and produce them. From HH, with radius HC or HD, describe arcs cutting the line HG. Produce at the points I, J, K, L. Lastly from GG, with radius GA or GB, describe arcs meeting those drawn from HH in IJKL, which will complete the ellipse.

To Describe an Elliptical Figure when one Diameter is given (Fig. 110).—Divide AB into four equal parts, and with radius CA or DB, and from C and D describe circles touching each other in E. With radius CD, and from C and D, describe arcs, meeting each other in F and G. Draw lines GC, GD, FC and FD, and produce them until they cut the circles in HIJ and K. With radius FK or GI, and from F and G, draw arcs uniting H with I and J with K, which will complete the ellipse.

To Construct an Elliptical Figure by means of Two Squares (Fig. 111).—Draw diagonals in each of the squares and obtain the points G and H. With radius BC, and from B, describe the arc CE. With the same radius, but from D, describe the arc AF, and with radius GC, and from G, describe the arc CA. With the same radius, and from H, describe the arc EF, which will complete the ellipse.

General Geometrical Problems.—

To Divide a Line into Any Number of Equal Parts by Aid of a Scale.—Assume that it is required to divide HH (Fig. 112) into eight equal parts. Through HH draw any two parallel lines; such as KK, KK, at right angles to HH. Then, with a scale of convenient unit length, adjust it as shown so that eight divisions are comprised between the two parallel lines KK. Mark the points of division along each, and then remove the scale and, through these points, draw lines parallel to KK, so that they meet HH in the required points.

To Divide a Line into Any Number of Equal Parts by Another Method (Fig. 113).— Assume that AB is the line to be divided, and then draw a line of any convenient length, such as CD, parallel to AB. Set out along CD a number of equal divisions equal to the number of divisions which AB is required to be divided into. Draw CA and 1OB, and produce both lines until they meet at E. From each of the points, at 2, 3, 4, and so forth, draw lines to E, which, passing through AB, will divide into eight equal parts.

ELEMENTARY SOLID GEOMETRY

As in the case of elementary plane geometry, it is thought necessary to deal only with elementary matters which will be suitable for application to problems arising in practical woodwork. Solid geometry deals with subjects that have bulk, such as cubes, prisms, cylinders, etc., and is different to plane geometry, which deals with the areas of figures only.

Cubes.—Fig. 114 depicts what is probably the simplest solid geometrical subject (the cube), drawn in isometric projection. It shows also objects made up of cubes. Each of the cubes has length, breadth and height.

Prisms.—A prism is a solid, bounded by plane rectilineal figures (Fig. 115), of which the two figures that are opposite are of the same shape, equal in size, and parallel to each other. The opposite ends or bases may be plane figures, of any size or shape, provided that they are identical to each other and similarly situated. The sides are composed of parallelograms, and when the faces of the prisms are at right angles to the bases, the parallelograms become rectangles, and the prism is said to be "right," and when at any other angle, the prism is "oblique."

Cylinders.—These are similar to prisms, but the ends are circles, and the sides are curved surfaces, as shown by Fig. 116, which depicts oblique and right cylinders.

To Draw the Development of the Lateral Surface of any Right Prism.—Fig. 117 represents a pentagonal prism, the base of which is shown by ABCDE. The rectangle A'AAA', having A'A equal to the perimeter of the pentagon ABCDE and A'A equal to the length of the lateral edges of the prism, will be the development of the prism.

Cones.—*A right circular cone* is as depicted by Fig. 118, upon which are shown its various parts, such as radius, slant and axis. A right cone is a solid figure formed by revolving a right-angled triangle about one of the sides contained in the right angle, the side of the triangle which revolves being the axis of the cone, the other side containing the right angle being the radius of the cone, and the hypotenuse the slant. The apex is the point of the cone, and the height is the length of the cone's axis. Oblique cones are depicted by Figs. 119 and 120.

The development of the curved surface of a right cone, where the height and diameter of the base are given, can be obtained as follows : Fig. 121 indicates a cone being so revolved on the plane surface that, after one revolution of its base, an imaginary

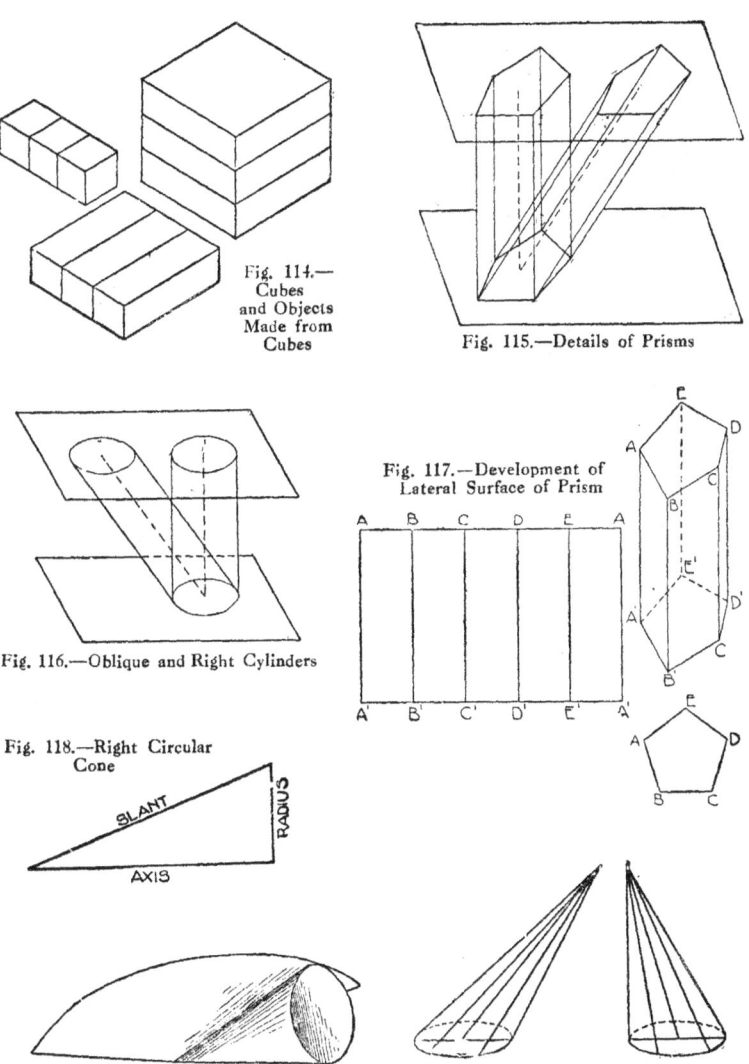

Fig. 114.—Cubes and Objects Made from Cubes

Fig. 115.—Details of Prisms

Fig. 116.—Oblique and Right Cylinders

Fig. 117.—Development of Lateral Surface of Prism

Fig. 118.—Right Circular Cone

Fig. 121.—Development of Curved Surface of Right Cone

Figs. 119 and 120.—Oblique Cones

surface, equal to the area of the curved surface, is shown on such plane surface. First consider Fig. 122 and find the slant OB. Describe a long arc BCD with OB as radius. Then with A as centre, and radius AB, describe B1, which gives a quadrant of the circumference of the base. Divide this quadrant into any number of equal parts—four in this instance (not too many parts)—giving points 2, 3 and 4. Next faces meeting at a point above the face, as shown by Fig. 123. A pyramid is either triangular, square, hexagonal, octagonal, etc., according to the shape of the base, the pyramid shown by Fig. 123 having a base with six sides being a hexagonal pyramid. A right pyramid is one having its apex perpendicular above the centre of the base, and an oblique pyramid is one which does not have its apex perpendicu-

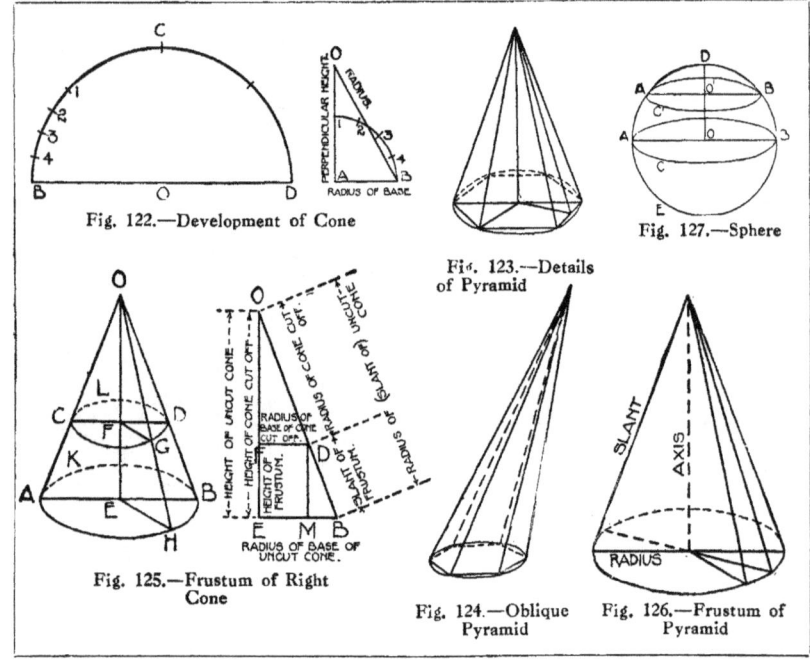

Fig. 122.—Development of Cone

Fig. 127.—Sphere

Fig. 125.—Frustum of Right Cone

Fig. 123.—Details of Pyramid

Fig. 124.—Oblique Pyramid

Fig. 126.—Frustum of Pyramid

mark off from B along the arc BCD four parts, each equal to one of the divisions of the quadrant. Take the length B1 as equal to the four parts (equal to the quadrant) and from B and from 1 set it off three times along the arc, as from 1 to C, and so on, towards D. The development required, OBCD, will be given by joining B to O and D to O.

Pyramid.—This is a solid having a base of three or more sides and triangular lar above the centre of its base, as shown by Fig. 124.

A *Frustum of a Right Cone* is depicted by Fig. 125 and is that part of a right cone containing the base AHKB, up to a plane parallel to the base, such as CGDL, or in other words is the lower portion of a truncated cone, the truncation being made parallel to the base. The part above the truncation, such as CGDLO, as shown by Fig. 125, is a complete cone.

DRAWING FOR WOODWORKERS

The names of the various parts of a frustum of a right cone are also shown by Fig. 125.

A *Frustum of a Pyramid* is depicted by Fig. 126.

Sphere (Fig. 127).—This is a solid generated by the revolution of a semicircle about its diameter, which remains fixed, and is also a solid having every part of its surface at an equal distance from the centre of the sphere. The diameter of a sphere is a straight line drawn from one surface, through the centre, to another surface. If any part of a sphere is cut so that a plane surface results, such plane surface is a circle. A segment of a sphere is formed by cutting it into two parts by a plane, the base of the segment being a circle formed by the intersection of the plane and sphere. Segments are shown at $A'DB'C'$, $A'EB'C'$ and $AEBC$. A hemisphere is a sphere cut into two equal segments.

DRAWING IN PERSPECTIVE AND BY ISOMETRIC PROJECTION

Perspective.—Drawings, such as plans, elevations and sections, are essential for working purposes and from which to obtain working dimensions, but they do not indicate fully, especially to the lay mind, exactly what an object will look like, as all the vertical and horizontal lines (apart from inclined lines) are shown horizontal and vertical on the plans, elevations and sections; whereas, truly to represent an object, vertical lines should be vertical, but the horizontal lines converge to points, in a manner as may be simply instanced by referring to the fact that a straight track of railway lines, if looked along, appear to converge to a point in the distance. Also, if a building, or any other rectangular object, is looked at from an angle, it will be noted that all the horizontal lines appear to converge to a point.

To explain fully all the principles of perspective drawing would entail much space, and as practical woodworkers would generally only require occasionally to make perspective drawings, it is only proposed to deal with quite elementary principles of perspective drawing; but the principles described will enable the subject to be fully grasped, and the more complicated subjects may be learned by obtaining any of the standard works dealing with perspective drawing.

Isometric drawing, which is a more simple matter to learn, is described later, and the difference between isometric drawing and perspective drawing is indicated by Fig. 128. Whereas it will be noted that in the perspective drawing of a simple cube all the vertical lines are drawn vertical and the horizontal lines incline and converge to points, in the isometric view of the cube it will be seen that the horizontal lines are parallel.

Definitions in Perspective.—Fig. 129 depicts a method of perspective drawing, and in relation to this figure the following definitions and descriptions will be understood :—

The *ground plane* is the plane on which the object would stand.

The *ground line* is the line where the ground plane meets the picture plane.

The *horizontal line* is a line drawn on the picture plane exactly at a level with the spectator's eye, and may also be termed a perspective representation of the horizon. When perspective drawings are to be prepared, and assuming that the object is to be looked at by a person standing on the ground, this horizontal line should be at about the height that the eye is above the ground line, i.e. about 5 ft. 6 in.

The *picture plane* may be termed an assumed vertical transparent plane, on which is drawn the perspective of any object lying behind it. This picture plane may be placed at any assumed position relative to the object; it may be placed well in front or at the back of the object, but for simple perspective work it is often assumed to be just touching the nearest vertical line of the object to be drawn, such as is indicated at D in Fig. 129.

The *principal visual ray* is a line drawn from the eye to meet the picture plane at right angles to it. It is the shortest line between the picture plane and the eye.

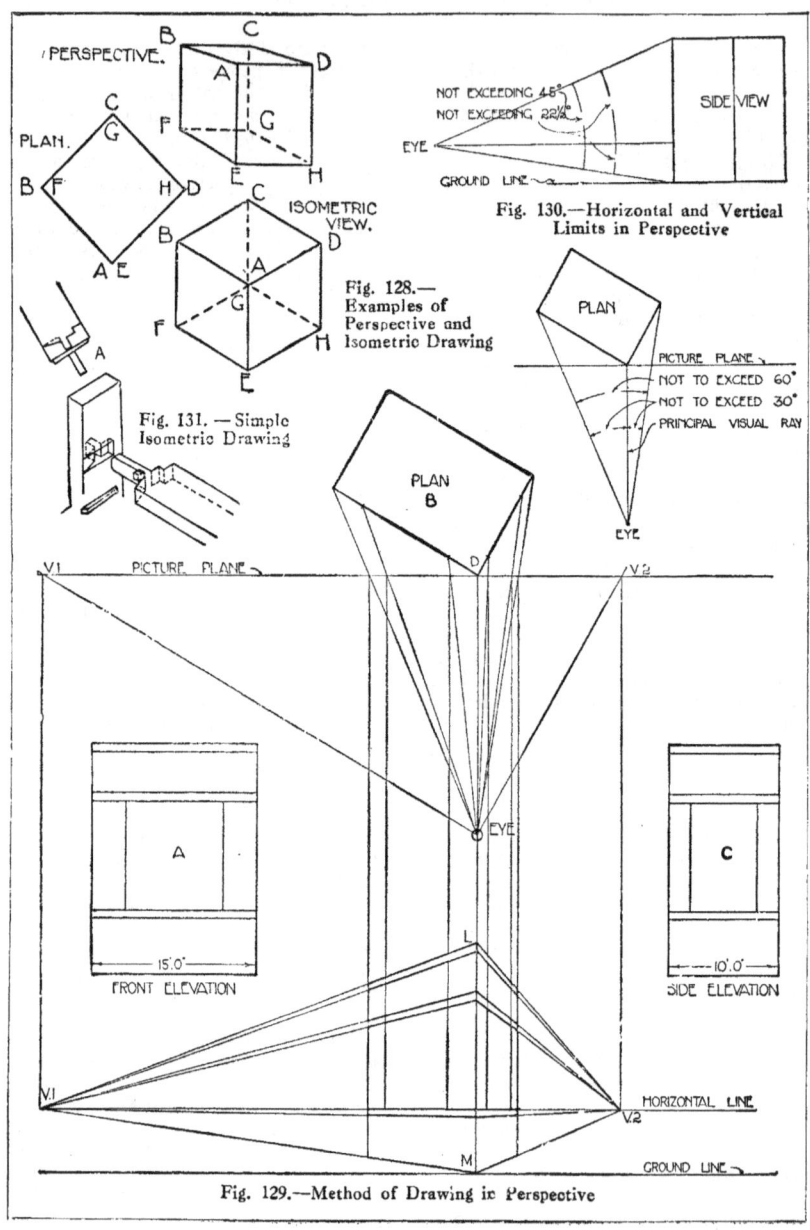

Fig. 128.—Examples of Perspective and Isometric Drawing

Fig. 130.—Horizontal and Vertical Limits in Perspective

Fig. 131.—Simple Isometric Drawing

Fig. 129.—Method of Drawing in Perspective

DRAWING FOR WOODWORKERS

The *centre of vision* is the point on the picture plane exactly opposite the eye.

The *eye level* is the position of the spectator, as marked on Fig. 129.

Vanishing points are those to which horizontal lines appear to converge, as marked v1 and v2 on Fig. 129.

The *measuring point* is a point by which measurements in perspective are obtained.

Selection of Point of Site.—So as to prevent distorted views, as a general rule no perspective view should include a horizontal angle of more than 60°, and not more than 30° should be on either side of the principal visual ray; a vertical angle of more than 45° should not be exceeded, of which not more than half of this angle should lie either above or below the horizontal line. These horizontal and vertical limits are shown by Fig. 130.

An Example of Perspective Drawing.— Fig. 129 shows, at A and C respectively, the front and side elevations of a rectangular solid, with lines inscribed on it. At B is depicted a plan of the above placed in connection with eye level (the eye of the spectator) in such a manner that the most convenient perspective view will be obtained. First draw the picture plane touching the nearest point of the object and at right angles to the principal visual ray. Next find the vanishing points, as follows: From eye level draw a line parallel to the front of the object until it intersects the picture plane, thus giving the line level, v1; then similarly draw v2, parallel to the side of the object. The point v1 is the vanishing point for all the horizontal lines in the front elevation, and v2 for those in side elevation. Draw lines from all the points in the plane, as shown, to eye level, these lines intersecting the picture plane. Draw the ground line and the horizontal line 5 ft. 6 in. to scale above it. Transfer vertically down to the horizontal line the points v1 and v2 and the other points as shown. Set out to scale on the line ML the horizontal lines of the object, and from these points draw the various horizontal lines to v1 and v2, thereby completing the outline of the perspective required.

Isometric Drawing.—Isometric projection is exceedingly useful, as it is possible to portray with one figure many, if not all, items shown by a plan, elevation and section; also, all the lines of the isometric drawing are to scale, and consequently may be measured. The vertical lines must be drawn vertical, and the horizontal lines in one plane must be drawn parallel to each other. A simple instance is shown by Fig. 131. It is usually convenient to draw horizontal lines with a 30° set-square.

TRACING

Tracings are often required, and may be made from either pencil or ink and sometimes lithographed drawings, and the tracing itself may be either in pencil or ink. The student should start by making a pencilled paper tracing of a simple inked-in drawing, as this will allow the black lines of the original drawing to be easily discernible through the tracing paper. A soft pencil should be used first and applied lightly; if a hard pencil is used, particularly on some of the common thin tracing papers, this would be apt to cut through such papers; therefore, to start with, a HB pencil may be used. Later, a hard pencil should be tried, and after a little practice it will be found that tracing is quite simple.

Before attempting ink work, a pencil tracing of a pencilled original drawing should first be made. Later, an inked tracing should be tried, and, generally, the same principles as explained for drawing with the T-square, set-square and ruling pen should be adopted, the first one or two tracings being made from inked-in original drawings, and, finally, inked tracings of pencilled drawings should be made, beginning with simple illustrations. As proficiency is attained, more complicated drawings may be done.

When preparing inked tracings, take care not to smudge the ink lines, and there is a certain knack to prevent this.

As an example, assume that it is required to prepare an inked tracing of the drawing shown by Fig. 47. If the horizontal lines of the elevation are drawn first, it will be found that the vertical lines cannot be drawn until such horizontal lines are dry, and often the inked lines on tracing paper, owing to the non-absorbent character of the paper, take rather a long time to dry, which, consequently, means a waste of time. To avoid this waste, the horizontal lines of, say, the plan may be drawn while the lines of the elevation are drying, and then, if it is not convenient to work back to the elevation again, the T-square could be left at the bottom of the board and some of the vertical lines of other parts of the drawing attempted.

When tracing cloth is used it will be found, unless precautions are taken, that, if a piece is cut off from the roll and immediately pinned down to the drawing board, it will stretch to a remarkable amount, and, consequently, if a tracing is commenced under these conditions, it will be seen that many of the lines on the tracing, which were originally truly made over the lines of the original drawing, will be considerably out. To avoid this trouble to a great extent, the tracing cloth should be cut off from the roll, the selvedge torn off, and then hung up on the wall or laid unpinned on the drawing table. It will be found that after, say, an hour all of the stretch will have taken place, and that no movement to an appreciable extent will occur.

PHOTO PRINTS

It often happens that one or more copies of a drawing are required, as, for instance, when an original drawing is prepared of an article of woodwork, from which it is intended to let one or more workmen operate. It may not be considered advisable to allow the original drawing to leave the drawing office, and therefore the question arises as to the best and cheapest method of preparing copies of the original drawing, for working or other purposes. As a general rule, blue printing provides the most economical and speedy method of obtaining the requisite number of copies.

The process of preparing photo copies of drawings is, in many cases, very similar to ordinary photography: the film, or plate, is the same as the original drawing; the blue printing or other paper is analogous to the photographic "printing out" paper; and the printing frame used for drawings is similar to the small printing frame used for photography. Photo prints may be taken by electric light, but as this process demands an expensive apparatus, and the number of prints required by a woodworker would generally be small, this system will not be described. The daylight process will be quite suitable, and is here described.

The Blue-print Process.—For this process, which gives a white line on blue ground, it will be necessary to obtain, or make, a printing frame as shown by Fig. 132. This consists of a rebated wood

Fig. 132.—Blue-print Printing Frame

frame, into which rebate the glass fits, and a back, fitting over the glass and into the same rebate. The back is rigidly held in position by clamps or springs. Part of the back is hinged, so as to allow inspection of the prints during exposure, in the same manner as the ordinary photographic frame. The drawing, which in all cases must be transparent, or at least sufficiently transparent to allow enough light to penetrate through it to ensure a clear definition of the print, must be placed on the glass with the side of the drawing or tracing on which the lines have been drawn face upwards, or next to the back. The printing paper is placed with its sensitive surface next to the tracing, a layer of soft felt is then laid over the printing paper, and, finally, the "back" is fixed in position. All the above operations should be done in a subdued light. The frame should then be exposed to the light for a varying period.

Exposure.—The time of exposure varies with the sensitiveness of the papers, the intensity of light, and the transparency of the tracings. Ferro-prussiate papers can be obtained of various degrees of sensitiveness. No definite rules can be laid down as to the time required for exposure, but after a little experience it will be found that a correct exposure can be gauged. A very good method of arriving at exact exposure is to use test strips, about 5 in. or 6 in. long by 1 in. wide, placed under a small tracing made of similar material to that from which the print is to be taken, and exposing these strips at the same time as the larger print, and in the same frame, with the ends protruding. These strips may be withdrawn and developed from time to time, until the process is complete. If rapid papers are used, or the light is very strong, it is better to turn the frame from the light while developing the test strips. If the test strips are not used, the sensitised surface of the paper should be examined occasionally, and when this is being done the frame must be turned away from the light and a part of the back and felt packing carefully removed, so as to permit examination; if the print is not sufficiently exposed, the whole must be very carefully placed back again and further exposure made.

Developing Blue Prints.—To develop ferro-prussiate papers, all that is necessary is to remove the print from the frame and thoroughly wash it in clean water until the lines become white. The print should be plunged into a bath or tray filled with water, with the face upwards, or it may be thoroughly flushed by means of an india-rubber pipe. When the lines are white, the print should be hung up to dry. Clean water should be used for every print. Under-exposed prints may be slightly intensified by using a weak solution of sulphuric acid, and over-exposed prints may be restored by using a tonic, which may be obtained from any drawing office supplies firm. If restorers, or intensifiers, are used, the prints must be thoroughly washed afterwards.

The Ferro-gallic Process.—By this process the paper is exposed in the same manner as described for blue prints, but the method of developing is different. Place the print face upwards in the bath or tray, having a depth of not less than 1½ in. of clean water; then carefully rub over the print to expel all air bubbles; leave for a few minutes until the lines become black and the ground white, flush off thoroughly with clean water and then dry by hanging up. If the print has a mauve ground, exposure to the light has been insufficient; if over-exposed, the ground will be white and the lines weak. For this process, originals must have lines with " body," as otherwise violet lines will result, owing to a proportion of light filtering through the lines and affecting the paper.

Developing Ferro-gallic Prints.—Ferro-gallic papers may be developed by an acid bath, made by dissolving ¾ oz. of gallic acid in boiling water, sufficient cold water being afterwards added to make up a gallon. This solution may be kept for a long time in a stone jar or bucket. To develop, lay the print face upwards on the glass bottom of the empty water bath and pour upon it a tumblerful of the developing solution, which must be distributed with a wide soft brush, and the solution kept on the surface of the paper until the yellow lines become quite black. Finally, the print must be thoroughly washed and then hung up to dry.

The Sepia Process.—With this process the sepia paper must be exposed exactly as if it were a very rapid ferro-prussiate paper. When exposure is complete, the lines show up light yellow on a brownish ground, before development. Under-exposure will result in a ground of insufficient density, and over-exposure will give broken lines. After removal of the print from the frame, it should be laid face upwards in the clean bath and thoroughly flushed with water for two or three minutes. After this, it must be fixed by throwing over the face a small quantity of a solution composed of ¼ oz. hypo soda and one pint water. This solution may be distributed with a soft camel-hair brush. The operation must be carried out quickly, and the print thoroughly washed in clean water. This process is extremely useful for making negatives from original drawings, in addition to the ordinary prints. When negatives are required, the image of the drawing must be reversed, so that when prints are made from the sepia print a correct reproduction of the original drawing will be given. A good negative should have a very dark brown ground, almost approaching to a black, and have very white lines. These papers print very rapidly, retain their sensitiveness for more than a year, and can be used to reproduce line prints, by means of thin paper negatives.

CARE AND INDEXING OF DRAWINGS

In drawing offices where drawings of a great number of different jobs are prepared, systems to guarantee the preservation, and also for indexing them (to allow for speedy reference), are essential. The average woodworker does not require any elaborate system, as the number of drawings prepared by him only necessitates a simple system, such as will, firstly, divide the drawings of each job into separate compartments or sections ; secondly, allow for speedy reference ; and, lastly, give particulars as to where the drawings (or copies of them) have been sent and the time of return. The drawings of each job may be kept in a simple manner by allocating one shallow drawer to several jobs, say, not exceeding six. A separate drawer for each job would probably be too expensive, and drawings for various jobs may be kept flat in one drawer, with divisions of either paper or millboard. Drawings that are being prepared, or are in constant use for jobs in hand, should preferably be kept flat, but as soon as the job is completed and the drawings are no longer required for immediate purposes, they may be neatly rolled up, labelled, and stacked away.

A drawings book (often called a " Plan Book ") should be kept, and this should be ruled with columns as shown by Fig. 133. Column (1) headed " Drawing No." would be used for the numbers of the drawings, and all numbers placed in this column should be consecutive. In column (2) would be given the date on which the drawing was completed. Column (3) would be used for the name of the job, and column (4) would be used for indicating, in a concise manner, the particulars of the drawing. Column (5) is an important one, and in it should be recorded all the movements of any particular drawing. Fig. 133 indicates that two drawings have been posted, and a perusal of this should make the objects and use of such a system of drawing indexing perfectly clear.

DRAWING No.	DATE COMPLETED	JOB	PARTICULARS	MOVEMENTS
245.	17.8.20	Oak Memorial Tablet Birmingham	General and detail drawings	(1) 17.8.20 1 Blue print J. Smith, Birmingham (2) 18.8.20 1 blue print to Shop. (3) (1) returned 20.8.20
246	22.8.20	Table: Lynton.	Detail drawings	(1) 23.8.20 2 Blue prints to Shop. (2) 24.8.20 1 Black & white print to Lynton

Fig. 133.—Particulars of Drawings Book

MOULDINGS

In recent times there has been a marked absence of any strict adherence to

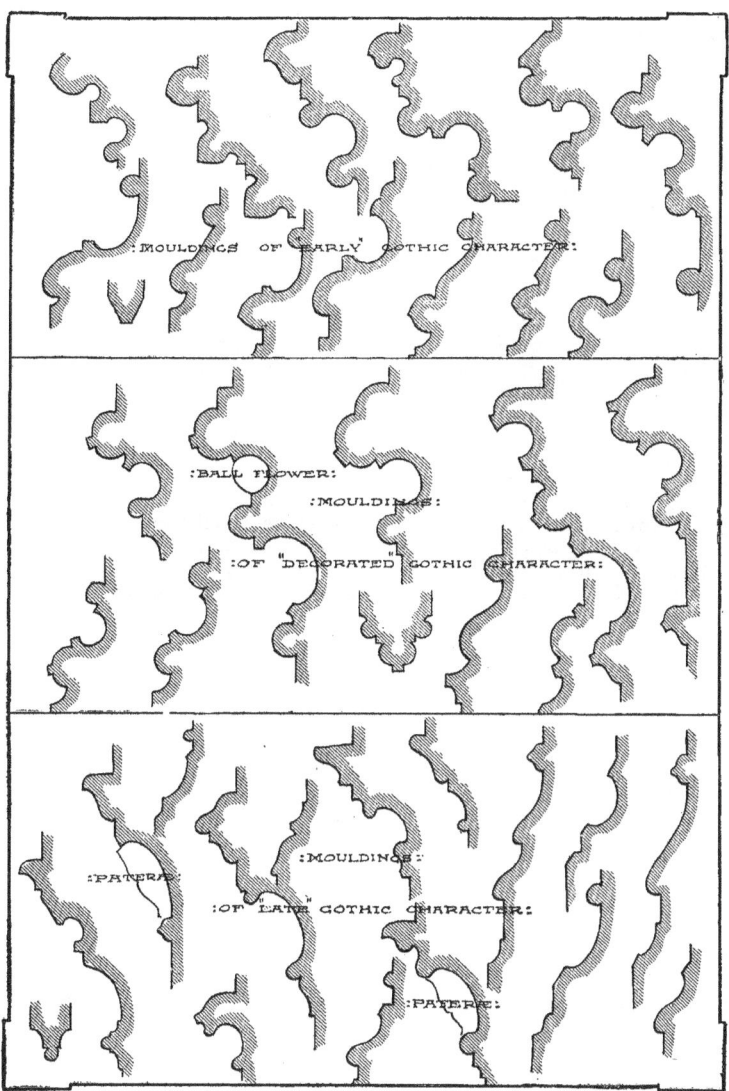

Fig. 134.—Examples of Mouldings for Execution in Wood

definitely established styles or " Orders," and such being the case any setting forth of the inflexible rules governing the graphics of the old Roman and Grecial mouldings —which by the way may be readily ascertained from rudimentary textbooks —is uncalled for. Only a few sets of sections such as may be found useful in connection with "up-to-date" work of the class have been here set forth.

On page 1514 is shown a diagram order, the surrounding sections being suggestions in variety for various mouldings thereof. Attention is drawn to the fact that all are of such members and proportions as are suitable for execution in wood. Where applied to stone or other like material all details would necessarily be of heavier proportions. On page 1515 is indicated such sections as will be found applicable to lighter finishings or joinery to interior of buildings. All sections indicated in Figs. 38 and 39 are suggested for fine grain hardwoods or painted work.

Particular attention is directed to the desirability of avoiding all *small* features or members in wood other than those which are of a *fine grain* or are to be painted, it being a frequently ignored fact that small sections being worked on oak and other bold-grained woods— particularly quartered oak—is unsatisfactory in a high degree, owing to such grain and small members clashing and nullifying each other.

In this connection is indicated in Fig. 48 (page 1522), flattened, broad members as seem to throw into prominence the invaluable charm of the natural grain and medullary rays of oak and other bold-featured woods. On lower part of Fig. 48 is also shown a limited selection of mouldings in the Neo-Grecian style, and the effect in a building consistently designed throughout is particularly pleasing, if and when desired a beautiful effect being economically obtained by the application of small rectangular blocks, pateræ or modillions at carefully studied intervals.

In Fig. 134 (page 1541) are shown Gothic mouldings, " Early," " Decorated " and " Late," as may be useful in connection with woodwork interiors of the respective periods, now almost exclusively adopted in ecclesiastical buildings, many examples of which are to be seen.

Timber: Varieties and Uses

THE following list of timbers is arranged in alphabetical order for ease of reference. The colour, characteristics and uses are given for each.

Acacia. Another name for the wood, Locust, which see.

Acajou. (*See* CEDAR, CIGAR-BOX, and MAHOGANY.)

Acle (*Pithecolobium acle*), a fine dark-brown heartwood, resembling walnut, with whitish sapwood. It is moderately hard and heavy, and has a decidedly peppery smell when worked. It is a native of India and the Philippines, where it is used for house- and boat-building; but, although as yet unknown in English trade, both it and several allied species of *Pithecolobium* would be well suited for furniture. It has been confused with the much heavier Pyingadu (*Xylia xylocarpa*).

Ailantus (*Ailanthus glandulosa*), native to Northern China, grown in Japan, in some parts of France and near Odessa, but in England and the Eastern United States for ornament only. Has a greyish-orange heart, much resembling ash when in cross section, is moderately heavy and hard, though somewhat brittle, and durable. It is used for firewood, charcoal, and joinery in France; but, having a beautiful satin-like lustre, is appreciated by cabinet-makers. It grows rapidly to a considerable height, but seldom reaches much more than 1 ft. in diameter. Its oriental name, "Ailanto," is said to mean "Tree of Heaven"; in French it is "Ailante" or "Vernis du Japon," in Russian "Pajasan," and in Chinese "Chou-chun."

Alder (*Alnus glutinosa*), with no heart, is a soft, smooth, and fine-grained wood. White when alive, it turns to a deep red or pink when cut, and dries to a pinkish brown. Weighing from 50 lb. to 60 lb. per cubic foot when green, it loses at least a third of its weight and about a twelfth of its bulk in drying, but does not subsequently warp, split, or splinter. It is recognisable by its pith, which in cross section is triangular with rounded angles; by the few broad, nearly straight compound pith-rays with very many fine simple ones between them; by the faint boundaries of the annual rings bending slightly inward at the broad rays; and by frequent brown pith-flecks that are often concentric. The wood seldom reaches large dimensions. It is liable to the attacks of the larva of a small beetle; but if wholly submerged is very durable. It is said to have been used in ancient times for boats. Vitruvius states that Ravenna was founded upon piles of this wood, and Evelyn says that those of the Rialto at Venice and those of Amsterdam were made of the same material. It is still so employed in Holland. Old trees full of knots, when cut into plank, have all the beauty of curled maple and the colour, though not the density or lustre, of mahogany. In Scotland this wood is sometimes immersed in peat water, to which lime is added, for some months, and is then used for table-tops which require varnishing. Newly felled alder can be readily stained to imitate ebony; or, being rich in tannin, will, if left long in peat, become equally black. Its non-splintering causes it to be used for the staves of herring-barrels, shovels, kneading-troughs, wheelbarrows, stone-carts and bobbins: the alder poles from the German Baltic ports were mainly bought by the Lancashire clog-makers; and in France, after being hardened and protected from the boring beetle by being smoked. The wood is suitable for turnery and plywood.

THE AMERICAN ALDER (*Alnus incana*) is a similar but inferior wood; and the large RED, OREGAN, or WESTERN ALDER (*Alnus rubra*) of the Pacific slope has a light brownish wood which is similarly employed. The name WHITE ALDER (*Platylophus trifoliatus*) is applied in Cape Colony to a hard, tough, durable, lustrous yellowish-white wood, often with a fine twisted grain, known to the Boers as "White Els."

Alerce. (*See* THUYA.)

Amaranthe. (*See* PURPLE-HEART.)

Amboyna-wood, the burrs of Kiabooca, probably *Pterospermum indicum*, native to Amboyna and other Molucca islands and New Guinea, known also as Lingoa-wood. The burrs are sawn off in slabs 2 in. to 8 in. thick, and up to 9 ft. in diameter, though generally much smaller, light reddish-brown to orange, beautifully mottled and curled, fragrant, very hard, and taking a good polish, and very durable, weighing about 39 lb. per cubic foot. Much used in the eighteenth century for inlaying, etc., but now rare and generally superseded by Thuya or Totara burrs from Algeria and New Zealand respectively.

Anjan (*Hardwickia binata*), native to Southern India, dark red streaked with black or purplish; one of the hardest, heaviest, and most durable of Indian timbers, is very strong and does not warp, but is liable to splitting; used for bridge-building, railway sleepers, etc., and, though resinous, also for cabinet work.

Apple (*Pyrus Malus*), a dark brown wood, generally with a red tint, with broad rings, invisible rays, and no pith-flecks, close-grained, very hard, and susceptible of a good polish, but brittle and warping badly in drying. It weighs about 50 lb. per cubic foot. As the fruit-bearing trees are now generally discarded whilst comparatively young, this timber is neither common nor of any considerable dimensions; but it is sometimes used for tool-handles, mallets, etc. The writer has known croquet-mallets and balls to be turned in this wood.

Ash (*Fraxinus excelsior*), the most valuable of European woods, is a light brown, much resembling light oak; but though its annual rings are well marked, the pith-rays are hardly visible. Of moderate weight and hardness, it is, when well grown, very even and close in grain, lustrous, and susceptible of a good polish, whilst it is the toughest and most pliable of European woods. Though the tree will grow in almost any soil, it produces the best wood when grown quickly in rich loam and in a moist climate. Few trees become useful so early, since it is fit for walking-sticks or whip-handles at four years' growth, for hop-poles or lances at five or six, for spade handles at nine, and reaches its full value per cubic foot when 3 in. in diameter. For small wood it is frequently coppiced, being then known as maiden or ground ash. In the Potteries it is largely used for crate-making, for which purpose it is cut every five or six years. As the wood can be steamed or heated and readily bent into any curve, without injury, it is invaluable for hoops. Larger wood is much used by the wheel-wright and carriage-builder, especially for felloes, and there is a constant demand for this wood in arsenals for the building of artillery wagons. Its combination of lightness, flexibility, and toughness makes it in great request for the construction of aeroplanes. For such a purpose, however, it is essential that the wood should be bright—a sign of soundness—and capable of standing the severest tests of its flexibility and strength. For this it should be valley-grown, winter-felled, and

TIMBER: VARIETIES AND USES

quickly converted into plank or board and seasoned. It is then very durable, but otherwise rapidly deteriorates.

The slower-grown Ash of Northern Europe, of mountains, or of poorer soils, is commonly darker in colour and may become " black-hearted," as also does the wood of pollard trees. In the north-east of England, wounds or " cankers " in the heart are attributed to bees, the wood being known as " bee-sucken ash "; and billets of ash imported from Austria and Hungary often exhibit contortion of the fibres, producing figure, known as " ram's-horn " or " fiddle-back " ash. Pyrenean Ash also exhibits figure, and is imported as veneers. These malformations detract from the flexibility, though not from the hardness of the wood. As ash does not splinter readily, it is admirable for chopping-blocks or shop-boards requiring frequent washing, or for billiard cues or oars ; but its flexibility unfits it for architectural work. In Russia the ash grows soft and kind, and is accordingly much used by the joiner and cabinet-maker in house-fitting and furniture. As there is no bitter principle in ash comparable to the tannin in oak, the wood is liable to be attacked by the larvæ of beetles, and requires, therefore, to be painted.

THE AMERICAN or WHITE ASH (*Fraxinus americana*) is the lighter-coloured wood of a quick-growing species which occurs from eastern Canada to Carolina in damp ground. It is about a third lighter than English Ash and fully as much less elastic, so that, although employed in America for all the purposes to which we put European Ash, the wood, when imported here, is put to very different uses. It comes, in part, from Quebec. in partly square logs 18 ft. to 35 ft. long and 10 in. to 18 in. square, or in planks, or partly manufactured, as oars, etc. The whitest logs, which are considered the best, are in great demand for bedroom and other furniture, carriage-panels, etc., and the inferior darker logs for carcase work and drawers, for which European Ash is never used. It is kind, soft, very easy to work, and stands well in panelling when thoroughly dried. Several other species are in use in North America, of which the best is, perhaps, the Blue Ash (*Fraxinus quadrangulata*) of the lower part of the Wabash Basin and the central United States.

ASH, BLACK. Another name for Cabinet Ash (*see below*).

CABINET ASH, the English trade name for the black-barked, or Nova-Scotia Ash (*Fraxinus nigra*), which grows in swamps from Newfoundland and Winnipeg southward, and yields a dark wood, inferior to white ash, and " burls," or wart-like swellings, forming valuable veneers ; and for the red or brown-barked ash (*F. pennsylvanica*), which is somewhat inferior.

JAPANESE ASH, the English trade name for a wood with some resemblance, but no real relationship to ash, known in Japan as " Sen," in China as " Tzu-Chin " (*Acanthopanax ricinifolia*), the plant being now common in our gardens and greenhouses, though there not of timber size. It reaches 60 ft. in height and 3 ft. in diameter, and its wood is hard, glossy, and fine-grained. It has been used for spears, tool-handles, the bottom-boards of boats, and for the fittings of railway carriages. A valuable true ash (*Fraxinus sieboldiana*), known as " Shui chü liu " in China, is not yet known in our commerce.

QUEBEC ASH. Another name for American or White Ash, which see.

Asp. (*See* ASPEN, below.)

Aspen (*Populus tremula*), a soft, light, dingy white or reddish-brown wood, which warps and cracks but little, does not splinter, and is fairly durable if kept dry, is tender and easily split or turned. It is imported in small quantities from the ports on the south side of the Baltic, mainly for cooperage, being used for milk-pails, butchers' trays, pack-saddles, and herring-barrels, and also for blindwood, clogs, matches, and paper-pulp. In France it is employed for sabots and for flooring. A similar North American species (*P. tremuloides*), often called the American or Quaking Asp, is used for cooperage, flooring, " excelsior " (wood-shavings used for packing), and paper-pulp ; but for this last purpose aspen is inferior to spruce.

Assegai-wood (*Curtisia faginea*), a South African species, sometimes known as "Cape Lancewood," or in Zulu as "Umguna" or "Umnoiso," though not in English trade, is a valuable wood. Bright red, but becoming dull on exposure, it is heavy, close-grained, strong, tough, elastic, and durable. The tree reaches 40 ft. to 80 ft. in height and 1 ft. to 4 ft. in diameter, and the wood is used for assegai-shafts, tool-handles, spokes, felloes, and wagon building. It might well be imported for turnery.

Basswood (*Tilia americana*), native to the east of Canada and the United States, not distinguished in commerce from White Basswood (*T. heterophylla*) of the Middle and Southern States, is very similar to the closely related Linden of Europe (*T. europœa*). It is white or light brown, sometimes with a reddish tinge, without the lustre of the maples, light, soft, close-grained, tender, and not strong, shrinking considerably in drying, but durable if kept dry. It is extensively used, especially in the northern United States, where the Tulip-tree does not grow, for the seats of Windsor chairs, carriage-panels, cheap office and bedroom furniture, toys, general carpentry, turnery and cooperage. It is also worked up by the rotary veneer machine into thin board as long as the log and as much as 100 ft. broad for the manufacture of three-ply wood. In the London cheap furniture trade this wood is often confused with canary whitewood.

Bay-wood. A trade-name for Mahogany (Honduras), which see.

Beech (*Fagus sylvatica*), native to Central and Southern Europe and to the southern parts of Britain, and giving their names alike to Bukovina, Buckingham, and Betchworth, is one of our more generally useful woods. It can be obtained in straight logs of considerable length and diameter and, though varying considerably in colour, has various uses for its different qualities. It varies, according to the soil upon which it has been grown, from red to yellow, or white, the redder, grown upon richer soil, being the better. In Germany the wood is known as red beech in contradistinction to that of the hornbeam, known there as white beech. Newly-felled beech is often reddened by steaming, as in the Sheffield tool trade. The annual rings are distinct and wavy, while the very wide pith-rays give a satiny lustre. The wood weighs from 41 lb. to 56 lb. per cubic foot, but usually 43 lb. to 44 lb. It is hard and as strong as oak, and even tougher—hence its use for wheel cogs—but it is much less stiff. It is close, even and silky in grain, cleaving readily along the rays, and is very suitable for turnery, being manufactured into tool-handles, wooden screws, shoe-lasts, wedges, tent-pegs, shovels, etc. The wrest-boards of pianos must be of English beech. The wood is grown and used on a large scale for the "Windsor" chair-making industry of Buckinghamshire and for the bentwood furniture of Vienna, its freedom from any oily secretion rendering it suitable for the staining usual in the latter trade. It is very durable under water, as is seen in the logs on which the foundations of Winchester Cathedral were laid in A.D. 1202; but it cannot, unless treated with preservatives, stand alternations of wet and dry conditions. Most of the complaints as to the perishability of beech—often attributed to soil or situation—are, in fact, due to the wood not having been seasoned or treated immediately after felling.

In France and Germany beech is considered the best of all woods, except walnut, for sabots and wooden soles; but for this purpose it is smoked over a fire of branches and chips of the same wood so as to become saturated with pyroligneous acid and very impermeable. In its natural state the wood, having numerous vessels, is very porous; it is possible to blow out a candle through a jack-plane of beech; and it is partly on account of this structure that beech forms so excellent a fuel, burning with a clear, bright flame; and for the same reason it absorbs large quantities of liquid preservatives. It is largely used for railway sleepers in France, after treatment with copper sulphate; and has been successfully used, after creosoting, for wood-paving.

In North America this species, though

TIMBER: VARIETIES AND USES

reaching large dimensions, has generally more sapwood, and—under the name of WHITE BEECH—is recognised as much inferior to the Red Beech (*Fagus ferruginea*), which is used for the same purposes as English beech, but is somewhat inferior to it.

Of allied southern species belonging to the genus *Nothofagus*, the evergreen NEGRO-HEAD BEECH or Myrtle (*N. Cunninghamii*) of Tasmania and Victoria reaches large dimensions and is a satiny reddish-brown wood, susceptible of an excellent polish, used for pier-decks, ballroom floors, piano carcases, furniture, fretwork, etc. Fine burrs occur on its stems. *N. betuloides*, another evergreen species, occurs from Tierra del Fuego northward, and is known in Argentina by the vague name Roble (Oak). Its handsome, fine-grained, easily-worked wood has been extensively used for the panelling of railway carriages.

For BLUE or WATER BEECH and the ORIENTAL BEECH, see HORNBEAM.

The name Beech is also applied to many woods, in different parts of the world, in no way related to the true beeches. Of these, the white beech of N.E. Australia (*Gmelina Leichhardtii*) is fine-grained, easily-worked wood used for decks, flooring and carving.

Beef-wood is a name applied to various deep red furniture woods. Of these, *Lophira alata* from Lagos and the Gold Coast, also known as African Oak, is very heavy, hard, and coarse-grained, weighing about 70 lb. per cubic foot. In Trinidad the name is applied to *Rhopala montana*, a valuable wood ; and in Australia to the allied proteaceous *Grevillea striata*, also known as Silvery Honeysuckle, *Banksia integrifolia* (or Coast Honeysuckle), and *Stenocarpus salignus* (or Silky Oak) ; and also to various species of *Casuarina*, also known as She-oak, Forest Oak, or Swamp Oak. Of these, *C. torulosa* (Forest Oak) is used for furniture and veneers, *C. suberosa* (Erect She-oak) for mallets and handles and formerly for boomerangs.

Birch (AMERICAN BIRCH) is the trade name for the imported wood which is the product of four or five species from Canada and the North-eastern United States, but chiefly of *Betula lenta*, which is variously known as Sweet, Black, Cherry or Mahogany Birch or Mountain Mahogany. This reaches larger dimensions than European birch. When first sawn the sapwood is distinctly yellow, the heart a brownish red ; but after seasoning the sapwood fades to a cream white and the heart to a pinkish red, though often darker in parts and handsome. The rays are wider than in other species, the pores large and pith-flecks rare, and the wood takes a beautiful satiny polish and presents the " roll-figure " seldom seen in any other wood. It weighs from 37·5 lb. to 48 lb. per cubic foot, and is hard, strong, close-grained, not very liable to insect attack, and, for a birch, fairly durable. It is largely used in America for furniture, being sometimes stained to imitate mahogany or cherry. It is imported in slightly waney logs, 6 ft. to 20 ft. long, and 1 ft. to 2½ ft. square, and in sawn planks seldom more than 9 in. wide, the best coming from Quebec. Here it is used in carriage-building, chair-making, and bedroom furniture. *Betula lutea*, the Yellow, Grey, Tall or Silver Birch, chiefly used for very small woodware, yields tough burrs from which mallets are made ; and *B. papyrifera*, the Canoe, White or Paper Birch, has a curl in the grain at the base of its branches which is in request for cabinet veneers in Boston ; but this and other perishable and weak species are mainly converted into paper-pulp.

EUROPEAN BIRCH (*Betula alba*) varies from yellowish or reddish white to light brown, with distinct rings and rays, and generally numerous pith-flecks near the centre of the stem. It weighs from 32 lb. to 49 lb. per cubic foot, and is moderately hard, even-grained, difficult to split, but easily worked. It is not a strong wood ; and, being rich in sugar when young and destitute of tannin or other bitter principle, is so liable to a fungoid fermentative decay or to the attacks of insects as to be far from durable. Occurring, however, as a rapidly-growing weed of timber lands throughout the north of Europe and Asia, it is in many lands the cheapest native hard wood, and is largely used for cooperage, turnery, furniture, fuel, and charcoal. In Yorkshire it is made into clogs, and in France it is one of the chief materials for sabots. Birch logs have been imported in considerable quantities from the Baltic, mostly with the bark on ; but are very apt, especially if felled in spring, left on the ground, kept too long on the voyage, or stored without ventilation, to become " doated " or foxed by incipient decay. A very extensive industry has arisen within recent years in the manufacture of ply-wood. The timber is cut rotarily, and two, three, or more thicknesses are then glued back to back with their grains in different directions so as to correct warping. This wood is largely exported to Ceylon and India, where soft wood is scarce, for tea-chests, and is now applied to a variety of purposes, such as carriage-building, where lightness combined with moderate stability is desirable. Burrs with a valuable marbled wood occasionally occur on the stems of birch ; in Lapland these are turned into cups. Unlike the wood, the bark of the birch is rich in tannin and very durable, and is used for an immense variety of purposes, boats, boxes, boots. cordage, baskets, dyeing and tanning, the coppice-wood, with the young bark on, being also put to many of these uses.

BIRCH, TASMANIAN. (*See* LIGNUM-VITAE.)

Blackwood is a name applied to several valuable woods in different regions. Indian Blackwood (*Dalbergia latifolia*), also known as Malabar Blackwood, or as Indian, Bombay or Rosetta Rosewood, has the smell of rose-water, and burns with a smoky flame smelling of tar. Its sapwood is narrow and yellow, the heart dark brown or purple to greenish-black, often with darker or lighter longitudinal streaks, taking a fine polish. It weighs from 46 lb. to 66·75 lb. per cubic foot, and is very hard, tough, close, and cross-grained, the difficulty of working it being intensified by calcareous secretions in the wood. It is used for sleepers, gun-carriages, cartwheels, agricultural implements, and toolhandles ; but is the best furniture wood in India. It is exported for furniture to Hong-Kong and Canton and, via Bombay, to London.

AFRICAN BLACKWOOD (*Dalbergia melanoxylon*), also known as Senegal Ebony or " Congo-holz " (the latter German), a native of Tropical West Africa, has a jet-black or brownish-black heart and is used as ebony in turnery.

TASMANIAN BLACKWOOD (*Acacia melanoxylon*), also known as Black, Silver, or Hickory Wattle, is one of the most generally useful of Australian timbers, an excellent substitute for American walnut. Dark brown, with a beautiful figure, sometimes fiddle-back, in the older wood, hard, close, and even in grain, but easily worked, it takes an excellent polish. When newly sawn it is sticky with resin-veins, and, unless very carefully seasoned, will warp. It is used for beer barrels, oil-casks, gun-carriages, gunstocks, and tool-handles, and the sounding-boards of pianos ; whilst the figured wood is cut into veneers for billiard tables and other furniture, or for railway-carriage panels.

In Cape Colony the name Blackwood, the Boer " Zwartbast " or Zulu " Umcaza " (*Royena lucida*), a small ebenaceous tree, is used in wagon-building, though it is fitted for higher uses in turning or for furniture-making.

Box (*Buxus sempervirens*). A light yellow wood, hard and difficult to split, more uniform in grain than any other known wood. With neither rings, rays nor vessels distinct, it is almost horn-like in its homogeneity, planing almost equally well in any direction. It only occurs in small dimensions, and is apt to split in drying. Box was used in ancient Rome for turnery and veneers, and was made into flutes, and it is still used for " strings " in inlaying. At St. Claude, in the Jura, where the largest boxwoods in Europe occur, the wood is turned into small boxes, beads, spoons, etc., for which purposes the wood is stored in the dark for from three to five years, soaked, boiled, and buried in bran. While box is invaluable for mathematical instruments, its chief use from the fifteenth to the nineteenth century was engraving. For this purpose it is chiefly imported from Asia by way of Constantinople, Smyrna, and Odessa in billets 3 ft. to 8 ft. long and 3 in. to 12 in. across. Large blocks for engraving were built up of small pieces. In spite of the general employment of other methods for engraving, there is still a great demand for box, and no completely satisfactory substitute for it has been found.

The Balearic species (*B. balearica*) is larger, but somewhat coarse in grain. The South African *B. Macowani* is suitable for turnery; but hardly for engraving. The name is also applied to Kamassi (*which see*) and to an excellent West Indian wood, *Tecoma pentaphylla*, the Jamaica Box, White Cedar, Cogwood, or Roble blanco of Tropical America. China Box (*Murraya exotica*), the Malay "Kamuning," growing in Queensland, the Philippines, Burma, and India, and used for tool-handles and walking-sticks, is a similar very heavy and hard yellow wood, suggested as a substitute. In Australia the name Box is applied to various species of *Eucalyptus*.

Box-Elder. (*See* MAPLE, ASH-LEAVED.)
Boxwood, CAPE and EAST LONDON. (*See* KAMASSI.)

Brazil-wood or Braziletto, is the hard, heavy, dark red wood of *Cæsalpina brasiliensis* and several allied Tropical American species. It takes a high polish and forms the material of violin-bows. These woods are mainly employed as red dyeing materials, and are imported from the Bahamas.

Butternut. (*See* WALNUT, GREY or WHITE.)

Buttonwood. (*See* PLANE.)

Calamander-wood or Coromandel-wood (*Diospyros quæsita* and allied species) is one of the most beautiful of cabinet woods. It is a native of Ceylon, belonging to the ebony family, but is now scarce. A red hazel-brown or chocolate colour, with handsome black stripes, and susceptible of a high polish, it is somewhat intermediate in appearance between the nearly allied zebra-wood and rosewood. It is intensely hard and close-grained, so as to be difficult to turn or work. It is light in weight for an ebony, weighing, as it does, 57 lb. per cubic foot. It is sometimes employed in veneer.

Camphor-wood (*Cinnamomum Camphora*), a native of China, Japan, and Formosa, of moderate dimensions, moderately hard, not very heavy, reddish, often prettily marked, rather coarse-grained but easily worked, fragrant, and, owing to the large amount of camphor it contains, durable. It was formerly used in China for coffins and the keels of junks, for sleepers, and even as fuel; but, being now scarcer, is used for high-class furniture, and, owing to its insect-proof character, for entomological cabinets. In Manila many cabinets are made of soft wood treated with camphor oil, in imitation of this wood.

The wood of the Bornean Camphor or "Kayu Kapor Barus" (*Dryobalanops aromatica*), a large tree, is light red, resembling bay-wood, not fragrant but straight-grained, and has been used for planks, beams, and piles and imported for wood-paving.

Canary Whitewood and American Whitewood are the English trade names for the wood of the magnoliaceous Tulip-tree (*Liriodendron tulipifera*) and the closely allied Cucumber-tree (*Magnolia acuminata*), often called Yellow or Virginian Poplar in the United States. It is a native of the Eastern States and reaches large dimensions. It is a light lemon-yellow, greenish olive-tinted or brownish, weighs about 25 lb. or 26 lb. per cubic foot, soft, close and straight in grain, firmer than most woods which are as soft, taking a satiny polish, stain, or paint very well, and easy to work. In America it is largely used as a substitute for pine in building, for joists, rafters, doors and wainscot, and for the seats of chairs, boxes, and turnery. Canary Whitewood is imported in waney logs and in large planks and boards, the latter being often planed on both sides to save freight. The planks and boards are often the somewhat harder and coarser cucumber-tree, which is also distinguishable by its wider sapwood. The wood is in great request for panelling, shop-fitting, carriage building, and cabinetwork, especially for ebonising or staining, but is often inexcusably confounded with basswood.

Cedar, a name applied in different parts of the world to a great number of woods, most of which are brown, even-grained, moderately hard, and easily worked and fragrant. They include many coniferous woods belonging to the genera *Cedrus Juniperus, Cupressus, Thuya,* and *Libocedrus,* and several entirely unrelated species of the meliaceous broad-leaved genus *Cedrela,* Lebanon Cedar (*Cedrus Libani*), with a pleasant odour obnoxious to insects, and therefore of great repute in ancient times for durability, but rather brittle; was used for coffins nearly three thousand years B.C., and later for internal work, carving and cabinets. In England it is only known as an ornamental tree; but at Warwick Castle there is a room panelled with the wood of wind-fallen Lebanon Cedars from the grounds of the Castle. The wood of the closely-related Mt. Atlas Cedar (*Cedrus atlantica*) of North-west Africa is the Numidian Cedar, of which the beams of the Temple of Apollo at Utica, stated by Pliny to have been sound after nearly 1,200 years, were made. It is known to the French as Lebanon Cedar. The Deodar Cedar (*Cedrus Deodara*), the chief timber of North-west India, is only known in England as an ornamental tree, it being introduced here in 1831.

PENCIL CEDAR in English commerce now means only *Juniperus Virginiana,* the Red Cedar of the United States. It reaches considerable dimensions, may be rose-red, and has no resin ducts. It was formerly much used for shipbuilding by the Spaniards in Florida, for coffins in the Southern States, for cooperage in Philadelphia, and even for railway sleepers and fencing, and in England until about 1860 for cabinets, work-boxes, etc. It is now, however, too dear for any use but pencil making, for which several million cubic feet are cut annually. Bermuda Cedar (*J. bermudiana*) and Barbadoes Cedar (*J. barbadensis*) are closely related forms, and Rocky Mountain Red Cedar (*J. scopulorum*) and Western Juniper or Yellow Cedar (*J. occidentalis*) have very similar woods, as also has the gigantic East African Cedar (*J. procera*), which occurs from Abyssinia to British East Africa.

WHITE CEDAR is a useful American trade name for the light brown woods of *Cupressus, Thuya,* and *Libocedrus.* Oregon or Port Orford Cedar (*Cupressus Lawsoniana*), reaching large dimensions, hard, strong, and durable, is one of the most valuable timbers of North America, and is largely cut for boat-building, fencing, flooring, etc. The white cedars of the Eastern States (*Cupressus thyoides* and the more fragrant *Thuya occidentalis*) are valuable timbers for many purposes, as also is the Californian Incense Cedar (*Libocedrus decurrens*); but perhaps the most important is *Thuya plicata,* otherwise known as *T. gigantea* or *T. Lobbi,* and as Western Red Cedar, Yellow Cedar, or Canoe Cedar. This species, which grows from Alaska to California, was the only wood used by the Red Indians of the North-west for their canoes; it is the chief shingle wood of the United States, nearly 75 per cent. of the 15,000 million shingles used annually on American roofs being of this wood; it is also used for internal fittings, coarse furniture and paving, and is now being very extensively planted. The Cedar of English commerce is, however, the Cigar-box Cedar (*Cedrela odorata*), also known as West Indian, Cuba, Havana, Honduras, Jamaica, or Mexican Cedar, which is a broad-leaved tree related to the mahoganies. This valuable wood, which can be obtained from 18 ft. to 40 ft. long and 1 ft. or 2 ft. square, is much softer than mahogany, weighs from 27 lb. to 47 lb. per cubic foot, is bitter, fragrant, but somewhat peppery in smell, and is now so scarce as only to be used for the boxes of the better qualities of cigars, African mahogany being used for cheaper brands. Few woods are more useful to the amateur craftsman than Cigar-box Cedar. Allied species, *C. guianensis* and *C. brasiliensis,* from the Guianas, Brazil, and the Argentine, are also used.

MOULMEIN CEDAR, Indian Mahogany or Toon, the Cèdre de Singapore or Cèdre rouge of the French, the Thitkado of Burma, or Calantas of the Philippines are

TIMBER: VARIETIES AND USES

names under which several valuable, closely-related, pale reddish, light and soft woods, durable and proof against termites, are confused. They are now referred to the genus *Toona* (*T. serrata, T. ciliata, T. febrifuga,* and *T. calantas*), nearly allied to *Cedrela* ; reach a large size ; and are fragrant, straight-grained, and easily worked. They sometimes exhibit a beautiful curl near the root or branches, suitable for furniture veneers, and are used for tea-chests, cigar-boxes, carving, and, in Queensland, for boat-planks.

The " Fragrant Chun," " Frêne odorant," or " Hsiang Chun," of China (*Cedrela sinensis*), lemon-scented, and beautifully marked with red bands on a yellowish brown, is an abundant, quick-grown, and valued allied species.

Cherry (*Prunus Avium*) is a moderately hard and heavy, light yellowish-brown wood, fine and even-grained, but not durable. After soaking for several days in lime-water the wood becomes a beautiful brownish red and can be used as a substitute for mahogany. It is used in inlaying, and is valued for turnery. The Perfumed Cherry, the fragrant, hard, red-brown, or green-streaked wood of *Prunus Mahaleb*, is grown in Austria for walking-sticks and the long stems of German tobacco-sticks ; and the larger but scarce American Wild Black or Rum Cherry (*P. serotina*) is a similar pink or reddish wood, moderately hard and durable and susceptible of a good polish, which is also stained to imitate mahogany and is employed with that wood for cabinetwork, furniture, and interior decoration.

Chestnut, often spoken of as Spanish Chestnut, to distinguish it from the unrelated Horse-Chestnut (*Æsculus Hippocastanum*), is the wood of a tree (*Castanea vulgaris*), sometimes reaching large dimensions, which is a native of the Mediterranean area, though long grown in England. It is brown, resembling oak, but distinguished from it by the absence of broad pith-rays. Though moderately hard, it is lighter and far softer than oak, for which reason it may be recommended to the wood-carver. It is rather coarse-grained, not very strong, but fairly durable. It is largely grown for hop-poles and fencing ; but as it takes glue well it is one of the best carcase-woods for veneering. The ancient roofs alleged to be of this wood, such as those of Westminster Hall, Beaulieu Abbey, Leycester's Hospital, Warwick, etc., are, without exception, oak.

The AMERICAN CHESTNUT of the Eastern United States (*C. dentata*) is closely related and a very similar wood, employed for a variety of purposes, but now threatened with extermination by the ravages of a fungoid disease. The smaller Chinquapin Chestnuts (*C. pumila*) and in the Western States *Castanopsis chrysophylla*, yield rather darker, heavier, stronger, and more durable woods, and there are allied species in the Eastern Himalayas and in Southern China.

The MORETON BAY CHESTNUT (*Castanospermum australe*) of North-east Australia, named from the resemblance of its seeds, is, however, in no way related. It is a dark brown, prettily-streaked wood, somewhat like walnut, used for gunstocks, veneers, and furniture.

Chikrassi. (*See* MAHOGANY, EAST INDIAN.)

" Christmas Tree." (*See* SPRUCE, COMMON.)

Cocobola-wood, a species of *Humiria*, from British Guiana, is a hard, heavy, coarse-grained wood of a deep orange colour with jet-black linear markings, which is used in Tunbridge Wells ware and other inlaying and turnery.

Cocus-wood, also known as American, Green, Jamaica, or West Indian Ebony (*Brya Ebenus*), is a very heavy, dark greenish-brown or purplish wood, very fine and even in grain, of small dimensions, used in the manufacture of flutes and flageolets, for inlaying, and, though not well fitted for the purpose, for bows.

Cornelian-wood. (*See* DOGWOOD.)
Co·omandel. (*See* EBONY.)
Cottonwood. (*See* POPLAR.)
Crocus-wood. (*See* SAFFRON-WOOD.)
Cucumber-tree. (*See* CANARY WHITE-WOOD.)

Cypress is not a wood often employed in Europe at the present day under that name. The fragrant, reddish, very fine-grained, and practically indestructible wood of *Cupressus sempervirens*, a native of South-west Asia and the Mediterranean area, was used by the ancient Egyptians for mummy-cases; for the doors of St. Peter's and for the gates of Constantinople, both of which were destroyed in the fifteenth century after some eleven hundred years' existence; and, according to Evelyn, for harps and organ-pipes.

The soft, reddish, fine-grained, durable wood of the DECIDUOUS CYPRESS of the Southern United States (*Taxodium distichum*), formerly used in Louisiana for canoes and house-building, is still extensively employed for roof-shingles, door and window frames, the drawers of mahogany furniture, fencing, and railway sleepers. It is closely similar in character and uses to the woods of the Redwoods (*Sequoia*) of the West.

Cypress-pine the general name for the species of the genus *Frenela*, the East Australian representatives of the Cypresses, brown woods, often with pinkish or darker streaks, and beautifully figured, with a camphor-like smell that renders them largely proof against termites and teredo. They are easily worked, take a good polish, and are durable. They are used for telegraph poles, piles, building, sleepers, and furniture. The chief species are *F. robusta*, *R. Endlicheri*, *F. rhomboidea*, and *F. Parlatorei*.

Dagame, or Degame Lancewood (*Calycophyllum candidissimum*), a native of Cuba, yellow, moderately heavy, and hard, and very fine and close in grain, is used as lancewood.

Date Plum. (*See* PERSIMMON.)

Deal, though now often used as a synonym for pine or spruce wood, is properly merely a name for 9-in. planks of such wood not more than 4 in. thick. The country of their origin and their colour is often indicated by a prefix. Thus the Northern Pine (*Pinus sylvestris*) yields Dantzic, Red or Yellow Deals; the Spruce (*Picea excelsa*) White Deals; and most Canadian and New Brunswick Spruce Deals are *Picea nigra*.

Dogwood in England is the name for two shrubs (*Cornus sanguinea* and *Rhamnus Frangula*), formerly used for skewers or "dags," and now largely employed for gunpowder charcoal. In North America the name is used for two larger species related to the first-named, *Cornus florida* and *C. Nuttalli*. *C. florida* is known commercially as Cornel, Cornelian wood, or Boxwood, and *C. Nuttalli* as Western Dogwood. Reddish-brown, heavy, very hard, and fine-grained woods, they are used for engraving, cogs, tool-handles, mallets, and turnery, In the manufacture of shuttle-blocks, blocks of these woods, measuring 2 in. square, are compressed by hydraulic power to $1\frac{5}{8}$-in. square, a test that very few woods can stand without rupture of their fibres.

Douglas Fir, or Oregon Pine (*Pseudotsuga Douglasii*), one of the most valuable and most widely distributed of American timbers, is native to the whole extent of western North America from the Tropic of Cancer to 55° N. lat., but reaches its greatest dimensions in Oregon, round the shores of Puget Sound, and in southern British Columbia. Reaching sometimes a height of 300 ft., free from branches for 200 ft. from the ground, and diameters of 6 ft. to 12 ft., or more, it comes to market in clean, straight spars 40 ft. to 110 ft. long and 9 in. to 32 in. in diameter. The wood resembles that of the larch or that of Canadian red pine (*Pinus resinosa*), its well-defined darker bands of autumn-wood placing it commercially with " hard pines " not only in appearance, but also in quality. The tree varies much in its rate of growth, according to situation, and tests made by the United States Forest Service show that rapidly grown wood (less than eight rings to the inch) is relatively weak, the best material having twelve to sixteen rings per inch, though that with twenty-four rings was the strongest. The wood with narrow growth-rings is known in its country of origin as " yellow fir," being reddish-yellow in colour, light, soft, easy to work, straight and fine in grain, uniform in texture, firm, tough, and elastic, but not at all liable to warp.

The more rapidly grown wood, known as " red fir," is a dark reddish colour. uneven in texture, with weak open spring-wood

TIMBER: VARIETIES AND USES

and flinty autumn-wood, coarse-grained, difficult to work, and heavier in weight. Employed in America for house-building, engineering work, and even for fuel, it is more used than any other wood down the Pacific coast of both North and South America. It is excellent for the lower masts, yards, and cross-arms of ships, and is largely used for sleepers.

The Californian or Pacific variety or Green Douglas Fir (var. *macrocarpa*) is grown in Britain in preference to the Colorado or Blue Douglas Fir (var. *glauca*), which is much slower in growth and is recognised by its shorter, stiffer, bluer leaves. The flagstaff at Kew, erected in 1861 with its butt end in a brick vault, but taken down in 1914 in an unsound condition, to be replaced by a larger one, is not perhaps a good advertisement of the durability of Douglas Fir.

Ebony, the very dense, hard, black heartwood of species of *Diospyros* and the allied genera *Maba* and *Euclea*. Any member of the family *Ebenaceæ* may furnish ebony if its heartwood is sufficiently developed, and it seems impossible to distinguish the woods of the various species microscopically. Many are so small as to be of little commercial importance. Some of the streaked woods, such as the Calamander-wood of Ceylon, already described, the Marblewood or Zebra-wood (*Diospyros Kurzii*) of the Andamans, and the Bolongeta (*D. pilosanthera*) and Camagon (*D. discolor*) of the Philippines, are more beautiful than the dead black; but they are less in demand and are sold as "bastard ebony." Most of the ebony of British India is the produce of *D. Melanoxylon*, known as "Coromandel" or "Godavery Ebony," reaching good sizes and sometimes beautifully streaked with purple. That of Ceylon is mostly *D. ebenum*, which also reaches a good size in that island, though seldom in India. Most of the ebony of the Philippines is the wood of the smaller *Maba buxifolia*; but it is stated that the streaked woods of Bolongeta and Camagon are rendered uniformly black by being buried in the salt mud of mangrove swamps. In Mauritius, ebony is the product of *D. tessellaria*; in Madagascar, of *D. haplostylis* and *D. microrhombus*; at Zanzibar, of *D. mespiliformis*; in West Tropical Africa, of *D. Dendo*; and in South Africa, of *Euclea pseudebenus*. The East African ebonies weigh from 50 lb. to 60 lb. per cubic foot; but the East Indian from 75 lb. to 80 lb. The fine-grained character of ebony and the filling up of its elements with a tannate of iron render the wood very free from shrinkage or warping, so that it is much used, not only for fine furniture, cabinetwork, inlaying, walking-sticks, and brush-backs, but also for pianoforte keys, the string-holder of violins, and foot-rules.

The Corsican ebony of ancient Rome, the false ebony of the French, is the dark greenish brown wood of the Laburnum (*which see*); and the green ebony of the West Indies has been described under its other name of Cocus-wood. The name ebony is extended in various countries to woods in no way related to the true ebonies, such as the leguminous Mountain Ebony (*Bauhinia acuminata*) of Indo-China, the Queensland Ebony (*Bauhinia Hookeri*), and some species of Acacia and Blackwood.

ARTIFICIAL, or GERMAN EBONY, is the dyed wood of box, pear, or yew, and can nearly always be distinguished by its much lighter weight, whilst its colour is usually only superficial. Holly is often "ebonised" for the handles of teapots, and Canary whitewood is stained black for furniture; but these imitations are hardly ever susceptible of the fine polish of true ebony.

EBONY, FALSE (FRENCH), (*see* LABURNUM).

EBONY, FIGURED (*see* MARBLEWOOD, ANDAMAN).

EBONY, GREEN (*see* COCUS-WOOD).

EBONY, SENEGAL (*see* BLACKWOOD, AFRICA).

EBONY, WEST INDIAN (*see* COCUS-WOOD).

Elm, the ENGLISH ELM (*Ulmus campestris*), is a handsome, strong, and in many respects valuable wood. It reaches a great height (80 ft. to 90 ft.) and a diameter of 3 ft. or more. The narrow yellowish sapwood is as strong and durable as the dark brown heart. This latter is hard, firm, tough, and susceptible of a high polish, and, when dry, 1 cub. ft. weighs about 44 lb. The wood, being sweet, is liable to be worm-eaten, and is, therefore, not suitable for building. As it wears smooth and does not splinter, it is used for butchers' blocks, pulleys, the naves of cart-wheels, the seats of chairs, and the sides of ammunition boxes. If kept thoroughly dry or wet it is so durable that hollowed elm-stems were formerly used as water pipes : the Rialto at Venice is said to be built upon 12,000 piles of this timber, and it is still used in building pumps. In China, under the name of "Yii," it is in request for tables, furniture, general turnery, axles, and other parts of carts ; but with us it is now chiefly employed for coffins. The loose hold the tree has upon the soil causes large numbers to be blown over by storms, so that the supply of the wood and its price are subject to considerable fluctuations. It is liable to twist while seasoning. Elm has also been most successfully employed for paving blocks where traffic is heavy, but it is too good a wood for such a purpose. Burrs are frequent on old elms and yield fine cabinet veneers.

AMERICAN ELM is a name under which, unfortunately, several species are imported indiscriminately. The small CORK-WINGED ELM (*U. alata*) of the south-east United States yields a light brown, heavy, fine-grained wood used for hubs and blocks, but seldom exported.

THE RED, MOOSE, or SLIPPERY ELM (*U. fulva*) of the north-eastern States and south-east Canada is larger, darker, coarser grained, readily split, and therefore used locally for fence rails and, when steamed, for the ribs of boats ; but little of it comes to England.

THE WHITE or WATER ELM (*U. americana*) of the eastern States has of late years been largely exterminated by the ravages of beetles. It is a very large, light-brown, coarse-grained wood, inferior to English elm, but employed for boat-building, wheel-hubs, tool-handles, and most of the purposes to which English elm is put in this country. When imported, however, it is used chiefly for keels.

ROCK or HICKORY ELM (*U. racemosa*), of Canada and the central United States, reaches less diameters than the last-mentioned, and is a slower-grown wood, averaging only 1 in. in diameter in fourteen years ; but, though less flexible than slippery elm, it is harder and probably much the best of American elms. It is imported in logs 20 ft. to 40 ft. long and 11 in. to 16 in. square, which are liable to split on drying. Used in America for chair-making, sleepers, door and window sills, and all the other uses of elm, it is largely imported to England for coach-building, wheels, and boat-building, being one of the best timbers for bending.

SCOTCH or WYCH ELM (*Ulmus glabra*) is a lighter coloured, softer, straighter-grained wood, more easily split than English elm. It is the common species north of the Trent. Many of the fine old linen-chests usually taken for oak are of this wood, " Wych " being apparently the early English " Hwæcce," the French " huche," a chest, our modern " hutch." At High Wycombe the wood both of this and of the last-mentioned species is used for the backs of Windsor chairs, and this species seems to be specially known as chair elm. Its wood is so flexible and tough that it was formerly used for long bows, and it is now used for shafts and many other purposes to which ash—a more costly wood—is applied, and, when steamed, for boat-building. It is distinguishable from oak by its narrower, less prominent, and darker-coloured rays.

Fir is a name used very loosely, both in commerce and in botany. White Fir or " Baltic White," and other species of *Picea*, are dealt with under the head of Spruce ; Oregon Fir or Pine has been treated under that of Douglas Fir ; and all the various names for our Scots Fir (*Pinus sylvestris*), derived mostly from the ports of shipment. such as Dantzic, Memel, Riga, Norway, Swedish, Red or Yellow Fir, come more suitably under NORTHERN Pine, where they will be found described. The name Fir is restricted to the genus *Abies*, and, though several of the species are well known in our arboreta as ornamental trees, and are employed locally in their native countries, the only kind at all important

TIMBER: VARIETIES AND USES

as a wood in use in England is the Silver Fir (*Abies pectinata*) of Central Europe. This is of a yellowish or pinkish-white, without distinct heart and with few resin-canals, but with regular circular, well-defined annual rings, light, soft, lustrous, easily worked, but not durable. As it takes glue well, it is used in its native countries for general carpentry, for toy-making, carving, paper pulp, and especially for packing-cases and small boxes which are largely exported from Switzerland and the Tyrol.

THE HIMALAYAN SILVER FIR (*A. Webbiana*) is used locally for building. *A. Veitchii*, the best Fir in China, is also used for telegraph poles, matches, and paper pulp; the tall SILVER FIR (*A. grandis*) of Oregon and British Columbia, and, better still, the RED FIR, LARCH FIR, or NOBLE FIR (*A. nobilis*), of the Western States, light, but hard, strong and durable, are used for internal carpentry.

For PRINCE ALBERT'S FIR (*see* HEMLOCK SPRUCE).

Fustic, the name applied to two entirely distinct woods, both mainly employed as yellow dyes. The smaller, "Young" or "Zante Fustic," is that of the Venetian Sumach or Wig-tree (*Rhus Cotinus*), well known as a garden shrub, belonging to the family *Anacardiaceæ* Old (that is, larger) Fustic, the "Fustete" or "Palo narango" of Spaniards and "Bois d'orange" of the French, is that of *Chlorophora tinctoria*, var. *Xanthoxylon* or *Maclura tinctoria*, a member of the mulberry family, native to Brazil, Guiana, the West Indies, and Bahamas. It reaches 20 ft. in length and 1 ft. in diameter, is a canary-yellow colour, light, tough, and hard, and is used for spokes and for the bellies of long bows. or the middle of three-wood bows.

Greenheart (*Nectandra Rodiæi*), a very valuable timber, native to the north-west of South America and the West Indies. It yields timber 40 ft. to 70 ft. long and 1 ft. to 2 ft. square; is dark greenish or chestnut in colour, often nearly black at the centre; is fine, even, and straight in grain, with indistinguishable annual rings, and is very heavy, hard, tough, strong, and durable. Its weight is usually from 60 lb. to 76 lb. per cubic foot. It is somewhat liable to heartshake, but its heartwood is very teredo proof. It is in request for dock-gates, jetties, piles, bridge-building, keelsons, etc. The lock-gates of the Manchester Ship Canal, the Panama Canal, and the Liverpool Docks are of this wood, and some of the latter have been found perfectly sound after thirty years' use. The imported logs are sometimes 60 ft. long and have "snape" or tapered ends to facilitate their being drawn out of the forest. These ends are useful for carriage shafts, motor-wagon spokes, fishing rods, etc.

The so-called AFRICAN GREENHEART from Nigeria, a species of *Piptadenia*, belonging to the entirely unrelated family *Leguminosæ*, has proved not to be durable, and is, therefore, worthless as a substitute for true greenheart.

Gum, the BLACK GUM (*Nyssa sylvatica*), of the eastern United States, is harder, heavier, and stronger than the related "Tupelo" or "Sour Gum"; but is used, as they are, for hubs, handles, and wooden shoes. They are imported in sawn boards and used for linings in cheap cabinetwork.

BLUE GUM (*Eucalyptus Globulus*), native to Victoria and Tasmania, and now largely planted, as a supposed preventive of malaria and as a quick-growing source of firewood or mine-timbers, in South Africa, California, the Philippines, etc. The tree reaches 200 ft. to 350 ft. in height and from 6 ft. to 25 ft. in diameter, and its wood is pale straw colour, grey or light brown, with darker streaks, hard, very heavy, moderately strong, tough and durable, partially immune from teredo, planing well but with a curled and twisted grain. It is used in India and Ceylon, whither it is extensively exported, for sleepers, bridge-building, and house-beams; and in its native country for fences, telegraph poles, carriage and ship-building. It is the most durable hardwood in Tasmania, and it is preferred to Jarrah or Karri for the piles driven in advance of the shield in tunnelling; in Dover harbour works piles of this timber 70 ft. to 100 ft. long and 18 in. to 20 in. square have been employed. The various gum trees of Australia are often wastefully felled at from 3 ft. to 12 ft. above the ground to save trouble; but their stumps often exhibit beautiful curled or wavy grain suitable for cabinet-work.

RED GUM (*Eucalyptus rostrata*), of Eastern Australia, known also as Flooded Gum, Yellow-jacket, and aboriginally as " Yarrah " (not to be confounded with Jarrah), is the most valuable hardwood in Victoria. It does not reach the gigantic dimensions of blue gum, but is a large tree. Its wood is dark red, often with a pretty curly figure. It is not quite as heavy as blue gum, but is exceedingly hard and most difficult to work when dry, which is against its use for furniture, although it takes a fine polish. Like most of the eucalyptus woods, it is liable to twists and shakes during seasoning; but is very durable, termite-and teredo-proof. It is the chief wood used for paving in Melbourne; is preferred to blue gum for sleepers; and is in request for piles, bridge and house-building, ships' beams, posts, etc. It must not be confounded with the next wood in the list.

SWEET GUM (*Liquidambar styraciflua*), belonging to the American Wych-hazel family (*Hamamelidaceæ*), and no more related to the Australian gum-trees than to the walnut, pine or hazel. It is known in America as " Bilsted " or " Red Gum," and reaches 100 ft. to 140 ft. in height, 4 ft. to 5 ft. in diameter, and weighs on the average about 38 lb. per cubic foot. The sapwood is cream-white; the heart irregular, reddish-brown, often beautifully marked with dark false rings, moderately hard, close grained, tough, free from knots but splintery, taking a satiny polish, but warping and twisting badly in drying, unless it be first steamed. Although little suited for paving, it has been sold for that purpose under the designation of Californian Red Gum; but it grows in the eastern States, especially in the Lower Mississippi Valley, and is shipped from New Orleans. In the timber trade it is commonly supposed that " Hazel Pine " is a trade name for the sapwood and " Satin Walnut " for the heart; but, as a matter of fact, the so-called hazel pine is the whole wood of the same species as satin walnut, but grown in low-lying swampy districts where the dark colouring-matter is not developed. It is the hygroscopic character of the gum that fills the vessels of this wood which makes it liable under changes of temperature both to longitudinal twisting and to transverse warping, for which reason it is better fitted for cheap bedroom furniture than for use in rooms in which fires are lit. The hazel pine is largely imported in planed boards which are used for the lining of cheap furniture, competing with the lower grades of canary whitewood. The satin walnut, which is undeniably a beautiful wood, makes handsome veneers.

Gurjun, or wood-oil tree (*Dipterocarpus turbinatus* and *D. alatus*), red, moderately hard woods of large dimensions, native to India and Burma, and used for house- and boat-building, are recommended for sleepers, and have some figure, so that when treated by the process known as Powellising they resemble African mahogany.

Hackmatack. (*See* LARCH.)

Hawthorn (*Cratægus Oxyacantha*) is a hard, heavy, flesh-coloured wood of slow growth and seldom of any size, known chiefly as used for walking-sticks, though it is the best substitute for box for the purposes of the engraver that has yet been discovered.

Hazel (*Corylus Avellana*), a reddish-white wood with no heart, resembling beech, but soft, very elastic, only of small dimensions and not durable, is used chiefly for barrel-hoops, walking-sticks, and alpenstocks. The TURKISH or CONSTANTINOPLE HAZEL (*C. Colurna*), native to the Balkan peninsula and much of Central Asia, reaches much larger dimensions and is suitable for small furniture work, for which purpose it is employed in China.

Hemlock Spruce (*Tsuga canadensis*), often spoken of simply as " Hemlock," or as " Eastern Hemlock," although specially valued for its bark, which yields a tanning extract, is an abundant and useful timber of eastern North America. It grows to more than 100 ft. in height and from 3 ft. to 6 ft. in diameter, and is

TIMBER: VARIETIES AND USES

a light reddish, lustreless grey or brown wood, with little distinction of heart and few resin-passages, light, soft, and stiff, but brittle, coarse-grained, splintery, shrinking and warping considerably in seasoning, wearing rough and not very durable, but retaining nails firmly, and employed for sleepers, laths, rafters, and fencing.

THE WESTERN HEMLOCK (*Tsuga heterophylla*), which grows from Alaska to Oregon and is known in arboreta as " Prince Albert's Fir " (*Abies Albertiana* or *A. Mertensiana*), is larger and yields a heavier and harder timber, which, however, is not so strong. The Chinese species (*T. chinensis* and *T. yunnanensis*) are both known as " Tieh sha," a name signifying Iron Fir, and are valued for planking and roof-shingles.

Hickory, the wood of species of the North American genus *Hicoria*, formerly known as *Carya*, which is nearly related to the Walnuts, though the woods are very different. When stripped of their characteristic barks, the hickories are not readily discriminated. They are slender trees, sometimes reaching from 70 ft. to 120 ft. in height, and 2 ft., 3 ft., or even 5 ft. in diameter. The sapwood is broad and white, the heart a reddish nut-brown, often not unlike ash. All the species are very heavy, ranging in specific gravity from ·75 to ·84, weighing, that is, from 47 lb. to 52 lb. per cubic foot; they are very strong, tough, and elastic, rather coarse, but smooth, and straight in grain, with large pith but indistinct rays. They dry slowly, shrinking and splitting considerably in the process; and, in addition, they are found to be very liable to insect attack and are not durable in contact with soil or exposed to the weather. The reddish-brown streaks often seen in the sapwood are due to the attacks of birds.

Hickory is unsuitable for house- or boat-building, but is of great value in carriage-building, for axles and spokes, axe and other tool-handles, screws for presses, chair-making, coach-whips, bows, and cask-hoops. It is harder, heavier, and tougher than ash, which it closely resembles in its general properties and uses. Nearly all American-made carriage-wheels imported into this country have their spokes and felloes of this wood, which, however, is better suited to the dry air of the States than to ours.

The best species are PIG - NUT or BROOM HICKORY (*Hicoria glabra* or *Carya porcina*), SHELL - BARK or SHAG - BARK HICKORY (*H. ovata* or *C. alba*), MOCKER-NUT HICKORY (*H. alba* or *C. tomentosa*), and BIG or THICK SHELL-BARK HICKORY (*H. laciniosa* or *C. sulcata*). These differ but little in value, and are hardly distinguished from one another commercially. Pig-nut Hickory is said to be the best for axles and axe-handles; Mocker-nut Hickory, for whip-handles and the back bows of Windsor chairs; and the Shell-barks are most largely imported for spokes, bows, etc. Mocker-nut Hickory is white when young, and the Thick Shell-bark is slightly lighter in weight and darker in colour than the others here named. The other species, of which the chief are the PECAN, NUTMEG, BITTERNUT, and WATER HICKORIES (*H. Pecan, H. myristicæformis, H. minima*, and *H. aquatica*, formerly known as *Carya olivæformis, C. myristicæformis, C. amara*, and *C. aquatica*), are lighter in weight, softer, and more brittle, and are chiefly used as fuel.

Holly (*Ilex Aquifolium*) does not reach a large size, seldom exceeding 40 ft. in height or 1½ ft. in diameter. It is a beautiful white wood, except in old trees, which are apt to be brownish, very fine, and close in grain, more nearly approaching ivory both in colour and texture than any other wood, and susceptible of a high polish. It weighs about 47½ lb. per cubic foot, and is hard, but readily turned. It is sometimes difficult to prevent its shrinking, warping, splitting, and becoming spotted or stained in drying. For this reason it should be cut into the form required, whether into veneer planks or round blocks for turning, as soon as felled and boiled in water for many hours. This removes the sap and enhances the whiteness of the wood. The pieces are then packed closely together and covered up for several weeks so as to cool and dry slowly, and are then stored in dry air, without being allowed to touch one another. Besides the use of small Holly for whip-handles, the wood is considerably used for engraving, especially in calico-printing and in veneer for inlaying, as in Tunbridge ware, and for white or stained strings in furniture and cabinetwork. For staining, dyeing, or ebonising, Holly is unequalled. The AMERICAN HOLLY (*Ilex opaca*) of the Eastern States is a very similar wood and is employed for the same purposes.

Honeysuckle-wood, a name sometimes applied in America to the wood of the Plane (*Platanus occidentalis*) when cut radially so as to expose the beautiful grain which makes it a first-rate wood for fretwork. In New Zealand the name is applied to the beautiful Rewa-rewa (*which see*); but it is, perhaps, most used for the Australian species of *Banksia*, *B. marginata*, *B. serrata*, and *B. integrifolia*. These belong mainly to the south-east, and are of moderate dimensions. They require careful seasoning, and are liable to become worm-eaten; but have beautiful figure, and are susceptible of a high polish. The two first named are a dark mahogany-like red; while the third, known as Coast Honeysuckle, is lighter-coloured. (*See also* BEEF-WOOD.)

Hornbeam (*Carpinus Betulus*), generally of moderate lengths and not more than 1 ft. in diameter, is a yellowish white, heavy, hard, close-grained, and somewhat lustrous wood which, owing in part to its wavy growth-rings, is of exceptional toughness. This renders it the best wood for the beaters of printers' rollers and for cogs, mallets, skittles, etc., for which purposes it is imported by us from France. It is also excellent fuel.

There is a species in the eastern Mediterranean region (*C. duinensis*) and one in eastern North America (*C. caroliniana*), with similar timber, though the latter is, perhaps, slightly inferior. All three trees are confused with the beeches from general resemblances of bark, bud, leaves and, to some extent, wood. Thus the German name for our species is "Weiss-buche," that is, White Beech; *C. duinensis* is sometimes dubbed Oriental Beech; and the American species is also called Blue or Water Beech.

The Hop-hornbeams of Southern Europe and the east of North America (*Ostrya carpinifolia* and *O. virginica*) are closely related woods, similar in structure, but browner or redder in colour, which are tolerable substitutes for the true hornbeams.

Horse-chestnut (*Æsculus hippocastanum*), a very quick-growing, light, soft, white wood, reaching considerable dimensions, and resembling willow or poplar in character. It has neither strength nor durability, and is grown chiefly for shade and ornament; but is a cheap substitute for other white woods. It warps but little, so is suitable for flooring and still more for the lining of carts and wheelbarrows, packing-cases, blind-wood in cabinetwork, moulds for castings, and the backs of scrubbing brushes. In France it is used for sabots, and might be employed, as are the woods of the related Buck-eyes in the United States, for artificial limbs. It is in no way related to the true, sweet, or Spanish chestnut.

Huon-pine (*Dacrydium Franklinii*), known also as Macquarie Pine, a light-yellow, coniferous wood from a Tasmanian tree 80 ft. or 100 ft. in height and 3 ft. to 6 ft. in diameter. It is light, close-grained, and tough, but easily worked, susceptible of a good polish, and often beautifully marked with dark wavy lines and small knots. It is, perhaps, tougher than any other pine; and when seasoned is harder than Baltic or American pine. It is durable, and very free from the attacks of insects, and has been used for bedroom furniture, and especially for boat-building; but is now quite scarce.

Ironwood, a name applied to many widely different woods in various countries, often to several in one region. As most of these woods have other local names, it will avoid confusion if, when they come into English commerce, this name be not used. In the United States it is sometimes applied to the Bitternut Hickory (*Hicoria minima*) or to the Hornbeam and Hop-hornbeam (*Carpinus caroliniana* and

TIMBER: VARIETIES AND USES

Ostrya virginica). In South and East Africa the name is applied to the Mopane (*Copaifera Mopane*); various species of Olive (*Olea*), the "Olivenhout" of the Dutch, dark, heavy, dense woods, nearly equal to Lignum-vitæ and used as guides for the stamps in gold-crushing, are known as Black Ironwood; and the name White Ironwood is applied to the Umzimbit (*Toddalia lanceolata*), and Mauritius White Ironwood or White Milkwood, to the very heavy greyish-yellow *Sideroxylon inerme*, used for telegraph poles and construction work. As the name *Sideroxylon* is merely the Greek equivalent of ironwood, the species of this genus have, perhaps, the best right to the English name. *S. nitidum*, in Java; *S. ferrugineum*, the "Tuaktuak" of the Malay Peninsula; and *S. tomentosum*, of the Coromandel coast, are known as Ironwood. The "Bilian" of Borneo (*Eusideroxylon Zwageri*); the "Tampinis" (*Sloetia sideroxylon*) of the same region; the "Nagesah" (*Mesua ferrea*), of India, Ceylon, and Malaya; the "Ipil" (*Intsia bijuga*), "Mirabow" (*Intsia Bakeri*), and "Pynkadu" (*Xylia xylocarpa*), allied dark-coloured leguminous woods, widely distributed in the East Indies, are among the chief "ironwoods" of the East Indies. In New Zealand the myrtaceous Rata (*Metrosideros robusta* and *M. lucida*) and the allied *M. tomentosa* are given this name, as is *M. vera*, the Kayu besi of Malaya or Nani of Amboyna.

In Australia the name Ironwood is applied to Marblewood (*Olea paniculata*); to the allied and similar Native Olive (*Notolœa ligustrina*); to several species of Wattle or Myall, such as *Acacia excelsa* and *A. stenophylla*; and to the Swamp Oak or Beef-wood (*Casuarina equisetifolia*), the Kayu ru of Malaysia. For Kaffir Ironwood, *see* UMZIMBIT. This by no means exhausts the list of ironwoods.

Jack (*Artocarpus integrifolia*), an East Indian wood, sometimes known from its colour as "Orange-wood," and used as a dye, is moderately hard and takes a good polish; but is coarse and crooked in grain, generally warping seriously, and brittle. It is used in the East for house- and boat-building, furniture, and the backs of musical instruments, and in this country in turnery, marquetry, and for the backs of brushes. It is much improved by being Powellised, its colour and figure being well brought out.

Jarrah (*Eucalyptus marginata*), perhaps the most valuable timber of South-west Australia, where it is fairly plentiful. Growing 90 ft. to 150 ft. high and 3 ft. to 5 ft., or even 10 ft. in diameter, it yields timber 20 ft. to 40 ft. long and 1 ft. to 2 ft. square, of a deep red mahogany-like colour, sometimes with some mottling and ornamental curl in the grain, very heavy, hard, close-grained, taking a good polish, working smoothly, very uninflammable, and, owing to the astringent gum it contains, very durable. It requires, however, careful seasoning, being liable otherwise to twist and split. In ship-building it can be used without copper sheathing, and can be imported into India at a cost below that of teak. It is largely used for piles, telegraph poles, sleepers, and especially for paving-blocks. Its chief drawbacks for such purposes are its liability to split during the process of conversion, and its wearing to a polished surface. The engineer must also bear in mind that the tree is often unsound at the centre and that large gum-cavities, which seriously affect the strength of the log in the round, also frequently occur. The ornamental varieties are used for furniture, and large and beautiful burrs sometimes occur.

Jarul (*Lagerstrœmia speciosa*) and other related species, known by this name in Bengal, as "Pyinma" in Burma, "Muruta" in Ceylon, and "Banaba" in the Philippines, is the most valuable timber of North-east India, and second in value only to teak in Burma. It reaches a large size, is moderately hard and heavy, reddish in colour, and durable, whether dry or under water. It is used in building, for gun-carriages, wagon-building, wheels, and boats, often yielding compass timber suitable for knees. It is also used in the east in wharf-building, for piles and for sleepers.

Juniper (*Juniperus communis*), little more than a shrub, yields wood of small dimensions, tough, durable, and fragrant when burnt. It is used on the Continent for whip-handles and for vine-stakes. The woods of this genus closely resemble those of the related genera *Cupressus* and *Thuja*, and produce similar ornamental burrs. *J. excelsa* may reach 100 ft. in height, and forms pure forests in the Crimea, the wood of which may prove valuable for sleepers. The nearly related Indian Juniper (*J. macropoda*), the only valuable timber near Quetta, is used both for building and carpentry. *J. pseudosabina* in Northern Turkestan and Siberia yields good timber, and several species are employed in China. The American species are alluded to under the name of Pencil Cedar.

Kamassi (*Gonioma Kamassi*), also known as Cape Boxwood, Knysna Boxwood, or East London Boxwood, names liable to confuse it with the similar but unrelated *Buxus Macowanii*, from the same region, is one of the best woods of South Africa, though only small. It is heavy, hard, close-grained, and tough, and is used for cabinetwork, planes, and other tools, but would also be suitable for engraving.

Karri (*Eucalyptus diversicolor*), from South-west Australia, huge timber, occurring over a large area between Albany and the Blackwood River, though not nearly so abundant as Jarrah. It reaches 300 ft. to 400 ft. in height and 12 ft. in diameter; but an average tree will be 200 ft. high and 4 ft. in diameter. It is a reddish wood, weighing from 50 lb. to 72 lb. per cubic foot, slightly wavy or curled in grain, but with no ornamental figure, hard, tough, strong, and elastic; but not so easily wrought as Jarrah, frequently having large gum-cavities and liable to star-shake, durable under water, but not between wind and earth, comparatively non-inflammable, but more liable to dry-rot than Jarrah. It is much used in Australia for wheels, boat-building, piles, bridge-building, and wagons, and is now largely exported and used almost indiscriminately with Jarrah for paving.

Kauri Pine (*Agathis australis*) has been described by an impartial expert as "undoubtedly the best of all soft woods." It unfortunately grows only in the north of the North Island of New Zealand, and is slow in growth. It reaches 120 ft. to 140 ft. or even 200 ft. in height, and 4 ft. to 10 ft. or even 15 ft. or 20 ft. in diameter at the base, so that planks 20 ft. long and 4 ft. to 5 ft. wide without knot or shake are readily obtainable. The wide sapwood is very resinous, copiously exuding the well-known Kauri gum. The heart is yellowish-white to brown, very clean, straight, fine and close in grain, moderately hard for a pine, very firm, strong, and elastic, generally sound or with only a slight heart-shake, shrinking very little in seasoning, planing up well, with a beautiful silky lustre like the plainer samples of satinwood, taking a good polish or staining well, and wearing even, without splintering. It is thus unrivalled for masts and spars, and, owing to its freedom from knots or splintering, for the decks of yachts. Except when exposed to the teredo, it is more durable than any other pine, and has been used for sleepers, telegraph poles, and house-building. Being sometimes richly curled in grain, it is also used for joinery and carving. It is imported in sawn planks; but its scarcity and the heavy freightage on soft wood brought from so great a distance limit its use.

QUEENSLAND KAURI, the allied *Agathis robusta*, and *A. Palmerstoni*, also known as Dundatha Pine, is a somewhat smaller tree with a yellower, softer, but useful wood, largely used in North-east Australia by joiners, cabinetmakers, builders and pattern-makers.

Laburnum (*Cytisus Laburnum*) is the Faux ebénier (False Ebony) of the French and the Corsican Ebony of ancient Rome. Its broad yellow sapwood contrasts markedly with its dark brown, slightly greenish heart. It is very hard and capable of a high polish, and is used in turnery and inlaying. In England the tree is so exclusively considered as an ornament to the garden that its wood is seldom seen in commerce.

Lacewood, a name sometimes applied in America to the wood of the Plane or Buttonwood (*Platanus occidentalis*) when cut radially so as to display the darker silver-grain against the lighter groundwork. It is also known as Honeysuckle-wood, and is cut into veneer and used for fretwork.

Lancewood, chiefly imported from Guiana, where it is known as "Yariyari," is *Duguetia quitarensis.* It is yellow, light, hard, elastic, and fine-grained, and is used for carriage-shafts, fishing-rods, bows and arrows. The closely allied *Guatteria virgata* of Honduras, known locally as "Yaya," is imported under the same name. See also under MYRTLE.

LANCEWOOD, CAPE (*see* ASSEGAI-WOOD).

LANCEWOOD, DEGAME (*see* DEGAME).

Larch, the rapidly grown, light, even-grained, soft, tough, and very durable woods of the ten or twelve species of the coniferous genus *Larix,* especially *L. europœa.* The common larch may reach 80 ft. or 100 ft., or even 120 ft. in height, with a diameter of 2 ft. to 4 ft. at its base. The heartwood is yellowish-white, or reddish-brown in alpine regions, generally straight-grained, and therefore easily split, though sometimes rather coarse. The annual rings are slightly waved and sharply defined by broad, dark autumn-wood. It shrinks and warps still more in seasoning, and afterwards, which militates against its use for boat-building; but its lightness, its great durability (owing to its richness in tannic and phenolic antiseptic substances), and its comparative non-inflammability have recommended its use for building from early times. Much of Venice was built originally on larch piles, which are still sound. It is largely used for sleepers, pit-props, scaffold-poles, and ladders; and, being more free from large and loose knots than spruce, is much in demand for carpentry. It works up fairly well and has a lustrous surface. Owing to the ravages of the larch canker-fungus (*Dasyscypha calycina,* formerly known as *Peziza Willkommii*), which, while only sporadic in the early ripened woods of the mountains, becomes epidemic in our lowland woodlands, the Japanese species, *L. leptolepis,* was recommended to British foresters as likely to prove quicker in growth and more immune from the attacks of this fungus than the European. This species, found chiefly in Nippon, is redder, heavier, and harder than European larch.

It has, however, been proved experimentally in Bavaria that, when twenty years old, the European species has outgrown *L. leptolepis* ; and experiments are consequently being carried out with the more northern *L. kurilensis.*

In Eastern Siberia and Manchuria there is a species, *L. dahurica,* apparently closely similar, which is employed for coffins, pillars in temples, masts and telegraph poles, as well as for sleepers, and is thought superior to Oregon Fir for shipbuilding. There are several species in China, of which *L. Potaninii,* of North-west Szechwan, is valued: the Himalayan *L. Griffithiana* is soft and not large, and but little used; whilst *L. sibirica,* of W. Siberia, is closely similar to the European species.

Larches in the United States are commonly known as TAMARACKS or HACK-MATACKS. *L. pendula,* also known as *L. americana, L. microcarpa,* and *L. laricina,* the Black Larch of the North-east United States or "Epinette rouge" of the French Canadians, is similar in dimensions, structure, and uses to European Larch, though lighter and perhaps harder. It has been described as resembling Hard Pine in appearance, quality, uses, equalling European Larch in strength and oak in durability. It is one of the best American timbers for sleepers; it is used for interior finish; its straight growth makes it valuable for telegraph-poles, though crooked pieces are available for ships' knees; and it is very durable when in contact with the soil.

The WESTERN TAMARACK, or Larch (*L. occidentalis*), the largest species in the genus, sometimes reaching 250 ft. in height and 4 ft. to 8 ft. in diameter, is stronger than all other American conifers, and redder, heavier, and harder but somewhat coarser in texture than *L. pendula.* Though used chiefly for sleepers, fencing, and fuel, it is sometimes beautifully coloured and is suitable for interior finish. It grows mainly in Montana, Idaho, Oregon, and Washington, extending into British Columbia, and accompanied by *L. Lyalli.*

Laurel, Cape. (*See* STINKWOOD.)

Letter-wood, or Leopard-wood, the "Lettre moucheté" of the French or

"Pao de letras" of the Portuguese, is the straight-grained specimens of the mottled wood of *Brosimum Aubletii* of Guiana. It is known in English commerce as "Snake-wood." The heart is very heavy and hard, and takes a splendid polish; but it only squares about 20 in., of which not more than 6 in. exhibits the characteristic mottling, and is difficult to work and full of defects. It is imported in very small quantity for the bellies of bows, walking-sticks, and inlay.

Lignum-vitæ, a name belonging properly to the Tropical American species of the genus *Guaiacum*, especially *G. officinale*, *G. sanctum*, and *G. arboreum*. The first named of these, native to Jamaica, Cuba, Hayti, Venezuela, and Colombia, shipped mainly from Jamaica and St. Domingo, is not a large tree, its height ranging from 20 ft. to 40 ft., with a diameter of 1 ft. or 2 ft. Lignum-vitæ is one of the heaviest known woods, ranging from 60 lb. to 83 lb. per cubic foot. The dingy yellow, non-resinous sapwood is as durable as the heart, and part of it is consequently left on, to preserve the rest from splitting. The heart is blackish, with a greenish tinge: the pith rays are indistinguishable and the annual rings nearly so, whilst, owing to the oblique direction of the fibres, both radially and tangentially, the wood can hardly be split. Though very close-grained and strong, it is liable to cup-shake when more than 10 in. in diameter. The presence of from 25 per cent. to 26 per cent. of the gum resin, which renders the wood so valuable medicinally as to have given it the names of Palo santo (holy wood) or Lignum-vitæ (wood of life), renders it almost imperishable. It is imported in lengths of from 6 ft. to 12 ft. up to 10 in. in diameter, or from 3 ft. to 6 ft. when wider. It is used for ships' blocks, pulley-sheaves, pestles, mortars, skittle-balls, police truncheons, croquet-mallets, rulers, string-boxes, etc.

BAHAMA LIGNUM-VITÆ (*G. sanctum*) occurs in Florida and the Bahamas, and is sometimes 26 ft. long, otherwise resembling *G. officinale*. MARACAYBO LIGNUM-VITÆ (*G. arboreum*), occuring from Paraguay to Venezuela, sometimes from 60 ft. to 70 ft. long, with a diameter of 1 ft. or 2 ft., is brown, but almost as heavy and hard as the other species. The name Lignum-vitæ is sometimes given by the French to the coniferous *Tetraclinis articulata* (see THUYA); in New Zealand to species of *Metrosideros* (see RATA), and in Australia to several different woods, including an Acacia (*A. falcata*), a Myrtle (*Myrtus acmenioides*), and a Gum-tree (*Eucalyptus polyanthema*).

As the true Lignum-vitæ is becoming scarce, mention may be made here of two of the most practicable substitutes for it, namely the myrtaceous *Xanthostemon verdugonianus* (see MANCONO), and the sapindaceous *Dodonœa viscosa*. This latter is a shore plant widely distributed throughout the tropics, but usually small. It is known as Ake-ake in New Zealand, as Birch in Tasmania, as "Banderu" in the Philippines, as "Apiri" in Tahiti, as "Varal" in Ceylon, and as "Switch-sorrel" in Jamaica. It has white sapwood and a dark-brown or greenish-black rose-streaked heart, very hard, close-grained and durable. It is used for walking-sticks, tool-handles, turnery, and engraving.

Lime. (See LINDEN, below.)

Linden, the preferable name for the wood of *Tilia cordata*, *T. platyphyllos*, or *T. vulgaris*, often known as Lime, a name corrupted from Line and belonging rather to one of the Orange tribe. It is pale yellow, white, or reddish-white, very light, weighing only about 30 lb. the cubic foot, soft and close-grained. It is liable to become worm-eaten, and will not stand exposure to weather; but stands fairly well when thoroughly dried and varnished or painted. Used in Japan for sandals, and on the Continent sometimes for sabots, Linden is chiefly turned into small boxes for druggists, carved into toys or used for the sounding-boards and blind-wood in pianofortes. For this latter purpose it is imported from Lithuania It might, however, be more extensively employed for furniture, coach-building, and ply-wood, being closely similar to the nearly related American Basswood (*T. americana*), which, as already mentioned, is

TIMBER: VARIETIES AND USES

largely used for such purposes. Leather-cutters' planks are of linden, and no wood lends itself better to carving in high relief for decorative work where light weight is an object. The beautiful work of Grinling Gibbons, best represented at Windsor, Chatsworth, Trinity College, Cambridge, and the choir of St. Paul's Cathedral, is mostly in this wood. Grinling Gibbons lived at one time in La Belle Sauvage Yard —where this work is printed and published. Here it was, according to Horace Walpole, that " he carved a pot of flowers which shook surprisingly with the motion of the coaches that passed by."

Lingoa Wood. (*See* AMBOYNA-WOOD.)

Locust, a name not often used in England. In the United States it is, with the names Black or Yellow Locust applied to *Robinia pseudacacia*, the tree commonly called the Acacia in this country. This species, a native of the south-eastern United States, reaches considerable dimensions and is of fairly rapid growth, forming heartwood in five-year-old shoots, which is, perhaps, earlier than any other tree. It is valued as a shade tree in North China, and for planting on railway banks on the continent of Europe, its moist foliage serving to quench sparks and thus protect forest from fire, while the coppice-shoots are eagerly eaten by cattle. The heartwood is yellowish-brown streaked with red and green, weighing about 46 lb. per cubic foot, hard, strong, tough, and very durable, especially in contact with soil. It shrinks considerably in seasoning, which unfits it for furniture or building; but it is used for sleepers, and especially for trenails, fence-posts, and wheel-spokes. As it has of late years been found very suitable for the spokes of motor-cars, it might well be grown more than it is. Fence-posts of this wood will last fifteen or twenty years.

The nearly allied HONEY LOCUST, or Three-thorned Acacia (*Gleditschia triacanthos*), from the same region, yields a similar wood, which, however, is not quite so heavy. In the West Indies and in Demerara the name Locust is applied to the allied but superior wood of *Hymenœa Courbaril*, also known as " Courbaril,"

or in Spanish as " Algarrobo," a fine reddish-brown wood with darker streaks, very heavy and hard, close and even in grain, easily worked, taking an excellent polish and not warping. It is used in shipbuilding, engineering, and cabinet-work, for trenails and for cogs.

Logwood (*Hœmatoxylon campechianum*), a native of Central America, naturalised in Jamaica, comes to market in logs from 3 ft. to 4 ft. long, of a deep dull brownish-red, very heavy and hard, and with a violet-like perfume; but is used exclusively as a red or black dye, or as an ingredient of ink.

Mahogany, a name belonging originally to the West Indian *Swietenia Mahagoni* and *S. macrophylla*, now known distinctively as Spanish or Cuba Mahogany, but extended in the East Indies and in Africa to numerous other members of the sub-family *Swietenioideœ* and sometimes to the West Indian genus *Cedrela* and the allied East Indian genus *Toona*, belonging to the sub-family *Cedreloideœ* in the same family, *Meliaceœ*, and (less justifiably) in Australia to certain species of *Eucalyptus* and similar woods. The Cedrelas and Toonas are often known as Cedars or Cigar-box woods, and the Australian woods ought at least to be distinguished as Bastard, Forest or Swamp Mahoganies.

The name BORNEO MAHOGANY is sometimes applied to Poon, and the trade name Philippine Mahogany is most misleadingly used for at least three entirely distinct woods, none of which is a true Mahogany, namely Calantas (*Toona calantas*), Padouk (*Pterocarpus indicus*, *P. dalbergioides*, *P. echinatus*, and *P. macrocarpus*) and Tanguile (*Shorea polysperma*).

TRUE SPANISH MAHOGANY reaches large dimensions, yielding accurately squared timber 18 ft. to 35 ft. long and 11 in. to 24 in. square, very solid at centre, rarely affected by cup- or star-shake, and with insignificant heart-shake. Its weight is about 53 lb. per cubic foot, which is very heavy, and it is very hard, close, and straight in grain, and susceptible of the most perfect polish, with a beautiful satiny lustre. When freshly felled it is a light reddish-brown, soon darkening on exposure to light to a cinnamon brown. Its fine but distinct pith-rays are deeply coloured, and a variety of wavy figures occur, yielding the valuable "roe." "mottle," "cross-mottle," "dapple," "fiddle-back," "plum-pattern," and "curl mahogany." It does not as a rule shrink or warp, and is, perhaps, superior to all other woods in taking a firm hold of glue. It is almost non-inflammable and very durable. Swietenia macrophylla is rather lighter and softer than S. Mahagoni.

From the early days of the Spanish Conquest down to the eighteenth century mahogany was used as an oak substitute in shipbuilding for beams, planks, and stanchions, whilst figured specimens soon attracted attention for furniture. Thus in Spain, in the Spanish Netherlands, as at Ghent, and in Spanish America, as at Lima, we see cathedral stalls of this wood. In England, whilst oak was used almost exclusively down to 1625, and from 1625 to 1688 or into the reign of Queen Anne there was the "Age of Walnut" in furniture (though that wood had been considerably employed on the Continent for two or three centuries), the "Age of Mahogany" is dated from 1688. The admirable designs of Chippendale, Heppelwhite, and Sheraton, mostly executed in mahogany, gave this wood the popularity throughout the eighteenth century in England that satinwood then had in France. Its very extensive use for dining-tables, piano-cases, wardrobes, and other large articles, although latterly these have been very generally veneered, rendered Spanish mahogany scarce and costly.

ST. DOMINGO MAHOGANY was similar in quality to the Cuban, or even harder and almost horny, and was mostly figured, presenting a rich curl at the bases of its branches ; but it was much smaller, being generally 8 ft. to 10 ft., though sometimes 25 ft., long and 12 in., 13 in., or rarely 15 in. square ; and it now appears almost exhausted

The mahoganies of the Central American mainland, which form the bulk of the shrinking American supply, and are known as Honduras, Tabasco, Bay-wood, Colombian, Panama, Mexican, or Bermuda mahogany, are all probably the woods of species of the allied genus Cedrela. They are considerably lighter than Cuban mahogany, often weighing not more than 35 lb. per cubic foot ; and they are also correspondingly softer.

HONDURAS MAHOGANY, shipped from Belize, Trujillo, and Tabasco (the largest logs coming from the last-mentioned port, but frequently affected by heart-shakes), yields logs 25 ft. to 40 ft. long and 12 in. to 24 in. square, or even larger. It is seldom figured, and is apt to become brittle and to develop star-shake on drying ; but under the general trade name of Bay-wood, it is largely used by cabinetmakers, especially as ground for veneers. Guatemalan mahogany is generally classed with, and sometimes sold as, Honduras ; but Mexican, though reaching the largest dimensions, squaring 36 in. or even 48 in., is generally somewhat soft and spongy at the centre.

AFRICAN MAHOGANY, first imported about 1833, and in rapidly increasing quantities since 1886, is the product of a considerable number of species of the genera Khaya, Trichilia, and Entandrophragma, all nearly related to the West Indian genus Swietenia, distributed down the West Coast from Senegal to Angola and represented also by newly discovered species, in which a trade may develop, in Central and Eastern Tropical Africa. The main difficulties as to the supply of this wood are the facts that the trees occur scattered among a host of less valuable species in the confusion of a tropical jungle, that their great weight makes it very difficult to get them to waterways, and that the coast surf in many places much hinders their shipment. The wood reaches England in logs hewn square from 10 ft. to 29 ft., but mostly 15 ft. to 20 feet long, and from 13 in. to 52 in., but mostly 20 in. to 30 in. square. It is mostly lighter in weight and often in colour than West Indian mahogany ; but it varies from yellow to brown, with dark zones : it is sometimes even a darker red-brown than that from Cuba, and it may be so beautifully figured as to fetch the very highest prices for veneers. Some of the finest veneer and counter-top

TIMBER: VARIETIES AND USES

wood comes from the French Ivory Coast ports of Assinee and Grand Bassam. Here, and in the neighbourhood of the Gold Coast ports of Axim and Sekondi, the wood is mainly the produce of *Khaya senegalensis*; from Lagos to Benin (South Nigeria), of *Trichilia Pricuriana*, excellent cabinet wood; and from Benin eastward to Sapeli, of *Entandrophragma Candolleana* or some other species of that genus, fine, large, well-squared, and scented like a cedar.

EAST INDIA MAHOGANY is a name generally used for *Soymida febrifuga*, a large tree of Central and Southern India, nearly related to the true mahogany, but yielding a darker blood-red wood, heavier and harder than that wood, somewhat cross-grained and brittle, but used for furniture and carving, though scarce. The name is also applied to the related and similar, but lighter and more cedar-like, Chikrassi (*Chukrassia tabularis*), a fragrant, hard wood with a fine satiny lustre, liable to warp in hot weather.

MAHOGANY, INDIAN (*see* CEDAR, MOULMEIN).

MAHOGANY, MOUNTAIN (*see* BIRCH, AMERICAN).

MAHOGANY, PHILIPPINE (*see* PADOUK).

Mancono(*Xanthostemon verdugonianus*), a myrtaceous wood, probably the heaviest and hardest wood in the Philippines, being about the same weight as, but even harder than, Lignum-vitæ, appears immune to the attacks of termites and teredo; and being of crooked grain and difficult to split, seems, on the whole, to be the best substitute for that timber as yet discovered.

Mango (*Mangifera indica*), widely cultivated in the East Indies and introduced elsewhere in the Tropics, yields the cheapest light wood obtainable in Madras. It is dull grey, becoming a light chocolate colour, and porous, and holds nails faster than any other wood. It can be readily treated with preservatives: when Powellised it takes an excellent polish and it can also be creosoted. It is used for planking, packing-cases, blindwood, ground for veneers, canoes, solid cart-wheels, etc.

Manzanita (*Arctostaphylos pungens*), a fine-grained, small, heavy reddish-purple wood, with lighter streaks, native to the United States and employed in turnery.

Maple, the wood of various species of the genus *Acer*, exclusive of *A. Pseudoplatanus*, the Sycamore. The only British species, the Common, Field, or Hedge Maple (*A. campestre*), is a small tree, rarely yielding wood more than 9 in. or 10 in. in diameter. This wood is light brown or reddish-white, heavy, hard, fine-grained, and tough, with a beautiful satiny lustre. It is sometimes marked by dark pith-flecks and not uncommonly has a curled or speckled (bird's-eye) grain. Besides its use for fuel or charcoal, the wood is valued in France for turnery and cabinetwork. The curled and bird's-eye specimens when cut into veneer by the rotary knife are equal to those imported from America. The wood of the root is often beautifully mottled and dark, and the handsome "mazer" bowls, formerly turned and mounted in silver, were probably mostly from this part of the tree.

The NORWAY or PLANE MAPLE (*A. platanoides*), widely distributed on the Continent, is a much larger tree, yielding a moderately hard, heavy, and tough wood, which is easily worked, takes a fine polish owing to the satiny pith-rays characteristic of the group, but is apt to crack and warp. It is used in turnery, for musical instruments, gunstocks, etc., and in wagon-building, being nearly identical with sycamore; but its greyish tinge detracts from its value, fashion decreeing that sycamore must be pure white.

Though there are species locally valuable in the Himalaya (*A. Campbelli*, used for planking and tea-boxes, and *A. lævigatum*, for beams), in Manchuria (*A. tataricum*, "Sê," used for furniture), and in Japan, and one species from the Pacific slope is important, eastern North America presents the greatest variety of maples.

OREGON or CALIFORNIA MAPLE (*A. macrophyllum*) is moderately heavy, hard, strong, and close-grained, and sometimes reaches 4 ft. in diameter. It is used locally for axe- and broom-handles, snow-shoe-frames, and furniture, the occasionally occurring "fiddle-back" curl being especially valuable for the latter purpose.

This waviness of the grain, though rarely noticeable in the growing tree or on a transverse section, produces transverse corrugations visible when the bark is removed and varying in width from one to several to the inch. On all planed longitudinal or oblique sections this figuring appears, and so closely resembles the light and shadow on an undulating surface that it is difficult to believe it smooth.

The most valuable species of eastern North America is *A. barbatum* (also known as *A. saccharum*), the ROCK, HARD or SUGAR MAPLE. This grows to a good size and yields a pale buff, heavy, very hard, fine, and close-grained tough wood, with a satiny lustre and susceptible of a fine polish. In New England it is used as an oak substitute, in preference to beech, birch, or elm, for boats' keels, house-frames, flooring and interior finish, chairs and other furniture, axles, spokes, shoe-lasts, saddle-trees, etc.; and also largely for fuel. Blister, landscape, bird's-eye or pin, fiddle-back, and curly figures all occur in this species, the first two being almost confined to it. " Blister " is produced by wart-like prominences on the wood beneath the bark. The minute pittings or rudiments of buds known as bird's-eye appear as "eyes" in a tangential section and in a transverse direction as "pins." These figurings seldom extend more than 6 in. or 8 in. from the surface. They are cut by a rotary lathe into veneers the length of the log and running spirally inwards, and these figured veneers are the chief form in which this wood is imported. They are now largely used to face three-ply wood for panelling.

A "bog maple," dug out of peat, of a beautiful pale blue colour, is also cut into veneer and used in cabinetwork.

The SILVER, WHITE or SOFT MAPLE (*A. saccharinum*) is a redder, lighter, softer wood than the last, sometimes curled, which is used for flooring, interior finish, cheap furniture, and turnery. The red-flowered SWAMP or WATER MAPLE (*A. rubrum*) produces a similar wood, used in chair-making and turnery and for fuel, or, when curled, for gunstocks and veneers; but it is rarely exported. The ASH-LEAVED MAPLE, or Box-elder (*Negundo aceroides*, formerly *Acer Negundo*), well known in a variegated form in our suburban gardens, produces in the United States a soft white or yellowish wood, chiefly employed for paper pulp. In Australia the name Maple is applied to some totally unrelated woods.

Marblewood, Andaman (*Diospyros Kurzii*), also appropriately known as Figured Ebony or Zebra-wood, is handsomely streaked black and grey in alternating layers, and is very heavy, hard, and durable. It has been used for handles, but is valuable for furniture or walking-sticks, as a substitute for the scarce Calamander wood derived from related species in Ceylon.

Milkwood, White. (*See* IRONWOOD.)

Mirabow (*Intsia bakeri*, formerly *Afzelia palembanica*), a shade lighter in colour than Shoondul or Ipil (*I. bijuga*), but otherwise indistinguishable, the wood of these two species being one of the best in the Malayan region. *I. bijuga* occurs on the coasts from Madagascar to the Sandwich Islands, whilst *I. bakeri* is an inland species of narrower range. These trees yield timber 30 ft. to 40 ft. long, from $1\frac{1}{2}$ ft. to $2\frac{1}{2}$ ft. in diameter, reddish-brown, very heavy, so hard as to be known as Ironwood, fine and even in grain, working freely and taking so fine a polish as to resemble mahogany, very tough, termite-proof, and otherwise durable, and sometimes prettily figured. It is in demand for bridge-building, telegraph-posts, the corner-posts of houses, and furniture, for which last purpose it is sent to Europe.

Molavé (*Vitex littoralis, V. pubescens*, etc.), yellow, reddish-brown, or olive-brown woods, very heavy and hard, close-grained, strong and durable, with a figure resembling satinwood and not shrinking or splitting in seasoning, are among the finest woods of the Indo-Malayan area, being apparently fully equal to teak for many structural purposes, bridge, dock, house and shipbuilding, piles, mine-props, joists, planking, sleepers, paving-blocks, wheels, axles, wedges, etc., while they might well be used in cabinetwork.

Mora (*Dimorphandra excelsa*), a native of Guiana and Trinidad, is a tree 100 ft.

TIMBER: VARIETIES AND USES

or more in height, yielding logs 18 ft. to 35 ft. long and 12 in. to 20 in. square. The wood is chestnut-brown or red, very heavy and hard, straight-grained, tough, strong and durable, but very subject to star-shake. It takes a good polish and has sometimes a beautiful curled figure. It is used for ships' beams, and, especially when red and figured, as a mahogany substitute for furniture.

Mulberry (*Morus alba*), a native of China, introduced into Europe, as a food for the silkworm, in the fifteenth century, is a tree of moderate size, having a yellowish-brown heartwood, somewhat similar to that of *Robinia*, but becoming reddish, like old mahogany, heavy, hard, tough, flexible, and lustrous. It is used by the Chinese for agricultural implements and furniture, and is occasionally used in Europe for veneers and inlay. The woods of *M. indica*, native from Japan to the Himalaya, used for tea-boxes and furniture, and *M. rubra*, of the Eastern United States, used for fence-posts and cooperage, are very similar to that of *M. alba*.

Myall, an aboriginal name applied in Australia to various species of wattle (*Acacia*), especially *A. pendula*, a small tree, native to the north-east of the continent. Its wood is a rich dark brown, beautifully marked resembling briar-root, very heavy, hard, close-grained, and, when unpolished, violet-scented, for which reason it is often known in England as Violet-wood. It is used for boomerangs, tobacco pipes, fancy boxes, and veneers; but is sometimes imitated by artificially scenting the wood of other species.

Myrobalan (*Terminalia belerica*), the Behara or Bohera of India, Bulu of Ceylon, or Thitsein of Burma, is a yellowish-grey wood, without heart, hard but not durable, readily becoming worm-eaten, though improved by steeping in water. It is used for coffee-boxes, packing-cases, planking, and canoes.

Myrtle, a name applied to the Evergreen Beech (*Nothofagus Cunninghamii*) of Tasmania and to various Australian myrtaceous trees. Of these the most important, perhaps, is *Backhousia myrtifolia*, the Scrub, Grey, or Native Myrtle of north-east Australia, also known as Lancewood, a small tree yielding a light yellow wood with pretty dark brown walnut-like streaks, hard, close-grained, tough, and durable. It is used for bows and turnery, mallets, tool-handles, etc.

Nan-mu (*Machilus nanmu*, with other species of the genera *Machilus* and *Lindera*) affords one of the most valuable woods in China. It was formerly obtained in logs 82 ft. long and over 4 ft. in diameter; but now reaches Shanghai in planks 8 ft. long and 14 in. across. It is greenish and brown, close-grained, easily worked, fragrant, and very durable, and has been used in building the palaces in Pekin.

Nettle-tree (*Celtis australis*), the "Micocoulier" of the French and "Zürgelbaum" of the Germans, is a tree of moderate size, native to the Mediterranean and Temperate and Tropical Asia, having a yellowish grey wood with dark streaks, heavy, hard, compact, strong, and elastic, taking a high polish, and, when cut obliquely, resembling satinwood. It was used for the early Greek statues of the gods, and is now employed to some extent for furniture, but chiefly for whip and tool-handles, walking-sticks, flutes, and other turnery.

Oak, a name which should be restricted to the woods of the species of the genus *Quercus*. Upwards of three hundred of these species are known to botanists, none of which occur south of the Equator, except in and near Java; but many of these are not used as timber even locally, while the number in general commerce is quite small. On the other hand, there are great variations in the quality of the woods obtained from the same species in different districts. Oak wood is generally yellowish-brown to brown, with distinctly visible pith-rays, either all fine or some wide and others narrow. It is moderately or very heavy and hard, with a strength that is exceptional in its proportion to the weight; but, as has been truly said, it is neither the hardest and heaviest, nor the most supple and toughest of woods, but it combines in a useful manner the average of these qualities. Oak, in most species, is subject to star- and cup-shakes and warps and shrinks slightly in the process of seasoning; but when once thoroughly dried, changes less than almost any wood. For fencing or staves, oaks generally split readily with a moderately smooth surface; and, for ornamental purposes, they are susceptible of a high polish, and may exhibit handsome mirrors or silver-grain if quartered.

The chief species of oak grown in North Africa and Europe—to adopt as the most convenient a geographical enumeration—are *Quercus Robur, Q. Ilex*, the Holm Oak; *Q. Cerris*, the Turkey or Mossy-cup Oak; and *Q. Mibeckii*, the Zeen Oak; though there are twenty others. The COMMON, BRITISH, or EUROPEAN OAK (*Q. Robur*) ranges from Mount Atlas and from Syria to lat. 60° N. It is a somewhat variable species, three somewhat inconstant types being recognised in Britain, namely, *pedunculata, sessiliflora*, and *intermedia*.

The PEDUNCULATE OAK (*Q. Robur pedunculata*) derives its name from the long stalks or peduncles to its acorns, for which reason also the Germans call it "Stieleiche," whilst from the situations in which it grows they term it "Thaleiche," Valley Oak, and from its early production and shedding of its leaves it is called "Früheiche," Early Oak, or "Sommereiche," Summer Oak. It is generally quick-growing, and its wood is denser, more compact, tougher, and lighter in colour than that of the other varieties, the French name "Chêne blanc" referring to this last characteristic.

The SESSILE-FLOWERED OAK (*Q. Robur sessiliflora*) has long stalks to its leaves, but not to its acorns, and is known by the French as "Chêne rouge," and by the Germans as "Rotheiche," "Bergeiche," or "Spateiche," Red, Hill, or Late Oak. It produces greater lengths of clear stem than *Q. Robur pedunculata*, but its wood is generally darker in colour, less dense, and more liable to shakes. From a supposed greater resemblance to the wood of the chestnut it is sometimes called "Chestnut Oak."

The DURMAST OAK (dark-acorned) (*Q. Robur intermedia* or *Q. Robur pubescens*) is uncommon. It has short stalks to both leaves and acorns, and its leaves are downy on their under surfaces. Its dark-brown wood is considered inferior; but it must be admitted that in the absence of any external evidence as to the source of the wood, timber-dealers cannot discriminate between the produce of these varieties. Slow-grown, unthrifty oak from poor soil or severe climatic conditions, though often beautifully figured, is generally softer than quick-grown thrifty wood from good soil and a favourable climate; while stunted, rock-grown trees or coppice-wood is often crooked in grain and difficult to split. There is, perhaps, greater difference between the oak of this species imported from various parts of the Continent than there is between the varieties just named. French oak, largely *pedunculata*, grown in Brittany and Normandy, is generally smaller, but shrinks and splits less in seasoning than does English wood; and, being equally strong, tough, elastic, and durable, would seem to be a better all-round wood.

DANTZIC OAK, largely *sessiliflora* mostly brought down the Vistula from Poland to Dantzic, Memel, or Stettin, but sometimes shipped from Odessa, is brown, straight, and clean in grain, and free from knots, and is sometimes so figured as to be classed as "wainscot-oak," for furniture. It comes to market either as staves for casks; in logs 18 ft. to 30 ft. long and 10 in. to 22 in. square; or in planks about 32 ft. long, 9 in. to 15 in. wide, and 2 in. to 8 in. thick. It is so pliable and elastic as to be capable, when steamed, of being bent into almost any curve without fracture, but is inferior in strength to good English oak.

RIGA OAK, from the Western Dwina, is a very similar wood, probably of the same variety as that from Dantzic; but only comes to market in wainscot logs of moderate dimensions for furniture or veneers, for which purposes it is the finest quality in the trade. Excellent oak, the product of this variety, occurs in Styria, Croatia, Hungary, Bosnia, Serbia, Rumania, etc., and is imported as "Adriatic" or Serbian.

Throughout Europe, and more especially in Britain, oak, mostly of this species, was employed for every purpose, both of naval and civil architecture, to the ex-

TIMBER: VARIETIES AND USES

clusion of all other woods, until about the beginning of the eighteenth century, when pine was first largely imported from the Baltic and North America. In our dockyards oak continued to be in large demand until about 1865, all other hard and heavy woods used in shipbuilding being compared with it as a standard and classed as " oak substitutes." With the introduction of armour-plating and steel ships, wood of any kind has become far less important in shipbuilding, and teak has largely superseded oak. In civil architecture, though the greater lightness, ease of working, and cheapness of coniferous timber have led to its being now generally preferred, oak is still in request where strength and durability are objects, though the picturesque partial collapse of old buildings is now avoided by the use of built-up beams in preference to those cut from the solid log, or, as the Americans term it, "boxhearted."

The durability of oak timber is undoubtedly much affected by the season at which it is felled, winter-felled wood containing least water and sap or fermentable matter. The "life" of a railway sleeper of good young oak, not treated with any preservative, is estimated at seven to ten years; if creosoted, at fifteen; or if treated with zinc chloride, at sixteen years; but the piles of Old London Bridge, sound when taken up in 1827 after six and a half centuries, or those sunk through the peat under Winchester Cathedral in 1079, probably without any preservative treatment, are still more striking evidences of durability. Bog Oak, blackened by the action of the iron salts in peat on the tannin of the wood—forming a natural ink—shows still greater periods of durability. The acid character of the wood, however, while securing it very largely from insect attack, has a very destructively corrosive effect upon iron in contact with it.

The harder qualities of oak are still largely in request for gate-posts, stair-treads, parquet floors, palings, and wheelwrights' work; whilst for wainscoting, furniture, and carving the softer, more figured varieties are required. For these purposes much American oak is now employed.

Veneers cut to the fortieth or fiftieth of an inch are sometimes used for wallpapers. Even when discoloured by the incipient decay of the aged but still growing tree, oak may fetch a high price for its deep coloured veneers, though, perhaps, in some cases this Brown Oak may be sound and owe its colour to the soil.

It may be suggested to the craftsman that, if he is not particularly anxious that his carvings shall endure for untold centuries, he may secure an effect almost equal to that of oak with about a tithe of the effort by working in chestnut. Attention has been directed to the widespread error of describing old roofs or buildings as chestnut which, on examination, prove invariably to be of oak.

The wood of the HOLM OAK (*Q. Ilex*), an evergreen species, native to the Mediterranean region, is not large, becomes with age a deep brown or jet-black, and is hard, horny, difficult to saw or work, and so liable to shakes as to be unsuitable for planks. Some Italian and Spanish oak formerly imported probably belonged to this species; but though common as an ornamental tree in England, its wood does not come into the market.

The TURKEY or MOSSY-CUP OAK (*Q. Cerris*) is a tall species with straight, clean stems producing a red-brown wood, which in the Mediterranean area is hard, but very liable to shakes and does not resist insect attacks. Some of the oak classed as Adriatic belongs to this species.

The ZEEN OAK (*Q. Mibeckii*) of Northwest Africa covers a large area in Tunis. It reaches a very large size; its wood is yellowish or reddish, with broad pith-rays, and is heavy, straight-grained, and very durable; and, like most evergreen species apparently, of a horny texture, but liable to shakes and warping. When winter-felled and well seasoned it is a valuable timber for bridge-girders, piles, railway sleepers, and barrel staves.

The North American oaks are numerous, and fall naturally and commercially into three groups—" white," " red " or " black," and " live," that is, evergreen.

WHITE OAK (*Q. alba*), a native of Southeastern Canada and the Eastern United

States, ranges from 28° to 46° N. lat., and reaches large dimensions. Its wood is reddish as compared with European Oak, heavy, hard, tough, close and straight in grain, and durable in contact with the soil. It is one of the most generally useful and commercially important of American hardwoods; but though the dominant species in extensive woodlands, its growing scarcity has made a market for Japanese wood.

QUEBEC OAK is the trade name for an excellent quality, fetching 20 per cent. more than the slower-grown Baltimore Oak, mainly because it reaches larger dimensions. The wood is largely used in boat- and house-building, for the frames, door-sills, and interior finish of houses, for barrel staves, railway sleepers, piles, fence-posts, carriage-building, agricultural implements, and fuel; whilst when quarter-sawn it is beautifully figured and largely employed for furniture. When steamed, it is so elastic that planks cut from it may be bent into almost any form, and it is free from knots and shrinks and splits very little in seasoning, though it may twist to some extent. It is shipped in logs 25 ft. to 50 ft. long and 11 in. to 28 in. square, or in thick or thin planks. It is inferior to the best European Oak.

BURR OAK (*Q. macrocarpa*), a rich brown though rather more porous than the last-named species, is more durable in contact with soil than any other American Oak, but is both used and classed as White Oak.

POST OAK (*Q. minor*), Chestnut Oak or Rock Oak (*Q. Prinus*) and Basket or Cow Oak (*Q. Michauxii*) are similar brown, heavy, hard, durable woods, classed and used as White Oak.

RED OAK (*Q. rubra*), so called from its leaf-tints, known in commerce as Canadian Red or Black Oak, reaches large dimensions, though it is a slow-growing species. It is light or reddish-brown with indistinct pith-rays, and is heavy, hard, and strong, though inferior to White Oak, both in strength and durability. It is coarse-grained, but easy to work, and shrinks moderately without splitting in seasoning, and is quite suitable for much constructive work; but is so porous as to be unfit for the staves of barrels to hold liquids. It is used for flour- and sugar-barrels, clap-boards, panelling and furniture, and is imported to England for the two last-named purposes.

The TEXAS RED or SPOTTED OAK (*Q. texana*), the Scarlet Oak (*Q. coccinea*), the Willow Oak (*Q. Phellos*), the Pin Oak (*Q. palustris*), and the Water or Punk Oak (*Q. aquatica*) are more or less similar oaks, varying in weight, which are classed as red oak and are at most not superior to it.

The LIVE OAK of the Southern States (*Q. virginiana*) reaches large dimensions and produces a dark golden-brown heartwood, with distinct pith-rays, which is very heavy, compact, hard, tough, strong, and durable, and takes a superb polish; but is often crooked in growth, somewhat twisted in grain, and consequently difficult to work. It is, perhaps, stronger than any known oak, and is used by wheelwrights and millwrights, and for interior finish, mallets, and tool-handles. The California Live Oak or Maul Oak (*Q. chrysolepis*) is similar.

Several species of evergreen oak occur in Southern Japan, including "Aka-gashi" (*Q. acuta*), dark red-brown, very hard and heavy; "Shira-gashi" (*Q. vibrayeana*), greyish-white; "Ichii-gashi" (*Q. gilva*), also light-coloured; and "Urajiro-gashi" (*Q. myrsinœfolia*). These are used in wagon- and boat-building. The genus is said to be represented by sixty species in China. On the Yalu River *Q. crispula* and *Q. dentata* reach a good size and yield hard, durable wood which used to warp and split considerably in seasoning, but is now steam-dried in Japan and is employed for shipbuilding, sleepers, casks, axles, oars, etc. In Southern China oak is found to be subject to termite attack, and none of the wood from this country appears to be equal in quality to *Q. Robur*.

In the Himalayas there are also a considerable number of species growing at altitudes of from 50 ft. above sea-level in Bengal up to 3,000 ft., 8,000 ft., and 10,000 ft., most of them being evergreen. Among them are the Holm Oak (*Q. Ilex*); the Grey or Himalayan Ilex (*Q. incana*); *Q. lappacea*, of the Khasia Hills, and *Q. lanceœfolia*, of the Garrow Hills, and Assam, which resemble English oak, but are harder; *Q. Griffithii*, of the Khasia Hills, Sikkim, and Bhotan; and *Q. serrata*, ranging into China and Northern Japan, brown woods much resembling English oak; and *Q. fenestrata*, at lower altitudes, which is somewhat inferior.

The SHE OAK, possibly a corruption of an aboriginal name "shiok," or possibly from some resemblance seen in the broad pith-rays, is a name applied in Australia to various species of *Casuarina*, by no means closely related to Oak. They are also known as Forest, Swamp, or Botanybay Oak, and some of them as Beef-wood or Ironwood. They are mostly a mahogany like, red or reddish-brown, often prettily mottled with dark longitudinal bands, heavy, hard, tough, close-grained, easily worked, and very durable, but liable to split in drying. Formerly used for boomerangs and for the forks used by Fijian cannibals, and now locally for roof-shingles (whence the name Shingle Oak), fences, and handles, several species, especially *C. stricta* and *C. torulosa*, are also employed for furniture and veneers.

SILKY OAK, the north-east Australian name for the red-brown, hard, close-grained woods of *Grevillea robusta* and some other related species of the Family *Proteaceæ*. They sometimes have a beautiful wavy figure, and, as they are now becoming scarce, are employed in veneers, or for walking-sticks.

For AFRICAN AND FOREST OAK *see* BEEF-WOOD.

Olive (*Olea europœa*), native to the Mediterranean region, seldom of any considerable size, is a heavy, very close- and fine-grained wood of a light yellowish-brown, without distinguishable annual rings or pith-rays, but with handsome, irregular, wavy dark lines and mottlings, resembling box in texture, but not so hard and rather brittle. It takes an excellent polish, and is chiefly employed in turnery and carving for small articles, such as fancy boxes, paper-knives, etc. The Indian species, *O. cuspidata*, is very similar, and several others are used in turnery in different parts of the world.

OLIVE, WILD (*see* SUMACH, VENETIAN).

Orange (*Citrus Aurantium*), probably a native of India, but now cultivated for its fruit in most tropical and sub-tropical countries, has small, light yellow, heavy, hard, close-grained wood, used in the West Indies for cabinetwork, and for tool-handles in Szechuan, made into toothpicks in Madeira and at Rio de Janeiro, and imported from Algeria for walking-sticks. "Black Orange" and "Congo Oak" are, however, names used in the walking-stick trade for the stems of the common Broom (*Cytisus scoparius*), imported from the same country. *See also* JACK.

OSAGE ORANGE (*Toxylon pomiferum*, formerly known as *Maclura aurantiaca*), from Arkansas and Texas, is known as Bow-wood (French, "Bois d'arc"), having been used by the Redskins for their bows, just as the related and similar wood of the mulberry was by the aborigines of China. The tree reaches a considerable size, and its wood is brown when cut transversely, yellow longitudinally, but soon turning greyish on exposure. It is very heavy, hard, flexible, and durable in contact with soil, but shrinks considerably in drying. It is used in America for sleepers, mine-props, paving-blocks, fence-posts, etc., and is not common in trade, but might be employed in turnery or for carving.

Orham-wood is a Canadian elm, brown, soft, coarse-grained, twisting badly in seasoning, and not durable, which has been considerably imported to Liverpool as a cheap cabinet-wood.

Padouk (*Pterocarpus macrocarpus*, *P. indicus*, *P. dalbergioides*, and *P. echinatus*), ranging from Southern India, Southern China and the Andaman Islands to the Philippines, Sunda, and Fiji Islands, and variously known as Andaman Redwood, Tenasserim or Philippine Mahogany, and Burmese Rosewood, are a series of large, very heavy, hard, red woods. They vary in colour, being either dark red, brick red, or streaked with black, and sometimes beautifully figured; are heavier than mahogany and slightly aromatic, susceptible of a high polish, durable, and termite proof. Some trees yield timber squaring 2 ft. in the side and 60 ft. in length, or they may be 5 ft. in diameter. The wood takes two years for natural seasoning, may fade somewhat on exposure to light, and does not take glue like mahogany. In India it has been used for gun-carriages and for furniture; in Burma for cart-wheels and for musical instruments; and in the United States in the building of Pullman cars, for parquet floors, counter-tops, and furniture. It is unquestionably one of the most valuable Eastern furniture woods. The wood of the roots and of some parts of the stem is sometimes exceptionally dark and variegated, and is manufactured into small ornamental boxes. The name "AFRICAN PADOUK" has been applied to *Pterocarpus erinaceus* and *P. angolensis*. (*See* ROSEWOOD, African.)

Pai'cha (*Euonymus Hamiltonianus*), a native of China, is a yellowish, soft, close, and fine-grained wood, used for carving and for wooden type.

Palisander-wood, imported from Bahia and other Brazilian ports, is a handsome chocolate-brown wood, marked by deep black veins and bands, very heavy and hard and somewhat brittle. Though, perhaps, once the bignoniaceous *Jacaranda brasiliana*, it is probably now *Dalbergia nigra*, or some species of the allied leguminous genus *Machœrium*, otherwise known from their faint rose-water smell as Brazilian rosewood. The best figured variety comes from Bahia in roughly hewn semi-cylindrical half-logs, never sound at the centre. That from Rio de Janeiro is less unsound and in round logs, but less figured. It is a very valuable wood, both solid and in veneers, for furniture and cabinet-work, especially pianoforte cases.

Pear (*Pyrus communis*), the comparatively small wood of the well-known fruit tree, has no true heart, but is a light pinkish-brown, moderately heavy, hard, close-grained-firm material, easily cut in any direction, taking a satiny polish, and very durable, if kept dry. It is highly valued for turnery, cabinetwork, T-squares, set-squares, calico-printing blocks, coarse wood engraving, or, when ebonised, for picture frames. As a kind of wood of pleasing natural colour and stable, it can be recommended to the craftsman. A Chinese species, *P. sinensis*, is used for wood engraving and for the manufacture of combs, which are dyed yellow with the fruit of a gardenia so as to resemble box.

Peppermint. (*See* REDWOOD.)

Persimmon (*Diospyros virginiana*), native to the Eastern United States, is a tall ebony, not exceeding 2ft. in diameter, with a very broad creamy-white sapwood, sometimes extending over sixty rings, and a sharply contrasted dark brown or black heart, very heavy, weighing 50 lb. per cubic foot, hard, close-grained, strong and tough, resembling hickory, but finer in grain and taking a fine polish. Known also as "Date Plum." It is used for wagon-shafts, mallets, shoe-lasts, planestocks, etc.

Pine should be a general name for the woods of the species of the northern genus *Pinus*, as distinguished from Spruce, the wood of the species of *Picea* and Fir, which should be that of *Abies*. It is, however, extended to the woods of such allied genera as *Sciadopitys* and *Pseudotsuga* in the northern hemisphere, and to *Agathis*, *Frenela*, *Araucaria*, *Dacrydium*, *Podocarpus*, and *Prumnopitys* in the southern. Curiously enough, also, the wood of the various local varieties of the Northern Pine (*Pinus sylvestris*) imported from Baltic ports, such as Dantzic, Memel, and Riga, is known in trade as fir or deal, while the name Pine is used for that of other species of the genus imported from North America.

Deal. it may be explained, should properly mean only wood in the particular form of planks 9 in. broad and not more than 4 in. thick. The relatively simple and uniform structure of the wood of the genus *Pinus* makes it easy to work. The different species occur in pure forests— forests, that is, made up mainly of a single species—over wide areas in the north Temperate zone or on the mountains of the northern tropics. Their woods are, also, quick-grown, and, for these reasons, are cheap. They season rapidly, but with little shrinkage; are never too hard to take a nail; are, when seasoned, protected by their resin from the attacks of boring insects and are otherwise durable; occur in long, straight-grown logs; and are, in proportion to their lightness, very stiff

TIMBER: VARIETIES AND USES

and strong. These reasons combine to render them the most generally useful, and by far the most extensively used of all woods. Although many of them are harder than some of the woods of broad-leaved trees, such as poplars, willows, horse-chestnut, etc., all coniferous woods are conventionally known as "soft woods"; but the Pines fall into two natural groups known as Hard Pines and Soft Pines. The Hard Pines are heavier, darker-coloured, ranging from yellow to deep orange or brown, and—owing to the autumn wood forming a much broader proportion of the annual ring—harder; while they also generally show a more abrupt contrast between heart and sapwood. This group includes the greater number of species, both in Europe and in North America, which latter area is the home of about three-fifths of the seventy species of the genus. The Soft Pines range in colour from white to light-red; are lighter in weight; and have a narrow zone of autumn wood merging gradually on its inner surface into the spring wood.

Deferring the description of the allied genera the wood of which is known as Pine, an arrangement will be followed as far as possible, both natural and geographical, beginning with the Hard Pines, and, among them, with those of Europe, but dealing only with the more important.

NORTHERN PINE is the best general name for *Pinus sylvestris*, the only species indigenous in Britain, where it is commonly known as Scots Fir. It has a wide range over Northern Europe, reaching altitudes of 700 ft. above sea-level in Northern Norway and 6,500 ft. on the Sierra Nevada of Southern Spain, and occurring as far as 68° N. lat. As its branches are in whorls the knots serve to distinguish the wood from larch, in which they are scattered. The characters and quality of the wood vary much, according to climate and soil. Conversely to what is the case with oaks, the more slowly grown pines of high latitudes or mountains, having narrower annual rings with a proportionally smaller amount of spring wood, are heavier, denser, and stronger than those of the south, or of plains, or from rich soils. English-grown pine of this species is thick-baited, carrying a large amount—often 4 in.—of sapwood, and is consequently of comparatively little value, not being nearly as durable as larch. Scottish-grown wood is of better quality and has been largely imported into the North of England, chiefly as mine-timber.

Pine imported from foreign countries is known by various names, such as Redwood, Red Deal, or Yellow Deal, or, according to its origin, as White Sea, Baltic, Petersburg, Riga, Memel, Dantzic, Gefle, Soderhamn, Swedish or Norway Fir. The White Sea wood, shipped from Archangel and Mezen especially to Peterhead and Leith, is close-grown, less resinous, but perhaps the strongest and most durable imported, though subject to heartshakes and surface-splitting. It is most suitable for joinery. Swedish wood from Gefle and Soderhamn is of high quality; but much of the wood from that country is yellowish white and liable to various shakes, whilst it seldom exceeds 35 ft. in length or 16 in. square. It furnishes much cheap building material, deals for rough carpentry, matchwood and firewood.

Most Norwegian Pine comes over in cheap prepared flooring, matchboarding, door and window frames, and firewood. Large, heavy, hard, resinous wood, good for sleepers, paving-blocks, masts, beams and planks, comes from the Southern Baltic ports. Riga Fir, from the Dnieper and Western Dwina, has few knots, but has a slight tendency to heartshake, making it more wasteful in conversion, and is lighter than, and on the whole inferior to, Dantzic. This last, floated down the Vistula, comes to market in lengths of from 18 ft. to 50 ft., squaring 11 in. to 20 in.; in deals from 2 in. to 5 in. thick, and in irregularly grown logs for sleepers. It is light, moderately hard, even and straight-grained, tough, elastic wood, easily worked, and useful for planking, beams, joists, scaffolding, masts, and spars. This pine is the chief timber used in house-building in the north of the continent of Europe. The houses are framed of hewn logs, the walls are built up of logs in the round, covered with clap-boards externally and with panelling within, all of this species. In Russia logs of it are used for corduroy roads, and it is used to an enormous extent as fuel on railways, and steamboats and in private houses.

Baltic Pine was imported to our east-coast towns for flooring, wainscoting, and joinery in the fifteenth, sixteenth, and seventeenth centuries, when oak was the chief timber employed over England generally. The high price of foreign timber during the Napoleonic Wars led to the clearing of the indigenous pine forests of Scotland and the north of England ; but the easy working and great durability of pine gradually broke down the prejudice in favour of oak and led to the great consumption of this timber, especially in Eastern Britain, and of the Yellow Pine (*Pinus Strobus*) of North America in the west.

The STONE or UMBRELLA PINE (*P. Pinea*) of the Mediterranean region is a whitish, very light, and moderately resinous wood, used locally. though the tree is most especially valued for its edible seeds or "nuts." It does not reach a very large size.

The CLUSTER PINE (*P. Pinaster*). sometimes known as *P. maritima*, of the same region, and also of moderate dimensions, yields a reddish, soft, coarse-grained, very resinous, but not very durable wood. Planted on the landes of Bordeaux to check the drifting of the sand-dunes, this tree is there a valuable source of turpentine, charcoal, and lamp-black ; but a million loads have been annually imported into South Wales for mine-timbers. The wood is also used for coarse carpentry, packing-cases, etc.

The AUSTRIAN PINE (*P. nigra*, var. *austriaca*), or black Austrian Pine, the chief source of pine wool and pine oil, yields timber much used for building on the Continent, similar to that of the Northern Pine, but rather coarse in grain and apt, when grown in poor soil, to be knotty.

The CORSICAN PINE (*P. nigra*, var. *Poiretiana*, often known as *P. Laricio*, or Larch Pine) is a closely related lofty species (growing to 80-100 ft.), producing wood which is creamy-white when freshly cut, but becomes brownish-yellow when seasoned, very resinous, durable, and obnoxious to insects, equal to Northern Pine of good quality.

The ALEPPO PINE (*P. halepensis*) of the Mediterranean region, which has been introduced into Australia, was used for the flooring, doors, and ceiling of the Temple at Jerusalem, and was probably the " Ash " or " Fir " of Isaiah xxxvii. 24, and xliv. 14. Its yellowish-white, fine-grained wood is now valued locally for telegraph-poles, joinery. turnery, and fuel, and the tree is also a source of turpentine. Largely used at one time for ships' decks.

The JAPANESE BLACK PINE (*P. Thunbergii*), the Sung-shu of Western China, O-matsu, or Kuro-matsu of the Japanese, occurring also in Corea, reaching large dimensions, and growing up to altitudes of 4,000 ft., has a close-grained and resinous wood which is durable only when grown at high altitudes. It is used in house-building. for furniture, and as fuel.

The JAPANESE RED PINE (*P. densiflora*), or " Aka-matsu," a somewhat smaller species, is used locally for all kinds of carpenters' work.

In the Philippines the SALENG (*P. insularis*) is a hard pine which is very resinous and of considerable local importance for house-building and planking.

Among American hard pines the best is, perhaps, the CANADIAN RED PINE (*P. resin, osa*), known as Norway Pine in Canada, as Yellow Pine in Nova Scotia, and in European trade as American Red. It reaches 100 ft. in height and 2 ft. to 4 ft. in diameter, weighs from 30 lb. to 44 lb. per cubic foot, and is a buff or straw colour to a pale reddish-tan colour, light, hard, tough, elastic, fine-grained, with a silky lustre, working up well and very resinous, and does not shrink or warp much in seasoning. When of small dimensions and consequently largely sapwood, it is not durable ; but the heart is so. The wood is excellent for piles, spars, boat-building, and flooring ; but, being more expensive than Baltic Pine, has never been very largely imported.

The CAROLINA or SHORT-LEAF PINE (*P. echinata*), of the Eastern United States,

TIMBER: VARIETIES AND USES

is commonly known as Yellow Pine in America, but as Carolina or New York Pine at Liverpool, to which port it comes from North Carolina. It reaches a good size; is a gold-ochre to a pale buff-yellow in colour, rather heavy, weighing 34 lb. to 38 lb. per cubic foot, hard, coarse-grained, compact, strong, not difficult to work, and durable, much resembling Long-leaf Pine—the pitch pine of our market—and little inferior to it in hardness or strength. It is used in house-building, flooring, and interior finish, and very largely in American dockyards for decks and spars.

The LOBLOLLY PINE (*P. Tœda*) of the Southern United States is generally confounded with the long-leaf pine, though it is softer, lighter, coarser in grain, wider in its annual rings, weaker, and less durable than that species. Its ready reproduction, rapid growth, easy felling and conversion, cheapness and suitability for many purposes, combine to render it the most valuable tree in Maryland, Delaware, and Virginia. It is so rich in resin as to be known as Torch or Frankincense Pine, and is, of course, excellent as fuel. It is known as Yellow Pine in the northern markets in the States.

The WESTERN YELLOW or BULL PINE (*P. ponderosa*) of the Western United States reaches a very great size, being sometimes 300 ft. in height and 15 ft. in diameter. In spite of its name it varies very much in weight, strength, and durability; but is generally hard, brittle, resinous, and not durable in contact with soil. It is the chief hard pine of the region and is largely used for sleepers, mine-timbers, building, and fuel. The AMERICAN BLACK PINE (*P. Jeffreyi*), growing at altitudes of over 6,000 ft. in Oregon and California, is a closely related wood generally confused with *P. ponderosa*.

The PITCH PINE (*P. palustris*), known in America as the Longleaf Pine or as the Southern or Georgia Pine, is the most abundant and commercially most valuable of American pines. It reaches a good size and weighs from 37 lb. to 45 lb. per cubic foot, which is often nearly twice the weight of Yellow—the American white—pine. It is exported from South Carolina, Georgia, and Alabama, being known, according to the port, as Savannah, Darien, Pensacola, etc., and comes in logs and planks, 20 ft. to 45 ft. long, squaring 11 in. to 18 in. or 3 in. to 5 in. thick and 10 in. to 15 in. wide. The wood is reddish, the redder quality—known as Red Pine in the northern American dockyards—being valued as more durable, especially against teredo. Though it resembles Northern Pine, it is somewhat heavier and more resinous, the broad zone of autumn wood having a somewhat greasy appearance. It is tough, compact, clean, and straight in grain, but varies from fine to a rather coarse texture; it is susceptible of a high polish, but is rather difficult to work, and often has heart and cup shakes. It is, however, stiff, hard, and strong to a higher degree than any other American species on the market, and is very durable especially when any shaky portions are removed by quarter-sawing. It is stated that in piles and jetties, exposed to sea-water and weather, it will last twice or thrice as long as Memel or Dantzic fir.

In America it is largely used for fencing, sleepers, mine-timbers, building, flooring, and rafters, wood-paving and fuel, as well as for decks, planking, and spars and other dockyard purposes. Three-quarters of the paving-blocks used in the States are said to be "Southern Yellow Pine." This may include Short-leaf, Cuban, and even Loblolly Pine, since there is no sure method of discriminating them except by a microscopic examination which is impracticable in commercial transactions; but the Long-leaf Pine is, undoubtedly, the species demanded. In England large quantities of this wood are used for wainscoting, church and school fittings, figured specimens being in request for cabinet-work. This species is the chief source of turpentine.

The CUBAN PINE (*P. heterophylla*) is smaller and coarser in grain, and has wider sapwood than the last named; but is classed with it in Florida and is but little inferior.

Among the Soft Pines of America, none of which are as heavy, as hard, or as durable as the Hard Pines, the FOX-TAIL PINE

(*P. Balfouriana*) of California is used for mine-timbers.

The SUGAR PINE (*P. Lambertiana*), of Oregon and California, the loftiest species of the genus, reaching a height of 300 ft. and a diameter of 20 ft., has a very light, soft, straight, but coarse-grained, compact, fragrant, white wood, easily worked, but not cracking or warping. It is not distinguished commercially from the woods of *P. monticola* and *P. flexilis*, all being known alike as Western White Pine. It is used for indoor carpentry, cooperage.

The WESTERN WHITE PINE (*P. monticola*) is a large tree, growing at high altitudes in Idaho and other Pacific States, valuable in local commerce, but inferior to the White Pine of the Eastern States (*P. Strobus*) which it closely resembles.

The FLEXIBLE PINE (*P. flexilis*) of the eastern slopes of the Rocky Mountains is a small tree, abundant and important locally.

The WHITE PINE (*Pinus Strobus*) is unquestionably the most important of all Soft Pines. It is known also in America as Pumpkin Pine and in our English timber trade as Yellow Pine ; whilst. when grown in England, it is called Weymouth Pine. from a Lord Weymouth, who planted it largely at Longleat about 1720. This species extends from Newfoundland and Quebec to Georgia, and has been known to reach 180 ft. in height, 100 ft. to its lowest branch, and from 6 ft. to 8 ft. in diameter. Its heartwood is pinkish-yellow to pinkish-brown ; its weight is only 20 lb. to 30 lb. per cubic foot ; and it is straight grown, very soft, compact, almost free from resin, easily worked, and susceptible of a fine polish, but liable to shakes and to a sponginess at the centre in old trees. and not durable in contact with soil. Its rapid growth, heavy yield of timber, easy management as a crop, and general utility render it the most valuable species of the Eastern United States. It is employed for every description of joinery, doors, sashes, blinds, interior finish, laths, roof-shingles, clap-boards, cabinetwork, and fuel. For masts or spars it is, however, much inferior in strength and durability to the Hard Pine of the Baltic ; it cannot be relied upon for more than eight or ten years, especially in the tropics, and should be carefully seasoned and then painted, the paint being renewed almost every year.

Sawmills having been started in 1623, and the exportation of this timber in 1635, all trees suitable for masts were protected by law in our American colonies early in the eighteenth century. A century later it is stated that 70 per cent. of the houses in North America were of wood, and that, of these, about 75 per cent. were built of this species. It has now practically disappeared from the States of New England and New York, and very nearly from Pennsylvania and other States, having been recklessly cut and burnt, so that the supply both in its own country and for exportation is much less than it was.

In the Himalaya the BHOTAN or BLUE PINE (*P. excelsa*), growing at altitudes of 6,000 ft. to 12,000 ft., is the most valuable species. Its light-red wood is light, moderately hard, compact, close-grained, very resinous and durable, and is used for railway sleepers and for planking. It should, however, be treated, sleepers lasting from two to two-and-a-half years when unprocessed, and ten or even thirteen years when creosoted.

The MANCHURIAN PINE of Northern China and Corea (*P. manchurica*) reaches 4 ft. in diameter, but does not exceed 80 ft. in height. Its reddish-white wood is used in house- and junk-building and for coffins, and in South China for piles and pit-props, but is found in that region not to be termite-proof or durable.

The CEMBRA PINE (*P. Cembra*), growing from Kamchatka to the Urals, Carpathians, and Alps, and known also as the Siberian Cedar or Swiss Stone Pine, though now valued mainly for its edible nuts, has wood very similar to that of *P. Strobus* and covers large areas of forest. It is used largely for wainscoting and turnery and lining chests.

The UMBRELLA PINE (*Sciadopitys verticillata*) of Japan, the native name of which is Kôya-maki, belonging to the Cypress group, produces a wood of good dimensions, varying in colour from nearly white to yellowish or reddish, straight-

TIMBER: VARIETIES AND USES

grained and strong, which is brought by water to the port of Osaka.

OREGON PINE (*see* OREGON FIR).

In the Southern Hemisphere, New Zealand is exceptionally rich in its variety of pine-like coniferous timbers, some of which have reached our markets in spite of the necessarily heavy freightage. For Kauri (*Agathis australis*) and Queensland Kauri (or Dundatha Pine (*A. robusta*) see KAURI. NEW ZEALAND WHITE PINE (*D. excelsum* and *D. ferrugineum*), related species of this genus of the Yew family, are known to the Maoris as Kahikatea. They reach 150 ft. or 180 ft. in height, sometimes 60 ft. to the lowest branch and 4 ft. to 5 ft. in diameter, yielding timber 20 ft. to 60 ft. long, squaring 12 in. to 30 in., and weighing 27 lb. to 35 lb. to the cubic foot. The wood is white, soft, straight and even in grain, easily worked, but not durable when exposed or in contact with soil. It is thus in many respects comparable to American White Pine (*Pinus Strobus*). Used locally for building, cheap furniture, packing-cases, and paper-pulp, it has come specially into request with the great Australasian demand for butter boxes ; and, as it can be obtained of a large size, it may well compete not only with white pine, but also with Canary whitewood.

For NEW ZEALAND RED PINE (*Dacrydium cupressinum*) *see* RIMU, and for MACQUARIE PINE *see* HUON PINE.

WESTLAND or SILVER PINE (*D. Westlandicum*) is heavier, harder, tougher, and more durable, and is well adapted for sleepers or piles. Its Maori name is "Manao."

BLACK PINE is a name applied in New Zealand to two woods, both of the Yew family, *Prumnopitys spicata*, of which the Maori name is "Matai," and *Podocarpus ferruginea*, the Maori "Miro." The former reaches 80 ft. in height and 2 ft. to 4 ft. in diameter, weighs 35 lb. to 49 lb. per cubic foot, and is a cinnamon-brown colour, close, smooth, and even in grain, easily worked, strong and durable. It is used for piles, sleepers, house-building, and millwrights' work. Miro is rather less in diameter, heavier, reddish-brown, hard, planing up well, and taking a good polish,

durable in contact with salt water but not with soil. It is sometimes nicely figured, and, though used for piles, suited for cabinetwork or turnery.

For the *Podocarpus Totara*, *see* under TOTARA.

CELERY-TOPPED PINE, or "Tanekaha" (*Phyllocladus trichomanoides*), is about the same size as Black Pine, yielding timber 18 ft. to 70 ft. long, squaring 10 in. to 16 in., yellowish-white, heavy, close and straight in grain, working up well, very strong and durable, and employed for piles, bridges, sleepers, mine-timbers, masts, decks, and building.

The CELERY-TOPPED PINE of Tasmania, also known as Adventure Bay Pine, is the allied and similar, but smaller and more slender *Phyllocladus rhomboidalis*.

For HUON PINE (*Dacrydium Franklinii*) *see* HUON PINE.

NORFOLK ISLAND PINE (*Araucaria excelsa*), reaching 200 ft. in height and 7 ft. in diameter, yields excellent timber, but is now scarce.

MORETON BAY PINE (*A. Cunninghami*), occurring in north-east Australia and New Guinea, reaches nearly an equal size, yielding spars 80 ft. to 100 ft. in length, weighing 30 lb. to 33 lb. per cubic foot. It is light-coloured, straight-grained, hard and strong, working easily and sometimes exhibiting a figure produced by small knots. It is durable if kept constantly wet or dry, and is the chief soft wood in Queensland, being in request there for flooring, carpentry, and even cabinetwork ; but it is not equal to European or American Pine.

For the Australian species of *Frenela* *see* CYPRESS PINE.

In South America the CHILE PINE (*Araucaria imbricata*), familiar in our gardens as the Monkey-puzzle, reaches 100 ft. in height and 6 ft. or 7 ft. in diameter at base, and yields a yellowish and sometimes beautifully veined wood, susceptible of a fine polish, used locally for masts. Another species, *A. brasiliensis*, is now being worked on a considerable scale in Southern Brazil. For the South African species of *Podocarpus*, *see* YELLOW-WOOD.

Plane, properly the wood of species of the genus *Platanus*. The wood of the

Levantine species (*P. orientalis* and its forms), a good-sized tree, valued for its shade, is but little used. It resembles beech, but is softer, very apt to warp and split and become worm-eaten. The American or Western species (*P. occidentalis*) and the Californian *P. racemosa* are rather more important, being also known as Buttonwood, or when cut radially as Lacewood or Honeysucklewood (*which see*). It is used for tobacco-boxes, wooden bowls, butchers' blocks, cooperage and blind wood in cabinetwork; but the cabinetmakers of Philadelphia object to it that it warps when in plank. This defect would probably be remedied by some years soaking under water. A good deal of confusion has arisen from this wood being sometimes known as Sycamore, whilst that of the Great Maple or Sycamore (*Acer Pseudo-platanus*) is known as Plane in Southern Scotland.

Plum (*Prunus domestica*), a small tree, probably native to Western Asia, has a deep brownish-red heartwood, resembling mahogany, heavy and hard, but not very durable, used in cabinetmaking and turnery.

Poon, an Indian trade name applied to the wood of several species of *Calophyllum*, especially when in the form of spars. Some twenty species of the genus are known in Malaysia as "Bintangor." The widely distributed *C. inophyllum*, the "Penaga" of Telugu and "Palo Maria" of the Philippines, occurs from Madagascar to the Fiji Islands, may exceed 80 ft. in height, and reach 5 ft. in diameter, and weighs from 35 lb. to 63 lb. per cubic foot. It is red-brown, with a pretty, wavy figure, whence its name of Borneo mahogany, fairly hard, coarse-grained, very strong and durable, and is used in India for sleepers, although suitable for joinery or furniture. *C. tomentosum*, of Ceylon, Queensland, etc., is similar, and is employed for tea-chests and spars.

Poplar, the wood of species of *Populus*, known in America, from their hairy seeds, as "Cottonwoods." These woods are very quick grown, white or pale grey, yellowish or brown, very soft and light, not splintering or splitting when nailed, but holding a nail well, and easily worked or turned. As they shrink in drying, they require prolonged seasoning, and are neither strong nor durable; but it has been found that they are much improved by Powellising. There does not seem to be much difference in the quality of the woods in different species, so that preference has been given in planting to those that give the most rapid yield. The wood is mainly used for paper pulp and cellulose, matches, packing-cases, sugar-barrels, and blind wood, but also for boards for winding silk; clothes-pegs, turned ware, pails, sabots, high heels for shoes, or the bottoms of brick carts and other wagons, churns, coach panels, brakes for railway wagons, etc. The polishing wheels used by glass-grinders are made of horizontal sections, across an entire stem.

The WHITE POPLAR (*P. alba*) is used for matches in Japan, and for building junks and carving in Shan-tung. On the Continent the GREY POPLAR (*P. canescens*) is considered superior. In Manchuria *P. suaveolens*, and in West Huepeh *P. villosa*, are used for building, furniture, and carving. In the United States the BALSAM POPLAR (*P. balsamifera*) and *P. grandidentata* are used; but the wood exported to Liverpool as cottonwood is mostly that of the so-called BLACK ITALIAN, CANADIAN or CAROLINA POPLAR (*P. deltoidea*). A hybrid recently raised by Professor Henry and named *P. generosa* promises to surpass all others in rapidity of growth. For VIRGINIAN and YELLOW POPLAR *see* CANARY WHITEWOOD. (*See also* ASPEN.)

Porcupine-wood (*Cocos nucifera*).—The wood near the outside of the base of the stem of the Coco-nut Palm being crowded with dense black-brown fibrovascular bundles resembling the quills of the porcupine, is very hard, strong, and durable. It has been used for spear-handles in India and for walking-sticks in England, but is generally seen as a veneer for work-boxes or other small fancy articles.

Purple - heart, Violet-wood, Amaranthe, or Paoroxo, the wood of several species of the leguminous genera *Peltogyne* and *Copaifera*, large trees native to Brazil, the Guianas and Trinidad, closely related and of nearly equal value and confused commercially. That from the mainland yields timber 20 ft. to 120 ft. long and squaring 18 in. to 30 in. ; that from Trinidad not more than 25 ft. long or 15 in. wide. The wood is brownish or a beautiful purple when freshly cut, but blackens with age. It is very heavy, hard, strong, easily worked, taking a fine polish, and durable. It is used for works of construction, house-frames, gun-carriages, furniture, and fretwork.

Quassia (*Picræna excelsa*), a native of Tropical America, yielding logs 6 ft. to 10 ft. long and 6 in. to 10 in. in diameter, of a yellow, light, soft, fine-grained wood, intensely bitter, used medicinally as a tonic, being sometimes turned into drinking-cups which impart their taste to water. Often called "Bitter-wood." It is also used as a garden remedy against aphides.

Queenwood, a name applied to two ornamental leguminous woods : *Daviesia arborea*, native to North-east Australia, streaked with pink, hard, close-grained, and susceptible of a fine polish, and *Piptadenia rigida*, a Brazilian species, also known as " Angico," reddish or dark brown with black lines, hard and suitable, as is the other, for cabinetwork and turnery.

Raspberry-jam Wood (*Acacia acuminata*), a native of West Australia, 30 ft. to 40 ft. high, and weighing 54 lb. to 78 lb. per cubic foot, reddish-brown, hard, close-grained, with a smell like raspberry jam. Sometimes called " Jam-wood," and " Myall." It has been used for weapons and fence-posts, but is now used for furniture.

Redwood, a name very variously applied in different countries. In the English timber market it refers to Dantzic Fir (*Pinus sylvestris*). The Californian Redwood (*Sequoia sempervirens*), having been unsuccessfully introduced as a furniture wood under this name, is now known as Sequoia (*which see*). In India, Andaman Redwood is a name for Padouk (*Pterocarpus*), and Coromandel Redwood or Indian Redwood for East India Mahogany (*Soymida febrifuga*). In Jamaica the name is applied to *Erythroxylon areolatum*), the scientific name of which has the same signification, a handsome mahogany-like wood, also known from its hardness as Ironwood, durable in water and used for cogs and mill-frames, though its figure entitles it to other uses. In Cape Colony this name, or its Boer equivalent " Roodhout," is given to *Ochna arborea*, also called Cape Plane, a small tree with a hard, strong, durable wood used for wagon-building and furniture. In Eastern Australia *Eucalyptus piperita* is variously known as Peppermint, Blackbutt, Messmate, White Stringybark, or Redwood. It is a large, very heavy, red wood, difficult to work, very subject to shakes, but durable, and is used for posts, roof-shingles, and rough building.

Rengas. (*See* ROSEWOOD, BORNEO.)

Rewa-rewa (*Rymandra excelsa*), a beautiful New Zealand wood, known also as Honeysuckle-wood. It is large and heavy, becomes foxy unless thoroughly seasoned, and will not stand exposure ; but on a radial section it is a lustrous golden-yellow with pretty warm, red-brown silver-grain, very effective in inlaying and cabinetwork. The finest figure is known as Tiger grain.

Rimu (*Dacrydium cupressinum*), or New Zealand Red Pine, is a fine tree, yielding timbers 20 ft. to 80 ft. long, squaring 10 in. to 30 in., chestnut brown at centre, lighter outwards, figured with light-red or yellow streaks, weighing 33 lb. to 45 lb. per cubic foot ; hard, fine, uniform and straight in grain, working well, and taking a good polish ; strong, but not durable in contact with soil. It is the most widely distributed tree in the Dominion and the most extensively used for beams, panelling, fencing, sleepers, paving-blocks, furniture, and carpentry. Working as readily as birch, but with a strength comparable with oak, it might well replace satin walnut, which it somewhat resembles, as a cabinet-wood, being far more reliable than that wood, so that it should have an assured future in our market.

Roble, though properly the Spanish for Oak, is very loosely used, especially in South America, where it is applied in Chile to the Beech (*Nothofagus obliqua*), and in Argentina to the evergreen *N. betuloides*. This latter is a small tree yielding a straight, very fine-grained, handsome wood, somewhat resembling American Oak, very easily worked and now extensively used for panels in railway carriages.

Rosewood, a name applied to upwards of thirty different woods, mostly tropical, heavy, and dark-coloured. Many of them belong to the *Leguminosæ*, especially to the genera *Dalbergia*. *Machærium*, and *Pterocarpus*, and some contain a resin or oil, the resemblance of which in perfume to rose-water is their only connection with the rose. Much of the rosewood in commerce comes from Brazil, including that of Bahia, the best, Rio, the second best, and San Francisco, and derived from *Dalbergia nigra*; or, in part, from *Machærium scleroxylon, M. firmum*, and *M. legale*, all four species being known as "Jacaranda." This wood comes in half-round logs 10 ft. to 20 ft. long, seldom more than 14 in. in diameter. It is dark chestnut or ruddy brown, richly streaked with black resinous layers, with the rose-water perfume, weighing 53 lb. to 65 lb. per cubic foot, taking a fine polish, but frequently hollow or with heart-shake and fading with age. It is a very valuable cabinet-wood, both solid and in veneer for furniture, especially pianoforte cases. Honduras and Nicaragua Rosewoods are apparently species of *Dalbergia*; and East Indian or Bombay Rosewood is *D. latifolia* and *D. Sissoo*. (See BLACKWOOD. INDIAN and SISSOO.)

BURMESE ROSEWOOD is Padouk (*Pterocarpus indicus*, etc.). AFRICAN or GAMBIA ROSEWOOD, known also as African Padouk, is *Pterocarpus erinaceus*, which reaches 70 ft. in height and 5 ft. in diameter, but has often a spongy centre. It is red-brown and hard; but fades on exposure to light. Unrelated rosewoods are those of Seychelles, Borneo, Austrália, and the Canaries. That of Seychelles is *Thespesia populnea*, a widely distributed Malvaceous tree of moderate size, known as "Faux bois de rose," "Bois de rose de l'Océanie," and other names. It is dark red or claret colour, resembling mahogany, smelling like roses when rubbed, hard, and strong; and is used in India for spokes, gunstocks, furniture, and carriage-building.

BORNEO ROSEWOOD, or Rengas, is the product of various species of the Anacardiaceous genera *Melanorrhea* and *Swintonia*, beautiful red woods with purple streaks, darkening with age, very hard and heavy, and used for furniture, but containing a dangerously poisonous dark gum. In Australia the name is applied to some of the Myalls, Pencil-cedars, and Bastard Sandalwoods, but especially to the Meliaceous *Synoum glandulosum*, of the north-east, a wood of moderate size, deep red, rose-scented when fresh, firm, easily worked, taking a fine polish, and long valued for furniture.

CANARY ROSEWOOD (which comes from the Canary Islands) is a very different material, being the rhizome or underground stem and base of the aerial stem of several species of *Convolvulus*, which have a strong scent of roses and are distilled for the ethereal oil of rosewood, an adulterant of attar of roses.

Sabicu (*Lysiloma Sabicu*), a large and heavy West Indian timber, coming in logs 20 ft. to 35 ft. long, squaring 11 in. to 24 in. and weighing 43 lb. to 62 lb. per cubic foot. It is dark chestnut-brown, sometimes with a curled figure, resembling rosewood, hard, strong, elastic, close-grained, seasoning slowly, but shrinking little in the process, working up well, taking a high polish, and durable. The staircases of the Great Exhibition of 1851 were of this wood, and wore well, and it was used in shipbuilding and for furniture, being imported from Cuba; but it is a wood of which little is heard to-day.

Saffron-wood (*Elæodendron croceum*), known also as "Safforan-wood" and "Crocus-wood"; a native of South Africa, of moderate dimensions, reddish-brown, beautifully grained like walnut, heavy, hard, and tough, used for furniture and for wagon- and boat-building, wheelwrights' work, beams, and planks.

Sal (*Shorea robusta*), one of the most valuable gregarious species of the *Dipterocarpaceæ* of the Indian region, forming vast forests, almost purely of the one

TIMBER: VARIETIES AND USES

species at the foot of the Himalayas from Assam to the Punjab and in Central India. Known also as "Saul." A large tree, 100 ft. to 150 ft. high and 7 ft. or 8 ft. in diameter, it yields timbers 20 ft. to 60 ft. long and from 1 ft. to 2 ft. in diameter, weighing 29 lb. to 52 lb. per cubic foot. The wood is brown, finely streaked with dark lines, hard, coarse, and cross-grained, elastic, tough, comparing favourably as to strength with teak, next to which it is classed in Lloyd's Register, warping and splitting considerably in seasoning, but almost unrivalled for durability, its whitish, aromatic resin protecting it from termites. It is the most extensively used timber in Northern India for piles, bridges, sleepers, beams, planks, gun-carriages, blocks, wedges, cogs, tool-handles, etc.; but, being too heavy to float, it is expensive.

Saleng. (*See* PINE.)

Sandalwood, the fragrant wood of *Santalum album* and other species of the genus, or of the nearly related genera *Fusanus, Exocarpus,* and *Osyris. Santalum album* occurs in India, chiefly in the south, and Malaysia. It reaches a height of 30 ft. and a diameter not exceeding 2 ft., and weighs 56 lb. to 71 lb. per cubic foot; but is sold in crooked billets weighing from 50 lb. to 90 lb. each. Yellowish-brown, heavy, moderately hard, close-grained, and fragrant, the heartwood increases in fragrance with age. It is largely used in India in the manufacture of carved and inlaid boxes, fans, walking-sticks, etc., burnt as a perfume, ground into powder as a cosmetic, and distilled for its oil. In the Sandwich Islands, *S. freycinetianum* and *S. paniculatum*; in Fiji, *S. Yasi*; in New Caledonia, *S. austro-caledonicum*; and in Eastern Australia, *S. obtusifolium* and *S. lanceolatum* are collected. The scarce *Fusanus spicatus* of Southern and Western Australia is not very fragrant, but is exported to Singapore and China.

EAST AFRICAN SANDALWOOD, from Portuguese East Africa, is the small, brown, heavy crooked wood of *Osyris tenuifolia.* It is sometimes called "Mucumite."

BASTARD SANDALWOOD, in Australia, is the small, but very fragrant, brown and beautifully mottled, hard woods of *Myoporum platycarpum* and the allied *Eremophila Mitchelli,* which take a fine polish and yield handsome furniture veneers. Known also as "Rosewood."

The Bastard Sandalwood of India is *Erythroxylon monogynum,* a dark brown, very hard and very fragrant wood, taking a fine polish. *E. laurifolium,* of Mauritius, and *E. australe,* of Queensland, are similar woods.

Two woods belonging to the *Meliaceæ, Epicharis loureiri* and *Lepidaglaia bailloni* are sold and used as Sandalwood in Burma and Cochin China.

Sanders Wood, Red (*Pterocarpus santalinus*), a native of Tropical Asia, known also as Red Sandalwood, to the Germans as Caliaturholz and possibly the Hebrew "Almug" of the Bible, is a small, deep orange-red wood, with lighter zones, turning to claret colour or black, very heavy and hard, fine-grained, and taking a beautiful polish. It is used for images, carving, furniture, turnery, etc., but chiefly as a source of the beautiful salmon-pink dyeing principle santalin, which is soluble in alcohol but not in water. The name is sometimes applied to *Adenanthera pavonina,* known also as Coralwood, Redwood, or Condori-wood, a large tree with beautiful coral-red heartwood with darker stripes when freshly cut, but apt to turn dark-brown or purple, like rosewood, on exposure, very heavy, hard, close-grained, and durable. It is used in house-building, for cabinetwork, and as a dye.

Sappan-wood (*Cæsalpinia Sappan*), a native of the East Indies, sometimes known as Redwood or Brazil-wood, small, dark, orange-yellow or brownish-red, very heavy, fine-grained, and taking a good polish, and thus useful for cabinetwork and inlaying, though almost exclusively used as a dye.

Sassafras (*Sassafras officinale*), a lauraceous tree of large dimensions, widely distributed in North America, with dull orange-brown heartwood and a slight characteristic smell; light, soft, weak, but durable. An essential oil is distilled from the roots. The name is extended in various countries to other *Lauraceæ* and to members of the allied Family *Monimiaceæ*, several of which are yellow and fragrant.

Satin Walnut. (*See* GUM, SWEET.)

Satine. (*See* WASHABA.)

Satinwood, in India and Ceylon, is the Meliaceous *Chloroxylon Swietenia*, a light orange wood of good dimensions, sometimes with a beautiful curl, heavy, hard, close-grained, taking an excellent polish, with the lustre that gives it its name, durable, but liable to darken unless varnished. Weight 49 lb. to 65 lb. per cubic foot. The wood is used in India for sleepers, oil-mills, agricultural implements and furniture, the beautiful figured variety being imported into Europe for the backs of hair-brushes, turnery, cabinetwork, strings in inlay and fretwork. In the eighteenth century it was fashionable for harpsichords, coach-panels, or cabinets. These were generally decorated by paintings, with which the names of Cipriani and Angelica Kauffmann are specially associated.

WEST INDIAN SATINWOOD (*Fagara flava*), a similar but entirely unrelated wood, being a member of the Rue Family, is imported in considerable quantity from Bermuda, the Bahamas, Porto Rico, St. Domingo, and Jamaica, in logs 10 ft. long, 8 in. wide, and 8 in. thick. In the Bahamas it is known as Yellow-wood, and its Spanish name is Aceitillo. It is hard, close, and even in grain, like box, and has a smell like that of coco-nut oil. It is used for high-class bedroom furniture, brush-backs, and cabin fittings.

AUSTRALIAN SATINWOOD, or Thorny Yellow-wood (*Zanthoxylum brachyacanthum*) is nearly allied to the last-mentioned.

AFRICAN SATINWOOD is a name applied to a bright canary-yellow wood from Southern Nigeria, derived from a large tree of the leguminous genus *Cassia*. It is close-grained and firm and suitable for cabinetwork.

Sequoia (*Sequoia sempervirens*), one of the most valuable of Californian softwoods, known in its native country as Redwood, is restricted to the coast range and has considerably appreciated from the heavy felling of the last thirty years. The tree may attain more than 350 ft. in height, and 75 ft. to 100 ft. to its lowest branch, commonly reaching 80 ft. in height and 16 in. in diameter in thirty years. Old trees reach 20 ft. in diameter. The wood is almost identical with that of the Deciduous Cypress (*Taxodium distichum*) of the Mississippi, a related but deciduous tree. It is maroon to terracotta or deep brownish-red, darkening on exposure, light, soft, brittle, close but short-grained, non-resinous, not strong, but very durable in contact with soil. It dries rapidly, losing all vitality, and is thus extremely stable. In California it is largely used for doors, panelling, and carpentry; sleepers, telegraph-poles, and furniture; but having no ornamental figure, it is too monotonous for a high-class furniture-wood in England, and is now used mainly for cabinet drawers and blind wood.

Service (*Sorbus domestica*), a small tree, native to Central Europe, known generally as "Cormier," but sometimes as "Sorbier," in France, yielding a fawn-coloured, very hard, fine-grained wood, resembling pear, but sometimes beautifully figured; in request for cabinetwork, turnery, cogs, screws, planes, and engraving.

Shoondul (*Intsia bijuga*), the Indian name for a moderate-sized tree, native to tropical shores from Madagascar to the Sandwich Islands, and yielding a valuable timber known under various scientific and vernacular names. It is the " Pyingadu " of Burma, " Ipil " of the Philippines, and " Vesi " of Fiji. A member of the Family *Leguminosæ*, it has dark reddish-brown wood, very hard, close-grained, termite-proof, and durable. In India it is employed for bridge- and house-building, sleepers, and electric-light poles; it is the best timber in the Fijis, where the natives use it for canoes, pillows, kava-bowls, and clubs, and it is exported to Europe as a furniture wood.

Silk-cotton (*Ceiba pentandra*), a large tree, widely distributed in the tropics, producing light, soft, white wood, weighing less than 18 lb. per cubic foot, and used for rafts, canoes, floats, packing-

TIMBER: VARIETIES AND USES

cases, and toys. The huge flat buttress-roots of this and other species are sometimes utilised for gold-pans by prospectors.

Siris, Pink (*Albizzia Julibrissin*), a moderate-sized leguminous tree of the Old World Tropics, yielding a dark brown to black wood, prettily mottled, very heavy, and capable and susceptible of a good polish, which is valued for house- and boat-building, and for furniture.

Sissoo (*Dalbergia Sissoo*), a large tree of Northern India, yielding logs 10 ft. to 15 ft. long. It varies from light brown to a dark red-brown with darker longitudinal veins, being at least as variable in colour as mahogany, very heavy, hard, close and even in grain, strong, elastic, seasoning well without warping or splitting, durable. It is rapid in growth and is one of the most valuable of Indian timbers. Being sometimes almost as beautiful as its relatives the rosewoods, it is valued for furniture; but it is unrivalled for the naves and felloes of wheels having to withstand heavy loads. It proved satisfactory for the spokes of heavy motor-wagons in the South African War, and is now being used in India in conjunction with Sundri-wood, but is unfortunately not plentiful.

Snakewood, in English commerce, is the crooked-grained condition of Letter-wood (*Brosimum Aubletii*), (*which see*); it is used for inlaying and the bellies of bows.

Sneezewood (*Pteroxylon utile*), the Boer " Neishout," perhaps the most valuable of South African timbers. It grows only 20 ft. to 30 ft. high, but reaches 2 ft. to 4 ft. in diameter, and weighs 65 lb. to 67½ lb. per cubic foot. The wood is handsome, with a beautiful grain resembling Satinwood, and takes a fine polish; but is not only very hard, but irregular in growth, so as to be difficult to convert. It is so little affected by moisture as to be superior to lignum-vitæ, iron, or brass for bearings, and is both termite- and teredo-proof, ranking with Jarrah and Greenheart as one of the most durable woods in the world. The gum-resin, which causes its dust to produce sneezing, renders it very inflammable. It is used for engineering work, furniture, agricultural implements, and carpentry.

Spindle-tree (*Euonymus europœus*), a British hedgerow shrub, producing a yellowish-white, hard, tough, fine-grained light wood; difficult to split and not splintering, but easily cut. It is used for shoe-pegs and spindles, and yields a fine crayon charcoal; but its poisonous character makes it unsuitable for skewers.

Spruce, a name originally applied to the European *Picea excelsa* from Pruce or Prussia, whence it was obtained, but now extended to all the score or so of species of the genus *Picea*, evergreen cone-bearing trees of the north temperate zone. Though varying in durability according to the soil upon which it is grown, the woods of the various species are closely similar. Of a whitish colour, with no distinct heart, light in weight, only slightly resinous, straight and even in grain, easily worked, with a fairly lustrous surface, elastic and resonant, they are generally superior to the firs and at least equal to the soft pines as timber, not very valuable as fuel, but useful for paper-pulp and unequalled as resonance-wood for sounding-boards and violins. In Europe the chief species is the Norway, or Baltic Spruce or White Fir (*Picea excelsa*), though there are also Serbian and Caucasian species; in Asia, though twenty species have been recorded from China and the Himalayan (*P. Morinda*), Siberian (*P. Maximowiczii*) and Thian-Shan species (*P. Schrenkiana*) are locally important, the Japanese and Yesso species (*P. hondoensis*) and (*P. ajanensis*) are, perhaps at present, of most consequence; but in North America the Red, Black, or Canadian White and Sitka species (*P. rubra, P. mariana, P. alba*, and *P. sitchensis*) are, for flooring, carpentry, and paper-pulp, among the leading woods of the Continent.

The COMMON SPRUCE (*P. excelsa*) ranges from the Altai and Urals to the Alps and Pyrenees, and is well known as a timber-tree in Britain, although not indigenous. Young specimens are familiar as Christmas trees. Reaching 125 ft. to 180 ft. in height and 3 ft. to 6 ft. in diameter, it is the loftiest of European trees. Its wood, known as Baltic whitewood, White Deal, or, in the musical instrument trade, as Swiss Pine or Violin-wood, is sometimes yellowish or reddish. When dry, it weighs only 28 lb. to 32 lb. per cubic foot. If often has many small, hard knots, and it shrinks and warps slightly in seasoning; but it contains some resin (known as Burgundy Pitch), and is durable. It is mostly imported from Norway, in logs 30 ft. to 60 ft. long and 6 in. to 8 in. in diameter, with the bark on; but that from Petrograd is the best; that from Riga, Memel, and Dantzig, large, but coarser; that from the White Sea excellent; whilst that from Moldavia and Transylvania is of great average length, but coarse in grain. Spruce is used for scaffolding, ladders, telegraph-posts, spars, roofing, packing-cases, the sounding-boards of pianos, the bellies of violins, dressers, and kitchen tables. In Central and Southern Europe it is commonly employed for flooring: for toys, specially wide-ringed, that is, quick-grown, wood is preferred; and in Saxony and elsewhere it is largely used for paper-pulp.

HIMALAYAN SPRUCE (*P. Morinda*), growing at from 6,000-ft. to 11,000-ft. altitudes, is not a durable wood, but is largely used in Simla for packing-cases, carpentry, planking, and fuel.

HONDO SPRUCE (*P. hondoensis*), from the mountains of Central Japan, known locally as "Tohi," and in China as "Sha," seldom exceeds 120 ft. in height. It is yellowish-red, very light and soft, fine-grained and glossy, and is used in house-building and carpentry, for masts, telegraph-poles, pillars, beams, match-boxes, and paper-pulp.

BLACK SPRUCE (*P. mariana*, commonly known as *P. nigra*) ranges from 53° N. in Alaska to Newfoundland, and 44° N. in the North-Eastern United States. It does not exceed 80 ft. in height. Its wood, exported as American, Canadian, New Brunswick, St. John's, or Double Spruce, or Spruce Deals, is a very light buff or ruddy, light, weighing about $28\frac{1}{4}$ lb. per cubic foot, soft, elastic, and compact, with a satiny lustre. It is tougher, stronger, more elastic, and more durable than Yellow Pine (*Pinus Strobus*); but, being only slightly resinous, is not so good as fuel. It is so similar to Baltic Spruce that in England each is used on that side of the country nearest to its origin, and the price of the one affects that of the other. The Canadian wood is, however, harder, more liable to loose knots and inferior in strength and durability to the European. The best is shipped from Quebec and St. John's, that from the lower ports being inferior. Trees with wide rings are confused by lumbermen with the White Spruce (*P. alba*). Black Spruce is used for flooring, spars, piles, and oars; the best, quarter-sawn, for pianos and violins; and immense quantities in Newfoundland for paper-pulp, for which it is, perhaps, the best material. In Manchester and Birmingham the wood is largely employed for packing-cases.

RED SPRUCE (*P. rubra*), of South-Eastern Canada and the Eastern United States, is said to be the most valuable timber of the district, being larger than the Black Spruce, reaching 80 ft. to 100 ft. in height and 3 ft. in diameter. Its wood is pale buff, light, soft, even-grained, but fairly strong. The best quality is used for the sounding-boards of pianos, the rest for flooring, carpentry, and paper-pulp; but in export trade it has been confused with the Black Spruce.

WHITE or SINGLE SPRUCE (*P. alba*), with a geographical range nearly identical with the Black, and extensively planted during recent years in Jutland, is a slightly inferior wood, pale yellowish buff in colour, reaching large dimensions (150 ft. in height and 4 ft. in diameter), but not strong and mainly employed for inferior finish or paper-pulp.

SITKA SPRUCE (*P. sitchensis*), said to be the best of the American Spruces, ranges from 57° N. in Alaska to 40° in California, ascending the Rockies to 2,300 metres, and sometimes called "Californian Coast Spruce." It sometimes attains 250 ft. in height and from 6 ft. to 12 ft., or even 15 ft. in diameter; but its wood weighs only $26\frac{3}{4}$ lb. per cubic foot. It is a light yellowish-brown, tinged with red, soft, straight-grained, compact, and strong, and is used in house- and boat-building, carpentry and cooperage; the lightness and elasticity render it peculiarly valuable in the construction of aeroplanes.

Stinkwood (*Ocotea bullata*), known also as Cape Laurel or Cape Walnut, reaches 70 ft. in height and 3 ft. or 4 ft. in diameter, and weighs over 50 lb. per cubic foot. It is a golden-brown, often mottled and resembling walnut, and sometimes iridescent. It gives off a strong, peculiar smell when worked, and is extremely tough, being little inferior to Teak in strength or durability, and more ornamental as a furniture-wood. Used in South Africa for house- and wagon-building and for gunstocks, but is now very scarce.

Stringybark (*Eucalyptus macrorrhyncha*, *E. obliqua*, and other species of Gum-trees of South-East Australia and Tasmania). *E. macrorrhyncha*, known also as "Ironbark," is 50 ft. to 100 ft. high and 2 ft. to 4½ ft. in diameter. Its wood is light brown, tinged with deeper red-brown, sometimes figured with yellow and brown stripes, hard, strong, close-grained, capable of a good polish, and durable. It is used for fencing, flooring, and carpentry, but is suitable for furniture. *E. obliqua*, which occurs in Tasmania, and is sometimes known as "Tasmanian Oak," is known in Victoria as "Mess-mate" from its resemblance to and association with the last-named species. It reaches far greater dimensions, even 250 ft. to 300 ft. in height and 15 ft. in diameter. It has been successfully introduced in the Nilgiri Hills. Its wood, like the last-named, weighs over 60 lb. per cubic foot. It varies from light to dark brown, with a wavy figure near the base of the stem; is hard, straight but rather coarse in grain, very strong, and tough. It is liable to shakes and gum-veins, and warps if not well seasoned, but is very durable. It is probably the most generally used of all Eucalypti, being employed for fencing, house-building, beams, joists, flooring, roof-shingles, docks, wharves, piles, bridges, girders, ships' keels, mine-timbers, railway sleepers, and paving blocks, and is exported for such purposes to India and South Africa. For WHITE STRINGYBARK, *see* REDWOOD.

Sumach, Staghorn or **Virginian** (*Rhus typhina*), a native of Canada and the North-Eastern United States, is small wood, citron-green to greenish gold-ochre, with darker autumn zones, handsome, slightly aromatic, soft, light and lustrous, used as a dye or in small pieces in inlaying.

VENETIAN SUMACH (*R. Cotinus*), known also as "Young" or "Zante Fustic," or "Wild Olive," is a Mediterranean wood of a similar character, but harder, imported from Greece as a yellow dye for leather or wool.

Sundri (*Heritiera fomes*), which gives its name to the Sunderbunds of Bengal, but ranges to Borneo, yields timber 15 ft. long and 1 ft. in diameter, weighing 50 lb. to 58 lb. per cubic foot, brown, very hard, elastic, strong, durable, and tougher than any other Indian wood. It is now used for handles, the spokes of heavy artillery wheels, and, in Calcutta, for firewood.

Switch-sorrel. (*See* LIGNUM-VITÆ.)

Sycamore, a name belonging originally to the Levantine Fig-Mulberry (*Ficus Sycomorus*), a shade-tree with strong wood, used from at least 1600 B.C. by the Egyptians for mummy-cases. In the sixteenth century the name was transferred in English use to the Great Maple (*Acer Pseudo-platanus*), a totally different, but shady, tree from the same region. This reaches 60 ft. in height and 3 ft. in diameter; and its white wood, which becomes yellowish with age, or slightly brown in the centre, weighs, when dry, 29 lb. per cubic foot. The fine, but distinct pith-rays, with the satiny lustre so general among maples, distinguishes it from linden-wood, and when cut radially this "fiddle-mottle" is in request for violins. The wood is compact, firm, fine-grained, and tough, though not hard; it is easily worked, and is susceptible of a high polish, but requires careful seasoning, as it shrinks a twelfth of its bulk and has a tendency to warp and crack. When seasoned, however, it is durable, if kept dry, and is generally left free from insect attack. When of large size, British-grown Sycamore commands a higher price than any British timber, except cricket-bat willow. Large wood is sought after for calico-printing rollers, and when quartered and white, for those of washing-machines. At Glasgow it is largely used for bread-platters, butter-dishes and moulds, reels, shoemakers' cutting-boards, coach-panels and bobbins; as veneer, it is employed for the interior of railway carriages; and on the Continent it is in request for turners, toymakers, and carvers. It is known as Plane in Scotland, whilst in New England the Plane (*Platanus occidentalis*) is called Sycamore.

Tallow-wood (*Eucalyptus microcorys*), known also as "Forest Mahogany," a large tree of Eastern Australia, producing an excellent yellow or yellowish-brown wood, strong and durable, though very greasy when freshly cut, liable to shakes, and generally hollow. It is used for piles, girders, ballroom floors, and wheelwrights' work, and is one of the best of Australian woods for paving.

Tamarack. (*See* LARCH.)

Tamarind (*Tamarindus indica*), the large and very heavy wood of the slow-growing Indian medicinal fruit-tree. It is yellowish-white, with an irregular heart of dark purplish-brown blotches resembling ebony or tulip-wood, and weighs 80 lb. per cubic foot. It is very hard and difficult to work, and the tree is apt to be hollow; but the wood is durable and free from insect attack, so that it is used for oil and sugar-mills, rice-pounders, mallets, and turnery.

T'an-mu, apparently a *Dalbergia*, is a reddish-black wood full of fine veins, very hard, tough and durable, used in China for wheels, shafts, and fine cabinetwork.

Teak (*Tectona grandis*), the most generally useful, durable, and valuable of Indian timbers, is a member of the verbena family, and is native to Southern India, Burma, the Shan States south of the Menam watershed, the Malay Peninsula, Sumatra, Java, and Celebes, whilst it has been largely planted in Ceylon and in parts of India where it is not wild. It may exceed 100 ft. in height and reach 8 ft. in diameter, yielding logs 23 ft. to 50 ft. long, squaring 10 in. to 30 in.

Its weight, when it is green, being more than that of water, is the reason for girdling the trees—that is, cutting a complete ring round the tree through its bark and sapwood, so as to kill it—some three years before felling them, so that they can be floated down to the port of shipment.

The wood is straight-grown, light straw-colour to a brownish-red, when fresh, but darkening on exposure. In the Deccan it is sometimes beautifully veined, streaked, and mottled, and old trees occasionally produce burrs resembling Amboyna-wood. When fresh cut, teak is very fragrant, so as to resemble rose-wood, owing to the presence of an oleo-resin which renders it obnoxious to insects and even keeps off rust from iron in contact with it; but, when seasoned, it has an unpleasant smell, like old shoe-leather. As at least a year usually elapses between the felling of this timber and its arrival in England, it arrives sufficiently seasoned and but very little shrunken, warped, or split; but the rapid drying induced by girdling is said to render the wood inelastic, brittle, and less durable, so that it splits too readily for use in gun-carriages. It is a moderately hard wood, clean, straight, and even in grain, but varies considerably according to the conditions under which it is grown, that of Malabar being darker, heavier, and rather stronger than that of Burma, although not so large. Though not splitting from their circumference, teak logs have nearly always a heart-shake, which, owing to a twist in the growth, may often be at right angles at the top of the tree to its position at the butt; this, however, while seriously interfering with conversion, may very little affect the use of the timber in bulk. In the shakes and larger vessels of the wood there is generally a secretion of white masses of apatite or calcium-phosphate, which will turn the edge of most tools. Teak owes its superiority for shipbuilding over pine and oak partly to its freedom, when once seasoned, from any change of form, even under the extremes of a monsoon climate.

As the Indian Forest Department plant several thousand acres annually, there is

TIMBER: VARIETIES AND USES 1587

little fear of the supply becoming exhausted, and the wood of cultivated trees is said to be better than that of natural forests. Teak is used in India for bridge-building, sleepers, and other purposes; but is little exported except to this country, where it is used for backing armour-plates, for deck-planks, railway wagons, greenhouses, etc. That from Moulmein, drawn from the valleys of the Salwen and Thungyen Rivers, is rather shorter, but less shaky, than that shipped at Rangoon from the Irawadi Valley; that from Java is excessively hard and gritty.

The name of so valuable a timber has naturally been applied to various very heavy and hard woods in no way related to it or to one another. The " Biji " of India, " Gammala " of Ceylon (*Pterocarpus Marsupium*), is known as Bastard Teak. It is a good-sized tree, with very heavy and hard yellowish-brown, dark-striped heartwood, taking a fine polish and very durable if not exposed to wet. It is heavier than most teak, and harder and darker than its ally Padouk; but is expensive to work. It is used for sleepers, furniture, etc.

JOHORE TEAK (*Parinarium oblongifolium*), a very heavy and hard, dark-brown, termite-proof rosaceous timber, used for piles at Singapore and exported to Colombo for the breakwater, is now unobtainable. So, too, is the so-called AFRICAN TEAK (*Oldfieldia africana*), a euphorbiaceous wood from Western Tropical Africa, formerly used in ship-building. For New Zealand Teak or " Puriri " (*Vitex littoralis*), see MOLAVE.

Tenasserim. (*See* PADOUK.)

Tewart (*Eucalyptus gomphocephala*), known also as " Tuart," " Touart," and " White Gum," of West Australia, reaching a height of 150 ft. and yielding timber 20 ft. to 45 ft. long, squaring 11 in. to 28 in., weighing 60 lb. to 78 lb. per cubic foot, is one of the strongest and toughest of known woods, hard, twisted, or curled in grain, so as to be difficult to cleave or work, but apparently imperishable. It is used for keelsons, capstans, piles, dock-gates, etc.

Thingan (*Hopea odorata*), the Burmese name of a valuable wood of great length ranging from India to Borneo. It is said to combine the good qualities of oak with the durability of teak. It is yellowish-brown, moderately heavy and hard, easily worked, and not subject to insect-attack, and is in demand for building. It and allied diptero-carpaceous woods form part of the Yacal used for sleepers in the Philippines and known as " Pallow " in the Singapore market.

Thuya (*Tetraclinis articulata*), a small Cypress native to Algeria and Morocco, producing reddish-brown, fragrant burrs, resembling Amboyna-wood. This very durable wood is the " Alerce " of the Alhambra and the roof of Cordova Cathedral, and is known as " Lignum-vitæ," by the French. The Thyine-wood of the Apocalypse and the enormously costly Citron wood of ancient Rome were probably the burrs, the name of which is pronounced in our English market as Thoo'ee.

Toon. (*See* CEDAR, MOULMEIN.)

Totara (*Podocarpus Totara*), or New Zealand Yew, next to Kauri the most valuable timber in the Dominion and far more abundant. It grows 40 ft. to 70 ft. or even 120 ft. in height, sometimes 40 ft. to its lowest branch and 2 ft. to 6 ft., or even 12 ft. in diameter, so that its timber is in 20-ft., 45-ft., or greater lengths, squaring 10 in. to 22 in. It weighs 28 lb. to 37 lb. per cubic foot. It is deep red, moderately hard, straight, close, fine and even in grain, very easily worked, not warping or twisting, strong, teredo-proof, and very durable. It is used for piles, sleepers, paving-blocks, telegraph-poles, bridges, and building; but might well be employed for interior finish or furniture, and should have a good future in our market. It sometimes produces Amboyna-like burrs.

Trumpet-tree (*Cecropia peltata* in Jamaica and *C. palmata* in Brazil and Guiana), small trees producing very light, resonant wood, used for floats and razor-strops, whilst hollow stems are converted into trumpets and drums.

Tulip-wood, in Europe (*Physocalymma scaberrimum*), a Brazilian wood, known locally as "Pao de rosa," rose-coloured, beautifully striped and used for inlay and turnery. In Queensland the name is given to the similar but unrelated black and yellow woods of *Harpullia pendula*, one of the *Sapindaceæ*, and *Owenia venosa*, one of the *Meliaceæ*. These handsome woods are heavy, hard, and close-grained; and, taking an excellent polish, are valuable for cabinetwork. (*See also* CANARY WHITEWOOD.)

Umzimbit (*Millettia Caffra*), an intensely hard leguminous wood in South Africa with yellowish-white, durable sapwood, contrasting sharply with the dark reddish-brown heart. Known also as "Kaffir Ironwood." It is used for walking-sticks, but will serve for machine-bearings, spokes, gunstocks, and furniture.

Violet-wood, a name sometimes applied, on account of its colour, to the Purple-heart (*which see*) of Tropical America, sometimes, on account of its perfume, to the Australian Myall.

Walnut (*Juglans regia*), a native of Northern and Western China and Persia, introduced in early times into Greece and Italy, and thence into the rest of Europe. It may reach 50 ft. in height and 3 ft. in diameter, and its wood, when dry, weighs 46 lb. or 47 lb. per cubic foot. The dark-brown or black-brown heartwood is often "watered," exhibiting dark wavy lines and zones of great beauty. It is hard, fine, and close in grain, splitting but little in the process of seasoning, but may be readily split artificially, taking a beautiful polish and singularly free from any tendency to splinter after being worked up. It is durable if kept dry, especially when dark or figured; but its sapwood is very liable to become worm-eaten. It can, however, be rendered resistant by being smoked over a beech-wood fire or by boiling in the juice of its own green fruits.

English-grown walnut, coming mostly from good soil in lowland situations, is pale, coarse, but little figured, and perishable; French is better; that from Austria, Serbia, etc., known as Black Sea, which is imported in waney logs 6 ft. to 9 ft. long, squaring 10 in. to 18 in., is still more valuable; whilst that from Italy, which comes in 5-ft. to 12-ft. planks, 10 in. to 16 in. wide and 4 in. to 9 in. thick. is the best. Walnut was considerably used in France for carving in the round during the fourteenth, fifteenth, and sixteenth centuries. At the beginning of the eighteenth century it became very fashionable as a furniture wood, its use being the first departure from the universal employment of oak.

The severe winter of 1709 killed most of the walnut trees of Central Europe, and the dead trees were bought up by the Dutch, who thus secured a "corner" in this wood. By 1720 it had become so scarce in France that its export was prohibited, and mahogany, imported by Dutch and Spaniards, largely replaced it as a furniture wood. No wood, however, equals walnut for the manufacture of gunstocks, so that the wars of the eighteenth century created a great dearth of this wood, and one reads of France consuming 12,000 trees a year in 1806, and of as much as £600 being paid for a single tree. European walnut is still in use for the best gunstocks; and Swiss carvings are mostly in this wood. Good walnut is used for repairing and copying Queen Anne furniture; plainer wood for the solid parts of furniture, turnery, musical instruments, etc.; but it is now so scarce as to be largely replaced for all purposes by the inferior American species.

Burrs, often 2 ft. to 3 ft. across and over 1 ft. in thickness, beautifully mottled and weighing 5 cwt. or 6 cwt., occur on Italian and Black Sea wood, and are highly valued for veneers for the pianoforte and cabinet trade. Before the war they were largely imported from Turkestan.

AMERICAN WALNUT (*J. nigra*), a larger tree, has wood more uniform in colour, darker, duller, less liable to insect attack, and, therefore, more durable. Formerly used for many unworthy purposes, it is now too valuable as a cabinet and veneer wood, and for rifle-stocks, to be employed for anything else. Before the middle of the last century it was only used in England for carcase work and frames for veneering; but now it is more used than European walnut, its uniform colour recommending it to shop-fitters as a basis for surface ornamentation in the cabinet trade. It is imported to Liverpool in 10-ft. to 21-ft. logs, squaring 15 in. to 50 in., in planks and in boards.

GREY or WHITE WALNUT, or Butternut (*J. cinerea*), is a very beautiful and durable American wood of good size, but lighter than the preceding, and is seldom imported.

MANCHURIAN WALNUT (*J. manchurica*) and JAPANESE WALNUT (*J. Sieboldiana*) cover large areas in Irkutsk, Transbaikal, and Yakutsk, and yield large, hard wood, suitable for gunstocks.

AFRICAN WALNUT is a Liverpool name for several woods from Tropical Africa of varying quality. One, *Boswellia Klainei*, is an inferior, light, coarse-grained wood. Another, from Benin, a species of *Trichilia* or *Pseudo-cedrela*, though a mahogany rather than a walnut, is a good but monotonous dark brown, easily worked furniture wood, of large diameter, weighing 32½ lb. per cubic foot. A third, also known as "Owowe," is a large species of *Albizzia*, similar to the next and quite a useful substitute for walnut.

EAST INDIAN WALNUT is a name given in the London market on account of its colour to *Albizzia Lebbek*, a leguminous wood of wide range in the Tropics from Africa to Australia, known as "Siris" in Bengal, "Koko" in the Andaman Islands, and "Ki-toke" in Java. It weighs 41 lb. to 56 lb. per cubic foot; is dark brown, with darker streaks and a wide, light sapwood; hard, coarse-grained, polishing well and durable; and is used for building, wheelwrights' work, and mill-rollers, as well as for cabinetwork.

For SATIN WALNUT, see SWEET GUM; and CAPE WALNUT, see STINKWOOD.

Washaba (*Ferolia guianensis*), a rosaceous wood native to Guiana, known also as "Satiné," "Bois de féroles" or "Bois marbré," and as "Washiba" or "Waciba." It is exported in logs 14 ft. to 28 ft. long, squaring 13 in. to 15 in., and is red or red-brown, splashed with yellow, hard, solid tough, elastic, and susceptible of a beautiful polish. It is used for bows, fishing-rods, and cabinetwork.

Wattle, the general Australian name for the species of *Acacia*, from their use by the early colonists in wattling their huts. Among them, *A. binervata*, unfortunately known as Hickory as well as Black Wattle, is valued for axe-handles and bullock-yokes in the north-east of Australia; *A. mollissima*, known as Black Wattle or Silver Wattle in the south-east, formerly used for boomerangs, mulgas, and spears, is now employed in Tasmania for cask-staves; but the only species reaching this country are those known as Myall (*which see*, also BLACKWOOD, TASMANIAN). Many of the species yield valuable Wattle Gum.

Whitewood. (*See* CANARY WHITEWOOD and SPRUCE.)

Willow, a name used only in Europe and America for species of the genus *Salix*. These hybridise freely among themselves, producing plants of very distinct characters. Many species and their hybrids are cultivated under the name of osiers for the manufacture of wicker-work. Others are treated as pollards, the small wood derived from their lopping being valuable for hurdles, hoops, hay-rakes, etc. Only two species are employed as sources of larger wood, the Crack Willow (*S. fragilis*) and several forms of the White Willow (*S. alba*).

CRACK WILLOW, also known as Openbark Willow, grows to heights of 50 ft. to 90 ft. and to diameters of 4 ft. to 7 ft. Its wood, when dry, is salmon-coloured, light, tough, and elastic, and is used for cricket-bats, but is inferior to Close-bark Willow.

WHITE WILLOW (*S. alba*) ranges from North-West India and North Africa north-westward, and reaches almost the same dimensions as the last mentioned. Its heart-wood has a brownish tinge and weighs from 24 lb. to 35 lb. per cubic foot. It is soft and smooth-grained, does not splinter, shrinks one-sixth of its bulk in drying; but is very durable, either dry or wet. It was formerly used for cottage flooring, and is still employed for wheelbarrows, especially in ironworks, as it does not split or warp when heated, or take fire readily on friction. It is also used for brake-blocks on railway wagons, for paddles of steamboats, the strouds of water-wheels, shoemakers' lasts and cutting-boards, toy-making, druggists' boxes, etc. The polishing wheels used by glass grinders are made of complete horizontal sections of the stem. By far the most important use of willow wood, however, is the manufacture of cricket bats. These should be made of the wood of the variety known as Close-bark Willow (*S. alba* var. *cærulea*) ; and large sound trees of this fetch very high prices.

Wych. (*See* ELM, SCOTCH or WYCH.)

Yellow-wood, though occasionally applied to Fustic and in Australia to various unrelated woods, is a name referring generally to South African woods of the Coniferous genus *Podocarpus*, especially *P. Thunbergii* and *P. elongata*, both of which are known as " Geel Hout " by the Boers ; but the former as " Umceya," the latter as " Umkoba," by the Zulus. They are tall trees, 2 ft. to 5 ft., or even 8 ft. in diameter, yielding pale yellow wood, weighing 30 lb. to 45 lb. per cubic foot, soft and close-grained, easily worked, but somewhat liable to warp and split. They are used for building, roof-shingles, flooring, and furniture, and, when creosoted, for railway sleepers. (For THORNY YELLOW-WOOD, *see* SATINWOOD, AUSTRALIAN.)

Yellow Jacket. (*See* GUM, RED.)

Yendaik (or **Yendike**) (*Dalbergia cultrata*), a moderate-sized leguminous blackwood in Burma, weighing 64 lb. per cubic foot, black with purple or light streaks, straight grown, very hard, tough, elastic, and durable, full of shakes, but not cracking or altering after conversion, sometimes called " Blackwood " and confused with Ebony. It is excellent for spokes, bows, tool-handles, spears, and carving.

Yew (*Taxus baccata*), generally of small height, but reaching 100 ft. in the Himalaya, and of all diameters up to 19 ft., produces a reddish-brown, non-resinous wood, resembling mahogany and weighing 40 lb. to 57 lb. per cubic foot. Often incorporating many ascending branches with separate centres in its stem, the resultant wood appears irregular in growth. It is very hard, close-grained, tough, flexible, and elastic ; is susceptible of a high polish ; and is insect-proof and more durable than any other European wood, it being proverbial that a post of yew will outlast a post of iron.

The twelfth-century framework of the feretory of St. Manchan at Boher in King's County, made of yew, is still quite sound. Yew was employed for the early Greek statues of the gods ; it is, however, as a material for bows, on account of its combined toughness and elasticity, that yew has been best known from early times. Though home-grown wood was used in England for this purpose in mediæval times, that imported by Venetian traders from Italy, Turkey, and Spain was of better quality. Small branches are used for walking-sticks, and the wood is employed to some extent in chair-making and on the Continent in turnery. It is also stained black as German Ebony. Old trees produce Amboyna-like burrs, veneers of which were commonly used towards the close of the eighteenth century for tea-caddies, punch-ladles etc. The wood of *T. cuspidata*, the Japanese form, was used by the aboriginal Ainu for bows, though nowadays chiefly employed for furniture and pencils.

Zebra-wood, a name applied to many different woods, mostly tropical, heavy, hard, susceptible of a good polish, and so striped or streaked as to suggest the name. They are mostly employed for walking-sticks or veneers. Among them are the very rare " Hyawaballi " of British Guiana (*Connarus guianensis*), a large tree, with reddish-brown wood ; the " Arariba " (*Centrolobium robustum*), a large, leguminous wood, exported from Rio ; the " Sea-coast Teak " (*Guettarda speciosa*), a small, Rubiaceous, light reddish-yellow wood, resembling box, known as " Ronron " in Honduras and as " Bua-bua " in Fiji ; the Andaman Marble wood (*which see*) or Figured Ebony (*Diospyros Kurzii*), beautifully streaked with black and grey ; and the " Cuius-cuius " (*Taxotrophis ilicifoliæ*) of the Philippines, belonging to the Mulberry Family, which is streaked with greenish dark-brown or almost black, with dark spots.

Index

(For names of various woods, consult the dictionary occupying pages 1543 to 1590)

"A.C.," or American cloth, 1419
Adam Brothers' mirrors, 942
Adze, using, 72
Aeroplane airscrew construction, 1287-1289
—— fuselage assembling, 1277-1281
——: interplane struts, 1286-1287
——: main plane, assembling, 1283
—— ribs : construction, 1283-1286
—— struts : finding length and bevel, 1287
—— wires, tension of, 1281, 1282
—— woodwork, 1275-1289
—— work, splayed scarf joint for, 266
Agate paper, 197
" Air-dry " wood, 128
Airer, clothes, hanging, 356, 357
Airscrew (see Aeroplane)
Algerian grass for upholstery, 1418
Alva stuffing in upholstery, 1417
American cloth, 1419
—— methods of wood finishing, 1409
Angle joint (see Joint)
Angles, equal, finding, on boards, 178, 179
——, measurement of, 1523-1525
——, mitre, 272, 273
——, oblique dovetail, 285, 286
——, right, and squares, testing, 34, 35
——, rounded, 162
—— of saw teeth, 61
Aniline dyes, staining with, 1405
Antiquarian (size), 1498, 1507
Aquarium, 1209-1214
Arbour, trellised, 550, 551
"Arc of contact" in machine belting, 1495
Arch, garden, 547-554, 564-567
Architrave joint, 270

Arkansas oilstone, 76
Arm-chairs (see Chair)
Auger, Gedge's pattern, 295
—— gimlet, 294
Austrian oak finish, 1404
Awl, marking, 32
Axe, sharpening, 80
——, using, 72

Baby's play-pen, 356-361
Back-flap hinge (see Hinge)
Backing cupboards and wardrobes, 290
Badger plane, 168
Bagatelle board, folding, 1218
—— table, 1215-1218
Bandings, inlaid, 1333
——, veneer, 1328
Bandsaw, adjusting, 1474
——, brazing, 1475, 1476
——: components, 1473, 1474
——, cutting with, 1475
——, fitting, 1474
——, repairing, 1475, 1476
——, setting, 1475
——, sharpening, 1475
—— teeth, shape of, 1475, 1476
——: tension required, 1474
——, testing, 1474
——: utility, 1473, 1474
Bar cramps, 710, 713
Barrow (see Wheelbarrows)
Basket or carrier, potato, 544
——, gardener's, 540-545
"Bastard" planks, 119
Bath cabinet, thermal, 350
—— seat, 349
——, wooden, 368-370
Bead, torus, 211
——, working, on edge of board, 211
Beaded work, tenons for, 258
Beading plane, 94, 95
—— with Stanley plane, 210
Beams cut from log, 189
—— —— square with tree, 189
——, getting, from log, 190
Bed screw, 156, 157
Bed-rest, adjustable, 1166, 1167
——, simple, 1165, 1166

Bedroom chairs (see Chair)
—— overmantel (see Overmantel)
—— suite, oak, 1119-1131
Bedside cupboard, 1129-1131
Bedstead, camp, 1185, 1186
——, inlaid, 1174-1178
——, mahogany, 1179-1182
——, oak, 1128, 1129, 1177-1180
—— "straining piece," 1184
——, temporary, 1183-1186
——, twin, 1182, 1183
Beehive and fittings, 399-406
Bell-tent floors, 630, 633
Belts for machinery, 1493-1496
Bench attachment for tables, 478-480
——, cabinet-maker's, 13-15
——, cabinet-maker's, with tool drawer, 14
——, carpenter's, 490-494
——, common type, 10-12
—— with drawer and cupboard, 17, 18
——, fitting iron bench screw to, 12
——, flap, portable, 501-503
——, folding, 481, 482
——, holdfasts, 711, 713
—— hook, 52-54
—— leg, construction, 12
——, organ, with music receptacle, 1036-1038
—— peg-board, 13, 15
—— for picture frames, 503-506
——, portable, 15, 17, 482-484
—— with side and tail screws, 484-489
—— stops, 21-23, 494, 496
——, timber for making, 10, 11
——, tool rack for, 498, 500, 501
—— top with vices, 480, 481
——, trough-top with leg vice, 11
—— vice for curved work, 20, 21
—— ——, fixing runner, 12
—— ——, improvised, 496, 497
—— ——, instantaneous grip, 19, 20
—— —— for small work, 20

INDEX

Bench, watchmakers', 494-496
——, wooden vice, fitting, 18
——, woodworkers' portable, 482-484
Benches, work, 478-506
Bending boards : natural direction, 703, 704
Bevel, adjustable, 36
——, angle of, 161
——, applying, to end of board, 178, 179
——, dispensing with, for rough work, 37
—— edge, developing, 700
— ——, marking out, 161, 162
——, testing edge with, 161
——, —— planed edge with, 179
——, using, 36, 160, 161
——, —— rule in place of, 37
Bevelled work, 698-707
Bevelling, 160, 161
——, complex system of, 161, 162
—— octagonal blocks, 162, 163
Bichromate, darkening oak with, 1404
Billiard bolt, 156, 157
—— table, full-size, 1219-1223
—— ——, small, for dining-room, 1223, 1224
Birdsmouth joint (see Joint)
Bit, centre, 298-301
——, —— sharpening, 298, 300
——, countersink, 301, 302
——, disc-cutting, 305, 307
——, dowel, 302
——, ——, sharpener, 305, 307
——, expansion, Clarke's, 303, 304
——, ——, Steer's, 303, 304
——, extension, 305-307
——, forked turn-screw, 303, 304
——, Forstner, 303-305
——, gauge, 304, 305
——, half-twist, 298, 299
——, nose, 298, 299
——, screw, 298, 299
——, screwdriver, 303, 304
——, shell, 297, 298
——, spoon, 297, 298
—— stock, angular, 297
——, twist, 300-302
——, ——, drill, 301, 302
——, ——: filing cutter, and nicker, 301, 302
Bits, case for holding, 307
Blackboard, making, 334
—— paint : recipes, 335
——, painting, 334
Block (metal) plane, 94, 96
Blooming, french polish, 1412
Blue-print process, 1538, 1539
Board, bagatelle, folding, 1218, 1219
——: dividing into three, 30
——, drawing (see Drawing board)

Board : lining-down with rule and pencil, 30
——, marking, for dowelling, 240
——, notice (see Notice board)
——, poster (see Poster board)
——, roll of honour (see Roll of honour)
Boarding : market sizes, 191
Boards, joining, 231, 232
——, louvre, 701
——: stacking after gluing, 232
Bolt, bed-screw, 156, 157
——, billiard, 156, 157
——, cheese-head, 156
——, countersunk-head, 156
——, cup-head, 155, 156
—— "eating" into wood, 156
——, flush, for double doors, 1389
——: gripping power, 156
——, gutter, 156
—— holes, boring, 156
——: measuring length of, 157
——, sinking, in woodwork, 157
——, washer for, 156
Bolts, handrail, and dowels, 269, 270
——: sizes, 156, 157
——: types, 155, 156
Bolting, 155-157
Book trough, 309
—— —— and stool, combined, 308
Bookcase bureau, 754-759
—— ——, simple, 759, 760
—— cabinet, fitted, 760-763
—— ——, curtained, with glazed cupboards, 737, 740
—— doors, 674
—— dwarf, 729, 732, 736
—— with glazed doors and cupboard, 750-753
——, movable shelves for, 727
——, open, with glazed cupboard, 739, 740
——, open-fronted, with cupboard, 748-750
——, revolving, miniature, 741
——, ——, three-foot, 742-747
——, sectional, 1256-1260
——, small, with rack, 731
——, tall, 748-763
—— and writing-desk, combined, 1101-1104
Bookcase-secretaire, recessed, 1098-1101
Book-rack with carved or modelled ornament, 723
——, hanging, easily-made, 719
——, simple, 718-724
——, sliding, collapsible, 717
——, small partitioned, 721
Bookshelves, pedestal stand with, 1107-1110
——, recess, 724
——, simple, 724-728

Boot and shoe racks, 311, 376
Boot-cleaning box pedestal, 362
——, chair-stools for, 901-904
Boring, eccentric, pulling shoulder into contact by, 151, 152
—— holes : measuring depth, 305
—— laths for roll-top desk, 1235
—— mitre, 307
—— with narrow chisel (woodturning), 1304
—— right angles to edge, 307
—— screw-holes, bit for, 299
—— tools, 290-307
"Bosting in" (woodcarving), 1349, 1350
Bow saw, 54, 55
Bowl, Norwegian knife-carved, 1379, 1380
—— with nut-crackers, carved, 1377-1378
Box, clothes, 456, 464
——, collection (see Box, donation)
—— construction, rough, 320-325
——, core, for pattern-making, 1443-1448
——, donation, 458, 460
——, dovetail, 274
——, dowel, 239
——, egg, 458, 459
——, fancy, 1052-1055
——, garden tool, 512, 513
——, hinges, fitting, 1388
——, letter, 314, 460
——, marquetry, 1304, 1342, 1343
—— ottoman, 914-916
—— pedestal for boot cleaning, 362, 363
—— pin joint, 279, 280
——, rough, 321, 322
——, ——: jointing methods, 323
——, ——: lock corners, 322
——, shrub, panelled, 1115, 1116
——, ——, for porch, 1112-1116
——, splayed, 161, 162
——, ——, irregular, 700
——, sprouting, for potatoes, 544, 545
——, stay, fitting, 1390, 1391
——, stopped butt hinge for, 1393, 1394
——, toilet-paper, 312, 313
——, tool, garden, 512, 513
——, ——, and garden seat, combined, 514, 515
——, ——, portable, 468-470
——, wooden, strong, 454, 455
Box-block, mincing or chopping, 313
Brace and bit, countersinking with, 151

INDEX

Brace: "crocodile jaws," 296
——, power of, 296
——, ratchet, 295-297
——, Scotch, 295, 296
—— and screwdriver bit, 155
——: sizes, 296
——, steel, ordinary type, 295
——, wooden, 295, 296
Bracket in pierced carving, 1358-1370
—— shelf for hall, 766
Bradawl blades, detachable, 292
——, boring action, 293, 294
——, driving, with hammer, 293
——: cutting edge, position of, 292
——, ferruled, 291
—— handle splitting, cause of, 293
——, ordinary, 291
——, sharpening, 292
——, sizes, 291
——, splitting with, 293
——, starting nails with, 291
—— toolpad, 292
——, using, 292
Brads, floor, 142-144
Brass countersink, 302, 303
Brazing bandsaw, 1475, 1476
Breaks in moulding, short, 270
Bridle joint (see Joint)
Bridled and tenoned joint, 256, 257
Brush polish (see Polish)
Brushes and colours for drawing, 1508, 1509
Buckets, wooden, 666
Buckled handsaws. 62
Built-up rim, wooden, 702
—— work (pattern-making), 1448, 1451-1458
—— —— (woodturning), 1307, 1308
Bull-nose plane, 92, 93, 160
—— steps: bending risers, 705-707
Bullet catch, fixing, 1389
Bull's-eye window, 686, 687
Bungalow, garden, 600-602
Bung-borer, 413, 414
Bureau, bookcase, 754-759
——, Jacobean oak, 1090-1094
——, oak, small, 1088-1090
Burrs, timber, 123
Butt joints (see Joints)
Butter churn, 667-669
Butterfly cabinet, 1004-1008
Buttoning upholstery, 1428

CABINET bookcase, fitted, 760
——, butterfly, 1004-1008
——, china, drawing-room, 984
——, coal, 820-824
——, coin, 1002-1004

Cabinet, corner, 976, 1374
——, Cromwellian, and modern variation, 988-993
—— with cupboards and shelves, 979-982
——, curio, pedestal, 986-988
——, dining-room, 993-999
——, ebony, 997-1000
——, egg-collector's, 1001-1002
—— for filing drawings, 1255
——, French, veneered and marqueteried, 1317
——, gramophone, 1021-1025
——, kitchen, or dresser, 788
——, music, 1009-1020
——, oak, sixteenth-century, 982-984
——, shaving, 1162, 1163
——, smoker's, 355, 967
——, thermal bath, 350
—— and writing-table, combined, 1094-1097
"Cabriole" legs, castors for, 1400
—— hammer, upholsterer's, 1416
Caddy, tea, converting into jewel-case, 1051, 1052
——, tea and sugar, 1049-1051
Calico for upholstery, 1419
Callipers, measuring diameter with, 1301-1304
Camp-bedstead, folding, 1185, 1186
Canadian box sleigh, 1269-1274
Canvas, artist's, joint for frame, 250, 251
——, upholstery (see Hessian and Scrim)
Carborundum wheel, 75-76
Card-tables (see Table)
Carpenters' benches, 478-494
Cart-wheel rims, construction of, 702-703
Carved corner cabinet, 1374, 1377
—— hall-stand, 1372, 1376
—— overmantel, 1374, 1377
—— work: removing polish and varnish. 1408
Carving, chip, 1370-1372
——, knife, 1377-1380
——, pierced, 1358-1370
—— tools, 1345-1347
——: woods used, 1345
Case, packing (see Packing case)
Casement windows, 683-685
Castors, fitting, 1399-1400
——, "socket," fitting, 1400
Catch, bullet, fixing, 1389
"Caul" veneering, 1321-1323
Cedar-wood, 126
Centre bit, 298, 299
Centring work for turning, 1298-1300
Chair: adjustable seat and back, 875-877

Chair, arm-, child's, 889-892
—— backs, Windsor, cutting, 1475
——, bedroom, 871-873
——, ——, oak, 1131
——, child's 885-892
——, dining-parlour, Sheraton, 873-875
——, dining-room, 868-871
——, dowelling, 242, 243
——, easy, 911, 912
——, ——, wing, 912-914
——, elbow, Sheraton-Heppelwhite, 873-875
——, Jacobean, small, 870-871
——, Queen Anne, 877-885
——, Sheraton, dining-parlour, 873-875
——, Sheraton - Heppelwhite elbow, 873-875
—— springs, putting in, 1421, 1422
——, three-cornered, 882-885
——, upholstering, 1421-1426
Chair-back frets, 1477
Chair-stools for boot-cleaning, 901-904
Chair-swing, garden, 533-535
Chair-table: seventeenth-century style, 891-893
Chalk line, using, 31-32
Chamfer, chiselling, 160, 161
——, cutting, 159
——, marking-out, 159, 160
——, meaning of, 158
——, ornamental. 160, 161
—— plane, 158, 159
—— stops, 158-159, 213
——, width of, 160
Chamfered surface, 158
Chamfering attachment for drawknife, 71, 72
——, bevelling and rounding, 158-164
—— gauge. 160
——, spokeshave for, 160, 161
Chamfers with Stanley plane, 211-213
Charnley forest oilstone, 76
Chessboard, marquetry, 1341
Chess table (see Table, chess)
Chest, carved, 1198, 1199
—— of drawers (see Drawers)
——, dressing, oak, 1123-1126
——, linen, carved, 1196-1199
——, old-style, 1194-1196
——, tool, patternmakers', 470
——, ——, woodworkers', 471
Chesterfield settee, 915-917
Chicken rearer, hot-water, 657
Child's chair, 885-892
—— cot (see Cot)
—— play-pen (see Play-pen)
China cabinet (see Cabinet)
Chip carving, 1370-1372
Chippendale colour, staining, 1403
—— corner cabinet, 976-978

101—N.E.

INDEX

Chippendale finish, 1406
Chisel, bevelled-edge, 66, 67
—— blade, 66
—— ——, grinding and sharpening angles, 67
——, coachmaker's, 70
——, countersinking with, 151
——, curved (see Gouges)
——, drawer-lock, 70, 71
——, firmer, 66
——, grinding, 74, 75
—— irons, 73
——, mortise lock, 70
——, mortising, 69, 70
——, paring, 66
——, pocket, 71
——, self-coring, 1462, 1463
——, sharpening, 77
—— sizes, 66
——, socket mortise, 70
——, spade, 1346
—— : types, 66
——, using, 68
——, woodcarving, 1346, 1347
—— in woodturning, use of, 1297
Chiselling corners, 68, 69, 163
—— mortise hole, 69, 70, 248
—— rebates, 166, 167
—— : removing waste wood, 70
—— slot, 67, 68
Chopping box-block, 313
—— plugs, 72
—— wedges, 72
Christiana timber standard, 191
Chucks, removal of (woodturning), 1311
Churn, butter, 667-669
Cinder-sifter, dustless, 364-366
Circles, drawing (see Drawing)
Circular desk-tops, 704
—— framing, 685, 715
—— louvre or ventilator, 687
—— mirror-frame, 936-940
—— ring of wood, 702
—— saw (see Saw)
—— table, small, 840, 841
—— veneering, 1325-1328
—— work, iron bands for, 715
Cistern, bolting ends of, 235
——, jointing boards of, 234
——, watertight joints for, 235
Clamp, dowelled and mitred, 289, 290
——, sub-tenoned and mitred, 289, 290
——, using on table, 21, 22
Clamped ends, 289
Clamping, mitred, 289, 290
Clasp, brass, for letter-case, 1344
"Clattering" plane, 90
Cleat holding boards while planing, 20, 22
Clock case, inlaid, 945-947
—— ——, old-style, 947-951
——, grandfather, 955-966
—— mantel, case for, 951-955

Cloister brown oak finish, 1404
Cloth, tracing, 1507
Clothes airer, hanging, 356, 357
—— boxes, 456, 464
—— rails, fixing, 695, 697
Coach screws, 155
Coal-boxes and cabinets, 817-824
Coconut fibre (see Coir)
Coffee table (see Table, coffee)
Cogged joint (see Joint)
Coin-collector's cabinet, 1002-1004
Coir (coconut fibre) for upholstery, 1418
Cold frame, garden, 603-605
Collectors' cabinets, 1001-1008
Colours and brushes for drawings, 1508, 1509
Compass plane (see Plane, compass)
—— saw, 55, 56, 61
Compasses, drawing, 1504
—— : scribing skirting board, 42
——, use of, in carpentry, 40-42
Concave surfaces in woodturning, 1309
Conductivity of wood, 126
Cones, drawing, 1534
Conifer cones, 121
—— shoots, 123
—— trees, 115, 194
Conversion of timber, 189
Cooker, fireless, 365-368
Coop for broody hens, 646, 647
Cord cramps, 709, 710
Core driver, 1462, 1463
Core-box for patternmaking, 1443-1448
Cores in patternmaking, 1442
Corner cabinet, Chippendale, 976-978
Cornering tool, light, 99
Corners, chiselling, 68, 69, 163
——, methods of forming, 164
——, rounded, 162, 163, 1453
——, veneering, 1327, 1329
Corrugated fastener, 149
—— iron, bolt for, 156
Cot, collapsible, 1192, 1193
——, folding, 1187-1191
Cote, pigeon, 379-385
Cottage porch, 554-558
Countersink for brass, 302-303
—— for iron, 302, 303
—— for wood, 301, 302
Countersinking, 151, 302-303
—— screws, 150, 151, 302, 303
Cracks in timber, 130
Cramp, bar or sash, 710, 713
——, cord or rope, 709, 710
——, dog, 711, 714
——, G-, 710, 713
——, gig, 710, 712
——, improvised, 708
——, Jorgensen, 710, 712
——, metal, 710-712

Cramp, mitre, 711, 714
——, screw mitre, 711, 714
——, wedge, 708, 710
——, wooden bar, 709, 711
——, —— screw, 709
Cramping, 263, 712-716
Crates, making, 323, 324
Crenelated steel square, 33, 34
"Crocodile jaws" (brace), 296
"Croid" glue, 136
Cromwellian cabinet (see Cabinet)
Cross-cut saws, 46-48
Cubes, drawing, 1532
Cup chucks (woodturning), 1301, 1302
—— shake in timber, 193
Cupboard, backing, 290
——, bedside, 1129-1131
——, glazed, with side shelf, 970-972
—— lock, fitting, 1388
——, medicine, oak, 975-977
——, office, 1258-1260
—— with shelves, fixing to wall, 695
—— and shelves, hanging, simple, 969-970
—— with shelves over, 970-974
Curb, fireplace, wooden, 361, 362
Curio cabinet (see Cabinet)
Curtain pole, joint for, 269, 270
Curved frame, hammer-headed joint on, 268, 269
—— ——, lapped and screwed joint in, 268, 269
—— head bolted with handrail bolts and dowels, 270
—— rebates, 169
—— scraper, 112-113
—— skirting, joint for, 271
—— and straight pieces, joining, 706-707
—— tops and covers, 703-705
—— work, 698-707
—— ——, screwed joints for, 268, 269
—— ——, tenons for, 257, 258
—— ——, veneering, 1322-1324
Curves, French, 1505
Cutlery drawer, tarnish-proof fitment for, 354, 355
Cutter block, 1478-1480, 1490
—— for marquetry work, 1333
Cutting, bandsaw, 1475
——, frets, 1477
——, marquetry, 1333
——, mouldings by machinery, 1481-1483
Cycle shed, 417, 418
Cylinders, drawing, 1532
Cylindrical articles, building-up (woodturning), 1307
—— patterns in patternmaking, 1452

INDEX

"DEALS," converting fir logs to, 190
Decagon, chip carving design based on, 1370
Decay, timber, preventing, 193
Density of wood, 127
Desk, double, inexpensive, 1241
——, office, for four, 1243-1247
——, roll-top, 1225-1237
——, writing (*see* Writing desk)
Desk-tops, circular, 704
Dibbers, 508-510
Dining tables, 850-867
Dining-parlour chairs (*see* Chair, dining-parlour)
Dining-room billiard table (*see* Billiard table)
—— cabinet (*see* Cabinet, dining-room)
—— chairs (*see* Chair, dining-room)
Dirigible toboggan, 1274
Disc, circular, cut out, 306
—— cutter, 305-307
Dividers, 1503, 1504
Dividing board in three widths, 30
Doatiness in timber, 194
Dog cramps, 711, 714
Dog kennels, 392-398
Dogs, steel, 232
"Dolly" vice, 12
Dolphin hinge (*see* Hinge)
Donation box, 458, 460
"Donkey" (stool) for marquetry, 1335
Door, bookcase, 674
—— with diminished and "gun-stock" stiles, 673
——, dowelling, 243
——, external, frame for, 676
——, framed and ledged, 671
—— frames, 676
——, garden, trellised, 676-677
——, grooved and tongued, with ledges, 288
——: joint between head and stile, 228
——, ledged and battened, 670
——, —— and braced, 671
——, letter-box for, 460-462
——, panelled, 671, 672
——, ——, setting out, 672, 673
—— rail, double tenon joint for, 255
—— sagging, 1398
——, small, hingeing, 1387-1388
—— warping, 1399
——: weather affecting fitting, 1397
Doorway, semicircular head joining, 706, 707
Double elephant (size), 1498, 1507
Dovetail, box, 274
——, coarse, carpenter's, 274, 275
Dovetail, different kinds of, 274
——, drawer, 281
——: driving home joint, 277
——, faults in cutting, 278, 279
——, gluing, 140, 276
—— grooves, cutting, 286
—— joints, plain, 275-280
——, lap, 281, 282
——, —— and secret, 281-287
——, mitred, secret, 283
——, oblique, 285, 286
——, ordinary, 274
—— pins, 275-279
——. "pins first" method, 277, 278
——, plain, 275-280
——, puzzle, 222, 223, 286, 287
—— saw, 53, 61
——: scribed, 275
——, secret, double lap, 282-284
——, —— mitre, 283-285
——, setting out, 274, 275
—— sockets, working, 275-278
—— tenon joint, 279
—— tongues, cutting, 286
Dovetailed box, 274
—— carcase of stand, 279
Dovetailing machine, 1487, 1488
——, simple, applications of, 279
Dowel bit, 302
——, boring marks for, 243
—— box, 239
——, cold glue for, 246
——, faults, 244
——, gluing, 246
——, handrail bolt and, 269
—— hole, boring, 244
—— ——, depth of, 245
—— ——, fitment for, 244, 245
—— ——, lathe fitment, using, 246-247
——, making, 239
——, marking felloes for, 243
——, —— for panelled work, 241
——, ordinary, 239
——, placing, in grooved work, 242, 243
—— plate, method of use, 240
—— pops, 240, 241
——, screw, for walking-stick, 270
—— sharpener, 305, 307
——, wheelwright's, 239
——, wood for, 239
Dowelled butt joint, marking for, 240
—— felloes, 243
—— joints, 238-246
—— panelling, length of, 241
Dowelling, boards, 240
—— chairs, tables, etc., 242
—— doors, 243
—— in patternmaking, 1458
——. setting out for, 241, 242
Dowelling template, 242, 243
Draughtsmanship, training in, 1497
——, academic or exact, 1519
Draughts table (*see* Table, draughts)
Draw-boring, 264
Drawer bottom, methods of securing, 174
——, cutlery, fitment for, 354
—— dovetails, 281, 466
—— front, setting out secret dovetail, 282, 283
—— lock, fitting, 1388
——, secret, clothes box with, 464, 467
——, tight-fitting, 1398
Drawers, chest of, 221, 1157-1161, 1252-1255
——, pedestal fitting with, 1171-1173
——, roll-top desk, 1227
——: weather affecting movement, 1397
Drawing : angles, measurement of, 1523-1525
——: arranging sets, 1519-1523
—— boards, 326-330, 1498-1500
——: circles, 1529-1531
——: colours and brushes, 1508
——: compasses, 1504
——: cones, 1534
—— cubes, 1532
——: curves, French, 1505
——: cylinders, 1532
——: dividers, 1503-1504
——: ellipses, 1531, 1532
——: enlarging, 1512, 1513
——: erasers, 1509
——: heptagons, 1529
——: hexagon, 1529
——: inks, 1508
——: instruments, 1497-1510
——, isometric, 1537
——: lettering, 1517-1519
——: lines, bisection of, 1523
——: ——, perpendicular, 1523
——: mouldings, 1512, 1522
——: of mouldings, freehand, 1512
—— octagon, 1529
—— papers, 1505-1507
——, parallelogram, 1527
—— pencils, 1507, 1508
—— pens, 1501-1503
—— pentagon, 1527
——, perspective, 1535-1537
——: photographic reproductions, 1538-1540
—— pins, 1505
—— plane figures, 1511, 1512
——, polygons, 1527-1529
—— prisms, 1532
—— pyramid, 1535
——, reading, 1519-1523
——, rectangle, 1527
—— rhombus, 1527
——: scales, use of, 1510, 1511

1596 INDEX

Drawing: sizes, doubling and halving, 1512, 1513
—— square about a circle, 1527
——: squares, set- and T-, 1500, 1501
—— sphere, 1535
——, tracing, 1538
——: tracing paper and cloth, 1507
—— trapezium, 1527
—— trapezoid, 1527
—— triangles, 1525-1527
Drawings, cabinet for filing, 1255-1256
——: care of and indexing, 1540-1542
Drawing-office chest of drawers, 1252-1255
Drawing-room cabinets (see Cabinet, drawing-room)
Drawknife, 71, 72
——, chamfering with, 71, 72
——, sharpening, 80
Dresser, kitchen, or cabinet, modern, 788-790
——, ——, with enclosed cupboards, 802, 803
——, ——, with glass doors, 793, 794
——, ——, improved, 794-799
——, ——, large, 799-802
——, ——, with mangle enclosed, 790-793
——, sideboard, 804-806
——, ——, alternative design, 807
——, ——, with sliding doors, 807-810
Dressing-chest, 1123, 1154
Dressing-table, 1149-1154
"Drift" when mortising, 70
Drill, hand, 297
——, seed, 507
Dry rot, 192-193
Dustless cinder-sifter, 364, 365
Dwarf bookcases, 729-740

EASEL, 336
Easel-stand, photograph, 310
Easy chairs (see Chair, easy)
Ebony finish, 1405
Edge bevels, 700
—— joints, 230-235
—— plane, 97
—— tools, sharpening and setting, 78-80
Eggs, box for transport of, 458
Elbow chairs (see Chair, elbow)
Electric motors, 1493
Elephant, toy, rocking, 1429
Elizabethan draw tables, 859
Ellipse, drawing, 1267, 1531
——, fixing joints of, 703
Emery cloth, 197
—— grinding machine, 1491
—— wheel, 74

Enamelling, stove, 1415
—— woodwork, 1414
"Ends," timber, 191
Erasers, drawing, 1509
Espalier, rustic, 559, 563, 564
Expansion bits, 303, 304

FACE-PLATE (woodturning), 1299
—— work, 1305-1307
Fastener, corrugated, 149
Feathered joint (see Joint)
Felloes, dowelling, 243
Fence, router, 1333
Fender, wooden curb, joint for, 269, 270
Ferret hutch, 390, 391
Ferro-gallic reproduction process, 1539, 1540
"Fifty-five" plane (see Stanley)
File: angle for saw-sharpening, 61
——, cutting action of, 195
——, half-round, 196
—— handle, adjustable, 197
——, length of, 196
—— manufacture, 196
——, metalworker's, 197
——, riffler, 197
——, saw, 60
——: special uses, 196, 197
—— teeth, 195
——, "three-square," 196, 197
——, wood, 195
——, woodworker's, various shapes, 196
Filing circular saw teeth, 1469
Fillers (french polishing), 1401
Filleted joint (see Joint)
Fillets in patternmaking, 1453
Fillister plane, 93, 168
Finger plates, inlaid, 1338, 1339
Finish, Chippendale, 1406
——, ebony, 1405
——, enamel, 1414
——, German, 1409
——, Japanese lac, 1410
——, oak (see Oak finishes)
——, rosewood, 1405
——, walnut, 1405
Finishing: American methods, 1409
Fir, Douglas, 119
—— "hand masts," 191
Fire-guard, folding wooden, 360, 361
Fireless (haybox) cooker, 365
Fireplace curb, wooden, 361
Fire-screens (see Screen)
Firmer chisel, 66, 67
Fish glue, 141
Fishing tent, portable, 629, 630
Fixing woodwork to walls, 689-697
Flap bench, portable, 501-503
—— stay, fall-down, fitting, 1391

Flemish oak finish, 1404
Flexibility of timber, 134
Floor polishing, 1413
——, bell-tent, 630-632
Floorboards: forcing edges together for nailing, 708
——: secret nailing, 147, 148
Flower vase, 1116-1118
Flower-stand, 1107-1110
Folding bagatelle board, 1218
—— bench, 481, 482
—— camp-bedstead, 1185, 1186
—— cots, 1187-1191
—— fireguard, 360, 361
—— see-saw, 537-539
—— steps, household, 410-412
—— —— stool, three-legged, 899
Footstool, old design, 906, 907
—— slipper box, 905, 906
Forest green oak finish, 1404
Fork centre: woodturner's lathe, 1298, 1299
Fountain, aquarium with, 1209
"Fox" (secret) wedging, 261
Foxiness in timber, 194
Fox-wedged mortise and tenon joint, 261, 262
Frame with bevelled halvings and diagonal braces, 222
——, door, 676
—— for external door, 676
——, garden, 603-612
——, hexagonal mitred, 273
——, lapped, with tee-stretcher, 219
——, photograph, inlaid, 1337
——, picture, 1290-1294
——, ——, bench for, 503-506
——, pier-glass, 923-925
——, rebated and beaded, 169
—— and sash windows, 679
——, sofa, 921, 922
——, ——, stuff-over, 918-921
Framing, circular, 685
——: oblique-tenoned braces, 252, 253
——, setting out rails for, 252
French curves, 1505
—— dibber, 508, 509
—— glue, 135
—— polish blooming, 1412
—— —— sweating, 1412
—— polisher's glaze, 1412
—— polishing, 1401-1403
Fretcutting, 1381-1383
——: glasspapering, 1383
——: overlays, 1383
—— patterns, pasting, 1381
——: saw, using, 1381-1383
—— tools, 1381
Frets, chair-back, 1477
——, cutting, 1477
Fretsaw, power: blade and blade speed, 1477
——, ——: examples and scope, 1477, 1478
——, ——: principle, 1476, 1477
Fumed oak finish, 1403, 1404

INDEX

Furniture, bedroom (see Bedstead, Wardrobe, etc.)
—— carcase work, dovetail for, 279
——, curved work in, 705
——, drawing-room (see Chair, Table, Cabinet, etc.)
——, graining, 1414
——, hall, 765-787
——, kitchen, paint for, 1405
——, office, 1225-1260
——, painting, 1414
——, upholstered, frames for, 911, 922

GADROONING decoration for tables, 853
Garden arch, 547-550
—— baskets, 540-545
—— bungalow for open-air life, 600-602
—— carpentry, 507-539
—— chair-swing, 533-535
—— dibbers, 508
—— door, trellised, 676
—— frames and lights, 603-612
——, propagator for, 610-612
—— room, 596-600
—— seat with canopy, 516
—— ——, high-backed, with screen, 521-524
—— ——, hooded, with table, 531-533
—— ——, modern design, 519, 520
—— ——, ornamental, 525-528
—— ——, rustic, 521, 522
—— —— and tool-box, combined, 514, 515
—— shelter or tool-shed, 423-425
—— shrub box, 1112-1116
—— swing, 535-537
—— table with hooded seat, 531-533
—— tent with extending canopy, 627-629
—— tool-box, 512, 513
—— wheelbarrow, 442-446
Gardener's trug or basket, 540
Gas plant for woodworking machinery, 1493
Gate-leg tables (see Table)
Gauge, bit, 303, 304
——, cutting, 40, 41
——, marking, 37-39
——, mortise, 40, 41
G-cramps, 710, 713
Gedge's twist bit, 301, 302
Geometry, plane, 1523-1532
——, solid, 1532-1535
German finish, 1409
Gig cramps, 710, 712
Gimlet, auger, 294, 295
——, advantages of, 295
——, boring action of, 294
——, half-twist, 294

Gimlet shapes, 294
——, shell, 294
——, splitting with, 295
——, using, 294-296
Glass (see also Mirror)
——, lobby, with coat hooks, 783-786
——, toilet (see Toilet glass)
Glasspaper, 197, 198
—— rubber, 198, 199
——, use of, 198
Glasspapering convex surface, 198, 199
—— fretwork, 1383
—— grain, 199
——, mechanical devices for, 199
—— turned work, 1310
Glaze, french polisher's, 1412
Glue, applying, 137
——, bad smelling, 135
——, boiling, 138
—— brushes, 136-138
—— : cake form, 135
—— : colour and condition, 135
—— : consistency, 139
——, "croid," 136
—— for direct use, 136
——, English, 134
——, "extra," 135
——, fish, 141
——, French, 135
——, heating, 137
—— : how made, 135
—— joints, 230
——, life of, 135
——, liquid, 136, 141
—— : "made off," 137
——, making, 137
——, marine, 141
——, ordinary, 136
—— in patternmaking, 1448
——, powdered, 138
——, preparing, quickly, 138
——, qualities of, 135
——, Scotch, 135
——, special, 141
——, squeezed-out, 139
—— sticks, 137
——, strongest, 135
——, varieties of, 135
——, waterproof, 141
Glue-pots, 136-138
Glued joints, 139, 140
—— ——, butt, 230
—— ——, dovetailed, 140
—— ——, end-grain, 139, 140
—— ——, nailing, 140
Gluing aeroplane woodwork, 1276-1277
—— broken joint, 139
——, clamping when, 140
—— crossing pieces, 139, 140
—— dovetails, 140, 276
—— dowels, 246
——, method of, 138
—— : pressure, 140
—— tongued joints, 232

Gluing : use of dog, 141
—— veneered work, 139, 1316-1318
Golden oak finish, 1404
Gouge, countersinking with, 151
——, firmer, outside ground, 71
——, grinding, 72, 75, 78, 80
——, paring, inside ground, 71
——, scribing, 258
——, —— joint with, 71
——, sharpening, 79, 80
—— : sizes, 72
——, woodcarving, 1346, 1347
—— in woodturning, use of, 1298
Grain, end, showing, avoiding, 290
—— fillers, 1401
——, importance of, in woodturning, 1304
——, straight, observing, 105
——, timber, 106
——, ——, effect on planing, 106
——, ——, planing, 105
——, ——, planing end, 107
——, wood, 106
Graining furniture, 1414
Gramophone cabinet (see Cabinet)
Grandfather clocks (see Clock)
Grecian ogee moulding, 214, 218
Greenhouse, portable, 613-620
——, span-roof, small, 620-625
Grinding chisels, 74, 75
—— circular saw, 1468-1470
—— : devices for holding tools, 74, 75
—— gouge, 75
——, inclination of tool, 79
—— machine, emery, 1491-1493
—— planing machine cutters, 1479, 1480
—— : proper method, 74
—— : screwdriver, 154
—— : sign of blade too hot, 73
—— tools, 73-83
—— wheels, artificial, 74
Grindstone, dark streaks on, 81
——, flaws in, 82
——, hand-driven, 80
—— : keeping wet, 73
——, life of, 81
——, mounting, 81
——, revolving, 73
——, selecting, 81
—— : setting true on axle, 83
—— spindle, 83
——, testing with thumb-nail, 82
——, treadle, 82, 83
——, using, 73
—— : various makes, 81
Groove, built-up, 174
——, cutting, 171
——, dovetailed, 173
—— by machinery, 172
——, shape of, 171

INDEX

Grooved joints, 171-176
—— work, tenon for, 257, 258
Grooving drawer bottoms, 174
—— panel, 174
—— plane, 94, 172
——, ploughing and tongueing, 171-176
Grounding (woodcarving), 1351-1352
Growth-rings, timber, 117
Guard, seed, 510, 511
"Gun-stock" stiles, 673

HAIR seating, 1420
Half-imperial (size), 1498, 1507
Half-lap joints (see Joint)
Half-twist bit, 298, 299
Hall furniture, 765-787
—— rack for sticks, 773, 774
—— seat, 774-780
—— settle, old style, 780-783
——, shelf bracket for, 766
—— stand, 774-776, 1372, 1376
—— table, 764, 767-773
—— wardrobe and hat rack, 773, 774
Hammer, "cabriole," 1416
——, claw, 64
—— handles, 63
—— head, tightening, 64
—— ——, wedging, 63
—— ——, working loose, 64
——, London, 63
—— marks, avoiding, 64, 146
——, upholsterer's, 1416
——, using, 64
——, various types, 63
——, veneering, 1318-1320
——, Warrington, 63
Hammer-headed key joint, 268
Hand drill, 297
—— light, garden, 607-610
"Hand masts," 191
Hand-mirror (see Mirror)
Handles, brass, 1160, 1161
Handrail bolts and dowels, 269
Handrailing joint, 269, 270
Hanging clothes airer, 356, 357
—— plate-rack, 373, 374
—— wardrobe, 1141-1148
Hard and soft woods, list of, 194
Hardwood, nailing, 145
Hardwoods, 115, 121
Hat rack, 773, 774, 776, 778
Hatchet (see Axe)
—— tube, 700, 701
Hay-box cooker, 365-368
Heart shake in timber, 193, 194
Heartwood, 120
Hen-coop for broody fowls, 646
Heptagons (see Drawing)
Hessian, upholsterer's, 1418
Hexagon, setting out (see Drawing)
Hexagonal tables (see Table)
High chair, child's (see Chair)

Hinge, back-flap, for table, 1391, 1392
——, butt, fixing, 1387, 1388
——, ——, stopped, for box, 1393
——, centre, for wardrobe, 1396, 1397
——, curved, fitting, 1395, 1396
——, dolphin, for secretaire, 1393, 1394
——, half-sinking, 1387, 1388
——, link joint, 1394, 1395
——, skew, 1397
——, strap, for writing-desk, 1391, 1392
Hinged table-flap, 317-319
Hinging box, 1388
—— door, 1387, 1388
"Hitting face" of mallet, 64
Hive (see Beehive)
Hobby-horse, 1431, 1432
Holding power of nails, 144
Holes, depth of, measuring when boring, 305
Hollow plane, 94, 95
Hollows with Stanley plane, 213, 214
Honour, roll of (see Roll of honour)
Hook, bench, 52, 53
—— tenon, 253, 254
Horse, towel (see Towel horse)
Horsehair stuffing, 1418
Hot-air incubator, 648-654
Hot-water chicken rearer, 657
—— incubator, 654-657
Housed joint, 171
Household steps, 407-412
Housing joint (see Joint)
—— shelves into bookcase, 226, 227
——, trenched, for stairs, 229
Hutch, ferret, 390, 391
——, rabbit, framed, 385-390
——, ——, simple, 385, 386
Hydro or hot-water incubator, 654-657

IMPERIAL (size), 1498, 1507
Improvised bench vices, 496, 497
"Inch masts," 191
Incising, wood, 1372-1376
Inclined struts, 701
Incubators, 648-657
Indexing drawings, 1540-1542
India oilstone, 76
Ink, drawing, 1508
Inlaid bedstead, 1174-1178
—— bookcase, dwarf, 732
—— clock case, 945-947
—— finger plates, 1338, 1339
—— mahogany jewel-box, 1045-1050
—— overmantel, 930-982

Inlaid photograph frame, 1337, 1338
—— trays, 1339-1341
—— woods, 1330
—— ——: transfer imitations, 1406
Inlay work, 1330-1344
—— ——: bandings and stringings, 1333
—— ——: colour treatment, 1330
—— ——: designs, 1331-1333
—— ——, polishing, 1411
—— ——, router for, 1333
—— ——: setting out, 1331
—— ——: woods used, 1330
—— work-box, triple, 1039 1042
—— work-table, 1072, 1073
Intensive poultry houses, 639
Ironing boards, 315, 316
—— table, 347, 348
Isometric drawing (see Drawing)

JACK plane (see Plane)
Jacobean chair, 870, 871
—— draw table, 850-856
—— oak finish, 1404
—— writing-bureau in oak, 1090-1094
Japanese lac finish, 1410
—— lacquered screen, 1056, 1057
Jardinière and aquarium combined, 1211, 1214
Jennings' twist bit, 300, 301
Jewel-boxes, etc., 1045-1052
Joggle halving joint, 267, 268
—— tenon, 252
Joint, angle, 230-235
——, —— butt, simple, 236, 237
——, ——, cutting, 235
——, ——, double, lap, 236, 237
——, ——, lap, 236, 237
——, ——, nailing, 235
——, ——, ornamental, 237
——, ——, plain mitred, 237
——, architrave, 270
——, bevelled and notched, 224, 225
——, birdsmouth, 224-226
——, bolted, invisible, 259, 260
——, box pin, 279, 280
——, bridle, barefaced, 224, 226
——, butt, 230
——, ——, beaded, 236
——, ——, with blocks, 236
——, ——, with fish plates, 265
——, ——, fixing more than two, 231
——, ——, glue for, 230, 231
——, ——, glued, strengthening, 232
——, ——: numbering, 231, 232

INDEX

Joint, butt, shooting board for, 231
——, ——, square-tongued, 236
——, ——, with stout and thin boards, 230
——, ——, trying plane for, 230
——, cogged, 223, 225
——, cross diagonal, 221, 222
——, curb fender, wooden, 266
——, curtain pole, 269, 270
——, curved skirting, 271
——, curved, tongued and grooved, 238
——, double-tenoned for transom rail, 256, 257
——, double-tongued, 173
——, dovetailed acute angle, 220
——, —— housing, 227
——, ——, marking, 220
——, ——, plain, 274-280
——, ——, sawing socket, 220
——, —— and stopped housing, 227
——, ——, wedged notching, 224, 225 (see also Dovetail)
——, dowelled butt, marking for, 240
——, draw-boring, 264
—— edge, 230-235
——, end-cogged, 224, 225
——, fastening halved or lap, 225
——, feathered, 232, 233
——, filleted, 233, 234
——, fox-wedged, 261
——, grooved, three types of, 173
——, grooved and tongued, 172
——, ——, ——, mitreing, 237
——, half-lap, angle, 218, 219
——, ——, bevelled, 219, 220
——, ——, chamfered and scribed, 222
——, ——, cross, 218, 219
——, ——, diagonal, 220
——, ——, double tee, 219
——, ——, dovetail, 220
——, ——, mitred, plain, 223
——, ——, moulded and mitred, 222, 223
——, ——, setting out, 219
——, ——, stopped dovetailed, 220
——, ——, —— and mitred, 223
——, ——, straight bevelled, 218-220
——, ——, tee, 218, 219
——, halved, 218, 219
——, hammer-headed, 268, 269
——, handrailing, 269, 270
——, housed and tenoned, 228
——, housing, clearing with router, 226, 227
——, ——, definition of, 227

Joint, housing, dovetailed and stopped, 227, 228
——, ——, full, 226
——, ——, plain, 226, 227
——, ——, stopped, 226, 227
——, ——, wedged, 228
——, joggle halving, 267, 268
——, key, hammer-headed, 268
——: keyed mitreing, 237
——, lock, 279, 280
——, longitudinal, double-halved, 268, 269
——, matched, 234
——, —— and grooved, 234
——, mortise and tenon (see Mortise and tenon)
——, mitred angle, 237, 2ᵃ8
——, ——, for desk top, 1234
——, ——, false tenon for, 273
——, ——, keyed, 272
——, ——, screwed, 273
——, notched, double, 223-225
——, —— and dovetailed for joist, 224
——, obtuse angle, rebated and tongued, 238
——, ovolo - moulded and rebated, 236, 237
——, patternmaking, 1448-1450
——: post housed to sill, 226
——, puzzle, double dovetail, 222, 223
——, puzzle dovetail, 286
——, rail and post, 226, 227
——, rebate, 258, 259
——, rebated, 165, 169, 232, 233
——, —— mitreing, 237
——, ——, in patternmaking, 1450, 1451
——, —— and tongued, 173
——, ——, tongued and moulded, 236, 237
——: "rubbing" glue, 231
——, rule, 1391-1393
——, sash-bar, 260, 261
——, scarf, double-splayed, 268
——, scarfed, in machine belting, 1493, 1494
——, screw dowelled, 270
——, screwed, for curved work, 268, 269
——, ——, portable, 260, 261
——: scribing moulding, 258
——, ship-lapped, 221, 222
——, slotted screw, 232, 233
——, square, grooved and tongued, 236
——, ——, for desk top, 1234
——, tabled, 267
——, table-leg, 259, 260
——, tapered, dovetailed and stopped, 227
——, tenon dovetailed, 279
——, tenoned and bridled, 256
——, toe, 224
——, tongued, 232, 233
——, ——, double, 233
——, ——, fixing, 175

Joint, tongued, gluing, 175, 221
——, —— mitre, 238
——, —— and moulded, 236
——, top-light mortise and tenon, 260, 261
——, trenched, 228
——, watertight, 234, 235
Jointing boards of cistern, 234
—— —— edge to edge, 173
—— plane, 94
—— rebated frame, 170
Joints, dowelled, 238-246
——, scarfing, 265-271
Jorgensen cramp, 710, 712

KEELER, washing, 663-666
Kennel, dog, indoor, 392-398
Key-plates, brass, 1160-1161
Keyed mitred joints, 272
Keyhole saw, 55
Kilns, timber-drying, 187
Knife carving, 1377-1380
Knives, marking, 32
Knot, "locking," 1422
Knots in timber, 123, 124

LAC finish, Japanese, 1410
Lace-box in marquetry, 1334
Lacquered screen, 1056, 1057
Ladder, 412-416
—— poles, 191
Lamp-stand, pedestal, 1107
Lathe, boring dowel holes in, 244, 245
——, copying, 1312
——: face-plate work, 1312
——: reeding on, 1313
Laths for roll-top desks, 1235
Laundry table, 347, 348
Leaded light, wardrobe with, 1132, 1133
Leather, imitation, 1419
Ledges, buttoned, 288
——, slot-screwed, 288
Leg, "cabriole," castor for, 1400
Leg-stool, adjustable, 908-910
Letter box, 314, 460
Letter-case, marquetry, 1343
Lettering drawings, 1517-1519
Levels, spirit, and plumb level, 43-45
Light, garden, 603-612
——, Yorkshire, 682-683
Linen, black, 1419
—— chests (see Chest, linen)
—— press, 1206-1208
Linen-fold pattern, 1198
Lining-down board with rule and pencil, 30
Linings, splayed, 700, 701
Link-plate locks, fitting, 1395
Liquid glue, 141
Lobby glass, simple, 783-786
Lock, cupboard, fitting, 1388
——, drawer, fitting, 1388

INDEX

Lock joint, 279, 280
——, link-plate, fitting, 1395
Locked tenons, 257, 258
Locking arrangement for roll-top desk, 1227
Logs (see Timber)
London hammer, 63
Longitudinal joint, double-halved, 268, 269
Louis XV screen, modern rendering, 1058-1060
Louis XVI cabinet, 1317, 1318
—— screen, modern rendering, 1057-1058
Louvre boards, 701
——, circular, or ventilator, 687, 688
Luggage stools (see Stool)
Lustre on wood, 125, 126

MACHINE belting, 1493-1496
—— dovetailing, 1487, 1488
——, emery grinding, 1491-1493
——, panel planing, 1488, 1489
——, sandpapering, 1490-1491
——, surface planing, 1478-1483
——, tenoning, 1489-1491
——, thicknessing, 1488, 1489
——, vertical spindle moulding, 1483-1487
Machinery, woodworking by (see Machine, mortising; Saw, circular, etc.)
Mahogany, Honduras, 123
Mallets, 63-65
Maltese grey oak finish, 1404
Mantel clock, case for, 951, 955
—— fitments, 1261-1267
Mantelpieces, wooden, 1261-1267
Marine glue, 141
Marker, seed, 509, 510
Marking awl, 32
—— gauges, 37-40
—— knives, 32
——, pin, double-pointed for dowelling, 240, 241
—— tools, 27
Marquetry box, 1342, 1343
—— chessboard, 1341, 1342
——, cutting, 1333
——, foundation for, 1336
——, French, 1334
—— letter-case, 1343, 1344
—— sawing, 1335, 1336
——, stool ("donkey") for cutting, 1335
—— veneers, 1335, 1336
—— ——, gluing and clamping, 1336
—— work, 1330-1344
Matched joints (see Joint)
Matching plane, 94, 172, 234
—— stains, 1408
Measuring, accurate, with rule on edge, 29
—— board's thickness, 29

Measuring diameter with callipers, 1301-1304
—— length with rule, 29
—— timber, 27, 191
—— tools, 27
Measuring-off board for length, 29
Meat safe, 352, 353
Metal fittings, fixing, 1387-1400
—— planes, 94-97
—— tongues, 175, 176
Mincing box-block, 313
Mirror, dressing-table, movements, fitting, 1389, 1390
—— frame design (pyrography), 1386
——, hand, 1045-1050
——, hanging, 927-929, 940
——, "landscape" in Adam style, 943
——, old-style, 940-944
—— and rack, 931, 932
Mirror-frame, circular, 936-940
Mission-room oak finish, 1404
Mitre angles, 273
—— blocks, 181-183, 1290-1294
——, boring, 307
——, box, ordinary, 181, 182
——, cramping, with handscrew, 715, 716
—— cramps, 711, 714
—— cuts, 182, 183
—— cutting, 181, 182
—— joints, 272, 273
—— keys, saw kerfs for, 272
——, making, 258, 259
——, shooting, 183
—— —— blocks, 183, 184
——, square and rule combined, 32, 33
——, templates, 36, 37, 258-260
——, tongued, 238
—— trimming machine, 182
Mitred clamping, 289-290
—— dovetail, secret, 283
—— frame, hexagonal, 273
—— tenon, 257, 258
—— joints (see Joint)
Mitreing on trimmer, 1463, 1464
"Mixed timber," 191
Model stage, 1435-1438
Moquettes (see Velvets)
Morocco for upholstery, 1419
Mortise, bored, 248
——, chiselling 248
——, closed, 247
——, cutting, 248
—— gauge, 40, 41
—— ——, using, 247
——, haunched, 251
——, ——, in table leg, 259-260
—— hole, chiselling, 69, 70
—— lock, compound double tenon for, 255, 256
——, making, by machinery, 1461-1463
——, slot, 266, 267
——, —— joint, 250, 251

Mortise : table-leg joint, 259, 260
——, unequal - sided, setting out, 254, 255
Mortise-and-tenon, adjustable slot, 250, 251
—— ——, closed, 247
—— ——, fox-wedged, 261
—— ——, hook, 253
—— ——, joints, 246-264
—— ——, oblique, 252, 253
—— ——, pinning joints, 263
—— ——: sash-bar joints, 260
—— ——, scarf, 266, 267
—— ——, slot, 250, 251
—— ——, top-light joint, 260
—— ——, wedging, 263
Mortising chisel, 69, 70
—— faults, 249
—— machine, 1461-1463
——, method of, 70
—— stile, 252, 253
—— stool, 24, 25
—— : tenons (see Tenon)
Motor cab, toy, 1433, 1434
—— van, toy, 1433-1435
—— wagon, toy, 1431, 1433
Motor-cycle shed, 421, 422
Moulding, bevelling off, 201
——, chamfering down, 201,202
——, combination, 215-217
——, curved, 201-203
—— cutters, planing machine, 1480-1483
——, cutting, 1481-1483
——, finished, 201-202
——, glasspapering, 199
—— iron, 203
—— in patternmaking, 1439
—— machine, vertical spindle, 1483-1487
——, making, 200-203
—— and moulding cutters, 1481-1483
——, ogee, Grecian, 214, 215
——, ——, hollow, 202
——, ——, reverse, 214, 215
——, ——, Roman, 215, 216
——, picture-frame, 1290
—— planes, 94, 202, 204-217
——, roughing out, 201, 202
——, sections of various, 200, 214, 215, 1514, 1515, 1541, 1542
——, short breaks in, 270
——, stages of working, 200
——, Stanley plane for, 214-217
—— for tray rim, 1340
Mouldings, easily-worked, 213
——, examples, 200, 214-215, 1514-1515, 1541-1542
——, freehand drawing of, 1512
——, scraper for, 112, 113
——, small, planes for, 94, 95
—— with Stanley plane, 214
Movable parts, allowances in fitting, 1397

INDEX

"Mullet," testing panel thickness with, 107, 108
Mullion windows, 681, 682
Muntins, setting out, for dowelling, 241, 242
Music cabinet, 1009-1020
—— stool, 1027-1038

NAIL, clinching, 145
——, clout, 144
——, cut clasp, 144
——, floor, 142-144
——, French, 144
——, hammering, 146
——, holding power of, 144
——, oval steel, 142, 144
——: panel pins, 142-144
——, rose-head wrought, 144
——, town clout-, countersunk head, 144
——, varieties of, 142-144
——, wire, oval, 142-144
——, withdrawing, 146, 147
——, wood fibres gripping, 144
——, wrought, 142, 144
Nailing, 144-147
——, "dovetailed," 145
——: punching, 147
——, screwing and bolting, 142-157
——, secret, 147, 148
——, slantwise, 145
Nail-punches, 147
Nail-sets, 147
Needle points, 144, 1416, 1417
Needlework, ornamental screen for, 1067-1071
Newspaper rack, 316, 317
Nose bit, 298, 299
Notched joint (see Joint)
Notice board, framed, 329
Nut-crackers, carved, 1377

OAK, bark and trunk of, 132
"——, brown," 125
——, colour finishes for, 1404
—— finish, Austrian, 1404
—— ——, cloister brown, 1404
—— ——, Flemish, 1404
—— ——, forest green, 1404
—— ——, golden, 1404
—— ——, Jacobean, 1404
—— ——, Maltese grey, 1404
—— ——, mission-room, 1404
—— ——, verde green, 1404
—— ——, weathered, 1404
——, fuming, 1403, 1404
—— log, converting to "silvergrain" panelling, etc., 189, 190
Oblique work, 698-700
Occasional tables (see Table)
Octagon, setting out, 164, 1529
Octagonal tables (see Table)
Office cupboard, 1258-1260
—— desk for four, 1243-1247
—— furniture, 1225-1260

Office pigeon-holes, 1250-1252
—— table, 1240-1241
—— wardrobe, 1258-1260
Ogee mouldings, 202, 214-216
Oil, red, for finishing, 1403
Oilcans, various, 76
Oilstone, Arkansas, 76
—— box, 76
——, Charnley Forest, 76
——, "combination" India, 76
——, "rubbing down" uneven, 76, 77
——, Turkey, 76
——: various kinds, 74
——, "Washita," 74
——, water v. oil for, 76
"Old woman's tooth" router, 227
Onion drill, 507
Open-air treatment, sanatorium for, 426-436
Organ stools, 1036-1038
Ottoman, box, 914-916
Overhand planing or shooting, 177
Overmantel, bedroom, 932-935
——, carved, 1374, 1377
—— with cupboards, 935, 936
—— with fretted ends, 935, 936
——, inlaid, 928-930
—— for low chimney-piece, 925
——, painted, 928-930
Ovolo plane, 94, 95

PACKING case construction, 320
—— circular saws, 1467, 1468
Packing-boxes, circular saw, 1467, 1468
Pad saw, 56, 61
Painted surfaces, varnishing, 1415
Painting and graining furniture, 1414
—— woodwork, 1413
Panel board, using, 108
——, carved, 1348, 1357
—— designs (pyrography), 1384-1386
——, flush, grooved, 174
—— "mulleting" piece, 107, 108
—— pins, 142-144
—— planing, 107
—— —— machine, 1488, 1489
—— saw, 50, 61
——, testing thickness with "mullet," 107, 108
Panelled work, dowels for, 241
Panelling, converting pitchpine log to, 190
——, tenoned joint for, 257, 258
Pantasote for upholstery, 1419
Pantry windows, 678
Paper, drawing, 1505-1507
——, tracing, 1507
Parallelogram (see Drawing)
Paring chisel, 66

Patternmakers' tool-chest, 470
Patternmaking: building up, 1451-1458
——: core-boxes, 1443-1448
——: corners, rounded, 1453
——: cylindrical work, 1439, 1452
——: dimensions, exactness of, 1438
——: distortion in cooling, 1438
——: dowelling, 1458-1460
——, easy, 1438-1460
——: fillets, 1453, 1454
——: general work, 1455-1458
——: glue, uses of, 1448
——: joints, 1448-1450
——: moulding, 1439-1442
——: prints and cores, 1442
——: ring, building, in segments, 1451
——: sand, use of, 1439
——: woods used, 1439
Pedestal, box, for boot cleaning, 362, 363
—— coal cabinet, 822-824
—— fitting with drawers, 1171-1173
Peg-board, bench with, 12, 15
Pegamoid for upholstery, 1419
Pencils, carpenters', 31
——, drawing, 1507, 1508
Pentagon (see Drawing)
Pergolas, 568-576
Perspective, drawing in (see Drawing)
Petersburg timber standard, 191
Photo prints (see Blue-print, Ferro-gallic, etc.)
Photograph stand, 310, 311
Picture frames, bench for, 503
—— framing, 1290-1294
—— rails: fixing to walls, 693
Pier-glass frame, 923-925
Pigeon cotes, 379, 585
Pigeon-holes, nest of, 1250-1252
Pigskin for upholstery, 1419
Pincers, 65
——, withdrawing nails with, 146, 147
Pinch-rod, method of using, 30
Pine tree, 117-121
Pinning by draw-boring, 264
—— tenon joints, 263
Pins, dovetail (see Dovetail)
——, drawing, 1505
——, panel, 142-144
——, veneer, 144
Pith of wood, 121
Plane "back iron," 85
——, badger, 168
——, beading, 94, 95
——, beech used for making, 84
——, block, 94, 95
——, bull-nose, 92, 93
——, chamfer, 158, 159

INDEX

Plane, "choking up," 89
——, "clattering," 90
——, compass, 91, 92
—— "cutter" (see Plane iron)
——, cutting action, 85
——, edge, 97
——, fastening wedge, 88
—— figures, drawing, 1511
——, fillister rebate, 93, 168
——, ——, sash, 93, 168
—— "fin," 94
—— geometry, elementary, 1523-1532
——, grooving, 94, 171, 172
——, hollow, 94, 95
—— iron, built-up blade, 67, 72, 85
—— ——, burr, removing, 78
—— ——, edges of, 86
—— ——, loosening, 86, 87
—— ——, replacing in position, 88
—— ——, round, wavy surface due to, 85
—— ——, sharpening, 77
—— ——, unscrewing, 86, 87
——, jack, 84, 85, 96, 97
——, ——, using, 101
——, jointing, 94
—— matching, 94, 172
—— ——, using, 234
——, medullary rays in, 85
——, metal, block, 95-97
——, moulding, 94
——, new, adjusting, 88, 89
——: oiling, before use, 84
——, ovolo, 94, 95
——, plough, 93, 94
——, rebate, 92, 93, 166
——, re-mouthing, 89, 90
—— for rough work, 84
——, round, 94, 95
——, "round sole," 91, 92
——, rounding, for staves, 414
——, scraper, double-handled, 112, 113
——, setting, 85, 105
——, "shooting," 90
——, sighting along sole, 89
——, simplest form, 84
——, smoothing, 91
——, ——, using, 104
——, Stanley "fifty-five" (see Stanley)
——: striking button, 89
—— surfaces, winding strips for, 102
——: taking apart, 86, 87
——, toothing, 91, 92, 1319
——, trenching, 171, 172
——, trying, 90, 91
—— and twisted surfaces, 101
——: various forms, 84
Planed surface, testing across, 101
Planing, 100-108
——: common faults, 101

Planing, direction of correct, 106
——, edge, with and without vice, 103
—— end grain, 107
——: face and edge marks, 103
—— machine, panel, 1488, 1489
—— ——, surface, 1478-1483
——, overhand, 177
—— panels, 107
——: squaring edge, 104
——: thickness correction, 104
—— thin strip, 107
——, twist in, 102
——: width correction, 104
Planks, "bastard," 119
Plant stand, 1110-1112
Plates, finger (see Finger plates)
Plate-rack, hanging, 373, 374
——, improved, 374-376
——, standing, 371-373
Play-pen, baby's, 356, 358, 359, 361
Plough plane, 93, 94, 172
——, cutters for, 172
—— fence, 173
——, using, 172
Ploughing, circular saw, 1471
—— with Stanley plane, 208
Plugging new work, 690, 691
—— walls, fixing after, 693
Plugs, chopping, 72
Plumb bob, screw, 45
—— rules, etc., 44, 45
Plumb-rule tube, 44
Plumbs, using, 43-45
Plushes for upholstery, 1420
Poker-work (see Pyrography)
Polish, bleached shellac, 1411
——, brush (french polishing), 1403
——, french, applying, 1402
——, old, removing, 1408
—— revivers, 1412
Polishing floor, 1413
——, french, 1401-1403
—— inlaid work, 1411
Polygons, 1527-1529
"Pops, dowel," 240, 241
Porch shrub box, 1112-1116
Porches, 554-562
Poster board, making, 332-334
Potato carriers, 544-545
—— dibber, 508, 509
—— sprouting box, 544, 545
Poultry houses, 634-646
Preserving timber, 193
Press, linen, 1206-1208
——, trousers, 1205
Prints in patternmaking, 1442
Prisms, drawing, 1532
Propagator, easily-made, 610
Provision safe, 353-354
Pulley rotation, reversing, 1495
—— speeds, 1495, 1496
Pulleys, machine, 1493-1494
Punching nails, 147

Puzzle dovetail joints, 286
Pyramid, drawing, 1535
Pyrography, 1383-1386

QUADRANT for writing fall, 1393
"Queen Anne" chairs, 877-885
—— —— chest of drawers, 1157-1160
—— —— mirrors, 940-942
—— —— stool, 907, 908

"RABBET," or "rabbit," 165
Rabbit hutch, 385-390
Rack, boot and shoe, 309, 376
——, domestic, 371-378
—— and mirror, 931-932
——, newspaper, 316, 317
——, stick, for hall, 773, 774
——, timber, 25, 26
——, tool for bench, 498, 500
Rail, clothes, fixing, 695, 697
—— joint, transom, 256, 257
——, segmental, tenoned joint for, 257, 258
—— set out by template, 243
——, setting out, for dowelling, 241, 242
——, towel (see Towel)
Rasp, cutting action of, 195
——, forms of, 196
——, teeth of, 195
Ratchet brace, 295, 296
—— screwdriver, 155
Reamer, iron, 303
——, wood, 302, 303
Rebate, box-lid, 169
——, built-up, 168, 169
——, curved, 169
——, cutting, 165-168
——, joints for, 258, 259
——, meaning of, 164
—— plane, 92, 93
—— ——, using, 166-168
——, shallow 169
——, stopped, 92, 93, 169, 170
Rebated frame, jointing, 170
—— joint, 165, 169, 232, 233
Rebating, 165-170
——, circular saw, 1465-1467
—— by machinery, 168
—— with Stanley plane, 208
Recess, bookshelves for, 724
——, measuring, 30
——, sideboard fitting for, 814
Red oil, 1403
Reeding on lathe, 1313
—— spokeshave, 98
—— tool, 99
Regulator, upholsterer's, 1416
Reproducing drawings: photo processes, 1538-1540
Revivers, polish, 1412
Rexine for upholstery, 1419
Rhombus (see Drawing)
Ribbon work, 1354, 1356
Rickers, 191

INDEX

Riffler file for curved work, 197
Rim, tray, moulding for, 1340
Ring, building, 702, 1451
Rip saw, 47-50, 61
Roanoid for upholstery, 1419
Rod, setting-out, use of, 262
Roll of honour, 330
Roll-top desk, 1225-1237
Roman ogee moulding, 216
Roofing felt, nails for, 144
Room, garden, 596-600
Rope cramps, 709, 710
Rosewood finish, 1405
Rot, wet and dry, 192, 193
Rounded angles, 162
—— corners, 162, 163
—— edges, 162, 163
Rounding with flat cutters, 162
—— poles, 164
—— rollers, 164
Rounds with Stanley plane, 213, 214
Router for inlaid work, 1333
Routers and spokeshaves, 98, 99
Rubbers, glasspaper, 198
"Rug-box" (see Chest, old-style)
Rule attachments, 42
—— joint, 1391-1393
—— measurement, methods of, 27-30
——: measuring length, 29
——, transferring measurement from, 27
——, using, 29, 30
——, various forms, 28, 29
Rule-joint stays, fixing, 1390
Ruling pens, 1501-1503
Runner shoes for sledge, 1268
Rustic arch, 559-564
—— garden seats, 521, 522
—— pergolas, 568-576

SAFE, provision, 352-354
Sanatorium for open-air treatment, 426-436
Sand for pattern-making, 1439
Sandpaper (see Glasspaper)
Sand-papering machine, 1490, 1491
Sapwood, 120
Sash cramps, 710, 713
—— and frame windows, 679
Sash-bar joints, 260, 261
Sash-moulding with Stanley plane, 209, 210
Sateens for upholstery, 1421
Satinwood, Ceylon, 123
Saw, band (see Bandsaw)
—— blade, thickness of, 46, 47
——, bow, 54, 55
——, buckled, 62
——, circular: cutting tenons, 1471
——, ——: filing teeth, 1469, 1470

Saw, circular: grinding and sharpening teeth, 1468-1470
——, ——: mounting, 1467, 1468
——, ——, operating, 1464-1466
——, ——, packing and packing boxes, 1467, 1468
——, ——: parts described, 1464, 1465
——, ——: ploughing, 1471, 1472
——, ——: position relative to fence, 1471
——, ——: rebating, 1465-1467
——, ——, setting, 1469-1471
——, ——: sizes, 1468
——, ——: speeds, 1471
——, ——: table, rising and falling, 1465, 1466
——, ——: tension, 1472
——, ——: what to avoid in sawing, 1472
—— clamps for bench vice, 59
——, compass, 55, 56, 61
——, cross-cut, 46-48, 61
——, dovetail, 53, 61
——, fret (see Fretsaw)
——, hand, 46, 47
—— handles, 47
—— "kerf," 46, 48, 62
——, keyhole, 55
——, pad, 56
——, panel, 50, 61
——, rip, 47, 48, 50, 61
—— screw, 53, 54
——, setting and sharpening, 56-61
—— teeth, angles of, 61
—— ——, dull-cutting, 47
—— ——, filed and set, 46, 48
—— ——, filing, 60
—— ——, number of, 47
—— ——, setting with hammer and vice, 58
—— ——, ——, with plier-type set, 57
—— ——, shape of, 46, 47
—— —— stamped out square, 46, 48
—— ——, topping, with flat file, 59
——, tenon, adjustable back, 52, 53, 165
——, veneer, 1319-1320
—— vice, 59
Saw-filer's vice, 59
Saw-kerfing, 706
Saw-set, 57
Saw-setting block, 58
—— hammer, 58
Sawing, accurate, 62
——: correct slope of saw, 50-52
——: cross-cutting long board near middle, 49
——, defective, 50, 51

Sawing end off board to prevent splitting, 49
—— —— of long board, 49
——, fretwork, 1381-1383
—— marquetry, 1335, 1336
——, methods of, 47, 48
——, mistakes in, 47
——: position of saw when starting, 50-52
——: ripping, 52
——: saw with too little slope, 51
—— stools, 24, 25
——: testing squareness when cutting, 49
—— in the waste, 62
—— in woodcarving, 1362, 1363
Scaffold poles, 191
Scales, use of, in drawing, 1510
Scarfing joints, 265-268
Scotch glue, 135
Scraper, action of, 109
——, curved, 112-113
——, handled, 112
——, kind of, 112, 113
——, making, 113
—— for mouldings, 112, 113
—— plane, double-handled, 112, 113
——, sharpening, 108, 109
——, using, various methods, 110-112
Screen, fire, 1066
——, folding, stencilled, 1062
——, inlaid Sheraton, modern, 1060-1061
——, Japanese lacquered, 1056
——, modern, based on Louis XVI period, 1057, 1058
——, modern rendering of Louis XV work, 1058
——, ornamental, for needlework, 1067-1071
——, Sheraton, modern, 1060
Screens, ancient and modern, 1056-1062
Screw bit, 298, 299
——, cramping action of, 150
—— gauges, table of, 149
—— heads, countersinking, 150, 151
—— holes, marking, 153
—— ——, sinking with countersink, 303
—— ——, wood plug for, 151, 152
Screwdriver, action of, 153
——, automatic, 155
—— bit in brace, 155, 303, 304
—— edges, 154
—— for fitting metalwork to wood, 1398
——, grinding, 154
——, holding, 154
——, long, advantage of, 154
——, ratchet, 155
——: types, 154
——, width of, 153

INDEX

Screwing cross pieces, 153
——— strips, battens, etc., 152
Screws, bed, 156, 157
———, boring for, 149, 150
———, brass, sizes of, 148
———, coach, 155
———, countersunk, 148, 149
———, diameter of, 149
———, dowel, 149
———, gutter, 148, 149
———, handrail, 148, 149
———, holes for, 149
———, iron, methods of finishing, 148
———, japanned, sizes, 148
———, raised-head, 148
———, round-head, 148
———: screwing, 148-155
———, sizes of, 148
———: slot, damaged, 153
———, spacing, 152
———, spout, 148, 149
———, starting difficult, 155
———: types, 148
———, withdrawing, 155
Scribing gouge, 258
———: Spiling method, 42, 43
Scrim, upholsterer's, 1419
Scullery fitment, 309, 310
——— side-table, 342
Seasoning timber, 185
Seat, bath, 349
———, garden, with canopy, 516
———, ———, high-backed, with screen, 521-524
———, ———, modern design, 519, 520
———, ———, ornamental, 525-528
———, ———, rustic, 521, 522
———, ———, and tool-box, combined, 514, 515
———, hall, and stand, 774-776
———, oak, for hall, 778-780
——— round a tree, 517, 518
———, stool (*see* Stool)
Secret dovetail joints, 281
——— ("fox") wedging, 261, 262
——— nailing, 99, 148
Secretaire, bookcase-, recessed, 1098-1101
Sectional bookcases, 1256-1260
Seed drill, 507
——— guard, 510, 511
——— marker, 509, 510
See-saw, folding, 537-539
Sepia process of reproducing drawings, 1540
Serges in upholstery, 1420
Set-squares for drawing, 1501
Settees, 780-783, 915-918
———, upholstering, 1426-1428
" Setting-in " (woodcarving), 1350-1351
Setting-out rod, use of, 262
Shafting, speeds of, 1496
Shafts, sleigh, 1272-1273
"Shakes" in timber, 130
Sharpening bandsaw, 1475

Sharpening bradawl, 292
——— centre-bit, 298-300
——— circular saw, 1468-1470
——— plane-iron, 77
——— scraper, 109-112
——— tools, 73-83 (*see also* Saw, Chisel, etc.)
——— trimmer knives, 1464
Shaving cabinet, 1162, 1163
Shaving-turning-up tool for secret nailing, 99
Shed, cycle, 417-420
———, motor-cycle and side-car, 421-423
———, tool, 423-425
Shelf bracket for hall, 766
Shell bit, 297
——— gimlet, 294
Shellac polish, bleached, 1411
Shelter, garden, 423-425, 570, 582
Shelves and cupboard, hanging, simple, 969, 970
———, movable, for bookcases, 727
Shelving : fixing to walls, 693-695
Sheraton music cabinet, 1009
——— screen, 1060, 1061
——— toilet glass, 1162-1165
Ship-lapped joint (*see* Joint)
"Shipping-dry" wood, 129
Shooting blocks, 178-181
——— ———, mitre, 183, 184
——— board, 177, 231
——— ———, donkey-eared, 1106
——— ———, metal, 184
——— ——— for picture frames, 1290-1294
——— ———: testing, 177
——— ——— warping, preventing, 178
———: breakages of corners, 180, 181
——— edges at an angle, 178, 179
——— end grain, 180, 181
——— ends at an angle, 181, 182
——— mitre, 183
——— and mitre cutting, 177-184
——— out of square, 178, 179
———, overhand, 177
——— square work, 176
Shoulder plane, 96
Shrinkage in timber, 131
——— of sawn-up log, 189
——— of wood in wood-turning, 1307
Shrub boxes, 1112-1116
Side rebate plane, 96
Side-table, scullery, 342, 343
———, semi-circular, small, 838
Sideboard dressers, 804-810
——— fitting for recess, 814-816
———, incised work, 1371, 1376
———, mahogany, 810-814
———, small, 802, 803
Sideboards and dressers, 788-816
Sizes (designs) : doubling and halving (*see* Drawing)

Skew hinges, 1397
Skirt ironing board, 316, 317
Skirting board, fitting, to uneven floor, 42, 72
———, curved, joint for, 271
Sledge, easily-made, 1268, 1269
Sleeve ironing board, 315, 316
Sleigh, Canadian box, 1269-1274
Slipper box, footstool, 905, 906
Slitting with Stanley plane, 209
Slotted screw joints, 232, 233
Smoker's cabinet, 355, 967
Smoothing plane (*see* Plane)
Sockets, dovetail (*see* Dovetail)
Sofa frame, 920-922
——— ———, stuff-over, 918-921
Soft woods, 118
Solid geometry, 1532-1535
Sphere, drawing, 1535
Spiling method of scribing, 42
Spiral turning, 1312, 1313
Spirit levels, 43, 45
——— varnish, white and hard, 1411
Splayed box, 162, 163
——— ———, irregular, 700
——— linings, 700, 701
Splitting, preventing, when nailing, 145
——— timber, 133
Spokeshave, adjustable, 98
———: best to use, 98
———, brass-plated, 98
———, flat-faced, 98
———, grain influences, 99
———, metal, 98
———, reeding, 98
———, round-faced, 98
———, using, 98
———, wooden, 98
Spoon-bit, 297, 298
"Spoon-bit" tool for woodcarving, 1355, 1356
Springs, upholstery, 1418, 1421
Sprouting box, potato, 544, 545
Square, adjustable bevel, 35
———, try, 32, 33
———, crenelated, 33, 34
——— edges, testing with try square, 35
———, horizontal, 448, 449
———, mitre and rule, combined, 32, 33
———, steel, 33, 34
———, tee, 1500
———, testing try, 33
———, using, 33-35
———, wooden, 33, 34
Squares and right angles, rule for testing, 34, 35
Stable wheelbarrow, 442-446
Stage, model, 1435-1438
Stain and varnish, combined, 1406
———, pyrography, 1385
———, water, 1404, 1405

INDEX

Staining Chippendale colour, 1403
—— with dyes, 1405
—— inferior woods, 1405
—— oak, 1403, 1404
Staircase bull-nose step, bending, 705-707
Stairs, trenched housing for, 229
Stand, flower-, with bookshelves, 1107-1110
——, hat and umbrella, 776-778
——, lamp-, pedestal, with bookshelves, 1107-1110
——, photograph, 310
——, plant, 1110-1112
——, umbrella, simple, in oak, 786-787
Stanley's "fifty-five" plane, 204-217
—— —— ——: arms, 205
—— —— ——: bottom, auxiliary centre, 204, 205
—— —— ——: cam rest, 205
—— —— ——: cutters and depth gauges, 206, 207
—— —— ——: cutters, regular, supplied with, 216, 217
—— —— ——: cutters, setting, 207
—— —— ——: cutters, special, 216, 217
—— —— ——: fences, 204, 205
—— —— ——: held correctly at right angles, 205
—— —— ——: holding, correct method, 207
—— —— ——: holding incorrectly causes slanted grooves, 205
—— —— ——: main stock, 204
—— —— ——: ogee cutter on runners, 206
—— —— ——: parts, 204, 205
—— —— ——: parts numbered and shown separately, 217
—— —— ——: runners, 206
—— —— ——: sliding section, 204
—— —— ——: tipping, effect of, 205
Star shake in timber, 193, 194
Staves, rounding, for ladders, 412-414
Stay, fall-down flap, fixing, 1391

Stay, rule-joint, fixing, 1390-1391
Steam plant for woodworking machinery, 1493
Steel squares, 33-34
Steps, making, 407-412
Stiles, diminished or "gunstock," 673
——, mortising, 252, 253
Stool and book trough, combined, 308
——, chair-, for boot-cleaning, 901-904
——, folding three-legged, 899-903
——, leg-, adjustable, 908-910
——, luggage, 895-898
——, making on lathe, 1313, 1314
——, mortising, 24
——, music, 1027-1038
——, octagonal, for jardinière, 1105-1107
——, organ, 1036-1038
——, plain, 894, 895
——, "Queen Anne," 907-908
——, sawing, 24, 25
—— seat, 900, 903, 904
——, three-legged folding, 899-903
Stopping nail-hole, 1414
Stops, bench, 21, 23, 494, 496
Stove enamelling, 1415
Straightedge, sizes, 31
——, testing accuracy, 31
"Straining piece," bedstead, 1184
Strap hinge (see Hinge)
Stringings, inlaid, 1333
——, veneer, 1328
Stub tenon, 252, 253
Stuffing materials, 1417-1419
Sugar caddy (see Caddy)
Suite, bedroom, oak, 1119-1131
Summer-house, extensible, 589-591
——, gable-fronted, 582-586
——, gable-roof with door at end, 588, 589
——, —— with pigeon cote, 585-588
——, open-fronted, 577-580
——, ——, alternative design, 580-582
——, revolving, 591-595
——, ——, portable, 595
—— tent, portable, 625-627
Swing, garden, 535-537
Swing-chair, garden, 533-535
Swivel window, 262
Sycamore wood, 125

TABLE, bagatelle, 1215-1218
——, bench attachment for, 478-480
——, card-, inlaid folding, 836-838

Table, card-, link joint hinges for, 1394-1395
——, chess and draughts, 827, 828
——, circular, constructing built-up rim, 702
——, ——, small, 840-841
——, coffee, 841-844
——: cramping with iron band and G-cramp, 712, 714
——, detachable, 343
—— with detachable legs, 340, 341
——, dining, extending top, 855-859
——, ——, telescopic screw operated, 863-866
——, dowelling, 242-243
——, draughts and chess, 827
——, draw, mediæval, 850-856
——, ——, screw-operated, 859-867
—, dressing (see Dressing-table)
——, Elizabethan draw, 850-853
—— flap, hinged bearer for, 289, 290
——, garden, with hooded seat, 531-533
——, gate-leg, oval, 845-849
——, hall, 764, 765, 767-773
——, hexagonal, 834-836
——, kitchen, 337, 343
——, laundry, 347-348
——, mediæval draw, 850-856
——, occasional, hexagonal, 834-836
——, ——, miniature, 839, 840
——, ——, small, 825-827
——, octagonal, 833, 834
——, office, 1240, 1241
——, oval gate-leg, 845-849
——, plain, 337-348
——, scullery (see Side-table, scullery)
——, side, small semi-circular, 838, 839
——, simple, 345
——, small, for hall, 764, 765
——, ——, with rising tray, 830-832
——, square fancy, 832
——, tea-, small, with panelled falls, 829, 830
——, telescopic dining, screw-operated, 863-866
—— top, attaching, 288, 289
——, typewriter, 1247-1250
——, work (see Work-table)
——, writing (see Writing-table)
Table-flap, hinged, 317-319
Table-leg joints, 259, 260
Tabled joint, 267
Tapered tenons, 254
Tapestries for upholstery, 1419
Tea caddy, 1049-1052
Tee square (see T-square)

INDEX

Template, dowelling, 242, 243
———, dovetail, 278, 279
———, mitre, 36, 37, 258, 260
——— for rounded corners, 162
——— square, using on glazing bar, 36-38
Tenon, barefaced, 251, 252
———, ——— tapered, 254
———: beaded work, 258
———, compound double, for mortise lock, 255, 256
———: curved work, 257, 258
——— cut, 247
———: cutting on circular saw, 1471
———, door frame, ordinary and barefaced, 252
———, double, 255
———, dovetail, 279
———: draw-boring, 264
———, false, for mitred joints, 273
———, fox-wedged, 261
———: grooved, beaded and moulded work, 257, 258
———, haunched, 251
——— haunching, secret, 251
———, hook, 253, 254
———, ———, mortise for, 253, 254
———, joggle, 252
——— joint, double, for door rail, 255
———, locked, 257, 258
———, loose, joint, 262
———, mitred, 257, 258
———, oblique, 252, 253
——— for panelling, 257, 258
——— ——— rebated work, 258
———: sash-bar joints, 260, 261
——— saw, 52, 53, 61
———, sawing, 249, 250
———, ———, faults in, 250
———, scarf, 266, 267
———: segmental rail, 257, 258
——— set out, 247
——— shoulder, faults in cutting, 250
———: slot mortise, setting out, 250, 251
———, starting, 248
———, stub, 252, 253
———, tapered, 254
———, tusk, 254
———, ———, mortise for, 254
———, unequal-sided, 254, 255
Tenoned braces, oblique, 252
——— and bridled joint, 256, 257
——— joint, double, for transom rail, 256, 257
Tenoning machine, 1489-1491
Tension, circular saw, 1472
Tent, bell, circular wood floor for, 632
———, ———, octagonal wood floor for, 630-632
——— fishing, portable, 629-630
———, garden, with extending canopy, 627-629

Tent, portable summer-house, 625-627
Thannette for upholstery, 1419
Thermal bath cabinet, 350-352
Thicknessing machine, 1488
Thills (see Shafts)
Three-ply wood, 1318, 1319
Timber (see also Wood)
———, air-dried, 128
———: alphabetical list of timbers, 1543-1590
———: ash in summer and winter, 125
———: beams cut square with tree, 189
——— for bench, 10
———, bird's-eye grain in, 123
———: boarding, sizes of, 191
———, coarse-grained, 122
———, coloured, 124, 125
———, conductivity of, 127
———: conversion, 189
———: ——— and seasoning, 185-194
——— cracks, preventing, 133
———: cup shake in balk, 193
———: curly effect, 122
———: darkening by exposure to air, 124
———: decay, 192
———: defects, 192
———: density and specific gravity, 127
———: diseases, 192
———: doatiness, 194
———: dry rot, 192, 193
———: even-grain, 122
———: figuring, 123
———, fine-grained, 122
———: fir log, converting to "deals," 190
———: flexibility, 134
———: foxiness, 125, 194
———: gloss or lustre, 125, 126
———: gnarled grain, 123
———, good, signs of, 193
———: growth and properties, 114-134
———: growth-rings, 117
———, hard and soft, 115, 118, 121
———: heart shake, 193-194
———: heartwood, 120
———: kiln-drying, 186
———: kilns for drying, 187
———: knots, various forms of, 123-124
———: ladder poles, 191
———, "load of," meaning of term, 191
——— log, beam and joist from, 190
——— ———: calculating contents, 191
——— ———, cup shake in, 193
———: ——— cut into planks and beams, 189
——— ———, measuring, 191

Timber, market sizes, 190-191
———, mechanical properties, 133
———, "mixed," meaning of, 191
———: moisture content, 129
———: odour, 126
———: origin, 115
———: piling, 186
———: pine logs, 119
———: pitch-pine log, converting to panelling, 190
———: pith, 121
———: planing and grain, 105
———: preserving from decay, 193
——— rack, 25
——— ———, metal cantilevers, 26
———: resonance, 126
——— rickers, 191
———: sapwood, 120
———: scaffold poles, 191
———, seasoning, 185-194
———: section of trunk, 129, 131
———: "shakes" or cracks, 130
——— shrinkage, 131
——— ———: effect on sawn-up log, 189
———: sources, 114
———: "spars and poles," 191
———: splitting, 132
——— standard, Christiana, 191
———, ———, Petersburg, 191
———: star shake, 193, 194
———: strain, 134
———: strength, 122, 134
——— ———: benching, 134
——— ———: crossbreaking, 134
——— ———: transverse, 134
——— stress, 134
——— strips, seasoning, 187
———, ———, apparatus for, 188
———: texture and grain, 121
———: toughness, 134
———: twisted fibres, 194
———: upsets, 194
———: waney edges, 194
———, weight of, 127, 128
——— weights, classification, 128-129
———: wet rot, 192, 193
———, winter felled, 130
Timbers, hard, list of, 194
———, pine and spruce, how sold, 190
———, soft, list of, 194
Tobbogan, dirigible, 1268, 1274
Toe joint, 224
Toilet-glass, Sheraton, 1162-1165
———, movements, fitting, 1389, 1390
Toilet-paper box, 312, 313
Tongued joint, fixing, 175
——— ———, gluing, 175, 253
Tongues: circular saw, 175
———, cross-grain, advantages of, 175
———, grain of, 175

Tongues, metal, 175, 176
——, use of, 174, 175
——, varieties of, 174
——, width of, 174
Tonguing, double, with Stanley plane, 209
Tool-box, garden, 512-515
Tool chests, 468-477
—— drawer, bench with, 14
—— rack for bench, 498, 500, 501
—— rest for woodturners, 1298
—— shed or garden shelter, 423-425
——, woodcarving, 1345-1347
Tool-grinding appliance for grindstone, 75
Toothing plane (see Plane)
Towel horses, 1167-1169
—— rail for wall, 1170, 1171
Toy hobby-horse, 1431, 1432
—— model stage, 1435-1438
—— motor cab, 1433, 1434
—— —— van, 1433-1435
—— —— wagon, 1431, 1433
—— rocking elephant, 1429-1431
Tracing, 1538
—— design (woodcarving), 1360-1362
Trailer, bean or pea, 511-512
Trammels, 41-43
Transfer imitation of inlaid woods, 1406
Transom rail, 256, 257
Trapezium (see Drawing)
Trapezoid (see Drawing)
Travelling trunk, 461-464
Tray, inlaid, 1339-1341
——, imaginary, 105
Tree, seat round, 517, 518
——, section of, 105
—— trunk cut obliquely, 105
—— —— cut to show figure, 131
—— ——, elevation and plan, 106
Trefoil, setting out, 309
Trellis arch and screen, 551-554
—— work, making and fixing, 546, 547
Trellised arbour, 550-551
—— porch with gable roof covered with weatherboarding, 558-562
Trench (see Groove)
Trenching plane, 172
—— with Stanley plane, 208
Triangles, drawing, 1525-1527
Trimmer: components, 1463, 1464
—— knives, sharpening, 1464
——, mitreing on, 1463, 1464
——, scope of, 1463
Trimmings, upholstery, 1421
Trousers press, 1205, 1206
—— stretchers, 1200-1205
Trug, gardener's, 540-545

Trunk, travelling, 461-464
T-squares for drawing, 1500, 1501
Tube, inclined, 700-701
Turkey oilstone, 76
Turning tools, 1295-1297
——, wood, 1295-1314
Turn-screw bit, forked, 303, 304
Tusk tenon, 254
Twin bedsteads (see Bedstead)
Twine, upholsterer's, 1418
Twist bits, 300, 301
Twisted and plane surfaces, 101
—— fibres in timber, 194
Typewriter table, 1247-1250

UMBRELLA stands, 776, 786
"Universal" plane, Stanley's "Fifty-five," 204-217
Upholstery: buttoning, 1428
——: chair, working on, 1421-1426
——: covering materials, 1419-1421
——: hair seating, 1420
—— hammers, 1416, 1417
——: "locking" knot, 1422
——: methods of working, 1421
—— needles, 1416, 1417
——: plushes, 1420
——: serge, 1420
——: settee, working on, 1426-1428
——: springs, chair, fixing, 1421, 1422
——: stuffing materials, 1417-1419
——: tapestries, 1419
——: trimmings, 1421
——: velvets, 1420
Upsets in timber, 194
Utrecht (see Velvets)

VARNISH, old, removing, 1408
——, spirit, white, hard, 1411
—— stain, 1406
Varnishing painted surfaces, 1415
Vase, flower, with repoussé panels, 1116-1118
Velvets for upholstery, 1420
Veneer, bending, 706
——: finding right side, 1320
——, gluing, 1316-1318
—— lines, bandings, and stringings, 1328
——, marquetry, 1334
—— pin, 144
——, saw, 1319-1320
——, saw- and knife-cut, 1316
Veneered mahogany work-box, 1042-1045
—— work, gluing, 139
Veneering, 1315-1329
——, "cane," 1321-1323
——, circular, 1325-1328

Veneering curved work, 1322-1324
——, decorative, 1324
—— hammer, 1318, 1320
—— woods, 1318
Venetian red and jelly size, painting with, 1405
Ventilator, circular louvre or, 687, 688
Verde green oak finish, 1404
Vertical spindle moulding machine, 1483-1487
Vice: back and front, 498, 499
——, bench, 17-21
——, —— top with, 480, 481
——, "Dolly," 12
——, improvised, 496, 497
——, instantaneous grip, 19, 20
——, saw-filers, 59
——: various types, 20-22

WADDING stuffing, 1418
Wait's rule attachments, 42
Walking-stick, screw dowel for, 270
Wall, fixing shelving to, 693-695
——, —— woodwork to, 689-697
——, plastered, fixing woodwork to, 692
Walnut finish, 1405
Waney edges in timber, 194
Wardrobe and hat rack for hall, 773-774
——, backing, 290
—— centre and hinge, fitting, 1396, 1397
——: fixing to wall, 696, 697
——, 4 ft., with mirror panels, 1141-1144
——, 4 ft. 6 in., 1133-1137
——, hanging, 1141-1148
——, oak, 1119-1123
——, office, 1258-1260
——, small, with leaded light, 1132, 1133
—— with drawers and trays, 1137-1141
Warping, buttoned edges to counteract, 288, 289
——, preventing when gluing, 140,-141
——, wood, 132
Warrington hammer, 63
Washing keelers, 663-666
"Washita" oilstone, 74
Washstand, 1152-1156
——, oak, 1126-1128
"Wasting away" (wood carving), 1349, 1350
Watchmakers' bench, 494
Waterproof glue, 141
—— joints for cistern, 235
Water stains, 1404, 1405
Weathered oak finish, 1404
Webbing chair, 1421

1608 INDEX

Webbing, damp, for veneering, 1326
——, upholsterer's, **1418**
Wedges, chopping, **72**
——, forms of, 263
Wedging, fox, 261-262
—— mortise and tenon joints, 263
Weights of wood, **127**
Wet rot, 192, 193
Wheel construction, 702, 703
——, dowelling felloes on, **243**
Wheelbarrow, easily-made, 440-442
——, ——, alternative design, 446-451
——, ——, modified design, **451-453**
——, garden or stable, 442-446
—— with movable sides, **450, 451**
Whiting mixture for cheap woods, **1414**
Winding strips for plane surfaces, **102**
Window, bull's-eye, **686, 687**
——, casement, 683-685
——, fast-sheet, **677**
—— frames, fixing, **696, 697**
—— —— out of parallel, **1399**
——, mullion, 681, 682
——, pantry, **678**
——, sash and frame, 679-682
——, ——, housed joint between stile and sill, **228**
——, swivel, 262
—— working tightly, **1398**
Windsor chair back, cutting, **1475**
Wires, aeroplane (*see* Aeroplane)
Wood (*see also* Timber)
—— countersink, 301, **302**
——: density, specific gravity and weight, 127-133
——, early, 118
——, elements of, 121
—— figuring, trunk cut to show, **131**

Wood finishing, painting and enamelling, 1401-1415
——, growth and properties of (*see* Timber)
—— incising, 1372-1376
——, late, 118
——, origin of, 115
—— for patternmaking, **1439**
——: pith, 121
—— reamer, 302, **303**
——, soft, 118
——, sources of, **114**
—— staining and fuming, 1403-1407
—— turning, 1295-1314
Woods, aeroplane, 1275-1276
——, alphabetical list of, **1543-**1590
——, hard (broad-leaf), list of, 194
—— for inlaying, 1330
——, mechanical properties of (*see* Timber)
——, soft (conifers), list of, 194
Wood-turner's tools, 1295-1297
Wood-turning, 1295-1314
Woodcarving, 1345-1380
——: boring holes, 1360-1362
——: "bosting in," 1349, 1350
——: bowl, Norwegian, 1379, 1380
——: bowl with nut-crackers, 1377, 1378
——: bracket in pierced carving, 1358-1370
——: carving back of work, 1369
——: chip carving, 1370-1372
——: contour, varying, 1355
——: corner cabinet, 1374, 1377
——: grounding, 1351, 1352
——: hall-stand, 1372, 1376
——: incised work, 1372-1376
——: knife carving, 1377-1380
——: knives, 1377, 1378
——: making up and finishing, 1369, 1370
——: modelling, 1352 - 1359, 1363-1367

Woodcarving: nut-crackers, 1377, 1378
——: overmantel, **1374, 1377**
——: panel, 1348-1357
——: preliminary work, 1347
——: ribbon work, entwined, 1354, 1356
——: sawing, 1362, 1363
——: "setting in," 1350, 1351
——: surface, finishing, 1367-1369
—— tools, 1345-1347
——: tracing design, 1360-1362
——: "wasting away," 1349
——: woods used, 1345
Woodware, domestic, 349-370
Woodwork exposed to weather, 1397
——: fixing to walls, 689-697
Work-boxes, 1039-1045
Work-table, carved, with open silk pocket, 1080-1082
——, inlaid, 1072, 1073
——, plain, 1078-1082
—— with fitted tray, **1076-1078**
—— —— sliding body, 1073-1076
Workshop: arrangement, 9-10
—— equipment, 9
——, lighting, 10
——, plan of, 10
——, portable, 436-439
——, small, typical, 9
—— windows, 10
Writing fall, quadrant for, 1393, 1394
—— furniture, 1083-1104
Writing-bureau, oak Jacobean, 1090-1094
Writing-desk and bookcase, combined, 1101-1104
——, oak, 1084-1087
——, strap hinge for, 1391, 1392
Writing-table and cabinet, combined, 1094-1097
——, pedestal, 1238-1241
——, small mahogany, **1083**

YORKSHIRE light, 682, 683

www.ingramcontent.com/pod-product-compliance
Lightning Source LLC
Chambersburg PA
CBHW031419150426
43191CB00006B/325